D1351621

INDIA'S RELIGIONS

OTHER BOOKS IN THE SERIES:

INDIA'S RELIGIONS
Perspectives from Sociology and History

Edited by
T.N. Madan

OXFORD
UNIVERSITY PRESS

OXFORD

UNIVERSITY PRESS

YMCA Library Building, Jai Singh Road, New Delhi 110001

Oxford University Press is a department of the University of Oxford. It
furthers the University's objective of excellence in research, scholarship,
and education by publishing worldwide in

Oxford   New York

Auckland   Bangkok   Buenos Aires   Cape Town   Chennai
Dar es Salaam   Delhi   Hong Kong   Istanbul   Karachi   Kolkata
Kuala Lumpur   Madrid   Melbourne   Mexico City   Mumbai   Nairobi
São Paulo   Shanghai   Taipei   Tokyo   Toronto

Oxford is a registered trade mark of Oxford University Press
in the UK and in certain other countries

Published in India
By Oxford University Press, New Delhi

© Oxford University Press 2004

The moral rights of the author have been asserted
Database right Oxford University Press (maker)

First published 2004

ISBN 0 19 566829 4

Typeset in Giovanni Book
By Eleven Arts, Keshav Puram, Delhi 110 035
Printed in India by Pauls Press, New Delhi 110 020
Published by Manzar Khan, Oxford University Press
YMCA Library Building, Jai Singh Road, New Delhi 110 001

For Cenu

I bring what you much need, yet always have ...
It is not to be put in a book, it is not in this book,
it is no further from you than
your hearing and sight ...

WALT WHITMAN

India is supposed to be a religious country above everything else ... I have frequently condemned [religion] and wished to make a clean sweep of it. Almost always it seemed to stand for blind belief and reaction, dogma and bigotry, superstition and exploitation, and the presentation of vested interests. And yet I knew that there was something else in it, something which supplied a deeper inner craving of human beings.

Jawaharlal Nehru, *An Autobiography* (1936)

Too much dependence on supernatural factors may lead, and has often led, to a loss of self-reliance in man and to a blunting of his capacity and creative ability. And yet some faith seems necessary in things of the spirit which are beyond the scope of our physical world, some reliance on moral, spiritual and idealistic conceptions, or else we have no anchorage, no objectives or purpose in life.

Jawaharlal Nehru, *The Discovery of India* (1946)

When the Indian progressive youth dismisses religion as opium, he is not only ignoring social facts, but [also] the historical process itself by which these have assumed the attached values.

Dhurjati Prasad Mukerji, *Modern Indian Culture* (1948)

A thoroughly post-Durkheimian society would be one in which our religious belonging would be unconnected to our national identity. It will almost certainly be one in which the gamut of such religious allegiances will be wide and varied.

Charles Taylor, *Varieties of Religion Today* (2003)

Contents

Preface

This is a book of readings about India's major religions from the perspectives of ethnography and history. It is not concerned with general theories of any kind, whether of the psychological origin or the sociological significance of religion, except indirectly, insofar as the authors whose work is included here may have had such interests. I have not even attempted to engage with questions such as how best to define religion, or whether a universal definition is at all possible. It may not be denied that social science theories of religion (including the Marxian) are marked in a variety of ways (in some cases in contrary ways) by presuppositions about the nature and significance of religion derived from Abrahamic religions, particularly Judaism and Christianity. This need not however prove a serious handicap so long as we do not allow such presuppositions (for example, the critical importance of the idea of the godhead to the conception of religion) to predetermine what beliefs, rites, and symbols will qualify as elements of religion.

Religion in this book is not a *defining* but an *identifying* term. Essentialism is largely eschewed, and the idea of a family resemblance (in the sense that a range of common concerns are randomly present) among religious traditions is preferred. Keywords derived from one tradition may be used as cues to explore the scope of another in respect of its repertoire of beliefs and rituals, which, going by ethnographic and historical evidence, are present everywhere although not identically related. The cultural traditions represented in this volume (including Christianity and Islam in the Indian environment) allow us to suggest that there is a discourse present in each about the place of the human being in a holistic framework that transcends but does not deny or exclude the mundane and the social. It is all a matter of relations and, at a higher (less concrete) level, of relations between relations.

A book about India's religions must obviously begin with the given dimensions of plurality as well as the ideologies of pluralism. This has been attempted in the introductory essay. In the following six parts, each beginning with prefatory remarks and comprising three readings, a number of key ideas and themes are explored. Each rubric after the first one is presented as an elaboration of those that precede it. In other words, the volume is not just a miscellany but has a structure. The epilogue returns to the themes of inter-religious understandings and syncretism.

Beginning with the concept of the sacred defined by its otherness (sacred places and performances), the book proceeds to explore how the hiatus that otherness creates may be overcome by bonding *via* piety and passion. The process of overcoming separation, or bonding, is universally facilitated by mediators of one kind or another, such as magicians, spiritual masters, or martyrs. These various aspects of the religious life are significant components of cultural traditions everywhere, which of course include other elements too. Traditions are constructed, preserved, and transmitted in a number of ways, that include the oral narrative and the literary text. This does not mean, however, that religious traditions are static. They in fact grow gradually and sometimes change radically (are transformed). This is understandable, even inevitable, because the category religious is not *sui generis*. The sacred and the secular (or profane) are, as was noted above, intertwined in principle. The manner in which these inter connections are made is the work of history. To repeat what was said earlier, it is all a matter of relations.

In an earlier book of readings, *Religion in India* (1991), which is still in print, and hopefully will remain available for some more years, I had focused on the idea of the sacred as the organizing principle. In this volume, a more comprehensive framework (described above) has been employed. Apart from the broader conceptual scope, *India's Religions* presents to readers selections from more recently published work: eleven of the eighteen readings are excerpted from books published between 1992 and 2001; three are from the 1980s and four from the 1970s. The two volumes together represent half a country of scholarly study of Indian religions by over three and a half dozen scholars, mostly social anthropologists or sociologists but including historians. Only three authors, besides myself, are common to both books.

I am pleased to have been able to include in this volume an oral narrative by an unlettered Tamil woman, presented here in English translation by an Indian and a French scholar. The study of Indian religions from social science perspectives is truly and happily a collective endeavour, and I have attempted to give recognition to this fact. The authors whose work has been included in *Religion in India* and *India's Religions* are from England, France, Germany,

India, Mexico, New Zealand, Pakistan, Sri Lanka, and the USA. Limitation of space has precluded presentation of the work of many other scholars who have made valuable contributions to the field. Also regretted is the inadequate attention, for the same reason, given to folk and tribal religious traditions. I would further like to point out that the materials included in the two volumes have been drawn in all but five cases from books. The fruits of research that appear as articles in journals are inadequately represented in them.

Also absent in the volume—as stated at the very outset—is any discussion of sociological and social anthropological theories of religion. The reader will find a brief discussion of these in the introductory essay in *Religion in India*. Besides, there are many excellent books on the subject in print, ranging from older textbooks such as Brian Morris's *Anthropological Studies of Religion* (CUP, 1988) or Bryan Turner's *Religion and Social Theory* (Sage, New Delhi, 1991) to Malcolm Hamilton's *The Sociology of Religion* (Routledge, London, 1995).

This volume bears testimony to the wide appeal and richness of the study of Indian religions from the perspectives of ethnography and history. I trust readers will find it as interesting to read as I have found it to compile and edit, and extend to it the same patronage as they have done to *Religion in India*. I would like to conclude by expressing my deep gratitude to all the scholars (many of them personal friends), and their publishers, who have readily granted permission for the inclusion of their work (in edited form) in this book. I regret it is not possible to convey my thanks to A.K. Ramanujan, who did so much to bring new information and precious insights into the study of Indian folklore and religious poetry, and who sadly left us prematurely. The summer he died (in 1993), Raman was to have come to India, and we were to talk about his first translations of the *vakh* (sayings) of the fourteenth century Kashmiri Shaiva mystic poetess Lalla (via Grierson's Sanskrit renderings). Alas, that was not to be.

Finally, a word about editorial procedure. Although the readings are excerpted from book chapters or journal articles, I have made a serious effort not to interfere too much with the authors' texts unless it seemed absolutely necessary to do so. Deletions of more than a word or two have been indicated by ellipses. The omission of references or footnotes has not been noted. Additions to fill gaps in the text, and references and footnotes supplied by me, have been placed in square brackets and/or marked by asterisks. Each author's preferences in respect of italicization of words and the use of diacritics have been generally respected.

T.N. Madan

Delhi
May 2004

Introduction
India's Religions: Plurality and Pluralism

T.N. MADAN

INTRODUCTORY REMARKS. DISTRIBUTIONAL PATTERNS

If the term 'religion' may be used to refer to particular aspects of India's cultural traditions (see below), the country can be said to have long been the home of all religions that today have a worldwide presence. Hinduism, Buddhism, Jainism, and Sikhism, called the Indic religions, were born here. Christianity, Judaism, Islam, Zoroastrianism, and the Bahai faith arrived here from abroad at different points of time during the last two millennia.

The plurality of religions in India is often obscured by the fact that Hinduism is generally regarded both as the demographically dominant and the culturally characteristic, even hegemonic, religion of the country, not only in popular imagination but also by official reckoning. According to the census, four out of five Indians are Hindus, and they inhabit the length and breadth of the land. From the cultural perspective, anthropologists and sociologists have provided details of the many components of culture and aspects of the social structure of the non-Hindu communities that have either been borrowed from the Hindus, or are survivals from their pre-conversion Hindu past, with or without significant alterations.

The foregoing popular view of the cultural scene in India, buttressed by official statistics, needs to be qualified in several respects. Unlike the other religions of India, Hinduism is a federation of faiths, which has a horizontal as well as vertical distribution, rather than a single homogeneous religion. Not only do the religious beliefs and practices of Hindus vary from one cultural region of India to another, Hindu castes in different areas are also characterized by differences of status and lifestyle even when similarly named. We will go into the details of such internal plurality among Hindus in section II below.

Suffice it to note here that, first, Hinduism has a long and eventful history, which has resulted in much internal diversity; and, second, there are communities today that are considered Hindu by others but who themselves no longer concur with this judgement. Most notably, the Scheduled Castes of official literature, including the Constitution of the Republic of India, who have traditionally comprised the bottom rungs of the caste hierarchy, and were called Harijan ('the Children of God') by Mahatma Gandhi (1869–1948), are today by self-description the Dalit ('the Oppressed'). If their claim that they are not Hindu (see, e.g. Ilaiah 1996) is accepted, the proportion of Hindus in the total population will fall significantly from four-fifths to two-thirds.

Further, clarification regarding the use of the term religion in the Indian context, anticipated at the very beginning of this introduction, may now be offered. Whether we have the Indic faiths in mind, or the major religions of non-Indian origin, notably Islam, religion in India is not a discrete element of everyday life that stands wholly apart from the economic or political concerns of the people. To assume that would amount to yielding to the temptation of words. The point is not that the religious domain is not distinguished from the secular, but rather that the secular is regarded as being encompassed by the religious, even when the former is apparently inimical to the latter. The relationship is hierarchical. In other words, religion in the Indian cultural setting traditionally permeates most aspects of life, not through mechanical diffusion, but in an integrated, holistic, perspective (see Radhakrishnan 1927). The processes of secularization are, however, gradually circumscribing the scope of the religious domain, particularly in urban areas.

A second clarification concerns the conception of divinity. The mono-theism characteristic of the Abrahamic religions (much more uncompro-misingly in Judaism and Islam than in Christianity) is either absent in the Indic religions (as in the case of Buddhism and Jainism), or we find in its place other conceptions, notably an abstract notion of 'Essence' or 'Being' as the source of all that truly exists (the Brahman of Vedantic Hinduism), or polytheism (as in Puranic Hinduism), or the exuberant 'spiritism' of folk Hinduism (see section II below).

The non-theism of orthodox Buddhism and Jainism, which was a major scandal in the eyes of the Vedic metaphysicians two thousand years ago, persuaded a modern European scholar of comparative religion, Emile Durkheim (1858–1917), himself born into the Jewish faith, to abandon belief in divine beings as an essential element in the constitution (or recognition) of religion anywhere. Instead, he focused on the conception of 'sacred things', that is, 'things set apart or forbidden' that contribute significantly to the constitution of society as a 'moral community'. The notion of sacredness is however itself problematic in several respects, but we will not go into that issue here (see Durkheim 1995).

Finally, it may be noted here by way of clarification, that the notion and word most widely used in India as a synonym for religion, namely the Sanskrit 'dharma' (from the root dhri), or its Pali equivalent dhamma, denotes the ideas of maintenance, sustenance, or upholding steadfastness and moral virtue. It is an idea that differs from the dependent bonding of the human being with supernatural powers conveyed by the term religion, which is of Latin derivation (religio, obligation, bond); it also denotes reverence, but in Lucretius it means 'fear of gods'. While the conception of a self-sustaining cosmo-moral order is found in all Indic religions, subtle differences of nuance notwithstanding, Islam literally stands for submission to the Will of God, conveyed through his Word as recorded in the Quran, which is to be read repeatedly as an essential act of piety (see section III below).

Bearing the foregoing observations in mind, we will now use the word religion here without further elucidation or qualification. Let us begin with the demographic picture (on the basis of the 1991 census). Hindus (including most of the Scheduled Castes, who account for 16.48 per cent of the total population) number 688 million, constituting 82 per cent of the total population of about 839 million. (The estimated population at the time of writing in 2002 is well above one billion, but the proportions by region are believed to be about the same as in 1991). Following the Hindus are the 102 million Muslims (12 per cent), and next in line are Christians (20 million, 2.32 per cent), Sikhs (16 million, 1.99 per cent). Buddhists (0.77 per cent), Jains (0.41 per cent) and others account for the balance of nearly 2 per cent of the population. Among the 'others', mention may be made of those tribal peoples who adhere to their own traditional faiths—earlier grouped together arbitrarily as animism under colonial rule—and of the Zoroastrians and the Jews. The total population of the Scheduled Tribes is about 68 million, or 8 per cent of the total population. Although figures for distribution by religion are not available, it is generally known that most of them either follow Hinduism of the folk type or are Christians; only a minority still adhere to their ancestral faiths. As for the Zoroastrians, the Jews and the Baha'is, they are counted in thousands only; the former two communities are threatened by declining birth rates and assimilation into other religious communities through intermarriage. Some Jews have migrated to Israel.

Distribution of the religious communities by state provides a picture of regional dispersal and variation. Hindus, spread over virtually the entire country, outnumber all the others in the states (percentages in parenthesis) of Himachal Pradesh (96), Orissa (95), Madhya Pradesh (93), Andhra Pradesh (89, Gujarat (89), Haryana (89), Rajasthan (89), Tamil Nadu (89), Pondicherry (86), Tripura (86), Karnataka (85), Delhi (84), Bihar (82), Uttar Pradesh (82), Maharashtra (81), West Bengal (75), Sikkim (68), Assam (67), Goa, Daman, & Diu (65), Manipur (58), and Kerala (57). Similarly, Hindus outnumber all the others in the Union Territories of Dadra & Nagar Haveli (95), Chandigarh (76), and Andaman & Nicobar Islands (68). They are the principal minority community in the states of Arunachal Pradesh (37), Punjab (34), Meghalaya (15), Nagaland (10), and Mizoram (5), in the Union Territory of Lakshadweep (5), and in Jammu and Kashmir.

The only other religious community with a perceptible countrywide distribution are Muslims. They are the majority community (percentages in parenthesis) in the state of Jammu & Kashmir (64 according to 1981 census) in the extreme north and in the Union Territory of Lakshadweep (94) in the south. They are the principal minority in the states of Assam (28) in the north-east; West Bengal (23) and Bihar (15) in the east; Uttar Pradesh (17), Delhi (9), Rajasthan (8), and Haryana (5) in the north; Maharashtra (10) and Gujarat (9) in the west; and Kerala (23), Karnataka (12), and Andhra Pradesh (9) in the south.

Christians are the majority community (percentages in parenthesis) in three north-eastern states, namely Nagaland (88), Mizoram (86), and Meghalaya (65). They are the principal minority in the states of Manipur (34), also in the north-east; and Goa, Daman & Diu (30) in the west; and in the Union Territory of Andaman & Nicobar Islands (24) in the south. Sikhs account for 63 per cent of the population in Punjab and are the principal minority in the adjacent state of Haryana (6) and the Union Territory of Chandigarh (20).

The state of Arunachal Pradesh in the north-east presents an interesting variation of the general pattern: the followers of traditional (tribal) religions at 36 per cent are about as numerous (percentages in parenthesis) as Hindus (37); Buddhists (13) and Christians (10) are in the third and fourth positions respectively. The only other places in the country where the Buddhists are a presence in demographic terms are the district of Ladakh (in Jammu & Kashmir), where they account for four-fifths of the population, and the states of Sikkim and Mizoram where their share in the population is 27 and 8 per cent respectively. Jains are concentrated in Rajasthan, Delhi, and the west coast states. Zoroastrians, more generally known as Parsis, four-fifths of whose estimated world population of 120,000 lives in India, are concentrated in the urban areas of Gujarat and Maharashtra. Far fewer than the Parsis are the Jews, who are, however, divided into three distinct groups, namely the

Baghdadi Jews of Calcutta, the Cochin Jews, and the Bene Israeli of Bombay. Only the last named group may be called a community; the other two are really clusters of families.

Detailed statistics about the distribution of the population of India by religion and domicile are given in the Table below, which is based on the Census of India 1991, Series-I, India, Paper I of 1995, *Religion*, pp. xii–xxiii.

We may parenthetically observe here that, among the countries of South Asia, Sri Lanka shares with India a greater contemporary plurality of religions than do the other countries. Although predominantly Buddhist, it harbours sizeable religious minorities, including Hindus, Christians, and Muslims. Nepal is more predominantly Hindu, but there are also Buddhists and Muslims, the latter in very small numbers. Bangladesh is predominantly Muslim (85 per cent), with Hindus and Buddhists as notable religious minorities. Pakistan and the Maldives are almost exclusively Muslim and Bhutan is primarily Buddhist.

In what follows, the focus is on the historical and organizational aspects of the religions of India. We are not concerned with their cognitive and ritual dimensions. The plurality of the major traditions is briefly outlined in sections II and III. Section IV examines, again briefly, the elements of pluralism in the traditions earlier described. Limitations of space have precluded any discussion of the so-called tribal religions and of Judaism and Zoroastrianism. Also excluded, regrettably, is an exploration of the interaction of the religious traditions and of the peaceful coexistence of religious communities (see, e.g. Gottschalk 2001).

INDIC RELIGIONS

Vedism and Hinduism

The beginnings of religious diversity in India go back to the country's proto-historic past. Arguably, there is material evidence of the existence of religious activity in the urban centres associated with the Indus Valley or Harappan civilization of about five thousand years ago, spread over vast areas in the north-western, northern, and western parts of the Indo–Pakistan subcontinent. It is reasonable to infer that religious beliefs and rituals of a somewhat different kind (e.g. shamanism) may have prevailed in the rural hinterlands. The Harappan religion in maturity was perhaps characterized by internal diversities reflecting social and theological divisions. Some scholars have written about a public religion, centred in temples, comprising ritual bathing (there is a 'great bath' in the citadel of Mohenjo-Daro), worship of gods and goddesses, fertility rituals, and perhaps animal sacrifice. The current consensus, however, denies the existence of temples. Apart from the public

TABLE 1: RELIGIONS OF INDIA (1991) CENSUS

	Total	Hindus	Muslims	Christians	Sikhs	Buddhists	Jains	Other	Religion not stated
India	838,583,988	82.41	11.67	2.32	1.99	0.77	0.41	0.38	0.05
Andhra Pradesh	66,508,008	89.14	8.91	1.83	0.03	0.03	0.04	n.a.	0.02
Andaman & Nicobar Islands	280,661	67.53	7.61	23.95	0.48	0.11	0.01	0.09	0.22
Arunachal Pradesh	864,558	37.04	1.38	10.29	0.14	12.88	0.01	36.22	2.04
Assam	22,414,322	67.13	28.43	3.32	.07	.29	.09	.62	0.4
Bihar	86,374,465	82.42	14.8	–	0.98	0.09	–	0.03	1.67
Chandigarh	642,015	75.84	2.72	0.99	20.29	0.11	0.24	0.01	0.01
Dadra & Nagar Haveli	138,477	95.48	2.41	1.51	0.01	0.15	0.38	20.59	–
Delhi	9,420,644	83.67	9.44	0.88	4.84	0.15	1.00	0.01	0.01
Goa, Daman, & Diu	1,169,793	64.68	5.25	29.86	0.09	0.02	0.04	1.67	–
Gujarat	41,309,582	89.48	8.73	0.44	0.08	0.03	1.19	0.03	0.02
Haryana	16,463,648	89.21	4.64	0.10	5.81	0.01	0.21	–	0.02
Himachal Pradesh	5,170,877	95.90	1.72	0.09	1.01	1.24	0.20	–	0.02
Karnataka	44,977,201	85.45	11.64	1.91	0.02	0.16	0.73	0.01	0.08
Kerala	29,098,518	57.28	23.33	19.32	0.01	–	0.01	0.01	0.04
Lakshadweep	51,707	4.52	94.31	1.16	–	–	–	–	0.01
Madhya Pradesh	66,181,170	92.80	4.96	0.65	0.24	0.33	0.74	0.09	0.19
Maharashtra	78,937,187	81.12	9.67	1.12	0.21	6.39	1.22	0.13	0.14

	Total	Hindus	Muslims	Christians	Sikhs	Buddhists	Jains	Other	Religion not stated
Manipur	1,837,149	57.67	7.27	34.11	0.07	0.04	0.07	0.77	–
Meghalaya	1,774,778	14.67	3.46	64.58	0.15	0.16	0.02	16.82	0.14
Mizoram	689,756	5.05	0.66	85.73	0.04	7.83	–	0.27	0.42
Nagaland	1,209,546	10.12	1.71	87.47	0.06	0.05	0.10	0.48	0.01
Orissa	31,659,736	94.67	1.83	2.10	0.05	0.03	0.02	1.26	0.04
Pondicherry	807,785	86.16	6.54	7.23	–	0.01	0.06	–	–
Punjab	20,281,969	34.46	1.18	1.11	62.95	0.12	0.10	0.01	0.07
Rajasthan	44,005,900	89.08	8.01	0.11	1.48	0.01	1.28	–	0.03
Sikkim	406,457	68.37	0.95	3.30	0.09	27.15	0.01	0.09	0.04
Tamil Nadu	55,858,946	88.67	5.47	5.69	0.01	–	0.12	0.01	0.03
Tripura	2,757,205	86.50	7.13	1.68	0.03	4.67	0.01	–	–
Uttar Pradesh	139,112,287	81.70	17.33	0.14	0.48	0.16	0.13	0.01	0.01
West Bengal	68,077,965	74.72	23.61	0.56	0.08	0.30	0.05	0.67	0.01

Note: There are no figures about Jammu & Kashmir in the table because census enumeration in 1991 was precluded by militancy related disturbances in the State. The results of the 2001 census on the religion-wise distribution of the population are not available yet (in February 2003).

(state) and private (domestic) rituals, differences reflecting clan-based cleavages also seem to have existed (see Ratnagar 2000: 69–77; Thapar 2002: 83–6).

The city cultures, it is generally believed, were overridden by nomadic Aryan-speaking peoples of central or west Asian origin around 1500 BC. They brought in their own religious beliefs and practices, and these focused on the creative and destructive powers of nature. According to this generally accepted view, the Aryans owed little in their religious life to the presumably Dravidian-speaking people they displaced from their homelands. Scholars who do not accept the general view, but consider the Harappan culture a continuing rather than a shut-down phenomenon, whether wholly internal or aided by a limited migration, maintain that the old and the new cultures coexisted, and the latter absorbed elements, both religious and linguistic, from the former (see Parpola 1994).

Vedic religion and Sanskrit took several centuries to acquire the forms in which we know them. The major source of our knowledge about the religious life of the Aryans, besides the numerous archaeological sites, is the body of sacred literature called the Veda ('knowledge', 'wisdom'), which is believed to be ever-existent (*sanātana*) and therefore lacking any human author (*apaurusheya*), and stretches over virtually a thousand years. The earliest of the Vedic texts is the *Rig*, which has been dated no later than 1200 BC (but is perhaps older). Its ten books of hymns in praise of divinities presumably represent ten family traditions among the Brahmans (rituals specialists) and took several centuries to compose. The *Sāma* and *Yajur Veda*s extend the scope of the *Rig* into music and ritual respectively. Finally, the *Atharva Veda* is believed to represent the absorption of folk religions into the vedic corpus, resulting in significant changes in it. These religions were encountered by the Aryans as they moved east into the Gangetic valley and adopted more settled ways. Indeed, the valley came to be called the home of the Aryas, *Āryavrata*. Thus, vedic divinities lost their supremacy and magical spells and rites became ascendant (see Flood 1996 and Brockington 1992).

The Vedas became the basis for immense textual efflorescence, comprising manuals of ritual performances (*Brahmanas*, *Āranyakas*), and later discursive speculative treatises (*Upanishads*), also called *Vedānta* (the culmination of the Veda) (see Olivelle 1998), all of which brings us close to 300 BC. Schools of Vedic learning and ritual, called 'branches' (*shākhā*), flourished, producing a cultural ambience of sometimes bewildering plurality within the vedic framework.

That however is not all; Vedism gradually made way for the emergence of what is generally called Hinduism on a subcontinental scale, which brought more texts on more varied subjects into existence, notably the *Grihya Sūtras*, which are guides to the performance of domestic rituals, and the *Dharma Sūtras* (see Olivelle 2000), which have social ethics and law as their subject matter. Besides, there are the *Shrauta Sūtras*, which are technical treatises on the correct procedures for the performance of vedic rituals of public significance. The *Grihya Sūtras* have a regional character: a text followed in one part of the country may be unknown in another. The Vedic corpus, considered revealed, is said to be based on *shruti* (that which has been heard, by the inner ear, as it were), and constitutes the first source of *dharma* understood as both the law and righteous conduct. After the *Sūtras* we come to the second source, namely *Smriti* (that which is remembered), and these texts are credited to human authors.

Later still than the *Sūtras* are the *Dharma Shāstras* which continue with the same themes but in much greater detail. The best known of these texts today is the *Mānav Dharma Shāstra*, attributed to a seer called Manu, and therefore also known as the *Manu Smriti* (see Doniger 1991). It is believed to have been composed between 200 BC and AD 300 which rules out single authorship. What stands out in this and other similar texts is the institutional framework for the conduct of both domestic life and public affairs.

In domestic life the key principles of *varna* (social class) and *āshrama* (stage of life) are adumbrated for the definition of appropriate rituals and worldly affairs. While universal norms (*sarva sādhārna dharma*) are not wholly eliminated, but retained as the foundation of all righteous conduct, it is the *varna*- and *āshrama*-specific rules that emerge as preponderant. It is thus that Hinduism has been defined as *varna–āshrama–dharma*, or a context-sensitive morality. Not only the householder, but the kings too, are bound by their respective duties defined in terms of varna and *āshrama* (see Lingat 1973). Even those who repudiated such divisions, notably the renouncers (sannyāsis), have been grouped into sects (*sampradāyas*) since at least the time of the composition of the *Mahābhārata* (c. BC 400–AD 400), and are guided by their own (*yati*) *dharma*. It is obvious that when variant regional, *varna* (including occupation), and *āshrama* identities defined the appropriateness of behaviour in particular situations, Hinduism could have been only a family of faiths and the behaviours that went with them and Hindu society a confederation of communities.

The speculative or philosophical concerns of the Brahmanical tradition were formulated as different systems of orthodox thought (*jnān*) and termed *darshana*, or 'visions', or 'views' (in both senses of the word, 'view' as something seen and also as a philosophical position) of life based on the Veda. Each of these *darshanas*, six in number, has its own authoritative texts. The thought (or reflections) that follows from each position is not exclusive in the manner of the various guides to ritual performance and social behaviour. The 'root' text of each *darshana* is concerned with extra-referential (*paramārthika*) knowledge, and transactive (*vyavahārika*) knowledge is built or grafted on it. Together they constitute what can only be called a complex totality aimed at deliverance from ignorance through true knowledge. The sotireological character of the *darshanas* is undeniable as are their theistic tendencies.

The six schools are: (i) Sāmkhya ('enumeration') which asserts the ontological duality of matter (*prakrti*) and the 'self' (*purusha*); (ii) Yoga ('joining', 'mixing') which constitutes a pair with Sāmkhya in terms of its metaphysics; (iii) Mimāmsa (vedic exegesis) which takes a pluralist view of reality; (iv) Vedānta ('culmination of veda'), grouped with Mimāmsa, which denies the reality of the many; (v) Nyāya (logic), and (vi) Vaisheshika (dialectics), considered a pair, which deal with logical, ontological, and dialectical issues within an empiricist, pluralist (more precisely atomist), framework (see Hiriyana 1993). The primacy which the monism of Vedanta has enjoyed in contemporary literature on India does little justice to the internal diversities of Brahmanical thought even when dealing with the same issues, or with its method of dealing with them to preclude mutual incomprehensibility.

The foregoing pluralities of scripture, metaphysics, and social organization that form the backdrop to Hinduism, and indeed partly constitute it, are characteristic of Brahmanical orthodoxy. This orthodoxy has not remained unchallenged. Indeed, the challenges came from within long before any major external threat materialized. The followers of public Vedic ritual, called the *Shrautas* (*shruti*, 'revelation'), first yielded space to those who gave precedence to domestic rituals, whether the Smārtas (followers of the Smritis or *Dharma Shāstras*) or the Paurānikas (those who organize their religious life on the basis of the Purānas, which are legendry accounts of the doings of gods, goddesses, and other supernatural beings as well as human beings like kings and ascetics). The latter two categories of Hinduism remain within the vedic fold.

It is the *Tāntras*, texts that are claimed by their followers, the Tāntrikas, to be revealed that are non-vedic. Traced to folk cults of Assam and Bengal, the eastern frontier of Vedic (Aryan) northern India, Tāntrism is characterized by enormous internal diversity including within its fold magical fertility rites as well as arcane metaphysics. The human body is the key site of Tāntrik practice; it reveals considerable variety, but is generally characterized by secret rituals, often performed at special sites, such as cremation grounds, and frequently at night. Thus, Tāntrik rituals that invoke the power of Shakti, the Supreme Goddess, are performed at night in the famous temple of Puri (Orissa), where worship of the god Jagannātha (an incarnation of Vishnu, the patron deity of Vaishnavas) and his divine consort, is performed publicly during the day (see Marglin 1985). The celebrated annual 'car festival' (*ratha yātra*) is dedicated to him.

We must pause here to mention two other important bodies of sacred texts, namely the epics, the *Mahābhārata* (c. 400 BC–AD 400) and *Rāmāyana* (c. AD 200), and the Purānas, which are post-vedic and fall into the category of the Smriti. They mark the transformation of the vedic Brahmanical religion into what has come to be known as Hinduism. Shiva and Vishnu, somewhat vague figures in the vedic pantheon, now emerge as the supreme gods, not always at peace with each other. Moreover, the notion of incarnation (*avatār*) is formulated within the Vaishnava tradition, Krishna (of the *Bhāgvata Purāna*) and Rāma (of the *Rāmāyana*) being the most notable among the nine or ten avatars generally recognized. The Purānas describe in great detail the deeds of the Hindu trinity (Brahmā the creator, Vishnu the preserver, and Shiva the destroyer) and other mythological personages. The Purānas were composed between the sixth and sixteenth centuries (see Dimmit and van Buitenen 1978).

While the worship of Vishnu is combined in the Smārta–Paurānika traditions with that of Shiva, Shakti or Devī, Sūrya (the sun god), and Ganapati (the lord of auspiciousness), in some parts of the country, particularly in the south, mutually exclusive and often hostile sects have emerged centred on the cults of the first two gods. These five deities together represent a syncretic movement in Hinduism, dating back to the ninth century, which sought to overcome sectarian and other divisions within Hinduism. Sūrya, and also Vishnu and Shiva, are of vedic origin; and Shakti represents the folk religious cults (see Bhattacharji 1988).

From as early as the fifth century, the Vaishnavas were divided into the sects of Panchārātras and Vaikhānasas. Similarly, the Pashupata, Kāpālika, and Kālāmukha sects were prominent among the Shaivas (see Bhattacharji 1988, Brockington 1992, Lorenzen 1972). Starting in the seventh century, the Vaishnavas and the Shaivas began to generate distinctive liturgical texts called the *samhitas* and *āgamas* respectively. Each sect claimed the supremacy of its own deity on the latter's own authority. In the development of these theistic traditions, from around the closing centuries of the last millennium BC, a number of elements from various sources, including the high Sanskritic and folk religious traditions, fused. Personal devotion (*bhakti*) to one's chosen deity (*ishta*), whether Vishnu in his various incarnations, including most notably those of Rama and Krishna–Vāsudeva, or Shiva, is a striking characteristic of these cults, and originated in the south and then spread to the north. This devotionalism found expression in emotionally surcharged poetry, particularly among the Vaishnavas, from the sixth century onward, and later also among the Shaivites, though the latter's devotion tended to be more austere (see Ramanujan 1973 and 1981).

Expectedly, the relationship of the devotee to the deity, whether expressed in human (anthropomorphic) terms or through abstract formulations, constitutes the core of the speculative thought of these religious traditions, ranging from absolute monism (*advaita*), associated with the name of Shankara (c. 788–820), to qualified non-dualism (*vishishitādvaita*) of Ramanuja (c. 1017–1137), and dualism (*dvaita*) elucidated by Madhva in the thirteenth century. The teachings of the latter two saints combine the metaphysics of the Upanishads with the theism of Vaishnava and Shaiva cults.

Associated with both of these is a third tradition, namely the worship of the great goddess, Devī, which emerged virtually independently as the Shākta (from *shakti*, 'power') tradition. Here too the roots go far back in time, perhaps to the Harappan culture, and later developments entail the amalgamation of Puranic, Tantrik, and folk goddess and ideas. As Lakshmī, the divine consort of Vishnu, the great goddess is presented as a benign bearer of auspiciousness; as Umā–Pārvatī, she is the divine consort of Shiva, mother of the universe; and as Durgā or Kālī, the highest manifestation of divine power, she is the fearsome destroyer of evil and greater than all the male gods through the pooling of whose powers she comes into being. At the village level she appears as the goddess who brings and removes illness and misfortune, such as Shītalā, the goddess whose visitations were held responsible for smallpox (see Hawley and Wulff 1996).

The Hindu religious tradition, we have seen, is characterized by strong pluralistic tendencies emanating from various sources and inspirations. Syncretistic tendencies have also been in evidence, as that, for instance, of the *smārta* worship mentioned above, believed to have been instituted by Shankara. Remarkably for his time and short life (he died at the age of 32), he is believed to have travelled from his home in Kerala to the banks of the Narmada river and then on to Varanasi, to Badrinath near the source of the Ganga in the Himalaya, and finally to Kashmir. Wherever he went, he engaged in disputations with rival seers, expounded his non-dualist philosophy (*dvaita*), and promoted non-sectarianism. His travels, deemed by his followers to have been successful, are remembered by them as his widespread victory (*digvijay*).

Hinduism has tended to absorb non-Hindu religious ideas and practices, including, in medieval times, elements of Sufi Islam (see Mujeeb 1967). It has dealt with internal dissent through accommodation, sometimes carried to the furthest extremes. Occasionally, this strategy has failed and resulted in breakway sects that in course of time grew into independent religions, such as Buddhism and Jainism, adding a new dimension to the religious plurality of India.

Buddhism

The most widely spread religion in Asia today, namely Buddhism, has adherents in the West too, but it is a minority religion in India, the country of its origin. Named after the title 'buddha', ('the enlightened one') of its founder, Gautama (c. 563–483 BC), Buddhism began as a revolt against the vedic preoccupation with the supernatural, rejecting the beliefs as well as the rituals that went with them. The rejection entailed repudiation of the authority of the Brahmans on the part of the Bauddhas. Gautama himself belonged to the Kshatriya (warrior) caste and, indeed, was the heir to a kingdom in the Bihar–Nepal area. Following his own awakening to knowledge and wisdom, his enlightenment, the Buddha attracted disciples whom he taught 'the four noble truths' that constitute the fundamentals of all schools of Buddhism (see Harvey 1990).

The first truth of life, the Buddha said, is sorrow (suffering); the second, the source of sorrow is ignorance and desire; the third, sorrow can be ended if desire is overcome; and the fourth, the way to the 'blowing out' (*nibanna*) of both desire and sorrow lies through 'the noble eightfold path'. This path, which is the path of righteousness (*dharma, dhamma*) consists of the right views, resolve, speech, conduct, livelihood, effort, mindfulness, and concentration.

The Buddha adopted a stance of silence on the issue of the existence of the divinity but denied the vedic gods any significance in human affairs, and concentrated on human agency. He did, however, retain the root paradigm of karma understood as the doctrine of agency and retribution. It is doubtful that the Buddha thought of himself as anything more than a reformer within the tradition, and his teachings as 'a new expansion, not against, but within Brahmanism'. Nevertheless, his teachings were said by the establishment to be negatory (*nāstika*), repudiating vedic revelation and the notion of divinity, and attacked as unforgivably heterodox. The Buddha's rejection of the *varna* system, ritualism, and techniques of self-mortification could not but have been aberrations in the judgement of the Brahmans.

Nevertheless, it is not unreasonable to believe that Gautama's concerns and dissatisfactions must have been shared by some other reflective persons. They chose, however, to work from within the tradition. The fact that the early Upanishads (c. 600–400 BC) are more or less contemporaneous with the beginnings of Buddhism would seem to support such a conclusion. Thus, the upanishadic notion of an abstract Brahman (with which the self, *ātman*, is identical) appears to stand midway between vedic polytheism and Buddhist atheism. With the passage of time Brahmanism and Buddhism came closer together; more about that below.

The Buddha originated the idea of the monastic community of monks and nuns (*sangha*), subject to a rigorous regime (*vinaya*), as the ideal arrangement for the pursuit of true knowledge. An easier way of life was envisaged for the lay community, with the *sangha* as their exemplar and refuge. Such was his confidence in this institution that the Buddha did not name a successor nor formalize or codify his teachings. He advised resolution of doubts on matters of common concern through discussion and consensus; in the event of failure to reach a consensus the majority view was to be respected. It was thus that the seeds of a plurality of belief and practice among the Buddhists were sown by Gautama himself.

The first great split is believed to have occurred a century after the Buddha's passing at a council of sanghas convened at Vaishali (Bihar) to settle contentious issues concerning monastic discipline and the character of the Buddha's personality. The opposing factions, namely the orthodox Sthaviras (Elders) and the Mahāsānghikas (upholders of the 'Great Community'), reached a temporary truce, but split formally four decades later. While the former held the Buddha to have been an enlightened human preceptor, the latter claimed for him the status of a transcendent being.

The foregoing and other issues continued to cause disagreements. In the process as many as eighteen viewpoints were formalized and collectively referred to as the Hinayāna, or the little (or lesser) vehicle (or approach). One of them, the school of Sthaviras, emerged as Theravāda (the Way of the Elders) in the second century BC in Sri Lanka, where it is now the state religion (see Gombrich 1988). It later spread to Myanmar, Thailand, Cambodia, and Laos. As for the Mahasanghikas, they were the progenitors of the adherents of Mahāyāna (great vehicle or approach) Buddhism that is today a major religion in the far east (China, Japan) and elsewhere. Mahāyāna arose between 150 BC and AD 250. Apart from moving in the direction of theism (the Buddha as a glorified, transcendent being), it also developed a new philosophical perspective, Shunyatāvāda, emphasizing the 'emptiness' of phenomena. The great teacher of this doctrine was Nagarjuna, who was born a Brahman, became a Buddhist, and founded the Mādhyamika (the Middle Path) school of Buddhism.

Mention may also be made of a later development (seventh century) in north India where a convergence of Buddhism and Tantrism occurred, resulting in what came to be called the Vajrayāna (thunderbolt vehicle). This in turn spread north into Ladakh (Jammu & Kashmir) and the kingdom of Bhutan (three-fourths of the people there are Buddhists), and Tibet where it absorbed further extraneous elements from Shamanism. In the north-eastern states of Tripura, Mizoram, and Arunachal Pradesh in India there are close to 200,000 Buddhists of the Theravāda school.

The presence of the Dalai Lama and settlements of refugees in India, since their exile from Tibet in 1959, has enhanced general awareness about Buddhism in its different expressions of doctrine and practice in India. The conversion of large numbers of low caste Hindus—who call themselves Dalits (the Oppressed) and are generally referred to as Neo-Buddhists—in 1956 under the charismatic leadership of B.R. Ambedkar (1891–1956) and thereafter, has contributed significantly to the same process. The population figures for all of India were under 200,000 in 1951 and about three-quarters of a million in 1991. It has, however, explicitly politicized Buddhist identity (see Zelliot 1996).

The virtual disappearance of Buddhism as a distinct religion from the country of its origin calls for comment. The early hostility of Brahmans has already been mentioned above. As Buddhism was finally driven out of India in the twelfth and thirteenth centuries, it would seem that, by itself, this hostility alone is an insufficient explanation. The emergence of Mahāyāna in fact opened the way for the incorporation of the Buddha within the Vaishnava tradition as an incarnation of Vishnu and the selective absorption into it of Buddhist ethics, metaphysics, and logic. This process continued into the Gupta and post-Gupta periods. There is ample evidence that the brahmanization of Bengal was at the cost of Buddhism which was transformed. There was much mutual borrowing and the two religions came very close to each other, particularly in the eyes of the common people (see Chakrabarti 2001: 109–64).

In addition to the complex Brahman–Buddhist relationship, there is a consensus among historians that the moral decline of the monastic communities, the withdrawal of royal patronage, and the decline of the support of the laity also were major causes. The final blow was the Muslim invasions: these were widespread (all the way from Kashmir to Bengal) and brutal (the destruction of Buddhist universities, notably Nalanda, and the accompanying massacres of monks were staggering events). The devastated Buddhist communities escaped to Myanmar and further east, and the Muslims occupied the cultural, religious, and political spaces that they vacated (see Thapar 1966: 263–4, Kosambi 1970: 176–82).

Jainism

Jainism too arose around the same time as Buddhism, in the same area (Bihar), for broadly the same reasons, and in a similar manner. There are however significant differences between the Buddhist and Jain visions of life. The terms Jainism and Jain (*jaina*, follower of the religion) are derived from *jina*, 'the conqueror' (of one's physical self and thus of karmic action). This title was bestowed on prince Vardhamana (c. 599–27 BC), also called Mahāvira, 'the great hero', to whom are attributed the basic teachings of the faith in their final form. Actually, he is regarded as the last of a line of teachers called *tīrthankara* ('ford maker'), who recovered time and again the perennial 'three jewels' of right faith, right knowledge, and right action. They also founded the Jain community comprising ascetics (monks and nuns) and the laity (householders). It is their community that is considered by the Jains a spiritual ford (*tīrtha*) to help all seekers to wash off karma and terminate the cycle of birth–death–rebirth (see Dundas 1992).

Sentiments such as desire, anger, greed, and attachment are the human failings that generate karma (fruit-bearing action). Karma is visualized as material: it contaminates the inner self and is the cause of suffering in one's own life and of injury to other living beings. The Jain ideal therefore is to be forever engaged in self-purification (through the suppression of all bodily appetites) and to assiduously refrain from injury to others (this is the ideal of ahimsā, 'non-injury'). Renunciation is highly valued and the final worldly goal for the ascetic is to end his/her life through abstinence from food and drink. For laymen, the householder's life, guarded by numerous rules and regulations, is the ideal.

Paradoxical as it may seem, the Jains in actual practice are also very successful merchants and visible in urban centres (see Laidlaw 1995). Although there are fewer Jains than Buddhists in India, it is they rather than the latter who are the more visible religious community. They share many religious practices, including fasts and festivals, with upper caste Hindus, and are often regarded by the latter as a sect of Hindu society rather than a separate religious community. Their original atheism and repudiation of vedic revelation had of course earned them, alongside the Buddhists, the opprobrium of being heterodox, in the judgement of the Brahmans.

Among the Jains themselves, heresies and sectarian schisms began to appear even while the Mahāvīra was alive. According to the mainstream Jain tradition, eight such deviations (*nihnava*, 'concealment' of the true teaching) occurred over a period of six centuries. The last of these resulted in the emergence of a heretical sect. Accounts of this schism are shrouded in rival legends of the so-called mainstream and the breakaway groups, the Shvetāmbaras (clad in white cloth) and the Digāmbaras ('clothed by the sky', naked).

The mode of clothing refers to the practices of ascetics rather than lay householders, but Digāmbara nuns do wear clothes; only men remain naked. The Shvetāmbaras use a bowl to receive food given to them, from which they also eat. Food is important because even those monks who have attained full omniscience (*kevalin*) must eat to survive. The Digāmbaras do not use a bowl but their cupped hands to receive alms, and it is from the hands so held together that they eat. They insist on absolute non-possession: no clothes and no alms bowls. In their judgement, true omniscience means, among other things, that one does not need to eat food any longer. Women are deemed unequal to the demands of total conquest of the passions leading to omniscience and deliverance from the fruits of karma.

The two sects are also separated by the scriptures that each acknowledges. On the fundamentals of Jain faith and knowledge, however, there is no serious difference. Sectarian differences seem to have taken very long to acquire their present rigidity and regional distribution—Shvetāmbaras in the north and the west and Digāmbaras in the south—seems to have contributed to it. The differences notwithstanding, the high value that all jains place upon non-violence has prevented the two sects from adopting aggressive measures to settle scores. Currently, sectarian conflict among Jains seems to focus on the issues of ownership of and access to places of worship rather than on matters of doctrine and practice. Regrettably, the same cannot be said about other communities.

Sikhism

The beginnings of Sikhism (*sikha*, disciple) early in the sixteenth century followed a major development in the history of religions in India over the previous eight-hundred years, namely the arrival and growth of Islam. This development is described in the next section, but is mentioned here because it contributed significantly to the making of the new faith. Like Vardhamana and Gautama before him, Nanak Dev (1469–1539), the founder of Sikhism, was an upper caste Hindu (of the Khatri jati of traders, originally Kshatriyas). From his experience and reflections, he developed an acute dissatisfaction with the ritualism, idol worship, magic, and miracles of the faith into which he was born, and with the stranglehold of the Brahmans over it (see McLeod 1968 and Grewal 1990).

Nanak also took a positive view of worldly existence generally and of the householder's life and productive labour in particular. He rejected caste distinction and the traditional ideal of renunciation. Above all, he extolled the virtue of the life of religious obedience and devotion focused on an abstract conception of the divinity and affirming this through 'name remembrance' (*nām simran*), that is, recitation and singing of hymns. Declaring that there were no true Hindus or Muslims to be found anywhere, he called for a third path comprising moral duty (*dharm*), human effort (*karm*), spiritual knowledge, truth, and divine benevolence.

In all this Nanak was carrying forward the medieval Sant tradition of syncretic religious devotionalism, which had given rise to many 'paths' (*panth*) or sects. The disciples who gathered around him and carried forward his teachings after his death came to be called the Nānak Panthī or, later, Sikhs. Some of his followers did not follow all his core teachings and, like his son who became a renouncer, founded other sects. Other changes and dilutions of dogma and practice, particularly the latter, occurred over the next two centuries, blurring the distinction between Sikhism and caste Hinduism, and rendering the Sikh identity somewhat 'misty'. Simultaneously, changing historical circumstances—which brought the Jats into the Sikh fold in large numbers, and also created suspicions in the minds of the Muslim rulers about the loyalty of the Sikhs—radically altered the pacifist character of the Sikh community.

The tenth guru of the Sikhs, Gobind Rai (1666–1708), intervened effectively on all fronts, theological, practical, social and political, and created a sharpened sense of identity among the Sikhs by instituting (in 1699) a ritual of initiation (called *pahul*), and laying down norms of conduct including, most visibly, the injunction to retain bodily hair unshorn. He also asked all Sikh men to uniformly substitute Singh ('lion', the caste name of Rajputs) for their various last names; the women were to call themselves 'Kaur' ('lioness').

The institution of these requirements also created unintended divisions amongst Sikhs between, (i) those who went through *pahul* and came to be called Amritdhāri ('bearers of nectar', the baptismal water); (ii) those who kept their hair and beard and were called Keshdhāri (bearers of hair); and (iii) those who affirmed Sikh identity but did not immediately follow the new injunctions, called the Sahajdhāri (bearers of the spontaneous, inner light). The first category also called themselves the Khālsā, or the 'pure' and 'the chosen of God', and were to play a hegemonistic role in the second half of the nineteenth century in defining Sikh identity.

A hundred years after Guru Gobind established the Khālsā, a Jat Sikh chieftain, Ranjit Singh (1780–1839) established the kingdom of Lahore, which did not, however, last long after his death. In the aftermath of the defeat of the Sikhs at the hands of the British in 1846, several reformist movements emerged amongst Sikhs.

Of these, the most notable were the Nirankārī and Nāmdharī (or Kukā) movements. Both were sectarian in character and acknowledged gurus subsequent to Gobind Singh, who had proclaimed closure of the line of personal gurus. The beliefs of these sects were therefore considered violative of the true Khālsā faith by orthodox Sikhs. The Nirankārīs called for a return to the teachings of Guru Nanak who had characterized the divinity as 'formless' (*nirankār*). The Nāmdhāris focused their attention on regenerating the Khālsā as instituted by Guru Gobind. A modernist version of the same effort (namely Khālsā rejuvenation) was the agenda of the so-called Singh Sabhas, which also had a considerable agenda of secular goals. Currently the Nāmdhāris are not very much in the news, but conflicts between the Nirankārīs and the orthodox Khālsā or Akāli Sikhs have resulted in violence and loss of life. The fundamentalist preacher Jarnail Singh Bhindranwale, who later came into conflict with the government on the issue of Sikh grievances, originally appeared in public (in 1978) as a fierce opponent of the Nirankārīs (see Kapur 1986).

From the foregoing account of developments in the long history of Indic religions, it is clear that pluralistic tendencies characterize them all, particularly Hinduism, which lacks a founder or a set of fundamentals of belief and practice or a 'church'. Even so, they share a concern for unity in diversity, or the Absolute transcending its myriad expressions. The notions of dharma and karma are key ideas in the metaphysical foundations of each, but the manner in which they are developed and articulated differs from tradition to tradition. While the relations of Buddhism, Jainism, and Sikhism to Hinduism are too complex to be discussed in a few pages, it is noteworthy that each of the new religions began as reformist movements. Their founders were aiming at the correction of corruptions rather than self-consciously founding new religions. Otherwise, why should the Buddha, for instance, have been concerned about the definition of a true Brahman (see *Dhampadda* Chap. 26)? Broadly speaking, each reformist movement began as a loosening of bonds and moved towards a rupture. Consolidation is the next phase, and then begins the process of internal fission within each tradition. Such pluralism is not, however, without its critics, the best recent example being the emergence of fundamentalism among the Sikhs in the 1970s (see Oberoi 1994, Madan 1997: Chap. 3).

CHRISTIANITY AND ISLAM

Christianity

Of the religions that originated outside India but found a home here, Christianity is the oldest. If tradition is to be believed, it was brought to Kerala by the Apostle St Thomas. Written records testify to the presence of Christians in Malabar from the fourth century onward. There is evidence that the persecution of Persian Christians through most of the fourth century led to the exodus of east Syrian refugees to south India in sufficient numbers to constitute a viable community. They do not seem to have undertaken missionary work immediately: this began in noticeable form from the sixth century and was mostly confined among the ritually clean castes. Further migrations of east Syrians occurred in the eighth and ninth centuries under the leadership of Nestorian prelates. Apparently they did not face any serious opposition from the Malabar rulers and people. Indeed, it is believed that they were accorded a high social status alongside Hindu upper castes. They themselves were divided into two major endogamous groups on the basis of ancestry and domicile (see Atiya 1968: 359–66 and passim). The Thomas Christians are also known as Syrian Christians for, apart from their origins, their liturgy was in Syriac, and they acknowledged the jurisdiction of the Syrian Patriarch of the East in Damascus (Syria). The community has remained confined to Kerala. It subscribes to various fundamentals of the Christian faith—such as Immaculate Conception and the divinity of Jesus—and practice (for example, celebration of the Eucharist: see Visvanathan 1993). One would have mentioned belief in the status of the Bible as revealed scripture, but this is not endorsed by the majority of non-Catholic clergy in India, let alone the laity (Oommen and Mabry 2000: 360–2).

It was only in the mid-sixteenth century that Franciscan missionaries made Goa their base, after it had become a part of the Portuguese colonial empire. They spread out to other parts of south India and Sri Lanka, and even ventured north. The Franciscans were followed by other Catholic groups, including the Dominicans, the Augustinians, and the Jesuits. Jesuit missionaries participated in the religious debates in Agra in the presence of Emperor Akbar (ruled 1556–1605). When they encountered the Thomas Christians, they asked them to sever ties with the Nestorian Church and come under the jurisdiction of Rome. This led to a series of splits among the Syrians: while about half the community complied, the rest resisted, and reaffirmed their loyalty to the Syrian Patriarch of Antioch. When some of those who had relented recanted and returned to Nestorianism, they suffered inhuman torture at the hands of the Inquisition, which had been extended to India on the advice of none other than St Francis Xavier (arrived in Goa in 1542), who is considered one of greatest and gentlest evangelists to have come to Asia (Atiya ibid.: 367). A long-lasting dissension among Thomas Christians and Jesuits was whether missionary activity was to be confined among the upper castes, and whether caste was to be deemed a religious institution and abolished, or only a secular social arrangement and therefore tolerated.

During the high noon of Portuguese power in Asia, the Vatican had played a subsidiary role but came into its own as the former declined. The area of missionary activity was expanded and Indian priests were trained to participate in it. A major event was the arrival of the Italian Jesuit Roberto de Nobili in the city of Madurai in Tamil Nadu in 1606. He focused his attention on Brahmans, from among whom conversions had been rather uncommon, presenting himself as a Roman Brahman who respected their high status, dressed as they did, and even wore the sacred thread. His success as a missionary was considerable and the 'saved souls' were counted in tens of thousands. Others followed, including, in about a hundred years, the Protestants who began their evangelical work in 1706. The range of activities also expanded. Bartholomew Zigenbalg, a Danish missionary, established the first printing press in India (at Tranquebar, Tamil Nadu) in 1712. He published from there a Tamil translation of Martin Luther's *Catechism*. In course of time (eighteenth and nineteenth centuries), other Protestant groups (such as the Anglicans, Lutherans, Methodists, Congregationalists, Baptists and Presbytarians) also came to India to evangelize Indians.

The arrival of the British in India in the mid-eighteenth century initially had no impact on the spread of Christianity as the East India Company, in deference to the wishes of the home government, did not permit missionary activity. It was only in the early nineteenth century that the British parliament removed the restriction and chaplains of the Company began to make converts. The Anglican diocese of Calcutta was founded in 1814. To begin with, Anglican chaplains administered to the spiritual needs of only the

British in India, but an Indian Church also had come into existence by the end of the nineteenth century. A close association of the Church with the state (under the colonial dispensation) was a liability and came to be loosened by the 1930s (see Gibbs 1972). Meanwhile, various Protestant denominations, representing both formal and non-formal societies had sent out missions, producing a plurality of churches and an interflow between congregations. Thus, some Thomas Christians clearly influenced by the theology and liturgical reform of the Protestant mission, especially the Anglicans in Kerala, established the Mar Thoma (Syriac for St Thomas) Church. The majority, however, remained loyal to the Syrian Patriarch, nominally acknowledging his spiritual authority, but otherwise independent. They are known as the members of the Jacobite or Orthodox Church (see Mathew and Thomas 1967).

In 1947, the year of India's independence, the Anglican, Methodist, and other Protestant churches came together to establish the Church of South India. Similar efforts in the north resulted in the establishment of a united Protestant Church, called the Church of North India, in 1970. The predominance of Roman Catholics (nearly 60 per cent) is a noteworthy feature of the Christian communities of India. Also noteworthy has been the search for Indian idioms of expression. Christians of all denominations have retained many of their pre-conversion beliefs, social attitudes, and liturgical practices, incorporating them into Christianity (see Bayly 1989; Robinson 1998). Diversities of pre-conversion origin (from among tribes, castes of varying social status, and different religious and speech communities) are responsible for much internal heterogeneity among them. However, evangelicalism too has remained alive and is indeed a cherished goal. The fundamental right to propagate one's religion, and not merely to profess and practice it, was written into the Indian constitution (Art. 30) to accommodate Christian sentiment on the subject. Whether propagation is for the edification of others or in fact implies the right to convert has been a matter of disagreement. The consensus of opinion is that propagation without conversion is an empty right. Conversions are therefore considered legitimate so long as force and fraud are not employed (see Madan 2003a).

Islam

The third and the youngest member of the family of Abrahamic religions, Islam ('submission to the will of God') is dated back to AD 622, when its promulgator, Prophet Muhammad (571–632) migrated from his native city of Makkah (in Arabia), where he did not receive the support he sought, to Madinah. In the latter city he established the first ever Islamic state. He accommodated resident Jews and Christians in it, as they too were judged to be in possession of books of divinely revealed knowledge and, therefore, entitled to protection.

The fundamentals of religious faith and practice among Muslims ('the submitters') are explicit and universally binding. They must affirm the oneness of God and the status of the Qurān ('the text to be read and recited') as the word of God. Besides, they must believe in god's angels and messengers (of whom Muhammad was the most perfect and therefore the last), and in the Last Day, when God will judge the actions of one and all, and despatch the pious to heaven and the sinners to hell (see Rahman 1979).

Moreover, every true Muslim must recite the creed (*kalimah*, 'the word'), which affirms the oneness of God and the finality of Muhammad's prophethood; say daily prayers (*namāz*) at the appointed times; observe the annual month of fasting by day (*rozah*) to burn away sins; give alms (*zakāt*); and, if circumstances allow it, go in pilgrimage to Makkah (*hajj*) so as to be there on Idul-Azha. (This day, it is generally believed, commemorates the willingness of Ibrahim (Abraham) to sacrifice his son Ismail (Ishmael) on God's command). It is noteworthy that Indian Muslims do not include the waging of war (*jihād*) for the extermination of unbelief and the propagation of Islam among the obligations of a Muslim, as is the case in many Muslim countries.

Islam is, however, more than the foregoing and similar other fundamentals of practice. Everywhere it incorporates much that is local and pre-Islamic, whether this be in the Arab heartlands or in distant places such as India. Students of Islam have commented on this internal tension owing to its character as a world religion that admits of no variation (e.g. the daily prayers are everywhere said in Arabic), and its regional, country, or national characteristics, like, for example, the worship of saints and relics, which is common in India (see, e.g. Khan 1994). It is arguable that the Qurān itself implicitly recognizes the possibility of some degree of internal diversity within the universal *umma* (community of true believers). Chapter 5, verse 3, of the Holy Book, addressed to 'true believers' informs them that Allah has in his mercy perfected their religion, Islam, for them to follow. There is, on the one hand, a paradigm of perfection that obviously admits of no variation. On the other hand, there are the believers who obviously come from diverse geographical, ethnic, linguistic, socio-cultural, and religious backgrounds. It is obviously impossible to completely wipe out these differences.

It is widely believed among South Asian Muslims that Prophet Muhammad had himself wanted to bring the people to India into the universal Islamic community. As Arab traders already had contacts with the western seaboard of India from pre-Islamic days (the Mapillas of Kerala were born of mixed marriages of Arab men and Malayali women), they must have been the first carriers of the new faith to the subcontinent. Islam arrived here as a political force in 712, when Sind was conquered on behalf of the Umayyad caliphate and incorporated in it. With the new rulers came the *ulamā*, their advisers on matters concerning Muslim holy law, the *shariah* (see Ahmad 1964, and Mujeeb 1967).

The numbers of the immigrants were naturally not large, and they were strangers who knew neither the culture, language, and religions (Buddhism and Hinduism were both in existence) of Sind, nor the prevailing system of governance. In the circumstances, local support was necessary, but this in turn entailed a conciliatory attitude towards Indians, which included the assurance that, by and large, there would be few restrictions on non-Islamic religions. In terms of strict Islamic orthodoxy, however, these religions could only be called ignorance (*jahālat*, incorrect belief). The long-term consequence of this initial compromise made for reasons of the state was twofold: firstly, it laid the foundations of multi-religious politics in which Islam and the Indic religions would coexist, much to the chagrin of the guardians of orthodoxy; secondly, it sowed the seeds of an Indian Islam, accommodating Indian cultural traits and forms of social organization (notably caste).

From the time of major incursions of political Islam into India, beginning with the invasions of Mahmud, king of Ghazni, in the early years of the eleventh century, two kinds of religious specialists became prominent. These were the *ulamā*, doctors of *shariah*, and the Sufi mystics in search of direct religious experience. The *ulamā* urged the kings to uphold *shariah* and to be vigilant on behalf of their own religion rather than tolerant of other misguided faiths. One such outstanding medieval scholar, Zia ud-din Barani (c. 1280–1360), was of the opinion that the Muslim kings could not be the refuge of Islam unless they completely destroyed unbelief, polytheism, and idolatory. If the kings cannot actually exterminate the unbelievers (because they are so many), they surely should deny them authority and honour, he advised (see de Bary 1959: 479–81 and passim). Such extremist opinions, however, never became general among the *ulamā* or ascendant in the ruling circles. The *ulamā* actually split into two categories: while some of them confined themselves to their specialized duties and kept aloof from statecraft, others opted for a close relationship with the kings. They supported the actions of the rulers even when these were grounded in statecraft rather than true faith as interpreted by those qualified to do so.

Islam spread throughout the length and breadth of India, less by the episodic coercion and violence of the kings, and more by the generally peaceful efforts of the *ulamā* and Sufis. In areas of mass conversion, notably East Bengal (or what is today Bangladesh) and the Kashmir valley, other factors too, including the ecological and the economic, contributed (directly or indirectly) to the phenomenon (see Eaton 1993). It is noteworthy, however, that at the time of Partition in 1947, after 800 years of Muslim rule, no more than a quarter of all the people of India (400 million) were Muslims. In the Gangetic valley, where Muslims provided enormous support to the demand for Pakistan, fewer than two out of every ten Indians professed Islam.

When Islam reached India, it was already marked by divisions of various kinds. According to Muslim tradition, Prophet Muhammad himself had prophesied that there would be more sects (*firqah*) in Islam than among the children of Isreal, but that they would all be sent to hell by God. Only those who followed the revelation and his words and deeds, and of his closest companions, would be saved (*najiyah*). They came to be called the Sunnī (from *sunnah*, customary way of life) or traditionalists, and account for the great majority of Indian Muslims. Their opponents are the Shiahs ('followers'), who came into being following Muhammad's death as the partisans of Alī the Prophet's cousin and son-in-law, whom they considered the legitimate successor (*khalīfah*) and leader (*imām*). It was not Alī, however, but Muhammad's father-in-law, Abu Bakr, who was chosen, resulting in the Sunnī-Shiah split which even today leads to violence in both India and Pakistan.

Besides the Shiahs, it is the Sufis who are excoriated by the traditionalists. A connection has been sought to be established between the two heterodoxies by claiming Alī as one of the founders of Sufism (*tasawwuf*). According to another view, Arabian philosophy derived from the teaching of al-Ghazali (1058–1111) was absorbed into Islam in the form of a mystical theology, but this locates Sufism late in the fifth century of Islam.

Some scholars, including the renowned early medieval historian al-Biruni (973–1048), found similarities between some key ideas of Sufism and the Brahmanical philosophy of Yoga or the magical Tāntra. Indeed, it has been suggested that Abu Yazid Tayfur of Iran (d. 874), a key figure in the development of Sufism, may have learnt the principles of Brahmanical and Buddhist mysticism from Abu Ali of Sind who himself may have been a convert to Islam. Be that as it may, two general observations can be made. First, a considerable number of Indic elements are recognizable in Sufism in India, but only some of these are pure borrowings, the others being adaptations of classical Islamic Sufi ideas in the Indian cultural environment. Secondly, Sunnī orthodoxy has always frowned upon both Shiahs and Sufis (see Rizvi 1978, 1982).

Four major worldwide Sufi orders—namely Chishtī, Naqshbandī, Qādirī, and Suhrawardī—are present in India. Besides, there are numerous local orders of seekers, faqirs and darveshs: while some of them are seriously devout, the devotion to higher spiritual goals among others, who are often given to excesses of various kinds, including drug abuse, is highly suspect. Among the former, mention may be made of the Rishī order of the Kashmir valley (see Khan 1994).

Islam was brought to Kashmir, it is generally believed, by the Kubrawī Sufi Sayyid Ali Hamadani late in the fourteenth century, but his efforts seem to have been confined to a small group of neo-converts in the city of Srinagar including the sultan. It was Shaikh Nuruddin (AD 1379–1442), the founder of the Rishī order, who carried the new faith to the masses. His success owed much, not only to his amiable disposition and peaceful methods of preaching, but also to his familiarity with and adaptation of prevailing Brahmanical religious ideas and practices (Kashmir Shaivism). His choice of the name Rishī (a Sanskrit word meaning 'seer') for his order is itself revelatory. He adopted vegetarianism for himself and his followers out of his compassion for animals, and thus abjured the universal Muslim practice of animal sacrifice.

While some historians have written of two types of Sufism in Kashmir, the immigrant and the native, or the classical and the folk, others have denied the existence of this dichotomy, pointing out that Sufīs of the Suhrawardi order, and even the Kubrawis, befriended and eulogized the Rishīs. According to the latter, the very rootedness of the Rishīs in Kashmir's old religious traditions, combined with their exposure to the ideas of classical Sufism, made them ideal agents for Islamization of the Kashmiri masses. It is noteworthy that Nuruddin claimed the Prophet of Islam himself as the real founder of his order, locating himself in shariah, the 'highway' of Islam.

It is not the Sufīs alone who have contributed to the culture of religious diversity in Indian Islam. The reputedly more stringent ulamā too have done so. Thus, in the late nineteenth century three groups of these doctors of the holy law of Islam led sectarian movements differentiated from one another by major issues (such as matters of belief and law) as well as minor (including minutiae of everyday life). The most influential of these were the ulamā of a famous seminary called the Darul Uloom at Deoband in north India (founded in 1867) (see Metcalf 1982). Their educational programme too was grounded in the traditional curriculum and thus opposed to the innovations and accommodations of western science that characterized the efforts of the modernists at the Mohammadan Anglo-Oriental College in Aligarh (founded in 1874).

Besides the Deobandis, the two other prominent reformist groups were the Ahl-i-Hadīs ('people of the tradition') and the ulamā of Bareilly popularly known as the Barelwis, who were opposed to both the other groups. In their disputations, one or the other of the four recognized schools of Islamic Law (Hanafī, Malikī, Shafiī, Hanbalī) were invoked, but the Hanafī school has always been the dominant in India (see Fyzee 1955).

Finally, mention must be made of the Ahmadiyah sect which was formally proclaimed to be heretical, and therefore a non-Muslim minority, in Pakistan in 1974. Its founder, Mirza Ghulam Ahmad (1839–1908) was born in

Qadiyan, a village in north Punjab. Not trained as a Sufi, he was a law clerk by occupation. He also claimed to be the recipient of divine revelation and therefore the messiah (*mahdī*) promised to the Muslims. Although Ahmad did not dispute the Islamic belief in the closure of prophecy with Prophet Muhammad, he asserted that he belonged to a line of secondary prophets. Provoked and influenced by the work of Christian missionaries and the activities of the Hindu revivalist Arya Samaj movement, he organized his response on similar lines, and gathered a considerable following. The sect called Ahmadiyah, or Qadiyani, continues to be recognized as Muslim in India reflecting a general attitude of tolerance rather than stern disapproval of diversity within the Islamic faith as well as among different faiths (see Friedman 2002).

RELIGIOUS PLURALISM AS IDEOLOGY

In the previous three sections we described the diversity or plurality of religions in India at two levels. These were, first, the global level, at which the major religions of India were in focus, and, second, the intra-religious level, at which sectarian or quasi-sectarian movements operate. We have seen that a native distinction between pluralist Indic religions and homogeneous (fundamentalist) Indian religions of foreign origin is wholly misleading. It is obvious that, whenever a religious community comprises many regional cultural groups, and also has considerable numbers, running into millions, internal plurality becomes inescapable. However, whatever is present empirically may yet be denied or deprecated ideologically. The question then is, has the long history of religious diversity in India produced serious arguments supporting and justifying the phenomenon? In other words, has plurality generated pluralism? (see Coward 1987).

Contemporary ideologues of secularism, understood as religious pluralism, speaking on behalf of or within the Hindu tradition, often claim that pluralism is as old as the oldest veda. It is recalled that the *Rig Veda* (I. 164.46) proclaims that 'the Absolute is one, although the sages have given it different names'. The oneness of the Absolute is the primary assertion here, but the fact that the wise sages choose to state it variously must imply worthiness of pluralism. This pluralism is, however, internal to the vedic tradition. It is silent on interreligious pluralism. Similarly, it is pointed out that the *Manusmriti* (ii.14) resolved the problem of conflict between contradictory revelations by laying down that they are all valid and must therefore be respected. Although revelation (*shruti*) enshrined in the vedas and other sacred texts is respected, it does not follow that it is widely known among Hindus, like, perhaps, the Bible is among Christians or the Quran among Muslims. In the absence of a single core text—the *Bhagavad Gita* has come to acquire such a position in relatively modern times—or a single founder, or a set of irrefutable fundamentals, or the practice of conversion from other religions, it is not surprising that the Hindu religious tradition has from its earliest beginnings been marked by pluralist tendencies. These have been in consonance with the cellular social organization based on the institution of caste and are essentially hierarchical in character (see Madan 1997).

A further observation is relevant. The making of the so-called Hindu tradition has been a gradual process of fusion. It has been documented by historians how the carriers of the Brahmanical tradition, as they travelled east and south, established their hegemonic position through give-and-take (propagation and accommodation) (see Chakrabarti 2001). Cultural anthropologists engaged in fieldwork in the 1950s wrote about the processes of parochialization (the downward flow and spread of elements of the Great Sanskritic Tradition) and universalization (the upward rise and spread of elements of the Little Folk Traditions) (see Marriott 1955). The homogenizing tendencies never had free rein and diversities have remained resilient and a distinguishing feature of later Hinduism (see Marriott 1976). In short, pluralism is said to be inherent in Hinduism in relation to its internal structure.

Such pluralism as is present operates within the Hindu tradition and is only derivatively applied to other religious traditions. Hinduism tolerates difference by incorporating and hierarchizing it: Buddhism, Jainism, and Sikhism are all considered inferior varieties of Hinduism. Moreover, conflict has not been altogether absent, as the record of the persecution of Buddhists and Jains by various Hindu groups, or of inter-sectarian conflicts between, say, the Shaivas and the Vaishnavas, shows. One can say, however, that the traditional Brahmanical notion of the legitimacy of the right of a group to its own way of life (*svadharma; adhikāra bheda*), without conceding that the different ways are of equal merit, is a form of pluralism.

In modern times, the Bengali mystic, Ramakrishna (1836–86) and his renowned disciple Vivekananda (1863–1902) are credited with promoting the ideology of religious pluralism by word and deed. Ramakrishna was no intellectual, but in his quest for spiritual experience he practised a simplified Islamic life for some time, withdrawing completely from his Brahmanical observances. He also disregarded sectarian differences among Hindus (see Sarkar 1993). Vivekanada formulated an ideology of pluralism, but it was based on tolerance of other religions rather than their acceptance as being equal to Hinduism. Indeed, within Hinduism itself, he raised Vedanta above all other creeds, calling it the mother of all religions and truer than any other religion. He was explicitly critical of Buddhism and Christiantiy. The ultimate goal of the Ramakrishna Mission, which he established, was the spiritual conquest of humanity (see Basu 2002). Often referred to as neo-Hinduism, this late nineteenth century development was a reversal of traditional internal pluralism, which was wide in range, and accompanied by such a diversity of belief and practice, that some Western scholars writing from the perspective of biblical religion, doubted if Hinduism could be called a religion at all (see Weber 1958: 23). In its place, an inter-religious pluralism, but within a hierarchical framework, was sought to be put in place. Both innovations had clear political implications: the forging of a national consciousness in the context of colonial subjugation, on the one hand, and the projection of Hinduism as a tolerant, universal religion, ready to provide spiritual leadership to the followers of all faiths, on the other.

While Bengal witnessed these developments, Punjab was the scene for the flowering of the Āryā Samāj movement, founded by Dayananda (1824–83) in Bombay in 1874. He not only rejected post-vedic forms of Hinduism as erroneous, and condemned what he called 'blind faith' (e.g. idol worship) and 'harmful customs' (e.g. practice of caste and gender discrimination), but also denied that Christiantiy and Islam could be considered divinely inspired religions. He made derogatory observations about them as well as Buddhism, Jainism, and Sikhism. The teachings of the Āryā Samāj represent the exclusivist strand of vedic Hinduism, and anticipate later, explicitly fundamentalist, developments (notably the thesis of Hindutva, or Hindu identity) and militate against pluralism as an ideology.

In the twentieth century, Mahatma Gandhi (1869–1948) put forward the most explicit formulation of religious pluralism when he announced on 30 May 1913 that, in his opinion, 'the world as a whole will never have, *and need not have* a single religion' (emphasis added). By acknowledging his indebtedness to Christianity and Islam, Gandhi implied that Hinduism could be enriched by incorporating in it some of the truths discovered by other religions. While he maintained that all religions were equally true, he added that, because of the limitations of human intellect, they were also equally imperfect. He refused to hierarchize the relationship between different religions, and thus moved in the direction of a genuine religious pluralism.

Writing in *Young India* in 1920 (11 August), Gandhi conceded that his critics were often right from their perspective in considering his ideas and actions wrong, while he was, from his own point of view, sure that he was right. Expressing his admiration for the Jain doctrine of 'many-sidedness' (*anekantavād*), he wrote: 'It is this doctrine that taught me to judge a Mussalman from his own standpoint and a Christian from his.'

According to Jain ontology, whatever exists has three aspects: substance (*dravya*), quality (*guna*), and mode of expression (*paryāya*). Substance is not matter, for even the soul is considered a substance. *Dravya* is the means through which qualities exist. These qualities are numerous and their modes are infinite. Therefore, no ordinary person can perceive the existent in its entirety or 'many-sidedness' (see Jaini 1979: 90–1). Hence the epistemology of *anekāntavād* or manifold aspects of reality. This doctrine has certain consequences, a notable one being conditional assertion (*syādavāda*). Absolute, that is unqualified, statements about existential reality cannot be made. Four specifications are required. These are: the specific being (*sva-dravya*), location (*sva-kshetra*), time (*sva-kāla*), and state of being (*sva-bhāva*) of the reality under reference (ibid.: 94ff.).

Buddhist pluralism is even wider in its scope, and nothing is expressed in unities. The four noble truths are at the very core of the Buddha's teaching. The first of these truths, namely the universality of suffering has many causes, notably worldly attachments (the second truth). The way to ending both (suffering, attachment) lies through the eightfold noble path (the fourth truth), which brings release (*nibanna*) (the third truth), of which there are at least two modes. For the laity, there are three refuges the Buddha, the Law (*dhamma*), and the community (*sangha*). According to Mahāyāna metaphysics, even the Buddhas are many.

Doctrines of ontological and epistemological pluralism within Jainism and Buddhism do not, however, translate into intersectarian toleration. The original teaching of the Buddha came to be regarded, as already noted above, as the lesser vehicle (Hinayāna) by the later Mahāyānists who virtually drove it out to Sri Lanka. Jain sects too are characterized by mutual exclusiveness.

Islam is, as we have seen, the second major religion of India. Except in Indonesia and Bangladesh, there are more Muslims in India today than in any other country. The attitudes of Muslims to the phenomenon of religious plurality are, therefore, of great importance for the future of the ideology of pluralism. Given the fundamental Muslim belief that Islam is the most perfect of all divinely revealed religions, and that the Qurān is the World of God, any attempt to project pluralism has to honour these beliefs. A careful reader of the holy book of Islam will find many passages on which an ideology of religious pluralism can be based. To give but one example: 'To you your religion and to me mine' (109.3), although this is often said to be applicable only to peoples with a revealed book.

In the mid-seventeenth century, Dara Shikoh, heir to the Mughal throne, disciple of a Sufi master and a Sanskrit scholar, made a close study of the Upanishads and even translated some of them into Persian. He concluded that they were revealed scriptures, anticipating the divine message of monotheism elaborated in the Qurān. He described Vedantic Hinduism and Islam as 'twin brothers': for this he was declared a heretic by the ulamā, and beheaded on the orders of his brother, Emperor Aurangzeb, who had usurped the succession.

In the twentieth century, the most elaborate effort to argue for religious pluralism on the basis of the Qurān itself was made by Maulana Abul Kalam

Azad (1888–1958), a profound scholar of religion and distinguished political leader. His many-stranded argument focused on, among other issues, the attributes of God and the true nature of divine revelation. He maintained that the manner in which 'divine providence' (*rububiyat*), 'divine benevolence' (*rahmat*), and 'divine justice' (*adālat*) are defined in the Qurān, it is obvious that Allah is God of all creation, and that the oneness of humanity is derived from the oneness of God. As for divine revelation, for it to be itself, it must provide guidance to everyone without distinction. Like Dara Shikoh, he detected significant common truths and insights in Islam and Vedantic Hinduism on the foregoing and other key issues. His effort, in the form of an exegesis of the Qurān, ran into difficulties with the ulamā who detected in it many serious flaws, including an alleged devaluation of the intermediary role of the Prophet and of the importance of formal prayer. In the event, Azad never brought his monumental undertaking to its conclusion (see Azad 1962).

Pluralism, as an ideological stance within the Hindu and Indian Muslim religious traditions, recognizes and respects plurality, but stresses the oneness of the ultimate goal of different expressions of the religious quest. It is an invitation to coexistence, dialogue, and even syncretism. Religious devotionalism (*bhakti*) of the medieval period in northern India, expressed through 'the voice of the seekers of the truth' (*sant vānī*), was echoed by the ecstatic mysticism of the Sufis. Nanak, the first Sikh guru, was a unique representative of the *sant* tradition. He sought emancipation from all external formalisms (rituals, customs, social distinctions) through a valorization of the inner spiritual quest. He dismissed the meaningfulness of the prevailing religious distinctions. More than a reconciliation or synthesis, his teaching presented a transcendent third path. The last of the Sikh personal gurus, Gobind, also declared that the true Sikhs or the Khālsā ('the pure' or 'the chosen') would have to be different from both Hindus and Muslims in physical appearance (unshorn and uncircumcized) as well as moral fibre (expressed through a code of conduct beginning with formal initiation or *pahul*). He too pointed to a higher path transcending not only the divide between Hinduism and Islam, but also the inner polarities of the former (e.g. domesticity versus renunciation). Like the Hindu and Indian Muslim perspectives on religious pluralism, the Sikh vision too is hierarchical. Moreover, as we move from Guru Nanak to the tenth and last personal guru, Gobind, there is an explicit tightening of the definition of Sikh identity, differentiating it from the Hindu identity and homogenizing it internally. In this context, the drawing up of the codes of conduct, *rahitnāmas* (see McLeod 1989) for the Khālsā is a significant development. For Sikhs generally, the only true source of spiritual knowledge is the *gurubānī*, the word of the Guru, as present above all in the Guru Granth Sahab. Those born to other religious traditions are welcome to embrace the Sikh faith and identity (hence the *gora* Sikhs of North America), but a Sikh who is lax in the observance of the Sikh way of life or, worse, follows the practices of other traditions is a lapsed or fallen (*patit*) individual. In short, the Sikh faith in its Khālsā version is exclusivist not pluralist. The Bhindranwale phenomenon showed that a fundamentalist turn too was possible (see Madan 1997: Chap. 3).

Within Christianity too, the theological trends of ecumenism and pluralism have been gaining ground worldwide. The efforts of scholars such as Raimundo Panikkar (1981), who is equally well conversant with the Brahmanical and the Christian traditions, to move from an exclusivist towards an inclusivist theological model of relating to non-Christian faith traditions are noteworthy. Moreover, a theo-centric conception of salvation, in place of a Christo-centric one, which also has a growing appeal among Christians everywhere, is bound to strengthen the pluralist orientation. These developments should obviously be of great interest to all liberal-minded persons and not to religious people alone.

The task of developing a well-argued ideology of religious pluralism on the basis of the religions of India awaits serious and competent attention. The emergence of state-sponsored religious pluralism, summed up in the slogan *sarva dharma samabhāva* (equal respect for all religions), and presented as Indian (in contrast to Western) secularism, does not go very far in strengthening inter-religious understanding and appreciation (see Smith 1963 and Madan 1997). These values are more profound than a working strategy of passive tolerance, and will have to be promoted by men and women of faith themselves. As Gandhi pointed out, the task of the secular state is to leave matters of religion to the people.

Contrary to the assumption of many modernists that religious faith is necessarily exclusive and therefore results in communal conflict, there is considerable historical and ethnographical evidence that the common people of India, irrespective of individual religious identity, have long been comfortable with religious plurality. They acknowledge religious difference as the experienced reality: they do not consider it good or bad. In other words, social harmony, or agreement, is built on the basis of difference.

The traditional élite of the nineteenth century were familiar with this folk pluralism, but considered it as no more than the ignorance of unlettered masses. Today's modernist intelligentsia have opted for the ideology of secularism. In its extreme version, it seeks to drive religion into the privacy of people's lives, if not altogether eliminate it. More generally and eclectically, secularism in India stands for mutual respect among the followers of different religions and a non-discriminatory state. This ideology envisages a pluralism that is a concomitant of structural differentiation in society. Needless to emphasize, the two pluralisms—the people's and the intellectual's—are different in several crucial respects. For example, and most notably, the former is wholly spontaneous—the lived social reality—but the latter is ideological, and in that sense self-conscious or constructed; the former is based on a positive attitude towards religion, but the latter is sceptical. Indeed, there is a hiatus between the two pluralisms, but this has not been so far examined with the seriousness it deserves (see Madan 1997).*

REFERENCES

Ahmad Aziz.
1964 *Studies in Islamic culture in the Indian environment.* Oxford: Clarendon Press.
Atiya, Aziz S.
1968 *A history of Eastern Christianity.* London: Methuen.
Azad, Abul Kalam.
1962 *The Tarjuman al-Quran.* Vol. 1. Ed. and trs. by Syed Abdul Latif. Bombay: Asia.
Babb, Lawrence A.
1996 *Absent Lord: Ascetics and kings in Jain ritual culture.* Berkeley: University of California Press.
Baird, Robert D., ed.
1995 *Religion in modern India.* New Delhi: Manohar.
Basu, Shamita.
2002 *Religious revivalism as nationalist discourse.* New Delhi: Oxford University Press.
Bayly, Susan.
1989 *Saints, goddesses and kings: Muslims and Christians in south Indian society.* Cambridge: Cambridge University Press.
Brockington, J.L.
1992 *The sacred thread: A short history of Hinduism.* Delhi: Oxford University Press.
Bhattacharji, Sukumari.
1988 *The Indian theogony.* Delhi: Motilal Banarsidass.
Census of India.
1995 *Census of India 1991*, Series I, India Paper 1 of 1995: Religion. New Delhi: Government of India.
Chakrabarti, Kunal.
2001 *Religious process : The puranas and the making of a religious tradition.* New Delhi: Oxford University Press.
Coward, Howard G., ed.
1987 *Modern India's responses to religious pluralism.* Albany: State University of New York Press.
de Bary, Wm. T., gen. ed.
1958 *Sources of Indian tradition.* New York: Columbia University Press.
Dimmit, Cornelia and J.A.B. van Buitenen, eds. & trans.
1978 *Classical Hindu mythology.* Philadelphia: Temple University Press.
Doniger, Wendy (with Brian K. Smith), trans.
1991 *The laws of Manu.* New Delhi: Penguin Books.
Dundas, Paul
1992 *The Jains.* London: Routledge.

*This is an expanded and corrected version of an earlier article on the subject (Madan 2003b). I would like to thank Professor T.K. Oommen and OUP's anonymous referee for helpful advice.

Durkheim, Èmile.
1995 *The elementary forms of religious life*. Trans. Karen E. Fields. New York: The Free Press.

Eaton, Richard.
1993 *The rise of Islam and the Bengal frontier, 1204–1760*. Berkeley: University of California Press.

Flood, Gavin.
1996 *An introduction to Hinduism*. Cambridge: Cambridge University Press.

Friedman, Yohannes.
2002 *Aspects of Ahmadi religious thought and its medieval background*. New Delhi: Oxford University Press.

Fuller, C.J.
1992 *The camphor flame: Popular Hinduism and society in India*. Princeton N.J.: Princeton University Press.

Fyzee, A.A.A.
1955 *Outlines of Mohammedan law*. Bombay: Oxford University Press.

Gibbs, M.E.
1972 *The Anglican Church in India, 1600–1970*. Delhi: ISPCK.

Gold, Ann Grodzins.
1988 *Fruitful journeys: The ways of Rajasthani pilgrims*. Berkeley: University of California Press.

Gombridge, Richard.
1988 *Theravada Buddhism*. London: Routledge.

Gottschalk, Peter.
2001 *Beyond Hindu and Muslim: Multiple identity in narratives from village India*. New Delhi: Oxford University Press.

Grewal, J.S.
1990 *The Sikhs of the Punjab*. Cambridge: Cambridge University Press.

Halbfass, Wihelm.
1988 *India and Europe: An essay in understanding*. Albany: State University of New York Press.

Harvey, Peter.
1990 *An introduction to Buddhism: Teaching, history and practices*. Cambridge: Cambrdige University Press.

Hawley, John Stratton and Donna Marie Wulff, eds.
1996 *Devi: Goddesses of India*. Berkeley: University of California Press.

Hiriyana, M.
1993 *Outlines of Indian philosophy*. Delhi: Motilal Banarsidass.

Ilaiah, Kancha.
1996 *Why I am not a Hindu*. Calcutta: Samya.

Jaini, Padmanabh S.
1976 *The Jain path of purification*. Delhi: Motilal Banarsidass.

Jones, Kenneth, W.
1989 *Socio–religious reform movements in British India*. Cambridge: Cambridge University Press.

Kapur, Rajiv.
1986 *Sikh separatism: The politics of faith*. London: Allen & Unwin.

Khan, Muhammad Ishaq.
1994 *Kashmir's transition to Islam: The role of Muslim rishis*. New Delhi: Manohar.

Kosambi, D.D.
1970 *The Culture and civilization of ancient India in historical outline*. New Delhi: Vikas.
Laidlaw, James.
1995 *Riches and renunciation: Religion, economy and society among the Jains*. Oxford: Clarendon Press.
Larson, Gerald James.
1995 *India's agony over religion*. Albany: State University of New York Press.
Lingat, Robert.
1973 *The classical law of India*. Berkeley: The University of California Press.
Lorenzen, D.N.
1972 *The Kapalikas and Kalamukhas: Two lost Shaivite sects*. New Delhi: Manohar.
Madan, T.N.
1997 *Modern myths, locked minds: Secularism and fundamentalism in India*. Delhi: Oxford University Press.
2003a Freedom of religion. *Economic and Political Weekly*, 15 March: 1034–41.
2003b Religions of India: Plurality and pluralism. In Veena Das, ed. *The Oxford India companion to sociology and social anthropology*. New Delhi: Oxford University Press.
Marglin, Frederique Apffel.
1985 *Wives of the god-king: The rituals of the Devadasis of Puri*. Delhi: Oxford University Press.
Marriott, McKim.
1955 Little communities in an indigenous civilization. In M. Marriott, ed., *Village India*. Chicago: University of Chicago Press.
1976 Hindu transactions: Diversity without dualism. In B. Kapferer, ed., *Transaction and meaning*. Philadelphia: Institute for the Study of Human issues.
Mathew, C.P. and M.M. Thomas.
1967 *The Indian churches of Saint Thomas*. Delhi: ISPCK.
Metcalf, Barbara Daly.
1982 *Islamic revival in British India: Deoband 1860–1900*. Princeton N.J.: Princeton University Press.
McLeod, W.H.
1968 *Guru Nanak and the Sikh religion*. Delhi: Oxford University Press.
1989 *Who is a Sikh?* Oxford: Clarendon Press.
Mujeeb, Muhammad.
1967 *The Indian Muslims*. London: Allen & Unwin.
Oberoi, Harjot S.
1994 *The construction of religious boundaries: Culture, identity and diversity in the Sikh tradition*. New Delhi: Oxford University Press.
Olivelle, Patrick.
1998 *The early Upanishads*. New York: Oxford University Press.
2000 *Dharmasutras: The law codes of Apastamba, Gautama, Baudhayana, and Vasishtha*. Delhi: Motilal Banarsidass.
Oommen, T.K. and H.P. Mabry
2000 *The Christian clergy in India*. Vol. 1. *Social structure and social roles*. New Delhi: Sage.
Panikkar, Raimundo.
1981 *The unknown Christ of Hinduism*. Rev. ed., New York: Orbis.

Parpola, A.
1994 *Deciphering the Indus script*. Cambridge: Cambridge University Press.
Possehl, Gregory L., ed.
1982 *Harappan civilization*. New Delhi: Oxford & IBH.
Roy, Asim.
1983 *The Islamic syncretistic tradition in Bengal*. Princeton N.J.: Princeton University Press.
Radhakrishnan, S.
1927 *The Hindu view of life*. London: Allen & Unwin.
Rahman, Fazlur.
1979 *Islam*. Second edition. Chicago: The University of Chicago Press.
Ramanujan, A.K.
1973 *Speaking of Siva*. Baltimore: Penguin Press.
1981 *Hymns for the drowning: Poems for Visnu by Nammalvar*. Princeton N.J.: Princeton University Press.
Ratnagar, Shereen.
2000 *The end of the great Harappan tradition*. New Delhi: Mahohar.
Rizvi, Saiyid Athar Abbas.
1978, 1982 *A history of sufism in India*. Vols. 1 & 2. Delhi: Munshiram Manoharlal.
Robinson, Rowena.
1998 *Conversion, continuity and change: Lived Christianity in southern Goa*. New Delhi: Sage.
Sarkar, Sumit.
1993 *An exploration of the Ramakrishna–Vivekananda tradition*. Shimla: Indian Institute of Advance Study.
Smith, Donald Engene.
1963 *India as a secular state*. Bombay: Oxford University Press.
Thapar, Romila.
1966 *A history of India*. Vol . One. Harmondsworth: Penguin.
2002 *Early India: From the origins to AD 1300*. London: Allen Lane.
Uberoi, J.P.S.
1996 *Religion, civil society and the state: A study of Sikhism*. Delhi: Oxford University Press.
Visvanathan, Susan.
1993 *The Christians of Kerala: History, belief and ritual among the Yakoba*. Delhi: Oxford University Press.
Weber, Max.
1958 *The religion of India: The sociology of Hinduism and Buddhism*. Glencoe, III.: Free Press.
Zelliot, Eleanor.
1996 *From Untouchable to Dalit*. New Delhi: Manohar.

PART
one

Setting Apart: Sacred Places and Performances

PREFATORY REMARKS

As already stated in the Preface, I have chosen the notion of the sacred, or sacredness, to open the present collection of readings about aspects of India's religions. The choice may seem arbitrary, but it is not misleading, for a considerable body of sociological and social anthropological writing on religion has been fruitfully constructed around this key concept. In his seminal and by now classic formulation, Emile Durkheim (1995) presented as the defining characteristic of religious life the observation that, while religion as a cultural universal is social in origin, a product of intense collective experiences, yet everywhere it stands apart from mundane, routinized, everyday life. Its location is in 'an ideal and transcendental mileu'. It is not therefore wholly accessible to the believers, whether as individuals or as a community, through empirical experience. For the sociologist, however, religious phenomena are externally observable as social facts that have coercive power and significant consequences, first and foremost among them being the preservation of social solidarity.

From the Durkheimian perspective, then, the sacred appears as a complex of beliefs and practices relative to beings, events, and objects that are set apart, in a sense even forbidden. It is present in all cultural settings, always and everywhere, in opposition to the profane: 'while the forms of the contrast are variable, the fact of it is universal' (Durkheim 1995: 36). This dichotomization is regarded as 'the distinctive trait of religious thought'. This does not mean that the two domains are unrelated or that the otherness of the sacred is absolute. Suffice it to note here that, as both Durkheim and Max Weber (1964), maintained, the sacred bestows legitimacy and meaning on the secular pursuits of everyday life. It is the source of moral values that sustain the social order, and also provides the basis for the evaluation of human actions as to their social function and intrinsic worth. 'Thus there is something eternal in religion that is destined to outlive the succession of particular symbols in which religious thought has clothed itself' (Durkheim 1995: 429).

The sacred is a multi-dimensional *and* holistic concept. It includes dogmas, myths, rituals, and ceremonies. People, places, and performances are imbued with the quality of the sacred. The sacred complex as an indivisible entity is well illustrated in the first reading in this section.

Susan Visvanathan writes about 'the core of worship' among a community of believers, namely the Syrian Christians of Kerala in south India. This consists of the service of the Eucharist 'as if it were a model of the life of Christ'. It is the dramatic replication of something that is believed to have happened two thousand years ago and is crucial to the Christian faith. A dramatic enactment needs a stage, a sacred event, a sacred space. This is of course provided by the neighbourhood church no less than a large cathedral. It also requires a text, and this is of course in the scripture but also in the community tradition. And it needs actors: these are the priests and members of the church. The Eucharistic liturgy has a conceptual and sequential (event) structure. Myth and rite are interrelated in and through the worship. Conceptually, the symbolism of sacrifice and thanksgiving lie at the very heart of the Eucharist. The service on any particular occasion consists of about fifteen steps, beginning with prefatory prayers and ending with thanksgiving and dispersal.

Religious life anywhere is hard to confine to particular places and times, although its 'effervescence' (to use a Durkheimian key term) is indeed more intense on particular occasions. Visvanathan's account brings out clearly how the Eucharistic celebration spills out of the church into the neighbourhood and individual homes. A critical element in this linkage is the communal eating of sacred food. This is not a profane act but a sacrament, and as such it has a moral significance. Through a series of spiritual and material gifts the quality of the spiritual life of the individual believer, the vigour of the institution of the church, and the social solidarity of the community are all maintained and enhanced.

The importance of the symbolism of food in religious as well as secular life is manifest in virtually all cultural settings. It is marked by an immense variety of expressions. This is well illustrated by R.S. Khare's detailed analysis of the sacred complex of food among selected Hindu castes in Uttar Pradesh in north India, presented in the second reading. His focus is on what he calls 'the food area', which is an area centred in the hearth and set apart from other parts of the home. It is internally differentiated and includes the domestic spaces where food is stored, cooked, and eaten, and where cooking and eating utensils are cleaned and then stored until further use. The data come from the homes of upper, 'twice-born', castes (Brahmans, Thakurs, Kayasths) and of some lower castes who enter into regular servicing relationships with the former. Both urban and rural households were studied. Khare points out that the system of culinary and commensal relations of upper castes has influenced the hearths and homes of the other castes.

The food area, Khare shows, is not merely a complex spatial category, but also a social and a moral space, where concrete inter-personal relations are worked out, and abstract ideas about ritual purity and pollution, and the physical and subtle qualities of food items, find expression. The food area is a convenient starting place for the study of the sacred complex of 'food cycles' under everyday and ceremonial conditions. One may, as a student of social life, choose any point of entry into the analytically isolable religious domain, its internal configuration eventually leading to a discovery of its interconnections with other domains. More about this in Part Six.

Visvanathan and Khare show how homes, hearths, places of worship, and neighbourhoods as social spaces may partake of the attributes of the sacred. This is also true of other social spaces, most notably of places of pilgrimage. These may be distant caves and river sources in the hills, confluences of rivers in the plains, or large bustling cities, such as Kashi in north India. Sacred spaces are often associated with life-cycle rituals, including death, as in Kashi.

Jonathan Parry's account of death and cosmogony in Kashi (the third reading in this section), illustrates the interrelationship of sacred space, sacred time, and sacred performance as phenomena set apart from the secular domain. Mythology (the close association of Kashi with the god Shiva) and metaphysics (e.g. the notions of *karman*, *samsara*, *purushartha*, or the four goals of the good life, and *moksha*) are invoked by the devotees of Kashi (including some of its citizens) to enlarge upon the sacred character of the city. It is indeed a city worthy of religious devotion, even as a divinity or its iconic representation is. Pilgrims circumambulate the city, as they would for instance a temple, taking five days to complete the fifty mile journey, with due ritual observance and solemnity.

In the eyes of the believers, Kashi does indeed stand apart from and is superior to the rest of profane space. Moreover, it includes within itself all other sacred centres of pilgrimage. Having come here one may be truly deemed to have been everywhere. Kashi is indeed the cosmos, but it is also identified with the human body, which too is in a variety of senses sacred; ultimately, after death, and after the impurities and sins attached to it are washed off in the holy waters of the Ganga (on whose western bank the city exists), it is a worthy sacrificial object. What makes Kashi a coveted place for the orthodox Hindu is that death within a certain area of the city is believed to grant liberation from transmigration (*samsara*). Death in Kashi is liberation (*moksha*) from the bondage of life, the ultimate *purushartha* that even today beckons millions of Hindus.

The readings in this first part of *India's Religions*, by Visvanathan, Khare, and Parry, show that sacred spaces as the sites for sacred performances and events are the ground, as it were, on which people everywhere and everywhen (to borrow a term from W.E.H. Stanner's studies of Australian aboriginal religion) have erected the edifices of their religious life.

REFERENCES

Durkheim, Emile.
1995 *The elementary forms of religious life*. Trs. by Karen E. Fields. New York: The Free
    Press.
Weber, Max.
1964 *The sociology of religion*. Boston: Beacon Press.

The Eucharist in a Syrian Christian Church

Susan Visvanathan

THE EUCHARISTIC LITURGY AND RITE[1]

The Eucharistic liturgy of the Syrian Christians of Puthenangadi [a neighbourhood in the town of Kottayam in Kerala] derives from the Liturgy of St James, which is apostolic in origin. This liturgy incorporates within it the body of religious knowledge that every practising Christian must possess, implicitly carrying the doctrines of Christianity regarding the notions of the Trinity, the Incarnation, Redemption, the place of Mary and the saints. The main elements of Eucharistic worship are:

    I The opening or prefatory prayers including censing and the Trisagion
    II The deacon's prayer preceding the apostolic reading
    III The reading of the Epistle by the deacon
    IV The gospel as read by the priest
    V The censing
    VI The creed
    VII The Kiss of Peace
    VIII The Invocation of the Holy Spirit

[1][The following account is based on the author's fieldwork and two textual sources: (i) *The Divine Liturgy of St James, according to the Rite of the Orthodox Syrian Church of Antioch* (abbreviated here as DL); (ii) *Qurbanakramam* (1981), the Service Book of the Holy Qurbana (QM). For further details, see the list of references.—Ed.]

Excerpted from Susan Visvanathan, The Eucharist and the person of Christ. In *The Christians of Kerala: History, belief and ritual among the Yakoba*, Madras: Oxford University Press, 1993. Chapter 5. © Oxford University Press.

My description begins by viewing the space of the church as the stage on which the Eucharistic rite is enacted. As the believers enter the church, they leave their footwear outside: 'In reverence will I enter Thy house and offer my prayers' (QM). Prefatory prayers and the Trisagion ('that God is thrice holy') follow. The Lord's Prayer is recited, as also a prayer to the Virgin Mary. The chancel is then unveiled and heaven revealed to the people. The *namaskaram* or prefatory prayers serve to prepare the laity for the moment of revelation. At this time, they are between *bhumilokam* (earth) and *akasam* (sky).

The priest enters the chancel to offer the *Qurbana*. He asks for leave to perform the sacrifice in Syriac-Aramaic: *Barekmore All Shub'kono* (Bless my Lord, for leave). Without divine grace, the sacrifice or Qurbana has no effect. The priest is, with the laity, human, and while in office, he is their leader. The chancel is again veiled so that the priest may prepare himself for the Eucharist. The deacons enter, and after asking for blessings while assisting in the sacrifice, one of them lights the candles. The priest places the objects to be used in the Qurbana on the altar. The *paten* (a shallow dish) cover, the sponge, and the spoon are placed on the celebrant's right. He places the chalice cover, the *sosafa* (a veil), and the cup for ritual ablutions on the left-hand side of the altar. The priest places the Host (the bread that is blessed and eaten at holy communion) in the *paten*, and looking upwards he prays that the sacrifice be accepted. ...

Here, the complexity of the Trinity, the nature of the Eucharist as sacrifice which replicates the original sacrifice, is clearly expressed. The priest offers to Christ the sacrifice which is at once a replication of the first sacrifice, and a new sacrifice. He mixes water with wine in the cup saying, 'O Lord God, as Thy divinity was united with Thy humanity, so unite this water with this wine' [DL: 6].

Pouring the wine and water into the chalice, he recollects that at the crucifixion of Christ, water and blood flowed from the side which was pierced by the spear, and these washed away the sins of the universe. A complex set of correspondences is made available here: water is equated to wine (in Cana) which is paralleled by wine which is synonymous to blood (the Last Supper). The celebrant covers the paten and the chalice. He then recites the Service of Penitence. This has one main theme: the priest offering the sacrifice is both mortal and a sinner.

The vesting of the priest in the sacred garments of his office takes place with special prayers. He removes his outer garments and puts on the *hamnikho* (stole), the *zunoro* (girdle), the two *zende* (sleeves), the *masnafto* (head cover) if he is a prelate, the *phayno* or cope, as well as the cross for the neck, the handcross, and the crozier or crook (if a prelate). Each of these symbolizes the power of the sacred over the profane life. The priest washes his hands, kneels down before the altar and prays inaudibly. He beseeches God for strength and purity, underlining that he is a servant of God, both mortal and sinful.

The priest once more kisses the altar and ascends the altar steps. Taking the covers off the paten and chalice, he takes the paten in his right hand and the chalice in his left. He stretches out his hands, crossed, right over left, and lifts them up above the *tablitho* (altar stone). In the general prayers that follow the priest 'commemorates at this time, upon this Eucharist that is set before us' the entire life of Christ:

His glorious conception and His birth in the flesh, His baptism in Jordan and His fast of forty days. His saving passion and His crucifixion, His life-giving death and His venerable burial, His glorious resurrection and His ascension into heaven, His sitting on the right hand of God the Father [ibid.: 12].

At this point, the persons for whom the *qurbana* is offered may be prayed for, and the intercession of Mary the Mother is requested.

The priest lowers the paten and chalice, placing the former to the east and latter to the west of the altar stone. The censer prayers follow, in which the priest, ascending the steps, raises the censer and swings it over the Mysteries (the bread and wine), east, west, north and south, and then in a circular motion, twice from the right and once from the left, intoning prayers for the acceptance of the sacrifice.

After the Trisagion, where the priest says three times 'Holy art Thou, O God, O Almighty, O Immortal', the Lord's Prayer and the Nicene Creed are recited.

The public celebration now begins. The sanctuary curtain is drawn aside, the priest burns incense and censing the altar, says loudly:

Mary who brought Thee forth and John who baptized Thee shall be supplicants unto Thee on our behalf. Have mercy unto us [ibid.: 20].

The people respond with exaltations, and with devotions to Mary, and the Trisagion is once more chanted.

The readings from the Epistles which follow are usually undertaken by the deacons. The reading of the Evangelion or New Testament is performed by the priest and is done in a very celebratory way. Two servers stand on

either side of the priest with lighted candles symbolizing the light brought
to the world by Jesus. The priest says:

With calm and awe and modesty, let us give heed and listen to the good tidings ...
[ibid.: 22].

The people respond with the prayer that they be made worthy. This
reading aloud of the Bible must have been of extreme significance at a time
when the Bible, being unprinted, had not been available to all, and thus it
is most elaborately framed with rituals, particularly in the way the Book is
ceremonially placed on the artistically engraved lectern in the centre of the
sanctuary. The priest now vests himself with a beautiful surplice.

The Blessing of the Chains of the censer takes place. It is an important
rite because it symbolizes that while the Trinity is one, it is simultaneously
three. This is particularly significant in terms of the role that the priest plays
in the Eucharist, because at different moments, he expresses the different
manifestations of the Trinity, and functions in the context of these differences.
He holds each of the three chains of the censer separately, with prayers to
God the Father, the Son, and the Holy Spirit, then he holds them together
symbolizing their unity.

After the prayers of the censer, the priest censes the sanctuary and the
congregation. The creed is recited by the people, and the deacon cries *Stomen
kalos* (stand well) for inattention is sacrilegious. The people respond with
Kyrie eleison (Lord have mercy).

The priest washes the tips of his fingers praying that the filth of his soul
may be washed away and 'that with pure conscience I may offer unto Thee
the living sacrifice that is well pleasing to Thy Godhead and is like to Thy
Glorious Sacrifice, Our Lord and Our God for ever' [ibid.: 31].

Here I would like to argue that there has been a subtle shift in the identity
of the priest. He has moved from the sinful mortal being who asks for leave
to perform the sacrifice to one who may offer the *living sacrifice* which is
similar to 'Thy glorious Sacrifice'. He is now the sacrificer and, therefore, in
function similar to God the Father. I argue here that the priest substitutes
at this point in the Eucharist liturgy for God the Father, not homologously
but analogously; and that in taking the place of God, he accepts not deification
of any kind but the sacred function of offering the sacrifice. Where God
sacrificed Jesus, His only begotten Son, the priest sacrifices the Mysteries,
which are not bread and wine merely, but body and blood as 'living'. By its
very nature, the offering is both sacrifice and oblation.

The Kiss of Peace follows. This is an ancient custom based on the words
of St Paul: 'Greet one another with a holy kiss' (II. Cor 13: 12). The priest
gives the *kaimuth* to the highest deacon, who passes it on to the other deacons,

who in turn pass it on to the people. On giving the hand of peace, each one says to the other. 'The Peace of our Lord and God'.

The priest then lifts up the great *sosafa* and waves it three times over the Mysteries. Having removed the veil that covers the Mysteries, he prepares the people for what is at the heart of the celebration, the partaking of the bread and wine.

After calling upon the heavens, the sun, the moon and all the stars, the earth, the seas, and the first-born, the angels and the seraphim to proclaim His holiness, the priest takes the Host from the paten with his right hand. He puts it on the palm of his left hand and, raising his eyes skywards, commemorates in a loud voice that moment when Christ blessed, broke, and gave bread to His disciples saying, 'Take, eat of it, This is My body, which is broken for you and for many, and is given for the remission of sins and for life eternal' [DL: 88]. Then the priest takes the chalice with both hands and similarly commemorates the moment when Christ said, 'Take, drink of it, all of you. This is My Blood which is shed for you'. [ibid.: 39].

Following this act of commemoration, the priest invokes the Holy Spirit upon the Mysteries by waving his hands like the wings of the dove that descended at the moment when Christ was baptized. Here, the function of the priest is similar to that of the Holy Ghost; the fluttering of his hands symbolizes the dove which descended on Jesus and was the bodily form of the Holy Spirit (Matt. 3: 13–17; Mark 1: 9–11; Luke 3: 21–2). The deacon says:

How full of awe is this hour, and how perturbed this time, my beloved ones, wherein the Holy Spirit from the topmost heights of heaven takes wings and descends and broods and rests upon this Eucharist here present and hallows it. In calm and in awe were you, standing and praying. Pray that peace may be with us and all of us may have tranquillity [DL: 40].

The priest cries loudly,

Hear me, O Lord, hear me, O Lord.
Hear me, O Lord, and have mercy upon us [ibid.: 41].

The priest is again clearly only the sacrificer, a mortal. Without divine intervention, the Qurbana cannot have meaning. He stretches out his left hand and waves his right hand over the Body and says,

May He (the Holy Spirit) abiding here make this Bread the life-giving Body, the Redeeming Body and the True Body of our God and Saviour Jesus Christ.

He repeats this formulaic prayer substituting blood for body, as he waves his right hand over the chalice.

After the consecration of the bread and wine which occurs secretly behind the veil come the diptychs. Here, kings, rulers, statesmen, prelates, saints, doctors of the Church, and the dead are remembered. Through the diptychs the Church as an institution is related to the social and political world around it. After the priest blesses the people, the veil is drawn over the sanctuary and the Mystery is hidden.

Behind the veil, the priest silently recites the Prayer of Fracture and Commixture:

Thus truly did the word of God suffer in the flesh and was sacrificed and broken on the cross, and His Soul was departed from His body while His godhead was in no way departed from either His soul or from His body. By His blood He reconciled and united the Heavenly hosts with the earthly beings, and the people with the Gentiles, and the soul with the body. The third day He rose again from the Sepulchre and He is one Immanuel, and is undivisible into two natures after the unity indivisible. Thus we believe and thus we confess and thus we confirm that this flesh is of the Blood and this Blood is of this flesh [ibid.: 49].

As Christ broke bread (Matt. 26: 26), saying that it was His body, so also the priest breaks bread symbolizing His suffering and crucifixion. Here he substitutes for Christ, replaying as actor the role of the central character. Christ is represented through the priest but is objectified in the bread and wine. The first is a relation of analogy and substitution, the second of homology.

In the rite of the Orthodox and Jacobite Syrians, the bread and wine are given together, not separately, symbolizing the unity of the body and blood which is the living Christ.

In the next prayer, the priest offers this living sacrifice to God, as sacrificer, mediator between the people and God:

O Father of Truth, behold Thy Son, the well-pleasing sacrifice. Accept Thou him who died for me that I may be forgiven through Him. Receive this offering at my hands and reconcile me unto Thee. And remember not the sin I committed before Thy Excellence.

Behold His Blood, shed on Golgotha by the wicked, pleads for me, for its sake receive my petition. As great are mine offences, so great are Thy mercies. Look upon the sins and look upon the offering for them, for the offering and the sacrifice are far greater than the sins [DL: 50].

In these two prayers, the priest clearly defines his own sinfulness. Yet again, by the power of his office and calling, the function of these, he has been made worthy of offering the supreme sacrifice to God himself. While the Trinity is indivisible, yet it is manifest as three. I interpret this sacrifice as the return, for it can only be understood within the framework of the gift and its inherent spirit (see Mauss 1974). Not everyone can take upon himself this function of returning to God what God has given man. They may participate in it, but cannot mediate the return.

The return which is the sacrifice or Qurbana is the institutionalization of memory. Only through this return can the gift of god (the sacrifice of His begotten Son) have meaning. The priest substitutes for God in his separate manifestations, yet he is never God. He makes the same sacrifice that God made, yet it is only because it was first made by God that the priest can in turn offer it. Because the Trinity is indivisible, God's sacrifice is also Christ's sacrifice; the priest who is neither God nor Christ is yet made worthy by his office to invoke the Holy Spirit and offer the sacrifice of the Living Christ. The priest says of the bread and wine,

Thou art Christ the God who was pierced in His side on the heights of Golgotha in Jerusalem for us.

Thou art the lamb of God that taketh away the sin of the world. Do then pardon our offences and forgive our sins [DL: 50].

Here he washes his fingertips and dries them. Then follows the litany of supplication. There are prayers by the people for compassion, tranquillity, and to be made worthy of partaking of the Mysteries.

The curtain or veil is drawn back. Prayers for preparation to receive the Mysteries follow. Incense is offered, and the elevation of the chalice and paten take place. The priest uplifts the paten ceremonially with both hands so all may view it. Then he puts it down slowly on the *tablitho* or altar stone. He repeats the same action with the chalice. There are prayers for Mary and the saints; for the dead who are always remembered in the Eucharist. The veil is again drawn over the sanctuary. The priest kneels before the altar and prays silently for forgiveness of sins after which communion takes place.

He ascends the altar steps taking the Gemourto (the particles of the Host) with the spoon. Receiving it, he says,

Thee I hold Who upholds the borders of the World; Thee I grasp, Who orders the depths; Thee, O God, do I place in my mouth; By Thee may I be delivered from the fire unquenchable [ibid.: 58].

He takes the Gemourto with the spoon from the paten, and puts it in the chalice. Thus the bread and wine are one. He fills the spoon from the chalice and drinks it, saying:

By Thy living and life-giving Blood which was poured on the cross, may my offences by pardoned and my sins remitted, O Jesus, Word of God, Who came for our salvation and will come for our Resurrection and of our race for ever and ever [ibid.: 59].

The priests and deacons in the sanctuary receive communication with prayers. The veil is drawn back once more. The prayers of the people are now joyous and triumphant rather than supplicatory.

In the ritual of communication the priest says to each one receiving bread and wine,

The atoning Gemourto of the Body and Blood of Christ, our God, is given to this faithful believer for the remission of debts and for the forgiveness of sins in both worlds [ibid.: 60].

The communicant responds with 'Amen'. Following this are the Prayers of Thanksgiving and then the Huthoma or the prayers of the exist. The priest blesses the faithful. The priest also asks the people to pray for him:

And may I, thy weak and sinful servant, be favoured and helped by your prayers. Glad and rejoicing, go now in peace and pray for me always.

The people say in turn,

Amen. May the Lord accept your offering and help us by your prayers [ibid.: 63].

The sanctuary is veiled, and the people leave the church. The priest must ceremonially consume whatever remains of the bread and wine. The sacred, awesome properties of the Mysteries are delineated here, which must not be reused or contaminated:

If there be a remaining particle, it remaineth to Thy knowledge, which created the Worlds, and if there be a member remaining, the Lord be its keeper and to me absolver and forgiver [ibid.: 64].

After several prayers accompanying the consumption of the contents of the paten and chalice, the priest washes the sacred utensils and wipes them. With prayers, he washes his hands, wears his ordinary garments, and takes farewell of the altar, kissing the middle, the right and the left sides.

The priest says:

Farewell, O holy and divine altar of the Lord. Henceforth, I know not, whether I shall return to Thee or not. May the Lord make me worthy to see Thee in the church of the First-born, Which is in heaven, and in this covenant do I trust [ibid.: 68].

With other similar prayers and hymns from the deacons signifying closure, the priest exits.

THE STRUCTURE OF THE EUCHARIST

The Eucharist must be seen as a construction positing a relation between three elements: myth, ritual, and liturgy.

The mythic dimension is that of the oral tradition. The origin of the liturgy, according to informants, is based on the crystallization of memory by those who shared the life of Christ (*Yesu Christue Kanda-varde Orma*). Informants speak of the first commemorative service that took place in which Mary, the Mother of Christ, also participated. Here, the apostles, disciples, and the Mother of Christ congregated 'in a small room' to carry out the wishes of Christ who had departed from their midst, but was yet ever present.

Such ideas are part of the structure of folk imagination, bricoleurian, hazy but in existence. However, the historical dimension of the formulation of the liturgy is not known to common people who treat the text synchronically and do not imagine that it is a piece which can be segmented according to the history of its development. In the same way, scriptural tradition represents a closure and is unquestioned veracity. It is the codification of memory, as opposed to the unstructured, open, mythic quality of apocrypha. ...

The Eucharistic service has meaning because it is related to the already existent idea that the Christian has about Jesus Christ. These derive both from scriptural and apocryphal traditions. It is because the Christian knows the history of the life of Christ that he can interpret for himself the liturgy and rituals which condense this life. Thus he relives Christ's birth with the opening phrases of the public celebration 'May Mary who bore You. ...' Later on in the invocation, the priest flutters his hands like the wings of the dove, and the people remember the Baptism and the Divine Acknowledgement of Sonhood. The central motifs of the Last Supper, crucifixion, and resurrection are re-enacted through the language of the rite (consecration, elevation, and communion).

Within such a framework, the myths underlying the practice of the Eucharist concern themselves with the person of Christ. These myths and legends pass down orally from generation to generation or are crystallized in the literate tradition through the offices of the colporteur. Church festivals, particularly, are occasions when tracts describing the life of the saints are sold to pilgrims. This again is reinterpreted by the people in their own idiom. History and myth often tend to coalesce in the conception of the present. There is complete lack of clarity in such accounts regarding geographical and historical detail. One woman insisted that Antioch was the land from which Jesus and Mary came, and thus it was the duty of Christians to revere the Patriarch, who came from Antioch too. Antioch and Nazareth can converge geographically because they are places of mythic rather than geographical importance.

The lay Christian views and interprets the person of Christ very differently from the theologian, and in terms of a paradigm born of lay experience. The latter results in a web of perception internalized over a long period of time, particularly through the many rituals (both individual and collective) that occur in a society where Christianity is still practised in a ritually effervescent manner.

People express ideas about the person of Christ primarily through conceptions about his mortality. Though theologically the unity of moral and divine are underlined, lay perception has its own ways of rendering comprehensible what may otherwise remain mysterious and inaccessible. Here, presumably, the corporeal explains what is otherwise too abstract to be understood. Questions of theology dealing with the indivisibility of the Trinity are not available in lay discussions. In fact, people resent being asked who Christ is or what constitutes the nature of his body. The answer invariably is that the ethnographer ought to ask such questions of theologians (*seminary le anchenmar*) and not devotees or even parish priests. However indirectly posed, the question reappears in term of people's narratives, where the life of Christ is often located in terms of the life of mortals like his Mother, Joseph, and the Apostles.

Besides liturgy and scripture, the people, in their attempt to understand the divinity and humanity of Christ, turn to the stories about Mary. She is the figure who is closest to Christ as only a mother can be to her son. If to some extent Mary can be visualized, then by that very exercise one is closer to an understanding of the nature of Christ. By referring for instance to the sorrow of Mary, the stories speak simultaneously of the mortal nature of Christ. Her deepest pain is known through the words of a song where she cries,

For how long I have brought you up;
If I had known the desire of Judas for silver
I would have given it myself.

By this rendering, Christ's crucifixion could have been avoided if his mother had satisfied Judas's greed. It is in this sense that the life of Mary re-echoes aspects of the life of Christ; visualized through her person, it is more clearly grasped.

Narratives are infused with empathy and describe how Mary gave birth in a stable, with no woman to attend on her, in such poverty that she had only rags in which to wrap the child. Of course, the absence of 'women to assist her' appears in the context of how women perceive birth even if this be divine birth. In fact, another narrative about the birth of Christ includes the presence of a midwife, but one who was so sceptical that she did not believe in virgin birth and, using her arm for purposes of gynaecological verification, came away a leper. According to another old female informant, the Christ child emerged from the thigh (thus unpolluted), and having given birth in purity, the thigh of the virgin was healed and no scar remained.

Similarly, Mary's emotions as she perceived her son dying are actually songs about Christ's Passion.

As he hung on the cross
The mother looked at her son;
Like a spear in her heart,
Her sorrow was felt
With tears in her eyes
She watched the death of her son
She asked him
Have you redeemed man of
the sin of his birth,
Of the sin of Adam, Eve and the Devil?
Born from my womb you have paid the debt.

Adam ate the Fruit of knowledge
And it is for that you must suffer now
And I must see you die.
If I had died first
I would not have to see this
You had told me earlier and
asked my leave
But now you are
Bathed in your own blood.
While you were near death,
You looked down on us on earth.
The earth was soaked with your blood
And the earth was freed.

This song, sung to me by a ninety-five-year-old woman, with tears in her eyes and a voice quavering with deep emotion, portrays how Christ's death is experienced by his mother as a physical rupture.

Both the canonical and the apocryphal sources of myth pertaining to the life of Christ contribute to the details about Christ as a person living in a particular culture and time. He is Jewish, born to Mary and sheltered by Joseph. He grew up in a carpenter's household, had brothers whose blood he did not fully share as they were, according to informants' accounts, sons of Joseph from an earlier marriage.

Even Christ's sojourn at the Temple of Jerusalem is perceived through the pain of Mary. Here, according to informants, is the moment when Mary realized that her son would be claimed by His Father. There is pain and pride, and a deep sense of loss because Jesus will not live by the decrees of ordinary life. Virgin birth, however, is the primary event that symbolizes Christ's difference from other mortals.

Lay informants accept virgin birth as an essential element of Christian dogma. Some Christians, referring to apocryphal literature, describe the conception of Mary herself as *shudh* (pure, untainted by the lust implicit in the sexual act). So also the conception of Christ is mystical, whereby the

word of God takes flesh. The relationship between Christ and God, Son
and the Father is a philological relation. It is the Logos that becomes flesh.
Christ is the male principle, the 'son' of God. In body, logically, Christ is
entirely of the substance of Mary. We have a principle here where the flesh
belongs to the mother and the spirit belongs to the Father. ...

In my analysis, the problem of sexuality, both in terms of the alleged
mystical conception of Mary and the conception of Christ, is conveyed here
as a continuing problem of the sin of Adam and Eve, which is transcended
by the birth of Christ. Christ stands in a relationship of correspondence to
Adam. As Adam was created without sexual union, so was Christ; as Adam
was banished from paradise and with him Man, in reversal with the death
of Christ, Man is allowed to re-enter paradise. If disobedience, sexuality,
and the loss of innocence was the condemnation of man and the rejection
from paradise, then celibacy, abstinence, suffering, and death become the
mode by which re-entry into paradise becomes possible, but through the
symbol of Christ. Christ is homologous to Adam but in reverse. Carnal
knowledge, childbirth, and suffering accompany Adam and Eve in their
expulsion from paradise. The spiritual union exemplified by the marriage
of Christ to the Church facilitates man's re-entry into paradise. This problem
of sexuality continues as a central theological motif centering around the
person of Christ both with reference to the ideas conveyed about blood
relations and their subjugation to the spiritual kinship arising from the
relation to the Father (Matt. 10: 37–8), and the symbolic centrality of the
celibate Christ (ibid.: 19:12). The celibacy of Christ in fact becomes a symbol
of the destruction of culture and temporality, the images of which conclude
in the Apocalypse. In the hereafter, nature and culture are destroyed, and
affinity is subsumed by the siblinghood arising out of the love of the Father
for all redeemed mankind; all are brothers and sisters in Christ.

Although Christ rejects the primacy of biological ties for spiritual ones
(ibid.: 12:48), the figure of Mary continues to remain central in a lay interpretation of Christ. Christ's rejection of Mary is explicit in the narrative
about the marriage at Cana and the changing of water into wine. Mary says
to Jesus, 'They have no wine'. Jesus answers, 'Woman, what have I to do with
thee? Mine hour is not yet come' (John 2:4).

This seeming rejection is seen by these Christians as characteristic of
the way in which sons may treat women in a patrilineal society. Here, verbal
rejection of the mother is not to be read as a denial of the love a man has
for his mother. Verbal contempt does not reflect the true nature of affectual
ties. As one informant said, whatever he may have said, the mother at once
bade the servants to do Jesus's will, knowing that a miracle would occur. In
the same context, love for His mother which at the end caused Jesus place
her in the care of His beloved disciple (ibid.: 19: 26–7), is treated as an index

of the personality of Christ. Similarly His anger at the Temple, His love for children, His compassion and knowledge are spoken of by the lay as if they are virtues of one known closely. The story of Christ is narrated too in terms of the details of His daily life; He is the son of Joseph in that He derives from the saintly protector (who is pater, not genitor), His lineage and occupation. He is a carpenter: Jesus of Nazareth, of the line of David; His brothers are the sons of Joseph from an earlier marriage. Mary in these accounts is immaculate and continues to be so because Joseph is both a widower and an elder whose role is to protect the mother and the child, born out of mystical union with the Logos. Jesus is then understood within the frame of two overlapping forms of experience: the empirical and the mystical.

The myths provide the narrative framework within which the Eucharistic rites may be understood; a reservoir for the purposes of the interpretation of any particular rite. Ritual becomes the mode of enactment of important aspects of the Christ's life; a theatre wherein the life is replayed. Both myth and ritual together appropriate time in several non-homogeneous ways. Time is not merely comprehended here as if it were historical, linear, and irreversible. Christianity takes into account an idea of time which is divided into mathematically notated divisions which are irreducible qualitatively, but yet, paradoxically juxtaposes mythic time at two ends of the continuum: Creation and Apocalypse.

In this sense, time is linear and event-based, counted both in terms of the passage of years and the actions of men. It expresses at once the mortality of man and the immortality of the soul. Good and evil are in existence in the very nature of man, and reward or punishment come at the end of time when man confronts eternity.

It is this notion of mythic time which gives quantitative time its meaning; which, in fact, introduces into the notion of the passage of quantitative time the vitality of ritual life. The sacred calendar in this sense becomes superimposed upon the secular annual schedule of time.

The cyclic, closed dimension of myth and ritual which captures the life of Christ through annual commemorations is also recapitulated in every Eucharist. The dissemination of Christ's life occurs through the Eucharist. It signifies that Resurrection is not closure but that Christ returns to Earth (mysteriously) embodied in the bread and wine. Without this mysterious return, the life of Christ in history can have no religious meaning. This is particularly so in a community where Christianity as it is practised is Eucharist-centred. The time of the Eucharist is thus simultaneously mythic, linear, and epochal. This multi-dimensionality of the nature of time occurs because myth, history, legend, and personal and traditional memories are caught within the same sacred framework. In both myth and ritual, in practice, there is very clearly a bricoleurian element, for variations in form at any one particular moment depend upon the elements chosen by the performer. In myth there is a greater emphasis on the need of the moment, and selection depends upon the audience that receives it. In ritual, there is a greater degree of codedness, but it must be affirmed that some priests say it 'better' than others: some chant in a higher pitch than others, some abbreviate, others do not. There is then an element of choice involved, though in principle the element is negated. What I wish to emphasize here is the performative aspect of ritual.

While myth and ritual are interrelated, they are yet mediated by the closed world of the liturgy which exists not only as the point of mediation but also of transformation. Here, in the text, the pure rule of synchrony dominates. It lies midway between the amorphousness of myth and the codedness of the rite. The liturgy, as text, excludes in its fixity of inscription the diachronic dimension. (This is true in spite of the fact that the text may be academically dismembered in terms of its historical evolution.) The text is a structured realm unlike the bricoleurian aspect that myth and ritual express. This closed structure of the liturgy best expresses itself in the synchronization of actors; by the learning of rules in the seminary. Standardization becomes here the primary principle.

Time, movement, and harmony are set along a scale which is rigidly followed. The interpretation of the liturgy becomes an unequivocal one, and charges of heresy are clearly made if there are modifications and changes. We know from the instances of the nineteenth century that the first signals of discord came from parishes divided over the reformed liturgy. Changes in the liturgy are thus difficult to bring about, take place over long periods of time, may result in schisms, and are made possible only through theological forms of discussion.

Just as the mythic dimension is codified and encapsulated in liturgy and enacted through ritual, changes brought about in the sphere of ritual (conversions, reform movements, ecumenicism) in turn affect the liturgy, leading to a change in the mythic consciousness. Thus the reform movements of the nineteenth century express this radical shift in the structure of the model. Changes in any one element are expressed in the transformation of the structure as a whole. ...

The Eucharist is the central motif of Christian ritual life. It represents the unity of event, the condensation of all the separate events that constitute the biographical rituals of the Christian calendar: the birth, baptism, works, death, and resurrection of the Christ. In that sense, the Eucharist is the model of the life of Christ. The Eucharist, which consists of the communication of the Mystery, culturally transforms itself into the symbols of eating and communion that occur in the family and the neighbourhood. Thus the Eucharist, or the experiencing of the bread and wine as body and blood, is a feast. The food of the Eucharist represents the body and blood of Christ. What bread and wine are to the physical body, Christ is to the spirit.

CHURCH, NEIGHBOURHOOD, AND HOUSEHOLD

There are three sets of signs which explicate the concept of the feast of the Eucharist. The Christian neighbourhood, the house and the Church, are to be seen as representing the table of life. Just as the Church provides a frame for the Eucharistic celebration, so also the neighbourhood during feast days can become after the Qurbana a centre of communal eating, with the house becoming a third locus.

This 'sacred food', clearly differentiated from everyday food, expresses itself in various ways, primarily in terms of the nature and logic of the gift. During church festivals, the people take pancakes (*appam*) to the priest for blessing after which they are distributed. Such communal feasts commemorate the death anniversaries of saints and holy men. During the rituals of celebration (as in the Festivals of Mary), they may be elaborate, consisting not only of cereals and vegetables, but also of *palharam* or festive foods. Similarly, the household enjoys a celebratory meal on Sundays and feast days after the Eucharist. Each of these is only a more elaborate level at the syntagmatic plane of the presentation of food. Food as spiritual sustenance, as sacrament, has the fewest possible elements; at the level of communal feasting, the elements are numerically fixed by the local church; at the level of the household, the greater the elaborateness of the meal, the greater the financial ability that is expressed.

The symbol of the table expresses, then, a morphological structure. The *tablitho* is the altar; it is also the cradle, the table, and the tomb of Christ. Similarly, the neighbourhood feasts present a metaphorical table where there is the communal preparation of food and communal eating. The household is also a table for the serving of celebratory food, with a fixed ritual place given to the head of the household, who like the priest (*Achen*, Father) blesses the food, which is eaten to celebrate a particular event.

Each of these separate morphological situations expresses a particular system of relations. The priest as head of the table is in a particular hierarchical relation with the servers and the lay. Similarly, the communal meal is an extension of the Eucharist, where the servers are like the deacons, assistants to the priest, and the trustees of the church. The food served here is sacred to the extent that it may not be arbitrarily disposed of, must be eaten then and there, or taken carefully home to be shared with those who did not come.

The two occasions when food as a meal is most definitively served at the neighbourhood table are the occasions of Passover (Pesaga) and Good Friday. During Passover, besides the Eucharist in which all must compulsorily participate, there occurs the distribution of *aviyal*. It is an elaborate preparation of vegetables which essentially symbolizes the condensation of the fully celebratory meal, and the Christian is invited to feast with the Christ.

On Good Friday, the Christian partakes of the food of mourning, commemorating the Crucifixion of Christ. This echoes the vegetarian meal associated with the death of a beloved person. On Good Friday, the Eucharist is not celebrated, and the food served both at the communally organized meal and at the house, symbolize death and bereavement. Rice, green pulses, *pappadam* (wafers), and pickles express the sorrow of the mourners who abstain from preferred culinary items such as flesh, fish, yoghurt, coconuts, and oil. When the Eucharist is celebrated, the family meal that follows is correspondingly celebratory. The father or head of the household blesses a meal that is elaborately and ceremonially non-vegetarian. A Sunday lunch is an *oon* (a feast) as opposed to *aaharam* (food as subsistence). It follows a period of fasting and the joyful celebration of the Qurbana.

The main event of ritual and communal feasting are in fact associated with Kanji Nercha (rice/gruel offering) which commemorates the establishment of Kurisu Palli with a new architectural design in the nineteenth century. On this occasion, the entire community of Orthodox Syrians contributes to the elaborate feast, bringing not only the raw materials required for cooking, but their knives and labour power as well. The communal effort involved underlines the joy that the residents feel in having Kurisu Palli in their midst. To that extent it may be interpreted as a sacred meal uniting an association of believers.

It is not merely on feast days and at the anniversary of the establishment of the church but also during saints' days that the Syrian Christians are integrated through the sharing of food while commemorating the death anniversaries of holy men. For Mary, St Thomas, and other important saints, *pal appam* (pancakes) is given to all who come to church. This is a transformation of the Eucharistic bread, and only the saints receive these white pancakes as gifts for redistribution through the office of the priest. The holy men who are not officially canonized receive cakes of a different shape which consist of jaggery and coconut and are similar to the cakes offered in the commemorative services of deceased parents.

Thus food and its sharing have always provided an important framework for mediating the rituals of integration. The Eucharist enjoins all those who participate in it in mystical union with Christ. The community meal, whether abbreviated in the form of pancakes for distribution, condensed in the *aviyal* or syntagmatically elaborate in the Kanji Nercha, define the nature of ritual relations that are in existence in the neighbourhood. When some of the Patriarch's party followers refuse to participate in the Kanji Nercha though they may be trustees of the church, they are making a statement about the affairs of the church, the nature of schism, and the consequent rupture in the association of believers. The sharing of food becomes an important index of the solidarity of the community. When the Christian does not wish to participate in the Qurbana by partaking of bread and wine (often he does not), he is in effect saying, 'I am not worthy to eat at the Lord's Table'. When the Patriarch's follower refuses to participate in liturgical events organized by the Catholicos, he also refuses to share in the communal extensions of the Eucharist.

Given that the Eucharist is the primary feast, when it is withheld (as during Lent) domestic and neighbourhood feasts also foreclose. On the other hand, on the day that Eucharist is celebrated after a long gap, such as after the fifty days of Lent before Easter, the meal that follows at the domestic table is a gargantuan one, symbolically expressing the closure of mourning and, through the consummation of the sacred, a return to a sacralized and more meaningful profane life.

Food is thus a central symbol of celebration and of closure as well as of liminality. The absence of certain elements and the abbreviation of the food code expresses mourning, ceremonial anticipation, or liminality. The converse symbolizes joyousness. Where the Eucharist is celebrated, the breaking of the fast is imperative, and this culminates in the elaborate meal or feast typified by the Sunday lunch. Where the Eucharist is remembered as instituted either through the Passover (Pesaga) or the establishment of the church, the event must be commemorated through the sharing of a meal. Where the Eucharist is withheld, as at the commemoration of Christ's crucifixion, the Christians are mourners around the newly interred body of the Christ.

Food symbolizes the nature of ritual relations which exist between the church, neighbourhood, and family. It separates the private from the public, the house from the neighbourhood, the ecclesiastical from the familial, the partaker from the observer, the server from the receiver, yet it interrelates the three levels of neighbourhood, church, and family in a system of continuities based on food and its distribution.

As is well known, Jewish sectarianism expressed itself through food. Thus in Christ's teaching and life, food became of central significance, and it was through several 'culinary disasters' such as eating with sinners, with unwashed hands and the like, that a new interpretation of life and divinity could be established. In this context it is both interesting and logical that Christ himself is analogized as food, implicit perhaps in the moment of his conception as flesh.

THE EUCHARIST: GIFT AND SACRIFICE

The Eucharist is perceived to be a thanksgiving, an offering, while at the same time it is Vishudha Qurbana or the Holy Sacrifice. It recaptures the life of Christ Who is understood through scripture to be given by God to Man in order to redeem him, and towards this end, underwent the sacrifice of His mortal life through crucifixion. Pain and suffering are for the Christian implicit in this life of Christ virtually enacted. Gift and sacrifice are inextricably interwoven: for, as the birth of Christ was a gift, His sacrifice was also a gift. As Marcel Mauss (1974: 71) would argue, this gift of God given to man has its own inherent spirit which makes the return obligatory. The commemorative service, the concrete form of which are the myths, rite, and liturgy, is the gift returned. Without this, the God would die. That the Hebrew *korban* corresponds somewhat to the English term 'sacrifice' while also meaning offering, shows this union between the two terms. The offering of bread and wine as the living sacrifice by the scarifiers (believers) and the sacrificer (God or the priest) is thus both return as well as a replica of the original sacrifice.

Through the Eucharist, memory is institutionalized, and from generation to generation the vicarious experience of the life of Christ is passed down. Through the experience of the Eucharist (participation by accepting the bread and wine), the soul is transformed and there is every effort logically to believe in the redemption of man through this second level (or ritual) participation.

Both Christ and the Christian are in a reciprocal relationship as giver and receiver. Christ receives the Christian, the Christian receives Christ. The gift received, however, is implicitly dangerous because it comes morally, physically, and spiritually from a person; in this case more so because it comes from the sacred person of Christ. Here, then, is the importance given to the 'pure state' that is required of the participant, whether he is priest, server, or lay, and to the prayers asking for compassion and mercy, for the receiver is a sinner. The act of repentance through confession is one where the Christian enters into a state of optimism. It is this optimism as opposed to a state of despair that signifies the true Christian. By committing oneself entirely into the hands of Christ through the Church, the Christian receives both peace and salvation.

In the same way, alms, both for the poor and in the form of gifts to the church and the priest, are typical of this relation of reciprocity. Material goods are in fact exchanged for blessings. The reciprocal nature of the gift relation in its legitimate and sacramental manifestations (tithes, alms, payments for blessing children, and the Eucharist fee) is the bond of culture and the base of the institutionalization of the church. It reflects the temporal dimension: the translation of ritual payments into concrete goods such as church property, expenditure at festivals, welfare institutions. The basis of the tithe—that grace will follow the giver—is the 'economic theology' that Marcel Mauss defines as being the subject of innumerable codes, epics, and cantos (ibid.: 55). The danger of the gift taking on the nature of contract is expressed in the nature of precautions taken. There is etiquette at every step: each stage in the process

The Eucharist (Sacrifice or Qurbana)

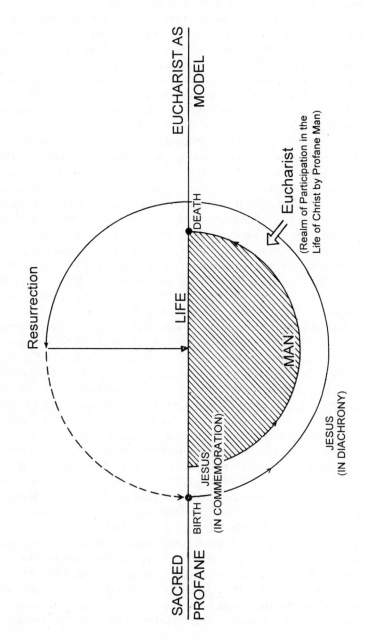

EUCHARIST AS MODEL

Eucharist
(Realm of Participation in the Life of Christ by Profane Man)

Resurrection

SACRED / PROFANE

DEATH

LIFE

MAN

BIRTH

JESUS (IN COMMEMORATION)

JESUS (IN DIACHRONY)

is regulated morally and economically (ibid.: 59). It is perfectly understood that money transactions can become corrupting.

Basically, there are two kinds of gift exchange: the gift of the Holy spirit, through invocation, where bread and wine become the body and blood of Christ, and simultaneously, the return made by man through the rites of commemoration. The two are inextricably linked and explain each other. The second is the material payment made to the church by devotees. Both kinds of gift exchange are understood only through the context of the sacrifice of Christ which occurred, by belief, in history, and is replicated through the liturgy and each ritual event of the Eucharist.

Sacrifice here consists of establishing a means of communication between the sacred and profane worlds through the mediation of a victim (see Hubert and Mauss 1973). The destruction—participation in the sacrifice does not result in taking upon oneself the dimensions of the sacrificed. The sacrificed is only one: the Christ, the sacrifiers are the believers and the sacrificers are God and the priest. The relation between God (as the Father who sacrifices His only begotten Son) and the priest (as one who performs the ritual sacrifice) is a relation of substitution, not of homology, as we saw. The priest is the mediator, and the sacred rite of sacrifice is one performed through grace which comes about only through ordainment. The most important function of the priest as it appears through the liturgical service is to gradually prepare the lay to face the overwhelming quality of the sacred.

This transition from profane to sacred is the essence of the performance of the sacrifical act. The Eucharist is a theatre, where the limen of enaction captures the moment between the profane and the sacred. To 'see' the Qurbana (Qurbana Kannuka) is not a perfect moment of ritual purity: it is to see the heavens open, but not a full participation in the world of the spirit. True participation is possible only through the 'experiencing of the Eucharist': by partaking of the bread and wine, and to believe thereby that the spirit of the Christ has entered one's soul. The movement from the profane to the sacred state through the participation in the Qurbana is not to become the Christ but to participate in the nature of Christ. The purpose of the inter-mediary, according to Hubert and Mauss, is 'that the two worlds that are present can interpenetrate and yet remain distinct' (ibid.: 93). Hubert and Mauss did not deny the existence of the 'other world', at least in terms of the logic of the social fact that ideas are things' (ibid.: 10).

The process of sacralization which sacrifice entails must perforce be accompanied syntagmatically by a process of desacralization. This is made possible by the act of returning to the profane world, explicated by the breaking of the fast after Qurbana. The ceremonies of exit in the sacrificial scheme prepare the sacrifiers for the return to the profane world since continued states of sanctity are not possible. Hubert and Mauss also argue that 'the religious condition of the sacrificer describes a curve symmetrical to the one traced by the victim'. But the curves thus described, while having the same general contours, are not the same (ibid.: 48). The sacrifiers and sacrificers may approximate the curve; they never attain it in the manner of the victim.

The return of the resurrected Christ as the sacrificial victim at the moment of consecration is a return to empirical time, resulting in a return to the earth, to the logic of ritual time which is a construct of culture. At the same time, the participants in the body of the Christ (*pars pro toto*) through the partaking of Qurbana return to the profane world carrying with them the sacred knowledge of Christ. It cannot be a perfect knowledge but an approximate one, and forms the basis of Christian life as a life of hope as opposed to despair. It is this opening of the heavens that Qurbana represents, symbolically stated by parting the *trisheela* or veil.

REFERENCES

DL.
1967 *The Divine Liturgy of St James*. Published by Metropolitan Mar Athanasius Yeshue Samuel, Archbishop of the Syrian Orthodox Church in the United States and Canada.
Hubert, Henri and Marcel Mauss.
1973 *Sacrifice: Its nature and function*. Chicago: University of Chicago Press.
Mauss, Marcel.
1974 *The Gift*. London: Routledge & Kegan Paul.
QM.
1981 *Qurbanakramam*. Thadiyoor: Oriental Publishing House.

CHAPTER
2

The Food Area in a Hindu Home

R.S. KHARE

This chapter ... will discuss the general structure of a typical north
Indian 'food area' mainly in terms of spatial, social, and ritual
categories and stages. The food area will be first considered under the
orthodox scheme, as normal domestic culinary relations become ritually
most elaborate under such an emphasis and provide a necessary 'normative–
typical' scheme for the region against which one compares wide-ranging
food transactions. We will begin with a definition of the term 'food area',
followed by a consideration of overlapping spatial, social, and ritual relations
that go to constitute the basic structure of a domestic food area.

Food area. The term 'food area', as used in this study, refers to all food-
related spaces within a homestead under both normal and ceremonial
circumstances. It is preferred over more restrictive terms like 'kitchen' and
dining area for its inclusiveness, especially since, as we shall soon discover,
the Hindu scheme may often require a discussion of both permanent and
temporary, institutionalized, and spontaneously organized food spaces and
their social activities. Since space, food, personnel, and rank order may jointly
determine what is a socially appropriate food area for a particular occasion
and what can be its possible spatial modifications, it is hard to find a
sufficiently inclusive word drawn from standard English usage. The term
'food area' ... can refer to all such spaces in which food is customarily handled,
whether for storage, or processing, or cooking, or eating. However, its precise

Excerpted from R.S. Khare, Food area: Spatial categories and relationships. In *The Hindu
Hearth and Home.* New Delhi: Vikas Publishing House, 1976. Chapter 2. © *R.S. Khare.*

scope and meaning will be determined by the immediate context in which it is employed. Finally, as an inclusive category, the food area, will be suitably subdivided to produce socially recognized sub-areas of food spaces within a homestead.

A place where cooking is done is normally called a *rasoi* or *chulha* in northern India, while the cooking and serving areas together are called *chauka* (cf. Madan 1965: 47–9). However, in practice the usage may not always be consistent among various caste groups. Some may use the term *rasoi* to cover both the cooking and serving areas, and *chauka* for cooking, serving, and food storage areas, while the *chulha* may be used to cover either cooking or serving areas or both. These terms may also have wide connotative meanings. For example, if a speaker is differentiating between the food and related domestic spaces, *chulha* and *rasoi* may be interchangeably used to refer to the spaces employed for cooking, serving, and eating. Normally, the area for raw-food storage is called *bhandar* or *bhandara* or *kothar*, and is differentiated from *chulha* and *rasoi*. In a less elaborate scheme, the latter terms may also include the storage space. Finally, if a person is specifically differentiating between a cooking area and the rest, he may employ both the terms, where *rasoi* refers to the actual hearth used for cooking and its immediate area, and the *chauka* for the rest (including the eating space utilized by the orthodox).

Under the indigenous scheme, the location of the food storage area (*bhandar*) is variable in conception as well as in terminological usage. Depending upon is physical location (i.e. whether it is in proximity to the cooking and serving area or separate), size, and elaboration, the storage space may or may not be explicitly included in the food area of a house. If it refers to a granary storing threshed grain within the house (but not in the immediate vicinity of the cooking and serving areas), the term *chauka* may be employed only to cover the cooking and serving spaces, leaving the storage area simply as a unit of normal domestic space. (This, as we will observe later, has certain practical advantages.) Such an arrangement is common in rural households where granaries are separately located from the cooking areas in rooms that constitute ordinary living spaces, and no special ritual procedures are therefore required to maintain the ritual rank of these 'uncooked' food storage areas. In comparison, in cities where the domestic space is often insufficient and provisions are brought from the market in limited quantities, the storage area is less elaborate, smaller in size, and located close to the cooking and serving spaces. In this scheme, *chauka* may often extend some of its ritual rank restrictions on the adjacent storage space, even if the latter is kept conceptually distinct in much the same way as in a rural house. Thus the question as to how the cooking and serving areas stand in relation to the store provides a clue to what can be given and received across them *without* affecting their ritual ranks. It follows from the brief discussion above that the food area among orthodox Hindus must be functionally subdivided into cooking (*chulha* or *rasoi*) and serving sub-areas (*chauka*).

A classification of the food area is also necessary because the eaten food must be separately stored from that not eaten, fresh food from (uneaten) leftovers, and inclusive food from exclusive. Accordingly, the storage area for the uncooked food will not be a suitable place for storing eaten and uneaten leftovers, for they belong to different ranks and must be separately stored.

WHAT IS INCLUDED IN A FOOD AREA

But if we extend the discussion of domestic food spaces a little more, some further questions emerge. For example, as the storage space for uncooked food in a house contains various edible materials, whether processed or not, should it be considered a part of the farms and fields where most of these foods grow, or does it belong to a significantly different rank? As a storage area accepts only uncooked food either directly from the field or processed by a lower caste member (often without any intervening purificatory step), it stands at a rank lower than that of the cooking and serving areas, which do not directly accept such foods until they are upgraded by washing, picking, sieving, etc. But if the rank of the storage area is lower than those of the cooking and serving areas, how is its rank regulated? Is it, then, true that anything and everything that is called 'food' can be stored in this space without any consequence to its rank? Obviously, this is not so. In practice, the rule of thumb is that only those food items that the household considers appropriate for cooking and eating will find their way into the storage area, and any item violating this guideline will render the storage area impure. Thus, obviously a household abstaining from consuming meat and eggs will not allow them to enter the storage area, for they will render the other food items impure.[1] Moreover, as not all foods are equally degraded when handled by a low ranked person, the type (i.e. the cultural taxonomy) of food is very important. Who would, for example, seek to wash and rinse ghee, milk, and flour before taking them inside the storage area? Even if they are touched and processed by lower caste members, they remain acceptable even to the most orthodox.

The major implication of such a discussion is to clarify how the storage area relates to the *rasoi* area in a northern Indian household. Should the storage space be included or excluded from the cooking space, especially

---

[1]Grains, pulses, lentils, and seeds are customarily processed by lower caste hired help (usually women) and are often allowed to be stored in the food area without any purificatory precautions. Such foods are not thought to contract impurity here.

as in many respects it may be found to be an ordinary domestic space? It may be hard to provide a single answer to such a question when the storage space, with its transactional peculiarities, and its close association with other ritual spaces, may significantly vary with the orthodoxy of the practitioner. Those who want to achieve and maintain higher ritual standards in their cooking, serving, and eating transactions try to integrate the storage space more completely with the spaces for cooking and serving than those not so concerned.

Typical spatial categories of a food area. Thus, as conceived under the orthodox Hindu culinary scheme, a food area is always physically located in an interior (and ritually pure) part of the house. It is accorded a definite priority in the planning of the domestic spaces and its place and orientation is guided by certain cultural rules. The characteristics commonly present in aligning a food area within a domestic space of the twice-born castes are:

(*a*) The food-related area (pure end) should be located at a place physically separate from waste disposal spaces (impure end), and nearer the worshipping place (purest end).

(*b*) As the food-related area is ritually purer (and ranks higher) than the living spaces not specified in (*a*) above, it should be physically demarcated from those spaces assigned either for sitting, or sleeping, or for receiving visitors.

(*c*) The specifications of (*a*) notwithstanding, a food-related area should be physically accessible to the Kahar (water carrier) for cleaning, washing, and water supply.

The above features[2] which guide the alignment of a food area with the rest of the domestic spaces lead to certain obvious, but important, propositions for our later analysis. First, all that is of appropriate rank for the food area is also appropriate for the worshipping place, for the two spaces are governed by similar rules of ritual purity and are often either contiguous or physically proximal. The above statement applies better to the orthodox scheme, because there is often an analogy drawn between the cooking area (the innermost part of a food area; see below) and the sanctum sanctorum (*garbha-griha*) of a Hindu temple. Second, as we will repeatedly observe, the physical expansion or contraction of a food area closely correlates with the ebb and flow of domestic life. Occasions of auspiciousness, festivity, and

[2]Granting that the above features also apply, with variations, to lower caste groups, the physical layout of a food area of a twice-born caste member may be found generally more elaborate, partly as a consequence of economic disparity and partly because of less lag between the claimed and the actual regard for the rules of orthodoxy, between the two types of groups. Even when the orthodox culinary style may be 'followed' by the lower caste groups changing under Sanskritization, the regularity, persistence, and detail of observances may still significantly fall short of the twice-born caste pattern.

celebration tend to elaborate and expand the food area as a spatial category, while those of tragedy, sorrow, and crisis cause it to contract, and even disappear (e.g. immediately after death). Thus, if the auspicious helps maintain and expand the food area, the inauspicious results in the opposite. ...

Third, even under the impetus of social change, the *basic* alignment of the physical spaces of the food zone may not be allowed to alter so long as the conflict is not too strong. While a food area may acquire several symbols of modernity (namely, ventilated hearths and gas stoves; Western-style stainless steel utensils, china-ware, crystal, and imported cutlery; and dining furniture), these additions are most often handled with appropriate regard for the rank and ritual properties of the orthodox section of the food area. The appearance of a *secondary food area* ... actually represent an adaptive strategy to maintain the basic culinary structure.

The food area itself minimally comprises three distinct sub-spaces: the cooking area (CA), the serving area (SA), and the storage area (ST). Each of them is specifically ranked in relation to the rest of the food area and the domestic space, and each of them carries a set of complementary relations, functions, meanings, and purposes. Considered in terms of the typical domestic plan, the ritual exclusion is strengthened as we move from the inner courtyard towards the food area. Within the latter, the order of ritual rank and exclusiveness increases from the ST to the CA.

In a typical plan, the CA is differentiated from the SA by a divider ranging from a low (six-inch high) boundary to simply a demarcating line. The CA may stand nearest to the native *chulha*, the commonly used word for it, although the term literally refers only to a hearth which is usually shaped like a 'u' turned down with three sides which are about a foot or so high (cf. Madan 1965). Fuel is fed from the open end. Most often a hearth is plastered on to a cooking platform made of clay (or brick), which is also used to accommodate fuel and some cooking pots. Variations of the traditional hearth are now common. There is one that has a rectangular plan with an arched opening in front for the fuel, and then there are indigenous stoves, *angithis*, that use coal, cow-dung cakes, and fuel balls made of charcoal, straw, cow-dung, and clay. The CA is normally spacious enough to allow for the free movement of the cook, although he or she sits while cooking. This cooking platform must also accommodate an assortment of cooking utensils, with or without cooked food. While the fuller significance of this area will become clear later, here we may indicate that the CA is obviously the sine qua non of the Hindu food area, mirroring most effectively the social and cultural world surrounding it at any particular moment. It is literally a structured space par excellence, where widely different relationships from myth, ritual, and kinship, denoting a host of different meanings, are sorted out and arranged unambiguously.

The close relationship between CA and SA cannot be overemphasized. A serving area is the appropriate eating area for the Hindu. The ritual rank of the CA is logically predicated upon the commensurate rank of the SA, because the food must be cooked according to the ritual demands of the eaters. It is a feature which is always emphasized in the Hindu scheme, both conceptually as well as spatially. Hence, the CA and the SA are traditionally located in close physical proximity so that the rank and purpose accorded to the CA gets easily extended to the SA as well.

The storage area, the third important zone of the food area, which is essentially a part of the normal living space within the domestic plan, as we have observed, is most often located near the CA and SA in homesteads for practical convenience. The rank and purity of the ST, therefore, must correspond with those of other living spaces. While it is higher than all waste and waste disposal areas of the house, it is lower than either the CA or the SA, or the worshipping place. The storage space may often be physically set apart in the households of the twice-born because the uncooked foods should be ranked above those foods (whether cooked or not) that are considered polluted, and below those that are being cooked in the CA. An independent access route to the ST is as important as it is to keep the CA, SA, and ST clustered together. A separate storage area normally ensures ritual separation and ranking of the 'cooked state' and the 'eaten state' from those 'uncooked' and physiologically 'raw'.

At this point, another important food-related space must be mentioned which helps to maintain the ritual ranks of the cooking, serving, and storage areas. It is the 'washing place', and usually refers to the area, in the corner of a courtyard, where the food area utensils are cleaned, and from which all other cleaning activities are performed by the Kahar. The 'place' is usually marked by a wooden or a stone platform and by appropriate cleaning materials, including ashes, mud, water containers, and coils of scouring grass (*munj*).

(*a*) *A paradigm for ranked spaces.* A typical food area[3] daily produces at least two complete cooking cycles, one in the forenoon and the other in the evening. These comprise well differentiated stages of cooking, eating, and

---

[3]When presenting the empirical details in this study, I shall throughout follow the north Indian food practices, because I am most familiar with them. However, the basic relationship that they exemplify could be of much wider relevance. What is a 'typical' food area for north India is a difficult question to settle, especially as I am leaning heavily on intensively observed case studies of higher caste groups, rather than on a statistical average or on a best representative quantitative model. My use of the term 'typical' is therefore partly based on observation and partly on intuitive generalization. My description of the 'typical' food area is most often based on the 'twice-born', 'middle income', rural–urban segment of Hindu society.

cleaning that are repeated everyday by observing a host of ritual rules for handling food. As indicated earlier, a Hindu's domestic space is ranked: the worshipping place and the food area represent the purest (highest) end; the living spaces, a ritually normal or 'neutral', ordinary, and non-sacred sector; and the places for refuse and waste disposal, a permanently impure end. This ranked alignment of domestic spaces closely relates with normative domestic spatiality (cf. Khare 1962). If the auspiciousness and purity of householders are sufficiently changed, the rank alignment of domestic spaces is altered. Realignments occur that could be either one-time or cyclical, temporary, or permanent. For instance, at birth the maternity area drops down from the ordinary ritual rank to one much lower, approximating that of the place for refuse and waste disposal, so that it is opened to the washerwoman (*dhobin*), the maternity nurse (*dai*, usually a Chamar), and a woman scavenger (*bhangin*)—all to be excluded by the twice-born householder. A person in an ordinary or neutral state accordingly becomes impure upon entering the maternity place. Logically, it follows that the pure end (the worshipping and food areas) or the domestic space would then move up and away from the maternity place. The worshipping area, therefore, bars entry to all those family members who are connected to the newborn by 'same particles' (*sapinda*) [blood ties], and the deity does not 'accept' any food prepared by them. This calls for special arrangements under which the deities are sent to a temple until the ritual 'recovery' of domestic spaces is complete. On the other hand, the food area, which must function to feed all domestic members, whether polluted or not by the birth, undergoes an organizational adaptation. Indeed, even a separate, temporary food facility is set up to cater to the needs of the mother and the child (those most polluted, almost 'untouchables'), while the permanent food area of the house continues to be used to cook for the rest.

Among the households of the twice-born, defiled sources are spatially separated according to the nature of defilement and appropriate purificatory processes are interpolated between the polluted and the pure 'ends' of the domestic space. The orthodox Kanya-Kubja Brahman, Thakur and Kayastha families of northern India follow this plan very closely, so that: (1) bathing facilities should be separate from (and not grouped with, as under the Western style) the latrine, but closely adjacent to it, for after defecation, the least time and distance should be taken in reaching the area of purification; (2) cooking and worshipping places should be as far away as possible from the foregoing but adjacent to each other (facilitating the offering of pure food to the domestic deity with, again, the least involvement of time and distance once the cooked food, symbolizing a transitional stage, is ready); and (3) the pure and impure spaces should be neither facing towards each other nor located on the same side, nor should they be in the same enclosure. ...

(b) *Ritual ranking of food area.* The term 'normal cycle' is used here to convey the repetitive and interconnected activities, events, arrangements, and meanings that are found to occur twice everyday in the food area of a twice-born caste home for the normal *kachcha–pakka* cooking and feeding done within a domestic group. The term remains applicable to all regular ceremonial, religious, and festive situations. The discussion of a normal cycle will be broken into a series of stages, each of which traditionally represents a specified group of relationships of the ritual rules outlined in the previous section. Each stage of a food cycle will demonstrate how the principles of inclusion and exclusion operates under normal domestic cooking. I shall describe, sequentially, how the food area is readied for *kachcha* cooking and then how through purification it is 'reborn' for another domestic food cycle.

STAGE I: INITIAL RANKING

To reach this ritual rank, the food area should be swept, washed, and plastered[4] beforehand. Its cooking and serving areas (CA and SA) should be very carefully cleaned, leaving no specks of leftover foods, whether eaten or not, from the previous cooking, 'for even one such speck would be sufficient to pollute the entire kitchen and the foods cooked in it'. Additionally, of course, all kinds of animal excreta (excepting cow dung) are impure; all soots, tars, and residues of fire which are in a solid or semi-solid state are also polluting. Hence, all items in, and all nooks and corners of, cooking and serving areas must be accessible for full ritual cleaning.

After the food area has been washed and plastered, and all the used utensils have been cleaned and placed again in either the serving or the cooking area (usually it is the former), and most importantly, *once these spaces have dried*, the food area [as a whole] has moved up in rank, only 'next' to the worshipping place. Now, therefore, the Kahar or Kaharin (artisan caste) who may have washed the higher caste food area only an hour or two before (as a paid domestic servant) cannot enter it without impairing its rank.

[4]Washing and plastering may be done with such materials as water and/or a thin paste of clay, straw, and cow-dung. In an urban, *pakka* (made of brick and plaster) food area, washing with water may mean a minimal application of clay and/or cow-dung paste for purificatory purposes; while in a rural, *kachcha* (clay and straw structure) kitchen, a thick paste of the same material is employed.

Stage I: Initial Ranking

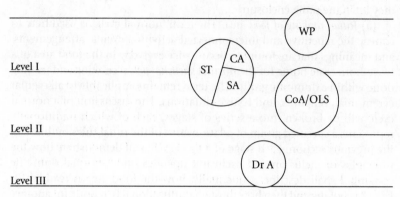

Key:
          CA = Cooking area
          SA = Serving area
          ST = Storage area
    CoA/OLS = Courtyard area/other living spaces
          WP = Worshipping place
        Dr A = Drainage and waste disposal

One approximate measure for determining the ritual rank of the food area (at any particular point of time) can be obtained by finding out what ritual objects, activities, situations, and relationships can either be included in it or excluded from it. This principle of graded inclusion and exclusion is most central to our discussion. Thus, when we find that a 'clean and dry' food area is just below the worshipping place (but is not of the same order), it entails specified ranges for both inclusion and exclusion of certain properties. They may be 'equal' in some ways and un-equal in certain others. For example, if the family deity is brought into the food area from the worshipping place (as both of these are usually in close physical proximity in an orthodox home), there will be some additional purificatory steps required for the food area. The footprints of the cook, who is otherwise pure, must be removed from the place by washing the area where the deity is to sit, although the food area is pure enough to send the food to the worshipping place for the deity's consumption there.

Further gradations of ritual ranks may be similarly obtained: the clean food area is higher than the courtyard area (CoA), for the former is more exclusive than the latter. Hence, any domestic member wishing to enter the cooking–serving area from the courtyard area must wash his hands and feet, even if he is in the state of ordinary ritual purity. What is ritually 'normal' for the inner courtyard may therefore be impure for the purified cooking–serving area. On the same basic criterion, the courtyard is purer than the domestic spaces for bathing, drainage, and waste disposal. As indicated earlier, the latter cluster symbolizes the opposite pole of the worshipping and food spaces and hence under no circumstances (except when being cleaned) will the latter extend into the former. However, under ceremonial circumstances, like marriage, the food area may encroach on a section of the courtyard (after appropriate purification) and/or any other living space, including the drawing (living) room (DrR). This is demonstrated in the fourth diagram because it is the most modernized end of the Indian domestic spaces [Khare 1970] and it may, especially among urbanites, subdivide and expand to produce a non-sacred pole for the food-handling facilities. Conceptually, all that is modern is not necessarily ritually impure. The principle of graded inclusion and exclusion applies to these non-sacred spaces (OLS). In practice, a modern dining or drawing room is of the same ritual rank as other ordinary living spaces; or, in other words, it is definitely higher than the waste disposal spaces, though less than the inner courtyard.

STAGE II: INTERNAL RANK DIFFERENTIATION

The food area enters the next stage of ranked exclusions when the *kachchi dal* [pulses], an item of daily food, is being prepared (this activity is called *dal dalna*). The food area again undergoes a suitable ritual rank differentiation, much more than under the first stage (compare diagrams I and II). In rural and urban orthodox homes, handling the preparation of *dal* normally sets apart whatever cooking activity has preceded from whatever has to follow to accommodate the exclusive nature of the *kachcha* foods. Significantly different measures of ritual purity are therefore applicable during and after *dal* preparation than before. By now the cooking area personnel have removed those utensils, objects, and vegetables that are not intended to be grouped with the *kachcha* food. Thus, the cooking area (CA) is further differentiated into CA_1 (for *kachcha* cooking) and CA_2 (for *pakka* vegetable cooking), where the former contains the central cooking hearth and its region, and the latter is designated as the additional (vegetable) cooking space, most usually located within the cooking area. Technically, the moment rice or lentil has begun boiling, CA_1 is ranked higher than CA_2.

In orthodox domestic groups this classification of the CA may be done to assure the observance of ritual rules for *kachcha* preparations in a way that is practically manageable. Thus CA_1 may be kept as the most exclusive part of the cooking area where the cook, foods, utensils, and even fire (as

Stage II: Internal Rank Differentiation

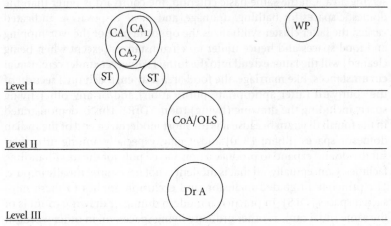

CA_1 = the hearth-innermost-area for dal cooking
CA_2 = a differentiation of the CA for 'vegetable' cooking

among the Kanya-Kubja Brahmans) may remain strictly confined to it. Whatever can be allowed to go inside CA_1 must be kept at the same ritual rank, which seriously limits contacts from the outside. ... In such a situation there are often two cooks, one operating exclusively in CA_1 and the other in CA_2; the zone of spatial movement for the CA_2 cook is much less restrictive, and he or she can freely move in and out of CA_2 to help the cook in CA_1. Such an arrangement is, especially, not uncommon in large-sized orthodox families, where more than one woman may be simultaneously involved in the cooking area.

In domestic groups of smaller size, CA_1 may not be spatially separated from CA_2 but the cooking of vegetables may be started *first at* CA_2 followed by the *kachcha* cooking of dal on the same hearth; thus CA_2 is converted into CA_1, or an inclusive spatial category into an exclusive one. The direction of rank differentiation is always from CA_2 to CA_1 and not vice-versa, because the ritual rank of CA_1 activities is more exclusive than those of CA_2. The food prepared in CA_2 is more inclusive so long as it is outside CA_1 because once CA_2 foods have entered CA_1, they become as exclusive as those cooked in CA_1. This distinction is cardinal for the *kachcha* and *pakka* categories of foods.

Briefly, therefore, in this stage, in comparison to stage I, the cooking area is further internally differentiated along the *kachcha* and the *pakka*; the serving area is drawn within the first level of ritual purity and CA_1 comes nearer still to the worshipping area.

STAGE III: RANK ORDERING FOOD EATING

As soon as the cooking has been completed,[5] more ritual distinctions are called for at all the three levels of domestic spaces for initiating serving and eating transactions. The first plate of the cooked food may be offered to the family deity (if there is one), or oblations may be made to the fire, or the first few morsels of food may be kept apart in order that they may be offered to a cow and a crow. (Such observances are followed as a part of 'the routine five sacrifices ordained by the scriptures for the twice-born individuals'). In this stage the emphasis is on a ritually appropriate mode of eating for the orthodox. This can be secured only by regulating the proper, one-way transfer of food from the CA (most exclusive) to the SA (less exclusive), by ensuring that the SA is appropriately internally ranked when there is such a necessity, and by emphasizing purificatory techniques for maintaining all ranked distinctions of the cooking and serving areas. Depending upon the size and age composition of the domestic group, an orthodox food area may differentiate the SA into I, II, and III spatial sub-categories, which are successively more inclusive zones, reserving 'the purest' (most exclusive) zone I for the most orthodox member of the domestic group and the 'least pure' (least exclusive) for an individual who does not care about the ritually pure state of foods. As an alternative, however, the SA may not be divided into spatial zones but may be used for successive eating, beginning with those most orthodox, who may eat first by sitting just outside the CA, while the less orthodox (in which category also fall modern educated youths) may eat either later on, or farther away from the CA, or even outside the SA. (Compare the logical similarity with intercaste commensality.)

Both of these zones of the food area may show some interesting adjustments to social change. The 'lines' demarcating zones within the SA are not normally fixed in a concrete manner; instead, these temporary demarcations (for example, chalk lines drawn on the floor) are recognized either according to the requirements of each cooking cycle and its ritual contingencies, or according to the needs of the ceremonial cycles.

The foods cooked and served in orthodox ways are eaten by both orthodox and unorthodox eaters; that is, the exclusive food can be eaten in an inclusive manner, while the opposite normally is not true. For instance, foods from the orthodox CA are carried out to a dinner table in the courtyard

---

[5]The ritual completion of cooking may be obtained when the cooked food is ready for making offerings to the household deities. Among Vaishnava sects, once the deity has been offered the food, the latter becomes *prasad*, a highly inclusive food for consumption. However, the actual cooking may not stop with that; side preparations may be continued along with the regular preparation of bread (roti) in the CA, making cooking, serving, and eating all simultaneous in the subspaces CA and SA.

Stage III: Rank Ordering Food Eating

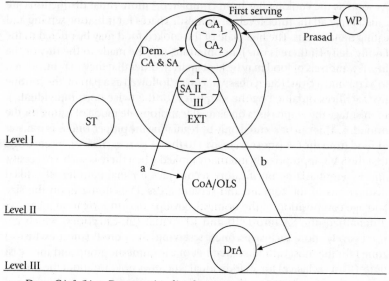

Dem. CA & SA = Demarcation line between CA and SA
        a = Food for unorthodox eaters, including children
        b = Food for unorthodox eaters

(instead of the traditionally provided washed floor) either for a family member wearing shoes (who is ritually polluted), or to a person of another caste. Thus, the ritually prepared food is non-ritually consumed by the unorthodox, without producing a confrontation either with the orthodox food area or with the orthodox members of the household. This also indicates that culinary orthodoxy ultimately rests with the individual and not necessarily with an entire household.

The structural alignment of the food spaces in this stage again logically reflects rank elaboration of those subspaces that are crucial to this stage. The ranked relations, which enter the climactic stage of 'transition' (comparable to a rite of passage) when the cooking is over, are appropriately consummated only after serving and eating.

STAGE IV: REINSTATING THE FALLEN FOOD AREA

Analytically, what happens to the food area after the cooking and eating have been completed is probably the most important means of demonstrating the complete nature of the domestic food cycle. Before serving and eating are over, all items, spaces, and activities of normal living acquire a rank lower

Stage IV: Reinstating Fallen Food Area

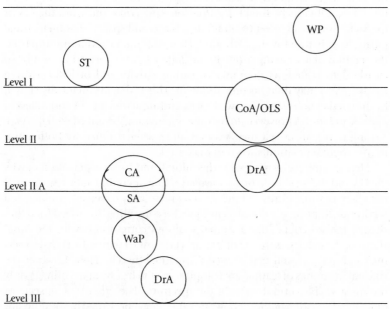

WaP = *kahar's* washing place
DrA = Drainage Area

than the food area, but subsequently it is just the opposite. The decisive nature of this ritual fall is depicted in diagram IV, where the CA and SA of the food area rank below the level of such other domestic areas as the courtyard. Now the food area comes into direct contact with the washing place (WaP), which is most often managed with a Kahar's help among the twice-born households.

However, the WaP is not of the same ritual rank as are the domestic areas of waste and refuse disposal because the artisan castes (e.g. Kahar and Bari) that will readily agree to clean the food area of the twice-born caste groups will refuse to render service in the zones of waste and refuse disposal. Hence, the latter must be attended to by another caste group (the Bhangi) which ranks lower than the artisans. With this distinction in mind, we may note that the ritual fall of the food area after each cooking and eating cycle is significant because it is neither ritually irrevocable, nor it is of the lowest ritual level.

As we notice in diagram IV, the CA and the SA are lowered from level I to III. The last level attempts to show the ranking between DrA and the Kahar's washing place (WaP). The ST, which remains unaffected and stationary in relation to both the highest (worshipping place: WP) and the lowest (WaP) markers on the diagram, indicates the extent of the lowered ranking of the food area. Obviously, therefore, a person now going out from the CA or the SA to the ST will lower (pollute) the objects and spaces of ordinary ritual purity. This is true for the orthodox. However, under modern influences, the relation of a 'drawing room' to the 'fallen' CA and/or SA may not be so clearly demarcated, as the ranks of eating activity and of leftover eaten foods (*jutha*) may then become different. This is diagrammatically shown by the overlap between these two spaces, cutting across the IIA and III levels. The CA and the SA however, do become synonymously ranked with the WaP so long as they are not cleaned, washed, and plastered. Once dry, both return to the original position shown in diagram I.

Here it is necessary to provide the cultural and social explanation of why the CA and the SA should be so 'lowered' while operating under the normal paradigm of ritual purity. While, as I have previously observed, cooking and serving are important cultural techniques for converting uncooked food into ritually ranked cooked food so that it always corresponds with the ritual status of the eater, it is the act of 'eating' (i.e. contact with saliva) that lowers the food space as well as the objects contained therein. Here, however, the cultural meanings of 'eating' are complex, in which ... human eating is only the most visible, middle part of the spectrum. The other two 'unseen' or hidden but ritually significant poles of 'eating' are represented by the domains of gods (auspicious) and of evil spirits (inauspicious). An evil spirit intrudes to defile the pure (cooked) food in one's food area, while a god, only when invited, participates. Hence, the cooking (the process) as well as the cooked food (the product) must be first raised high enough for the gods to participate. Secondly, they must be guarded against invasions by evil spirits. The deities and divine agencies (especially fire and water) are considered most helpful in establishing auspiciousness. Offering the cooked food to a deity, the continued presence of the fire in the hearth, and of the cook in the CA help the foods and the food area in retaining their higher rank and auspiciousness.

Inclusion and exclusion of leftovers. Besides cultural considerations, the ritual paradigm of 'eating' can also be explained at the social level. Again, the principle of inclusion and exclusion is found useful and the common rule is: the higher (more exclusive) the eater, the less polluted (more inclusive) will be his partially eaten, leftover food, and therefore it will still be fit for wider consumption. For example, when the domestic Vaishnava deity (most exclusive) has 'eaten' the food (which is only a symbolic act, but by faith the highest kind of 'eating'), the leftover food still remains unsullied in relation to the human world, and hence it is appropriate for the widest consumption. When one's guru, who is more exclusive than the disciple but less than the deity, has eaten the food, once again the victuals remain pure for the entire domestic group of the disciple. Here, the principle of pollution by saliva is superseded for maintaining a higher value. In contrast, if the cooked food is first eaten by a caste or kin member ranked lower than oneself, the food spaces involved and all the objects therein are immediately lowered.

The above discussion allows us to propose that the lowering of leftover eaten food is always commensurate with the rank of the eater. Unless the latter is ranked lowest, the lowering of leftover food is always only relative to those who rank higher than the eater. It also follows that the commensal rules appear as a logical extension of culinary rules observed by the givers as well as the receivers of foods. The orthodoxy of a food-giver is not a limiting factor in setting commensal rules unless it is lower than that of the intended receiver (eater) of the cooked food.

Against the background of the above implications of eating in stage IV, one may understand why a food area while involved in cooking ranks next to the worshipping place and why the same food area, after the eating is over, opens itself to lower intercaste contacts and services. All eating places within the house must be purified or cleaned after every cooking–eating cycle, as the aftermath of eating is always polluting under the orthodox Hindu scheme.

The preceding discussion allows us to observe that the food area of an orthodox Hindu home is characterized by well-regulated durations and ranks between spaces, events, and actors, and that the precise stages, durations, and repetitive sequences of activities and relationships provide the essential structural framework for the entire food area. It is therefore these properties that enable the *kachcha* cooking activity to be distinguished from the *pakka*, the cooking from the serving, the eaten from the uneaten, the fresh (*taza*) from the stale (*basi*). ... The food area for the orthodox is a very comprehensive and precise locus classicus for maintaining one's individual religiosity.

(*c*) *Food area of lower caste households.* The basic categories of the food area, particularly the CA and the SA, are also consistently found among urban lower caste groups. In principle, the food area undergoes the same cyclical rise and fall that coincides with cooking and eating; only the elaboration of the orthodox, high caste scheme is absent. There is seldom a food area serviced by a hired hand: women members of the household do the chores. Economic constraints most of all reduce the food area to a few pots and pans, to a small *chulha* tucked away in a corner of a verandah or of a small room (with no demarcation between the CA and SA spaces), and to only one full cooking cycle every day. Eating *basi* (un-eaten, leftover food) is therefore much more frequent. Vegetables, being costly, remain rare, while tea has pervasively become their popular drink. It may sometimes replace a meal for the want of money to buy regular foodstuffs. ... Ambitions to follow the normal pattern of the high castes find little expression in a daily cooking cycle, for the emulation requires money. Such ambitions have a better prospect of realization during festivals and ceremonies, and although it is the women more than the men who hanker after it, they often lack the means to translate their hopes into practice. Emulation of higher caste models is therefore erratic, especially when their hearth, the most stable centre of their house, is poorly provided. The small rented quarters (or huts) of the urban lower castes leave little place either for display or for secrecy. If the quarters are too small, and the weather agreeable, the serving and eating may be done in a nearby lane; this usually becomes their courtyard when some festive occasion arrives, requiring communal feeding. Ritual rules that classify domestic members, spaces, foods, and activities in the twice-born caste scheme here give in to the basic pressures of survival. Thus, while the distinction between the pure and the impure may exist, the provision for its consistent separation is absent.

However, the entire onus cannot be placed on the economic factor. Thus, for example, when the domestic hearth of a poor Brahman is compared with that of a Kahar, the physical appearance is not strikingly different but the culinary behaviour is. The separation between the pure and the impure is more clearly and consistently maintained throughout a food cycle by a Brahman household, although elaboration may be sacrificed at every step, giving the appearance of makeshift arrangements to cope with adverse circumstances. Hence, if the suggestion here is that culinary orthodoxy presupposes availability of enough money, it is also true that money alone is not a direct condition for either observance or non-observance of culinary and commensal rules. An additional point to be made is that the physical layout of a food area is only a qualified indicator of what happens there in practice.

REFERENCES

Khare, R.S.
1962 Ritual purity and pollution in relation to domestic sanitation. *The eastern anthropologist* xv, 2: 125–39.

1970 *The changing Brahmans: Associations and elites among the Kanyakubjas of north India*. Chicago: University of Chicago press.
Madan T.N.
1965 *Family and kinship: A study of the Pandits of rural Kashmir*. Bombay: Asia Publishing House.

Death and Cosmogony in Kashi

JONATHAN P. PARRY

THE SCENE OF COSMOGONY

Kashi, the 'Luminous', the City of Light, is the pious Hindu's name for the sacred city of Banaras, now officially known as Varanasi.

When Babylon was struggling with Nineveh for supremacy, when Tyre was planting her colonies, when Athens was growing in strength, before Rome had become known, or Greece had contended with Persia, or Cyrus had added lustre to the Persian monarchy, or Nebuchadnezzar had captured Jerusalem, and the inhabitants of Judaea had been carried into captivity, she had already risen to greatness, if not to glory ... While many cities and nations have fallen into decay and perished, her sun has never gone down; on the contrary, for long ages past it has shone with almost meridian splendour (Sherring 1975: 7–8; originally 1868).

[The city's] present life reaches back to the sixth century BC in a continuous tradition. If we could imagine the silent Acropolis and the Agora of Athens still alive with the intellectual, cultural, and ritual traditions of classical Greece, we might glimpse the remarkable tenacity of the life of Kashi. Today Peking, Athens, and Jerusalem are moved by a very different ethos from that which moved them in ancient times, but Kashi is not (Eck 1983: 5).

Whatever their historical justification, from the perspective of the extensive eulogistic literature on the city which its priests and other sacred specialists invoke for the instruction of the pilgrims and mourners they serve, such statements are but a bland understatement of a far more venerable religious truth. Kashi is as old as time itself. As the site of cosmic creation, it is the place where time itself began. As cosmogony is here a ceaselessly repeated event, its present time is also the primordial time of origins.

In this chapter I focus on the place of death in this 'divine vision' of the city. Those with the eyes to see know that Kashi is both the origin-point and a microcosm of the universe; that it stands outside space and time yet all space is contained within it; and that it provides for the attainment of all the four conventially enumerated goals of human existence (the *purusharthas*): in life for the fulfilment of moral and religious duty (dharma), material and political advantage (*artha*), and of the sensual appetites (*kama*), and, above all, in death for the attainment of salvation (*moksha* or *mukti*). The keystone of this symbolic construction, I argue, is death as an act of cosmic regeneration. It is the city's association with death that provides it with an immunity to the degenerative flow of durational time, and renews its capacity to encompass the rest of creation.

The celebrated ghats of Banaras are defined segments of river frontage between 30 and 200 yards in length. Most have been constructed to form a series of stone terraces and stairs running down into the sacred waters of the Ganges. Many are themselves important places of pilgrimage, none more so than Manikarnika ghat. Manikarnika is one of the city's most important bathing ghats, the focus of a wide variety of ritual activities and, however pressed the pilgrim, a sine qua non of every pilgrimage. For present purposes, however, its most salient attributes are that it is not only the site of the sacred tank beside which Lord Vishnu performed his cosmogonic austerities, but also the site of the most important of the city's two cremation grounds. As I understand it, the conjunction is of crucial symbolic significance.

The ghat is located at a point roughly midway along the Ganges between the confluence of the Asi and the Ganges, which marks the southern boundary of the sacred city, and the confluence of the Varuna and the Ganges which marks its northern boundary (see map). It stands at the dividing line between two equal divisions (*khand*s) of the city: Shiva *khand* to its north and Vishnu *khand* to its south. While in India the cremation ground is generally on the periphery or outside the area of human settlement, in Kashi it is the city's focal point. Just as India is said to be the 'naval' (*nabhi*) of the world, and Kashi the naval of India, so Manikarnika is the navel of Kashi. As the site of creation itself, it is the very hub of the entire universe.

I paraphrase here the *Kashi Khanda*'s account of cosmogony (chapter 26). This text is the most important in the whole corpus of 'praise' literature which eulogizes the city.[1]

---

[1]Unless otherwise stated, my citations from *the Kashi Khanda* are from Baikunthnath Upadhyaya's translation from [the original Sanskrit] into Hindi.

During the period of cosmic dissolution (*mahapralay*) all creation was destroyed and all was darkness. There was neither sun nor moon nor stars, no form or sense perception, and no cardinal points. All that existed was *Brahman* which cannot be apprehended by the mind or described by speech, and which is without shape, name or colour or any physical attribute. This undivided one (*advaita*) desired to become two and accomplished this by his own divine play (*lila*). 'I [Shiva] am the material form of that immaterial *Brahman*. Oh Parvati, together we created the sacred area of Kashi.'

Wandering in this forest of bliss, Shiva and Parvati desired to create another being to whom they could hand over the burden of the whole [of the rest] of creation, which would leave them free to bestow 'liberation' on all who die in Kashi. Shiva turned his gaze full of nectar on his left side [i.e. Parvati] and a beautiful being was instantly created. This was Vishnu whose breath was the Vedas, through which he was omniscient, and according to which he was instructed to perform his task. Vishnu dug a tank with his discus and filled it with the sweat of the terrible austerities he performed by its side for 50,000 years [in order to construct the universe]. At the end of this time Shiva and Parvati came there and saw Vishnu burning with the fire of his asceticism. Shiva was entranced, and with the violent trembling of his delight his ear-ring dropped off into Vishnu's tank, which Shiva decreed should henceforth be known as Manikarnika ('jewel of the ear'). Aroused with difficulty from his austerities Vishnu was told to demand a boon. He requested that he should always behold the divine couple as at that moment; that he should take the form of a black bee perpetually drinking the nectar of Shiva's lotus-like feet, and that since Shiva's ear-ring had been

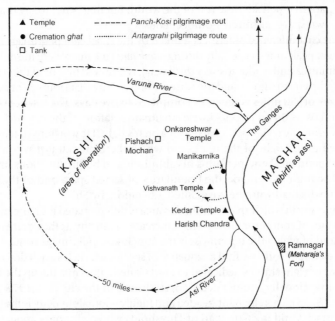

Map of Kashi

studded with *mukta* (pearl), this sacred place (*tirath*) should confer *mukti* ('liberation'). Shiva agreed and added that for those who reside in Kashi it will always be the *Satya yuga* (the Age of Truth), the [auspicious] time of the summer solstice (*uttarayan*) and a festival day; and that pious deeds performed here will result in immortality.

Manikarnika, then, is the place where the genesis of the universe occurs at the beginning of time. But it is also the place where the corpse of creation will burn at the end of time (*pralay*). Kashi (in its entirety) is known as the 'Great Cremation Ground' (*mahashamshan*) because it is there that the five great elements which compose the world (earth, water, fire, air and ether) arrive as corpses (Kane 1973:4:627). Only the city itself survives this universal holocaust for it exists outside (normal/profane) space. At the time of cosmic destruction it becomes a light or halo in the sky; or, in the more robust idiom of my informants, is raised up above the general conflagration like an umbrella. But Manikarnika ghat is not only the scene of the genesis and dissolution of the world at the beginning and end of each cosmic cycle. It is also, I argue, the case that these cosmic events belong to a kind of eternal present and are perpetually reactualized on the ghat.

IN AND OUT OF TIME AND SPACE

Kashi, then, exists in a time and space that is radically distinct from the time and space that pervades the rest of the world. But that is not to say that the city's own space is entirely homogeneous.

The circumference of Kashi is marked by the *Panch-kosi* pilgrimage route which at peak times, especially during *adhik mas* (the intercalary month that the Hindu calendar adds to every third year), is followed by tens of thousands of pilgrims from the city and the surrounding districts. The journey of nearly [five *kos*, or] 50 miles is generally completed in five days. The essence of the Panch-kosi is that it is a clockwise circumambulation of the city such that the pilgrim always keeps the sacred area on his right. He worships in temples located to the right of the road (and which therefore fall just within the sacred perimeter) and performs his ablutions and bodily functions on the left. The route thus marks the boundaries of sacred space and of the area within which all who die are granted 'liberation' by Shiva.

One way in which space within this area is differentiated is on the model of a series of concentric circles which increase in sanctity as they decrease in size, and of which the outermost is the Panch-kosi pilgrimage route. In its most elaborate form we find a sequence of seven such circles, each described by a set of eight shrines dedicated to Lord Ganesh, thus making up the fifty-six conventionally enumerated Ganesh shrines of the city (Eck 1978:179; 1983: 187–8). This elephant-headed and highly anomalous deity is the Lord of Obstacles and the Guardian of Thresholds who commonly appears on doorways or temple-gateways, who is worshipped on entry into or exit from sacred time at the beginning and end of life-cycle rituals, and who in this context appears as the protector of Kashi's sacred space. At the focal point of the whole series is the most sacred and renowned of all of the city's temples, that dedicated to Shiva as Vishvanath, the Lord of the Universe. The pilgrim thus passes through seven protective rings in order to penetrate the sacred core of the city.

Not only the city however. The numerology equates it with the cosmos, the seven circles representing the seven layers of the atmosphere (Rana Singh 1986); the eight shrines round each circle guarding the eight points of the compass. What seems to be marked out, then, is the totality of space, at the centre of which stands the Lord of the Universe. Given the repeated equivalence we shall find postulated between Kashi and the cosmos, and between both of these and the human body, the whole scheme is moreover suggestively reminiscent of the yogic idea that in order to attain union with God, the adept's life-force must cross through the seven centres or circles ranged along his spine [Eliade 1969: 241ff, Beck 1976].

A slightly different ground-plan is of a division into four circles, of which the outer and most inclusive is marked by the Panch-kosi route, and the inner and least inclusive by the *Antargrahi* ('inside the house') pilgrimage around the heart of the city. We will later see that, according to one theory, the fate of the deceased's soul depends on which of the four he died in.

Kashi is apart from the rest of space. Being really gold, the very earth on which it stands is different. According to the *Kashi Khanda*, the city is not attached to the ground but is suspended in the sky, though this can only be seen by those with the 'divine sight' (*divya drishti*) of the yogi. It is popularly said to balance above the earth on the trident (*trisul*) of Shiva. As an elderly funeral-priest explained it,

Kashi was once just jungle. One day when Shiva and Parvati were sitting there, Shiva suddenly announced, 'O.K. Parvati ji, I am going to leave you for twelve years.' 'But Maharaj,' protested Parvati, 'I always serve and worship you. How am I going to live without you?' Well, you know that God Shankar [i.e. Shiva] is *arbhangi* [one who follows his whims with truculent intransigence]. So Shiva said, 'No, I am going; it is my wish', and disappeared with a 'we'll see' when Parvati swore to find him before twelve years were up.

Separately, both of them remained in this jungle. Every midnight Shiva would plant his trident in the earth, and stick Mount Kailash [his Himalayan abode] on top of it. All the gods would come there to sit and chat until morning.

There was an old woman who lived in that jungle. Nobody knows what caste she was ... On the very day before Shiva would have completed his twelve years' absence, she happened upon Parvati wandering alone in that dense and desolate forest. Parvati explained her plight, and the old woman promised to guide her to Shankar's court that night ... So it came to pass that Parvati found the great god playing his *damru* [two-sided drum] with his left hand; in his right hand was his trident, and from his matted locks flowed the Ganges. Just as dawn was about to break, and Shiva was on the point of uprooting his trident, Parvati came up behind him and caught him by the wrist. 'Leave go', he ordered angrily. But Parvati refused. 'If I do', she said, 'and if you uproot the trident, then how will people in the *Kali age* [our present degenerate epoch] "swim across" [i.e. obtain salvation]?' 'Are you crazy?' asked Shiva. 'If I leave my trident here those people will profane (*apavitra kar dena*) Kailash; they will wash their arse-holes and spit in the Ganges, insult the gods and fuck in the temples. Is that a good thing?' 'Well,' said Parvati, 'you should close your eyes and enjoy it, for everybody will be worshipping you. Just listen, don't look.' With that, morning came, the trident remained where it was and the gods were unable to leave.

The shaft of Shiva's trident is implanted below the Vishvanath temple, such that the temple itself stands on its middle prong. The two outer prongs support the Kedar temple in the extreme south of the city, and the temple of Onkareshvar Madadev in the extreme north. These three temples give their names to three divisions (*khands*) of Kashi; and again we shall find that these are of eschatological significance, for it is widely held that those who die in Kedar *khand* are granted a more immediate and unconditional 'liberation' than those whose death occurs elsewhere. The three prongs are also said to represent the three *gunas* or 'qualities' from which all substance is composed, and the three 'worlds' (*loks*) of heaven, earth and the netherworld—once more equating Kashi with cosmos.

The gulf which divides the city from profane space is again underlined by the maxim that it stands *apart* from the three *loks*, the fourteen *bhuvans* ('worlds' of which seven are above and seven below), and the nine *khands* (regions of the earth). Kashi constitutes a tenth *khand*. Now clearly this formulation reiterates the theme of separation. But it also implies the notion of englobement. When, for example, the *Satapatha Brahmana*, one of the most venerable texts on sacrifice, claims that there are thirty-three gods and that Prajapati is the thirty-fourth, this is to be understood to mean that Prajapati 'is greater than the thirty-three gods and encompasses them and all other beings within himself' (M. and J. Stutley 1977:230). By the same token, Kashi is not only separate from, but is superior to, and contains the rest of space. Apart from the three *loks*, it subsumes them. Hence, not only do all the gods reside in Kashi, but so do all other places of pilgrimage. There is consequently no need for its inhabitants to visit other sacred centres for they are present as physically identifiable locations within their own city. They are not only here, but they were created and will be destroyed here. Similarly, space itself was given form in Kashi where the deities who preside over the eight directions were assigned their jurisdiction [Eck 1978]. As Kashi can be said to encompass the rest of space, the Panch-kosi pilgrimage is not just a circumambulation of the city but also a circumambulation of the universe.

But if Kashi is the cosmos it is also symbolically identified with the human body. The five ghats which are visited in the course of the *Panch-tirath* pilgrimage are sometimes explicitly equated with the five elements (*panch-tattva*) of which the body is composed. In popular thought the model which is most often suggested is that of the gross (physical) body (*sthul sharir*). The city is described as a prone figure with its head on the southern boundary at Asi, its loins at Manikarnika, and its feet at Varuna in the north. The *Kashi Khanda* (chapter 55) would seem to suggest that this body is that of Shiva himself. In the literary sources, however, the postulated homology is more often with the centre of the subtle anatomy (Kashi is the spot between the nose and the eyebrows), or with the subtle body as a totality. On this last theory, the rivers Asi and Varuna at the extremities of the city, and a third river which flows through the centre, are identified with the three main veins of the yogic body—respectively with the *ida, pingala* and *sushumna* [Kane 1973:4:625–6, *Kashi mahima prakash*, p. 36]. This last is associated with the transcendence of duality and the achievement of *moksha* [Eck 1983: 299]. Synonyms for it are *brahmanadi* and *shamshan* (cremation ground); and it is significant that those of my informants who know this yogic theory generally identify the *sushmna* with the Brahmnal (= *brahmanadi*), a small rivulet of which there are now no obvious traces, but which is supposed to issue into the Ganges at Manikarnika. According to this identification, then, the central vein of Kashi's mystical body terminates at the cremation ground, equating it with the highest centre of the yogic anatomy.

As we have seen, one of Shiva's boons to Vishnu was that Kashi perpetually remains in the *Satya yuga*, the golden age of original time. All time is auspicious there, and not even the worst planetary conjunctions should prevent the pilgrim from setting out for the sacred city. As it is always the Satya yuga in Kashi, the time in which it exists is immune to the degeneration to which time elsewhere is subject. It is said that there are three powers which can never enter its precincts: Yamraj (the god of death), *yamdut* (his messengers) and the Kali Age (the degenerate epoch into which the rest of creation has sunk). Time here does not so much run down as stand still. It remains as it was at beginning of things. Kashi is therefore free from the progressive decay and doomsday destruction to which our world is otherwise subject. Shiva's city thus takes on Shiva's own characteristics as the 'Conqueror of Death' (Mahamritunja), and as the only one of the gods who is truly indestructible (*avinashi*) and who survives the dissolution of the cosmos.

According to the doctrine of karma, all actions, sinful or meritorious, are held to have more or less inevitable consequences which the actor will harvest in this or future lives. Now, although *karma* theory can be, and in popular thought commonly is, placed within the framework of cyclical time (by, for example, making the murderer suffer an appropriate fate at the hands of his victim in the next life) the doctrine would a priori seem to imply a durational notion of time flowing inexorably on into a future in which the actor will reap the fruits of his past actions. But in a timeless world, actions have no future consequences; and this may perhaps help us to understand why people often talk as though the laws of karmic retribution are suspended in Kashi, where saint and sinner alike are equally eligible for release from the cycle of rebirths. If duration is denied, so too are the karmic consequences of conduct.

But this, of course, is only one side of a much more complicated picture. Karma doctrine is not completely abandoned; nor is Kashi's immunity to the insidious effects of time unequivocally upheld. The same informant who reaffirms the dogma that all time in Kashi is equally auspicious and belongs to the Age of Truth is likely to attribute the uninhibited venality of daily life to the exigencies of a degenerate epoch, and to be as fastidious as the next man about consulting an astrologer before scheduling his daughter's marriage. 'Where Kashi is, the Kali Age is not,' says Sita Maharaj, only to admit ruefully that something of its 'influence' nevertheless 'falls' on the city, and that even here one who dies under an inauspicious lunar asterism (*nakshattra*) is unlikely to obtain the 'highest state'. In the Kali Age, people explain, the soil of Kashi no longer looks like gold to mortal eyes; the *ling* (the phallic emblem of Siva) in the Kedar temple which was made of nine jewels in the *Satya yuga*, of gold in *Treta* and of silver in *Dvarpara* is now mere stone; and even the shape of the city has changed and contracted in size. Originally 84 *kos* (about 168 miles) and in the form of a trident in Treta its perimeter shrank to 52 and became like a discus, in Dvarpara it was 32 *kos* and in the shape of a chariot, and it is now just 25 *kos* and like a conch shell. The change is so palpable that when an ascetic who had been meditating in a secret cave since the time of Lord Ram was disturbed by the rebuilding of Sindhia ghat, he opened his eyes, looked about him in dismay, exclaimed that the *Kali yuga* must have arrived, and disappeared into the Ganges. Even in Kashi, one is forced to concede, creation has been tarnished by time. It could hardly be otherwise, for here too the world is manifestly imperfect.

My informants were generally content to live with the contradiction between the notion that Kashi is preserved from the ravages of time, and the admission that even here time has taken its toll. But in many of their statements they nevertheless imply a resolution to it by suggesting that it is not Kashi itself which has degenerated, but man's ability to perceive it. The soil *is* gold, the city *is* suspended in space, and Shiva *does* wander in it daily; and if we cannot see all this it is because we do not have the 'divine sight' of the yogi. 'This Kashi', as Anant Maharaj explained, 'is like the sun behind the clouds. I know it is still there although I cannot see it.'

The more radical conclusion which is sometimes drawn is that this Kashi of bricks and mortar is not the real one. The real Kashi is in the heart, and this external one is merely an aid to its realization. If this realization is achieved, then there is no need to go to the physical *tirath* (place of pilgrimage), for it will come to the worshipper. Thus Shiva came to Kashi from Kedarnath in the Himalaya, and established himself in the form of the *ling* in the Kedar temple, as a reward for Rishi Mahandatta's devotions. As the popular saying has it: 'If the heart is good, the Ganges is in the [shoemaker's] wooden bowl; if the heart is true, Mecca is in the shit-house'.

But whether the real *tirath* is considered to be in the mind or on the ground, the overwhelming consensus is that the physical Kashi puts the worshipper in direct contact with the transcendental world. Transmission conditions between the sacred and profane worlds are, as it were, optimal; and the place itself is a kind of transitional zone between the two. The term *tirath* derives from the Sanskrit root signifying the idea of crossing over, and refers not only to a 'place of pilgrimage', but also to a 'ford' or 'crossing point'. It thus implies a literal and symbolic transition. The term *tarak* has the same etymological provenance [Eck 1983: 332] and is the name of the mantra Shiva whispers in the ear of those who die in Kashi in order to enable them to 'swim across' and obtain salvation. In myth, it is the place where the *ling* of Shiva is made to span the three worlds like a giant column, and thus to join the different cosmic planes [Eck 1978].

'A *tirath*', as one informant defined the term, 'is a place where you can settle to religious practice and immediately reap the fruits of it.' It is like sinking a well for water, he went on. In certain kinds of terrain you can dig and dig without success, while in others your efforts are almost immediately rewarded. Kashi belongs to the spiritual equivalent of the second. Meritorious actions performed there yield fruits a thousandfold greater than the same actions performed elsewhere; while such deeds performed during the Panch-kosi are magnified ten million times. The pilgrimage to Kashi is a sure way of expiating even such monstrous crimes as cow-slaughter, and it is said that all the pilgrim's past sins drop away as he crosses the Panch-kosi road. For such expectations there are impeccable precedents. When Bhairav chopped off Brahma's fifth head with the nail of his little finger, the skull clung irremovably to his hand, and until he came to the tank at Kapalmochan on the city's boundary, he was forced to wander the three *lok*s in search of a means of ridding himself of the sin of Brahmanicide. Similarly, Ram and Sita performed the Panch-kosi in order to expiate the Brahmanicide of Ravana.

Kashi boosts the consequences of actions, with the result that merit performed here is powerfully magnified. But this quality is double-edged. The repercussions from *sins* committed there are also heightened. According to the *Kashi mahima prakash* (chapter 22), such sins earn the sinner a lengthy spell as a *rudrapishach* (the most terrifying of demons). Popular tradition takes a more optimistic view by allowing them to be expiated on the Panch-kosi, the performance of which mitigates 'the sufferings of Bhairav' inflicted at the time of death (p. 29). Sins perpetrated during this pilgrimage, however, are recorded in the 'thunderbolt writing' of Vishnu—that is, they are ineradicable. A slightly more elaborate formula, much quoted by the pilgrimage-priests (*pandas*), postulates a whole hierarchy of locations, the superior deleting sins of the inferior. Thus, those committed elsewhere are destroyed by visiting a *tirath*; those committed in a *tirath* are destroyed in Kashi; those of Kashi on the Antargrahi pilgrimage; those of the Antargrahi on the Panch-kosi, while the latter are written with the thunderbolt of Vishnu, unless, some *pandas* add, they are offered the gift of a cow at Manikarnika ghat as the final act of the pilgrimage. Since this last dispensation is in some doubt, the rules which should govern conduct on the Panch-kosi are particularly austere, for at all costs the pilgrim must avoid the merest hint of lust, anger, and envy, or the unintentional destruction of the insects beneath his feet. The near impossibility of doing so, and the dire consequences of failure, are often casuistically invoked by the *pandas* themselves as justification for their own reluctance to undertake the rigours of the journey.

A FULL LIFE AND A LIBERATING DEATH

Not only does the sacred area contain the rest of space, but it also encompasses the four goals of human existence (the *purusharthas*). All are fulfilled in Kashi (*Kashi mahima prakash*, chapter 64). Hence the desire for salvation no longer excludes the politico–economic pursuits of *artha* or the sensual pleasures of *kama*. When Brahma weighed Kashi against heaven and the other *loks*, Kashi was heavier on account of the combined weight of the *purusharthas* (*Kashi khanda*, chapter 30). Again, an inscription outside the main shrine of the Kedar temple claims that the *ling* bestows *moksha*, *dharma*, *artha*, and *kama*, and that one who worships there will never lack grains. In Kashi, Parvati frequently assumes the form of Annapurna whose very name suggests her inexhaustible bounty as a giver of sustenance. She provides for the physical well-being of the city's inhabitants, while her consort, Shiva, provides for the salvation of their souls (cf. Eck 1983: 161). Kashi is likened to a huge storehouse, and it is said (despite some rather intrusive evidence to the contrary) that nobody ever goes hungry there.

Since tomorrow will provide for itself, the 'true' Banarasi whiles away the day at the pan shop at the corner, doing body-building exercises at one of the city's innumerable wrestling schools, indulging his fancy for music or caged birds, or merely sitting on his roof in a pleasurable hemp-induced haze of bhang. A burping, pot-bellied, pan-spitting jocularity or a muscle-bound devil-may-care assertiveness provide the predominant stereotypes for those who work and live by Manikarnika ghat, rather than the morbid moroseness one might perhaps associate with people who spend their lives in an atmosphere perpetually permeated by the smoke and smell of the funeral pyre. Their self-image is above all summed by the words *mast* and *phakkarpan*. The meaning of the first is hard to capture adequately in English but conveys the idea of an intoxicated joy and amusement at the divine comedy of the world, while the second has the sense of a carefree eccentricity (cf. Sukul 1974: 325; Saraswati 1975: 49; Kumar 1988: 83ff). Both are pre-eminently characteristics of Lord Shiva himself. Just as Shiva reveals himself in the nature of his chosen city, so he reveals himself in the character of its inhabitants. It is tempting to go further. If, as Kumar's (1988) study would suggest, an ultimate 'good' in the Banarasi value scheme is a sense of freedom from constraint, then it is not only Shiva who provides the role model, but also Shiva who is seen as making it possible. In life, his city as a storehouse of plenty assures freedom from want; while in death, it assures an ultimate freedom.

As the much quoted Sanskrit tag proclaims, *Kashyam marnam mukti*: 'death in Kashi is liberation'. Those who die in one of the other six sacred cities (*puris*) of India are reborn in Kashi, and thus enhance their prospects of salvation next time round. Even the gods desire death here, and several Puranic texts advise the pilgrim to smash his feet with a stone on arrival lest he be tempted to leave for another *tirath* (Kane 1973: 4: 566–7). Although it is close to where he lives, an old Dandi Svami ascetic of my acquaintance will not so much as cross the Asi into the modern quarter of Lanka, for Lanka lies on the wrong side of the sacred boundary, and who knows but that death may overtake him there.

'Liberation' is granted to those who die within the sacred area enclosed by the Panch-kosi pilgrimage route. The course of the Ganges, as it passes through Banaras, is particularly auspicious: it flows from south (the direction of death and of the kingdom of Yamraj) to north (the direction of rebirth). The sacred city itself is built entirely on the western bank of the river, which forms one of its boundaries; while the eastern bank is known as Maghar and is an especially inauspicious place to die. The reason for this is explained by a number of myths which recount how the sage Veda Vyas attempted to establish Ramnagar on the far side of the river as a centre to rival Shiva's city. Jealous of his initial success, Shiva dispatched Ganesh to scotch the threat, and by various stratagems Ganesh tricked the sage into writing in the scriptures that those who die in Maghar will be reborn as assess (cf. Sherring 1868: 173). Since there is no gainsaying the veracity of these texts, the pious inhabitant of Ramnagar hopes to be spared time to move across the river into Kashi when death approaches.

Characteristically, however, there is a mitigation. According to some variants of the story, Ganesh had come to Vyas in the guise of one on his deathbed. When, having accomplished his mission, he then died, Shiva and Parvati were distraught at the prospect of such a rebirth for their son. What was written was written; but to it Shiva insisted on the proviso that those who die in Maghar during that particular month, the month of Magh, will obtain the same rewards as those who die in Kashi.

Conventionally there are said to be three different routes to salvation: the paths of knowledge, works, and devotion. Although at first sight the dogma that 'death in Kashi is "liberation"' would seem to provide a fourth alternative, in fact this is not the case. Those who die here achieve gnosis at the moment of death when Shiva gives them the *tarak* mantra generally believed to consist of the sacred syllable 'Aum' which destroys the fruits of past actions 'as a single match burns ten thousand kilogrammes of cotton'. A vision of this scene was vouchsafed to Swami Ramakrishna Paramhams who, as he passed Manikarnika in a boat, saw the goddess Annapurna sitting with a corpse in her lap and Shiva bending over to whisper in its ear (cf. Sukul 1974: 219). Shiva thus acts in precisely the same way as the Brahman who, by whispering the *gayatri* mantra to the initiand at the sacred thread ceremony, converts him into one of the Twice-born (Eck 1983: 331). In the fullest sense of Hertz's phrase (1960: 80), then, 'death is an initiation' with Shiva as the preceptor.

One way of ensuring that death is met with in Kashi is, of course, to take matters into one's own hands. We know that a tradition of religious suicide in pilgrimage centres goes back at least as far as AD seventh century [Bharadwaj 1973: 76]. The practice is sanctioned by the *Skanda* and *Padma Purana*s (Kane 1973: 4: 607), and is associated with several *tiraths* [Dave 1959: 95]; (Morinis 1984: 297). Bishop Heber, who visited Banaras in 1824, described how every year:

Many scores ... of pilgrims from all parts of India, come hither expressly to end their days and secure their salvation. They purchase two large Kedgeree pots between which they tie themselves, and when empty these support their weight in water. Thus equipped, they paddle into the stream, then fill the pots with the water which surrounds them, and thus sink into eternity. Government have sometimes attempted to prevent this practice, but with no other effect than driving the voluntary victims a little further down the river; nor indeed, when a man has come several hundred miles to die, is it likely that a police-officer can prevent him (Heber 1861: 168).

In the oral 'history' of my informants, however, this tradition of religious suicide is above all associated with the Kashi Karvat temple. It is significant though that here matters were supposedly not left entirely up to the pilgrim himself. It is said that in a less corrupt age a *karvat*, or saw, was suspended from the roof of the shrine and would spontaneously fall on those on whom

Shiva chose to bestow his blessing. What this story reveals (and resolves) is a certain ambiguity in the attitude to religious suicide, which seems to smack of the victim's reluctance to submit himself passively to the divine will. The texts, as Kane notes (1973: 4: 604ff), are equally ambivalent and sometimes attempt to lay down stringent conditions under which such action is permissible. Certainly today, suicide in Kashi is regarded with equivocation, and some of my informants held that it is sanctioned by penalties ten times as severe as those which apply elsewhere. When, during my fieldwork, an old man tried to drown himself in the Ganges off Manikarnika ghat, the Boatmen promptly fished him out, and nobody I spoke to seemed to think that they had done his soul a grave disservice, or that their action revealed a want of faith.

But while the idea of travelling to Kashi in order to commit suicide is generally discountenanced, there is no question about the rewards which await those whose object is to die a natural death. We can distinguish between two broad categories of such people: those who have come for Kashi-*vas* ('residence in Kashi') and those who have come for Kashi-*labh* ('the profit of Kashi'). Kashi-*vasis* have moved to the city in order to lead the religious life during their declining years, and to await death with the confidence provided by the guarantee of Shiva's grace. Those who come to reap 'the profit of Kashi' are those who are carried here on their deathbeds, the majority of them being catered for in one of several charitably founded hospices specifically intended for the dying.

Far larger numbers of corpses of those who have not been fortunate or deserving enough to die in the city are brought for cremation on the ghats, often from very considerable distances. Although the doctrine generally upheld as orthodox by the Brahman specialists is that it is only by actually expiring in Kashi that 'liberation' is achieved, many people maintain that cremation here is sufficient. In fact these two views are not entirely incompatible, for it is often asserted that the vital breath (*pran*) does not leave the body until the chief mourner cracks open the deceased's skull with a stave when the body has been half-consumed by fire. According to this theory, then, death does not occur at the cessation of physiological functioning, but during the last rites, and consequently all who are cremated in Kashi may be said to have died there.

An even greater number of bundles of ashes of corpses cremated elsewhere arrive in Banaras for immersion in the Ganges. The saying is that the deceased will reside in heaven for as long as any portion of his mortal remains is sanctified by Ganges water (cf. Kane 1973: 4: 243); for it is recalled that Raja Bhagirathi brought the sacred river to earth in order to inundate the bones of his forbears, and thus secure their immortality. ... An alternative theory is that those whose ashes are immersed in Kashi will be reborn in the city, with the implication that they will attain 'liberation' at the end of their next incarnation.

Ashes can be taken out into the river by boat from anywhere along the ghats. At present, however, cremation is confined to Manikarnika and Harishchandra ghats. Throughout most of this century, the former has been by far the more popular of the two, accounting for around three-quarters of the total number of corpses disposed of at the burning ghats each day (around eighty at the time of my fieldwork). As a result, the funeral pyres burn uninterruptedly throughout the day and night at Manikarnika, a fact so palpable that my informants' constant reiteration of it seemed over-determined. Persons of real distinction are cremated right next to the footprints which Vishnu left at the very spot on which he performed his cosmogonic austerities; others to one side of the ghat.

Though in an admittedly weaker form, an association between cremation and cosmogony is again made with regard to Harishchandra ghat. Harishchandra abuts on to Kedar ghat, and although at present a hundred yards or so separates the latter from the pyres of the cremation ground, I was frequently told that formerly there was no gap at all. Now the tank known as Gauri *kund* at Kedar ghat is commonly described as the 'original (*adi-*) Manikarnika'; and it is claimed by those associated with this part of the city that it was here that Vishnu 'really' performed his cosmogonic austerities, and that the Manikarnika tank is merely a replica. In this way the Harishchandra cremation ground is also identified with the place of creation.

What the pilgrims and mourners who come to the ghat are far more likely to know, however, is the story of the righteous raja for whom it is named. There are several rather different textual variants, but the following version (told by a funeral-priest) is typical of the oral tradition of the ghats. Several of its most prominent themes will crop up again in subsequent chapters: in particular, a characteristic element of cynical self-parody in the portrayal of even a heavenly priesthood; and a stress on the vital significance of various types of prestation.

In the time of the *Satya yuga* Raja Indra (the king of heaven) decided to perform a sacrifice and summoned the sage Vashishth to preside. But Vashishth sent word that he was engaged in an important *shraddh* (mortuary) ritual, and that Indra should invite somebody else. Accordingly, he called upon Vashishth's great rival, Vishvamitra.

Before Vishvamitra could get started on the sacrifice, however, Vashishth showed up at Indra's court having completed his previous engagement. This was a considerable embarrassment as Indra now had two (notoriously rivalrous) priests to preside over the same ritual. Moreover, the sages had immediately started to squabble about which of them was the more knowledgeable. 'Well,' Vashishth challenged, 'who is the most truthful being in the whole world? Tell me that.' Conscious of who was providing the gifts (*dan*) associated with the sacrifice, Vishvamitra unhesitatingly nominated Indra himself. But Vashishth stoutly insisted that it was Raja Harishchandra of Ayodhya. 'Having thrown the bone', Indra remarked to his wife, 'the two dogs quarrel.' The dispute, it was agreed, should be resolved by putting Harischandra to the test.

So it was that Vishvamitra—in the guise of an impoverished Brahman—appeared to the raja that night in a dream. Being the king that he was, Harishchandra pressed him to accept *dan* of a thousand gold coins, and told him to demand whatever else he had need of. 'I require your kingdom,' said the sage.

On waking, Harishchandra sent all his servants and soldiers in search of that Brahman; and when Vishvamitra was eventually brought before him, he made the *sankalp* (the binding ritual resolution) for the donation (*dan*) of all his possessions. But no sooner had the gift been gifted than Vishvamitra pointed out that 'on top of every *dan* there is a [supplementary] *dakshina*' [a gift or 'fee' which completes the original donation]. 'Where', he demanded to know, 'is that?'

Well, of course, Harishchandra had nothing left to give. So he set out on foot with his wife [Taramati] and son [Rohit] for Kashi. In order to realize the *dakshina*, he there sold Taramati and Rohit to a malevolent and grasping Brahman from the neighbourhood of Jangambari. In that house Taramati was put to grinding flour and washing dishes, was treated with unremitting harshness, and at one stage was even accused of being a witch who ate the livers of young boys. Meanwhile, the raja had sold himself as a servant to Kalu Dom, the then Dom Raja. (The untouchable Doms are a caste of funeral attendants who preside over the construction of the pyre and the incineration of the corpse and who levy a 'tax', or *kar*, for providing the fire with which it is ignited).

Piqued by his lack of success thus far, Vishvamitra one day turned himself into a snake and bit Rohit as he plucked flowers for the Brahman's puja. As her son lay dying, Taramati begged her cruel mistress to summon some man knowledgeable in the cure of snakebite, shrewdly appealing to her self interest by pointing that if he died they would lose their original investment. But all her mistress could do was to kick her in the arse and demand to know how Taramati proposed to reimburse them for their loss.

Thunder crashed all about her on that dark, rain-driven night when Taramati carried her son's limp corpse to the cremation ground where Harishchandra worked as a watchman. At first he did not recognize his wife and child through the murk; nor did he identify Taramati's grief-choked voice when she protested that she had no money to pay the *kar* on which he insisted. But even when a flash of brilliant lightning had illuminated his wife's features, and realization had dawned on both of them, he resolutely refused to cremate the corpse until his master had received his due. 'Who is Taramati? Who is Rohit? This is my *karam* [work, destiny, *karma*]. Without the tax I cannot burn.' Now the one thing which Taramati still possessed was a ring which Raja Harishchandra himself had given her, and this she now offered as *kar*. But the Dom's perquisites also include a shroud off the bier. Rohit, however, had neither shroud nor bier; and again, Harishchandra was immovable. So Taramati began to unwrap her sari to offer the Dom in lieu.

Before her nakedness was revealed, however, a dazzling light appeared in the sky, and a heavenly aeroplane raining petals of flowers swooped down on the ghat. On one side sat the chastened Vishvamitra; on the other the triumphant Vashishth. The righteous raja and his rani were taken aboard; Kalu Dom clung on to the tailplane and the three of them were carried off to heaven, where Harishchandra was offered, but declined, the throne of Indra. Rohit, who had been restored to life, ruled Ayodhya for many years as the true son of his truthful father.

THE DIALECTICS OF 'LIBERATION'

'Death in Kashi is "liberation"'. But what is 'liberation'? I employ the term as a rough equivalent for *mukti* or *moksha* (which are used interchangeably). The verb *mukti hona* means 'to be free of', as in the phrase *rin se mukt hona*, 'to be free of debt'. The noun forms *mukti* and *moksha* thus commonly signify 'freedom' from some encumbrance. Tonsure, for example, is a procedure for getting *moksha* from sin; while the world gets *moksha* from the evil effects of an eclipse when it is over.

The problem starts as soon as one enquires what death in Kashi is a liberation *from*. The range of responses to this question is extremely wide. The commonest is that it is a 'cessation of coming and going', that is, of rebirth. You no longer 'have to bear the pain of the womb', or have 'to wander between the 840,000 kinds of life-form'. But what kind of state this absence of rebirth is held to imply is highly variable and often only vaguely formulated. My theologically more sophisticated informants often claimed that it is a permanent extinction of the individual soul which is 'absorbed into the Universal Spirit as water mixes with water'. But a funeral-priest with a reputation for being the most learned member of his community in such matters held that you become a star which eventually disintegrates into the five elements once your merit is exhausted. By far the most prevalent view, however, is that *mukti* entails a perpetual and sybaritic residence in heaven. As one informant, a man of apparently limited aspirations put it: 'if you feel like a *rasgulla* [a variety of sweet] then one will appear before you'. Another visualized heaven as a kind of antithesis to the world of economics as defined by Lionel Robbins. In heaven, he said, 'the ends are few and the means are many. On earth the means are limited and the needs are many.'

The most knowledgeable pandits distinguish a hierarchy of four different types of 'liberation': *salokya* (residence in the same world as God), *samipya* (living in close proximity to God), *sarupya* (acquiring the form of God) and, the highest, *sayujya* (complete union with God 'as water mixes with water'). We have seen that the sacred area of Kashi is sometimes represented in terms of a model of four concentric circles, of which the innermost (marked by the Antargrahi pilgrimage route) encloses the area of greatest sanctity. In some of the texts this spatial hierarchy is made to interlock with the hierarchy of types of *moksha*, such that *sayujya* is attained only by those who die within the Antargrahi, and *salokya*, the lowest form, by those who die in the outermost ring bounded by the Panch-kosi road (Sukul 1977: 39 after the *Padma Purana*).

Many people, however (*including* a number of prominent priests), interpret the doctrine that 'death in Kashi is a "liberation"' as a promise of a happy and prosperous *rebirth*, a distinctly uncanonical view. A handful go so far as to repudiate explicitly the notion that it leads out of the endless cycle of existence on the grounds that if all the people who die in Kashi were regularly eliminated, the world would soon come to an end. Some are unwilling to say anything more precise than that 'from it one gets a good state'; and others combine these different theories: *moksha* means different things in different parts of the city. Those who die in Kedar *khand* are released from the cycle of rebirths, while those who die elsewhere are reborn 'in a good house'.

But whatever 'liberation' is, there is almost complete unanimity that all who die in Kashi get it. Shiva's grace is indiscriminately extended to all, whether they be Brahman or Chandal (untouchable), raja or beggar, dog, insect, Muslim or *mleccha* (foreigner). Not only is caste made irrelevant to one's prospects of salvation, but so too is karma. Here in Kashi Shiva bestows his blessing even on sinners, 'just as a mother takes a dirty child onto her lap'. The story is told of a certain Brahman who had lived the most infamous of lives and who was killed by a tiger. A vulture scavenged a bone from the corpse; and in mid-flight right over Kashi a second vulture tried to snatch it away, with the result that it fell into the Ganges below. Now at that very moment the messengers of death were dragging the deceased's soul into the most terrible of hells. But as soon as the bone made contact with the water, they were forced to release their victim who went straight to heaven (*Kashi Mahima Prakash*, chapter 22). Kashi, it is often said, is for him whose salvation can be obtained nowhere else. ...

We have earlier seen that in Kashi time stands still. What we are now in a better position to appreciate is that, according to the more orthodox view of *mukti*, it is not only the city which is outside time, but also all those who have died there. Death becomes liberation from time and impermanence. Shiva's city holds out to the dying the promise of its own, and his own, immunity to temporality.

Taken literally, it is clear that all this radically subverts a whole gamut of doctrines generally regarded as fundamental to 'orthodox' Hinduism. It not only implies a suspension of the laws of karmic causation, but also puts in serious question the significance of the sacerdotal function of the Brahman. The rituals at which he officiates becomes an irrelevance to the salvation prospects of his patrons. This conclusion is in fact drawn by many of the sacred specialists themselves, who will on occasion concede, or even volunteer, that in Kashi the mortuary rituals are merely outward form, and are not strictly necessary to the fate of the deceased's soul. The dilemma of the Banaras Brahman who makes his living out of the traffic of pilgrims and mourners seems to be this. If *mukti* is subject to the qualifications of karma, then the greatness of Kashi (on whose reputation his livelihood depends) is undermined, for it can no longer cater to the miserable sinner in search of a sure salvation. But if he insists that *mukti* is available to all regardless of their ritual conduct, then the Brahman declares himself redundant. Further, this same doctrine simultaneously constitutes an oblique challenge to the institution of renunciation, to the idea that an ascetic withdrawal from the world is prerequisite for salvation. It too is deprived of any ultimate significance, since for those who expect to die in Kashi *moksha* is attainable *without* abandoning the world, and is no longer incompatible with the sexual and material pursuits of the householder.

Even the position of the gods is subverted (as they themselves are quick to realize), for when all are liberated who will make them offerings? As a result they are not a little ambivalent about Shiva's munificence, and it is they who petition him to revoke his boon that a mere visit to the *ling* in the Kedar temple is sufficient qualification for *mukti*. Again, it is in response to the representations of the gods that the Asi and Varuna rivers are instructed to prevent the grossest sinners from entering the city (*Kashi Khanda*, chapter 30). Even Shiva himself is forced to recognize the problem. Exiled from Kashi during the reign of the righteous king Divodas, and abandoned by nearly all the gods who have been seduced by the glories of the city, he sourly reflects on the difficulty of commanding obedience when even death is without menace (*Kashi Khanda*, chapter 52). The path of devotion (*bhakti*) as the pre-eminent route to salvation is again discouraged: the problem which apparently preoccupied the medieval mystic poet–saint Kabir when he insisted on being moved *out* of Kashi into Maghar on his deathbed. As his much-quoted verse explains, 'If Kabir dies in Kashi, what homage will he render Ram?'

Although nearly all my informants assert that 'liberation' is bestowed on all who die in the city, and although this would seem to abrogate the inevitability of karma, few of them maintain this position entirely consistently. Despite the complete eschatological significance to which such a theory condemns them, the mortuary rituals *are* (usually) performed; and, even though they died in Kashi, the souls of those for whom they are not are believed to wander the city as malevolent ghosts. Moreover, there is a natural reluctance to admit that the scoundrel gets off scot-free, and it is generally supposed that in some form or another he will be confronted by the fruits of his past actions. 'If you planted an acacia tree then how will you eat mangoes?' There is also the disturbing consideration that if literally everybody were eligible for 'liberation' in Kashi, the population of the world would soon be depleted, and the ordained order of things disrupted. 'If all the donkeys go to heaven, how will the Washerman live?'

The problem, then, is how to have it both ways: how to maintain the dogma that death in Kashi is *always* 'liberation' without abandoning the theory of the immutability of karma. For those who hold that the real Kashi is in the heart, there is of course no difficulty. It is by reaching the *internal tirath* that *mukti* is attained; and this can only be done by those who have escaped the bondage of desire. For others, however, the problem remains; and a whole range of possible resolutions to it are attempted.

One is to claim that retribution is exacted in *this* life. Sins will catch up on the sinner in the form of a lingering and gruesome end, or of a miserable existence before it. But a much more general solution is to propose that only those with good karma are privileged to die in Kashi. Endless instances are given of people who had come to await death in the city, but who, on account of their insufficient accumulation of merit, expired on some brief expedition outside the sacred precincts. The tale of the Brahman reprobate, whose just punishment was rescinded after the vultures had dropped one of his bones in the Ganges, is matched by the parable of Dhananjay, the moral of which is diametrically opposed to that of the first story. Dhananjay was the dutiful son of a wicked mother. On her death he brought her ashes to Kashi for immersion; but owing to a whole chapter of accidents, they were stolen before he could complete the task. The lesson explicitly drawn is that even in Kashi karma cannot be cheated.

Even more frequently, however, the difficulty is met by postulating a period of expiatory suffering immediately after death and before the soul is granted 'liberation'. So, for example, it may be said that the sinner is condemned to a term as a demonic *rudrapishach*, or must pass through nine existences as a stillborn foetus. But the commonest and most elaborated theory is that he is first subjected to *Bhairavi yatna*, 'the sufferings of Bhairav', who is Shiva's ferocious and terrifying chief-of-police (*kotval*) in Kashi. The punishment is much less protracted than that meted out to those who died elsewhere, but is much more intense. The *Kashi Khanda* (chapter 31) quantifies its severity as thirty-two times greater than that experienced at the hands of Yamraj. *Bhairavi yatna* is described as purifying the soul in preparation for *mukti* as gold is purified by melting it in fire. The punishment 'burns up the sins, after which the gift of Shiva is obtained'.

Given such a retribution, it might appear somewhat misleading to speak of the law of karma being 'suspended' or 'abrogated' in Kashi. This would be so were it not for the fact that the dialectics of 'liberation' are taken a step further. We have seen that according to one scheme, Kashi is divided into three zones, or *khands*. Now even those who insist most stridently that sins must inevitably be paid for by 'the sufferings of Bhairav' are apt to claim exemption for those who die in Kedar *khand*. For them, it is held, 'liberation' is direct, immediate, and unqualified. The inevitability of karma is thus once more subverted—on occasion only to be propped up again with the plea that it is exclusively those of exceptional merit who are permitted to die in this quarter of the city. Such submissions, however, bear the marks of an impromptu sophism with which even the sacred specialists themselves are not entirely comfortable; for it is hard to suppress the suspicion that not all the acknowledged scoundrels who died here were really saints. The underlying contradiction cannot be so easily disposed of; and is perceived not only by the anthropologist but also by many of his informants.

DEATH AND COSMOGONY

This belief that salvation is guaranteed to those who die at the pilgrimage centre is, of course, familiar from other world religions. Those who die at Mecca, Jerusalem, or Compostella go straight to heaven. But in the case of Kashi the association with death and its transcendence is given a pivotal place in the sacred identity of the city; and my contention is that this association is inseparable from the set of sacred characteristics which I have outlined in the previous sections of this chapter.

At the outset we saw that Kashi is the place where the universe is created and destroyed at the beginning and end of each cosmic cycle. What I would now like to suggest is that at Manikarnika ghat this process is kept in perpetual motion by the constant stream of cremations which are staged here.

A recurrent theme in Hindu religious thought is the homology which is held to exist between the body and the cosmos (e.g. Eliade 1959: 172ff). Kashi itself establishes a link between them, for as we have seen, it is not only a microcosm of the universe, but also a macrocosm of the body. Body and cosmos are governed by the same laws, are constituted out of the same five elements and everything that exists in the one must also exist in the other. Thus, all the gods and the whole of space are present within the human body, a notion which is explicitly elaborated in the *Garuda Purana* (part 15), to which the Banaras sacred specialists continually refer. The homology is also one of the basic principles underlying the architectural theory of the Hindu temple, which is constructed on the plan of a cosmic man (Beck 1976); while many forms of worship involve a cosmicization of the body of the worshipper (cf. Gupta 1979).

Body and cosmos are thus equated; and this would seem to imply a further equivalence between cremation which destroys the microcosm of the physical body and the general conflagration which destroys the macrocosm at the end of time (*pralay*). Etymologically, *pralay* is 'a process (*pra*) of melting (*laya*) (M. & J. Stutley 1977: 231), but it is generally represented as a two-phase destruction by fire and flood resulting in a return to a state of complete undifferentiation. A corpse is similarly subjected to fire (through cremation) and water (through the immersion of the ashes)—in some of the Puranic texts an individual death being classified as *nitya* ('daily' or 'constant') *pralay*. According to these same sources, Shiva (as Rudra) presides over the conflagration phase, while Vishnu (as Narayana) presides over the deluge.

Cosmic dissolution, however, is not only an end of the universe; it is also a beginning, a necessary prelude to a new world cycle and hence a renewal of time. Similarly, we shall find that cremation is not just a destruction of the deceased's body, but an act of regeneration through which he is reborn. So just as the world's annihilation by fire and flood is a precondition for its recreation, so the deceased is cremated and his ashes immersed in water in order that he may be restored to life. Since the body is the cosmos, the last rites become the symbolic equivalent of the destruction *and rejuvention* of the universe. Cremation is cosmogony; and an individual death is assimilated to the process of cosmic regeneration.

It was by his prolonged austerities (*tapas*) that Vishnu created the world. *Tapas* generates heat, which is in many contexts represented as the source of life and fertility. Through the heat of his austerities the ascetic acquires a super-abundant sexual potency; through the cremation pyre the seven storm-gods are born (O'Flaherty 1973: 109), and through bathing in the tank of Lolark in Banaras fecundity is conferred on barren women—the tank being sacred to the sun, the source of heat. Of a piece with this, Vishnu burns with the fire of his *tapasya* in order to create the cosmos at Manikarnika ghat. Cremation is sometimes explicitly described as a kind of *tapasya*, and certain of the texts clearly represent it as such (Knipe 1975: 132). It is no coincidence, then, that the most celebrated cremation ground in India is also the scene of cosmogony. By entering the pyre here the deceased, as it were, refuels the fires of creation at the very spot where creation began.

That this association is symbolically meaningful is illustrated by Baikunthnath Upadhyay's comments following his rendering of chapter

26 of the *Kashi Khanda*. In recent years, he notes (p. 57), there has been a move to persuade the authorities to shift the burning ghat away from the centre of the city. But this, he argues, would be quite improper as it is *essential* that corpses be burnt by Charan Paduka on Manikarnika ghat, the marble sandals marking the very spot on which Vishnu performed his austerities.

Another way of developing the same argument would be to show that cremation is a kind of sacrifice (cf. Knipe 1975: 132–4; Das 1982: 120–6), and that sacrifice is a re-enactment of cosmogony. With regard to the second of these connections, and to invoke a different account of the origins of the world, *every* sacrifice is held to replicate the primal act of Prajapati who produced creation by the sacrificial dismemberment of his own body: 'any sacrifice is ... the repetition of the act of Creation, as Indian texts explicitly state' (Eliade 1965: 11). Or, as Heesterman (1959: 245ff) puts it, 'the sacrifice may be described as a periodic quickening ritual by which the universe is recreated ... The pivotal place is taken up by the sacrificer: like his prototype Prajapati he incorporates the universe and performs the cosmic drama of disintegration and reintegration ...' Prajapati is recreated 'in order that he may repeat the cosmogony and that the world may endure and continue' (Eliade 1969: 109).

A proper elaboration of the first proposition, that cremation is a kind of sacrifice, will [be found in Pary 1994, chapter 5]. Some preliminary indication of its plausibility is perhaps suggested by the fact that in the Sanskritized Hindi of my informants, cremation is *antyeshti* or 'last sacrifice'; that the manuals of mortuary practice regularly explicitly equate it with fire sacrifice, and that both are represented as resulting in rebirth. The ritual procedures described on both occasions reveal moreover some remarkable parallels: in terms, for example, of the preparation of the site, the treatment of the victim and the divine status it is accorded, the offerings to the fire and the idea of being engaged in an act of dangerous and polluting violence.

My argument, then, is that since cremation is a sacrifice, since sacrifice regenerates the cosmos, and since the funeral pyres burn without interruption throughout the day and night at Manikarnika ghat, creation is here continually replayed. As a result it is always the *Satya yuga* in Kashi, the beginning of time when the world was new. That it is because of the city's sacredness that people come there to die and be cremated is an obvious truism. What is less obvious perhaps is that the ideology itself implies that Kashi *is* sacred precisely because they come for this purpose, for it is death and cremation that keep the city at the navel of the universe yet outside space and time. It is no accident, then, that the scene of cosmogony is also the site of unceasing cremation; or that especially important corpses should be burnt on that very spot where Vishnu sat for 50,000 years alight with the fire of the austerities by which he created the world.

REFERENCES

Beck, B.E.F.
1976 The symbolic merger of body, space and cosmos in Hindu Tamil Nadu. *Contributions to Indian Sociology* (n.s.) 10, 2: 213–43.
Bharadwaj, S.M.
1973 *Hindu places of pilgrimage in India: A study in cultural geography*. Berkeley: University of California Press.
Das, Verma.
1982 *Structure and cognition: Aspects of Hindu caste and ritual*. Delhi: Oxford University Press.
Dave, J.H.
1959 *Immortal India*. Vol. 2. Bombay: Bhartiya Vidya Bhavan.
Eck, D.
1978 Kashi, city and symbol. *Purana* 20, 2:169–92.

———
1983 *Banaras: City of light*. London: Routledge & Kegal Paul.
Eliade, M.
1959 *The sacred and the profane: The nature of religion*. New York: Harcourt Brace Jovanovich.

———
1965 *The myth of the eternal return*. Princeton NJ: Princeton University Press.

———
1969 *Yoga: Immortality and freedom*. Princeton, NJ: Princeton University Press.
Gupta, S.
1979 Modes of worship and meditation. *In* S. Gupta, D.J. Hoens, and T. Goudriaan, *Hindu tantrism*. Leiden: E.J. Brill.
Herber, Reginald
1861 *Narrative of a journey through the upper provinces of India*. 2 vols. London: John Murray.
Hertz, R.
1960 *Death and the right hand*. London: Cohen and West.
Heesterman, J.C.
1959 Reflections on the significance of daksina. *Indo-Irananian journal* 3:241–58.
Kane, P.V.
1973 *History of Dharmsastra*. Vols. 3 and 4. Poona: Bhandarkar Oriental Institute.
(Shri) Kashi kanda.
n.d. *Complied and rendered into Hindi by Baikunthnath Upadhyay. Varanasi: Shri Bhragu Prakashan.*
Kashi mahima prakash.
n.d. Complied by Kashinath Jha. Varanasi: Master Kheladilal & Sons.
Knipe, D.M.
1975 *In the image of fire: The vedic experience of heat*. Delhi: Motilal Banarsidass.
Kumar, Nita.
1988 *The artisans of Banaras: Popular culture and identity, 1880–1986*. Princeton, NJ: Princeton University Press.
Morinis, E.A.
1984 *Pilgrimage in the Hindu tradition: A case study of West Bengal*. Delhi: Oxford University Press.

O'Flaherty, W.D.
1973 *Asceticism and eroticism in the mythology of Siva*. Oxford University Press.
Saraswati, Baidyanath.
1975 *Kashi: Myth and reality of a classical cultural tradition*. Simla: Indian Institute of Advanced Study.
Sherring, M.A.
1975 (1868) *Benares: The sacred city of the Hindus*. Delhi: B.R. Publishing Corporation.
Singh, Rana P.B.
1986 Shiva's universe in Varanasi. *In* T.P. Verma, D.P. Singh, and J.S. Mishra, eds., *Varanasi through the Ages*. Varanasi: Bhartiya Itihas Sankalan Samiti.
Stutley, Margaret and James.
1977 *A dictionary of Hinduism*. London: Routledge & Kegan Paul.
Sukul, Kubernath.
1974 *Varanasi down the ages*. Varanasi: K.N. Shukul.
_____
1977 *Varanasi Vaibhav*. Patna: Bihar Rashtrabhasha Parishad.

PART two

Bonding Together: Piety and Passion

PREFATORY REMARKS

Within its own domain, which may or may not be constitutive of society in its totality, religious life usually tends to be holistic: things that have been set apart must eventually be brought together. Thus, in Islam, absolute otherness defines Allah. He is the stern lord who will preside over the day of judgement, meting out reward and retribution to the arisen dead. He is, however, also the most merciful and beneficent God to whom the pious pray for guidance as to 'the straight path' (*al-sirat mustaqim*) in human affairs. Prayer (*abadat*) and mercy (*rahmat*) bind Allah and the believer. Among the various Latin roots of the word religion, the verbs *religere* (noun *religio*) and the later *religare* respectively denote the ideas of reverential bonding and intimate attachment between human beings and divinities (or the supernatural generally). In short, setting apart and bonding are mutually implicated ideas: one does not make sense without the other.

Prayer and passion (from the Latin *passio*, suffering) as the means of religiousness obviously must not be conceived of in matter-of-fact, instrumental, terms. The underlying attitude in whatever one does is one of piety (from the Latin *pietas*, meaning 'devout behaviour towards both human beings and divinities'). Georg Simmel defined piety as 'a disposition of the soul, an integral part of life ... [that] colours the soul even in the permanent absence of a religious object' (1997: 23). It is an integral condition but ruthlessly non-egoistic. It is the projection of this altitude that, according to Simmel, constitutes religion (ibid.: 161).

Piety in its most intense forms is imbued with feelings of longing and suffering that result from the inability to connect, conveyed by the Sanskrit word *viraha* (pangs of separation) common to most Indian languages. Perhaps the simplest and the most widespread ritual of devotion and bonding amongst Hindus and Jains is *puja*, the highly formalized and respectful worship of icons and images, at home or in a temple. (The word *'puja'* may be of Dravidian origin, indicative of the offering of flowers and anointing with holy paint or powder as acts of homage.) It comprises symbolic acts of adoration, decoration, feeding, etc. and the recitation of verbal formulae (mantra) and hymns (*bhajan*). Buddhists too have a conception of *puja*, but this may on occasion consist only of verbally seeking the threefold refuge (*trisharana*) of the Buddha, the *dhamma*, and the *sangha* (monastic community). Congregational prayer in Sikh *gurdwaras*, although not called *puja*, shares some features with it, most notably formal expression—through hand gestures, bowing, and singing—of piety and reverence.

The first reading in this section is a condensation by Christopher Fuller of a large body of ethnographic material bearing upon Hindu worship. He discusses, among other things, the nature of divine images, the settings, structure, and meaning of *puja*, and the symbolic exchanges, most notably of consecrated food, between the worshipper and the deity that may be regarded as the consummation of the ritual of bonding. Fuller illustrates some of these aspects of *puja* from his own ethnographic study of the celebrated Minakshi temple in Madurai in south India. He also discusses the sociological aspects of the ritual, focusing on the connection between *puja* and social hierarchy. Finally, he analyses the relationship of *puja*, social precedence, and kinship.

Puja usually has the individual worshipper as its subject, but it could also take the form of the collective *arti* (a sound-and-light celebration involving bells, conches, ghi lamps, and the burning of camphor and incense). It usually comes at the end of the evening *puja*, or the last *puja* of the day, and is led by a designated temple priest. It has a highly formulized structure and offers little scope for individual innovation.

Within the Hindu traditions of worship, the impatience of the individual devotee with formalism has found expression in *bhakti*, which is the spontaneous, ecstatic expression of the devotee's love for his or her chosen deity (*ishtadeva, ishtadevi*), and of his or her longing for union with the divine. This tradition is perhaps of Vedic origin, but has over time come to be regarded as an alternative to formal expressions of veneration, disdainful of priests and other functionaries, and the most personal form of devotion. *Bhakti*, it may be noted, is derived from the root *bhaj*, 'to share, be loyal', or *vibhaj*, 'to separate'.

A good example of the *bhakti* attitude is provided by Basavanna's hymn with which the second reading by A.K. Ramanujan opens. In it the devotee sings of the superiority of the human body over the temple as a site of devotion. Ramanujan offers his interpretations of *bhakti* on the basis of songs called *vachans* composed by the saints of the Virashaiva tradition of south India, who were radical heretics. They rejected the 'great traditions' of Hinduism as well as the established 'little traditions', the Vedic fire sacrifice as well as image worship.

The core idea that these seekers cherished was that of the spontaneous 'outbreak of love' for the divine that knows no limits and follows no rules. Longing for union with one's chosen deity lies at the very core of mysticism across religious traditions. It carries with it intense suffering, which is particularly characteristic of women devotees such as Mahadevi whose *vachana*s too are discussed by Ramanujam. Employing a structuralist framework, he contrasts the 'structure' of the established religious traditions with the 'anti-structure' and protestation of *bhakti*.

The motif of suffering does, however, also occur prominently in the 'great traditions' of major religions. The Passion of Jesus, culminating in his crucifixion has already been alluded to in Susan Visvanathan's discussion of the Eucharist. Shia Muslims the world over symbolically participate in the suffering and martyrdom of Imam Husain, Prophet Muhammad's grandson, through rituals of mouring during the first ten days of Muharram, the first month of the Islamic calendar (see Saiyid in Madan 1991). These rituals include self-flagellatilon. The holy city of Karbala in Iraq, where Husain met his death, has a particular appeal to Shia pilgrims anywhere, and their willingness to make sacrifices for undertaking the pilgrimage is well known.

The third reading in this part is Akbar Ahmed's account of a tragic incident of faith leading to death reported from Pakistan about twenty years ago. Inspired by what they believed to be a series of revelations received by a young Shia woman, a group of her relatives and co-villagers disposed of their worldly possessions and arrived in Karachi to enter the sea in the firm belief that, as revealed, they would be miraculously transported to the port of Basra in Iraq, from where they would proceed on pilgrimage [which is a mode of bonding *par excellence*] to Karbala. In the event, half of the 38 pilgrims were drowned.

Ahmed's analysis of the incident throws light on a number of critical issues such as the nature of inter-sectarian differences in Islam, the place of women in Muslim society, the concept of death, and the power of sacrifice, suffering, and, above all, martyrdom. These traditional religious themes combine in interesting ways with contemporary social institutions and social change to create situations such as the one discussed in the third reading here.

REFERENCES

Saiyid, A.R.
1991 Moharram. *In* T.N. Madan, ed., *Religion in India*. New Delhi: Oxford University Press.
Simmel, Georg.
1997 *Essays on religion*. New Haven: Yale University Press.

Hindu Worship

C.J. FULLER

*P*uja, 'worship', is the core ritual of popular theistic Hinduism. Every
day, in temples and homes throughout India, puja is being performed
before the deities' images by both priests and lay people. *Puja* in a
large temple, especially in the blackness enveloping the inner-most shrines,
has a powerful sensual impact, often amplified by the press of a large crowd
of devotees in a hot, confined space. Frequently, there is a deafening and
even discordant sound as the music of pipes and drums combines with
ringing bells and the chanting of sacred texts. Scented smoke pours from
the burning incense and camphor, and the heavy perfume of sandalwood,
jasmine, and roses hangs in the air. The bright silks and gold, silver, and
jewels covering the images scintillate as priests wave oil lamps through the
darkness. And when the ritual reaches a climax, devotees lift their hands in
the *namaskara* gesture to show their respect to the deities whose names they
loudly praise.

In a small temple or house, where *puja* is performed with fewer people
present, the ritual is usually more restrained, so that its personal and almost
homely aspect is more apparent than in a large temple. In *puja*, the deity in
its form as an image is typically welcomed with a drink of water; it is undressed
and bathed, and then clothed again, decked in jewellery and garlanded with
flowers. A mirror may be provided so that the deity can gaze upon its own
beauty. The deity is offered a meal, ideally of sumptuous splendour, and

Excerpted from C.J. Fuller, Worship. In *The camphor flame: Popular Hinduism and society
in India*. Princeton, N.J.: Princeton University Press. Chapter 3. © Princeton University Press.

entertained by music, singing, and dancing; incense is wafted over it and decorated lamps are waved before it. At the end, the deity is bade farewell with the standard gesture of respect. In a temple in the early morning, a deity may be gently woken and at night put to bed, perhaps alone with a lullaby, perhaps with its consort to the accompaniment of erotic hymns. *Puja*, at its heart, is the worshippers' reception and entertainment of a distinguished and adored guest. It is a ritual to honour powerful gods and goddesses, and often to express personal affection for them as well; it can also create a unity between deity and worshipper that dissolves the difference between them.

THE NATURE OF DIVINE IMAGES

Like other rituals addressed to the deities of popular Hinduism, *puja* is normally conducted with images (*murti; vigraha*). ... All larger temples, as well as many domestic shrines and other places of worship, contain sculptured images. ... Sculptured images are athropomorphic (or sometimes theriomorphic) representations of deities, carved in stone, cast in bronze, or made out of wood, terracotta, or other materials. Sometimes images are made out of painted clay, so that they disintegrate when thrown into the river or sea at the end of a festival. In almost all large temples, the majority of images are stone or bronze, and they are often exquisitely beautiful. In a temple, the immovable image (*mula murti*, 'root image') of the presiding deity, generally made of stone, is housed in the main shrine; around it stand images of subsidiary deities, sometimes placed inside shrines and sometimes not. Movable images (*utsava murti*, 'festival image') of the presiding (and subsidiary) deities, which are usually cast in bronze, are used in festival processions and other rituals performed away from the immovable images. Although most sculptured images are anthropomorphic or theriomorphic, the aniconic *linga* of Shiva is an important exception.

Plainly, since many images represent gods and goddesses with several heads, eyes, or arms, and a host of other fantastic features, they are not designed to be exact likenesses of ordinary people or animals. The deities have powers and attributes transcending those of earthly beings, which their images are intended to display. However, the design of sculptured images (including *linga*s) is strictly governed by traditional iconographic rules, which in principle define precisely their proportion and shape, as well as the features particular to the deity whose image it is. Thus, the number of arms or the weapons and animals held in their hands are specified uniquely for each deity or form of a deity, who can easily be identified once the rules of Hindu iconography are known.

Images are normally man-made artifacts. They are not usually considered to be sacred objects until they have been consecrated by installing divine power within them. However, some aniconic images are actually uncarved rocks. The *linga*s in many of Shiva's grandest temples are believed to have emerged naturally from the ground, 'self-existent' and already full of divine power. A comparable example is the special type of fossil known as *shalagrama*, considered sacred to Vishnu. As it is imbued with Vishnu's powers, it can be revered just like any other image of the god. The same applies to the dried berry of a shrub (*Elaeocarpus ganitrus*), known as *rudraksha*, which is sacred to Shiva. Various other 'naturally' sacred mineral and vegetable objects are treated similarly.

In the category of aniconic images, we can also place the unhewn or perhaps roughly etched stones, sometimes painted red, that serve as little village deities' images throughout India; they are either housed in crude shrines or left standing under a tree or in the open air. These stones serve exactly the same function as the sculptured images and *linga*s found in larger temples, even though they do not fit the classical iconographic rules. The same applies to other representations, such as the metal tridents or pots that stand at small shrines in some areas of India. Pots in particular, when filled with water in which a deity's power has been installed, are often used as the functional equivalents of sculptured mobile images at little deities' temples.

Frequently, a picture of a deity substitutes for an image. Pictures have probably always been used, but the advent of cheap colour printing has made an enormous selection available in contemporary India. Carved images are relatively expensive, and in millions of poorer homes the household shrine contains only pictures of the family's favourite deities, which are consecrated and worshipped just like images.

Completeness requires us to stretch the category of images still further to embrace, for instance, natural phenomena such as rivers, as well as animate beings. For example, although any deity may be installed in a water-pot, the consecration ritual is generally said to turn the water into the water of the river Ganges (Ganga), the phenomenal form of the goddess Ganga. The Ganges (and indeed all rivers) are both 'images' of Ganga and Ganga herself. In some contexts, much the same holds true for the soil in relation to the goddess of the earth, Bhudevi. A comparable but distinct example is the burning oil lamp, commonly identified with the goddess Lakshmi. Among living beings, various animals can be understood in a similar way. The cow is probably the best known example; it is frequently, although not invariably or exclusively, identified as an 'image' of Lakshmi and Lakshmi herself. And most important, in the final analysis, the same can apply to a human being. For example, when a priest becomes a form of Vishnu or Shiva during temple worship, his body is really an animate image; a literally anthropomorphic form of the god and, as such, the priest worships himself just as he worships the deity in its image. The case of the human 'image' is important for understanding the relationship between a deity and its image, but let us first go back to ordinary sculptured images.

THE RELATIONSHIP BETWEEN DEITY AND IMAGE

When Hindus visit a temple, just gazing on the images for a 'sight' or 'vision' (*darshana*) of the deities is one of the most important things that they do. *Darshana* brings good fortune, well-being, grace, and spiritual merit to the seeing devotees, especially if they go to the temple early in the morning just after the deities have woken up. But *darshana* is not merely a passive sight of the deity in its image form; the deity is also gazing on the devotee with eyes that never blink, unlike those of human beings. Hence, in *darshana* there is the 'exchange of vision' (Eck 1981: 6) that is so central to Hindu worship before images. In Hindu iconography, the eyes have a special place, and painting on or 'opening' an image's eyes is frequently said to vivify it in an essential preliminary to consecration and worship. Shiva in particular is often represented with a third eye in the centre of his forehead, from which his fiery power flows out, but on all divine images (as well as on men and women) the mark above the bridge of the nose symbolizes the third eye, the point from which power emanates. Thus, when devotees look at images, they are also standing in the field of the deities' power and absorbing it like light through their own eyes.

So in the act of *darshana* what exactly is a Hindu looking at? Is it the deity, its iconic representation in an image, or something in between? The answer is not easy, but it is crucial for understanding popular Hinduism.

We can begin by saying that a deity is *in* an image. It may be there because it has been installed by a consecration ritual, as with a manufactured image, or it may be 'naturally' there, as with a self-existent image or *linga*. The deity may be permanently present in the image, as is generally said to be true in temples, or it may be there only temporarily, as with images made for a festival and discarded afterwards. A distinction between a deity and its image is plainly presupposed in many contexts. For example, the consecration ritual itself is premised on the notion that the image is 'empty' before the deity is installed. By some more theologically sophisticated Hindus, ... the relationship between a deity and its image is commonly explained in terms of the power, *shakti*, possessed by all deities, even though *shakti* itself is personified as feminine. According to this explanation, the image actually contains some or all of the deity's power, so that the purpose of consecration is to install that power in a particular location, the image. There is no limit to the number of separate images within which the deity's power can be installed and the deity is never shackled by locating its power in images. Hence, an image itself cannot be equated with its corresponding deity; the object of worship is not the image, but the deity whose power is inside it. Devotees who gaze upon an image do not directly see the deity, although they are touched by the power flowing out of the image. Certainly, much Hindu ritual is most consistently and economically explained by treating the image as a repository of divine power and, therefore, by distinguishing clearly between the image and its corresponding deity.

Yet this distinction between container and contained must not be over-played. It is true that the identification of an image can be disputed, so that different people disagree about which deity's powers are in an image; sometimes, too, the accepted identification of an image changes over time. Nonetheless, if an object, sculptured or otherwise, is a divine image, it must in principle be the image of a particular deity (or occasionally deities). Hence an image, unlike an ordinary container, is defined precisely by what it contains—the power of a particular deity—so that in the final analysis there can be no absolute distinction between an image and its corresponding deity. Thus people commonly point to an image and observe that it is, say, Vishnu or Shiva, of whom they have had *darshana*; this is not a metaphorical but a matter-of-fact statement that identifies the image as a specific, named deity. Similarly, the term *murti* is widely employed to denote a deity's form (especially Shiva as Dakshina-murti, Nataraja, etc.) as well as a deity's image. Consequently, we must understand the relationship between a deity and its image in a double sense, for the deity can either be distinguished from the image or identified with it, so that the image itself is then a 'bodily' form of the deity, made concrete and visible in mundane time and space. Thus worship is addressed to a deity whose power is *in* an image and also to a deity *as* an image.

The double relationship between deity and image is particularly striking in the case of the human 'image'. Take for example the priest who, in south Indian Shiva temples, should install Shiva's powers in himself before he worships the god; according to the Shaiva ritual texts known as the Agamas, 'only Shiva can worship Shiva'. Plainly, the formula implies that the only perfect worship is the one performed by the god for himself, but here on earth it is commonly taken to mean that the priest must become, at one level, Shiva himself. As a form of the god, the priest then worships himself as part of Shiva's worship in the temple. At another level, though, the priest is a man who can be distinguished from the god Shiva, like a container from the contained. Hence, in these temple rituals, Shiva assumes a form as the priest, but he is also the god whose power is in the priest; his animate image. In general terms, the same applies to anyone identified as divine, whether it is someone possessed by a village goddess, or a bride and groom treated as deities on their wedding day, or a holy man widely revered as a living god. In all these cases, to identify a person as a form of a deity also implies that that person is an 'image' of the deity, for every image is also a divine form.

Finally, let me note that because no deity is constrained by its embodiment in images, a deity can be, and sometimes, is, adored in imageless form; specifically, the divine 'without qualities' (*nirguna*) is worshiped instead of the divine 'with qualities' (*saguna*) made visible iconically. Some religious virtuosi, as well as Hindus opposed to so-called idolatry, have persistently argued that material images are needed only by the simple-minded and spiritually immature, who cannot turn their minds to the godhead without visible representations on which to focus. Muslims in India have long decried the Hindus' reverence for images, but in the last two hundred years or so, partly in reaction to Christian censure during the colonial period, image worship has been increasingly criticized by reformist Hindu intellectuals as a superstitious deviation from the true, original religion of the Vedas, which only marginally refer to the ritual use of images. But apart from some adherents of movements like the Arya Samaj in northern India, which has vigorously opposed image worship since its foundation in 1875, the vast majority of ordinary Hindus have been untroubled by criticism of their 'idolatry'. They know, as any sympathetic observer must also recognize, that in popular Hinduism devotion and respect for the deities are not diminished but most completely expressed through the use of images in worship.

THE CONTEXTS OF *PUJA*

Hindus perform *puja* in a wide range of settings. In temples, where priests are usually responsible for performing it before the deities' images, *puja* should be carried out regularly. Typically, in the great deities' major temples, it is done at least once a day, but in very grand and well-endowed ones, the daily cycle of worship includes a number of separate acts of worship, held at different times of day. In small and poorly funded temples, by contrast, worship may be done no more than once a week or even less often, and at the simple shrines of little deities, it tends to be sporadic. Worship at public temples is classically said to be 'for the benefit of the world', because it is addressed on behalf of all to the deities who protect the whole population and preserve the entire socio–cosmic order. At private temples belonging to particular families, kin groups, castes, or other social units, worship is mainly intended to benefit those who own the temple. When worship is performed by priests, especially in public temples, ordinary devotees have no active role and the value of the ritual is unaffected by the presence or absence of an audience. In all public temples, however, worship can also be performed for the deities either by individual devotees themselves or by priests acting on their behalf, although most ordinary people are usually content simply to salute the deities with the gesture of respect and to have *darshana* of them.

In addition to the worship conducted regularly, a temple's ritual cycle normally includes a range of periodic festivals (*utsava*) as well. ... In very large temples, many different festivals occur weekly, fortnightly, monthly, and annually, whereas in smaller temples there may be at most only one annual festival. During festivals, various kinds of rituals take place, such as processions, dramatic performances, dancing by the divinely possessed, and, at some temples, animal sacrifice. Festivals always incorporate acts of *puja* as well and in its basic structure worship during festivals does not differ from worship performed on other occasions. At public temple festivals the rituals, including the *puja*, are again for the benefit of all, whereas the beneficiaries of private temple festivals are particular groups.

Besides, temples, *puja* is performed in many other institutions, such as monasteries, as well as in Hindu homes, normally at the household shrine where images or pictures of the deities are kept. Ideally, worship at home is done regularly, daily, or perhaps weekly; although men do participate, especially during the more important festivals, domestic worship is often mainly the responsibility of women. ... Some richer, high-caste households employ Brahman domestic priests to conduct their *puja*s, at least at major festivals, but the vast majority of domestic worship is done by ordinary householders. The principal purpose of domestic *puja*, of course, is to protect the household, but in addition many people perform personal worship at home, often addressing it to their own favourite deity (*ishta-deva; ishtadevata*).

In each and every context, *puja* is often one component of a longer sequence, so that it is performed in conjunction with hymn singing, offering oblations into a fire, festival processions, animal sacrifice, and or a host of other rituals. Naturally, *puja* can also vary enormously in its elaborateness and, correspondingly, in the quantities of time and money spent on it. Between the spectacular worship conducted during a major festival at a great temple and the minimal rite held in a simple shrine or a poor home, there is a wide and obvious divergence. But despite this, and despite significant variations in the style of worship among different groups of Hindus in different regions of India, all rituals of *puja* have the same fundamental structure. ...

WORSHIP IN THE MINAKSHI TEMPLE

Let us begin with one particular example of *puja*, which comes from the Minakshi temple in Madurai. Rituals of worship in the Minakshi temple vary considerably. The one to be described is neither as elaborate as some, nor as simple and almost perfunctory as many others. I should make it clear that I shall not describe one specific event. Instead, I shall present a composite account of a ritual that occurs repeatedly in almost exactly the same way on similar occasions, mainly during major festivals for Minakshi and Sundareshwara (Shiva), the presiding deities of the temple.

At such a ritual, movable, festival images are the objects of worship. Minakshi's movable image, which is about two feet high, represents her standing alone, like her larger immovable image. Sundareshwara's movable image, of similar size, is not a *linga*, but an anthropomorphic image of Somaskanda, which represents the god sitting beside a female consort (Uma), with a small figure of their son Skanda between them.

Before a festival procession, the two images are normally placed side-by-side in a hall inside the temple complex. They are clothed, Minakshi in a sari and Somaskanda in a white cloth, but these garments are rarely neat, and the few garlands draped on the images have obviously been there for some hours. Priests and other temple officiants, including musicians, wait near the images and a small crowd of devotees sits or stands in front of the hall. At the start of the *puja*, a curtain is drawn in front of the images to shield them from the gaze of onlookers, but it is usually easy to see round the curtain and no one really objects.

Parenthetically, I should note that a *puja* of the kind to be described is rarely preceded by a preparatory ritual of purification. The latter is generally omitted in the Minakshi temple, although it is recognized that it always ought to be performed, as it is before certain very important rituals. The preparatory ritual is made up of a sequence of several separate rites. The priest states his earnest intention (*sankalpa*) to perform the main ritual that will follow, and he worships Ganesha, lord of beginnings and obstacles, to ensure success. In the course of the rites that complete the sequence, the priest, the site, and the instruments of worship (the lamps, vessels, and the like, in addition to any special object to be used in the main ritual) are successively more highly purified. Charged with the power of the deities that has been installed in them, the priest and the instruments of worship are then worshipped as well.

Puja begins when the musicians start to play and a chanter, a Brahman officiant who is not a priest, starts to recite mantras (ritual formulas) in Sanskrit. The mantras derive from the Agamas and almost all rituals performed in the Minakshi temple include their recitation. The priest presiding over the ritual, assisted by others, first removes the clothes and garlands from the images of Minakshi and Somaskanda in preparation for the bathing ritual, known as *abhisheka*. He pours or rubs over the images a series of mostly liquid substances, such as (in this order) sesame-seed oil, milk, curds, a sweet confection known as *panchamrita*, green-coconut water, and finally consecrated water into which divine power has been invoked beforehand by the chanting of mantras. When this water is poured, the musical accompaniment reaches a climax, signalled by loud and rapid drumming.

The next stage is the decoration ritual, *alankara*, when the images are dressed in new clothes, given new sacred threads, sprinkled with perfume, and adorned with jewellery and fresh garlands of flowers. (Although Minakshi is a goddess, she, like her husband, wears over her shoulder the sacred thread that is the prerogative of adult male Brahmans.) A dot of red powder (*kunkuma*), symbolizing the goddess, is placed above the bridge of the nose on the images, and three stripes of white ash (*vibhuti*) are drawn horizontally on their foreheads, so that the images themselves bear the Shaivas' distinctive mark. The decoration during a major festival is often highly elaborate: an expensive, coloured silk sari for Minakshi and a white silk cloth for Somaskanda, immensely valuable ornaments of gold and precious stones for both images, and several heavy garlands of flowers.

After decoration comes the food-offering ritual, *naivedya*. A covered plate of food, normally plain boiled rice (although there are alternatives), is held before each image in turn by a Brahman assistant to the priests. The presiding priest continuously rings a bell while sprinkling water around the plate, whose lid is slightly raised by the assistant. In this way, the priest offers the food to the god and goddess. The food (to be consumed later by priests or other temple officiants) is then taken away, and the curtain that has screened the whole of the worship thus far is drawn back. Its purpose is partly to protect the deities, especially Minakshi, from prying eyes while they are bathed and dressed, and partly to hide them from evil spirits, who are particularly jealous of the deities' splendid fare and always try to snatch it during the food offering.

Removing the screen lets all the devotees see the final stage, the display of lamps, *diparadhana*. In this ritual, the priest waves a series of oil lamps, and finally a candelabra burning camphor, in front of the images. On various occasions, different lamps are used, but a typical series comprises five oil lamps, each with its own design and number of wicks. The closing candelabra has seven camphor flames (one on each of its six branches and one in the centre; although not strictly part of the *diparadhana*, we can include the candelabra here. Although there are variations in style among priests, it is generally agreed in the temple that the lamps should be waved separately before the head, body, and feet of an image, each time describing in the air the almost circular shape (as written in Tamil) of the ancient mystic syllable *om*, which represents the totality of the universe. The priest, facing the images, waves the oil lamps with his right hand and continuously rings a bell with his left; he does lay down the bell to take the camphor candelabra in both hands. Usually, the candelabra is waved with special care, high in the air, so that everyone can see it; at the same time, the musicians drum very loudly and rapidly to signal the culminating climax of the worship. At this point, many watching devotees raise their hands to gesture in salutation and call out the praises of the god and goddess. Many of them crowd round the priest, who will bring them the still burning candelabra, so that they can cup their hands over the flames before touching their eyes with the fingertips. From the priest, devotees also accept red powder or, more usually, white ash to put on their own foreheads. They then start to walk away, and the priests and their assistants begin to move the images in readiness for the next event in the festival.

Ideally, just as every *puja* should be preceded by a preparatory ritual of purification, so it should also be completed with a sacrificial fire ritual. Briefly, this involves kindling a fire, invoking the deity, in this case Shiva, in the fire, and worshipping him there, pouring oblations of clarified butter and other foodstuffs into the flames (the rite known as *homa*), and then making offerings to the temple's guardian deities around the fire, including an extra offering to the guardian deity of the north-east quadrant, who is himself a form of Shiva. Like the preparatory ritual, the fire sacrifice is carried out in conjunction with acts of worship during certain very important rituals, but otherwise it is omitted. In a *puja* of the kind described, the distribution of powder and ash to devotees normally completes the ritual.

THE STRUCTURE AND MEANING OF *PUJA*

In theory, we might uncover the general structure of *puja* and elucidate its meaning by comparing a series of ethnographic accounts, for which my description of the Minakshi temple *puja* would be one starting point. However, there is a better and simpler approach. The Agamas, which in principle govern the ritual in Shiva's south Indian temples, belong to a body of Sanskrit texts that are treated as authoritative because they contain the deities' own directions for their proper worship. But these texts, since they are the products of an indigenous intellectual desire to abstract and systematize, also provide us with paradigmatic descriptions of *puja*. Only for the worship of the great deities, notably Vishnu, Shiva, and Devi in major temples served by Brahman priests, are texts like the Agamas taken as authoritative. Elsewhere, especially for little village deities worshipped by non-Brahman priests, even putative reference to ritual texts is rare. Nevertheless, the evidence shows that all *puja* rituals share the same fundamental structure and that structure is most clearly laid out in the paradigmatic descriptions contained in the Sanskrit texts.

According to the texts, *puja* consists of an ordered sequence of offerings and services, each of which is known as an *upachara*. Different texts contain variant lists of offerings and services, but their overall sequence is always much the same and the most common total number is sixteen. Jan Gonda

(1970: 186, n. 196) provides a typical list of the sixteen *upacharas* in order, which I reproduce with some added clarifications in table 1.

The sixteen items in this sequence can be grouped into partly distinct phases. First, the deity is invoked (or invited to enter the image) and then installed there (nos. 1–2). Second, water for washing is offered (nos. 3–5). Third—the heart of the ritual—the image is bathed, dressed, adorned, shown incense and a lamp, and offered food (nos. 6–13). Fourth, after a series of gestures of respect, the deity is bidden farewell (nos. 14–16).

The Minakshi temple *puja* described above comprises four rituals that are separately identified: bathing, decoration, food offering, and waving of lamps. These four rituals are normally considered to constitute the full *puja* for Minakshi and Sundareshwara both during festivals and in daily worship, when *puja* is performed before their immovable images. Each ritual is classified as an *upachara* and they correspond—comparing them with the list in table 1—to bathing (no. 6); dressing, putting on the sacred thread, sprinkling with perfume, and adorning with flowers (nos. 7–10); offering food (no. 13); and waving an oil lamp (no. 12). Quite often the lamp service is immediately preceded by waving a censer of incense as well (no. 11). In the Minakshi temple, the rest of the offerings and services (nos. 1–5, 14–16) are usually omitted, to leave only the central, third phase (nos. 6–13).

Does this mean that the Minakshi temple *puja* is incomplete and therefore imperfect? The answer is certainly not. In Hinduism, ritual abbreviation and simplification are ubiquitous procedures that are allowed by the texts themselves, and the practice in the Minakshi temple is entirely conventional.

TABLE: THE SIXTEEN OFFERINGS AND SERVICES OF *PUJA*

1. Invocation of the deity
2. Offering a seat to or installation of the deity
3. Offering water for washing the feet
4. Offering water for washing the head and body
5. Offering water for rinsing the mouth
6. Bathing
7. Dressing or offering a garment
8. Putting on the sacred thread
9. Sprinkling with perfume
10. Adorning with flowers
11. Burning incense
12. Waving an oil lamp
13. Offering food
14. Paying homage by prostration, etc.
15. Circumambulation
16. Dismissal or taking leave of the deity

Admittedly, temple officiants, if directly questioned, sometimes concede that the missing offerings and services should be included, although they often plead as well that because the images are permanently installed in the temple, they always contain the power of the deities, whose invocation and dismissal are therefore redundant. Arguments of this sort, though, are largely beside the point. A full series of sixteen offerings and services is best, but a shorter sequence, albeit less good, still constitutes a properly performed ritual of worship. Moreover, although the 'full' worship in the Minakshi temple comprises only four rituals, which leaves out at least eight of the sixteen textual *upacharas*, it is common practice merely to offer food and wave the lamps. This is done for Minakshi and Sundareshwara on many occasions and for the subsidiary deities almost always. None of this is peculiar to the Minakshi temple, and in most temples, which the former dwarfs in size and resources, a *puja* as full as its four rituals is fairly unusual. Frequently, in the Minakshi temple and elsewhere, *puja* is further reduced to no more than the showing of a one-flame camphor lamp with a plantain on the side as a food offering. Hindus commonly refer to the lamp service, and especially the camphor flame display, as *arati*, a term widely used throughout India as a synonym for *puja*. In the final analysis, the camphor flame, as the culmination of worship, stands synecdochically for the entire ritual. Synecdoche, indeed, is a basic principle of all Hindu ritual, including *puja*. As ordered parts of the whole, short and simple rituals, even if they are described as less good, still reproduce the structure and meaning of their fuller homologues.

It should now be clear that *puja* is, in the first place, an act of respectful honouring and that this meaning is inherent in its structure as an ordered series of offerings and services, most fully displayed in the paradigmatic textual model, but no less present in the Minakshi temple worship that I have described, as well as in more attenuated versions of the ritual. Honour is shown to the deities by presenting offerings and services to their image forms that are (or should be) as luxurious, sumptuous, and delightful as possible, and they should also fit the preferences that each deity is believed to have (for example, elaborate bathing rituals for Shiva and beautiful decorations for Vishnu). That worship is an act of homage to powerful, superior deities is explicitly understood by priests in the Minakshi temple and by many, if not most, Hindus throughout India.

It is common to liken the honour shown to deities with that due to kings, and Gonda's interpretation is echoed by other writers: *puja* 'originally and essentially is an invocation, reception and entertainment of God as a royal guest' (1970: 77). Certainly, the idea that the deities are royal guests is important, especially in major temples where they are actually proclaimed as sovereign rulers. On the other hand, it would be wrong to conclude that *puja* always represents deities as supereminent kings. As I remarked earlier,

Hindu worship has a personal and homely aspect too, and Diana L. Eck rightly observes that it can reveal 'not only an attitude of honour but also an attitude of affection' (1981: 36). Gods and goddesses are often the honoured guests of humble worshippers, and the offerings and services of *puja* closely resemble the acts that ordinary people perform for each other or their guests at home. Respectful honouring is the first meaning and purpose of worship, but it elaborates the hospitality of the home as much as the grandeur of the palace, even if the latter is more striking in great temples.

THE DEITIES' NEEDS AND THEIR RESPONSE TO WORSHIP

Plainly, it is men and women who worship; they have to honour the deities. But do the deities need to be honoured, and do they need the offerings and services rendered to them? Eck points out that worship is shaped by human ideas about honouring guests, rather than being a response to 'God's necessity' (ibid.: 37). She is right and it is crucial that *puja* compromises neither the deities' power nor their other attributes. Nonetheless, the question of divine needs is not simple and there are divergent answers to it, which also suggest that worship, despite its fundamentally uniform structure, can have varying significance for different groups of Hindus.

In the Minakshi temple ritual, as in the vast majority of *puja*s, the images have a key role because the various offerings and services are actually made to them. The images of Minakshi and Somaskanda are physically bathed and decorated, real food is placed before them, and lamps illuminate them. Inasmuch as the images are forms of Minakshi and Sundareshwara, the divine couple themselves accept the offerings and services, or at least they are presumed to do so.

Yet it does not follow that the deities really require these ministrations. In the Minakshi temple, I was repeatedly told that *puja*, like other rituals, is designed 'to please the gods'. If worship, especially in public temples, is performed properly and does please the deities, they can be expected to respond by protecting the whole community so that it flourishes; if worship is not performed properly so that the deities are displeased, they are likely to withdraw protection, causing distress and misery. Many Minakshi temple priests blame contemporary India's problems on what they see as persistently poor performance of temple ritual. That in turn is put down to excessive interference in temple affairs by the Tamil Nadu government, whose control over the temple they fiercely resent. However, even when temple worship is performed properly, divine protection cannot be guaranteed because the deities cannot be directly induced to act beneficently by honouring them in worship. Ultimately, the action of deities is determined by their own will, not that of mortals on earth.

But for my informants in Madurai, the impossibility of compelling divine action also depends on the premise that the deities' pleasure does not derive from the offerings and services in themselves. Gods and goddesses do not actually need offerings and services, because they never are dirty, ugly, hungry, or unable to see in the dark. Hence, the purpose of worship is not to satisfy non-existent divine needs, but to honour the deities and show devotion by serving them *as if* they had such needs. By this method alone can human beings adopt a truly respectful attitude towards the deities. Such an explanation of how *puja* pleases deities is logically consistent with a relatively emphatic distinction between a deity and its image, the container of divine power, because then the deity itself is not directly touched by the offerings and services made to its image. The outlook of Minakshi temple officiants is intellectually consistent and echoes the Agamic ritual texts, which make it clear that Shiva never requires anything from human beings. Many Hindus share a perspective close to the temple officiants' on the purpose of *puja*, the deities' needs, and the role of images, even if they articulate it less systematically.

Yet there is an alternative view, which is more consistent with the tendency to play down the distinction between container and contained, so as to equate an image with the deity of which it is a form. This view is more prevalent among Vaishnava, notably devotees of Krishna, who tend to insist more forcefully than many Shaivas that the image is fully a form of the deity. Correspondingly, in the Vaishnava tradition, the god himself is often thought to need the offerings and services provided for him in worship. Devotees typically portray Krishna, especially in his form as a child, as willingly dependent upon them, so that the god, and the image that is his physical manifestation, actually suffer if they are not worshipped. In other words, Krishna has bodily needs that must be met by the offerings and services of *puja* and he is, in the form of the image receiving them, pleased because his worshippers meet those needs.

Even in this case, though, Krishna's need are satisfied by human beings because he permits it, thereby expressing a mutual dependence between god and devotee that is more prominent in Vaishnava than Shaiva cults. It is all part of Krishna's 'play' (*lila*) in this world; he has chosen to make himself dependent on his worshippers most patently as a child, but his choice implies no qualification of his divine power. As John S. Hawley says, Krishna 'allows us the game of feeding him for our benefit; it is symbolic action and would have no value but for the belief, the mood with which it is infused. God dines on our love, not our food' (1981: 18). Consequently, whether worship is addressed to Vishnu, Shiva, or any other deity, its fundamental purpose is human ministration to *putative* divine needs, in which the action of offering and serving, rather than the offerings and services themselves, is critical.

Furthermore, Vaishnavas are equally insistent that worship does not constrain the deities. Therefore, irrespective of whether a deity actually has needs, or an image actually receives the offerings and services, *puja* is still an act of respectful honouring whose objective is to please a deity in the hope or expectation but not the certainty, that it will protect and favour human beings.

Not all Hindu worship however, is so high-minded, and it frequently is motivated by a conscious intention to persuade or induce a deity to bestow reciprocal favours on the worshipper. Many Hindus, like the priests in the Minakshi temple, insist that it is always wrong to worship in such a spirit, as well as counter-productive, because the deities will be displeased by worship done with blatant ulterior motives. In some regions, especially western India where Vaishnava devotionalism is influential, a linguistic distinction is made between *puja* and *seva*. *Puja* is an exchange, a transaction 'made in connection with benefits for the worshiper', whereas 'worship through *seva* ... represents the "loving care" of those devoted to the deity without thought of benefit or return by the latter' (Mayer 1981: 167). Elsewhere, the term *puja* rarely carries this negative connotation, but the distinction identified by Adrian C. Mayer is a more general one, and *puja* (to revert to the one term) often is performed by or on behalf of individuals or groups, who want to win boons from the deities. For instance, ordinary Hindus in Madurai have often told me that they regularly worship deities in connection with specific requests. Some deny that they bargain, and say that they ask a priest to do the worship while simultaneously praying to the deity, but other people frankly admit that they try to make a deal. Some people even ask first and only offer worship afterwards if their request is met, arguing that it is senseless to spend time and money worshipping deities who will not demonstrate that they can help.

There is no doubt that the great deities, especially Vishnu and Shiva, are generally held to be unresponsive and even angered by futile efforts to persuade them to act in specific ways. Many little deities, by contrast, notably deified malevolent spirits, are thought to voice particular demands, and to be open to more or less direct bargaining about what they will do if such and such an offering is made during worship. In such cases, respectful homage is almost completely overshadowed by the real and assumed motives of worshipper and deity, respectively. Yet other deities—for example, many forms of the goddess—are not thought to take the lofty attitude of Vishnu and Shiva, but are still impervious to blatant cajolery. All these assumptions about the deities are themselves significant elements in the ideological discourse of evaluation, for superior deities are partly distinguished from inferior ones precisely by their ostensible refusal to enter into demeaning bargains with men and women about possible favours. Similarly, as part of the same discourse, educated, high-caste Hindus are generally more inclined to dismiss and condemn attempts to bargain with deities than uneducated low-caste people, although the latter certainly do worship deities without ulterior motives as well; we must be careful not to endorse wholesale élitist disparagement of the faith of the lower strata. It is, however, clear that there is considerable variation among Hindus about the feasibility and morality of seeking personal benefits from worship. *Puja* is first of all an act of respectful honouring, and this is plainly inscribed in its structure. Yet how and why it is such an act, and whether honouring the deities excludes treating with them, are issues on which real differences of opinion exist among Hindus themselves.

THE ACHIEVEMENT OF IDENTITY BETWEEN DEITY AND WORSHIPPER

Let us now turn to one of the most important and distinctively Hindu aspects of *puja*. This is the movement toward identity between deity and worshipper, which is partly revealed by the sequential logic of the ritual as it unfolds.

In the words of Penelope Logan, whose analysis of domestic worship in Madurai I draw on here, a fundamental process in *puja* is 'embodying the deity and disembodying man' (1980: 123). In this process, the image plays a crucial role. Worship, whether in the home or elsewhere, is normally performed before an image precisely because the deity is then represented 'with qualities' discernible by people and it takes on a tangible, fixed, and embodied form, proximate to the human being's condition. In its form as an image, the deity, so to speak, has come 'down' toward the human level; through the performance of worship, the worshipper goes 'up' toward the divine level to achieve, finally, identity with the deity.

In the course of most of the offerings and services that constitute worship, the deity is treated like a human guest embodied in its image, and the ritual reinforces the deity's embodiment in a physical form resembling the worshipper's own. Moreover, since the offerings and services are enjoyed by the deity alone, the separation between deity and worshipper has not yet disappeared. The partial exception to this is the display of lamps, an intangible service seen by both deity and worshipper. In many acts of worship, the lamp service precedes the food offering (as in table 1); in many others, as in the Minakshi temple and most south Indian cases, it follows it. Very frequently, however, in the ritual as performed by Hindus today, *puja* is closed by waving a camphor flame either by itself or in conjunction with other lights.

Showing the camphor flame is the climax of worship and, as mentioned above, it synecdochically represents the entire ritual. Quite commonly, an *arati*, a service of lights that includes a camphor flame, is performed by itself as a standard temple ritual. It is true that a camphor flame is not always shown and the lamp service may include only lamps, or sometimes long wicks, burning oil, or ghee. Nonetheless, as Logan argues (ibid.: 124), camphor has particularly powerful symbolic properties because it burns with a very strong light and fragrance. The flame symbolizes both the deity's embodiment during *puja*, by appealing directly to the physical sense, as well as the deity's transcendence of its embodied form, for the burning camphor, which leaves no sooty residue, provides an intangible display of incandescent light and fragrance. As the all-consuming flame acts upon the senses of the worshipper, as well as of the deity, it simultaneously symbolizes the total disembodiment of the human worshipper. And although the deity was and remains in an embodied form, to be treated like a human guest, this state is now partly dissolved, so that both deity and worshipper together can transcend their embodied forms. When a camphor flame is shown at the climax of *puja*, therefore, the divine and human participants are most fully identified in their common vision of the flame and hence in their mutual vision of each other: the perfect *darshana*. God has become man, and a person, transformed, has become god; they have been merged and their identity is then reinforced when the worshipper cups the hands over the camphor flame, before touching the fingertips to the eyes. By this means, the deity's power and benevolent, protective grace, now in the flame, are transmitted to the worshipper and absorbed through the eyes, again the crucial organs. In principle, moreover, all who see and touch the flame participate in the identification, for they also benefit from the transformation undergone by the worshipper who is often, as in a temple, a priest whose place cannot be taken by ordinary devotees.

Light, most especially the camphor flame, is thus an extraordinarily potent condensed symbol of the quintessentially Hindu idea, implied by its polytheism, that divinity and humanity can mutually become one another, despite the relative separation between them that normally prevails in this world where men and women live and must die. So it is fitting, too, that the camphor flame, through which the identity of deity and worshipper is achieved, should also stand for the whole ritual of *puja*.

THE *PRASADA*

At the end of the Minakshi temple worship, the priest brings the camphor flame to the waiting devotees and also gives the white ash or red powder, which they normally apply on the forehead, although a little ash may be swallowed. The priest usually keeps a stock of ash and powder in a little bag, but ideally he has taken them from the images' feet. The ash and powder are kinds of *prasada*, literally meaning 'grace', and the distribution of *prasada* is the indispensable sequel to all acts of worship in popular Hinduism.

There are several different types of *prasada*. Ash and powder are normally handed out in south Indian temples of Shiva and his consort, but in Vishnu's temples the principal item is a little consecrated water, some to be sprinkled over the head and some to be swallowed. Water and other liquids used in bathing rituals are similarly taken by devotees to be sprinkled or sipped, and flowers that have been placed on the images during worship may be presented to devotees at the end. Other examples could be added, but in many contexts—in temples, houses, on elsewhere—the main type of *prasada* is food that has been offered to the deity during worship and is subsequently eaten by priests, attending devotees, lay worshippers, or indeed anyone else, such as absent friends or relatives to whom it has been sent. In the literature on popular Hinduism, *prasada* is often defined as sanctified food, but this is an error; *prasada*, despite the undoubted importance of food, comprises a wide range of sanctified substances.

Prasada is the material symbol of the deities' power and grace. During *puja*, different substances—ash, water, flowers, food, or other items—have been transferred to the deity, so that they have been in contact with the images or, as with food, have been symbolically consumed by the deity in its image form. As a result, these substances have been ritually transmuted to become *prasada* imbued with divine power and grace, which are absorbed or internalized when the *prasada* is placed on the devotee's body or swallowed. Whenever *puja* is concluded by waving a camphor flame, taking in the *prasada* is a process that replicates and consolidates the transfer of divine power and grace through the immaterial medium of the flame. Hence the flame and *prasada* together divinize the human actor to achieve the identity between deity and worshipper (including non-participatory devotees), which completes the transformation initiated by the offerings and services made during *puja*.

Because food *prasada* is actually eaten, it most strikingly symbolizes human internalization of divine qualities and the 'physiological engagement' between deity and devotee, to borrow from a slightly different setting a phrase of Lawrence A. Babb (1987: 69). No doubt, the powerful and patent symbolism of eating explains the prominence of food as *prasada*. In some Vaishnava cults in particular, the offering of food and its consumption as *prasada* are highly elaborated. But other items can be swallowed as well, and all *prasada* is absorbed by the body, literally or figuratively, so that food *prasada* has no unique efficacy. Moreover, the ritual in its entirety—the *puja* plus the taking of *prasada*—is required to effect the ideal merging of deity and worshipper.

The structure of Hindu worship also suggests that the identification of deity and human is sustainable for only a short period, despite the mutual vision through the camphor flame and the divine power and grace absorbed from the *prasada*. The normal temporariness of the state of identity is aptly marked by the impermanence of almost all the main materials used. Liquids used in bathing rituals drain away; flowers on the decorated images quickly fade and lose their scent; incense, oil, and camphor all disappear in smoke; foodstuffs are consumed; and the ash, powder, or water smeared or sprinkled on the person at the end rapidly rub off or evaporate. Taking *prasada* does not prolong the identity of the divine and human for very long. The whole ritual then has to be repeated and, in a sense, there is so much repetitive worship in Hinduism precisely because it has so much obsolescence built into it. Hence, although *puja* ideally brings about identification between deity and worshipper, the very need for the ritual and its repeated performance are themselves testimony to the relative differentiation of the divine and human that is an ever-present reality for most people most of the time. In the divine world, we are told, flower garlands do not fade, but in this world, where men and women blink and die, they do. ...

WORSHIP AND SOCIAL HIERARCHY

All Hindu rituals ... are about relationships among members of Indian society, as well as between them and their deities, *Puja* is obviously no exception, and how different sets of social relationships among priests, lay worshippers, and devotees are reflected, expressed, and constructed through worship could be discussed from many angles. However, I shall focus on two particular problems that have stimulated anthropological discussion: the connection between *puja* and social hierarchy, and the relationship of *puja* with precedence and kingship.

The terms of the first problem are initially given by the importance of purity and pollution in Hindu society. With more or less analytical sophistication, some writers have argued that the relationship between deities and worshippers in *puja* is homologous with that between the higher castes, particularly Brahmans, and the lower castes: in short, that deities are to people as pure high castes are to impure low castes. ...

The crucial element in this comparison is ritual pollution and its removal; however, infringing the rules of purity offends deities much like any mis-performance of worship, but it does not necessarily mean that deities themselves are seriously affected by pollution, whereas all human beings are, irrespective of their status.

Moreover, although some deities are said by some Hindus to suffer from death or menstrual pollution, no deity is subject to the day-to-day pollution caused by ordinary bodily functions. The Brahmans' purity partly depends on lower castes removing such pollution from them, but the deities' does not depend on Brahman priests acting in like fashion. Thus, the relationship between deity and worshipper is not homologous with that between pure and polluted persons—specifically Brahmans and the lower castes—and *puja* does not express any such homology. ...

Another argument regarding the homology focuses on food transactions and exchanges in *puja*, but in fact there is no real 'transaction in foods' at all during *puja*. The deity is not given food, which it has to reciprocate with a 'counter-prestation' of *prasada*. Instead, the deity is served a meal, which the worshipper later consumes. The food *prasada* is not a return gift, but the same food transmuted, like all other substances that become *prasada*, by its contact with the deity in its image form. There are no food transactions and prestations in *puja*, because they are not what the food offering together with the receipt of *prasada* amount to.

Furthermore, food exchanges between castes do not mirror any salient dimension of *puja*. The rules that traditionally govern intercaste food exchanges, now greatly weakened in much of contemporary India, are complicated. They vary according to the kind of food involved and they are not the same for all groups everywhere in the country. In general, however, ordinary boiled foods such as rice and vegetable dishes, which typically constitute the core of a meal offered to the deities, are subject to the tightest restrictions, because these foods are thought to transmit pollution to the eater most easily. Consequently, to protect their own purity, nobody will traditionally accept such food if it is cooked and served by someone of a lower caste. The very refusal to accept is itself an assertion of higher-caste status. Deities, however, self-evidently accept food cooked by human beings, who are nevertheless their inferiors. Thus deities do not act in relation to people as the members of high castes act in relation to those of low castes and *puja*, inasmuch as it is about the offering of food to deities, does not obey the rules governing food exchanges within the caste system. Once more, we see that the relationship between deity and worshipper is not homologous with that between high and low castes.

Far more pertinent is the relationship between husband and wife. In most households, the wife cooks and serves food to her husband, so that he takes it from his inferior partner; in the same way, the deity takes food from the inferior priest or lay worshipper. In temples, food is often prepared by someone other than the priest; but obviously the cook is also the deity's inferior. When we recall that the closest analogue to eating the deity's leftover food is a wife's consumption of her husband's, it makes good sense to say that a worshipper stands in relation to a deity as a wife to her husband. Such a comparison is indeed drawn in many contexts, so that priests and devotees are commonly described as wifely servants of the gods and goddesses. That in turn is consistent with the fact that *puja* is really about honouring a respected guest, for the quality of hospitality in a Hindu home always depends on a wife's work in her kitchen. Thus, in a real sense, it is the institutionalized hierarchical inequality between husbands and wives, not between castes, that is most patently reflected in the ritual of *puja*.

WORSHIP, PRECEDENCE, AND KINGSHIP

Let me now take up the second problem, the relationship among *puja*, precedence, and kingship, which has attracted considerable attention in recent scholarship. Especially in temples, worship frequently provides the context for displaying and establishing distinctions of rank, and this occurs in two main ways, the first being the order of *prasada* distribution. At a temple, the priest normally gives *prasada* to the person of highest rank first. He (or occasionally she) may be the temple's patron or manager, who has overall supervisory responsibility for its affairs and must ensure, among other things, that its rituals are properly conducted. In the past, particularly at an important temple, the patron was often a king, and even today there are many temples at which an ex-king or his descendant retains the supervisory role. In most smaller temples, the patron was and is a local magnate, often a village or dominant-caste headman, acting in his role as a petty ruler. Especially in south India, most large and many small temples are now controlled by the state, so that the government official in charge assumes the patron's role. Although much temple ritual is paid for by funds controlled by patrons, particular events are often sponsored by outside bodies, such as families or caste associations, and then the leading party who receives *prasada* first is the senior representative of the sponsoring body. Sometimes, too, the sponsor is a wealthy individual. From time to time, the highest-ranking person in attendance at worship is a dignitary visiting a temple, such as a government minister, an influential holy man, or even a famous film star. Often, of course, nobody important is present at ordinary temple worship, so that the priest just goes to the nearest person first. But if there are several people of high rank, the priest distributes *prasada* in their order of precedence before turning to anybody else. In India today, distinctions are rarely made among ordinary members of the public in temples, but in the past, at some major temples, *prasada* was carefully given to Brahman devotees first and then casually handed out to the lower castes or even, as in Suchindram (southern Tamil Nadu), just thrown on a platform for them.

The second way to signal rank, particularly in south Indian temples, is by the receipt of 'honours' (*mariyadai* in Tamil). Honours come in various forms, but one of the most common is a silk cloth, which is draped across the image's shoulders during worship and then tied by the priest, like a turban, round the recipient's head at the end of the ritual. This cloth is usually the principal honour given to a ritual's sponsor; if several representatives of the sponsoring body are entitled to cloths, they are tied in order of seniority. Normally, the recipient of the first (or only) cloth was also, immediately beforehand, the first recipient of *prasada* as well, so that his primacy is doubly marked. *Prasada* and honours have some similarities, but there are also crucial differences; in particular, honours are restricted in number and always single out dignitaries, whereas *prasada*, although, distributed in rank order, can be offered to everyone.

To many Hindus, again especially in south India, the order of precedence at temple worship is of paramount importance, because it publicly confirms the rank of individuals, the offices they hold, or the groups they represent. For this reason, powerful men, on behalf of themselves, their offices, or their groups, have long competed vigorously and even bitterly for precedence in temple worship. Frequently, in temples great and small, disputes over precedence have actually ended in absurd stalemate. ...

But why do people go to such lengths over precedence at temples? Although the distribution of *prasada* allows everyone to receive a deity's power and grace, someone given *prasada* first, and an honour as well, is openly singled out as the deity's first worshipper. That in itself is constitutive of superior status and authoritative rights within the temple, principally because the first worshipper can claim to be the highest-ranking subject of the deity in its capacity as a sovereign ruler. In other words, precedence as emergent from worship depends upon the idea that the deity is quintessentially honoured as a king, whose worshippers form a court arranged in order of rank according to their proximity to him. ...

CONCLUSION

Puja, to conclude, is an act of respectful honouring for powerful deities, which comprises a series of offerings and services. The ritual owes as much to notions of domestic hospitality as it does to obeisance in the king's court. In general, the worshipper is as much a deity's wifely servant as its royal subject. Correspondingly, an attitude of devotion, as well as deference to a powerful superior, is commonly central in worship, although there are also contexts in which respectful honouring largely gives way to interested bargaining for favours from the deity. A ritual that always has the same fundamental structure can therefore be variously interpreted and modified by Hindus, so that its emphasis tends toward homage, devotion, or negotiation.

Participation in *puja* plainly expresses and constructs relationships between powerful deities and their worshippers, and also among worshippers themselves. Such people are often unequal, as we have just seen. Sometimes inequality is most dramatically displayed by complete exclusion from the assembly of worshippers, as in the case of Harijans who were formerly kept out of public temples. Moreover, the constitution of social groups as communities with shared qualities and interests is itself significantly shaped by their common participation in worship, notably worship offered to deities who protect a particular group, such as a family or village. ...

Finally, let me stress again that fundamental to *puja* is the ideal achievement of identity between deity and worshiper; it is inherent in the ritual's internal sequential logic and it is consolidated by the taking of *prasada* afterwards. Ethnography shows that this identity is not explicitly sought by all ordinary Hindus whenever they perform *puja*, and I do not mean to imply that every act of worship is motivated by this lofty objective; more pragmatic ends, such as seeking divine aid in times of trouble, are often far more in evidence. Yet this movement toward identity is worship's most distinctively Hindu aspect and it must be given due significance in understanding the ritual. Through worship, an inferior, less powerful mortal here on earth potentially transcends the human condition to become one with a deity present in its image form. Like *namaskara*, the gesture of respect made to the deities, but more elaborately, *puja* expresses the principle of hierarchical inequality between deity and worshipper. But the ritual simultaneously, even if only temporality, can also overcome the relative separation between divinity and humanity.

REFERENCES

Babb, Lawrence A.
1975 *The divine hierarchy: Popular Hinduism in central India*. New York: Columbia University Press.

1987 *Redemptive encounters: Three modern styles in the HIndu tradition*, New Delhi: Oxford University Press.
Eck, Diana L.
1981 *Darśan: Seeing the divine image in India*, Chambersburg: Anima.
Fuller, C.J.
1984 *Servants of the goddess: The priests of a south Indian temple*. Cambridge: Cambridge University Press.
Gonda, Jan.
1970 *Viṣṇuism and Śivaism: A comparison*, London: Athlone Press.
Hawley, John S.
1981 *At Play with Krishna: Pilgrimage dramas from Brindaban*. Princeton: Princeton University Press.
Logan, Penelope.
1980 *Domestic worship and the festival cycle in the south Indian city of Madurai*. PhD Thesis, University of Manchester.
Mayer, A.C.
1981 'Public service and individual merit'. In Adrian C. Mayer, ed., *Culture and morality*. Delhi: Oxford University Press.

CHAPTER
5

Virashaiva Devotion

A.K. RAMANUJAN

The rich
will make temples for Śiva.
What shall I,
a poor man,
do?   5

My legs are pillars,
the body the shrine,
the head a cupola
of gold.

Listen, O lord of the meeting rivers,   10
things standing shall fall,
but the moving ever shall stay.

asavaṇṇa was the leader of the medieval religious movement,
Vīraśaivism, of which the Kannada *vacanas* are the most important
[spoken] texts. If one were to choose a single poem to represent the
whole extraordinary body of religious lyrics called the *vacanas*, one cannot
do better than choose the above poem of Basavaṇṇa's. It dramatizes several
of the themes and oppositions characteristic of the protest or 'protestant'
movement called Vīraśaivism.

Excerpted from Introduction. In A.K. Ramanujan, tr., *Speaking of Śiva*. Harmondsworth:
Penguin Books, 1973. © Penguin Books.

For instance: Indian temples are traditionally built in the image of the human body. The ritual for building a temple begins with digging in the earth and planting a pot of seed. The temple is said to rise from the implanted seed, like a human. The different parts of a temple are named after body parts. The two sides are called the hands or wings, the *hasta*; a pillar is called a foot, *pāda*. The top of the temple is the head, the *śikhara*. The shrine, the innermost and the darkest sanctum of the temple, is a *garbhagṛha*, the womb-house. The temple thus carries out in brick and stone the primordial blueprint of the human body.

But in history the human metaphor fades. The model, the meaning, is submerged. The temple becomes a static standing thing that has forgotten its moving originals. Basavaṇṇa's poem calls for a return to the original of all temples, preferring the body to the embodiment.

The poems as well as the saints' legends suggest a cycle of transformations: temple into body into temple; or a circle of identities; a temple is a body is a temple. The legend of saint Ghantākarṇa is a striking example: when the saint realized that Śiva was the supreme god, he gave himself as an offering to Śiva. His body became the threshold of a Śiva temple, his limbs the frame of the door, his head the temple bell.

The poem draws a distinction between *making* and *being*. The rich can only *make* temples. They may not *be* or become temples by what they do. Further, what is made is a mortal artifact but what one *is* is immortal.

This opposition, the standing *v.* the moving, *sthāvara v. jaṅgama*, is at the heart of Vīraśaivism. ... *Sthāvara* that which stands, a piece of property, a thing inanimate. *Jaṅgama* is moving, moveable, anything given to going and coming. Especially in the Vīraśaiva religion, a *Jaṅgama* is a religious man who has renounced world and home, moving from village to village, representing god to the devoted, a god incarnate. *Sthāvara* could mean any static symbol or idol of god, a temple, or a *liṅga* worshipped in a temple. Thus the two words carry a contrast between two opposed conceptions of god and of worship. Basavaṇṇa, in the above poem, prefers the original to the symbol, the body that remembers to the temple that forgets, the poor though living moving *jaṅgama* to the rich petrified temple, the *sthāvara*, standing out there.

The poem opens by relating the temple to the rich. Medieval south Indian temples looked remarkably like palaces with battlements; they were richly endowed and patronized by the wealthy and the powerful, without whom the massive structures housing the bejewelled gods and sculptured pillars would not have been possible. The Vīraśaiva movement was a social upheaval by and for the poor, the low-caste, and the outcaste against the rich and the privileged; it was a rising of the unlettered against the literate pundit, flesh and blood against stone.

The poem enacts this conflict. Lines 1–5 speak of 'making temples'. 'They' are opposed to 'I', the poor man, who can neither make nor do anything. In lines 6–9 the poet recovers from the despair with an assertion of identities between body and temple: legs are pillars, the body a shrine, the head a cupola, a defiant cupola of *gold*. From 'making' the poem has moved to 'being'. Lines 10–12 sum up the contrasts, asserting a universal: What's *made* will crumble, what's standing will fall; but what *is*, the living, moving *jaṅgama*, is immortal.

The first sentence of the poem has a clear tense, placing the making of temples in time and history. The second movement (lines 6–9) asserting identities, has no tense or verb in the Kannada original, though one has to use the verb *to be* in the English translation for such equations, e.g. 'My legs are pillars'; Kannada has only 'My legs themselves, pillars'. The polarities are lined up and judged:

the rich	:	the poor
temple	:	body
make	:	be
the standing (*sthāvara*)	:	the moving (*jaṅgama*)

The *sthāvara/jaṅgama* contrast is not merely an opposition of thing and person. The Vīraśaiva trinity consists of guru, *liṅga*, and *jaṅgama*: the spiritual teacher, the symbolic stone-emblem of Śiva, and His wandering mendicant representative. They are three yet one. Basavaṇṇa insists, in another poem, '*sthāvara* and *jaṅgama* are one' to the truly worshipful spirit. Yet if a devotee prefers external worship of the stone *liṅga* (*sthāvara*) to serving a human *jaṅgama*, he would be worthy of scorn.

Jaṅgama in the last sentence of the poem is in the neuter (*jaṅgamakke*). This makes it an abstraction, raising the particular living/dying *Jaṅgama* to a universal immortal principle. But the word *jaṅgama* also carries its normal association of 'holy person', thus including the Living and the Living-forever.

VACANAS AND HINDUISM

Anthropologists, like Robert Redfield and Milton Singer speak of 'great' and 'little' traditions in Indian civilization; other pairs of terms have been proposed: popular/learned, folk/classical, low/high, parochial/universal, peasant/aristocratic, lay/hieratic. The native Indian tradition speaks of *mārga* ('classical') and *deśi* ('folk'). The several pairs capture different aspects of a familiar dichotomy, though none of them is satisfactory or definitive. We shall use 'great' and 'little' here as convenient labels. Reservations regarding the concepts and the dichotomy will appear below.

The 'great' tradition in India would be inter-regional, pan-Indian; its vehicle, Sanskrit. The 'little' tradition would consist of many regional traditions, carried by the regional languages. It should not be forgotten that many of the regional languages and cultures themselves, e.g. Tamil, have long traditions, divisible into 'ancient' and 'modern' historically, 'classical' and 'folk' or 'high' and 'low' synchronically. Such languages have a formal 'high' style and many informal colloquial 'low' dialects. These colloquial dialects may be either social or sub-regional. Cultural traditions too tend to be organized similarly into related yet distinct subcultures socially and regionally. Even the so-called 'great' tradition is not as monolithic as it is often assumed to be. Still, taken in the large, one may speak of pan-Indian Sanskritic 'great' traditions and many regional 'little' traditions. But traditions are not divided by impermeable membranes; they interflow into one another, responsive to differences of density as in an *osmosis*. It is often difficult to isolate elements as belonging exclusively to the one or the other.

A Sanskrit epic like the *Mahābhārata* contains in its encyclopedic range much folk material, like tales, beliefs, proverbs, picked obviously from folk sources, refurbished, Sanskritized, fixed forever in the Sanskritic artifice of eternity. But in a profoundly oral culture like the Indian, the Sanskrit *Mahābhārata* itself gets returned to the oral folk-traditions, contributing the transformed materials back to the 'little' traditions to be further diffused and diffracted. It gets 'translated' from the Sanskrit into the regional languages; in the course of the 'translations', the regional poet infuses it with his rich local traditions, combining not only the pan-Indian 'great' with the regional 'little', but the regional 'great' with the regional 'little' traditions as well. Thus many cycles of give-and-take are set in motion. ...

For the sake of exposition we may speak of several parallel components in the 'great' and 'little' traditions in Hinduism. We may consider these under four tentative heads: (a) social organization, (b) text, (c) performance, (d) mythology. For the 'great' traditions they would be respectively, (a) the caste hierarchy, (b) the Vedas, (c) the Vedic rituals, (d) the pan-Indian pantheon of Viṣṇu, Śiva, Indra, etc.

We may recognize elements parallel to these four for the 'little' traditions. Instead of the Vedic texts there would be *purāṇas*, saints' legends, minor mythologies, systems of magic and superstition—often composed in the regional languages. These are mostly local traditions, though they may seek, and often find, prestige by being rewritten in Sanskrit and absorbed into the pan-Indian corpus. Parallel to the Vedic rituals, every village has its own particular kinds of 'cultural performance': local animal sacrifices, magical practices, wakes, vigils, fairs. The social organization of the 'little' traditions would be the local sects and cults; the mythology would centre round regional deities, worship of stone, trees, crossroads, and rivers. (See diagram on p. 139).

*Vacana*s are *bhakti* poems, poems of personal devotion to a god, often a particular form of the god. The *vacana* saints reject not only the 'great' traditions of Vedic religion, but the 'little' local traditions as well. They not only scorn the effectiveness of the Vedas as scripture; they reject the little legends of the local gods and goddesses. The first of the following examples mocks at orthodox ritual genuflections and recitations; the second, at animal sacrifice in folk-religion:

See-saw watermills bow their heads.
So what?
Do they get to be devotees
to the Master?

The tongs join hands.
So what?
Can they be humble in service
to the Lord?

Parrots recite.
So what?
Can they read the Lord?

How can the slaves of the Bodiless God,
Desire,
    know the way
    our Lord's Men move
    or the stance of their standing?

                Basavaṇṇa

The sacrificial lamb brought for the festival
ate up the green leaf brought for the decorations.

Not knowing a thing about the kill,
it wants only to fill its belly:
born that day, to die that day.

But tell me:
    did the killers survive,
    O lord of the meeting rivers?

                Basavaṇṇa

Religions set apart certain times and places as specially sacred: rituals and worship are performed at appointed times, pilgrimages are undertaken to well-known holy places. There is a holy map as well as a holy calendar. If you die in Benares, sinner though you are, you will go straight to heaven. [See chap. 3 above.] The following *vacana* represents the contempt of the saint for all sacred space and sacred time:

To the utterly at-one with Śiva
there's no dawn,
no new moon,
no noonday,
nor equinoxes,
nor sunsets,
nor full moons;

his front yard
is the true Benares,

O Rāmanātha.

Dāsimayya

In his protest against traditional dichotomies, he rejects also the differences
between man and woman as superficial:

If they see
breasts and long hair coming
they call it woman,

if beard and whiskers
they call it man:

but, look, the self that hovers
in between
is neither man
nor woman

O Rāmanātha

Dāsimayya

The Vīraśaiva saints, unlike exponents of other kinds of Hinduism, and
like other *bhakti* movements of India, do not believe that religion is
something one is born with or into. An orthodox Hindu believes a Hindu
is born, not made. With such a belief, there is no place for conversion in
Hinduism; a man born to his caste or faith cannot choose and change, nor
can others change him. But if he believes in acquiring merit only by living
and believing certain things, then there is room for choosing and changing
his beliefs. He can then convert and be converted. If, as these saints believed,
he also believes that his god is the true god, the only true god, it becomes
imperative to convert the misguided and bring light to the benighted. Missions
are born. *Bhakti* religions proselytize, unlike classical Hinduism. Some of
the incandescence of Vīraśaiva poetry is the white heat of truth-seeing and
truth-saying in a dark deluded world; their monotheism lashes out in an
atmosphere of animism and polytheism.

How can I feel right
   about a god who eats up lacquer and melts,
   who wilts when he sees fire?

How can I feel right
   about gods you sell in your need,
   and gods you bury for fear of thieves?

The lord of the meeting rivers,
self-born, one with himself,
he alone is the true god.

Basavaṇṇa

The pot is a god. The winnowing
fan is a god. The stone in the
street is a god. The comb is a
god. The bowstring is also a
god. The bushel is a god and the
spouted cup is a god.

Gods, gods, there are so many
there's no place left
for a foot.
   There is only
one god. He is our Lord
of the Meeting Rivers.

Basavaṇṇa

The crusading militancy at the heart of *bhakti*[1] makes it double-edged, bisexual, as expressed in poems like the following:

Look here, dear fellow:
I wear these men's clothes
only for you.

Sometimes I am man,
sometimes I am woman.

---

[1] The *vacanas* often divide the world of men between *bhakta* (devotee) and *bhavi* (worldling), men of faith and the infidels, reminiscent of Christian/Heathen, Jew/Gentile, divisions. One amusing legend speaks of a Śaiva saint who lived in the world, devoting his energies to converting worldlings to the Śaiva faith, by any means whatever: bribes, favours, love, and if needed physical force, coercing or persuading them to wear the Śaiva emblem of holy ash on the forehead. One day, Śiva himself came down in disguise to see him. But he did not recognize Śiva and proceeded to convert him, offering him holy ash, trying to force it on him when he seemed reluctant. When his zeal became too oppressive, Śiva tried in vain to tell him who he was, but was forced down on his knees for the baptism of ash—even Śiva had to become a Śaiva [a devotee of Śiva].

O lord of the meeting rivers
I'll make war for you
but I'll be your devotees' bride.

Basavaṇṇa

THE 'UNMEDIATED VISION'

Why did the *vacanakāras* [composers of *vacanas*] (and certain other *bhakti*
traditions in India and elsewhere) reject, at least in their more intense moods,
the 'great' and 'little' traditions? I think it is because the 'great' and 'little'
traditions, as we have described them, together constitute 'establishment'
in the several senses of the word. They *are* the establishment, the stable,
the secure, the *sthāvara*, in the social sense. In another sense, such traditions
symbolize man's attempt to establish or stabilize the universe for himself.
Such traditions wish to render the universe manipulable, predictable, safe.
Every prescribed ritual or magical act has given results. ...

Ritual, superstition, sacred space and sacred time, pilgrimage and temple-
going, offerings to god and priest, prayers and promises—all forms of
'making' and 'doing'—all of them are performed to get results, to manipulate
and manage carefully the Lord's universe to serve one's own purposes, to
save one's soul or one's skin. Salvation, like prosperity, has a price. It can be
paid, by oneself or by proxy. The 'great' and 'little' traditions organize and
catalogue the universe, and make available the price-list.

But the *vacanakāras* have a horror of such bargains, such manipulations,
the arrogance of such predictions. The Lord's world is unpredictable, and
all predictions are false, ignorant, and worse.

Thus, classical belief systems, social customs and superstitions, image
worship, the caste system, the Vedic ritual of *yajña* as well as local sacrifices
of lambs and goats—all of them are fiercely questioned and ridiculed.

Vacanas often go further and reject the idea of doing good so that one
may go to heaven. Righteousness, virtue, being correct, doing the right things,
carry no guarantee to god. One may note here again that making and doing
are both opposed to being or knowing (in a non-discursive sense).

Feed the poor
tell the truth
make water-places
and build tanks for a town—

> you may then go to heaven
> after death, but you'll get nowhere
> near the truth of our Lord

And the man who knows our Lord,
he gets no results.

Allama

All true experience of god is *kṛpa*, grace that cannot be called, recalled, or commanded. The *vacana*s distinguish *anubhāva* 'experience', and *anubhāva* 'the Experience'. The latter is a search for the 'unmediated vision', the unconditioned act, the unpredictable experience. Living in history, time, and cliché, one lives in a world of the pre-established, through the received (*śruti*) and the remembered (*smṛti*). But the Experience when it comes, comes like a storm to all such husks and labels. In a remarkable use of the well-known opportunist proverb ('Winnow when the wind blows'), Chowḍayya the Ferryman says:

Winnow, winnow!
Look here, fellows
winnow when the wind blows.

Remember, the winds
are not in your hands,

Remember, you cannot say
I'll winnow, I'll winnow tomorrow.

When the winds of the Lord's grace lash,
quickly, quickly winnow, winnow,
said our Chowḍayya of the Ferrymen.

      Chowḍayya of the Ferrymen

A mystical opportunist can only wait for it, be prepared to catch It as It passes. The grace of the Lord is nothing he can invoke or wheedle by prayer, rule, ritual, magical word, or sacrificial offering.[2] In *anubhāva* he needs nothing, he is Nothing; for to be someone, or something, is to be differentiated and separate from God. When he is one with him, he is the Nothing without names. Yet we must not forget that this fierce rebellion against petrification was a rebellion only against contemporary Hindu practice; the rebellion was a call to return to experience. Like European Protestants, the Vīraśaivas returned to what they felt was the original inspiration of the ancient traditions no different from true and present experience.

Defiance is not discontinuity. Alienation from the immediate environment can mean continuity with an older ideal. Protest can take place in the very name of one's opponents' ideals.

We should also remember that the *vacana* ideals were not all implemented in the Vīraśaiva community; the relation of ideals to realization, the city of god and the city of man, is a complex relation, and we shall not embark here

---

[2]Though the saints generally reject external ceremony, the Vīraśaivas have developed their own ceremony and symbols; but they are nothing as elaborate as the Vedic. ...

on an anthropology of the contemporary Lingayat community, for it would require no less to describe the texts in context.

What we have said so far may be summarized in a chart. The dotted lines indicate the 'permeable membranes' that allow transfusion.

HINDUISM

	STRUCTURE		ANTI-STRUCTURE
	Establishment: *'Public' Religion*		*Protest:* *'Personal' Religion*
	Great Tradition	Little Tradition	
Text	Vedas etc.	Local Purānas, etc.	
Performance	Vedic ritual	Local sacrifices, etc.	*v.* Bhakti
Social organization	Caste- hierarchy	Sects and cults	
Mythology	Pan-Indian deities	Regional deities	

Following Victor Turner in *The Ritual Process*, I am using the terms structure and anti-structure. I would further distinguish between anti-structure and counter-structure. Anti-structure is anti-'structure', ideological rejection of the idea of structure itself. Yet *bhakti*-communities, while proclaiming anti-structure, necessarily develop their own structures for behaviour and belief, often minimal, frequently composed of elements selected from the very structures they deny or reject. The Vīraśaiva saints developed in their community, not a full-scale 'Communitas' of equal beings, but a three-part hierarchy based not on birth or occupation but on mystical achievement: the Guru, the Elders, and the Novices. ... The saints are drawn from every social class, caste, and trade, touchable and untouchable—from kings and ministers to manual workers—laundrymen, boatmen, leatherworkers. Such collapsing of classes and occupations in the new community of saints and saints-to-be, however short-lived, led to Vīraśaiva slogans like *kāyakavē kailāsa* (Basavanna), 'Work is heaven', 'to work is to be in the Lord's Kingdom'. Kāyaka could also mean the work of ritual or other worship; here I think it means 'labour, work'. Furthermore, in the new community, instead of the multiple networks of normal social relationships, we have face-to-face dyadic relations with each other, with the guru, especially with God. Such dyads are symbolized by intimate relationships: lover/beloved, father/son, mother/child, whore/customer, master/man.

There are many varieties of *bhakti*;[3] here we refer only to the kind exemplified by the *vacanas*. In the Northern traditions, Kabir's poems would be a parallel example. The 'great' and the 'little' traditions flow one into the other, as in an osmosis. They together constitute the 'public religion' of Hinduism, its 'establishment' or 'structure' as defined above. Bhakti as anti-structure begins by denying and defying such an establishment; but in course of time, the heretics are canonized; temples are erected to them, Sanskrit hagiographies are composed about them. Not only local legend and ritual, but an elaborate theology assimilating various 'great tradition' elements may grow around them. They become, in retrospect, founders of a new caste, and are defied in turn by new egalitarian movements.

Vīraśaivas were protesters not only against the Hinduism of their time, but also against Jainism, the powerful competitor to Hinduism. Basavanna's and Dāsimayya's lives were desperate struggles against both Brahminism and Jainism. The Jainas were politically powerful in the area and represented privilege. Ideologically, their belief in *karma* was absolute; the individual had inexorably to run through the entire chain of action and consequence, with no glimmer of grace. To this absolute determinism, the Vīraśaiva saints opposed their sense of grace and salvation through *bhakti*. Yet they shared with Jainism and Buddhism the doctrine of *ahimsa* or nonviolence towards all creation, the abhorrence of animal sacrifice and ritual orthodoxy. Śaivism in general, and Vīraśaivism even more so, has been rightly described as 'a revolt from within, while Buddhism and Jainism were revolts from the outside'. Some Vīraśaivas, however, disclaim all connections with Hinduism.

THE *VACANA* FORM AND ORAL POETICS

The Sanskrit religious texts are described as *śruti* and *smṛti*. *Smṛti* is what is remembered, what is memorable; *śruti*, what is heard, what is received. Vīraśaiva saints called their compositions *vacana*, or 'what is said'. *Vacana*,

[3]Two kinds are broadly distinguished: *nirguṇa* and *saguṇa*. *Nirguṇa bhakti* is personal devotion offered to an impersonal attributeless godhead (*nirguṇa*), without 'body, parts or passion'; though he may bear a name like Śiva, he does not have a mythology, he is not the Śiva of mythology. By and large, the Vīraśaiva saints are *nirguṇa bhaktas*, relating personally and passionately to the Infinite Absolute. *Saguṇa bhakti* is *bhakti* for a particular god with attributes (*saguṇa*), like Krishna. The woman saint Mahādēviyakka, in this selection, comes close to being a good example, though not a full-blown one, for she speaks little of the mythological or other attributes of Śiva, say, his divine consort Pārvati or his mythic battles with evil demons. Yet she is in love with him, her sensuality is her spiritual metaphor. Vaiṣṇava *bhakti*, *bhakti* for Krishna or Rāma, generally offer the best examples of *saguṇa bhakti*.

as an active mode, stands in opposition to both *śruti* and *smṛti*: not what is heard, but what is said; not remembered or received, but uttered here and now. To the saints, religion is not a spectator sport, a reception, a consumption; it is an experience of Now, a way of being. This distinction is expressed in the language of the *vacanas*, the forms the *vacanas* take. Though medieval Kannada was rich in native Dravidian metres, and in borrowed Sanskritic forms, no metrical line or stanza is used in the *vacanas*. The saints did not follow any of these models. Basavaṇṇa said:

I don't know anything like timebeats and metre
nor the arithmetic of strings and drums;

I don't know the count of iamb and dactyl.
My lord of the meeting rivers,
as nothing will hurt you
I'll sing as I love.

It is not even he that sings; the Lord sings through him. The instrument is not what is 'made', but what one 'is'. The body can be lute as it can be temple.

Make of my body the beam of a lute
    of my head the sounding gourd
    of my nerves the strings
    of my fingers the plucking rods.

Clutch me close
    and play your thirty-two songs
    O lord of the meeting rivers!
                    Basavaṇṇa

The *vacana* is thus a rejection of premeditated art, the *sthāvaras* of form. It is not only a spontaneous cry but a cry for spontaneity: for the music of a body given over to the Lord.

The traditional time-beat, like the ritual gesture, was felt to be learned, passive, inorganic; too well organized to be organic. Here too, the *sthāvara*, the standing thing, shall fall, but the *jaṅgama* shall prevail. The battles that were fought in Europe under the banners of Classical/Romantic, rhetoric/ sincerity, impersonal/personal, metre/*vers libre* were fought in Indian literature in genres like the *vacana*.

But then 'spontaneity' has its own rhetorical structure; no free verse is truly free. Without a repertoire of structures to rely on, there can be no spontaneity. In the free-seeming verse, there are always patterns that loom and withdraw, figures of sound that rhyme and ring bells with the figures of

meaning. It is not surprising that ... the apparently metreless metre of the
vacanas has a *tripadi*-base. *Tripadi* is a popular 3-line form of the oral tradition
used widely both in folk song and in folk epigram.

[Many scholars] have studied the techniques of oral verse-making in
folk-epics. They have paid little attention to shorter forms. Several features
noted for heroic oral poetry do appear in the *vacanas*: in particular a common
stock of themes that occur in changing forms, repetitions of phrases and
ideas, the tendency to cycles or sequences of poems. But the extensive use
of formulae and substitutes in the strict sense and a distinct given prosody,
both characteristic of the oral bardic traditions, are generally absent in the
vacana, a genre of epigram and lyric.

The *vacanakāras*, however, did use stock phrases, proverbs, and religious
commonplaces of the time. This stock, shared by Southern and Northern
saints, the Upaniṣads and the folk alike, included figures, symbols, and
paradoxes often drawn from an ancient and pan-Indian pool of symbology.
Bhakti saints, like the *vacanakāras*, have been called the 'great integrators',
bringing the high to the low, esoteric paradox to the man in the street,
transmuting ancient and abstruse ideas into live contemporary experiences;
at the same time, finding everyday symbols for the timeless.

They also travelled within and across regions, claimed kindred saints of
other regions in their geneological tree of gurus. Thus the Vīraśaiva saints
named the 63 Tamil Saints among their forebears. Śaivism knits faraway
Kashmir with south India, and within south India the saints of Tamil,
Kannada, and Telugu. Both Kābir of the Hindi region, and Caitanya of Bengal,
were inspired by southern precedents. Chronologically, from the seventh
century on, century after century, *bhakti* movements have arisen in different
regions and languages, spanning the whole Indian subcontinent, in Tamil,
Kannada, Marathi, Gujarati, Hindi, Bengali, Assamese, and Punjabi, roughly
in that order. Like a lit fuse, the passion of *bhakti* seems to spread from
region to region, from century to century, quickening the religious impulse.
Arising in particular regions, speaking the local spoken languages, it is yet
inter-regional: both 'parochial' and 'universal'. Even modern urban *bhakti*
groups include in their hymnals, songs of several languages and ages. ...

Yet it should not be imagined that the common stock was used in exactly
similar ways. Only the components were the same; the functions, the emerging
meanings, were often startlingly different. For instance, the image of the insect
weaving a web out of its body is an ancient one. The *Bṛhadāraṇyaka Upaniṣad*
has this description of Brahman, the creator:

As a spider emerges (from itself) by (spinning) threads [out of its own body] ... so
too from this self do all the life-breaths, all the worlds, all the gods, and all contingent
beings rise up in all directions.

Mahādēviyakka has the following:

Like a silkworm weaving
her house with love
from her marrow,
     and dying
in her body's threads
winding tight, round
and round,
     I burn
desiring what the heart desires.

Cut through, O lord,
my heart's greed,
and show me
your way out,

O lord white as jasmine

Mahādēviyakka

Note the startling difference in the feeling-tone of these passages, the coolness of the Upaniṣad and the woman-saint's heart-rending cry for release. The classical text describes the object, the Cosmic creator; the *vacana* describes the subject, the speaker's feelings towards herself. The one describes creation by and out of the creator; the other describes the self trammelled in its self-created illusions. One speaks of the birth of worlds, awesome, wondrous, nonhuman; the other speaks of a death, small, calling for compassion, all too human. ...

The oral origins and qualities of this poetry are demonstrated and reinforced by the never-failing vigorous tones of speech, the imperatives (Basavaṇṇa 162), instructions (500), warnings (212), pleas (350), curses (639), questions and answers (97), oaths (430), vocatives (848), outcries (8), chatty talk (703), and the recurring invocation to Śiva, the eternal addressee. [The numbers are of the *vacanas* in *Speaking of Śiva*.]

Linguistically too, the *vacana*-poets were the first to use the changing local sub-standard spoken dialects of their birth-places in poetry, while contemporary poets wrote in a highly stylized archaic language, preferring again the *jaṅgama*s of language to the *sthāvara*s. In fact *vacana*s and inscriptions are the most important witnesses to the dialectal speech of medieval Kannada country. In their urgency and need for directness, they defied standard upper-class educated speech and stylized metrical literary genres, as they defied ritual and orthodoxy. Such untrammelled speech in poetry has a fresh 'modern' ring to it in imagery, rhythm and idiom—a freedom that modern literary writers in Kannada have not yet quite won.

The common language of the *vacana*s did not exclude Sanskrit words (and even common Sanskrit quotations); instead the *vacanakāra*s used Sanskrit with brilliant and complex effects of contrast, setting it off against the native dialectal Kannada. To take one instance, Mahādēvi (quoted on p. 143) opens with the sentence:

teraṇiyahulu tanna snēhadinda maneya māḍi tanna
nūlu tannanē sutti sutti sāva teranante

Like a silkworm weaving
her house with love
from her marrow,
          and dying
in her body's threads
winding tight, round
and round ...

In that Kannada clause, there is only one Sanskrit-derived word *snēha*, meaning in common usage 'friendship, fondness, love, any attachment'; but etymologically it means 'sticky substance' like oil or marrow (in my translation of the un-translatable I have tried to suggest both by 'love' and 'marrow'). The word stands out ... gathering double meanings to itself. The sticky substance out of which the worm weaves its threads, as well as the attachments in which humans trammel themselves, are suggested and inter-related in one stroke by the word *snēha*. Furthermore, here as elsewhere in the *vacanas*, the use of Sanskrit itself becomes symbolic; symbolic of abstraction. The god's names are partly Sanskrit: e.g., in Cennamallikārjuna, *cenna* 'lovely' is Kannada, the rest Sanskrit. But, because of the transparent Kannada, the Sanskrit too is never opaque or distant for long; it becomes double-faced as in the case of *snēha* above, by etymological recovery: even linguistically the Body stirs in the Temple. The etymologies of the Sanskrit names are never far from the surface, and often participate in the poetry. The proper name Guhēsvara 'Lord of Caves', is appropriate to Allama: his favourite imagery is of dark and light. Mallikārjuna ('Arjuna, Lord of goddess Mallikā'—the god's name including His beloved—or literally, 'Lord White as Jasmine'), is appropriate to Mahādevī whose metaphor is love itself, and who is ever thrilled by the lord's beauty. Rāmanātha, or Śiva as worshipped by Rāma as his lord, is right for Dāsimayya who urges the greatness of Śiva over all other gods. With his water-imagery and themes of merging social differences, Basavaṇṇa's god is Kūḍalasaṅgamadēva, the Lord of the Meeting Rivers. Interestingly enough, the last name combines in itself both Kannada (*kūḍalu*, 'meeting of rivers') and Sanskrit (*saṅgama*, synonymous with *kūḍalu*). Such quickening of etymologies in the poetry is one reason for translating attributive proper names io literal English—hoping that by using them constantly as a repetitive formula they will keep their chanting refrain quality and work as unique proper names.

THE 'LANGUAGE OF SECRECY' (SANDHYĀBHĀSA)

The range of *vacana* expression spans a pan-Indian stock of figures, homely images of everyday experience, the sense and idiom of the earth, as well as an abstruse esoteric symbolism. The esoteric *vacanas* are called *beḍagina vacana* (fancy poems), more riddle than poem and, often, with a whole occult glossary for key. This glossary is made up of a common pool of symbols and concepts drawn from yogic psychology and tantric philosophy. Allamaprabhu, the most metaphysical of the *vacanakāras*, has many *beḍagina vacanas*, and we have included a few. For instance:

They don't know the day
is the dark's face,
and dark the day's.

  A necklace of nine jewels
  lies buried, intact, in the face of the night;
  in the face of day a tree
  with leaves of nine designs.

When you feed the necklace
  to the tree,
    the Breath enjoys it
in the Lord of the Caves.

The paradoxical images of this poem have a surrealist brilliance in themselves. To a learned Vīraśaiva, the poem would mean the following:

The night and day are obviously ignorance and awareness. It is in the experience of the ignorant that we find the jewel of wisdom, a necklace of nine *liṅgas*. In awareness is knowledge and discrimination (the tree), carefully nurtured. But only when the wisdom of the ignorant experience is fed to the discrimination of the aware, the *Liṅga* of the Breath finds true joy.

Such a dark, ambiguous language of ciphers (*sandhyābhāṣa* or 'intentional language') has been much discussed by scholars of *yoga* and *tantra*. Riddles and enigmas were used even in Vedic times. In the heterodox and esoteric cults, such systems of cryptography were intended to conceal the secret doctrine from the uninitiated and the outsider. But riddle and paradox are also meant to shatter the ordinary language of ordinary experiences, baffling the rational intelligence to look through the glass darkly till it begins to see. (Just as often, it may degenerate into a mere mental gymnastic.) It is 'a process

of destroying and reinventing language' till we find ourselves in 'a universe
of analogies, homologies, and double meanings'.

A related device is a favourite with *vacanas*: extended metaphor, a simile
which projects a whole symbolic situation suppressing one part of the
comparison, as in Basavaṇṇa [see *vacana* 111 in the book]. One of the most
moving uses of the extended analogue is Mahādēviyakka's love of God,
where all the phases of love become metaphors for the phases of mystical
union and alienation. For instance:

I have Māyā for mother-in-law;
The world for father-in-law;
three brothers-in-law like tigers;

and the husband's thoughts
are full of laughing women:
    no god, this man.

And I cannot cross the sister-in-law.
But I will
give this wench the slip
and go cuckold my husband with Hara, my lord.

My mind is my maid:
by her kindness, I join
my Lord,
    my utterly beautiful Lord
    from the mountain-peaks
    my lord as white as jasmine

and I will make Him
my good husband.

                        Mahādēviyakka

Mahādēviyakka's poem explicitly takes over conventions of Indian love-
poetry (available in Sanskrit as in the regional languages). An *abhisārikā*, a
woman stealing out of a houseful of relatives to meet her lover, is the central
image. The method is the method of allegory, explicitly equating, one-
for-one, various members of a household with various abstractions: *Māyā*
or Primal Illusion is the mother-in-law, the world is the father-in-law. Some
of the equations are implicit, and they draw on a common background of
philosophical concepts. For instance, the three brothers-in-law are the three
guṇas, the three ultimate components which make all the particulars of nature
what they are; these three are inescapable as long as one is part of nature,
they keep a tiger-vigil. The husband is *Karma*, the past of the ego's many
lives. The sister-in-law, who also keeps the speaker imprisoned, is apparently

the *vāsanā*, the binding memory or smell' that the *Karma*-Past carries with it. The kind confidante or maid is the Mind, who alone helps her meet her Lord and keep the tryst.

Note how all the relationships mentioned are those 'made' by marriage. The house is full of in-laws, acquired, social ties. Not one person is related to the woman by birth. (The mother-in-law in a south Indian family of this region could be a blood-relation, a paternal aunt. This only adds a further nuance, the conversion by ritual of a blood-kin into an in-law). A net of marriage rules and given relations binds her. These are what you make and enter into, not what you are born with. This elaborate build-up of social bonds is shattered by the cuckolding climax of the poem, with the Lord as the adulterous lover. Here a vulgar Kannada word is used to speak of the 'cuckolding', the 'fornication'. The whole poem, written in a colloquial, vigorous speaking style, moves toward the word *hādara* or fornication, enacting by linguistic shock the shock of her explosive desire to shatter the entire framework of so-called legitimacies. Elsewhere also Mahādēviyakka rejects outright all notions of modesty as a virtue. She is supposed to have thrown off her clothes at one point, in defiance of the indecent pruderies of the society around her.

This stresses the view that love of God is not only an unconditional giving up of all, but it is necessarily anti-'structure', an anti-social 'unruly' relationship: unmaking, undoing, the man-made. It is an act of violation against ordinary expected loyalties; a breakdown of the predictable and the secure. Some such notion is at the heart of this complex of metaphoric action. The Lord is the Illicit Lover; He will break up the world of *Karma* and normal relationships, the husband's family that must necessarily be violated and trespassed against, if one should have anything to do with God.

Such a poem is an allegory with no need for a key. Sometimes in the *vacanakara*'s quest for the unmediated vision, there comes a point when language, logic, and metaphor are not enough; at such points, the poet begins with a striking traditional metaphor[4] and denies it at the end:

Looking for your light,
I went out:
    it was like the sudden dawn
    of a million million suns,

    a ganglion of lightnings
    for my wonder.

[4]*The Bhagavadgītā* xi, 12 'If in [bright] heaven together arise the shining brilliance of a thousand suns, then would that perhaps resemble the brilliance of that [God] so great of Self.' Tr. Zaehner, 1969.

O Lord of Caves,
if you are light,
there can be no metaphor.

                                    Allama

CONCLUSION

In describing some of the general characteristics of Vīraśaivism through the
vacanas, we have also described aspects of other *bhakti*-movements in India.
The supreme importance of a guru, the celebration of a community of
saints, worship as a personal relationship, the rejection of both great and
little traditions (especially caste barriers), the wandering nature of the saint,
the use of a common stock of religious ideas and symbols in the spoken
language of the region, and the use of certain esoteric systems, these are only
some of the shared characteristics. Such sharing actually makes for one more
pan-Indian tradition, *bhakti*, with regional variations.

Both the classical (in Sanskrit and in the regional languages) and folk
literatures of India work with well-established languages of convention, given
personae, and elaborate metrical patterns that mediate and depersonalize
literary expression. The literary ideal is impersonality. But *vacanas* are personal
literature, personal in several senses:

(a) Many of them express the real conflicts of real persons, represent a
life more fully than anything in the older literature. For instance, Basavaṇṇa
speaks of himself as the minister of a non-Vīraśaiva king, accused by his
own men of betraying his god for a king.

(b) They are uttered, not through a persona or mask, but directly in the
person of the poet himself, in his native local dialect and idiom, using the
tones and language of personal conversation or outcry.

(c) Even the few given conventional stances of *bhakti* are expressed in
terms of deeply-felt personal relations; the loves and frustrations of *bhakti*
are those of lover and beloved (e.g. Mahādēvi), mother and child, father
and son, master and servant, even whore and customer.

(d) Compared to other Indian religious literatures like the Vedic hymns,
the *vacanas* describe the devotee's state directly and the god only by
implication; the concern is with the subject rather than the object (of worship).

Furthermore, *bhakti* religions like Vīraśaivism are Indian analogues to
European protestant movements. Here we suggest a few parallels: protest
against mediators like priest, ritual, temples, social hierarchy, in the name
of direct, individual, original experience; a religious movement of and for
the underdog, including saints of all castes and trades (like Bunyan, the
tinker), speaking the sub-standard dialect of the region, producing often
the first authentic regional expressions and translations of inaccessible
Sanskrit texts (like the translations of the Bible in Europe); a religion of

arbitrary grace, with a doctrine of the mystically chosen elect, replacing a social hierarchy-by-birth with a mystical hierarchy-by-experience; doctrines of work as worship leading to a puritan ethic; monotheism and evangelism, a mixture of intolerance and humanism, harsh and tender.

The *vacana*s express a kin-sense and kindness for all living things—not unknown to classical Hindu religion, but never so insistent and ardent—a love of man, beast, and thing, asserting everywhere that man's arrangements are for man and not man for them. Basavaṇṇa cries out:

They say: Pour, pour the milk!
    when they see a snake image in a stone.
But they cry: Kill, kill!
    when they meet a snake for real.

His most-quoted saying in Kannada asks, 'Where is religion without loving-kindness?' A poignant example of such loving-kindness towards all creation was the saint named Dasarēśwara. He did not even pick flowers to offer them to a god; he gathered only blossoms that fell of themselves:

Knowing one's lowliness
in every word;

the spray of insects in the air
in every gesture of the hand;

things living, things moving
come sprung from the earth
under every footfall;

and when holding a plant
or joining it to another
or in the letting it go

    to be all mercy
    to be light
    as a dusting brush
    of peacock feathers:

such moving, such awareness
is love that makes us one
with the Lord
Dasarēśwara.

REFERENCES

Zaehner, R.C. tr.
1966 *Hindu scriptures*. New York: Oxford University Press.
1969 *The Bhagavadgita*. New York: Oxford University Press.

Faith and Suffering in Shia Islam

Akbar S. Ahmed

In this chapter I have examined the relationship between attitudes to death and the social order through a recent case-study from Pakistan: the Hawkes Bay case. Various social factors that may help to explain the incident are discussed, including tensions arising from changing contemporary values, local attitudes to leadership, and the kinship connections of the participants. The case also raises important issues about concepts of death, sacrifice, and martyrdom among Shia and Sunni Muslims, and shows how ideas about the status of the individual in the afterworld may effect social behaviour in this one. ...

In late February 1983, 38 Shia Muslims entered the Arabian Sea at Hawkes Bay in Karachi in response to revelations received by one of their number. The women and children in the group, about half the number, had been placed in six large trunks. The leader of the group, Sayyed Willayat Hussain Shah, pointing his religious banner at the waves, led the procession. Willayat Shah believed that a path would open in the sea which would lead him to Basra, from where the party would proceed to Karbala, the holy city in Iraq. A few hours later, almost half the party had lost their lives and the survivors emerged in varying stages of exhaustion and consciousness.

Pakistan was astonished and agog at the incident. Religious leaders, intellectuals, and newspapers discussed the event threadbare. ... Some

Excerpted from Akbar S. Ahmed, Death in Islam: The Hawkes Bay case. In *Pakistan society: Islam, ethnicity and leadership in South Asia*. Karachi: Oxford University Press, 1986. Chap. 4. © Akbar S. Ahmed.

intellectuals saw the episode as evidence of 'insanity'. ... Sunnis dismissed the matter as yet another Shia aberration from orthodox Islam. The Shias, on the other hand, pointed to the event as a confirmation of their faith. Only the Shias, they argued, were capable of such extreme devotion, of such a sacrifice. It was, undoubtedly, a case rooted in Shia mythology, which preconditioned the community to respond to, and enact, the drama. The Shia, in our case, lived in Chakwal Tehsil, in Punjab.

CHAKWAL TEHSIL

Willayat Shah's family lived in a small village, Rehna Sayyedan, about 10 miles from Chakwal Tehsil in Jhelum district. Located on the main Grand Trunk Road, Jhelum is about 70 miles from Chakwal Tehsil. A population of about 250,000 live there. Chakwal and Jhelum are rainfed agricultural areas, unlike the canal colonies in Punjab—Lyallpur, now Faisalabad, and Sahiwal, with rich irrigated lands. The population of the village itself is about 2,000, consisting primarily of the Sayyeds—the upper, and Arain—the lower social group. The latter are challenging the authority of the former through new channels of employment, hard work, and frugality. The village is somewhat isolated from the rest of Pakistan. Electricity has only recently arrived and the road to Chakwal Tehsil is not yet metalled. This is one of the hottest areas in the country. Winters are short and the rainfall is unreliable. Poor harvests have pushed people off the land to look for employment outside Chakwal Tehsil. Many have joined the armed services: the district is a rich recruiting ground for the Pakistan Army. From the sixties, the Arab states offered opportunities for employment. Willayat Shah, after his service as a junior officer in the Pakistan Air Force, left to work in Saudi Arabia. He returned to Pakistan in 1981 after a stay of four years.

Rehna Sayyedan is self-consciously religious. Its very name announces a holy lineage, that of the Sayyeds, the descendants of the Holy Prophet, and means 'the abode of the Sayyeds'. Many of the Shia actors in the drama bear names derived from members of the Holy Prophet's family: Abbass and Hussain for men, and Fatima for women. But there is tension in the area between Shia and Sunni, a tension made more acute by the fact that their members are equally balanced. The economic subordination of the Sunni by the Shia reinforces the tension. Conflict between Shia and Sunni easily converts into a conflict between landlord and tenant. This opposition also runs through the local administration. ... Even families are divided along Shia–Sunni lines. Where individuals have changed affiliation, relationships have been severely strained. ... The tension is exacerbated by the current emphasis on Sunni forms of religion by the Government of Pakistan. The Shias, about 20 per cent of Pakistan's 90 million people, resent this emphasis.

The Jamaat-e-Islami, the major orthodox Sunni political party of Pakistan, is active in the area. In the background is the larger ideological tension between the Shias and Sunnis in Pakistan. From 1980 onwards, this tension became severe and erupted into clashes between the two, especially in Karachi. ...

Willayat Shah was living in Saudi Arabia when Imam Khomeini returned to Iran at the head of his revolution in 1979. Being a devout Shia, he would have been inspired by the message and success of the Imam, but Saudi Arabia was no place to express his rekindled Shia enthusiasm. He would, however, have been dreaming around the themes of the revolution: sacrifice, death, change, and martyrdom. His first act on returning home was to begin the construction of a mosque.

THE HAWKES BAY CASE

On 18 February 1981, Willayat Shah had been engrossed in supervising the construction of the mosque. Late that evening, Naseem Fatima, his eldest child, entered his bedroom and announced she had been visited by a revelation (*basharat*). She had heard the voice of a lady speaking to her through the walls of the house. The apprehensive father suggested she identify the voice. For the first few days, the voice was identified as that of Bibi Roqayya, close kin of Imam Hussain, the grandson of the Holy Prophet, buried in Karbala.

Some handprints next appeared on the wall of Willayat Shah's bedroom. They were made with henna mixed with clay. A handprint has highly emotive significance among the Shia Muslims. It is symbolic of the five holiest people in Islam: the Holy Prophet, his daughter, Hazrat Fatima, his son-in-law, Hazrat Ali, and his grandsons, Hazrat Hassan and Hazrat Imam Hussain. The news of the handprints spread like wildfire in the area. The impact on the village was electric. It was described thus by an informant: 'for the next fifteen days or so the usual business of life came to a halt. People gave up their work, women even stopped cooking meals. Everyone gathered in the house of Willayat Hussain to see the print, to touch it, to pray, and to participate in the mourning (*azadari*) which was constantly going on' [Pervez 1983]. The *azadari*, a recitation of devotional hymns and poems in honour of, in particular, Hazrat Hussain, was a direct consequence of the handprints. It created a highly charged and contagious atmosphere among the participants.

Sunnis, however, were cynical about the whole affair. They would remain adamant opponents of Naseem's miracles (*maujza*). Opinion was divided among the Shia Muslims. Established families like the Sayyeds scoffed at Naseem and her miracles and, at first, both Willayat Shah and his daughter had their doubts. As if to dispel these doubts, Imam Mahdi, or Imam-e-Ghaib, the twelfth Imam, himself appeared in the dreams of Naseem. Earlier,

Bibi Roqayya had announced that the Imam rather than she would communicate with Naseem. The Imam wore white clothes and was of pleasing appearance. All doubts in her mind were now dispelled, and he addressed her as Bibi Pak (pure lady).

The Imam, with whom she now communicated directly, began to deliver explicit orders (*amar*). One commanded the expulsion of the carpenter who was working for Willayat in his house and who had overcharged him by a thousand rupees, in connivance with the contractor. ... The orders increased in frequency. They soon included matters of property and marriage. The family, at least, no longer doubted the miracles. They obeyed the divine orders without question. During the revelations, Naseem would demand complete privacy in her room. Her condition would change. She would quiver and tremble. Noises would sound in her head before-hand and the trauma of the revelations often caused her to faint afterwards. The orders would come to her on the days the Imams died or were made martyrs. 'The Imam', according to her father, 'had captured her mind and heart'.

Local Shia religious leaders and lecturers (*zakirs*) acknowledged Naseem and visited her regularly. Of the three most regular visitors, one, Sakhawat Hussain Jaffery, was particularly favoured. Naseem claimed that she had been especially ordered by the Imam to single him out. They were often alone for long periods. Naseem began to organize *azadari* regularly. These meetings were charged with emotion and created devout ecstasy in the participants. They were held next to the local primary school. Many people attended, with such noisy devotion, that the school had to close down. Naseem now completely dominated the life of the village. Before moving to the next phase of the case, let us pause to examine the effect of the revelations on some of the main actors in the drama.

Naseem was a shy, pleasant looking girl, with an innocent expression on her face, who had a history of fits. There was talk of getting her married. Although she had only studied up to class five, her teachers recall her passionate interest in religion, especially in the lives of the Imams. She had a pleasing voice when reciting *nauha*s or poems about Karbala, many of which she composed herself. After her revelations there was a perceptible change in Naseem. She began to gain weight, wear costly dresses and perfumes. She became noticeably gregarious and confident. In a remarkable gesture of independence, especially so for a Sayyed girl in the area, she abandoned the *parda* or veil. According to Shia belief, any believer may become the vehicle for divine communication. Naseem turned to the dominant person in her life, her father, upon receiving communications and he interpreted them in his own light.

Willayat Shah, about fifty, strong and domineering, now reasserted himself in village affairs after an absence of years. His daughter's religious experience had begun soon after his retirement from Arabia. He had an older brother to whom, because of the traditional structure of rural society, he was subordinate. His period in Saudi Arabia had enhanced his economic, but not his social position. Because of the miracles and revelations of his daughter, however, he gained a dominant position in the social life of the area. Sardar Bibi, Naseem's mother, was dominated by her husband and daughter and identified wholly with the latter. She was said to have been a Sunni before her marriage, and this created an underlying tension in the family. In an expression of loyalty to her husband, she severed relations with her parents and brothers because they disapproved of her conversion. She blindly obeyed her daughter's revelations.

Another actor in the drama was Sakhawat Jaffery, a *zakir* of Chakwal Tehsil. He was not a Sayyed and his father was said to be a butcher. He had thus risen in the social order. Willayat Shah rewarded him for his loyalty with gifts: refrigerators, televisions, fans, etc. When he needed money for a new business he was presented with about 20,000 rupees. With this sum, he opened a small shop selling general goods. He was given such gifts on the specific orders of the Imam to Naseem. In turn, he was the only one of the three *zakirs* who personally testified to the authenticity of Naseem's miracles. Naseem was regularly visited by Sakhawat Jaffery and she reciprocated. In a gesture of affection, contravening social custom, Naseem named Sakhawat's male child, a few months old, Rizwan Abbass. Such names, deriving from the Holy Prophet's family, were traditionally reserved for Sayyeds.

Most people were cynical about the relationship between Naseem and the *zakir*. Sakhawat's own wife, who had complete faith in Naseem, said people had spread 'dirty talk' (*gandi baten*) about Naseem and her husband. In spite of his belief in the revelations, Sakhawat Jaffery did not join the pilgrimage to Hawkes Bay. He had recently opened his shop and explained that abrupt departure would ensure its failure. Naseem was understanding: 'this is not a trip for *zakirs*. We want to see you prosper'.

After the visions, Naseem's followers bestowed on her the title already used by the Imam, Pak Bibi, or pure lady. The transformation in her appearance and character was now complete. She radiated confidence. Her following spread outside the village. In particular, she developed an attachment to the people of a neighbouring village, Mureed, who were recently converted Muslims, *sheikh*s, and who whole-heartedly believed in her. Most of them were *kammi*s, belonging to such occupational groups as barbers and cobblers. Naseem, as a Sayyed, represented for them the house of the Prophet, while her father, being relatively well off, was a potential source of financial support. Seventeen of the villagers of Mureed would follow her to Hawkes Bay.

The normal life of the village was disrupted by the affair. The Shia Muslims, in particular, 'whole heartedly accepted the phenomenon' but, not unnaturally, 'the regular routine life of the village was paralysed'. In particular, 'women stopped doing their household jobs'. Some placed obstacles in Naseem's path, teasing members of her family, especially children on their way to school, and dumping rubbish in front of her house. The Sayyeds, who did not believe in her, ill-treated her followers from Mureed.

Meanwhile, a series of miracles were taking place which riveted society. Blood was found on the floor of Willayat Shah's bedroom. Naseem declared this to be the blood of Hazrat Ali Asghar, the male child of Hazrat Hussain, martyred at Karbala. On another occasion, visitors were locked in a room and told that angels would bear down a flag from heaven. When the door was opened, there was indeed a flag. On one occasion four children disappeared, to appear again later. But the greatest miracle of all remained Naseem's constant communication with the Imam. Supplicants would pray in front of Naseem's room, expressing their demands in a loud voice. The Imam would be consulted not only on profound matters but also on trivial ones, such as whether a guest should be given tea or food. Naseem, who received many of her orders during fainting fits, would then convey a reply on behalf of the Imam.

There came a time, however, when Naseem's authority was disputed. Doubts arose first from the failure of certain of her predictions and, second, from the public refusal of her kin to redistribute their property according to her orders. Naseem had been making extravagant predictions regarding illness, birth, and death. Some of these came true, others did not. In one particular case, she predicted the death of a certain person within a specified period. He did not die. In another case, the elder brother of Willayat was asked to surrender his house for religious purposes which he refused to do. A cousin also refused when asked to hand over his property to Willayat. In yet another case Naseem, perhaps compensating for a Sunni mother in a Shia household, ordered the engagement of her cousin to a non-Shia to be broken; it was not.

Naseem and Willayat responded to such rebellion with fierce denunciation. The rebels were branded as *murtid*; those who have renounced Islam and are, therefore, outside the pale. Their relatives were forbidden to have any contact with them. In some cases, parents were asked not to see their children and vice versa. While taking firm measures against those who did not believe, the followers were charged with renewed activity, calculated to reinforce group cohesiveness. The frequency of religious meetings increased as did visits to shrines. Participation was limited to believers.

Naseem's physical condition now began to correspond with the revelations: she lost weight and her colour became dark when she was not receiving them; she glowed with health when she was. People freely equated her physical appearance with her spiritual condition. She lost *noor*, divine luminosity, in her periods of despondency, and regained it when receiving revelations. For her believers, it was literally a question of light and darkness. But the crisis in Naseem was reaching its peak; so was the tension in the community.

Exactly two years after the first communication began, Naseem asked her father a question on behalf of the Imam: would the believers plunge into the sea as an expression of their faith? The question was not figurative. The Imam meant it literally. The believers were expected to walk into the sea from where they would be miraculously transported to Karbala in Iraq without worldly means. Naseem promised that even the 124,000 prophets recognized by Muslims would be amazed at the sacrifice.

Those who believed in the miracles immediately agreed to the proposition. Willayat was the first to agree: he would lead the party. There was no debate, no vacillation. They would walk into the sea at Karachi, and their faith would take them to the holy city of Karbala. Since the revelations began, Willayat had spent about half a million rupees and had disposed of almost all his property. He now quickly disposed of what remained to pay for the pilgrimage. The party consisted of 42 people, whose ages ranged from 80 years to 4 months. Seventeen of them were from Mureed and most of the remaining were related. ... Willayat, his brother, and cousin, distributed all their belongings, retaining only one pair of black clothes, symbolic of mourning. They hired trucks to take them to Karachi. With them were six large wooden and tin trunks. They also took with them the Shia symbols of martyrdom at Karbala: *alam* (flag), *taboot* (picture of the mourning procession), *jhola* (flag), and *shabi* (picture of the holy images).

Stopping over at shrines for prayers in Lahore and Multan, they arrived in Karachi on the third day. Karachi was in the throes of anti-government demonstrations and the police had imposed a curfew. The tension in the city directly reflected the conflict between Shia and Sunni Muslims in Pakistan. In spite of this, the party was not stopped as they made their way to Hawkes Bay. For them this was another miracle. At Hawkes Bay, the party offered two prayers, *nafil*, and read ten surahs from the Holy Quran, including al-Qadr, an early Meccan *surah*, which states 'the Night of Destiny is better than a thousand months'. The verse was well chosen: for the party, it was, indeed, the night of destiny.

The Imam then issued final instructions to Naseem. The women and children were to be locked in the six trunks, and the virgin girls were to sit with her in one of them. Willayat was asked to hold the *taboot* along with three other men. Willayat's cousin, Mushtaq, was appointed chief (*salar*) of the party. He was ordered to lock the trunks, push them into the sea, and throw away the keys. He would then walk into the water with an *alam*.

At this stage four young people from Mureed, two men and two girls, became frightened. This fear, too, 'was put in their hearts by the Imam'.

Naseem, therefore, willingly exempted them from the journey. The remaining 38 entered the sea. Mothers saw children, and children saw old parents, descending into the dark waters. But there 'were no *ah* [sighs] or *ansoo* (tears)'. Those in five out of the six trunks died. One of the trunks was shattered by the waves and its passengers survived. Those on foot also survived; they were thrown back on to the beach by the waves. The operation which had begun in the late hours of the night was over by early morning when the police and the press reached Hawkes Bay. The survivors were in high spirits: there was neither regret nor remorse among them. Only a divine calm; a deep ecstasy.

The Karachi police in a display of bureaucratic zeal arrested the survivors. They were charged with attempting to leave the country without visas. The official version read: 'The Incharge, FIA Passport Cell, in an application filed in the court said it was reliably learnt that one Willayat Hussain Shah, resident of Chakwal Tehsil, along with his family had attempted to proceed to a foreign country "Iraq" without valid documents through illegal route i.e., Hawkes Bay beach'. The act came within the offence punishable under section 3/4 of the *Passport Act 1974*. The accused were, however, soon released.

Rich Shias, impressed by the devotion of the survivors, paid for their journey by air for a week to and from Karbala. In Iraq, influential Shias, equally impressed, presented them with gifts, including rare copies of the Holy Quran. Naseem's promise that they would visit Karbala without worldly means was fulfilled.

SOCIAL CHANGE, LEADERSHIP, AND KINSHIP IN CHAKWAL SOCIETY

In an attempt to find a sociological explanation of the Hawkes Bay case, I shall begin by putting forward a thesis ... [that] suggests that Pakistani workers, returning from Arab lands with their pockets full of money, are no longer prepared to accept the status quo of the social order from which they had escaped. The returnees demand more social status and authority in society. In their own eyes, they have earned the right to be respected by their long and usually hard periods abroad. But they may have little idea how exactly to go about changing society, or even whether they wish to move it 'forward' or back to older, more traditional, ways. Their new social confidence, backed by economic wealth and combined with frustration at the slow pace of change, may result in tension and dramatic developments, of which the Hawkes Bay case is an example.

Consider Willayat Shah. Belonging to the junior lineage of a Shia family and with a Sunni wife, he escaped to Arabia determined, it may be assumed, to make good on his return. After four hard years there, he returned with considerable wealth, but society had remained the same and there was no perceptible change in his social position. Willayat's immediate family were acutely aware of his predicament. His closest child and eldest daughter, fully grown and intelligent, and herself under pressure to get married, responded to the crisis in their lives with a series of dramatic, divine pronouncements. In her case, social crisis had triggered psychological reactions. The revelations were calculated to disturb the social equations of the village forever. Naseem dominated not only the social but also, and more importantly for the family, the religious life of the area. Willayat Shah had finally arrived. Both he and Naseem now reached out towards the better, truer world that, for Muslims, lies beyond death. Through their deaths they would gain an ascendancy which would be final and unassailable. They would triumph through the Shia themes of death, martyrdom, and sacrifice.

For the actors in our case, society provided the stress but failed to suggest cures. We know that at least four individuals closely related to the key actor, Naseem, suffered from tension due to mixed loyalties in the Shia–Sunni line up: her grandmother, her mother, her uncle, and her aunt's husband were rumoured to have been Sunni in the past. It was known that her grandmother's family were Sunni. By assuming the role of Shia medium, Naseem was socially compensating for the Sunni connections in her family. Under such complex pressures, religion is the most convenient straw to clutch. The stress thus assumes a form of illness, but the illness is both mental and physical and 'in its expression culturally patterned'. One must look for cultural acts and symbolic forms which have local significance, including sacrifice and martyrdom. This case is certainly patterned by the religious sociology of Chakwal Tehsil.

Willayat Shah compared the sacrifice of his family to that of Karbala because 'he and his group had been assigned a duty to save the religion and the faith'. In an interview given to Tariq Aziz on Pakistan Television he explained why Karachi was selected. He could have died in a pond in the village, he said. But the world would not have known of their faith. The prediction of his daughter had indeed come true. The world was amazed at the miracle of Hawks Bay and people would talk of them as martyrs forever. Throughout the interviews he remained proud and unrepentant. His perception of those hours at Hawkes Bay are revealing. He 'insisted that he had been walking on the sea all the while like a truck driving on flat road'. He felt no fear, no regret. Most significantly, he remained convinced that the revelations would continue, even after the death of Naseem, through a male member of the family. Willayat's wife, Sardar Bibi, reacted with a fervour equal to that of her husband. 'If the Imam tells us to sacrifice this baby too,' she said, pointing to an infant she was feeding during an interview, 'I'll do it'.

Willayat's eldest sister, Taleh Bibi, divorced and living with her brother, lost one daughter in the incident. She herself survived because she was in the trunk that did not sink. She, too, believes the miracle will continue through a male member of their family. In relation to the Islamic concept of death, it is significant that she had mixed feelings about her own survival. Although relieved to be alive, and although she gives this as another proof of the miracle, she is nonetheless envious of those who died and thereby gained paradise.

Was the psychological condition of Naseem cause or effect of her religious experience? We know that her peculiarities of temperament became acceptable after the revelations. Her fits, her rapture, her ecstasy now made sense. She was touched by the divine. Even her acts defying tradition in Chakwal Tehsil, such as abandoning the veil or being alone with a man, expressed her transcendent independence. Examples of trance, spirit possession, and ecstatic behaviour have been recorded among Muslim groups ... [in Pakistan and elsewhere]. It is commonplace that highly gifted but disturbed individuals adapt religious idioms to consolidate their social position or to dominate their social environment. Women have heard voices before, all over the world. Joan of Arc's voices advised her to lead her nation into fighting the English. Naseem's urged her to lead her followers into the sea. In order to understand the motives of those involved in this case, we need to combine an appreciation of religious mythology with an examination of certain sociological factors. There was more than just *jazba* (ecstasy) at work in Chakwal Tehsil. What did the followers think was awaiting them at Karachi?

Both local leadership and kinship helped to determine who would be on the beach that night. The importance of a leader in an Islamic community, Shia or Sunni, is critical. The group is judged by its leadership. In different ways Willayat, Naseem, and Sakhawat Jaffery played leading parts in the drama, but we look in vain for a Savanarola figure in either Willayat or Sakhawat. Leadership was by consensus. They were all agreed upon Naseem's special role in the drama. She led, as much as she was led by, her father and the *zakir*. The followers were responding not to one leader in their immediate community but to the concept of leadership in Shia society. They were responding to symbols centuries old and emotions perennially kept alive in Shia society. What is significant is the lack of ambivalence in the majority of the followers. Even the call for the ultimate sacrifice evoked an unequivocal response among most of them. Asad's [1983] interesting question, 'how does power create religion?' may, therefore, be turned around. The Hawkes Bay case provides an interesting example of how religion may create power.

Willayat Shah was a forceful person who mobilized public opinion behind his daughter. The *zakirs*, especially Sakhawat Jaffery, supported him and he, in turn, assisted Sakhawat Jaffery financially. Apart from assisting the *zakirs*, Willayat also paid sums to a variety of other people. Among the beneficiaries were members of the traditionally lower social class, mostly artisans, barbers, and blacksmiths. The seventeen people from Mureed who were prepared to walk into the sea were from this class. In fact, four of this group backed out at the last minute, and although thirteen entered the sea, only three of them died. The people of Mureed were recent converts to Islam and, like all converts, they were eager to exhibit their religious fervour. They looked to Willayat Shah for religious and financial support. For them, he was both a Sayyed and a man of means, and they were enraptured by his daughter. Through him and his daughter, they found access to a higher social level.

Whatever the levelling effect of religion, and the loyalties it created, the Sayyeds rarely allowed their genealogy to be forgotten: the rural Punjab class structure was recognizable despite the experience at Hawkes Bay. Even in death, class distinctions remained: three of the four men who held the *taboot* as they stepped into the waters were Sayyeds, and the non-Sayyed was swept into the sea. Later, with a strange twist of logic, Willayat explained this by suggesting that his faith was weak. His faith was weak because he was not a Sayyed, while the three Sayyeds who survived did so because their intentions were pure. And yet, he also argued that those Sayyeds who died did so because of their purity. Sayyeds, obviously, won whether the coin landed heads or tails. The Sayyeds, of course, provided Willayat's main support and many of them were his relatives. Of those who walked into the sea, twenty-five, were related. ... For these, Willayat was the elder of the family: father to one, brother to another, and an uncle to others. Of the eighteen who died, fifteen were his near relatives, while ten of his kin survived. Religious loyalty was, here, clearly buttressed by ties of kinship.

There was, however, structural resistance to Naseem and her revelations. The Sunni dismissed them out of hand, and even the Shia were not unanimous in supporting her. The Sayyeds, senior in the Shia hierarchy, ill-treated Naseem's followers, especially the poorer ones, teased her family, and even dumped rubbish on her doorstep. The older, more established, Shia lineages felt threatened by the emergence of Naseem since she challenged their authority. Willayat's own brother, Ghulam Haider, suspected of having Sunni affiliation, kept away from the entire affair. The *zakir*, himself a close confidant and beneficiary of Naseem, but worldly wise, chose not to accompany the party on some pretext. And at the last moment, by the sea, four followers backed out. But, although there was opposition and resistance at every stage, thirty-eight people were prepared to sacrifice their lives on the basis of Naseem's commands and revelations. The explanation for their behaviour partly lies, as stated earlier, in the forces of social change, leadership, and kinship in Chakwal society. But there are also other, more ideological and mythological dimensions to consider.

DEATH, SECTS, AND WOMEN IN MUSLIM SOCIETY

There is no substantial difference between the core theological beliefs of Shia and Sunni. Both believe in the central and omnipotent position of

Allah and both accept the supremacy of the Holy Prophet as the messenger of Allah. The Holy Quran is revered by both as the divine message of Allah, and its arguments relating to notions of death and the afterworld are accepted by both. Discussion of death is indeed central to the Holy Quran, which has many verses on the theme that 'every soul must taste of death'.

Death in Muslim society is seen as part of a natural, pre-ordained, immutable order, as directly linked to the actions of the living and as part of a continuing process in the destiny of the individual. Humans 'transfer' from this to the next world (the word for death in Urdu and Arabic, *inteqal*, derives from the Arabic *muntaqil* to 'transfer'). It becomes, therefore, a means to an end, 'the beginning of a journey'. The Holy Quran warns 'unto Him you shall be made to return' [al-Ankabut: 21]. On hearing of someone's death, a Muslim utters the words: 'from God we come, to God we shall go'. For Muslims, there is no escaping the consequences of death. ...

Islamic history, Shias maintain, began to go wrong when Hazrat Ali, married to Hazrat Fatima, daughter of the Prophet, was not made the first caliph after the death of his father-in-law. To make matters worse, Hazrat Ali was assassinated. Hazrat Ali's two sons, Hazrat Hassan and Hazrat Hussain, following in their father's footsteps, opposed tyranny and upheld the puritan principles of Islam. Both were also martyred. Hazrat Hussain was martyred, facing impossible odds, on a battlefield, with his family and followers, at Karbala. Among those killed at Karbala, was Hazrat Hussain's six month old son, Hazrat Ali Asghar (who appeared to Naseem in Chakwal Tehsil). The Prophet, Hazrat Fatima, Ali Hassan, and Hussain are the five key figures for Shia theology and history. These are the *panj tan pak*, 'the pure five', of Shias in Pakistan, including those in Chakwal Tehsil. Since three of them were martyred in the cause of Islam, death, martyrdom, tears, and sacrifice form the central core of Shia mythology. Members of the Shia community are expected to respond with fervour (*jazba*) to a call for sacrifice by the leadership. A sense of sectarian uniqueness of group loyalty, faith in the leadership, readiness for sacrifice, devout ecstasy during divine ritual, characterize the community. It has been called 'the Karbala paradigm' and would have been exhibited in Chakwal Tehsil. ...

An appreciation of the five central figures of the Shias also helps us to understand the role of women in that community. The position of Hazrat Fatima is central. Her popularity among the Shia in Chakwal Tehsil may be judged by the fact that seven women in Willayat Shah's family carry her name. Two of these are called Ghulam Fatima, or slave of Fatima. Always a great favourite of her father, Hazrat Fatima provides the link between her father and husband and between her sons and their grandfather. The Sayyeds, those claiming descent from the Prophet, do so through Hazrat Fatima. So do the twelve Imams, revered by the Shia. In addition, Fatima's mother and the Prophet's first wife, Hazrat Khadijah, is also an object of reverence. Two other women feature in Shia mythology, but neither is a popular figure. They are Hazrat Ayesha and Hazrat Hafsa, both wives of the Prophet. The reason for their unpopularity is linked to the question of Hazrat Ali's succession. Ayesha was the daughter of Abu Bakar and Hafsa of Umar, the two who preceded Ali as caliph. Ayesha is singled out as she actively opposed Ali after her husband's death.

Thus, one of the five revered figures of the Shia is a woman. Among the sunnis a similar listing—of the Prophet and the first four righteous caliphs—consists entirely of males. In other matters, too, Shia women are better off than Sunnis. Shia women, for example, often inherit shares equal to that inherited by male kin, whereas among educated Sunni, women receive, at best, one half of what a male inherits. In the rural areas, they seldom inherit at all. Shia women also play a leading role in ritual. The organization of *marsya*s and *azadari*, the enactment of the death drama of Karbala, all involve the active participation of women.

Of the 18 people who died at Hawkes Bay, 10 were women, a notably large number in view of the fact that only 16 of the 42 who set out on the pilgrimage were women. Willayat Shah lost both his mother and daughter. It may be argued that the women were unequivocally committed to sacrifice. By locking themselves in trunks they had sealed their own fates. For them there was no coming back from the waves. Their sense of sacrifice and passion for the cause were supreme. ... The idea of sacrificing life and property for Allah exists both in Shia and Sunni Islam and is supported in the Holy Quran. Sacrifice and its symbolism are part of Islamic religious culture. Ibrahim's willingness to sacrifice his son Ismail, for example, is celebrated annually throughout the Muslim world at Eid-ul-Azha. But for the Shias, sacrifice holds a central place in social behaviour and sectarian mythology. Here, it is necessary to distinguish between suicide: throwing away life given by God; and sacrifice, or dedication of that life to God. Suicide is a punishable offence in Islam. Sunnis, therefore, seeing the deaths at Hawkes Bay as suicide, disapproved. They saw the episode as a throwing away of valuable lives, whereas Shias saw it as a sacrifice which would confirm their devotion. Willayat Shah was convinced his mission was divine and that he had proved this through a dramatic act of sacrifice. Reward, he was certain, would be paradise in the afterworld. In interviews after the event, he expressed his wish to be martyred (*shaheed*). There was no remorse; there was only *jazba*. To a remarkable degree Shia tradition, and the practice of death and sacrifice, coincided in this case. For the Shia in Chakwal Tehsil, text and practice were one.

Suffering thus became as much an expression of faith as of social solidarity. 'As a religious problem, the problem of suffering is, paradoxically, not how to avoid suffering but how to suffer; how to make of physical pain, personal loss, worldly defeat, or the helpless contemplation of others' agony something bearable, supportable—something, as we say, sufferable' (Geertz 1973: 19). Suffering, martyrdom, and death, the Karbala paradigm, create an emotionally receptive social environment for sacrifice. Death in our case, therefore, became a cementing, a defining, a status-bestowing act for the community. It consolidated the living as it hallowed the memory of the dead.

REFERENCES

Asad, Talal.
1993 Anthropological conception of religion: Reflections on Geertz. *Man* N.S. 18, 2: 237–59.
Geertz, Clifford.
1973 Religion as a cultural system. *In* Michael Banton, ed., *Anthropological approaches to the study of religion*. London: Tavistock.
Pervez, S.
1983 *Hawkes Bay incident: A psyco-social case study*. Islamabad: National Institute of Psychology.

PART
three

Mediations: Charisma and Spiritual Power

PREFATORY REMARKS

Knowledge about material and spiritual things within a religious tradition is usually marked by much internal complexity, including apparent contradictions, and, at the same time, holism. It is not enough to note that religious traditions recognize fundamental binary oppositions as between the sacred and the profane, good and evil, righteousness and wrong-doing (sin), and the like; one must also appreciate that such oppositions are ultimately overcome through some kind of transcendence, which posits a higher level of cognitive awareness, and is not merely a compromise or reconciliaton between categories at the same level at which the opposition between them is seen to exist. Thus, the *Bhagavad Gita* (2. 45) says that one should overcome the dualities that characterize the material world and states of consciousness, and abide in 'goodness' which is an undifferential state.

By such advice, this scriptural text, like many others, introduces the idea of mediation and of the spiritual teacher or guru—moral preceptor or exemplar—who helps one to rise to a higher (transcendental) level of consciousness. In the *bhakti* tradition (see Part Two), the guru may be exalted even above god, because he shows the devotee the path that leads to god—and self-realization. In some traditions, most notably Buddhism, the emphasis is on transcendence through meditation and self-perfection or yoga (which is primarily a matter of moral discipline rather than physical control). In the doctrine that the Buddha is believed to have taught, one is expected to achieve moral perfection through personal endeavour without anyone's mediation.

The idea of mediation and the role of the mediator are, however, found widely among religious traditions; if not in the mainstream, then in a subculture or an alternative tradition, as for instance among the Sufis who attach the highest importance to the role and power of the spiritual master (*pir*) who initiates the disciple (*murid*) and guides him in his spiritual quest. The Sufi master's role is direct to the point of being possessive. Other kinds of mediators may inspire by their example, as does a martyr who lays down his life in defence of the truths that he holds sacred. All mediators, be they personal teachers or impersonal exemplars, are believed to be gifted with divine grace and have the spiritual power to influence others or the course of events in a particular case. Similarly, persons with magical powers, obtained through esoteric practices or learnt from a master, are also believed to be able to directly exercise extraordinary powers.

In the three readings comprising this section, we have an account of, first, the ritual subculture of magical monks among Shvetambar Jains of north India; secondly, the institution of *piri-muridi* in the Chishti order of Sufis, again of north India; and finally, the Sikh tradition of martyrdom.

Magical powers are exercised by the Shvetambar Jain monks of Jaipur, who are the subject of Lawrence Babb's essay, but here the source is not a divine gift but asceticism. The manner of its exercise is distinctive, with the emphasis upon *prachar*, or formal promulgation of the tenets and practices of the faith. These monks are systematic teachers as well as powerful exemplars of virtue. They have miraculous powers. When an ascetic dies he, now called a Dādāguru, could become the object of worship, and his anthropomorphic image, or more commonly the image of his feet, would be installed in a temple.

It is noteworthy that the most sacred beings among the Jains are the great masters of the past, the Tīrthankars ('fordmakers'), but certain classes of ascetics, such as the magical monks under reference, have in some ways attained greater prominence. Babb's essay brings out how this has happened. The Dādāgurus are considered worshipful because they are powerful magical mediators who could, when propitiated, provide assistance in worldly matters such as (most prominently among Jains) business enterprises. The Jains are conspicuous for the paradoxical combination of the values of wealth and renunciation (see Laidlaw 1995). Babb shows how, in the worship of the Tgirthankars and the Dādāguru, these contradictory values are reconciled; the opposition here is not exactly transcended.

Frederic Pinto's essay is based on a first hand study of the master–disciple relationship at the famous shrine (*dargah*) of Khwaja Nizamuddin in Delhi. Beginning with the persona of the *pir* and his principal duties, the essay discusses in some detail the nature and exercise of his powers. This power is basically a gift and not something achieved, but in practice a lot of teaching and learning go with it. In Sufi terminology, it is *bariqah*, lit. refulgence, or the inner enlightenment, and comparable to the notion of *tejas* in Hindu thought. Max Weber called it 'charisma', the gift of God (see Weber 1948: 52 and passim). Those thus gifted have the capacity to receive revelations, perform magical acts, or heroic feats of valour. Baffling success certifies the person's stature; failure is his ruin (Weber ibid.: 52). *Bariqah*, or *baraka*, leads to *barakat* which stands for bounty. The cult of amulets is shown to be part and parcel of the institution of *piri*. It is through the actual exercise of his powers that the *pir* initiates and trains his disciples. In course of time the disciple takes over from the master and thus is the chain (*silsila*) established.

As already stated above, while the Sufi *pir* and the Jain monk are active mediators, the martyr in the Sikh and the Shia traditions is essentially an exemplar with the unintended, unselfconscious, power to inspire others. As in the former two cases, martyrs are also bearers of divine grace. On their side, they stand before their God as witness to the Truth of their faith, and indeed die for it willfully, thereby gaining immortality in the eyes of their co-religionists. Martyrs are then messengers who bear witness to the power of true faith. [See chap. 6.]

Louis Fenech's essay traces the ideal of martyrdom in the Sikh tradition from the first guru, Nanak Dev, himself, who embodied the basic virtues of a martyr, namely unyielding resistance to injustice and untruth and total fearlessness in the conduct of his life. Self-respect entails self-surrender, absolute obedience to God's command, not as an act of pride but that of humility. The *shahid* attains liberation in a manner that is the opposite of the Brahmanical notion of *sannyasa* (renunciation), inasmuch as his courageous act is intended to be creative and meaningful, that is, it should have significant social consequences.

Drawing upon the oral and the textual traditions, Fenech takes us through the principal details of the lives of the Sikh gurus who became martyrs, namely Arjun and Teg Bahadur. What they stood for was the teachings of Nanak. Guru Teg Bahadur exemplified the martyr's role as the protector of the right of the oppressed to their faith. A critical question is whether the tenth and the last of the personal Gurus, Gobind Rai, who was assassinated, was a martyr too. The majority of the texts of the Sikh tradition, the author maintains, do not grant this privileged status to him, but it is conceded by everyone that he put the seal of fulfilment on the ideals of social and spiritual life enunciated by Guru Nanak. What is historically most significant, however, is the fact that Guru Gobind has been considered the supreme exemplar by all the recognized Sikh martyrs since his time. The frequent claims to the status of the martyr that have in recent times been made on behalf of various individuals raise basic questions of once again stating the criteria of a true call to martyrdom, but that is another matter (see Uberoi 1996: 112–34).

REFERENCES

Laidlaw, James.
1995 *Riches and renunciation: Religion, economy and society among the Jains*. Oxford: Clarendon Press.
Uberoi, J.P., S. Uberoi.
1996 *Religion, civil society and the state: A study of Sikhism*. New Delhi: Oxford University Press.
Weber, Max.
1948 *From Max Weber: Essays in sociology*. Trs. & eds. H.H. Gerth and C.W. Mills. London: Routledge & Kegan Paul.

CHAPTER
7

Jain Monks

LAWRENCE A. BABB

The Śvetāmbar Jain temple complex at Mohan Bāṛī in Jaipur dedicated
to ... Pārśvanāth's five-*kalyāṇak pūjā* ... is not the community's most
important temple, but it is of great interest to us because it exhibits a
range of diverse ritual sub-traditions in close physical juxtaposition. The
main shrine is dedicated to Ṛṣabh: here he is represented (unusually for a
Tīrthankar) by a pair of feet (*caran*s) carved in stone. The other structures in
the complex do not contain representations of the Tīrthankars* at all; rather,
they are shrines dedicated to various monks and nuns of the past. ...

The temple complex at Mohan Bāṛī encourages us mentally to rotate the
cult of the Tīrthankars slightly so that we see it at an unaccustomed angle.
At first glance the worship of the Tīrthankars seems discontinuous with
any wider ritual context at all. Such a view is encouraged by the tradition's
own habitual emphasis on the idea that the worship of the Tīrthankars is a
kind of physical enactment of soteriological ideas and values. Mohan Bāṛī
teaches us that this impression is in some ways quite misleading, at least
for the image-worshipping Śvetāmbar Jains of Jaipur. We see that to the
sensibilities of those who constructed and use this temple, the worship of
Tīrthankars has a natural home among mortuary cults—indeed that it *is* a

Excerpted from Lawrence A. Babb, Magical monks. In *Absentee lord: Ascetics and kings
in a Jain ritual culture*, Berkeley: University of California Press, 1996. © The Regents of the
University of California Press.

*[Tīrthankars, 'fordmakers', are omniscient teachers who promulgate the Jain faith.
Ṛṣabh was the First Tīrthankar of the present era, Pārśvanath, the twenty third.—Ed.]

particular kind of mortuary cult, albeit one with exceptional characteristics.

This chapter deals with the worship of deceased ascetics who are not Tīrthankars, and in particular with the cult of the Dādāgurus. ... [It] will show that, as sacred personae, the Dādāgurus are in some ways quite Tīrthankar-like. If we focus specifically on transactions, however, we see that their relationship with worshippers is very different from that of the Tīrthankars. This difference supports, and is supported by, a symbolic surround that shares some similarities with the cult of the Tīrthankars but is strikingly different in its orientation toward worldly values. The cult of the Dādāgurus is, I therefore suggest, a ritual subculture with a regional (Rajasthan) and ascetic-lineage (the Khartar Gacch) focus. It utilizes many of the ritual idioms and usages ... [found in other settings], but it does so in ... a context in which overt recognition is given to the worldly ambitions and desires of devotees. If ascetic and worldly values are in tension at the tradition's highest levels, in this ritual subculture they are brought into a far more stable relationship. ...

ASCETIC CAREER AS RITUAL CHARTER

We normally think of hagiography as the portrayal of exemplary lives, and this is certainly true of the abundant Jain hagiography. These materials typically concern ascetics' lives that embody the tradition's central values and highest aspirations. But in some of the hagiography of the Khartar Gacch there is also a sub-theme of great interest. The main dish is the ascetic's life, but also important is his death and its aftermath. As were the Tīrthankars, these figures were ascetics, but of course they were in no sense at the same spiritual level. As did the Tīrthankars, they departed this world, but of course in no sense was their departure as complete. And just as the Tīrthankars left something behind, so did they. They left a continuing pattern of helpful response to the supplications of devotees.

To illustrate this principle I now present a highly abstracted version of a posthumously written biography (Jinharisāgarsūri 1948) of a distinguished Khartar Gacch monk named Chagansāgar. The biography was written by one of his disciples, Jinharisāgarsūri, and it shows us how in this tradition hagiography can become a charter for ritual.

An Ascetic's Life

Chogmal (his original name) was born on Mahāvīr Jayantī in 1839 CE in the town of Phalodī in what was then Jodhpur State (Marwar). His father belonged to the Golechā clan (*gotra*) of the Osvāl caste. Our biographer reports that Chogmal's birth was preceded by an augury. One night his mother was awakened by a remarkable dream of the sun. In the morning his father asked his guru to interpret the dream. The guru said that a son as lustrous as the sun would be born in his house, one whose brightness would light up *saṃsār* [the world of endless passage].

Our author tells us ... that Chogmal married the daughter of a wealthy merchant, and that after his father's death he entered business with his two brothers and began the life of a householder. Unfortunately, business went badly and the brothers fell out and separated. Chogmal then decided to depart Phalodī and seek his fortune elsewhere. He left his wife behind, and, after many difficulties on the road, he found his way to a village named Bārsī. For three years he worked there in the shop of a man named Rangājī. He then returned to Phalodī, where he stayed for a year and begot a son. After this he made his way back to Bārsī, and later ... he again returned to Phalodī. After his wife bore him a second son, he took to the road once again, this time to Hyderabad. ...

It was in Hyderabad ... that his life began to change. Here he began to associate with pious individuals with whom he engaged in a variety of ascetic exercises and ritual activities. His ... spiritual life flourished along with his financial affairs, and ... his life became a 'model' of religion (*dharm*) and prosperity (*dhan*). Later, he again returned to Phalodī, and during this stay he came under the influence of a leading Khartar Gacch ascetic named Sukhsāgar. ... Chogmal asked him for initiation. Sukhsāgar was encouraging but counselled delay because, as he put it, Chogmal still had some 'enjoyment' (*bhog*) *karmas'* remaining. Chogmal then had another son. After the birth of this son he and his wife took a vow of celibacy. He also arranged the marriages of his two older sons and his daughter.

His initiation was finally precipitated by hearing a sermon delivered by a well-known Khartar Gacch nun of those days. Inspired by what he heard, he asked his wife for permission to leave the householder's state and begged her pardon for any hardships he might have caused her. In response she expressed the wish to become a nun. ... Chogmal received initiation from Sukhsāgar. As a monk, his name became Chagansāgar, and he became a member of Sukhsāgar's *samudāy* [sub-lineage]. ...

At the direction of Sukhsāgar, Chagansāgar became the companion of a senior monk named Bhagvānsāgar. Their first journey together was to the village of Khīcand near Phalodī where Chagansāgar began his period of studies prior to final initiation (*baṛī dīkṣā*). ... [This] was performed by Sukhsāgar in the village of Lohāvaṭ (about 16 miles from Phalodī) ... in the year 1885. Bhagvānsāgar and Chagansāgar then set out together on their ascetic wanderings; they would continue to travel as a pair until Bhagvānsāgar's death in 1900.

The biography now becomes an account of their travels. This record need not be summarized in detail; it is enough to say that they visited villages, towns, temples, and pilgrimage centres, and they took the *darśan* of many important images. They also participated in important pilgrimage parties organized by laymen, and they undertook notable fasts. Chagansāgar achieved particular fame for his ascetic practices, and as a result became generally known as Mahātapasvījī (practitioner of great austerities). As the author puts it, they 'obtained *lābh* (benefit)' by means of these activities, and they 'gave *lābh*' to the people as well. Their travels were punctuated by their rainy season sojourns, which our biographer clearly sees as defining episodes in their careers. He puts great stress on the role of laymen's entreaties in bringing them to a given locale for the rainy season retreat and on the benefits their presence bestowed on the communities in which they stayed.

Lying below the particular details in this account are certain recurrent themes. Perhaps the most important of these is the biographer's constant emphasis on the role played by the two ascetics as instigators of lay piety. As the author puts it, the two constantly engage in the *pracār* (promulgation) of religion. This they accomplish by means of their discourses and also by the powerful example of their learning and asceticism. We are told how they inspire laymen and laywomen to take the twelve vows of the *śrāvak dharm* (or *grhasth* [householder's] *dharm*). They inspire people to give up cannabis and tobacco. They induce some to take vows of celibacy. They inspire laymen and laywomen to undertake ascetic practices (such as fasts) and also to take initiation as ascetics. ... many others, some of whom became quite well known as ascetics, for example, a Maheśvarī of Pireu (in Marwar), took initiation from him in 1906. His ascetic name was Navnidhisāgarjī, and he became quite famous, with many disciples of his own. Many nuns were also drawn to initiation because [apparently Chagansāgar had] much 'influence' (*prabhāv*) ... over Jains and non-Jains alike.

Another strong theme in this account is that of the powerful ascetic as the protector of Jainism. Examples are abundant in the text. In the town of Meḍtā, Chagansāgar successfully debated an erudite Brāhman who claimed that Jains were atheists (*nāstik*). In Kolāyatjī, a Vaiṣṇava pilgrimage centre, he debated another distinguished Brāhman scholar, and did so in Sanskrit; the Brāhman was 'influenced' (*prabhāvit*), and declared, or so our biographer says, that in future he would hold Jain teachings in his honour and that he regretted his past opinion that Jains were atheists. In Bikaner, Chagansāgar debated a famous Terāpanthī ascetic named Pholmaljī, and defended the practices of charitable giving and *dravya pūjā* (the worship of images with material things). He also defended *dravya pūjā* in a debate in Deśnok. On this occasion he stated that the materials and items used in worship are produced by householders for their 'enjoyment' (*bhog*), and that enjoyment is what makes the world go round (*bhog se saṃsār baṛhtā hai*). Thus, by using these things in devotion to the Lord instead of enjoying them, the householder is in fact engaged in world renunciation. His point, of course, was that worship is properly seen as a form of asceticism. ...

Another theme is that of the miraculous. Chagansāgar possessed great supernatural power and performed a large number of miracles. Our author is careful to state that he performed miracles only for the ... glorification of Jainism. Early in his career he and Bhagvānsāgar had gone to Mt. Abu, and there he practiced special kinds of meditation and obtained certain *siddhi*s (accomplishments; in this context, magical powers). After this, he saw a lion on the pathway. 'Influenced' by Chagansāgar's new power, the lion bowed humbly and departed. In Pālī, where he and Bhagvānsāgar spent the 1890 rainy season, the people were being tormented by *ḍākiṇīs* (malign female supernaturals). Once, while Chagansāgar was delivering a discourse there, a woman lost consciousness as a result of possession (*praveś*, literally 'entry') by a *ḍākiṇī*, and began to dance. He quelled the disturbance by putting *vāskṣep* powder on her, and she was never troubled again. Indeed, on numerous other occasions he benefited individuals by means of what our author calls his 'miraculous (*camatkārik*) *vāskṣep*'. He relieved many victims of ghost-possession (*bhūtāveś*). For example, he once encountered a Rājpūt and his wife on the road from Nāgaur to Khīvsar. She had become possessed by a ghost, and the Rājpūt begged for his assistance. Chagansāgar said that if the Rājpūt would give up meat and liquor, all would be well. The Rājpūt did so, and his wife recovered completely. In Pīpad, he quelled a cholera epidemic. He even relieved Nāgaur of a drought.

Because of Bhagvānsāgar's increasing age and frailty, Chagansāgar and he spent the rainy season of 1893 in Lohāvaṭ, and in nearby Phalodi in 1894. From this point on they spent the rains in one or the other of these places. In 1900, Bhagvānsāgar died, and Chagansāgar thereupon became his successor. Bhagvānsāgar had succeeded Sukhsāgar upon the latter's death in 1885, and so Chagansāgar became the third leader of this *samudāy*.

Chagansāgar continued his travels and work as before. Eventually, however, his own advancing age and the entreaties of local Jains persuaded him to spend the rains only in the vicinity of Phalodī and Lohāvaṭ. In 1908 and 1909 he spent the rainy season in Lohāvat, and, at the beginning of the 1909 retreat, while doing *caturmāsik pratikramaṇ* [a ritual of confession and expiation] with members of the community, he sneezed—highly inauspicious during *pratikramaṇ*, and an ill omen. That evening in a special vision he became aware of his impending death. When his death came it was directly related to his propensity for austerities. After rigorous fasting during that year's Paryuṣaṇ [a period of religious observances during the rainy season], and despite the entreaties of the community, he extended his *saṃvatsarī* fast (the fast on the final day of Paryuṣaṇ) for an extra day. ... He died on the day after this; after blessing the community he passed away while meditating on the five *parameṣṭhin*s [supreme deities].

The community, our author says, felt the pains of separation deeply. Chagansāgar's obsequies took place near a local *dādābāṛī*, and a certain Ray

Badrīdāsjī Bahādur of Calcutta built a *chatrī* on this spot. The term *chatrī* refers to the umbrella-like memorial cenotaphs with which deceased individuals of distinction are commemorated. The custom of marking the cremation sites of the dead with these structures is associated especially with the Rājpūt aristocracy, but religious figures of note are also memorialized in this fashion. In the latter case the deceased individual is symbolized by an image of his or her feet. Chagansāgar's feet were duly installed in his cenotaph, and here they are still being worshipped.

Our author ends his narrative with a series of crucial assertions. Local Jains, he says, sponsor an annual ceremony at the *chatrī* on the anniversary of Chagansāgar's death. In Jaipur, Jodhpur, Bikaner, Phalodī, Lohāvaṭ, and elsewhere, devotees perform puja, *tapasyā* (austerities), and *jāgraṇ* (all-night singing of devotional songs) on bright sixths (that is, the day of the month on which he died) and on the bright sixth after Paryūṣaṇ. Every year, he adds, devotees come to Lohāvaṭ to this memorial, which is located just in front of the Campāvāḍī railway bridge. Chagansāgar was peripatetic in life ... but now his devotees come to him. This great monk, says our biographer, had miraculous powers in life (that is, he was '*camatkārī*'), but *now too* his miracles occur for the faithful. In times of trouble (*sankaṭ*), meditation on Chagansāgar can help. Happiness, good fortune, health, progeny, and an increase in wealth can be obtained by invoking his name. ...

Virtue and Power

Jinharisāgarsūri's biography of Chagansāgar teaches us an important lesson about Jain ascetics. A distinguished ascetic is certainly an exemplar of virtues. But he may also be a wielder of great magical power. Indeed, in Chagansāgar's career these two things seem to blend nearly seamlessly.

We note first that his career, as portrayed in our biography, echoes themes found in the lives of the Tīrthankars. This important idea is signalled early in the account when we learn that before his birth his mother had a dream of the sun, a dream that was interpreted—or so we are told—as an augury of his future greatness. The parallel with the fourteen dreams of the mother of the Tīrthankar-to-be is obvious. We know, too, that just as the Tīrthankar develops equanimity toward the pleasures of the world, indeed toward the pleasures of heaven, prior to his renunciation, Chagansāgar likewise became detached from the world. His biographer is eager to show us that, for Chagansāgar, world renunciation was never a virtue made of necessity. He had everything that truly matters to the worldly: progeny and wealth. His life as a layman was a perfect blend of wealth and piety (*dhan* and *dharm*), but in the end he gave up everything. His career as an ascetic was likewise a model career. He was scholarly, influential, a protector of Jainism, a teacher, and an able custodian of the virtue and piety of the lay community. He was also a great master of ascetic practices.

All this provides an important context for the fact that Chagansāgar also possessed and exercised great magical power. In his biography this power has been completely embedded in Jain values and aspirations, and in this way has been legitimized in Jain terms. To begin with, the power is clearly associated with his virtuosity in Jain ascetic praxis. Furthermore, his use of the power is connected always with two linked goals: to protect Jainism and Jains, and also to increase the glorification (*prabhāvnā*) of Jainism. Finally, our biographer reminds us at the very end of his account that Chagansāgar was connected, by disciple succession, to the ultimate source of all legitimacy in the Jain world, namely, the Tīrthankar himself. Chagansāgar's power was a Jain power, legitimately employed to help Jains and Jainism.

When Chagansāgar dies, this power crystallizes into a *ritual effect*. The legitimacy of the power is guaranteed by the original paradigm of its application: to help Jains and Jainism, to glorify the Jain creed. Its efficacy is guaranteed by its association with a recurrent time (the lunar day of Chagansāgar's death) and permanent place (the site of his death rites). In fact, to this day the anniversary of his death continues to be noted in Khartar Gacch almanacs. In this way, hagiography is refocused into a charter for a mortuary cult. The relationship between Chagansāgar and his followers is *preserved* in the form of a pair of permanently available ritual roles: powerful monk and lay follower in need of assistance. The Tīrthankars are, of course, departed ascetics too. But a crucial difference in the case of the Tīrthankars is the fact that, because of the fifth *kalyāṇak* (liberation), this relationship cannot truly be preserved; thus, as we have seen, the core of worship must be emulation, not connection. With Chagansāgar, however, connection remains a post-mortem possibility.

Jinharisāgarsuri's biography thus discloses an alternative possibility for ritual action in Śvetāmbar Jainism: the veneration of ascetics who wield power on behalf of devotees in need of assistance, and whose power becomes posthumously available in the form of an institutionalized pattern of worship. This is the general principle underlying the ritual subculture of the Dādāgurus.

DĀDĀGURUDEVS*

The worship of deceased ascetics of note is a central feature of the religious life of Śvetāmbar Jains associated with the Khartar Gacch. Of these the most important by far are the figures known as Dādāgurus or Dādāgurdevs. The Dādāgurus are past Khartar Gacch *ācāryas* who are singled out from others because of their roles as defenders and reformers of Jainism, and as miracle workers and creators of new Jains. The four are: Jindattsūri (1075–1154 CE),

---

*Dādā, paternal grandfather, *guru*, spiritual guide.—Ed.

Jincandrasūri 'Maṇidhāri' (1140–1166), Jinkuśalsūri (1280–1332), and Jincandrasūri II (1541–1613). These figures are the focus of a widespread cult.

Most temples affiliated with the Khartar Gacch contain images of the Dādāgurus. There are also many shrines (called *dādābārīs*, 'gardens of the Dādā') dedicated specifically to them. The temple complex at Mohan Bāṛī is, in fact, a large *dādābāṛī*. Even in *dādābārīs*, however, images of the Tīrthankars are present—as we see in the case of Mohan Bāṛī—and, in theory, are the primary objects of worship. *Dādābārīs* are basically mortuary structures. Although many of them have been enveloped by urban growth, the ideal is for *dādābāṛīs* to be away from population centres, as would be appropriate for a place where funerary rites take place. The complex at Mohan Bāṛī functions in this way today. ...

The Dādāgurus are usually worshipped in the form of foot images, but anthropomorphic images have become more common in recent times. It is clear, however, that footprints are more fundamentally in character for the Dādāgurus than anthropomorphic images, because even when there is an anthropomorphic image there are usually footprints too. The structures in which the Dādāgurus' images are housed are modelled on the funerary cenotaphs that are so common a feature of Rajasthan. Even where temple-like buildings have been erected for the Dādāgurus, their images, whether footprints or anthropomorphic figures, are usually housed in cenotaph-like shrines within.

We may say that deceased ascetics constitute a general class of objects of worship. The Dādāgurus are different in degree from other deceased monks, not different in kind. They are the most beloved, respected, and powerful of them all, but, as we have seen in the case of Chagansāgar, other ascetics have achieved post-mortem recognition. As I have already suggested, the Tīrthankars can also be seen as members of this class, but this statement requires qualification. The distinction between the Tīrthankars and ordinary deceased ascetics is never in doubt; the Tīrthankars have achieved omniscience and liberation, whereas even ascetics as distinguished as the Dādāgurus have not. The *namaskār* mantra* established a clear hierarchy among ascetics, with the Tīrthankars unambiguously at the top. But at the same time, Tīrthankars are deceased ascetics too. As noted before, Ṛṣabh is represented at Mohan Bāṛī by feet, not by an anthropomorphic image. Moreover, these footprints are stationed under a *chatrī*-like structure. This is an unusual arrangement, but the fact that it is a plausible arrangement suggests that in some respects the Tīrthankars are thought of as belonging to the same category as other deceased ascetics. The physical homologies seen in the

---

*The most popular verbal homage to Tīrthankars, liberated souls, and ascetics.—Ed.

arrangements at Mohan Bāṛī suggest a common conceptual substratum. Ṛṣabh is a deceased ascetic too, who has left footprints behind.

The Dādagurus are absolutely central to the beliefs and practices of Śvetāmbar Jains associated with the Khartar Gacch. They are objects of worship, and in some ways are ritually more prominent than the Tīrthankars themselves. To understand their role we must learn something about their place in history, and this in turn requires that we learn something of the history of the Khartar Gacch.

Reformers

The Khartar Gacch was at first a reform movement among ascetics (see Dundas 1992: 120–2). In medieval times, possibly as early as the eighth century CE, ascetics known as Caityavāsīs, 'temple-dwellers', had become prominent in western India. These were ascetics who, contrary to the Jain ideal of the peripatetic mendicant, lived in permanent establishments. Their leaders were learned, were held in high esteem at court, and in general exercised great influence over the Jain laity. But the Caityavāsīs had their critics as well, and the Khartar Gacch began as a protest movement against what was viewed by critics as the stagnation and backsliding of these false ascetics.

The story begins with a late tenth- to early eleventh-century ascetic named Vardhmānsūri. He was initiated originally as a Caityavāsī, but ultimately left the Caityavāsīs because of his growing disgust at their lax ways. He then became the student of a learned ascetic named Udyotansūri, who taught him 'true' Jain doctrine. He later went forth to propagate teachings opposed to those of the Caityavāsīs, and died in 1031 CE. His most important disciple was Jineśvarsūri, one of the truly great figures of Śvetāmbar history. Said to have been of Brāhmaṇ origin, Jineśvarsūri and his brother apparently met Vardhamānsūri while still boys and were quickly initiated by him. Both went on to distinguished ascetic careers.

Jineśvarsūri was an able scholar and powerful debater, and his most celebrated deed was the defeat of the Caityavāsīs in a famous debate. Vardhmānsūri had decided to confront the Caityavāsīs on their own ground and had gone to Pāṭan with his disciples. This city, the capital of Gujarat, was a great centre for the Caityavāsīs. Because of the Caityavāsīs' influence in the city, Vardhmānsūri and his followers had difficulty finding a place to stay. In the end, however, the scholarly Jineśvar so impressed the king's chief (Brāhmaṇ) priest with his Sanskrit learning that the priest invited the monks to stay with him. The Caityavāsīs then put it about that they were spies dressed as mendicants. When word of this reached King Durlabhrāj he called his priest, who defended the mendicants. The Caityavāsīs then decided that the best way to get rid of this threat would be to challenge and defeat them in a debate.

The debate was joined in the presence of King Durlabhrāj in a Pārśvanāth temple in the year 1024 CE. Sūrācārya, the leader of the Caityavāsīs, sat with eighty-three other local Caityavāsīs. Vardhmānsūri and his followers were summoned. When they arrived, the king offered them betel, which apparently the Caityavāsīs were quite accustomed to taking. In response, Vardhmānsūri produced a couplet from the Śāstras that said that for celibates, mendicants, and widows, taking betel is equivalent to the sin of eating beef.

As the debate then unfolded, Jineśvar (who carried the burden of the debate) asked the king whether he, the king, followed new political policies or those of his ancestors. The king replied that he followed the policies of his ancestors. Jineśvar pointed out that the followers of Vardhmānsūri were simply trying to do the same thing, namely, to follow the original teachings of the Tīrthankars. Jineśvar then reminded the king that he and his fellows had come from far away and noted that they did not have the books they needed to debate properly. He asked the king to have books brought from the Caityavāsīs' *maṭh* (monastery). The bundle of books was duly produced, and when it was opened the first thing that came to hand was the *Daśavaikalikasūtra,* and from this book of the first thing that met the eye was a stanza that read: 'An ascetic (*sādhu*) must live in a place that is not specifically for ascetics but which is designed for any other purpose, and in which there are facilities for eating and sleeping, and in which there is a proper designated place to urinate and defecate, and from which women, animals, eunuchs, etc. are forbidden.' The king, who was an impartial judge, found this extremely convincing. The king then asked for thrones to be brought for Jineśvar's group to be seated upon. Jineśvar responded that it was improper for monks to sit on thrones and backed up the assertion with a couplet from the *Śāstras*. In the end, Jineśvar's victory was total, and the king took him and his companions under his protection. The Caityavāsīs left the temples and the kingdom, and were replaced with Brāhmaṇ temple priests.

This dissident reforming sect, founded by Vardhmānsūri and consolidated and propagated by Jineśvarsūri, was at first known as the *vidhimārg* (the path of [proper] method). However, it is said that at the time of the great debate the admiring king Durlabhrāj applied the term *khartar* ('fierce') to Jineśvar. This sobriquet later became the name of the *gacch*.

Jindattsūri

Vardhmānsūri and Jineśvarsūri had many illustrious successors. Among them, however, the ones who stand out most in the ritual life of Jains associated with the Khartar Gacch are the four Dādāgurus. And of the Dādāgurus, none is of greater importance than the first, Jindattsūri.

Jindattsūri was born in 1075 CE at a place called Dholkā. His clan was Humbaḍ and his given name was Somcandra. When he was a small boy he once accompanied his mother to discourses being given by some Khartar Gacch nuns. They noticed auspicious marks on the boy, became convinced that he was destined for greatness, and sent news of their discovery to a senior monk named Dharmdevjī Upādhyāy. This monk then came to the village and asked the boy's mother if she would be willing to 'give the boy to the *sangh*' (the conventional expression for allowing a child to be initiated). Parental permission was given, and the boy's initiation occurred in 1084 when he was only nine years old.

Somcandra demonstrated cleverness and great independence of mind from the start. His education was put in the hands of an ascetic named Sarvadevgani. Dharmdevjī told Sarvadevgani to educate the boy in every particular of the mendicant's life, and even to take the boy with him to the latrine. Somcandra, however, was very young and ignorant of the rules of ascetic discipline. Knowing no better, he uprooted some plants in a field there. In his exasperation, Sarvadev took away the boy's mouth-cloth and broom and told him to go home. The boy responded that if Sarvadev wanted him to go, he'd go, but first he'd like the hair that had been taken from his head (in his initiation ceremony) returned. Sarvadev was highly impressed by this spunky response, as was Dharmdevjī when it was reported to him.

After his studies were completed, Somcandra began his wanderings from village to village. He impressed everyone with his learning, meditation, and piety. As time passed his reputation grew to such an extent that, when Jinvallabhsūri, the leader of the Khartar Gacch at that time, passed away, Somcandra was his logical successor. He attained the status of *ācārya* at Cittaur in the year 1112, at which point he acquired the name Jindattsūri and assumed the leadership of the Gacch.

Wishing to know where he should go in his wanderings, the newly elevated Jindattsūri engaged in a programme of meditation and fasting. According to the hagiographies, a deceased ascetic named Harisinghācārya came to earth from heaven in response. He told Jindattsūri that he should go to Marwar and places like it. Jindattsūri followed this advice, first going to Marwar and then to Nagpur, and later through countless villages and towns. He taught, he protected the Jain faith, and he converted many non-Jains to Jainism. His rainy season sojourns were sources of inspiration in the communities in which they occurred. He performed numerous consecrations of images and initiations of ascetics. He was also a great reformer. Under his influence, large numbers of Caityavāsī *ācārya*s abandoned their former ways and took initiation with him. He had many admirers among great kings and princes. Arṇorāj, the then-ruler of Ajmer, was one of the kings of the period who numbered among his devotees.

He seems to have been tough-minded and earthy, qualities of character that probably served him well in a pattern of life that was surely merciless in its physical and psychological demands. Once in Nagpur a certain rich man presumptuously tried to advise Jindattsūri on how to gain more followers. The monk responded with a verse that reveals a man with a short fuse who did not suffer fools gladly. ...

He was, above all, a great worker of miracles, as were all the Dādāgurus. It is extremely important to emphasize that the hagiographies insist that these miracles always had a higher purpose than merely solving someone's worldly problem. From the standpoint of Jainism's highest ideals, ascetics are not supposed to be magicians. As we have already seen in the case of Chagansāgar, the hagiographers must therefore legitimize this power by establishing a Jain context for it. One legitimizing strategy is to accentuate the point that the miraculous power is associated with its possessor's asceticism. Another strategy is to stress that the purpose of the miracles was always to glorify Jain teachings or to help Jainism flourish. The miracle-working ascetic protects Jain laity, defeats Jainism's enemies, and often aids non-Jains, who may become Jains as a result. ...

In Jindattsūri's case, however, the hagiographies establish yet another legitimizing frame of reference for magical power. It seems that Vajrasvāmī, a legendary ascetic from centuries earlier, had written a book of ancient knowledge (presumably magical). Because he lacked any disciple who could make proper use of this knowledge, he secreted the book in a pillar in the fort at Cittaur. Others had tried and failed to obtain this book, but by means of his own yogic power (*yogbal*) Jindattsūri was able to acquire it and derive powers from it. This tale makes the point that Jindattsūri's power derives both from sources internal to himself (his own yogic ability) and from an interrupted tradition of magically potent ascetics. Legitimacy is conferred on this connection, in turn, because it is embedded in the longer line of discliplic succession connecting Jindattsūri to Lord Mahāvīr.

Many of Jindattsūri's miracles ... involved subduing non-Jain powers. An example is his victory over the five *adhiṣṭhāyak pīr*s of the five rivers of Punjab who once tried to disturb him in meditation. It is said that because of his powers of concentration they found it impossible to budge him, and as a result the five *pīr*s conceded defeat by standing before him with hands joined, after which they became his servants. The fact that these non-Jain powers are depicted as *pīr*s [see chap. 8], which refers to Muslim saints, may reflect the fact that Muslim influence was particularly strong in this region. It is also said that he subdued fifty-two *bhairav vīr*s (forms of the deity Bhairav), who also became his servants. Bhairav (or Bhairava) is a form of Śiva, and this episode may mirror Jain conflict with the Śaivas, which was ongoing at the time.

Another example was his defeat of sixty-four *yoginī*s: malicious, non-Jain, female supernaturals. The incident occurred in Ujjain, where Jindattsūri had begun a public discourse. He told his listeners that the sixty-four yoginīs were coming in order to create a disturbance, and that they should spread sixty-four mats and seat the *yoginīs* on them. The sixty-four arrived disguised as laywomen, and were duly seated on the mats. Jindattsūri cast a spell on them by means of his special power, and then resumed his discourse. When the other listeners rose at the end, the *yoginīs* were unable to leave their seats. They then were ashamed and said to Jindattsūri that although they had come to deceive him they had in fact been deceived themselves. They begged forgiveness and promised that they would assist him in propagating Jainism. This episode possibly reflects Jain opposition to cults of *tantric* goddesses and may also echo the theme of the taming of the lineage goddesses, which will be explored in the next chapter.

He also used his miraculous powers against Jainism's human opponents. Once, at a place called Baḍnagar, some Brāhmaṇs tried to disgrace Jindattsūri and the Jain community by having a dead cow placed in front of a Jain temple. In the morning the temple's *pujāri* discovered the outrage. He told the tale of the chief businessman of the city, who in turn told Jindattsūri. By means of his knowledge of how to enter other bodies Jindattsūri caused the cow to rise, walk, and expire again in front of a Śiva temple. Here the opponents are both Brāhmaṇs and Śaivas. In another version of the same story, the Brāhmaṇs put the corpse of a Brāhmaṇ in front of a Jain temple, and Jindattsūri caused the Brāhmaṇ corpse to rise and expire again in front of a 'Brāhmaṇ' temple.

Jindattsūri even defied the fury of nature on behalf of Jainism. Once, in Ajmer, a fearsome stroke of lightning in the evening threatened a group of laymen performing the rite of *pratikramaṇ*. Jindattsūri caught the lightning under his alms bowl and the rite was able to proceed.

Jindattsūri is said to have had the title of *yugpradhān* (spiritual leader of the age) bestowed upon him in a miraculous fashion. It seems that in order to find out who was the *yugpradhān*, layman named Nāgdev (Ambaḍ in some accounts) went up to the summit of Girnār and fasted for three days. Pleased by his austerities, the goddess Ambikā Devī appeared and wrote the *yugpradhān's* name on his hand, saying, 'He who can read these letters, know him to be the *yugpradhān*.' Nāgdev travelled far and wide and showed his hand to many learned *ācāryas*, but nobody could read the letters. In the end he went to Pāṭan, where he showed his hand to Jindattsūri. The monk sprinkled *vāskṣep* powder on the letters and they became clear. It was a couplet that read as follows: 'He at whose lotus feet all of the gods fall in complete humility, and who is an oasis-like *kalptaru* (wish-fulfilling tree), may that *yugpradhān* who is Śri Jindattsūri be ever-victorious.'

Jindattsūri's life ended at Ajmer in 1154 CE. When he realized that the end was near, he ceased taking nourishment and died on the eleventh day of the bright fortnight of the month of Āṣārh. At the time of his cremation, his clothing and mouth-cloth failed to ignite, and they are said to be preserved to this day in Jaisalmer. His successor, Jincandrasūri 'Maṇidhāri', established a memorial on the spot on which his body was burned, and this was later made into a proper temple.

After death Jindattsūri became a god. According to one account. ... Sīmandahr Svāmī (a Tīrthankar currently active and teaching in the continent of Mahāvideh) was once asked by his guardian goddess (śāsan devī) where Jindattsūri had been reborn. The omniscient Sīmandhar replied that at the present time he was in devlok (heaven), and that after a sojourn there he would take birth in Mahāvideh and there achieve liberation. ...*

A RITUAL SUBCULTURE

Worship of the Dādāgurus is extremely popular among Jaipur's Śvetāmbar Jains. In fact, their worship is the principal religious activity of many Jains, and even members of the non-temple-going sects (the Sthānakvāsīs and Terāpanthīs) sometimes visit their shrines. Although in some ways Jinkuśalsūri [third in the chain of succession] is the most popular of the four, they in fact blend into a single, generic Dādāgurudev.

The reason for the Dādāgurus' popularity is simple: They are powerful beings to whom one can appeal directly for assistance in one's worldly affairs. Moreover, there seems to be little effort to disguise the goal of gaining assistance in worldly matters from the Dādāgurus. Although some of my Jaipur friends claimed to worship the Dādāgurus solely for such reasons as 'peace of mind', most devotees spoke with unembarrassed candour about the material benefits of worshipping the Dādāgurus. The general view of the Dādāgurus is that they will give you wealth, health, success in business, or any of your heart's desires (manokāmnās). In verses of praise they are often compared to the kalptaru, the wish-fulfilling tree, or to the fabled cintāmaṇi, the jewel that grants all desires. I have been told by tough, capable businessmen that everything they have they owe to the Dādāgurus.

The Dādāgurus are able to render assistance to their worshippers because, unlike the Tīrthankars, they are unliberated and can therefore engage in transactions with worshippers. They, are, one might say, vastly magnified versions of Chagansāgar. They too, are powerful and virtuous ascetics with whom ritual relationships can be maintained after death. When they died they ascended to the realm of the gods; after a sojourn there they will return to human bodies and achieve final release. Most Jains are not clear about exactly where the Dādāgurus currently are or what their status is, and the

*The author, L.A. Babb, next presents brief accounts of the lives of three other Dādāgurus.—Ed.

average devotee will simply say they are in 'heaven'. But the important thing is that although they are bound for liberation, they are not liberated yet; in the meantime they can and do dispense divine aid to their worshippers. ...*

Ascetics as Gods

If we focus solely on the worshippers, there is hardly any difference at all between the worship of the Dādāgurus and the Tīrthankars. Here those who worship are the same laymen and women playing the same role as admirers and supporters of ascetics. We are dealing, that is, with the same basic ritual culture. But there is nonetheless a striking contrast. The Dādāgurus are in some ways very Tīrthankar-like. However, because of their unliberated status, their relationship with worshippers is very different, as are the meanings that are assigned to that relationship. To put it otherwise, the cults of the Dādāgurus and the Tīrthankars are truly quite different in content and spirit, despite their formal similarities. For this reason, the cult of the Dādāgurus emerges as a subordinate and partially separate ritual subculture.

Perhaps the most striking difference is that soteriology is displaced by the miraculous fulfilment of worldly desires. As we have seen, normative interpretations of the eightfold worship stress the theme of liberation. The text of the Dādāgurus' worship, however, is focused on magic. As in the case of Chagansāgar, this is sanitized magic, legitimized in Jain terms. In the hagiographies the magic tends to be rationalized as a means of promulgating and protecting Jainism. In the cult of the Dādāgurus this same magic is refocused as a source of aid to individuals. Long ago the Dādāgurus came to the aid of Jains (or Jains-to-be) in times of difficulty. The position of the worshipper now is analogous to that of those whom the Dādāgurus aided then; they too hope for the Dādāgurus' miraculous assistance. Typical phrasings from the hagiographies expressing this idea are *bhay se mukt karnā* (to liberate from fear) and *dukh se mukt karnā* (to liberate from sorrow). The term *mukt*, of course, can also mean 'liberated' in the soteriological sense. It is therefore possible to say that liberation from worldly fears and problems replaces liberation from the world's bondage as a central theme in the Dādāgurus' cult.

The theme of world renunciation is also given a different context in the cult of the Dādāgurus. In modern hagiographies the Dādāgurus' magical abilities are directly associated with asceticism; their power, for example, is called *yogbal* (power of yoga) or *tapobal* (power of asceticism). Thus we see that their asceticism has been decoupled from direct association with the

---

*Babb next describes the modes of worship at the *Dādābārī* temples, and elaborates the character of the cult of Dādāgurus as a ritual subculture distinct from that of the Tīrthankars.—Ed.

path of liberation and instead has been linked with magical power. This magical power, in turn, is connected directly with the worldly well-being of those whom the Dādāgurus assist. This, indeed, is the whole point of their cult. While worship of the Tīrthankars tends to be rationalized as an act of renunciation (*tyāg*), worshipping the Dādāgurus is based on the desire for miraculous intervention in one's worldly affairs; it is about getting things, not giving things up. ... [Babb concludes his discussion of the differences between Tīrthankar worship and the cult of Dādāgurus with reference to the temporal frames of the two.—Ed.]

REFERENCES

Dundas, Paul.
1992 *The Jains*. London: Routledge.
Jinharisagarsuri.
1948 *Mahatapasvi jivan-charitra*. Lohavat: Parakh Indrachand Jain.

Muslim Spiritual Masters

DESIDERIO PINTO

[The Persian word *pir* literally means an elder; *piri* is old age. Within the Sufi tradition in India, and indeed all of South Asia, a *pir* is a religious guide (*murshid*) who shows his disciples (*murid*, one desirous of being instructed) the straight path (*rashid*) to spiritual fulfilment. In this context *piri* is the calling of the *pir*. The account that follows is about the institution of *piri* within the Chisthi Sufi order based on a study made at the *Dargah* (tomb, shrine) of Nizamuddin Awliya in New Delhi.—*Editor*.]

THE *PIR*'S PERSONA

... The *pir*'s external appearance is typical of a traditional Muslim gentleman. But he is much more than a gentleman. This hidden aspect of the *pir* is indicated by the rings with stones of different colours that adorn all the fingers of his right hand, the place where he sits (usually the precincts of a *dargah*), the instruments of his trade (*tawiz* [amulet] paper, inks and pens, books on astrology and *tawiz*, etc.), and by the reverence displayed by the persons who visit him. The *pir* himself and the more advanced *murid*s invite the novice to discover this hidden aspect of the *pir* by telling him to consider the *pir* as a short examination question that requires a lengthy answer. That the *murid* usually does not have access to any written tradition that explains

Excerpted from Desiderio Pinto, The pir in the Nizamuddin dargah, In *Pir–Muridi relationships: A study of the Nizamuddin dargah*. New Delhi: Manohar, 1995. © Desiderio Pinto.

what the *pir* is, is no impediment, however, as the *pir* and more advanced *murid*s discourage the *murid* from using the written word as a means of understanding the *pir* (or answering the question). They advise him to come to an understanding of the *pir* by attending to his own personal experience of him; and they explain how he should use this experience to gain the required understanding of the *pir*; he has to use this experience in the same way as he uses his experience when solving riddles. The *murid* contrasts and compares his experience of the *pir* with his other everyday social experiences in order to arrive at definitions of the *pir*, which he constantly revises as his familiarity with his *pir* and his acquaintance with the beliefs and practices (*adab*) surrounding the *pir* increases. These definitions are expressed in stories and statements of belief.

The *pir* is compared and contrasted with the *murid*'s experience of his own father. The *pir* is father, in the sense that he commands respect and obedience, is ever watchful in order to save the *murid* from troubles and difficulties, constantly cares for, helps, and educates him. But he is more than a father because his responsibility over the *murid* extends even after death until the final judgement on the last day. The *pir* is also compared to a *maulvi* who teaches the faith; but unlike the *maulvi*, he practices his faith. Hence, he knows the difficulties involved in putting that faith into practice and the ways of overcoming them. Thus, he has power, not possessed by the *maulvi*, that comes from this constant practise of the faith. Since the experience of the *maulvi* as guide and teacher is not adequate to understand the *pir*, the *pir* is further compared to Mohammed, the Prophet, who received the revelation, the Quran, and showed the revealed way of putting it into practice, the *Sunnah*. The *pir* is, however, subservient to the Prophet because far from bringing any new revelation and practice, he is restricted by the Quran and by the *Sunnah* (practice) of the Prophet. Hence, he is compared to the flying horse, Buraq, that took Mohammed into the presence of God (the *miraj*, 'ascent'). Just as that flying horse took the Prophet into the presence of God, the *pir* takes the *murid* to the Prophet, and also into the presence of God.

Finally, the *pir* is called the hands, feet, eyes, and ears of God (i.e. the concrete manifestation of God) ..., because he is a friend of God. As a friend of God he is in constant contact with God and does only what He wills (i.e. he has no ego and, thus, mediates between God and the *murid*). Hence, he can also take the *murid*'s needs and requests to God and have them granted: he is an intercessor and is compared to the secretary who takes a visitor's request to ... [say] the prime minister of India. The power that comes from this intimate relationship is, however, also frightening for some *murid*s because it can also destroy the good fortune they enjoy. Hence, the *pir* has to be kept at a distance and, when necessary, approached with gifts and great respect. ...

The *pir* is described as having two major characteristics: worship and service. Worship seems to mean the process of becoming the possession of God. This process involves a number of other characteristics like following the *sharia* (law), being [grateful to] God even in the midst of great adversity, fasting, and service. Service is an aspect of worship and involves attracting people so that one can lead them to God. He accepts everyone, irrespective of caste and religious affiliation; displays an understanding, helpful, forgiving, and merciful attitude; gives something (material things and also spiritual things like blessing, spiritual advice, *tawiz*, etc.) to all visitors, clients, and *murids*; and displays a sense of responsibility for all those who come and visit him.

The *murids* understand the [significance] of worship (the process of becoming a possession of God) to be like being ground in a mill into flour. They explain their own experience of the *pir*'s attitude of service in terms of a mother's selfless devotion to her child.

The main duty of the *pir* is to lead the *murid* to God. ... The *pir* has to love his *murids* ... and must be gracious to and help all who come to him, be they poor or rich. ...

THE *PIR*'S POWER

Hardly anyone speaks of the *pir* without some comment on his power. To the *murid*, this power is of utmost importance, not only within the *piri–muridi* relationship but also when he is in the process of choosing a *pir*, as we shall see later. For many *murids*, it is also an important personal goal. The *pirs* and *murids* describe this power in different ways.*

There is something called *karamat*. ... It is like one's knack of cooking [which comes from experience rather than cookery books].

We have the Quran, the Hadith, the *sharia*, etc. They tell us what to believe and what beliefs to practise. But nothing happens only by reading them. One has to think of ways of believing in what they say, and find ways to practise these beliefs. In the effort to believe and in the process of practising the beliefs, one gets practical experience. The *pir* has this practical experience. This gives him his power. He knows how to believe in what the books say, and how to practise these beliefs. Hence, he is successful while the ordinary people are not. The *pir* has gained this experience by submitting to guidance. ...

There is a particular method of getting experience. The method is *piri–muridi*. The *pir* has gone through this process. He who has used this method and gained experience is the one who has power. He is the *pir*.

*[All quoted paragraphs in what follows are drawn from the author's interviews with the *pirs* and the *murids* at the Nizammuddin Dargah in New Delhi—*Editor*.]

The power of the *pir* is only this: his prayer is heard ... quicker than other people's. God listens to everyone, but to the *pir*. He listens more quickly. Others will cry out to Him for one month, and may still not be heard. But the *pir* has to pray only once and he is heard.

Sometimes, by the grace of Allah, whatever I say happens immediately. At other times it takes time. I should not be proud. I cannot tell you that everything I say comes about. Sometimes, even work that is lawful takes a long time to take effect. If someone asks me for a *tawiz* [talisman] for someone to fall ill, for an enemy to get robbed, or for a husband to divorce his wife, I cannot help him. Such work is possible but not allowed. I can do only good work like bringing about love between an estranged couple. ...

The *pir*'s power concerns knowing the special way in which the spirits and *jinn* [genii] can be controlled. This special method has to be learnt. It is learnt from heart to heart. Besides this, one has to accept certain restrictions. One must not eat meat, fish, eggs, onions, spices, etc. One must follow the *sharia* and spend one's life in doing good works.

Learning 'from heart to heart' is another way of saying that the *murid* learns by observing the *pir* in the course of living with him and keeping him company. In this way the *murid* accumulates ways of understanding and doing things without any deliberate or conscious effort. He is socialized into a particular way of life.

When you come here and meet me, I may say nothing. You also may say nothing. But our eyes meet. We sit before each other. Heart to heart contact is taking place. You may not realize this, but all the same it is taking place. Then when I talk to someone, you listen. Then we drink tea together. When it is time to leave, you take my permission. Heart to heart contact has taken place but you do not know this.

The *pir*'s power, it is commonly believed, is gifted, never achieved.

One can get this power only by becoming a *murid* of an authentic *pir*. A *pir* who does not have this power is not a true *pir*. One does not have to do special studies to attain it. The *pir* does not give it by teaching the *murid*. He knows when he will die. When the moment comes, he will call his *murid* and embrace him. At that moment, his power will flow from his chest to the *murid*'s. That power coming from above [charisma] will be transferred to the *murid* in all its fullness. The Prophet Mohammed transferred his power to Ali [his cousin and son-in-law and the fourth *khalifa*: his partisans were the Shias], Ali passed it on to the heads of the various *silsilah*s [unbroken traditions, or orders, among the Sufis; Nizamuddin Awliya belonged to the Chisti order], who did the same thing with the other *pir*s. In this way that power has travelled down from Mohammed to today's *pir*s.

To receive this gift may call for great effort. The *murid* may have to undergo great asceticism or serve the *pir* in an extraordinary way.

A *pir* worshipped for twelve years. He did not eat anything in those twelve years. But that was not enough. Even then his worship was not over. He tied a stone to his stomach. He even tied a cooking vessel to his stomach and did many spiritual exercises for those twelve years. Even so he did not attain the knowledge. So, what did he do? He hung himself upside down in a well for another twelve years. During this time a crow used to come and perch on his body. And he used to tell the crow, 'Eat whatever part of my body you find tasty, but do not touch my eyes. These eyes are reserved for the Beloved'. When the twelve years were over, he came out of the well. He saw birds flying about. He said, 'Die'. And they all fell dead. Then he said, 'Fly'. And all the birds came to life again and flew away. He then said to himself, 'I have received some knowledge'.

As he walked away, he felt thirsty. He went towards a well. There he saw a woman drawing water and throwing it on the ground. When he asked her for a drink she did not hear him. The *pir* repeated his request. She then told him that she would quench his thirst after putting out the fire in her mother's grave. The eyes of the *pir* followed the course of water. It led to a grave out of which huge flames were leaping up. He also saw that the water was putting out the flames. When the fire was put out, the woman called to him and offered him water. But he said, 'I will drink only after you tell me how you knew that there was fire in that grave'. She replied, 'I have the power. My husband who was a *pir* gave it to me. One night he asked me for a glass of water. But when I returned with the water, I found him asleep. So I stood by his side all night with the glass of water in my hands, waiting for him to awaken. When he opened his eyes in the morning he asked me why I had not kept the water by his side and gone to sleep. I told him that I had brought the water because he had asked for it. But since I found him asleep on my return and did not want to disturb him I waited by his side. Then he looked at me and opened my eyes and my heart.' Then Baba Farid recalled all the efforts he had made to attain the same amount of power for the last twenty-four years and marvelled at this woman who, with just one night's service, had received all that he himself had.

Asceticism and service in itself may not be enough to attain this power. The *murid* has to be given a special kind of knowledge to attain it.

This power is obtained by doing *chilla*. *Chilla* is reciting a particular divine name—any name—for forty days at certain fixed times. One must also say all the five daily prayers, the *namaz*. Then one must give alms, do good deeds and fast. One must not eat salt, spices, fish, meat, etc. Of all the allowed foods, only one kind is allowed. For instance, if you drink tea on the first day, you have to survive only on tea for all the forty days. Water is allowed. Then one will begin to experience the effects of *vazifa* [daily lesson, often a part of the Quran]. You will get power. But this is a very difficult thing to do and very few people do it. ...

The power comes with learning the way of reciting *vazifa* and writing *tawiz*. My *pir* taught me. How else would I know! Besides, whenever I see a faqir [someone leading a religious life] I go to him. It does not matter whether people go to him or not. What matters is that he is sitting there and reciting a name of Allah. Naturally, he has gained some knowledge. Who knows, he may have spent thirty or forty years reciting a name. And with this constant roaming about, he has seen and heard much. Hence, I go and serve him. I give him money and anything else that he may need. Then, if he tells me to recite a particular formula, I begin reciting. One has to recite ten *lakh* times, sometimes a thousand *lakh* times. My *pir* sometimes calls me and gives me a new *vazifa* and *tawiz*, and he makes me recite and write it out in front of him. He then tells me how many thousands of times I have to continue writing and reciting it. In this way my knowledge and power increases.

It may well be that the service, which involves dying to oneself and becoming aware of one's being a servant, convinces the *pir* that one is capable and responsible enough to handle the power.

If the *murid* serves the *pir*, he will give him the power. The *murid* has to do all the work that the *pir* gives him. He has to make the place where the *pir* sits comfortable, attend to his guests, and look after his every need, like taking his children to school, doing the shopping for his wife, picking up his lunch and serving it to him in the office, looking after the old and sick members of his family, running errands for his important guests, etc. Only then will the *pir* give him this power.

The power can be attained if one is able to forget one's rights and only think of one's duties. Take Nizamuddin. He fasted all his life. When he forgot to fast and sat down to eat, he used to think of all the friends of God who were poor and hungry— and he used to vomit out all that he had eaten. He remained hungry all his life. But he used to give food to all those who went to him. The most important thing is to kill one's *nafs* [physical wants]. Then one will get ... the power of the *pir*.

The spiritual power does not come to one just like that. It requires many years of practice. The *murid* has to pass spiritual tests. When he passes the tests he receives the power—and more power as he passes further tests. He does not receive power just like that. ... Spiritual powers are not given to one who is not fit to have them. He who receives power must be capable of handling it responsibly. Someone irresponsible would use such power to trouble someone [else]. One's sense of responsibility is examined through tests. This power is meant to help people, not to give them trouble.

A good number of *pirs* and *murids* also accept that the *pir's* power depends only on his experience, personal holiness, influence with God and ability to write *tawiz*. The attitude of the *murid* or the one who will experience this power is extremely important if the power is to be effective and demonstrable.

The power of a *pir* cannot be understood by talking about it. It can only be demonstrated in action. It happens just like that. When the eyes meet, love is born. The eyes meet without planning. But after the eyes meet, the heart begins to do its work. If the eyes do not meet, the heart cannot do its work. There will be no love. In the same way, first, the *murid* has to surrender himself completely to the *pir*. Only then will the power of the *pir* manifest itself to the *murid*. It manifests itself automatically. If the *murid* does not surrender himself, the power will not manifest itself. I can show you this power if you surrender yourself to me.

The power works of itself. The *pirs* themselves do not know that they have brought about a certain thing through their power. When someone is in trouble we may just say, 'Go, everything will be all right'. And everything does become all right. The power has worked by itself. The *pir* is not even aware of it. Often I am surprised when someone tells me what has happened to him. But I cannot show my surprise. If I do, my *murids* will lose faith in me.

It would seem that the faith of the *murid* in his *pir* is very important, if not the most important factor in the demonstration of the *pir's* power.

As far as the *murid* is concerned, the *pir* is a *pir*. Whatever the *pir* does is his own affair. It does not concern the *murid*. In the eyes of the *murid*, his *pir* cannot do wrong. Otherwise, the *pir's* power will disappear.

If the *murid* does not believe in the *tawiz* I give him it will be ineffective. It is of utmost importance that he believe in what I give him.

Sometimes we have to make a big *tamasha* [demonstration] to convince the client. We may surround him with lighted joss sticks. Then we call out the *jinn*. The *jinn* has to leave him because of what we are reciting. Suppose people have brought me a woman troubled by a *jinn*. If I just tell them that the *jinn* has left her, they will not believe me. So, we light a lamp, act as if we are catching the *jinn* with our hands and flinging him into the fire. Then we tell them that the *jinn* has been burnt and will not trouble her again. It is most important that they are convinced. If they doubt, nothing can be done to help them. The work is done without all this *tamasha*—but the *tamasha* is necessary to convince people.

This dependence on the faith of the *murid* is explained as resulting from the freedom of man.

Allah has not written that we should do evil. But we do evil. And when there is a lot of evil in the world Allah begins to give us trouble. We do the evil and bring down the trouble on ourselves. Allah has written good works. He has decreed that we should not rob, not kill, not commit adultery, etc. If Allah wanted He could have made us do good works. But He has also decreed 'freedom'. He has written, 'Do what you want to do'. We will be rewarded according to what we do. If Allah wants, He can destroy us in one minute. So all that Allah has done is to make man free. It depends on us to decide whether to walk on the right or the wrong path. He will not prevent you from doing evil. He never stops anyone from doing anything.

Since the faith of the *murid* in the power of the *pir* is of utmost importance, a great deal of effort is exerted to convince him, through stories, the sharing of experiences of this power, by predictions and magical tricks, and by making him experience the effects of *vazifa*. Stories and the experiences of power are shared by the *pirs*, the more advanced *murids* visiting Sufis, and clients.

... The founder of the Bahamani sultanate was a landless labourer. He did not even have enough to eat. His mother once told him that she had heard of Nizamuddin, who made people's lives easier through his power and prayers. When the king of Delhi was leaving the presence of Nizamuddin, this man arrived at the door of his *khanqah* [hospice]. His clothes were dirty and muddy. Nizamuddin said, 'One king is dead and another has come'. Everyone there began to wonder what he was talking about. It was true that a king had just left. But where was the next king? So Nizamuddin called to the poor man standing at the door. The people said, 'His clothes are dirty and torn. And you say that he is a king!' Nizamuddin said, 'Let him come to me'. Anyone who went to Nizamuddin, always received something from him. At that moment Nizamuddin had a *chapati* in his hand. He gave the *chapati* to the man saying, 'I am giving you the canopy of a king'. The poor man thought to himself, 'What kind of *pir* is this? What is he talking about? I do not have enough to eat and he says I will become a king'. None the less, he took the *chapati* and returned to his mother. He said to her, 'I went so far, and what did I get? A dry *chapati*. I still have it with me. When giving it to me he said that I would become a king'. She said, 'If he said that you will become a king you certainly will become one. Whatever comes from the mouth of a *pir* always comes true. Do not try to find out why he says peculiar things. Just believe'. From that day he began to prosper. And he became a king. His dynasty lasted three hundred years. This is the power, and it remains with the *pir* always. God tells the *pir* what to say. The *pir* says everything with full faith. He does not say meaningless things.

When Moinuddin Chisti [the founder of the Chishti order, d. 1236] first went to Ajmer, he began living on an open ground meant for the king's animals. The king's men told him to leave, because, they said, the place was reserved for the king's animals. Moinuddin Chisti said, 'Alright, let the animals sit. I am going'. And all the animals that sat there refused to get up. The king's men went to Moinuddin Chisti and complained that the animals refused to get up. Moinuddin said, 'Very good. You threw me out so that they may sit. Now they are sitting.' This is the power of the *pir*.

Thousands of such stories are current, illustrating the power of the *pir*. But this may not be enough to convince a *murid* of the power of his *pir*. To demonstrate his power to him, the *pir* may resort to magical tricks. For instance, he may apply some sticky substance to one end of a clove when the *murid* is looking elsewhere. Then he will draw the attention of the *murid*, mutter something, and pick another clove with the clove that is in his hand. This done, he will separate the cloves and shake them up in a tin of cloves. Once, after displaying this trick, the *pir* explained,

This was possible because of my power. When I said something with my mouth, the power travelled from my mouth to my arm, then down my arm to the clove in my hand. The power then travelled from the clove to the next one. That is why the other clove stuck to it and could be picked up.

This over, the *pir* showed him all the *tawiz* he had so far prepared for the different diseases and difficulties people experience, and told him how he was always busy writing *tawiz* and reciting *vazifa*. He said,

All the power of the *tawiz* is within myself. Hence, my *tawiz* are immediately effective. If they do not work immediately, it is because their recipient does not have a pure intention.

... The *pir* also convinces his *murids* that he has power by making predictions. [Predictions are often made with the help of information that the *pir* acquires accidentally without his interlocutors knowing this.] A *pir* may also demonstrate his power by making his *murid* recite a verse from the Quran, or a particular divine name, and wait for him to experience the effects. ...

Predictions, magical tricks, and the effects of *vazifa* serve to increase the *murids*' faith in their *pir*s. A *murid* says,

My *pir* has the power to capture your spirit. He can take away your spirit. He can lessen your breath. He has such power. Whoever has such power is a real *pir*. One who has this spiritual knowledge, the ability to control the breath of other men, and one to whom Allah has given such power is the true *pir*. It is useful and profitable to become his *murid*. Even if I get nothing in this world I will one day go to paradise because of my *pir*.

The *murids* not only believe everything the *pir* says, but also obey him: if not out of love, then out of fear as will be seen later. The power of the *pir* also places grave responsibilities on his shoulders.

A lot of desperate people come here. I have to give them advice and confidence. If I do not encourage them and make them believe that I can really help them, they may go and commit suicide. If I do not help them, tomorrow Allah will say, 'That man came to you yesterday. Why did you not help him? Did you not have the hands to embrace him? Did you not have the sense to understand what he needed?' Hence, it is extremely important to help the people who come here in every possible way. Otherwise I, myself, will become a sinner before God.

If the *pir*s did not have this power, the people who rule the earth would have destroyed it by now. They would have wiped out the poor who have no one else to help and support them. The ruling élite are selfish. They care for no one but themselves. The *pir*s limit their destructive influence. That is why rulers fear them. They fear their power. The *pir* is nothing. He may sit naked under a tree. He has no money. And yet, kings fear his word. This is a matter of recorded history.

To recapitulate: There are different explanations for the power of the *pir*. Some say that it is the expertise resulting from many years of putting into practice the Quran, *Sunnah* [the sayings or doings of the Prophet] and Sharia [the holy law], and from the constant recitation of *dhikrī* [the name of Allah as an act of remembrance and piety] and *vazifa* under the instruction of someone (a *pir*) who has himself learnt and practised those things at the hands of another experienced person. To many *murids* who do not understand it, it is a mysterious something (much desired, but greatly feared) that is gifted to the *pir* by his *pir* or a saint. To others it is a gift that is given only after the practice of great asceticism, the giving of much whole-hearted service to a *pir* and in such a way that he notices it, the recitation of many *vazifas*, taking instruction in the way of writing of *tawiz*, and performing *chillas* (forty-day retreats during which a person recites a particular *vazifa* prescribed by his *pir*, abstains from certain foods like meat, fish, onions, etc. which are considered hot and as leaving a bad smell in the mouth, and fasts). While doing all this, the *murid* has to demonstrate forgetfulness of self, and the negation of his ego to a remarkable degree.

The power itself is described as nothing more remarkable than the ability to have God answer one's prayer for others more quickly than is usual for the ordinary run of men. Or it is described as the ability to give meanings (of words of the Quran or the divine names ...) and influence existent things to manifest their effects and properties as demonstrated in *tawiz*. Some, however, say that the *pir's* power is an illusion made possible by his close relationship with God. The relationship results in his knowing what God will do at each successive moment and he agrees to do only that which God is going to do. Thus, people believe that the *pir* has power when in actual fact only God has power.

In actual practice, the *pirs* who are believed to have power invariably showed ignorance about the manifestations of their own power. Usually *murids* attributed their psychological, imagined, and accidental physical experiences to the intervention of the *pir*. The *pirs* concerned said that they do not as a rule contradict such *murids* because it is important to retain their faith if *piri–muridi* is to function at all. Also, their power is manifest only when someone either surrenders himself to a *pir* (i.e. becomes a *murid*), or when someone believes that a *pir* really has the power to affect his life for better or for worse. Hence, the *pirs* expend much energy to make clients and *murids* believe that they possess the power. They use tricks, citing predictions and stories about people who have suffered or benefited as a result of this power, for this purpose.

Some *pirs* justify these tactics when confronted in private by pointing to desired ends: to frighten a *murid* into giving up a bad habit, to make people believe that their problem can be solved so that they find the courage to do something about it, to make themselves available to people who would rather suffer than go to a psychiatrist or a relative to have a problem solved, and for many other such good ends.

The *pirs* and *murids* also explain this power to novices and clients by using different images drawn from the *murids'* and clients' life experience, for instance, from cooking. The wife can produce a very good meal with ordinary ingredients, but the husband will produce a meal that no one can eat with the very same ingredients and even with superior ones. This expertise of the wife is like the power of the *pir*. A *pir* or a *murid* may also explain this power by using the example of our normal way of looking at things. If we look at a female human being we may see different things or roles. At one moment she is a woman, at another she is a mother, then a daughter, and finally a wife. Or she may be all these things to different people looking at her at the same moment. But her correct image at any particular moment can only be one of these. The *pir* knows her correct persona at a particular moment. Hence, he can deal correctly with her at each moment. In this lies his power. Sometimes the power of a *pir* is described as a *tamasha* (a big show) that creates faith in him so that the watchers open themselves to his good influence and go away feeling better.

THE *PIR*'S CONCEPTION OF HIMSELF

[The discussion ends with an account of the *pir*'s conception of himself as a link in the chain of *pir–murid–pir/murid–pir–murid* stretching all the way back to Nizamuddin Awliya (d. AD 1325), the 'benefactor of all'.—Ed.]

REFERENCES

Currie, P.M.
1989 *The shrine and cult of Muin al-din Chishta of Ajmer*. Delhi: Oxford University Press.
Weber, Max.
1948 *From Max Weber: Essays in sociology*. Trans. and eds., H.H. Gerth and C. Wright Mills. London: Routledge & Kegan Paul.

Sikh Martyrs

Louis E. Fenech

THE MARTYROLOGICAL INTERPRETATION OF GURU NANAK'S HISTORY AND THEOLOGY

The Tat Khalsa-aligned accounts ... [of martyrdom] begin by characterizing the late fifteenth and early sixteenth centuries as a period in which oppression and tyranny had free reign. This common description is, they maintain, based on the many compositions of the first Guru himself. ...

Despite the continual assertions of [reputed scholars] that what Guru Nanak left behind for the benefit of posterity was his theology and not a description of his period, the vast majority of texts continue to subscribe to the above interpretation of the first Guru's age. ... In the Sikh martyr tradition, the first Master's severe response to a regime described as draconian underscores his courage and defiance far more than a response to the abstract, cosmic age of degeneracy does. Harsh criticism directed towards the regime would have certainly put the Guru's very life in danger from authorities. ...

We should note that where, in the martyr tradition's interpretation of hymns such as the Bābur-vāṇī, the focus rests upon the courage of Guru Nanak, many texts which do not deal specifically with this tradition, although unwilling to dismiss the notion emphasized in it, will rather highlight the

Excerpted from Louis E. Fenech, Theology and personnel. In *Martyrdom in the Sikh tradition: Playing the game of love.* New Delhi: Oxford University Press, 2000. Chapter 3.
© Oxford University Press.

Guru's sensitivity and anguish at the wanton destruction wrought by the invading hordes, placing such hymns within a recognizably theological context. The primary message in these hymns is straightforward. Humanity must look to Akal Purakh for protection, submitting itself to his will (*hukam*) and devoutly remembering his name (*nām*). Of course, within the martyr tradition this message is not discounted. For it, however, Guru Nanak becomes imbued with the many characteristics that all martyrs possess: defiance, resistance, courage, and fearlessness. It is these virtues, moreover, that his hymns extol and these that Guru Nanak enjoins his disciples to embody. ...

Again, it is worth reiterating that the authors do not knowingly mislead their readers, nor write that which they consider to be untrue. For them Guru Nanak was truly heroic. Despite the fact that the Guru was not a martyr, he possessed all the characteristics of one. He was, one may say, a potential martyr. This is an interpretation of Guru Nanak's life and teachings that saturates the society in which the majority of our texts were produced. ... When we examine the martyr tradition specifically, we note that the relationship between scripture and tradition is dialectic. The martyr tradition provides a framework to interpret the Adi Granth (as well as other texts within the Sikh canon) which, in turn, provides the material for the martyr tradition. Each feeds into the other in a continuous and circular process. When our authors approach the hymns of the first Guru, therefore, an interpretative model is already in hand.

The specific interpretation that tradition engenders attempts to bring all the teachings of scripture within its boundaries. It is tradition, in other words, which supplies the pious with a conceivable means by which to gain access to and make sense of the vast contents of scripture. This is a basic fact, but one which must nevertheless be borne in mind. The tradition of martyrdom supplies an interpretation which presents the teachings of Guru Nanak as directed towards a single goal; the defence of truth. ...

Our texts imply, moreover, that this goal is commensurate with both the martial piety so characteristic of seventeenth- and eighteenth-century Sikhism and Guru Nanak's theology of liberation. The affinity with the former is evident, so our texts state, in Guru Nanak's description of Akal Purakh as *asur saṅghār*, the 'destroyer of demons', and in the heroic stories from Puranic and epic mythology, which the Guru notes in his hymns, that stress divine chastisement. Our authors make it clear that the Khalsa itself was created to manifest just this purpose. These imply, moreover, that such references on the part of the first Guru anticipate Guru Gobind Singh's deification of the sword, with which the Bachitar Nāṭak begins (*DG*: 39).

The martyr tradition incorporates Guru Nanak's theology of liberation by maintaining that all martyrs cultivate those qualities on which emphasis is placed in the *bāṇī* of the fist Master: selfless service, truth, patience, courage, self-surrender, humility, and self-respect, to name a few. These are, after all, virtues to which all martyrs in today's popular martyrologies ascribe. Unlike other Sikh traditions, however, the martyr tradition attempts to take all these virtues to their natural limit: the death of the individual. It, therefore, makes concrete the potential which is implied in other Sikh traditions. That is, the heroic tradition in Sikhism will refer to the Sikh hero's potential for dying in upholding Sikh ideals. The martyr tradition highlights the fact that the martyr has actually died for such ideals (McLeod 1997: 128–31).

The Guru's stress that liberation is not the monopoly of those people who renounce the world is unmistakable. Guru Nanak denounces these ascetics and the lifestyle they follow in strong terms, affirming in their place the reality of the world and a life of disciplined worldliness. The martyr tradition qualifies this affirmation of abiding pure within an impure world. Guru Nanak's rejection of the ascetic lifestyle becomes the Guru's command that all people must accept the responsibilities that living within the world peacefully entails. These include sacrificing one's life to ensure that all people are allowed their rights and that none suffer oppression, acts which are also noted as very profound forms of *sevā* or selfless service. ...

Two very important points emerge from this conclusion. The first is that the destruction of tyranny is an expression of the 'Will of God'. For texts dealing with the tradition of martyrdom, this is very much in accord with the thought of Guru Nanak, who foresaw divine retribution for those kings who acted oppressively. The term for 'will' ... is *hukam* (order), a word that designates, along with *nām*, *śabad*, *gurū*, *sach*, and *nadar*, the divine self-expression in the *bani* of Guru Nanak. According to the theology of the first Master, one who devoutly practises *nam simran* cleanses the *man* of *haumai* or 'self-centredness', the root of all evil in Sikhism, and thus attunes oneself to the *hukam* (AG: 1). Through this practice of *nam simran* and the grace (*nadar*) of Akal Purakh, the devout progress through a series of five stages or realms (*khaṇḍs*), the pinnacle of which is *sach khaṇḍ*, the Realm of Truth. It is in this realm that the pious end their journey for it is here that one is perfectly and absolutely in tune with the divine order (AG: 8). It is here that one is 'God-realized', the perfect *gur-mukh* (lit. 'facing the [Eternal] Guru').

The belief that the *gur-mukh* is fully integrated with the *hukam* indicates that the *gur-mukh* comes to inherit this order and will thus act as the will of God dictates. The *gur-mukh* becomes, in other words, the 'instrument of God' because in this state he is God-like. ... As Akal Purakh chastises those who oppress, so, too, is the *gur-mukh* unable to sit by idly in the face of oppression. Inactivity in such cases is the prerogative of those who have not realized the *hukam*, the *man-mukh* ('facing towards the [uncleansed] *man*'). It may be discerned, therefore, that only those who rid themselves of *haumai*, through both the sustained, devout practice of *nam simran* and the grace of Akal

Purakh, can battle the forces of evil and achieve martyrdom, acting selflessly in defence of others with no desire whatsoever of reward in the hereafter. The texts acknowledge that all Sikh martyrs are liberated from the cycle of existence, yet these also tacitly note that only the liberated can become martyrs. ... Where in other religious traditions, martyrdom is an act which redeems, our texts imply that in Sikhism only the redeemed are capable of martyrdom. And thus, the realization of *sach khand* is not the end of one's spiritual journey, according to the Sikh tradition of martyrdom.

The accounts, in keeping with the first Guru's emphasis on both a disciplined worldiness and selfless service, further imply that not only must these *gur-mukh*s cleanse themselves of *haumai*, but that they must also destroy the social and institutional manifestations of this evil if such an opportunity presents itself. ... The very idea of liberation or *muktī*, then, becomes intentionally transformed by Guru Nanak to mean liberation from fear. ... We should by all means note that although the liberated alone possess the ability to become martyrs in the Sikh tradition, the inverse of this, that only martyrs are liberated, is not acceptable. All *gur-mukh*s are potential martyrs, willing to sacrifice their lives if circumstances warrant such action. When death in this manner occurs, it seals the perfection which the *gur-mukh* has already attained. One can, therefore, assume that as liberation is a gift from Akal Purakh, so, too, is martyrdom.

The way in which the tradition of martyrdom interprets Guru Nanak's treatment of suffering (*dukhu*) reinforces these conclusions. It is mentioned that Guru Nanak acknowledges two levels of suffering: that suffering which is innate to all human beings by virtue of their entanglement in the cycle of existence (*samsāru*) and the suffering which is encountered in everyday life as a result of hunger, distress, tyranny, and so on. To overcome the latter, one need, according to Guru Nanak, interpret all such occurrences as the will of the divine, and bear such suffering in a spirit of resignation. Along the lines one finds in Indian philosophical discourse, Guru Nanak maintains that the suffering which is innate to all humans can be eradicated by ridding oneself of its root (desire, or in the specific Sikh sense, of *haumai*) by fixing one's heart, mind, and soul on the Divine. According to Guru Nanak, the sustained and devout practice of this will transmute all suffering to bliss (*Asa di var* 12: 1; AG: 469).

The authors are unanimous in their claim that all martyrs have their souls fixed on God while either undergoing various tortures or battling for righteousness. The texts further state that although these men and women do suffer physically, they do not suffer spiritually for they have eradicated the greatest of sufferings; detachment from Akal Purakh. By implication, therefore, these people are among the liberated. In his *bani* the Guru makes it abundantly clear that this supreme suffering is very real and very poignant.

He implies, moreover (as far as our texts are concerned), that this spiritual suffering is much worse than any type of physical punishment that can be inflicted by an oppressor. For this reason, state the texts, the torment that martyrs suffer at the hands of tyrants is undergone cheerfully. First, it is the will of God and, second, this form of physical torture is nowhere near as great as the agony of being absorbed in *haumai*. ...

The martyr tradition takes this ability to bear torment cheerfully and indicates that through such action, Sikh martyrs attempt to embody the Guru's teaching that suffering must be 'meaningful and creative' (Talib 1969: 232). In other words, rather than physically suffer through the mortification of the flesh by fasting or sexual renunciation, as was commonly practised among Hindu sannyasis and renunciates for their own individual liberation (practices against which as we have seen, Guru Nanak spoke), the martyr must suffer in public and bear it cheerfully, so that through example he demonstrates that the truth to which he is a witness (*shahid*) will prevail. Through the spectacle of martyrdom, he silently but forcefully indicates that evil can be resisted; that in suffering and in death he triumphs over his slayers. For the tradition of martyrdom, this is a creative and meaningful suffering. ... Indeed, the physical suffering the martyr undergoes is a form of selfless service to the Panth. The demonstration that a person of flesh and blood can undergo a painful physical death for Sikh ideals facilitates the recruitment of those who would also be willing to dedicate their lives to ensure that the ideals for which the martyr died are implemented. ...

The virtue of fearlessness is among the most important themes in the teachings of Guru Nanak, with respect to the tradition of martyrdom. It is not fearlessness as itself that the Guru enjoined his followers to embody, but that fearlessness which results from the fear of God. The two are very strongly interconnected in Sikh theology and form a recurrent theme in the *bani* of Guru Nanak. ...

We mentioned above that our texts interpret liberation to mean an emancipation from fear. For these texts, the fear of God is one of the essential characteristics that Sikhs, particularly Sikh martyrs, must possess. Once one inculcates this fear, nothing else is held in terror, particularly tyrants, and the painful death they can inflict. Once one becomes fearless, according to tradition, one is liberated. Again, the martyr tradition takes this theme to what it considers the limit of fearlessness. ...

One thing remains to be said. Because the interpretation the martyr tradition puts forth is just that, an interpretation, it does not necessarily mean that it is an incorrect view of the history and meaning of the Guru's hymns. There is no single 'correct' interpretation of scripture, despite the Singh Sabha's efforts to convince Sikhs to the contrary. ... Yet, as the Gurus themselves note, the meaning contained in *gurbani* is limitless. It is obvious that the meaning which a Khalsa Sikh will appropriate from the first Guru's hymns will be different from that which a Nirmala or an Udasi Sikh extracts. ...

MARTYRDOM AND THE SIKH GURUS IN POPULAR HISTORY

We may now state what the texts generally assume. ... Akal Purakh, hearing the cries of a world overburdened by tyranny and ritualism, sent Baba Nanak down to earth to bring light to this all-enveloping darkness. Preaching a radically new faith which denounced the traditional Indian path of asceticism and renunciation, Guru Nanak enjoined his followers to recognize God as one, do away with caste and rituals, view all humanity as equal, and to seek liberation while living within the world. With no small amount of courage and defiance, he fearlessly converted Muslims to the Sikh faith and criticized both contemporary politics and social conditions, commanding his disciples to be willing to sacrifice their lives for the betterment of humanity if such a sacrifice was required. Of course, Guru Nanak was not asking his followers to seek out death or to simply throw their lives away. For our texts, the Guru was quite concerned with the preservation of life, but only life lived with honour, justice, and self-respect. It was when these values were threatened that his disciples were ordered to liberate people from their antagonists or die in the attempt, and this only as a last resort. This is the mission for which Guru Nanak had inspired and prepared his disciples. ... The spiritual path which Guru Nanak elaborates in his compositions was indeed plagued with the most harsh hazards: one that the Guru himself describes as

A path sharper than the edge of a double-edged sword. [*Maru Solahe* 8(10); AG: 1028.]

For our sources, it was only natural that the successors of Guru Nanak travelled along this same hazardous path. After all, it was the divine light of Nanak that was passed on to each of the Gurus who followed him. This belief has been incorporated into the Adi Granth as each Guru whose hymns are included in it has the sobriquet 'Nanak'. ... Logically, therefore, that same courage, defiance, and fearlessness manifested by Guru Nanak becomes embodied in his immediate successor, Guru Angad.

According to tradition, while residing in his ancestral village of Khadur, Guru Angad was visited by the Mughal emperor, Humayun, who was on his way to Iran after having been defeated in 1540. When Humayun came to the Guru to seek his blessings, Guru Angad was unable to meet the emperor immediately. Enraged by this, the emperor grasped the hilt of his sword and attempted to draw it out of its scabbard. One version of the story maintains that through a miracle effected by the Guru, the sword would not come out of its sheath. The Guru then chastized Humayun, indicating that he should have drawn his sword against Sher Shah rather than against a defenceless man of God. A second version discards the miracle and holds that Humayun's temper abated, after which he apologized and sought the Guru's forgiveness. For the tradition of martyrdom, both versions demonstrate the Guru's fearlessness and patience in the face of mortal danger. ...

The tradition maintains, moreover, that it was Guru Angad who placed an emphasis on the physical development of his Sikhs through the preparation of a wrestling ground at Khadur. ...

The tradition continues that Guru Angad also emphasized the virtues of physical fitness in order to prepare his Sikhs to actively engage in truth. Naturally, strength and endurance are critical for those who wish to travel along the hazardous path which Guru Nanak outlined above. In his famous composition, *Anandu*, Guru Angad's successor, Amar Das, also describes this spiritual path in terms that echo Guru Nanak's *Mārū solahe* 8 noted earlier. For the third Guru, this is a path.

Sharper than a dagger's point and thinner than a hair [*Anandu* 14, AG: 918].

Within the tradition of martyrdom, this verse is more than just an echo of Nanak's description; it is an affirmation of Guru Nanak's ideals. As the first Nanak enjoined his disciples to act decisively when confronted with injustice, so, too, did the third Nanak demand a steadfast commitment from his Sikhs to be willing to accept death so that truth and justice prevail. He explicitly asserted that the true Sikh must live in the world and accept all the responsibilities this entails, including the destruction of evil. It is with this in mind that Guru Amar Das, according to the standard narrative, directly opposed the state in its attempt to levy pilgrimage taxes from the Hindus of the Punjab, an act which the third Master considered unjust.

The fourth Guru, Ram Das, also enjoined his followers to embody those virtues on which Guru Nanak spoke. In fact, for the tradition, an injunction representative of the Guru's teachings in this regard is extracted from within Guru Ram Das' famous *Sūhī chhant* 2, a hymn that is today recited as the couple circumambulate the sacred scripture during the Sikh wedding ceremony, *Anand Kāraj*. The Guru here emphasizes that the purpose of one's life is to do all that is possible to ensure that righteousness prevails. Guru Ram Das fulfilled this injunction, so the tradition implies, in the creation of the *masand* system. *Masand*s became more than just the Guru's authorized agents to distant *sangat*s, Sikh preachers, and the collectors of pious offerings. Rather, theirs was a status akin to that of the nobility and their creation was deemed a step towards the formation of a 'righteous government', a clear alternative to the Mughal administration and an act of open defiance. This is the precursor to ... the premeditated 'institution' of *sachchā pādśāh* (true king).

Sacha Padshah, as its very name implies, was to be a union of spiritual and temporal authority. It was to be the embodiment of the values for which

Sikhism stood, as opposed to all political authority based on injustice, oppression, and exploitation. This ideal was not only set up, but was also institutionalized. It is widely held, for example, that Guru Arjan used to hold assemblies which seemed like royal darbars.

Before dealing with Guru Arjan, the first Sikh martyr, we should pause to examine some of the inconsistencies which are readily apparent in the martyr tradition's formula. Is it enough to say that Guru Nanak was a potential martyr? In an age characterized along lines similar to those that distinguish the eighteenth century in Sikh historiography, in which people were persecuted for their beliefs and observances, why did the first Guru not act upon his very own words? Within the tradition, he is shown to exhort his followers to sacrifice themselves for the truth, yet both he and his disciples seem to avoid such action. How do the texts explain this apparent lapse? Was the infamous jizya tax so often mentioned in Sikh martyr tradition any less discriminatory in Guru Nanak's period? Were the authorities much less intolerant? Obviously, the texts emphasize that this was not the case. Why, then, did not such a harsh regime persecute the Guru for preaching activities that both violated the precepts of Islam and criticized the government? ...

The tradition which the vast majority of other texts narrate acknowledges that the Guru did not [always] act as might be expected, but it does not accept any suggestion that this was due to fear or to an unwillingness to act on is part. Instead, the tradition emphasizes Guru Nanak's keen wisdom, rationalizing his apparent inaction with relative ease: Guru Nanak did not volunteer himself for martyrdom because he realized that he must first 'morally and spiritually uplift' the oppressed. Once they were elevated, political upheaval would automatically follow. Rather than fight for political and social change with the sword, the Guru, therefore, chose to do so through his ideas. The essence of the response is similar to that of later Sikh martyrs; the means of responding, however, is not. Moreover, the texts allow us to infer that Guru Nanak was well aware of the fact that his Panth would be unable to expand if it was known for the death of its members. For his 'reforms' to take effect, the Panth required a much larger number of adherents. The texts thus offer another reason. The Guru was kept from acting because he had too few followers supporting him to bring about a serious change. ...

What the rest of the world may regard as an unwillingness to put into practice the doctrines the Guru himself taught is transformed into a conscious, intermediary stage of preparation: one which aimed at destroying the entrenched caste system and its attendant notions of inequality, thus wakening people to their responsibilities towards the world and society. Once done, the active, altruistic response to repression which the Guru implied in his hymns (so the tradition continues) would come about.

One may infer, as do our texts, that such was the case with Nanak's three successors. Although none of these Gurus had to contend with as harsh a political regime as had the first Guru, due to the tolerant policies of the enlightened Mughal emperor, Akbar, on the one hand, and the Panth's relatively insignificant numbers, on the other, their period was by no means hazard-free. According to Sikh tradition, these Gurus were forced to deal with treachery from a number of sides: the sons of the previous Gurus who would not acknowledge the choice of their fathers and the present Guru's claim, orthodox Brahmans who felt that both their prestige and income would suffer as a result of the Gurus' teachings on equality and interior religion, and petty Muslim and Hindu nobles 'blinded by authority'. In some cases, the three combined to accuse the innocent Gurus with some form of transgression, thus bringing the latter into direct contact with the Mughal administration in Delhi. Tradition narrates, for example, that on one occasion while in Lahore, Akbar himself had summoned Guru Amar Das from Goindwal to address the false charges directly.

Yet these Gurus, like Nanak, take no overt action in response to aggression. The same questions which were posed earlier in regard to Guru Nanak are, therefore, applicable here. As may be expected, the texts deal with the next three Gurus in a way reminiscent of their treatment of Guru Nanak. When the son of Guru Angad, Datu, kicked Guru Amar Das in the midst of the gathered *sangat*, for example, the tradition emphasizes the third Guru's humility and forbearance rather than his inaction. This is again the case when Guru Amar Das responded to Sikh complaints against Muslim oppression. In this case, the texts again stress that the period of the first four Gurus was one of preparation. ...

Once again, the implication that there were insufficient Sikhs to precipitate a serious change is offered.

We may now return to the narrative. Although our sources are by no means in agreement on the machinations involved in Guru Arjan's death, they all acknowledge that this death was a martyrdom. This is despite the fact that Guru Arjan may have been tortured and met his death in private. The tradition that this execution was kept from public view may well have contributed to the controversy which surrounds the death of Guru Arjan and may, moreover, aid in explaining why Guru Arjan's martyrdom receives the least attention of all popular Sikh martyrdoms in the eighteenth- and nineteenth-century *gur-bilas* literature. That the administration in Lahore purposefully chose this line of action is not implausible.

It is, however, popular tradition with which we are dealing, and according to that tradition, the fact that Guru Arjan's death lacked the public spectacle seems to be irrelevant. What is significant here is that a number of factors came together to persuade the new, less tolerant emperor, Jahangir, to put a stop to the fifth Guru's work at Goindwal. Along with the dramatic expansion of the Panth's size and influence, Sikhs began to appropriate a terminology to describe the Guru's situation that was similar to that commonly used by the Mughals. Moreover, Guru Arjan received considerable amounts of money from his *masands*. Our authors suggest that this was indeed a government which was parallel to that of the Mughals, a state within a state (see Narang 1912: 95). Secondly, a Hindu official, Chandu Shah, whose daughter was rejected by the fifth Guru as an appropriate spouse for Arjan's only son, combined with Guru Ram Das' eldest son, Prithi Chand, who also harboured a strong dislike for the then present Guru, and complained to the emperor of Arjan's allegedly anti-Islamic activities. Third, the head of the orthodox Naqshbandiyya order, Shaikh Ahmad Sirhindi, was in a strong position to influence the emperor and did so in regard to Guru Arjan. Finally, when it was felt that the fifth Guru aided in the campaign of the emperor's disloyal son, Khusrau, Jahangir saw this as the perfect opportunity to act against him.

In response to all this, the emperor initiated a violent change in Sikh fortunes, beginning the enmity between the Sikhs and the Mughal administration which was to occupy much of the Panth's energies in the seventeenth and eighteenth centuries. According to tradition, Jahangir ordered Guru Arjan to accept Islam as his faith and to include within the Adi Granth hymns in honour of Prophet Muhammad or be killed. The Guru refused, and though horrifically tortured he remained steadfast, reciting hymns while sitting on a red-hot iron plate in the scorching heat of the Indian summer. Although the Sufi saint, Mian Mir, asked the Guru to allow him to intercede with the authorities, the Guru refused, stating that he bore this torture to set an example for his Sikhs, an assertion that dramatically expresses confidence in the victory over tyranny and persecution. For the tradition, the theme of self-sacrifice is brought out by the Guru's refusal to allow his suffering to be alleviated despite Mian Mir's ability to do so. The tradition interprets this as the precise adherence to Guru Nanak's command for self-sacrifice so that righteousness might prevail. ...

The tradition implies, moreover, that in the Guru's stoic response to Mian Mir, one detects an attitude towards suffering which is similar to that of the first Guru. Indeed, Guru Arjan had physically suffered under his captors, but as tradition maintains, this extreme torment was bearable for the Guru interpreted it as the will of God. As he was being tortured, tradition continues, the fifth Guru was constantly reciting his own *Āsā* 93, a hymn which underscores the belief that all must accept the will of God with cheerful resignation:

Whatsoever your will ordains is sweetness to me. All I require is the wealth of God's name. ...

With the eradication of the greatest suffering, physical torment poses no challenge. When the Guru finally died, his blistered body swept away in the currents of the Ravi River, Sikhism had its first martyr; one who embodied the truth of which Guru Nanak spoke. It was this event, according to tradition, that changed forever the course of Sikh history, for it was the martyrdom of Guru Arjan which led to the transformation of the Sikh Panth. From mere farmers and shopkeepers to brave warriors, this new Panth had a *mālā* or garland in one hand and a sword in the other.

The tradition implies that by the time of the fifth Guru, the period of preparation was over. Not only were there Sikhs across the entire subcontinent, but they were also found outside India, as far west as Baghdad and as far south as Sri Lanka. Amritsar and Tarn Taran were thriving towns filled with many Sikhs of all castes. The villages surrounding these towns were populated by large numbers of Sikhs, particularly Jat Sikhs, who pursued agricultural occupations. These were a people who often resorted to violence to settle disputes over honour and land, a natural tendency, so the texts state, considering the fact that the Punjab was the gateway through which all would be 'conquerors' to India had to pass.

Due to the execution and the dying injunctions of his father, the sixth Guru, Hargobind, girded himself with two swords at his investiture: the swords of temporal and spiritual authority (*mīrī/pīrī*). This made manifest his decision to arm the Panth so that it would be able to defend itself and all others from the might of the oppressive Mughal empire. Although this new burden was by no means light, it was desperately required. According to one pious Sikh, in order for the Sikh orchard to continue to fructify, a protective edge of thorny *kikkar* trees was essential. To build up this perimeter, the Guru, therefore, harnessed the militant nature of the Jats, infusing it with a new courage; a courage which stemmed from goals of which Baba Nanak would have certainly approved: the defence of truth and conscience.

This was the same for both those Sikhs who were not Jats and the highwaymen and robbers who had joined the Guru's army in pursuit of booty. Military exercises, physical training, the erection of Fort Lohgarh in Amritsar, and the continual sound of both *rāg*s from the Adi Granth and martial music within the precincts of Harimandir Sahib and before the newly erected Akal Takht ('the Eternal Throne', the Sikh seat of temporal authority) were all designed to instil in these Sikhs martial qualities, a desire to defend the helpless, and to ensure with their lives, if need be, that truth always prevailed. When the time came for battle with the empire, therefore, these Sikhs were more than prepared. They had been moulded by their charismatic Guru into a force which blended in a unique harmony the courage and loyalty of the soldier with the spirituality of the saint. They were, in other words, the embodiment of the Sikh ideal: the *sant-sipāhī* (saint–soldier), warriors who, out of love for Akal Purakh and fellow beings, battle and die to destroy tyranny, protect the poor, and establish social harmony.

According to tradition, Guru Hargobind was the first of the Sikh Gurus to manifest in his dress and person the purpose clearly enunciated in the hymns of Guru Nanak, to ensure that righteousness prevailed. Not only were the battles that the sixth Guru and his Sikhs fought against the emperor's troops devoted to this scheme (battles which produced numerous Sikh martyrs), but such altruism is seen in the Guru's conduct off the battlefield as well. The contemporary tradition makes clear that it was not Islam against which the sixth Guru fought but the Mughal government. If this were otherwise, why would he have built a mosque for his Muslim brothers and sisters at Kiratpur? Moreover, as Guru Nanak after his imprisonment by Babur's forces obtained the release of numerous fellow captives, so too, did Guru Hargobind refuse to leave the fort of Gwalior until his incarcerated prison-mates were given their freedom. This poignantly demonstrated the Guru's ability to sacrifice his interests for those of others and to suffer for their rights. It was this act, states tradition, which bestowed on Guru Hargobind the title *bandīchhor*, liberator of captives.

As in most of Sikh tradition, the seventh and the eighth Gurus, Hari Rai and Hari Krishan, figure only insofar as they pursue the ideas elaborated by their predecessors. Of these two Gurus, the seventh is, however, more prominent in the tradition of martyrdom. Although he did not engage in battles himself, he did keep a retinue of 2200 warriors, an injunction he was asked to honour by his grandfather, the sixth Guru, prior to the latter's demise. Despite the tradition which emphasizes the compassion of Guru Hari Rai, one so deep that he wept at the sight of a flower on which he had trampled, the seventh Guru was willing to assist with troops anyone who he felt was unjustly threatened, regardless of their caste and status. The military aid he bestowed upon the brothers Kala and Karam Chand, for example, as well as the offer of help to Shah Jahan's mystically inclined son, Dara Shikoh, against Aurangzeb are all viewed in this light. These were again attempts to restore righteousness (see Gopal Singh 1979: 237–9). ...

Of all the martyrs the Sikh faith has produced, none has received the attention that it given to Guru Tegh Bahadur. One would assume that the reason for this is due to the fact that he was not just a martyr but also a Guru. This explanation, however, fails to take into account Guru Arjan, who is perhaps the Sikh martyr whose story has seen the least print. One need not search far for the reason behind the ninth Guru's popularity. Firstly, Tegh Bahadur's martyrdom is interpreted as one of the major events which led to the creation of the Khalsa in 1699, believed to be a watershed in Sikh history. Secondly, the majority of books and articles dealing with the Guru's death were produced around the mid-1970s, close to or after the three-hundredth anniversary of Guru Tegh Bahadur's slaying.

Although there are sources which present slightly different versions of the Tegh Bahadur narrative, the standard history may be reconstructed as follows. Born in 1621 to the great warrior Guru, Hargobind, Tegh Bahadur, according to the poet Sohan, was destined to become a great warrior in his own right. Following his destiny, the young Tegh Bahadur demonstrated a rare piety, while excelling in both horsemanship and the use of arms. His skill in the latter he displayed in 1635 during the skirmish between his father's Sikhs and the Mughal army, now referred to as the battle of Kartarpur. At this time he was in his fourteenth year. In his later years, he is shown to embody that humility of which Guru Nanak spoke. Unlike other members of his family, notably Dhir Mal, Tegh Bahadur gracefully acknowledged his father's choice of Har Rai, Baba Gurditta's youngest son, as the seventh Guru (despite the protestations of Tegh Bahadur's own mother) rather than bolster his own claims and torment the legitimate line of Gurus. After Guru Hargobind's death he left for Bakala, where he spent the next twelve years engaged in *nam simran*.

The tradition is quite clear that Tegh Bahadur was not an ascetic during his residence at Bakala. He fulfilled his duties as a householder and occasionally enjoyed a hunt. Although living some distance from Guru Hari Rai's location, the future Guru was kept abreast of events relating to the Panth by his brother-in-law, Kirpal Chand. After twelve years, Tegh Bahadur visited his nephew, Guru Hari Rai, at Kiratpur, after which he began his missionary tours. While on these tours, he was made aware of Ram Rai's apostasy and the latter's friendly relations with the empire, as well as the death of Guru Hari Rai. The future Guru's humility was again displayed on his acceptance of the seventh Guru's choice of successor, Tegh Bahadur's very young grand-nephew, Hari Krishan. Yet a few years later, Tegh Bahadur had returned to Bakala and soon heard news of Guru Hari Krishan's death. The time for his guruship had dawned. The accounts maintain that Tegh Bahadur's very acceptance of this mantle was an act of tremendous courage for he knew full well that it was bound to have repercussions, particularly within the Mughal administration. Aurangzeb, who had summoned the two previous Gurus to his court in Delhi, had decided that the right to arbitrate the succession to the guruship was his (see Gupta 1973: 3–24).

According to tradition, Tegh Bahadur's life as Guru was fraught with tremendous difficulties; problems to which he gave expression in his compositions. From the very day he became Guru, he was harassed by both family and state. In Bakala, his cousin, Dhir Mal, had attempted to assassinate the newly declared Guru by instructing his loyal *masand*, Shinan, to fire a shot at Tegh Bahadur. After this attempt had failed, Dhir Mal and his followers then ransacked the Guru's house. Moreover, the heretical Mina Guru, Harji, grandson of the infamous Prithi Chand, denied the Guru access to Harimandir on the latter's first visit. Despite the incredible setbacks with which he had to contend, Guru Tegh Bahadur travelled extensively, tirelessly proclaiming his message of hope to scattered *sangats*, inspiring all people and encouraging them to bear their daily tribulations. The extant *hukam-nama*s make both this and the high regard in which he was held by his followers all too clear. ...

Following the tradition, we note that this form of protest had given him a reputation throughout the subcontinent as a protector of the helpless and oppressed, as well as awarded the Guru a month-long custody in Delhi in 1665. But in spite of this he carried on. It was ten years later, while residing in his new centre of Makhowal, that a deputation of Brahmans visited the Guru from Kashmir. Before him they narrated their tale of the dreaded persecution which their co-religionists unwillingly entertained. Deeply concerned for many years with the state of the oppression in northern India, Guru Tegh Bahadur now decided finally to confront the authorities in Delhi and there defend the right of all people to practise their religious beliefs in freedom and good conscience. He had the Brahmans send word to the Mughal emperor that if the administration could succeed in converting him to Islam, then all the non-Muslims of India would follow. If not, Aurangzeb must desist from his policy of religious tyranny (TGK I: 720 ff).

Upon entering Delhi, the Guru and his companions were arrested and imprisoned. After the group had refused to adopt Islam and thus abandon their faith, they were brought to Chandni Chauk, the main market square near the Red Fort. The Guru was then placed in an iron cage and forced to watch as his three closest companions, Bhais Mati Das, Sati Das, and Dayal Das, were tortured to death before him, an act designed to impress upon the Guru the consequences that one who remains a Sikh must suffer. Unperturbed by this public display, the Guru again refused to abjure his faith and was subsequently beheaded in a large public spectacle on the morning of 11 November 1675.

The sources are unanimous in their claim that the life and sacrifice of the ninth Guru made manifest many of the teachings found in the *bani* of Guru Nanak. From many sources Tegh Bahadur's life and death are interpreted as the culmination of the ideology enunciated by the founder of Sikhism. One would expect that the narratives which deal with Guru Tegh Bahadur would often make reference to the first Sikh martyr, Guru Arjan, since in many ways the deaths of these two Gurus were under similar circumstances. According to the tradition, the recalcitrant sons of the previous Guru (Prithi Chand in Guru Arjan's case and Ram Rai in Tegh Bahadur's) had informed on the present Guru's anti-establishment activities. Both Gurus were executed by the Mughal emperor for their unwillingness to embrace Islam and both Gurus are believed to have followed the injunctions of Guru Nanak precisely, passively offering themselves for execution as a demonstration that righteousness will always prevail. Although some sources will briefly mention the fifth Guru's sacrifice, the tradition places far more emphasis on the relationship between the first and the ninth Gurus in relating Tegh Bahadur's narrative. When the tradition interprets an act of the ninth Guru, for example, an allusion to either one of his hymns or a hymn of Guru Nanak is always applied, rather than a reference to a hymn from Guru Arjan's *bani*.

In fact, a close analysis demonstrates that Tegh Bahadur is presented along lines similar to those we find applied to Guru Nanak. Since the tradition is clear that Guru Tegh Bahadur was the ninth Nanak, such a practice seems only logical. Within the narrative we find, for example, that upon being presented to his father, the infant Tegh Bahadur was described as the very incarnation of the spirit of Guru Nanak (Chawla 1991: 17–18). Moreover, as Guru Nanak had gone on numerous missionary tours, so, too, did Tegh Bahadur, the second longest in terms of distance after Guru Nanak, as the tradition reminds us. On these tours, both Gurus spread their message of hope and encouragement in an age of insecurity and oppression. The texts thus imply that Tegh Bahadur's tours were indicative of that same concern for humanity that Guru Nanak evinced by simply choosing to proclaim his message of liberation.

Although the texts draw on a considerable amount of material in their construction of the standard Tegh Bahadur narrative, the pattern in which an emphasis is placed on the ideological relationship between the first Guru and the ninth may be traced to the account one finds in the *Bachitar Nāṭak*, probably the first source in which mention is made of the ninth Guru's sacrifice. This should elicit no surprise, for this text is believed to have been written by Guru Gobind Singh, the son and successor of Guru Tegh Bahadur. An exceptional degree of sanctity is thus attached to it.

The verses in question are numbers four to sixteen in the fifth canto (DG: 53–4). Here, we note that the number of verses that Guru Nanak receives is surpassed only by those devoted to Tegh Bahadur. One can easily detect that for the author of this passage, there is a special relationship between Guru Nanak and his eighth successor which is denied to the other successors of the first Guru. In this passage, only Guru Nanak and Guru Tegh Bahadur act beyond the mere reception and subsequent transmission of the single mystical flame. The main importance of the other seven Gurus is that they serve as the transmitters of this essence or divine light between Nanak and Tegh Bahadur.

Of course, the passage does not detract from the importance of Gurus Angad to Hari Krishan. We are made very aware of the belief that all the Gurus are the single manifestation of the one divine light. Yet to understand the relationship between the first and the ninth Guru within this passage, it must be placed within the context of the entire *Bachitar Nāṭak*, a text which attempts to understand the legacy inherited by Guru Gobind Singh and his position within it (see Grewal 1982: 71–7). As the next canto implies, after the death of the ninth Guru, the light of Nanak is passed on to the tenth Guru. It begins by stating that it was in his previous life that Gobind Singh was appointed by Akal Purakh to continue spreading that righteousness which Guru Nanak brought into the world, and for which his father had died (DG: 54–7). In the description of the battles in which Guru Gobind Singh participated, it is evident that this righteousness was foremost in the Guru's mind, both upheld and employed in the fighting. For the author of the *Bachitar Nāṭak*, the two most important Gurus before the tenth Master are the first and ninth, and one may clearly infer the author's implication that it is these two Gurus who have had the greatest influence on Nanak's last human successor. In this case, however, the greatest influence on the tenth Guru is the martyrdom of his father. This is implied by both the presentation of Tegh Bahadur only in his capacity as martyr and the relatively lengthy account of the sacrifice. Within the passage, the ability to sacrifice life to ensure the righteousness which the first Guru brought into the world would continue belonged to the ninth Guru alone.

Since the verses above, describing the sacrifice of the ninth Guru, are amongst the most celebrated in Sikh literature, it is only logical that the relationship between Guru Nanak and Tegh Bahadur implied here would figure in the Tegh Bahadur narrative, particularly when the verses are often directly embedded within our texts. In fact, the way the martyrdom is understood today seems to be a direct result of this passage. With this in mind, the tradition's attempt to demonstrate that Guru Tegh Bahadur followed the ideals of Guru Nanak precisely elicits no surprise. Within the compositions of the ninth Guru, the dominant theme is one which also permeates those of the first Master, the absolute certainty of Akal Purakh's protective embrace in the midst of the most trying circumstances. The strong belief that many of these hymns were composed just prior to his execution in 1675 is firmly buttressed by this theme. It is Guru Tegh Bahadur's strong insistence on the conquest of fear that is often noted as a loud echo of that same concern in the *bani* of Guru Nanak. The ninth Guru's *slok* 16 often appears in this capacity:

Nanak says, 'Listen O mind, that person who fears nothing nor gives anyone cause to fear has alone obtained [the] true knowledge [of the divine]' (AG: 1427).

Hagiography presents many episodes that underscore the belief that the ninth Guru exemplified this maxim. According to tradition, Guru Tegh Bahadur miraculously caused the shackles binding those of his fellow Sikh prisoners, who were unable to go through the terrifying ordeal, to unfasten. That he chose to remain in spite of his power to escape is indicative of his fearlessness. In this light are interpreted three other incidents commonly found within the martyrdom narrative of the ninth Guru: Tegh Bahadur's refusal to be released in exchange for a miracle, the stoic composure he exhibited during the slaying of his more stalwart companions, and the famous incident with the paper around his neck. For the ninth Guru, the tradition continues, only Akal Purakh could annual fear within his devotees. Following Gur Tegh Bahadur's *slok* 33, the tradition notes that only those in a state of fearlessness are liberated (AG: 1428).

In the martyrdom of Tegh Bahadur the tradition also notes that Guru Nanak's injunction that righteous people must defy and resist tyranny (an injunction based on the tradition's interpretation of Nanak's *Vār malār* 19, AG: 1286), is a command which the ninth Guru personified in his choice to take on the plight of the Kashmiri Brahmans. According to S.S. Chawla (1991: 6), this was the fulfilment of Guru Nanak's concept of a single humanity as expressed in his famous pronouncement, 'There is neither Hindu nor Muslim'. Moreover, the theme of a disciplined worldliness and its corollary of social responsibility, which recurs throughout the hymns of the first Guru, is also applied to the ninth Master. ... For example, the ninth Guru could not turn the Brahmans away, for Guru Nanak himself had stated, while confronted with the ravages wrought by Babur's hordes:

If a powerful person were to beat upon another powerful person it is no matter for anger. [Refrain.] But if a lion were to fall upon a herd of cows, it is their master who must answer for it [*Asa* 39; AG: 360].

According to the tradition, the Brahmans from Kashmir were like a herd of cows set upon by the ferocious Mughal government which was attempting to deny them their right to practise their faith and wear their religious symbols.

As the martyrdom of Guru Arjan led to a drastic change in the Sikh Panth, so, too, was the martyrdom of Guru Tegh Bahadur responsible for a most dramatic shift. According to tradition, this event played a considerable role in the creation of the Khalsa. The tradition states that amongst the crowd which had gathered to view the ninth Guru's execution, there were many Sikhs present. Rather than step forward and publicly note their objections to the slaying of their Master, however, these men and women chose to blend into the crowd and pass as non-Sikhs for fear of their lives. It was in the light of this cowardly action that Tegh Bahadur's successor, Gobind Singh, had vowed to create a group of Sikhs who would be both unable and unwilling to hide in the face of similar circumstances. No longer would Sikhs accept a baptismal *amrit* stirred by the toe of their Guru and take on names like Das ('slave'), both of which imply servitude. To inspire these Sikhs to act in the face of injustice, a new name and a new preparation were required; ones which infused into the noviciate the sweetness that had come to be associated with the Sikhs of old and the vigour and courage that the harsh times had necessitated.

The name would be 'Singh' (lion) and the *amrit* would be one prepared with sugar and water, stirred with the double-edged sword, (*khaṇḍe dā amrit*). According to tradition, those who accepted the invigorating nectar and the name Singh saw themselves transformed. Donning five symbols indicative of this transformation, these new Sikhs chose to dedicate their lives to establish the righteousness for which the martyr–Guru had given his life and for which the tenth Guru had been born. Swearing at initiation to be loyal to their Guru to the death, and to live and die if required to destroy tyranny, the new Khalsa would forcefully act in the face of injustice.

The notion of martyrdom that permeates all Khalsa narratives begins with the very story of the order's creation. As we noted earlier, the first five men who were initiated into the order intended to give their lives for the Guru on that very day. The tradition suggests that the men and women who would afterwards join would always be willing to give their heads to the Guru, fighting each battle to the death solely for the defence of those ideals which Guru Nanak had issued two hundred years before and which Guru Gobind Singh had continued. As the Sikhs of Guru Hargobind were loyal to their last breath, so, too, were the Khalsa Sikhs of Gobind Singh. Numerous anecdotes emphasize the belief that these Sikh warriors would often argue amongst themselves in determining who would be the first to sacrifice his life for the Guru. We must reiterate that the interpretation we are presenting is aligned with the Singh Sabha rendering of Sikh history, a view which strongly implies that the blood of martyrdom flows only through the veins of the Sikhs of the Khalsa. From this, one may assume that it is only these Sikhs who have access to liberation.

The man who animated and enthused the Khalsa has as revered a role in the tradition of martyrdom as the élite order he created. We may now turn to Guru Gobind Singh. Though not himself a martyr, the tenth Guru figures very prominently in the tradition of martyrdom. Lakshman Singh provides what is the standard understanding of the Guru's role. Acknowledging the fact that the tenth Master's death is not interpreted as a martyrdom, Lakshman Singh states the reason for his decision to include Gobind Singh within his famous monograph.

[Guru Gobind Singh] was at once a leader and follower, a prophet and a seer, a poet and scholar, an intrepid soldier and an astute tactician—most heroic in times of danger, most amiable and lovable in the days of peace, most loving and sacrificing, and most selfless in all that he did. Hence this brief history would be incomplete if it did not contain a brief memoir of this *prince of martyrs*, whose example it was that pre-eminently inspired most of the Khalsa to seek the crown of martyrdom [1989: 71-3.)

Although there are accounts which present the Guru's death as a martyrdom at the hands of a Pathan assassin, the majority of texts will not concede this status. Instead, they imply that like Guru Nanak and all liberated

Sikhs, the tenth Guru was a potential martyr. The difference here is, of course, the fact that Guru Gobind Singh fought battles to defend Sikh ideals, tradition implying that it was his skill as commander, swordsman, and archer, as well as his endurance on the field, which kept him from falling in battle. As we will see, the tradition's interpretation of the many compositions attributed to the tenth Master strongly support the belief that the Guru's ideal death would be that of the martyr. Within the tradition of martyrdom, Guru Gobind Singh is described as the exemplary *sant–sipahi*, embodying all those virtues that martyrs possess: courage, loyalty, endurance, defiance, and altruism. The tenth Master had not only sacrificed all his belongings, among which were included his writings and those of the previous Gurus, in order to ensure that his mission to defend righteousness would continue, but his beloved family as well (Teja Singh 1942: 49). Could anything less be expected from the ninth man within whom the divine spirit of Nanak dwelled?

Sikh tradition maintains that the tenth Guru brought to a fulfilment the very ideals which began with Guru Nanak. Indeed, in the various battles that the tenth Guru fought, and in his creation of the Khalsa, Guru Nanak's ideals were fully realized (Grewal and Bal 1966: 126). These are interpreted as the constant struggle to ensure that truth prevails and that all humanity realizes its duty to praise the one and only God. Tradition maintains, incidentally, that these violent battles in no way altered the religion of Nanak. The words of Khushwant Singh's popular *History of the Sikhs* are often mentioned in this regard:

The only change Gobind brought in religion was to expose the other side of the medal. Whereas Nanak had propagated goodness, Gobind Singh condemned evil. One preached the love of one's neighbour, the other the punishment of transgressors. Nanak's God loved his saints; Gobind's God destroyed his enemies [1963: 88].

The religion of Gobind Singh was the religion of Nanak, and all the latter's battles were ones which attempted to restore the righteousness on which Nanak's *bani* elaborates. According to Grewal and Bal, in the *Bachitar Nātak*

we find Guru Gobind Singh convinced of his providential role to fulfil, in his own way, the mission of Nanak, and also conscious that he could not do so without meeting obstruction and opposition. His problem was to defend the claims of conscience against external interference [1966: 112–13.]

Tradition also notes that although the Sikhs of the previous Gurus were indeed brave and willing to commit themselves to ensuring the victory of righteousness, they had yet some distance to proceed before they would be up to the requirements that the new, harsh situation demanded. It continues that Guru Gobind Singh was very aware of this predicament years before he had chosen to create the Khalsa. Even as a child, for example, he would inspire his young companions and followers to show an interest in martial activity. As a young man, the Guru was determined to transform his Sikhs into the bravest of warriors. To further instil in Sikhs a strong desire to defend righteousness, the tenth Guru composed a series of hymns and epics which were to be brought together in the early eighteenth century as the *Dasam Granth*, or the Book of the Tenth King, by his boyhood companion, Mani Singh. Tradition states that Guru Gobind Singh

discovered that from reading the Ad[i] Granth the Sikhs became feeble-hearted. Therefore [he said], I myself will prepare such a Granth that the Sikhs from reading it will learn the art of ruling, the use of weapons and other skills, so that they will become fit for warfare. [See Loehlin 1971: 19.]

As the tradition implies, the creation of the Khalsa was the final step in the process.

Tradition also interprets that the wars detailed in the *Dasam Granth* were *dharam yudh*s (righteous wars). Although these wars were glorious ones, the decision to engage in such battles was not meant to be capricious or unprovoked. Only as a last resort must such a war be declared. This is clearly indicated in a famous extract from the tenth Guru's *Zafar-nāmā*, the Epistle of Moral Victory, a letter which was apparently written for the Mughal emperor, Aurangzeb.

When all alternatives have failed it is lawful to draw the sword from its scabbard [DG: 1390].

Only when righteousness and truth have been attacked may be sword be drawn for their protection, and this only after all other manners and methods to resolve the situation have been explored. Tradition maintains that Sikhs must always be defenders, not aggressors. All Sikh martyrs, of course, fall into the former category.

It is no wonder, therefore, that for the tradition of martyrdom the Khalsa and the overwhelming majority of famous eighteenth-century Sikh martyrs drew their inspiration from both the character and hymns of this altruistic, saintly warrior. Sikhs of this period joined the Khalsa and were willing to undergo, and succeeded in undergoing, various privations, including death, to institute the tenth Guru's ideal of righteousness. In the words of one nineteenth-century observer, 'Guru Gobind Singh had made himself master of the imagination of his followers' (Cunningham 1990: 66).

Tradition is clear that it was with the tenth Guru in mind that the vast number of Sikh martyrs went to their deaths. Many eighteenth-century Sikhs acquired the status of martyr in the battles the Guru and his Khalsa fought. ... Among the most hallowed names appear those of the heroic elder sons of the Guru himself, Sahibzade Ajit Singh and Jhujar Singh, who [were] struck down in the thick of battle. Although mere boys, tradition maintains that they acquitted themselves in the conflict as true warriors, fighting to the very death. To heighten the poignancy of their deaths, one often comes across many a tender account of Guru Gobind Singh lovingly clothing his sons in battle attire.

REFERENCES

AG: Adi Granth
Chhabra, G.S.
1971 *Advanced history of the Punjab*. Jullundur.
Chawla, S.S.
1991 *Martyrdom of Guru Teg Bahadur: Message for mankind*. New Delhi.
Cunningham, J.D.
1990 (1849) *A history of the Sikhs*. Delhi.
DG Chattar Singh et al., eds.
1988 *Sri Dasam Granth Sahib Ji*. Amritsar.
Gopal Singh.
1979 *A history of the Sikh people 1469–1978*. Delhi.
Grewal, J.S.
1969 *Guru Nanak in History*. Chandigarh.
1982 *From Guru Nanak to maharaja Ranjit Singh*. Amritsar.
Grewal, J.S. and S.S. Bal.
1966 *Guru Gobind Singh*. Chandigarh.
Gupta, H.R.
1973 *History of the Sikhs*. Vol. 1, Delhi.
Khushwant Singh.
1963 *A history of the Sikhs*. Vol. 1. NJ: Princeton: Princeton University Press.
Lakshman Singh.
1989 *Sikh Martyrs*. Ludhiana.
Loehlin, C.H.
1971 *The Granth of Guru Gobind Singh and the Khalsa brotherhood*. Lucknow.
McLeod, W.H.
1997 *Sikhism*. London.
Narang, Gokul Chand.
1912 *Transformation of Sikhism*, Delhi.
Talib, G.S.
1969 *Guru Nanak: His personality and vision*. Delhi.
1976 The concept and tradition of martyrdom in Sikhism. *In* G.S. Talib, ed., *Guru Teg Bahadur: Background and supreme sacrifice* . Patiala.
Teja Singh.
1942 *The growth of responsibility in Sikhism*. Lahore.
Teja Singh and Ganda Singh.
1989 *A short history of the Sikhs*. Patiala.
TGK Gian Singh.
1987, 1933 *Tavarikh Guru Khalsa*. 2 Vols. Patiala.

PART four

Traditions: Oral Narratives and Canonical Texts

PREFATORY REMARKS

Most of he readings in the previous three parts of this volume bring out, among other things, the processual character of religion. Whether one uses the term 'evolution' to describe the processes concerned or not (this is not the place to address that question), it is undeniable that religions as collective sacred complexes, or as individual personal faiths, tend to change. Beliefs and practices, and even supernatural beings, may be dropped or acquired over time.

The sudden emergence and decline of the cult of the Hindu goddess Santoshi Ma in the second half of the twentieth century is an interesting example (see Das 1981). Wilfred Cantwell Smith perhaps expressed it somewhat dramatically, when he wrote that no one can say today what a Hindu may do tomorrow (1978: 145), but his point about the processual character of Hinduism is historically valid. Even religions that claim to be based on unalterable revealed foundations, such as Islam, have not been non-responsive to changes of domicile or the passage of time. As Clifford Geertz (1968) has shown, Javanese Islam differs significantly from the Moroccan. Similarly, the character of Islamic movements in Iran and elsewhere in the last quarter of the twentieth century is marked by emphases, such as that on jihad ('holy war'), which are not exactly orthodox.

One must also discard the naive notion that the so-called pre-modern societies are characterized by unchanging religions. Actually, as some societies in the past lacked literacy and therefore written records, it was not really possible to say for certain that their religious life was static even when it may have been conceded that the pace of change could only have been gradual. The notion that custom was king in such societies was an invention of the ethnographer who usually made but one fieldwork visit to a relatively inaccessible community, and rationalized the absence of a temporal dimension in his or her data by invoking the ethnographic present as 'all-time'. In short, religions are best regarded as cumulative traditions [see Smith 1978] rather than fixed stocks, although not all religions have written histories. And whatever else they may be about, they are about life-styles.

Oral traditions imply chains of transmission. The transmitter, such as a bard, usually performs a culturally defined role of preservation through transmission. He or she generally is seen as a mouthpiece, as it were, of the tradition, which is by definition a collective thing. The life story of a gifted narrator may, however, combine in subtle and creative ways personal experiences and opinions with collective expectations and perspectives. This is well illustrated by the first reading in this section excerpted from a book-length oral autobiographical account, recorded over a period of ten years by an Indian ethnomusicologist and presented here in a text prepared by her jointly with her geographer husband, a Frenchman.

Viramma belongs to the Periyar caste, which is the largest Dalit group among the Tamils. Resident of a village near Pondichery, she came from a family of agricultural labourers as did her husband. Despite the lowliness of caste status as a pariah, acute poverty, and a life of unavoidable hard labour, Viramma found ways to bring some cheer into her life and the lives of others similarly deprived. Gifted with a receptive mind, gregarious nature, keen capacity for observation, and retentive memory, Viramma became a storehouse of folklore, of tales of demons, magic and miracles, and developed a reputation as a singer. Her attitude to life was one of fortitude born of rustic fatalism. She attempted to understand the world around her in terms of many ideas derived primarily from the local, low caste belief system, but also from hegemonic Brahmanical notions such as a morally grounded scheme of life (*dharma*) designed for the 'dark age' (*kaliyuga*) in which a struggle for emancipation is an alien idea, but one that beckons many of her Dalit sisters and brothers.

The chapter from her book included here describes the folk cult of mother goddesses who cause sickness but also grant recovery. Such cults are found virtually all over India and have, through processes of upward 'universalization' and downward percolation ('parochialization') of beliefs and rites, established composite sacred complexes everywhere.

In the process of being absorbed into larger regional, even countrywide, sacred complexes, folk cults are incorporated into literary religious traditions. The Vedas were composed by seers (*rishis*) who considered themselves not as authors but as inspired agents for the recovery of eternal (*santana*) truths. The recovery was through an internal process of listening and comprehending ('seeing'); hence the notion of the Veda ('sacred knowledge') as *shruti* ('that which is heard'). What the seers recovered over a long period of time, beginning about three and a half millennia ago, was orally transmitted for centuries before it was committed to writing.

Both kinds of transmission were carried out by Brahmans who emerged as custodians, interpreters, and teachers of sacred knowledge and as adepts of liturgy (priests). To begin with, the Vedic corpus comprised hymns of invocation and praise (*mantras*) of deified powers of nature (fire, wind, water, etc.) and ritual manuals (Brahmanas). The corpus grew and expanded, and in course of time (from about the middle of first millennium before the common era and onward) came to include the speculative (philosophical, mystical) texts called the Upanishads and known as Vedanta, or the culmination of the Veda, centred around the abstract concept of an impersonal Absolute (*Brahmana*). The Brahmanical religious tradition continued to grow in response to various developments, including the challenge of heretical movements, notably Jainism and Buddhism, that denied the sacred character and authority of the Brahmanical tradition.

Central to all three traditions is the key concept of *dharma*, denoting both the cosmic moral order and the modes of righteous action that sustain it. The second reading traces the idea of *dharma* from the Vedic times onward, lists its literary sources, and discusses its social contexts (*varna–ashrama–dharma*) as well as the value orientations that have come to be associated with it, be these about the goals of life (*purushartha*) or grades of ritual purity or moral well-being. It may be noted here that, although it is common to use *dharma* as a synonym for *religion*, it is obviously a far more complex concept. However, the manner in which the term is sometimes used in contemporary, popular discourse (in vernacular, e.g. Arya dharm), it does comes close to carrying a connotation similar to that of the word religion.

Like the Jains and the Buddhists, the Sikhs also subscribe to the notion of *dharma* (*dharm*). To begin with, at the beginning of the sixteenth century, the followers of the teachings of the first Guru of the Sikhs ('disciples'), Nanak Dev, were called Nanak Panthis ('*panth*', pathway). By the time of the death of the tenth Guru, Gobind Rai, in 1708, who declared the closure of the institution of personal (human) gurus, the Sikhs had grown in numbers but had not consistently maintained their distinctiveness from the religion of the Brahmans. A real turning point in the evolution of the Sikh religious tradition was the institution of the ritual of initiation (*pahul*) in 1699 by Guru Gobind and the promulgation by him of requirements of external identity markers (unshorn hair, carrying of the *kirpan* on one's body, bearing the last name Singh or Kaur) to go with the state of internal purity attained through the drinking of baptismal water (*amrit*) and sustained through meditation (*nam-simran*) on the one true God (Akal Purakh) and other means.

The Sikhs were now the Khalsa, 'the purified' or 'the elect', and their life was to be governed by many prescriptions as well as proscriptions. The totality came to be called *Rahit*, or *Rahit Maryada*, 'code of discipline'. Soon enough a proliferation of the norms of conduct occurred, and these were written down as *Rahitnamas*. The process continued into the twentieth century. A consolidated *Rahit Maryada* approved by the Shri Gurdwara Prabandhak Committee (the supreme body in such matters) in 1945 was published five years later. The third reading in this section is a discussion of the Khalsa and its Rahit by W.H. McLeod.

REFERENCES

Das, Veena.
1981 The mythological film and its framework of meaning: An analysis of *Jai Santoshi Ma. India International Centre Quarterly* 9, 1: 43–56.
Geertz, Clifford.
1968 *Islam observed: Religious development in Morocco and Indonesia.* Chicago: University of Chicago Press.
Smith, Wilfred Cantwell.
1978 *The meaning and end of religion.* New York: Harper & Row.

Folklore

VIRAMMA, JOSIANE RACINE, AND JEAN-LUC RACINE

When Mariatta moved into the *ceri* [hamlet], I had a child in my arms. Don't ask me which one, I don't remember any more. I remember it as a girl, not very old: I was still breastfeeding her and she had *mariatta*. You know what *mariatta* is, it's chickenpox or smallpox. In the country we call it *mariatta*, because it's Mariamman, the Mother, who comes in this form to make people give her a jar of gruel. She goes from person to person, from house to house, from *ceri* to *ceri*, and everywhere she goes she takes one or two people. And when everybody has made her an offering, when everybody has given her what she wants, she leaves this world.

Mariamman came to earth one day when her husband Isvaran was furious and drove her out, covering her with twenty-one types of spot. He cursed her and said, 'Peuh! You're not worthy of my household! Get out of here! Sow the spots all around you and live on what people will give you to be cured! Poor people like us saw this woman arriving all naked and covered in spots, and wondered who she was. Some launderers at the wash house quickly soaked a white cloth in turmeric water and gave it to her to cover herself and treat her spots. Then she saw some cobblers. They prostrated themselves at her feet and gave her a pair of sandals so she could go round the world without hurting her feet. A bit further on, people from our caste were harvesting rice. They quickly picked a few ears, made flour out of them, offered that to the Mother in an unpolluted coconut shell and gave her *kuj*

Excerpted from Viramma, Jociane Racine, and Jean-Luc Racine, Mariamman and Kali. In *Viramma: Life of a Dalit*. New Delhi: Social Science Press, 2000. Chapter 10. © Social Science Press.

[millet gruel] to drink. And the Mother carried on her way, granting good favour to everyone who offered her underskirts, saris, *kuj*, and balls of flour. So then temples were built everywhere to honour her and that's why, when you have *mariatta*, you go and get gruel from the launderer and cooked rice from the cobbler. Normally we wouldn't touch food cooked by them: they're lower than us. As for the launderers, they wash our dirty clothes. They work for us, basically! Mariamman is a very important goddess for them. She has given them the power of the drum. They come and play in front of houses and sing invocations to Mariatta so that she'll leave quickly.

The possessed warn us when the Mother storms into the *ceri*. One of the gods comes down, not just on anybody but on someone in their favour. The possessed starts dancing and announces to us, 'Dei! Dei! Mother has arrived! Dei! Mother's just entered your *ceri*! Dei! Pay attention everybody! Above all no uncleanliness! Behave yourselves well! Nothing unclean!' He goes through the streets, stops at the crossroads, shouting like that. All of us leave our houses and crowd round him to listen and find out if Mariatta is in the *ceri* or the village. Yes, those people always cover it up when Mariatta's reaches them. They're too afraid, too ashamed to say it. But the possessed tells us and then we take our precautions. The old woman of Kuppam or other old people from the *ceri* question the possessed, 'Mother, Mother Mariatta! How long will she stay in this village? When will she leave the *ceri*? In ten or twelve days? In five or seven days? Will she cause losses on the land? Should we hold sacrifices? Will Mother leave if we carry out *puja* to the gods of the territory?'

The toothless man from Guardian Street used to ask the most questions. But quite a few of us burst out laughing whenever he talked—now he's dead—because he'd lost his front teeth and so every word was followed by a *pfeu*! 'Mother *pfeu*! Mother *pfeu* Mariatta *pfeu*!' When we made fun of him, the men insulted us, 'Aye! Bastards! Whores! Monkey bitches! Shut it!' Then the possessed did a jump and screamed, 'Pariah dogs! Your language! Your language! You've got lost, Dei! Be careful!' The elders apologized and we'd put the fold of our sari in front of our mouths and snigger. You laughed when you heard him, Sinnamma. It's true, he was really funny with his empty mouth. Sometimes when we women were on our own, we'd strike up conversation with him and make him sing: hearing him always made us burst into mad laughter. So he'd stand up, adjust his turban and walk away, telling us, 'She-asses *pfeu*, she-asses *pfeu* on *pfeu* heat *pfeu*!' That made us laugh even more. We'd catch up with him to calm him down and give him betel and areca nut to chew. He'd take it, happy as anything, still saying, 'Bunch *pfeu* of *pfeu* whores *pfeu*!' I couldn't control myself when I was young, even at very serious times like the announcement of Mother Mariatta's arrival. Anyway, later on, Toothless wasn't allowed to talk in public any more, because he made the young laugh too much and even the old found it difficult to be serious. But he was still asked for advice; he knew a great deal and people listened to him a lot. It was his way of speaking that made people laugh; even girls as little as bees.

To get back to the possessed, he answers all the questions and says what has to be done. 'The frontiers have to be marked out'. Then he collapses: the god has left him to return to the mountain. We bring him round with water and prepare the *karagam*. The possessed stands up. Margosa branches are tied all over his body and, inspired again, he sets off with the two drums of Mariamman and about ten men to support him because Mariatta won't give in: she'll fight to stay there. The possessed fears her a little because she is very powerful. She can slap him and break his limbs like you break a stick. But he is under the gods' protection: he carries the *karagam* [jar filled with water] on his head, walks to the limits of the village territory, and at the eight cardinal points he plants a flag, shouting, 'Govinda! O Govinda! Remove Mariamman from this village, Govinda!'

The next day we all club together—ten or twenty *paice* per house—to carry out he thread *puja*. We buy a ball of thread, which we soak in turmeric water, and offer to Mariamman in her temple. Then the possessed goes through every house and ties a piece of the thread on everyone's wrist to protect them. He even ties the thread on babies born that night and on the cows, oxen, and goats. That won't stop Mariatta staying or doing what she has to do, but it means she'll do less damage.

You can be a maharaja's son or the son of a Koravan but if Mariatta has decided to come down on you, she'll come. No one can escape her. I'll tell you a story that everyone knows here.

A woman only had one son and she didn't want Mariatta to take him. So she says, 'My son, Mother is playing in our *ceri*. Go and hide at your grandmother's. Mother won't touch you there in the other *ceri*!' And the child set off. But someone's waiting for him under a banyan before he gets to his grandmother's. Yes! Mariatta, under a banyan tree! Seeing this boy coming, she took the form of an old woman trembling all over. When the child passed in front of her, she called him, 'Who goes here? Stop a while! Come here! I'm a poor old woman. Which town are you going to, Sami? My head is itching very badly; will you pick out my lice? Be kind, little brother, pick out all these beasts for me and scratch me hard, I'll grant you a favour, a good favour!' The child agreed to pick out her lice. He put down his bundle, started unknotting the old woman's hair, and then all he saw was eyes, eyes, countless eyes like holes in a flour sieve. The child took fright and said, 'Grandmother, I can only see eyes on your head, eyes everywhere! I'm afraid!'

'Don't be afraid,' the old woman said to him, 'I'm Mariatta herself. You wanted to run away from me, but I can be in front of you wherever you go!

I am everywhere and I see everything!' Taking a tuft of his hair in her hands and shaking his head, she said to him, 'I promised you one favour and this is it: you will only have five pearls on your forehead, no more, and ycu will not suffer!' Then she disappeared. The boy reached his grandmother's *ceri* with a high fever and only five spots on his forehead. That's why we call those five spots 'the pearls of duty'.

Even now when she enters a house and wants to stay there, Mother Mariatta still chooses her victims by pulling their hair and shaking their heads. If the hair tears off and comes away in her hand, she goes away. But if it doesn't, she gives the usual spots, well spread out over the body and shining brightly. If she isn't crossed she'll just give what she has to and they look pretty. The spots will bud a few days later and even the smallest will grow enormous. Towards the fifth day, the pearls on the forehead will burst and the others will quickly follow. On the ninth day Mariatta will get down from the body and leave only scars.

You never go out when you've got *mariatta*. Even children stay shut up until the last bath. You have to wait for the Mother to leave before you can put your head outdoors otherwise the evil eye or meeting an unclean person could drive Mariatta into a rage, and then she'd mark us for life! You mustn't go near anyone who's had relations not even the place where a man and a woman have been together. Unclean food or other uncleanlinesses don't bother her. But she doesn't put up with the pleasures of the mat! You know why, Sinnamma [Jaciane Racine]! This mother was never happy with her husband. She was innocent, but Isvaran cursed her and that's why she wanders from country to country.

When Mariatta came down on my baby, she also settled in on me. The poor little thing was covered with spots and sticky as glue because of the milk coming out of all the spots. 'Mariatta's milk' is like cashew milk. I couldn't take the little one in my arms, we were both so sticky! My mother-in-law handed me the baby wrapped up in a banana leaf for breastfeeding. I had a pot of cow's urine mixed with turmeric beside me: I sprinkled the little one with that to soothe its irritated skin. I had begged Mariamman: I'd promised to pour a jar of gruel one Friday in her temple if she'd leave peacefully. I hummed the invocations of the *kumbam* [water jar] myself. Kalimuttu, our launderer, normally ought to come three times a day to sing praises to the goddess, but he didn't have enough time. He was accompanying supplicants to Mariamman's temple to make offerings of gruel, and he was running from one house to another with his drum. He came by the house once, in the morning. He started his rounds here and he said to my mother-in-law, 'Sister, you can sing, you've got a voice: your daughter-in-law has as well.

Sing lullabies to Mariatta yourself: she is bound to hear you. I'll come every morning with my drum. I don't know where to go any more; that Mother has moved in everywhere!'

My mother-in-law said to him, 'Go on! Off you go! Now you can make the most of it!'

The fifth day arrived, but Mariatta still didn't seem to want to go. I said to my mother-in-law, 'Ayo! That pighead is still here, eating the launderer's broth and the cobbler's cooked rice!'

My mother-in-law, having paid homage and done penitence ten times in front of the *kumbam*, begged the goddess, 'Ayo, Mother! You make us suffer, you keep on staying with us, you put us to the test, Mother! We trust you, we love you. You've come to my house: that's enough, now. Leave here, go somewhere else!'

And I kept on protesting, 'Ayo! I've got such a young baby, and that widow has come and moved in on us! How am I going to fill my belly! I am poor! How can I stand her being so stubborn?'

I cursed her. While she was there we didn't light any camphor in the evening. We didn't draw *kolam* [auspicious floor design] in front of the door. We didn't make sweet things, like rice with molasses. The lamp stayed out and the house was dark.

Round about the ninth day, Mariatta said to herself, 'Ayo! I've come to this cursed woman's house who won't even burn ten *paice* of camphor for me! There's no point staying here. Let's leave!' Yes, Sinnamma, if you treat her like that in every house, she ends up by leaving the *ceri*.

By the ninth day, at last, the pearls on the forehead had burst. Gradually the others did as well. Towards the eleventh day, the *mariatta* had completely disappeared, but of course there were some scars left. The bath had been prepared. My mother-in-law had gone and bought a new jar from the potter. She decorated it with turmeric and red dots, then filled it with water which she'd left to heat up in the sun. She'd gone to pick margosa leaves and couch grass roots. Margosa trees are stripped bare at these times, Sinnamma! Everyone picks their leaves; they eat them to clean out their intestines; they use them in the bath, to heal the skin and help with the itching; and they purify their houses with them after Mariatta has passed. So my mother-in-law made a big lump of turmeric, margosa, and couch-grass paste. She took a little bit of it, mixed it in water heated in the sun and purified the whole house with it. The baby was given a bath first. Then it was my turn. I was covered with plenty of oil and washed with the paste, carefully rinsed with warm water from the jar and finally wrapped in a white cloth. All damp, with a margosa branch in my hand, I set off to raise a collection. I stopped and asked at each house, 'Alms for Mariatta! Alms for Mariatta!' I went round the whole *ceri* like that collecting gruel from each house. People gave very thick gruel: no one refuses. Coming back here, I poured it all into a big rice jar and added water to bring it to the consistency of a normal gruel. Meanwhile my mother-in-law had prepared 'Mariatta's flour'.

When a child has *mariatta*, you offer flour. When an adult does, you offer gruel. We offered both since my baby and I had had *mariatta*. Kalimuttu came with his drum to go to Mariamman's temple with us. We sang some prayers and dedicated our offerings to Mariamman. The baby was given a little flour and a mouthful of gruel to eat, as we said 'Mariatta, eat this flour and drink this gruel, Ma!' Then we shared out the gruel with everyone else, starting with children, the old, widows and sterile women. I was entitled to a good meal: white rice, fish sauce with aubergines, and drumstick beans.

One year Mariatta played a long time in our *ceri*. We'd stripped I don't know how many margosa branches to cover the whole courtyard of Mariamma's temple; a real mattress, as thick as that! The adults with spots were taken there packed tight in rows. They were all naked. The men didn't have their talisman any more, the women had taken off their jewels. Each had a coconut shell to eat their gruel out of. A *kumbam* was put at the temple entrance. Kalimuttu, Uncle Murti, and Grandfather Vellai started describing Mariamman, singing her story. Night and day, all three sang praises of Mariamman. But Mariamman had some children and two adults on her list, one at Naliveliya's and one in the street of Perumal's temple. She didn't want the rest; she kicked them and then left. ...

Nothing was done for the ones who went to *vaikundam* [Gods abode]. You mustn't do anything for those dead: no tears, no songs, no music, no flowers. They are simply rolled in a yellow cloth and handed over to the gravediggers. Even the mother of a child who dies of *mariatta* is not meant to shed tears. You can ask anybody, Sinnamma. No, no! You must never cry for those dead because that would only make Mariatta more furious and she would do even more damage.

There are several kinds of *mariatta*: little spots, which we call coriander seeds; black ones like palmyra fruit; *mariatta* with plaits where you can see three feet which weave in and out of each other: others which are all flat like my earrings. The *mariatta* of the throat is very painful: the goddess and her husband come and sit each side of the ears. Your throat swells up as big as that and you can't move your head or swallow anything, not even your own spit. There's no cure for that, you have to wait. You just use poultices made out of margosa, turmeric, and couch-grass paste to relieve it a bit, that's all.

To tell the truth, Mariatta only comes because she desires the *tali* [necklace of a married woman]. The gold's what makes her come. You know that she hasn't enjoyed her *tali*. Paramasiva drove her out. He even cut off her head and cursed her. 'All your desires will be granted by the people on earth until your time comes', is what he said to her. And that's why she comes like this, in all her different forms, to ask us for what she wants. To satisfy her, we take a white cord and dye it yellow with turmeric water. We thread a new *tali* on it decorated with a red spot, and after dedicating it to Mariamman we tie it round the neck of Mariatta. Satisfied, she goes on her way immediately. But you have to be very careful, and especially not go where a couple have been together, or else this Mother will assume her terrifying form and maybe suffocate us in one go. What you must do is wait piously without making her furious, so she'll leave as she came, peacefully.

Everything's changed now. Doctors go through the villages with the *mariatta* injection. They catch the little ones most of all to inject them; even those who aren't a foot tall yet. They say that this injection is a protection against Mariatta like the thread you put on your wrist. But the doctors don't make any offerings: they catch us like calves, do the injections, and go away! No one can stop Mariatta coming but you could say that she wasn't playing as much as before in the *ceri*. At first we hid when the doctors came to the *ceri*. We were afraid their talk would provoke Mariatta and she'd turn against us. The world has changed with time. But even now there are still people who flee the doctors. In the past I hid Anban during the time of *mariatta*: when the doctor did his rounds, I said to him, 'No one's got *mariatta* in my house, sir!' I didn't want my boy to be taken to hospital! Do you think we poor have got the time to go with someone to hospital and stay sitting there next to him, just like that? And who'll do the work here? There are plenty of other sicknesses worse than that. We can understand that people are taken to hospital for them. A few years ago there was an outbreak in the *ceri* of what we call 'local fever'. That one's horrifying. People who catch it die every time. Last time at least five people died and that was only here. Next to all those sicknesses, *mariatta* is nothing. She turns up, does her duty, gives what she has to give, and goes away. She's not like cholera which kills without counting.

Govinda! O Govinda! Sinnamma, you're much too young to have experienced cholera. I was still at Velpakkam when it struck. I saw five or six people die every day with my own eyes! Everything started at Velpakkam with Nayagam's son. It got him very early in the morning. He kept on being sick and having diarrhoea. He couldn't take any more, the poor boy: he was almost old enough to marry. His mother had called the family and showed them her son, when they heard, 'Govinda! O Govinda! Govinda! O Govinda!' I remember that it was in the month of Markaji, and our priest had been playing the gong in the village. Everyone had rushed outside to see what was happening. The old man of Pombur was in a trance. He shouted, 'Dei! Wake up! Build the fire to drive away the spirits! Cholera has come to us! Build the fire to drive away the spirits! Burn everything! Govinda! O Govinda!' Ejeumalaiyan had come down on this old man to warn us.

Cholera is Mother Kali. They say that she comes down to earth with a jar filled with dark blue oil in a woven basket. She goes into every house looking for the ones she wants to take: men, women, children, or animals. She pours a spoonful of oil in their mouths and goes away. The old man of Pombur showed us that cholera was there, because he was in a trance: how would we guess otherwise?

Hearing what the old man was saying, we immediately went off shouting, 'Govinda! O Govinda!' We rushed to the margosa trees. Everyone had a branch in their hands and shouted, 'Govinda!' We met up in every street, at every crossroad, to build fires out of everything we could find: palms twigs, whatever. We ran in every direction knocking into each other and shouting, 'She's over there!—No! She's here, that widow!' It was as if the *ceri* had burst into flames. It was burning in every corner. They say that when you start fires like that, Mother becomes afraid and runs away to another village. If fires were started everywhere she'd leave this earth!

But it turned out differently at Velpakkam. The *ceri* over there is to the north: that's to say it's higher than the *ur* [village]. I don't know what asshole built it like that, but anyway, he put the *ur* to the south. So, when there's an epidemic of *mariatta* or cholera, what direction do you expect Mother to run away in, eh? Well, when the fires are lit in the *ceri*, Kali can only run away ... into the *ur*! That's exactly what happened! They started to get cholera in the *ur*. They made fires too to drive Mother away, but she hid by a drumstick tree. They sent for the old man of Pombur. He went into a trance and, accompanied by the musicians and scores of people, he went to dig up the jar of oil and the basket and the spoon. Of course the goddess of the village, Draupadi, helped him drive Kali away. She drives out Mariatta and other evil spirits: she protects our village.

Only the possessed can approach the jar of oil. No one else, because Kali would slap them and that would be the end of it—we could all take the road to *vaikundam*. When he'd dug it up, the old man of Pombur took the jar a long way away to a tamarind tree by the pond. There he broke it and burnt it: the fire lasted until sunset. Since then I've had children, two sons-in-law, grandchildren, but thanks to God, cholera hasn't come back here again.

All this was after the seventh month ceremony during my first pregnancy. We were hulling cotton at the house in Velpakkam when we learnt the news. My father rushed towards the cotton husks and threw them into the street to burn them with anything else he could find. We all went back into our houses and shut the door. Only the people with cholera were in the temple courtyard, totally naked, without their talismans. Their bodies had been rubbed with white ash. The poor things were emptying out through their mouths and their bottoms. They were wasting away from day to day. We could see it was this Mother's work: oily diarrhoea was coming out—basically just oil; the oil Mother had poured into them. That's why you always have to sleep on your stomach to catch Kali out. If she comes in, she takes us for a tree branch and rejects us with a kick, saying, 'Pah! That's nothing but a piece of wood!' But if you sleep on your back, she has no trouble realizing that she's dealing with humans: she pours her oil into your mouth and runs away. That's how you catch cholera. ...

But it's all written, Sinnamma! Look how crowded our *ceri* is! I've had twelve children: how would I have fed them and brought them all up? And it's the same in every family! How many people would there be in this *ceri* if everyone had stayed alive? That's why Mother goes into the *ceri* each year. She gives cholera to some and *mariatta* to others. She takes five or ten people in each *ceri*, and about ten more in each *ur*. She does that in every *ceri* and every *ur* in the world and that means there's that many fewer people to feed!

CHAPTER
11

Dharma

GAVIN FLOOD

D uring the late vedic period, by the time of the composition of the
Śatapatha Brāhmaṇa and the early Upaniṣads, Aryan culture had
become established in the Ganges plain; we know that the Śatapatha
Brāhmaṇa and Bṛhadāraṇyaka Upaniṣad were composed in the Videha region.
Larger kingdoms replaced smaller ones and a process of urbanization began.
This was a formative period in the history of Indian religions, which saw the
rise of the renouncer traditions, particularly Buddhism, and the establishment
of brahmanical ideology. Between the Mauryan dynasty (c. 320–185 BCE)
and the Gupta empire (320–500 CE), there was a politically unsettled period
prompted by incursions from the north-west. The last Mauryan king,
Bṛhadratha, was assassinated by his Brahman general Puśyamitra Śūṅga in
185 BCE. The Śūṅga dynasty (c. 185–73 BCE) lost much of its empire to Greek
invaders from Bactria under King Demetrios who founded an extensive
empire, the most important king of which was Menander (c. 166–150 BCE).
After Menander's death the kingdom broke up to be eventually replaced by
the Śāka empire, established by Sai-Wang tribes from central Asia (c. 140
BCE–78 CE). With a slight decline in Śāka power, the Kuṣāṇas (Kuei-shang)
invaded, and established an empire which extended along the Ganges plain
to beyond Varanasi, culminating in the rule of Kaniśka (between 78 and
144 CE). Finally the Gupta empire was founded by Candragupta I (c. 320 CE)
and spread across all of northern, and much of central, India.

Excerpted from Gavin Flood, *Dharma*. In *An introduction to Hinduism*, Cambridge:
Cambridge University Press, 1996, Chapter 3. © Cambridge University Press.

Political support for religions varied with different dynasties and with different kings. Aśoka (268–233 BCE) was favourable to Buddhism, as was Kaniśka (first century CE), though both kings seem to have been tolerant of other religions within their realms. Candragupta Maurya may have been a Jain. With the death of the last Mauryan, his assassin Puśyamitra favoured a return to vedic sacrificial religion and performed the horse sacrifice and seems to have performed a human sacrifice at the city of Kausambi, perhaps in celebration of a victory over the Greeks. Although official patronage of religions varied, brahmanical ideology grew in importance and established itself as the centre of a socio–political religion, intimately allied to the status of the king; an ideology central to the Guptas (320–600 CE) and to later dynasties. This brahmanical religion was concerned with the ritual status of the king, the maintenance of boundaries between social groups, and the regulation of individual behaviour in accordance with the overarching principle of *dharma*. With the rise of the kingdoms culminating with the Guptas, *dharma* becomes an ideal operating in the domestic realm of the high-caste householder and in the political realm of the Hindu state.

The brahmanical ideology of *dharma* was articulated by the vedic traditions or schools (*śākhā*) in texts concerned with the performance of vedic ritual and social ethics, and expressed in the domestic realm by the figure of the ideal Brahman and in the political realm by the figure of the ideal king. These two figures, the Brahman and the king, were intimately connected. It was the king who legitimized the Brahman's power through his patronage, yet it was the Brahmans who performed the ritual consecration of the king. The ideology of *dharma* was articulated at the level of the court, embodied in the figure of the king, and manifested in the social world in rules of interpersonal interaction and ritual injunction. In this chapter we shall examine the institutions of *dharma* as they are developed in the Dharma literature and as they became expressed in Hindu history.

THE IDEA OF *DHARMA*

The term '*dharma*' is untranslatable, in that it has no direct semantic equivalents in any Western languages which convey the resonance of associations expressed by the term. It has been variously translated as 'duty', 'religion', 'justice', 'law', 'ethics', 'religious merit', 'principle' and 'right'. More particularly, *dharma* is the performance of vedic ritual by the Brahmans. It is 'the ritualistic order of Vedic sacrifice' (Heesterman 1985: 3), which refers especially to the performance of the 'solemn' rites (*śrauta*) enjoined on all Brahmans, to the domestic rituals (*gṛhya*), and to obligations appropriate to one's family and social group. *Dharma* is an all-encompassing ideology which embraces both ritual and moral behaviour, whose neglect would have bad social and personal consequences. The philosopher of the Mīmāṃsā school, Jaimini, defines *dharma* as that of which the characteristic is an injunction (*vidhi*). This means that *dharma* is an obligation, declared by the Veda, to perform ritual action (*karma*), which brings of itself no reward other than that its non-performance would be 'that which is not *dharma*' (*adharma*) and result in retribution or 'sin' (*pāpa*). The rituals, particularly the solemn rites, are for their own realization: it is ritual for ritual's sake, though it does create reward in heaven for the ritual patron. A Brahman can also perform supererogatory rituals for gaining wealth and happiness in this world and the next, but these are not obligatory. *Dharma* is identified with vedic obligation, which is eternal, and with action which is particular: the transcendent *dharma* is expressed or manifested at a human level in ritual action in order to produce that which is good.

The Sources of *Dharma*

While the source of *dharma* is ultimately the Veda, oral texts were formulated between the eighth and fourth centuries BCE, within the vedic traditions (*śākha*), concerned with ritual and law. These texts, the Kalpa Sūtras, form part of a body of knowledge, the auxiliary science, known as the 'limbs of the Veda' (*vedānga*). The Vedāṅgas are:

  śīkṣa, correct pronunciation of vedic texts;
  kalpa, the correct performance of ritual;
  vyākaraṇa, the study of grammar;
  nirukta, etymology of vedic words;
  chaṇḍas, prosody;
  jyotiṣa, astrology.

The *Gautama Dharma Sūtra* says that the Veda is the source of *dharma* and also of the traditions which flow from it. There are three sources of *dharma* according to he Dharma Sūtras: revelation (i.e. the Veda), tradition (*smṛti*), and the customs or 'good custom' of the virtuous or those learned in the Veda. The *Manu Smṛti* or *Mānava Dharma Śāstra* adds to these three 'what is pleasing to oneself' which might be rendered as 'conscience' (see Doniger 1991).

The Kalpa Sūtras, the second source of *dharma*, are categorized into three groups:

  — the Śrauta Sūtras, texts dealing with the correct performance of the solemn or public rites;
  — the Gṛhya Sūtras, dealing with domestic rites;
  — the Dharma Sūtras, dealing with law and social ethics.

While the Veda is revelation, the Kalpa Sūtras are tradition or secondary revelation, 'remembered' texts (*smṛti*) composed by human sages within the various vedic schools, though regarded as inspired and extraordinary humans.

Each sage is thought to have composed a text in all three classes, though in fact only three sages, Āpastamba, Hiranyakeśin, and Baudhāyana, have Śrauta, Dharma and Gṛhya Sūtras attributed to them. In all of these texts we see how *dharma* was seen very much in terms of ritual; to perform *dharma* correctly is to fulfil one's ritual obligations.

The Śrauta Sūtras

These texts, called *śrauta* because they follow from *śruti*, lay down the rules, in a highly technical form for the performance of public, vedic ritual. The actual *śrauta* rites are primarily focused upon Agni and Soma, to whom vegetarian and non-vegetarian offerings are made into three or five fires established upon altars. These public rituals are older and more complex than the simpler, domestic rites, and surprisingly have survived political upheavals and social changes throughout India's long history. During the Gupta period they underwent a revival and are preserved in present times among the Nambudri Brahmans of Kerala. The Śrauta Sūtras are ritual manuals which lay out the rules for the performance of *śrauta* rites. The earliest is by Baudhāyana (sixth century BCE or earlier) whose text is the first example of the *sūtra* style. A *sūtra*, literally 'thread', is a pithy aphorism which states a principle or rule. These rules are cumulative, the later rules assuming the earlier. Thus, in an injunction to make an oblation, an oblation made with ghee is understood. The Śrauta Sūtras are technical manuals comprising rules and metarules for what Frits Staal (1989) has called a 'science of ritual'. This science of ritual has close parallels to the science of language which developed a little later, but which uses the same *sūtra* style. This science is furthermore distinct from the Brāhmaṇa literature which preceded it, in not speculating about the hidden meanings of ritual, but rather concentrating on the rules by which it should be performed. These texts, as Staal has shown, are also distinct from the later Mīmāṃsā philosophy which is concerned with arguing a viewpoint, particularly against the Buddhists.

The Gṛhya Sūtras

The Gṛhya Sūtras describe different kinds of ritual (*yañña*) to be performed in the home. These domestic rituals may have been permitted for all twice-born classes in the earlier vedic period, but came to be restricted to the Brahman class. A Brahman could perform them for himself or for the other twice-born classes. These texts contain instructions on kindling the domestic fire which it is incumbent upon the Brahman to keep; rules for ritual purity; and rites of passage, particularly birth, initiation, marriage, and death. Indeed, a household might employ a Brahman to perform domestic rituals only for rites of passage, classified as 'occasional rites' (*naimittika-karma*) rather than 'daily rites' (*nitya-karma*). Concern for ritual became supplemented in the

Dharma Sūtras with a concern for regulating and defining social relationships within and between groups. It is interesting to note that at the level of self-representation, ritual procedures took precedence over social considerations, though the two spheres became intimately connected: to perform one's ritual obligations was to act in accordance with one's social status which was to act ethically. That is, from the perspective of *dharma* there is no gap between ritual performance and social or ethical obligation, an idea which the renouncer traditions, particularly Buddhism, were to reject.

The Dharma Sūtras

These texts develop material found in the Gṛhya Sūtras and are concerned with customs and correct human conduct. In contrast to the Śrauta Sūtras, the Gṛhya Sūtras demonstrate the domestic concerns of the Brahman householder, laying emphasis on domestic rituals and codes of acceptable behaviour. The most important of the Dharma Sūtras are ascribed to the sages Gautama, Baudhāyana, Vasiṣṭha, and Āpastamba, whose texts contain rules for performing domestic rites, jurisprudence, and rules pertaining to the four stages of life (*āśrama*). The significance of these texts is that they lay down rules for the performance of *dharma* for the Aryan householder, and lay the foundations for the important traditions of the Dharma Śāstra.

THE DHARMA ŚĀSTRAS

The Dharma Śāstras are a slightly later group of texts, though they contain older material, which elaborates upon the topics of the Sūtra literature. While other texts of human authorship were regarded as *smṛti*, particularly the Epics (*itihāsa*) and narrative traditions (*purāṇa*), it is the Dharma Śāstras which are particularly associated with *smṛti* and are, indeed, sometimes simply referred to by that name. The Dharma Śāstras differ from the earlier Sūtras in that they are composed in verse in contrast to the prose or mixture of prose and verse of the Sūtras. The subject matter is the same, though the Śāstras give more explication where the Sūtras are silent, and contain more material of a juridical nature, particularly pertaining to the role of the king [see Lingat 1973: 73–4]. It is these texts which are particularly important as sources of *dharma* and which provide clear indications for the high-caste householder as to what duties he should perform, what was expected of him, what was prohibited, and how these rules relate to a wider, cosmic sense of law and duty. The Brahmans who followed the teachings of these texts were known as Smārtas, those who followed the *smṛtis*, and were particularly concerned with *dharma* in respect to caste and stage of life, the *varṇāśrama-dharma*.

The rules of *dharma* in the Dharma Śāstras merge into jurisprudence and they become important texts in Hindu legislation and litigation, even during the period of British rule in India. Indeed, one of the first Sanskrit texts 'discovered' by the British was the *Manu Smṛti* or *Mānava Dharma Śāstra*, first translated into English by the founder of Indology, Sir William Jones, and published in 1794. While the *Manu Smṛti* is the oldest and most important text of this genre, composed between the second century BCE and third century CE, other Dharma Śāstras are important for their legal material, particularly the *Yājñavalkya Smṛti* and the *Nārada Smṛti*, probably composed during the Gupta period (320–500 CE). The Sanskrit commentaries are also important, particularly Medhātithi's commentary on the *Manu Smṛti*. These texts contain a doctrine of *dharma* as a universal, all-encompassing law, which is yet flexible and adaptable to different circumstances and a variety of situations. They were used particularly by assemblies of Brahmans throughout the history of Hinduism to help decide legal matters. We know something of their use from twelfth-century epigraphic evidence. In one inscription, the caste of Wheelwrights, the *rathakāras* (lit. 'cart-makers'), are disputing their position in the vedic social hierarchy. With questions from a number of Sanskrit sources, including the *Nārada* and *Yājñavalkya Smṛti*s, the stone records the decision that there are two types of wheelwrights, one group born from 'respectable' or hypergamous marriages of the twice-born classes, and another, menial group, born from the marriages of high-caste women with low-caste men.

Such inscriptions show that the Dharma Śāstras were important and were used in an advisory capacity to help settle ambiguous legal matters. In quoting from a wide range of textual sources, not only from the Dharma Śāstras, the inscriptions suggest an awareness of a scholarly Hindu tradition and a high degree of assertiveness and self-awareness among lower social groups. These inscriptions also show us that texts were open to a continuous process of interpretation in the light of contemporary social events. The Śāstras reflect the dominant brahmanical ideology and a vision of social order in which the Brahmans, the class with the highest status, had an important place as the upholders of ritual and moral purity and the conveyors of the sacred traditions.

THE CONTEXT-SENSITIVITY OF *DHARMA*

While *dharma* has been an important concept associated with kingship and has pervaded all classes of Hindu society, the law books have been mainly concerned with the obligations of Brahmans. To fulfil his *dharma* a Brahman's ritual action must be pure (*śuddha*). Although there is some debate concerning the importance of purity in Hinduism, whether the status of purity is subordinate to political power or superior to it, purity is undoubtedly a very important concept. The body, which is polluted every day by its effluents, should be in as pure a state as possible through ritual purification, principally by water. There is, however, a deeper level of pollution which is a property of the body and differentiates one social group from another. The polarity of purity and pollution organizes Hindu social space, a principle recognized in the Dharma Śāstras which view social ethics as the maintenance of order and the boundaries between groups and genders as governed by degrees of purity and pollution. The Brahman, by virtue of being the highest class of person, is excluded from certain kinds of interaction with other classes; rules of commensality and strict marriage regulations ensure the clear maintenance of boundaries.

At a universal level *dharma* refers to a cosmic, eternal principle, yet it must also relate to the world of human transaction. At a particular level, *dharma* applies to specific laws and the contexts to which they are applied. One of the sources of *dharma* according to Manu, is 'custom'. This means that *dharma* can be adapted to particular situations and particular applications of it were decided by a local assembly of a number of learned men; as Wendy Doniger [ibid.: xlvi] has observed, *dharma* is 'context sensitive'. The Dharma Śāstras provide us with examples of this. The religious obligations of men differ at different ages and vary according to caste (*jāti*), family (*kula*), and country (*deśa*). A king, for instance, must judge according to the customs and particular duties (*svadharma*) of each region. This idea of *svadharma* is important in understanding that *dharma* is relative to different contexts: what is correct action for a warrior would be incorrect for a Brahman, what is correct for a man may be incorrect for a woman, and so on. Manu says: 'one's own duty, [even] without any good qualities, is better than someone else's duty well-done'.

VARṆĀŚRAMA-DHARMA

Two concerns in particular dominate the Dharma Sūtras and Śāstras, one's obligations (*dharma*) with regard to one's position in society, that is, class (*varṇa*), and obligation with regard to one's stage of life (*āśrama*). These two concerns together became known as *varṇāśrama-dharma* whose fulfilment was a sign of brahmanical orthopraxy and, indeed, part of an essentialist definition of a Hindu. While it should be remembered that some Hindu traditions have rejected this model, its influence has been substantial in terms of Hindu self-perception and self-representation, and in terms of the West's perception of Hinduism. It has been integral to brahmanical ideology and many Hindu traditions, such as tantric traditions, have defined themselves against this brahmanical norm.

Class (*Varna*) and Caste (*Jāti*)

Vedic society, as we have seen, was divided into four classes, the Brahmans, the Nobles or Warriors (*rājanya, kṣatriya*), the Commoners (*vaiśya*) and the

Serfs (*śūdra*), the top three classes being called the 'twice-born' (*dvija*) because boys underwent an initiation (*upanayana*). This system was part of a larger 'chain of being', fitting into a cosmical hierarchy in which various categories (*jāti*) were arranged in varying degrees of subtlety and purity and associated with each other [see Smith 1994]. Only the twice-born classes were allowed to hear the Veda and, while in an earlier period all twice-born were eligible to learn it, only the Brahmans came to be its guardians, learning it and reciting it during rituals. The *Viṣṇu Smṛti* states clearly that the Brahmans' duties are to teach the Veda and to sacrifice for others, the Kṣatriya's is to practise with arms and protect the people, the Vaiśya should tend cattle, practise agriculture and money lending, and the Śūdra should serve the other classes and practise art. The term translated as 'class' is *varṇa*, 'colour', which refers not to any supposed racial characteristics, but to a system of colour symbolism reflecting the social hierarchy as well as the qualities (*guṇa*) which are present in varying degrees in all things. The Brahmans were associated with white, the colour of purity and lightness, the Kṣatriyas with red, the colour of passion and energy, the Vaiśyas with yellow the colour of the earth, and the Śūdras with black, the colour of darkness and inertia.

While the term *varṇa* refers to the four classes of vedic society, the term *jāti* ('birth') refers to those endogamous sections of Hindu society which we know as 'castes'. Castes are characterized by the following features:

— castes are arranged in a hierarchical structure in any region, with the Brahmans at the top, the Untouchables (Harijan, as Gandhi called them; Dalits as they call themselves) at the bottom. Between these are a wide array of other castes.
— the caste hierarchy is based on the polarity between purity and pollution, the Brahmans being the most pure, the Untouchables the most impure.
— the caste of any individual is inalienable; it is a property of the body and cannot be removed (except according to some traditions by initiation).
— there are strict rules of caste endogamy and commensality.

The term *jāti* refers not only to social classes, but to all categories of beings. Insects, plants, domestic animals, wild animals, and celestial beings are all *jātis*, which shows that differences between human castes might be regarded as being as great as differences between different species. Members of a *jāti* share the same bodily substance; substances which are ranked hierarchically [see Daniel 1984: 235–6]. This 'substance' has been regarded by some anthropologists as something which is exchanged in transactions: social actors constantly emit and absorb each other's substance and so are not autonomous individuals [see Marriott 1976]. The human *jātis* are a highly complex social reality which incorporate within them many sub-divisions. Indeed the Brahman and Kṣatriya *varṇa*s are also taken to be *jātis*. The caste system, while having changed through time, as do all human social institutions, has nevertheless retained a continuity. It is probable that the caste system was complex even at the time of Manu, and fluid in the sense that different castes can change their rank relative to each other in any region over a period of time by, for example, creating a pure, legendary origin. The *varṇa*s on the other hand, provide a stable model for a stratified social order in which each group is clearly defined and functions as part of an organic whole: as part of the body of society which is also the body of the primal person or being, sacrificed at the beginning of time, as the *Ṛg Veda* states.

The exact historical relationship between *varṇa* and *jāti* is unclear. It is not certain that the 'castes' or *jāti*s developed from the *varṇa* system. Indeed, philosophical texts do not consistently distinguish between the two terms and, according to Halbfass, *jāti* is used in the sense of *varṇa* in the Dharma Śāstra literature. The traditional view is that the jātis represent a proliferation of social groups from the *varṇa* system. Manu could be attempting to make sense of a pre-given social stratification in terms of the clear ideology of the vedic classes, when he attempts to explain the proliferation of *jāti*s in terms of miscegenation amongst the *varṇa*s, against the dangers of which he warns the twice-born. Indeed Manu prescribes some severe penalties for 'sexual misconduct'. A Brahman who sleeps with a Śūdra woman goes to hell and loses brahmanical status upon the birth of a son; homosexuality is punished by loss of caste, and adultery by the woman being 'eaten by dogs in a place frequented by many' and the man 'burnt on a red hot iron bed' (Doniger, ibid.: 191–2).

It is not certain whether such severe punishments were ever actually carried out, but these examples certainly have rhetorical impact and Manu clearly makes the point that sex outside the boundaries of marriage prescribed by *dharma* is not to be tolerated by an ordered society. Yet while Manu presents a clear vision of social ethics based on caste hierarchy, there are nevertheless subtleties in *dharma* which accommodate various human situations. For example sex outside caste-restricted marriage is wrong, yet there is the institution of the temporary *gāndharva* marriage for the satisfaction of desire, and while killing is wrong, there are circumstances in which it is permitted. *Dharma*, the universal moral law, must be adapted to human situations and to the everyday reality of the householder.

Although cross-caste marriages are condemned by Manu, if they are to occur, then those in which the man is of higher caste than the woman, marriages 'with the grain' (*anuloma*), are better than marriages of low-caste men with high-caste women, marriages 'against the grain' (*pratiloma*). The *jāti*s, according to Manu, are the consequences of such mixed marriages. For example, three of the lowest or outcast groups—the castes of carpenters, carvers, and the 'fierce' Untouchables (*caṇḍāla*)—are born from the union of Śūdra women with Commoners, Warriors, and Brahmans respectively.

The 'fierce' caste, the *caṇḍāla*s, whom Manu classifies as a group whom he contemptuously calls 'dog-cookers', are taken as exemplifying the lowest social groups highly polluting to the higher castes, and so becoming known as 'untouchables' in the West, though the actual term *aspṛṣṭa*, 'untouched', is not much used in Sanskrit sources. There was never a literal caste of 'dog-cookers'; this is merely Manu's rhetoric for groups identified with the most impure of creatures, cocks, dogs, and pigs. If a Brahman is touched by a member of one of these groups, amongst others such as one fallen from caste or a menstruating woman, he should purify himself with a bath.

Although untouchability is now legally prohibited in India, Untouchable castes constitute about a fifth of India's population. They were totally excluded from vedic society and high-caste ritual traditions, 'outcaste' beyond the system of the four classes (*avarṇa*). Even the Śūdras were within the class system, though forbidden to hear the Veda and outside the twice-born designation, but the Untouchables had no place within the higher social orders, living on the outside of villages, as Manu directs, and living by performing menial and polluting tasks such as working with leather and sweeping excrement from the village. The fifth-century Chinese Buddhist pilgrim, Fa-hsien, mentions the Untouchables as having to strike a piece of wood before entering a town as a warning for people to avoid them. The untouchable classes almost certainly go back into the first millennium BCE. The dating of Manu is unsure, though it is earlier than the third century CE and probably far older. There is evidence, cited by Dumont, of untouchable castes several centuries before the common era, from the Buddhist Jātakas, stories of the previous lives of the Buddha, and Dumont (1980: 54) not implausibly suggests that both Brahmans and Untouchables were established at the same time, for the impurity of the Untouchable is inseparable from the purity of the Brahman; they are at opposite ends of the status hierarchy.

The *Āśrama* System

The second concept in the ideology of *dharma* is that of life's stages or the *āśrama*s. These are codifications of different elements present in vedic society and an attempt to integrate them into a coherent system. The four stages are: that of the celibate student (*brahmacārya*), householder (*gṛhastha*), hermit or forest dweller (*vanaprastha*), and renouncer (*samnyāsa*). Patrick Olivelle (1993) has shown that the *āśrama* system, as a theological construct within the Hindu hermeneutical tradition, should be distinguished from the socio-religious institutions comprehended by the system. The *āśrama*s are a theological entity whose object of reflection is the social institution, or institutions, which the system reflects upon.

The *āśrama* system arose during the fifth century BCE as a result of changes within the brahmanical tradition. Initially the term referred to a 'hermitage' (*āśrama*, the source of the anglicized 'ashram') and came to be applied to the style of life of those Brahmans who lived there. The brahmanical 'hermits' who lived in an *āśrama* were householders within the vedic fold, performing the domestic sacrifice, who pursued a religious life, probably in areas removed from towns and villages. The term, as Olivelle has shown, referred to this special category of brahmanical householder. The meaning of the term came to be extended, referring not only to the place where the brahmanical householder–hermits dwelt, but to the style of life they led, and eventually came to refer to other brahmanical styles of life as well. In the Dharma Sūtras the *āśrama*s are not regarded as successive stages through which a man must pass, but as permanent possibilities—or lifestyle choices—open to the twice-born male after completing his studies. The twice-born boy would be separated from childhood by the vedic initiation. He would then become a 'student' in the house of a teacher, during which time he would learn about the duties and responsibilities of each of the four *āśrama*s. At the end of this period of study he would choose one of the *āśrama*s that he would wish to follow for the rest of his adult life. Thus, he could choose a life of study and continue as a 'student' or *brahmacārin*. By the time of the Dharma Śāstras, the *āśrama*s have solidified into successive stages through which the twice-born should pass, and much space in the Śāstras is devoted to describing the demands of each stage. As with the *varṇa* system, the *āśrama*s are a model, this time concerned not with the ordering of society but with the diachronic ordering of the individual's life: they are a paradigm of how the high-caste man should live.

The celibate student stage of life (*brahmacārya*) refers to the traditional period after the high-caste initiation (*upanayana*) when a boy would go to the home of his teacher (*ācārya, guru*) to learn the Veda. The student of the Veda or *brahmacārin*, 'one who moves with or applies himself to brahman', is known as early as the *Atharva Veda*, where he has all the characteristics of the student portrayed in the Dharma Śāstras: he begs for food, practises penances, wears an antelope skin, collects fuel and practises heat-generating austerity (*tapas*). Yet, unlike the contemporary idea of the student, the *brahmacārin* is in a holy condition in which he is identified with Prajāpati, the creator deity in the Brāhmaṇas, and is under a strict rule of celibacy. Indeed the term *brahmacārin* can mean 'one who is celibate', the idea behind this, common to all Indian religions, being that to remain celibate is to be unpolluted by sex and to control sexual energy which, usually understood as the retention of semen, can be sublimated for a religious purpose. According to Manu, this state would last between nine and as many as thirty-six years, during which time the student would learn all, or a number of, the Vedas. After this the student would undergo a homecoming ritual and would soon be married and entered upon the householder's life.

When a householder is wrinkled and grey and sees his grandchildren, then, says Manu, he should retire and become a hermit or forest-dweller (*vanaprastha*). In this stage a man, along with his wife if he so wishes, retires from householder's duties to live an ascetic life in the forest and to devote himself to ritual. Here, in the words of Manu, 'constantly devoting himself to the recitation of the Veda, he should be controlled, friendly, and mentally composed; he should always be a giver and a non-taker, compassionate to all living beings' (Doniger ibid.: 117). He is not a complete renunciate and has not given up fire for cooking and, more importantly, for making the daily offerings into the three sacrificial fires. Nevertheless, from the descriptions of this stage in the Dharma Śāstras, we can see that *vanaprastha* practised severe bodily asceticism, eating only certain kinds of food such as vegetables, flowers, roots, and fruits, and even practising extreme austerity such as sitting surrounded by five fires in the summer or wearing wet clothes in winter, in order to generate spiritual energy or 'inner heat' (*tapas*). The significant difference between this stage and that of the total world renouncer is the use of fire. The renouncer has gone beyond the vedic injunctions of maintaining his sacred fires; living entirely by begging he does not cook his own food. If fire and cooked food are symbols of culture and raw food of nature, as Lévi-Strauss has suggested, then the renouncer, in relinquishing fire, has, in a sense, relinquished culture; he is attempting to transcend culture for a pure, trans-human realm of spiritual liberation.

If a Brahman follows through the stages of life, says Manu, and has paid his three debts (*rṇa*) of vedic study to the seers (*ṛṣi*), of ritual to the gods (*deva*), and of begetting sons to make funeral offerings to the ancestors (*pitṛ*), then he may aim at attaining liberation (*mokṣa*). However, if he has not fulfilled his social obligations then he goes to hell, making it clear that while renunciation and the goal of liberation are valid, they must be deferred until social obligations have been met: here, *dharma*, in the sense of social obligation, is clearly superior to *mokṣa*.

Of the *āśrama*s the householder and renouncer stages are clearly the most important both ideologically and in terms of concrete historical developments. These two stages, or rather the figures of the householder and the renouncer who pass through them, reflect the distinction between socio-political religion and soteriology. While throughout the history of Hinduism there are attempts to reconcile the householder and the renouncer ideals, the two images, and two institutions, remain in tension.

The Dharma Śāstras favour the householder's life. Manu explicitly states that, of the four stages, the householder's is the best because the householder supports the others and his activity is the supreme good. The text presents a picture of the Brahman as a learned man, a model of rational self-control who restrains his senses 'as a charioteer his race-horses' (Doniger ibid.: 50), and who performs the correct ritual activity. He abides by the ritual injunctions (*vidhi*) of the Veda, namely the performance of obligatory daily rituals (*nitya-karma*), occasional rituals (*naimittika-karma*)—such as the life-cycle rituals (*saṃskāra*) of birth, high-caste initiation, and death rites—and rites performed for a desired result (*kāmya-karma*) such as going to heaven. This is in contrast to the renouncer, who has given up home, the use of fire for ritual and cooking, and who cultivates total detachment, treating everything with equanimity and going beyond attachment to the material world.

The image of the renouncer might be contrasted not only with the Brahman but also with the image of the king, the ideal householder, who, unlike the renouncer, possesses political power, and, unlike the Brahman, does not possess brahmanical purity, being lower in the *varṇa* hierarchy and having corpse-pollution due to war and punishment. The relation between the images of the renouncer, the Brahman householder and the king, has been contentious. Some scholars, such as Louis Dumont [1980] have regarded the renouncer and the householder to be the central contrast with Hinduism, while others, notably Jan Heesterman [1985] have argued for the similarity between the renouncer and the Brahman and have emphasized the contrast between the Brahman and the king. ... [See also Madan 1982.]

GENDER ROLES

All these stages are characterized by different regimens of the body, particularly the control of diet and sexuality. The first and last *āśrama*s are explicitly celibate; celibacy is a defining characteristic of *brahmacārya*, the central ascetic idea being that sexual power contained in semen can be redirected to a spiritual end and, indeed, be stored in the head. The forest dweller and the renouncer, like the *brahmacārin*, are seeking to transcend and transform sexual power for the purposes of the higher goal of liberation. Only the householder can express and explore his sexuality as a legitimate goal of life (*kāmārtha*), concerning which there is an extensive literature, the Kāma Śāstras, and the most notable text, Vatsyāyana's *Kāma Sūtra*, a text to which, exceptionally, women had access. Sexual enjoyment was regarded as the foremost of pleasures, and a man of wealth, particularly a king, would experience *kāma* with courtesans trained in the arts of love. Yet even the Brahman's sexuality stands within his rational control; a control which orders his world according to the principles of maintaining ritual purity and of controlling elements within it which threaten to disrupt that purity, particularly his own desire and its focus, namely his wife and other women of his household.

That physical love (*kāma*) is a legitimate purpose of life is significant in demonstrating a strand in brahmanical ideology which was generally positive towards the body and sexuality. Sex is not inherently sinful but can be legitimately explored and expressed within the correct caste-specific boundaries, especially by men with wealth and power. Even Manu, a text which in the light of contemporary Western sensibilities seems oppressive of women's rights, recognizes the need for the mutual sexual satisfaction of husband and wife. This is also the case in Hindu erotic literature where women are not simply the instruments of male desire. As Biardeau (1989) observes, love (*kāma*) was a traditional art which women handed down to one another through the generations; love was a woman's *svadharma*, or more correctly her *strīdharma*, 'woman's duty', and a realm of human experience which is legitimized in the Smṛti literature. However, sexuality beyond rational control, that is outside of caste restrictions and pollution controls, was anathema to the orthodox Brahman for it threatened his ritual purity and threatened the stability of society and the family.

Manu's attitude to women expresses the ambivalence of the general brahmanical ideal. Women are to be revered and kept happy by the house-holder in order that the family may thrive, yet women are also polluting to the Brahman male during menstruation. According to Menu, women are to be subject to male control throughout their lives. A high-caste woman must do nothing independently (*svatantra*), but must be subject to male authority: as a child to her father, as a married woman to her husband, and as a widow to her sons [see Doniger ibid.: 115]. By leading a life subject to male authority, a woman's virtuous behaviour will be rewarded by heaven upon her death. In later brahmanical tradition, a 'good woman' (*satī*) is one who dies on her husband's funeral pyre if he predeceases her, a practice which had developed by the fourteenth century though it was not known to Manu, and although now illegal, still sometimes occurs in contemporary India.

An eighteenth-century dharmic text, Tryambaka's *Strīdharma Paddhati*, gives details of the wife's duties towards her husband, who is treated by her as a *deva*, and his expectations of her. Above all, obedient service to her husband is her primary religious duty, even beyond regard for her own life [see Leslie 1989]. However, probably the text which best portrays the ideal high-caste woman is not a technical law book, but the Hindu epic poem composed perhaps as early as the fifth century BCE, the *Rāmāyaṇa* [and its later versions, see Richman 1994]. In this narrative the god–king Rāma is banished to the forest with his brother [Lakṣmaṇa] and his wife Sītā. Sītā is demure, modest, beautiful and dedicated to her Lord Rāma, yet she is also strong in herself, endures great hardship, and displays great devotion to her husband. She is the ideal high-caste wife.

In examining Hindu literature on *dharma* we are dealing with brahmanical self-representations and idealized images of gender roles. In Manu we have the brahmanical view of how things should be: a clear picture of brahmanical ideology, but the degree to which this reflected social reality is unclear. Women probably wielded power within the home, within the realm of domesticity, but wielded little power in the realms of public office, administration, and politics, a situation which, in India as elsewhere, has only begun to change in the twentieth century.

PURITY AND AUSPICIOUSNESS

Two distinctions have been important in the history of Hindu society: on the one hand the distinction between purity (*śauca, śuddhi*) and pollution (*aśauca, aśuddhi*), and on the other, the distinction between auspiciousness (*śubha, maṅgala*) and inauspiciousness (*aśubha, amaṅgala*). The scale of purity and pollution is a scale of status hierarchy which corresponds to the caste hierarchy, with the Brahmans at the top and the Dalits at the bottom. Hindu society is arranged around this scale. Auspiciousness and inauspiciousness, on the other hand, is a scale of the degree to which events, times, and relationships are conducive to the well-being of the society or individual. Astrology is particularly important here in determining the degree of auspiciousness for a particular event such as a marriage.

The degree of purity and pollution is concerned with status, the degree of auspiciousness and inauspiciousness concerned with power, particularly political power. While purity has been the predominant concern of the Brahman, auspiciousness has been the predominant concern of the king and the local dominant caste. While the Brahman creates a ritually pure environment, so the king must create an auspicious kingdom; one in which there is good fortune and prosperity. The ability to create auspiciousness in the kingdom is a function of the king's divinity. The king, like the icon in a temple, might be regarded as a channel for divine power and the level of prosperity in the kingdom related to the degree to which he lives up to this responsibility.

[Flood next discusses *artha*, the second *puruṣārtha* (goal of life according to the tradition), the first and the third being *dharma* and *kama* respectively, which stands for the rational pursuit of political and economic ends. He focuses on the king's duties (*dharma*) and his complex relationship with the royal priest. Village-level economic arrangements (*jajmani* relations), involving asymmetrical inter-caste exchanges of goods and services, are also briefly mentioned. Transcending the pursuit of the worldly goals of *artha* and *kama* within the framework of *dharma* is the ultimate goal of freedom *moksha*. One who achieves such a level of awareness is a *jivan mukta*, 'free though alive'. See also Madan 1982.]

REFERENCES

Biardeau, Madeleine.
1989 *Hinduism: The anthropology of a civilization*. New Delhi: Oxford University Press.
Daniel, E. Valentine.
1984 *Fluid signs: Being a person the Tamil way*. Berkeley: University of California Press.
Doniger, Wendy, trs.
1991 *The laws of Manu*. Harmondsworth: Penguin.
Dumont, Louis.
1980 *Homo hierarchicus: The caste system and its implications*. Chicago: University of Chicago Press.
Heesterman, Jan C.
1985 *The inner conflict of tradition: An essay in Indian ritual, kingship and society*. Chicago: University of Chicago Press.
Leslie, Julia.
1989 *The perfect wife: The orthodox Hindu woman*. New Delhi: Oxford University Press.
Lingat, Robert.
1973 *The classical law of India*. Berkeley: University of California Press.
Madan, T.N. ed.
1982 *Way of life: King, householder, renouncer*. New Delhi: Vikas.
Marriott, McKim.
1976 Hindu transactions: Diversity without dualism. *In* B. Kapferer, ed., *Transaction and meaning: Directions in the anthropology of exchange and symbolic behaviour*. Philadelphia: Institute for the study of Human Issues.
Olivelle, Patrick.
1993 *The āśrama system: The history and hermeneutics of a religious tradition*. New York: Oxford University Press.
Richman, Paula, ed.
1994 *Many Ramayanas: The diversity of a narrative tradition in South Asia*. New Delhi: Oxford University Press.
Smith, Brian, K.
1994 *Classifying the universe: The Ancient Indian varna system and the origins of caste*. New York: Oxford University Press.
Staal, Frits.
1989 *Rules without meaning: Rituals, mantras and the human sciences*. New York: Peter Lang.

The Khalsa *Rahit*

W.H. McLeod

To be a Sikh at the beginning of the seventeenth century meant adherence to the Nanak-panth. This involved a professed veneration for Guru Nanak, continuing obedience to his legitimate successors, and regular association with others who acknowledged the same loyalty. Those who shared the same Nanak–panthi allegiance constituted local groups or *sangat*s which gathered regularly in *satsang*s to sing the Gurus' hymns. Such gatherings took place in *dharamsalas*. Amongst the devout no caste barriers obstructed membership of the Panth or participation in its developing rituals, although caste identities were still recognized by Sikhs within the larger Punjabi society to which they belonged. A substantial majority of Sikhs were rural folk, most of them belonging to trader, cultivator, or artisan castes.

Special festival days had been appointed for observance by the Panth, and on such occasions Sikhs would reverently visit the Guru or gather at places which had acquired pious associations. One location was regarded with particular respect by the end of the sixteenth century. This was Ramdaspur or Amritsar, and it was there that the fifth Guru supervised the compilation of a sacred scripture for the Panth. The Guru remained the key figure within the Nanak-panth, the object of devout veneration and source of continuing guidance.

Early in the seventeenth century that guidance seemed to be undergoing a significant change. Hargobind had succeeded his father Arjan as Guru in

Excerpted from W.H. McLeod, The Khalsa and its Rahit. In *Who is a Sikh? The problem of Sikh identity*. Oxford: Clarendon Press, 1989. Chapter 3. ©W.H. McLeod.

1606 and the ever-faithful Bhai Gurdas reflects the concern which soon developed within the Panth. In a famous stanza from his *Var 26* (*Varan Bhāī Gurdas*) he gives expression to criticism which the sixth Guru evidently attracted.

The earlier Gurus sat peacefully in *dharamsalas*; this one roams the land.
Emperors visited their homes with reverence; this one they cast into jail.
No rest for his followers, ever active; their restless Master has fear of none.
The earlier Gurus sat graciously blessing; this one goes hunting with dogs.
They had servants who harboured no malice; this one encourages scoundrels.

These are the criticisms. They are immediately followed by an assertion of the author's own continuing loyalty.

Yet none of these changes conceals the truth; the Sikhs are still drawn as bees to the lotus.
The truth stands firm, eternal, changeless; and pride still lies subdued.

Guru Hargobind had adopted a new policy: one which tradition dramatically expresses in the donning of two symbolic swords. One sword represented the continuing spiritual authority (*pīrī*) which he had inherited from his five predecessors. The other proclaimed a newly assumed temporal power (*mīrī*). The Panth was to become more than an assembly of the devout, and its Guru was thereafter to wield an authority more expansive than that of his predecessors (Nabha 1960: 198).

A new building is also believed to have symbolized the same change. No one can be sure precisely when Akal Takhat was first erected, but Sikh tradition insistently maintains that it first appeared during the time of Guru Hargobind and that it has ever since represented the same ideal as the doctrine of *mīrī-pīrī*.[1] Akal Takhat faces Harimandir (the Golden Temple), and, whereas Harimandir symbolizes the spiritual message of the Gurus, it is Akal Takhat which represents their temporal authority. Together with the appearance of weapons, horses, dogs, and hunting expeditions, Akal Takhat also serves to represent the growing militancy of the Panth. The dual concept, whatever its actual origin, is traditionally located in the period and in the intention of Guru Hargobind. In its developed form it was to reflect a transformed Panth.

---

[1]The traditional date is AD 1608–9. The modern Akal Takhat was destroyed by the Indian Army in its attack on the Golden Temple complex in June 1984, and Jarnail Singh Bhindranwale was killed while defending it. It was immediately rebuilt, ostensibly by a Nihang chieftain Santa Singh but in fact by covert government assistance. Sikhs opposed to the central government immediately tore down the new building and erected a much bigger one.

The actual reason for this significant shift in the nature and policy of the Panth remains a subject of debate. Tradition delivers one answer, and there can be no doubt that the traditional answer is at least partly correct. The sixth Guru, witnessing the increasing tyranny of the Mughal rulers, assumed an enlarged authority and armed his followers in order to resist their evil deeds. A modified version of the tradition views it as an essentially defensive move. Both variants offer Mughal threats as the reason and both interpret the change as a deliberate decision by the Guru to arm a Panth which had hitherto been peaceable and weaponless.

There is no evident reason why this response theory should be denied. There is, however, good reason for introducing a supplementary cause, and it is this additional element which has generated some controversy in recent years. The supplementary claim focuses on the undeniable presence of Jats in the early Panth and it suggests that in becoming Sikhs they will have remained Jats. In other words, they are most unlikely to have shed the militant traditions which they certainly inherited as a major feature of their Jat culture (McLeod 1976: chaps. 1 and 3).

It accordingly seems necessary to assume that militant traditions were already present within the Panth by the time Hargobind became Guru in 1606. If this is correct, it means that the standard explanation can be accepted only in the sense that a decision by Guru Hargobind represented a formal adoption of militant means and a corresponding change in the Guru's own lifestyle. In an informal sense, militant traditions were already well represented within the Panth and the Guru's change of policy served to harness these traditions to a developing need rather than introduce them for the first time. Contemporary circumstances thus encouraged a process whereby the traditions of a significant segment within the Panth increasingly became the acknowledged policy of the Panth as a whole. To this extent the traditional explanation seems eminently plausible. Alone it remains inadequate.

During the middle decades of the seventeenth century the threat receded, and during this period the Panth continued to live a life resembling that of its early experience. Serious trouble returned during the later years of Guru Tegh Bahadur (1664–75). This involved renewed and increasingly serious hostility on the part of the Mughals, a condition which Sikh tradition attributes directly to the bigoted policy of Emperor Aurangzeb. According to the dominant tradition, Guru Tegh Bahadur decided to confront Mughal power in response to a plea from Kashmiri Brahmans threatened with forcible conversion to Islam. He allowed himself to be arrested and executed in order that Mughal tyranny might stand revealed and that brave men might rise against it (Harbans Singh 1982). [See pp. 207–12 above.]

Three themes are implicit in this tradition. The first is that Mughal rule spelt oppression and injustice. Though initially restricted to the Mughals, this theme was later to involve hostility towards Muslims as such. The second theme is the need to protect time-honoured conventions, notably those associated with Hindu tradition. The third, which is denied by the Guru's action but which follows as a deduction, is the ultimate need for force as a means of combating extreme injustice.

The tradition thus legitimizes the developments which were soon to follow. The protection theme is modified in that the rampart becomes *dharma* rather than Hindu rights; and *dharma* is variously conceived as the pattern of belief embodied in the Panth or as the moral order generally. With this amendment, the three themes together supply the traditional interpretation of the crucial century which lies ahead. The moral order has been assaulted by evil men and, because the attack is fierce, those who would defend dharma must do so by means of the sword (*Zafar-nāmā* 22, Dasam Granth: 1390). The assailants are Muslims, first Mughals and then Afghans. The defenders are to be Sikhs of a very special kind.

Here (as always) we are involved in the counterpoint of history and tradition, in the reciprocal interchange between the actual course of events in all its complexity and the comparatively simple interpretations with which those events are glossed. This is not to suggest that we should dismiss the latter and concentrate our attention only on the former. For present purposes that would be altogether inappropriate. If we are seeking answers to the question 'What is Sikhism?' or 'Who is a Sikh?', the double focus must be maintained. Traditional interpretations can be just as important as the actual facts, and typically they are the more important. This is an axiom which needs to be kept clearly in mind as we venture upon the founding of the Khalsa and its development during the eighteenth century.

Tradition offers three interconnected reasons for the founding of the Khalsa. The first derives directly from the scene of Guru Tegh Bahadur's execution, where, it is maintained, the Sikhs who were present shrank from recognition for fear that they might suffer a like fate. Guru Gobind Singh, having learnt of their cowardice, determined to impose on his followers an outward form which would make them instantly recognizable. This would ensure that never again would Sikhs be able to take refuge in anonymity (McLeod 1987: section 166, p. 168).

The second of the traditional reasons focuses on the general problem of tyranny and injustice rather than on the specific instance provided by the ninth Guru's execution. According to this variant tradition, Guru Gobind Singh had realized that his Sikhs were mere sparrows; weak and timorous creatures who could never be trusted to face armed injustice without taking instant flight. The problem could be traced to the docile beliefs and customs which they had inherited, to traditions which might be appropriate in times of peace and order but which could never withstand the assaults of violent tyranny. Steel was needed; steel in their hands and steel in the soul of the Panth. [Indeed, they had to become warriors and bear the name 'Singh', lion.] ...

The third reason concerns the internal administration of the Panth. As we noted earlier, the problem of increasing numbers and geographical dispersion had been met first by developing the *manji* system and then by delegating authority to deputies called *masands*. A century later many of the *masands* had acquired corrupt ways and an overweening arrogance. The Guru accordingly decided to disestablish the *masands* and summon all Sikhs to place themselves under his own direct supervision. As such they would become members of his *khālis* or *khālsā*, that portion of the royal domain which remained under the direct supervision of the central authority.

Although there is nothing intrinsically implausible in any of these reasons, or in a selective combination of all three, we must nevertheless maintain our insistent distinction between history and tradition. We are here dealing with tradition, with *post facto* interpretations which express a later understanding and which recast earlier events in the light of subsequent developments. The distinction between history and tradition must be maintained notwithstanding the fact that one feature of the composite explanation can be strongly argued on the basis of etymology and other objective evidence. This concerns the role of the *masands* as a possible reason for the founding of the Khalsa as a formal order (Grewal 1972: 60-1). With the possible exception of this item, we must deal with obscure history on the one hand and clear if variant tradition on the other.

The contrast becomes even more marked when we move from the reasons for the event to the actual event itself. From the traditional narratives we receive singularly dramatic accounts of what took place on Baisakhi Day 1699. The Guru is said to have circulated instructions that the regular Baisakhi Day assembly should be regarded as a particularly important one on this occasion. In response to the message a vast concourse gathered at Anandpur, eagerly awaiting the appearance of the Guru. When he stood before them he shocked all present into stunned silence by demanding the heads of five loyal Sikhs. His insistent demand finally produced a volunteer who was led into a nearby tent. A thud was heard and the Guru, emerging with a bloodstained sword, called for a second head. Eventually he secured five volunteers, each of them taken into the tent and there apparently dispatched.

The Guru then drew back the side of the tent, dramatically revealing five living Sikhs and five decapitated goats. The Sikhs were the *pañj piāre*, the 'cherished five' who had so convincingly demonstrated their total trust and loyalty. These were then initiated as the first members of the Khalsa order, and having completed the ceremony Guru Gobind Singh himself received initiation from their hands. For the ceremony he had provided an iron pot containing water into which one of his wives cast soluble sweets. The sweetened water, stirred with a two-edged sword, was the *amrit* with which each entrant was initiated. Some of the *amrit* was applied to the face and hair and some was drunk. All were thus required to drink from the same vessel regardless of caste, and subsequently all were given *kaṛāh praśād* from a single iron pan. The rejection of caste distinctions, inherited from Nanak and transmitted by his successors, was thus given ritual expression in the *pāhul* or initiation ceremony of the Khalsa (Gian Singh 1970: 856–61).

Properly told in all its vivid detail, the story is an unusually dramatic one, and it would seem churlish to suggest that it cannot be entirely true. If we are writing one sort of history, the obligation to do so is inescapable and the task has been very effectively discharged in a masterly essay by J.S. Grewal (ibid.: chap. ix). Grewal does not deny that an important event took place at Anandpur Sahib on Baisakhi Day 1699, nor does he reject all the details traditionally associated with the occasion. He does, however, criticize the manner in which the available source materials have been used by other historians. Having shown that some features must certainly be discarded, he concludes that judgement should be suspended on many other points pending careful research which has yet to be done.

Another sort of history (and a perfectly legitimate one) frees us from this obligation. If we are seeking to understand the fashioning of a Sikh identity, we can remain uncommitted as far as most of the details are concerned. It matters little whether five volunteers were actually summoned or whether five goats were actually slain. The overriding fact is that in its essential outline the story is firmly believed and that this belief has unquestionably contributed to the subsequent shaping of conventional Sikh attitudes.

Having thus evaded a significant portion of the historian's usual responsibility, we must acknowledge that our quest for Sikh identity requires us to examine one particular feature of the Anandpur event in some detail. According to the traditional narratives, Guru Gobind Singh included in the inaugural ceremony a sermon, and in this sermon he is said to have enunciated the way of life which each initiant was thereafter to follow. The injunctions supplied in this sermon supplemented certain key items incorporated in the actual *pāhul* ceremony. Together they constitute the substance of the Rahit, the only significant additions being those which the Guru delivered immediately prior to his death in 1708 (Khushwant Singh 1963: 83–6, 95). Such at least is the traditional view, and, because the Rahit is so intimately related to the question of identity, it is an aspect of the traditional account which plainly we cannot avoid.

'Rahit' is one of those words which, because it expresses a fundamental concept, deserves to be much better known.[2] Indeed, it deserves (like 'Panth')

---

[2]The word derives from *rahaṇā*, 'to live'. The word is sometimes spelt 'Rahat' or 'Rehat'. The former transcribes a variant Punjabi version. The latter is incorrect.

to be a part of standard English usage, at least for anyone interested in the Sikhs and their tradition. Kahn Singh (Nabha 1960: 760) defines the word as follows: 'The systematic statement of Sikh principles; the way of life lived in accordance with the principles of the Sikh religion.' This is an interestingly inaccurate definition. It is significant because it draws us back to the problem which so persistently frustrates all attempts to produce a simple comprehensive statement of Sikh identity. Kahn Singh was committed to the view that authentic Sikhism was represented by the Khalsa mode, and he accordingly uses the terms 'Sikh' and 'Sikh religion' where correct usage requires 'Khalsa' and 'Khalsa tradition'. If, however, we make these substitutions, his brief definition can be accepted. It is the way of life enunciated by the Khalsa tradition which is summarized in the word 'Rahit', and non-Khalsa Sikhs sustain a separate identity precisely because they decline to observe some key features of the standard Rahit.

The Rahit is thus the Khalsa way of life; the system of belief and distinctive behaviour which all who accept Khalsa initiation are expected to observe. Since the eighteenth century various attempts have been made to express the Rahit in written form and the manuals thus produced are called *rahit-namas*.[3] Some of these manuals are very brief, concentrating on particular features of the Rahit as understood by their authors at the time of writing. The comprehensive *rahit-nama* endeavours to cover all aspects of the Rahit and may venture into such areas as denunciation of the faithless or promises of a glory yet to come. In a comprehensive *rahit-nama* we can expect to find four recognizable elements, distinct in themselves yet closely related as aspects of the total Khalsa tradition.

The first element consists of the fundamental doctrines which an orthodox Sikh of the Khalsa is expected to affirm. These include such basic items as belief in Akal Purakh, veneration for the personal Gurus, and recognition of the mystical presence of the eternal Guru in the pages of the *Adi Granth* (the *Guru Granth Sahib*). This is normally the least conspicuous part of a *rahit-nama*. Such doctrines are obviously crucial features of the Khalsa faith and identity, and all that follows must necessarily be perceived as strictly compatible with these basic beliefs. As far as the *rahit-namas* are concerned, however, they can be largely taken for granted. For the purposes of enunciating the Rahit, a summary statement is usually accepted as adequate.

In passing, we should note that this portion of a *rahit-nama* will typically incorporate much that the non-Khalsa Sikh can accept. Both Khalsa and non-Khalsa can affirm a certain range of common doctrine: a range which essentially corresponds to the earlier Nanak-panthi foundation. It is when we come to the three remaining components of a comprehensive *rahit-nama*

[3]There are nine such works which date from before the middle of the nineteenth century.

that the critical differences emerge. These portions modify and extend the range of doctrine, building upon it an impressively detailed structure of personal behaviour and *panthic* ritual.

Rules for personal behaviour constitute the second component of a *rahit-nama*. These rules (which may be very detailed and specific) include instructions concerning the devotional obligations of a Khalsa Sikh, the outward forms by which Sikh men and women proclaim their identity, a variety of practices which are proscribed, and a list of particular groups with which a Khalsa should not associate. In a more developed *rahit-nama* the detail can be very considerable indeed, with injunctions covering a wide range of behaviour from personal devotion to elementary hygiene. Predictably, there is a strong emphasis on features which express the militant aspect of the Khalsa identity; features which so obviously reflect the social constituency of the Panth and the experience of warfare which it encountered during the eighteenth century.

Some of the typical *rahit-nama* prescriptions derive from earlier Nanak-panthi practice and are thus congenial to all who claim to be Sikhs. They include an insistent emphasis on the personal performance of a specific daily liturgy (the *nit-nem*) and regular attendance at a gurdwara, there to pay one's respects and participate in corporate *kirtan* with other members of the gathered *sangat*. Other items define the distinctively Khalsa identity. All *rahit-namas*, regardless of their age or provenance, stress the paramount obligation of retaining the hair uncut, and as the tradition works its way through early uncertainties this provision eventually becomes one of the celebrated *pañj kakke* or Five Ks. These are five items of external appearance which all Khalsa Sikhs must wear, each beginning with the letter 'k'. In addition to the uncut hair (*kes*), the cluster comprises a wooden comb worn in the hair (*kaṅghā*), a steel bangle (*kaṛā*), a sword or dagger (*kirpān*), and a pair of breeches which must not reach below the knee (*kachh*) (McLeod 1987).

Conspicuous amongst the practices to be avoided is smoking tobacco, an injunction which was originally aimed at the hookah but which now includes the European pipe and cigarette. The origin of this particular ban is not altogether clear. A possible reason could be the fact that a hookah would encumber a soldier and that the prohibition should accordingly be understood as one of the many military injunctions incorporated in the Rahit. Alternatively, the hookah may perhaps have been identified as a distinctively Muslim artefact. If this latter theory is correct, the item becomes one of the numerous anti-Muslim injunctions of the Rahit.

Muslims and their distinctive practices provide an explicit target for the early *rahit-nama*s and some other surviving injunctions can be traced to this particular source. The most obvious is the ban on *halāl* meat. For the Khalsa, meat is permitted, provided that it is not beef and provided also that it comes from an animal killed with a single blow (*jhaṭkā*). This eliminates the possibility that it may have been polluted by Muslim ritual, for animals slain by the *halāl* process must bleed to death.

In the modern *rahit-namas*, this eighteenth-century attitude towards Muslims has been greatly softened, but a few remnants of its earlier prominence still survive. *Jhaṭkā* meat provides a rare example of one which still proclaims its origin. Usually the origin is concealed by a recasting produced in response to later circumstances. An early prohibition of sexual contact with Muslim women thus becomes a commandment directed against adultery in general. It seems probable that, in like manner, an original ban on the Muslim hookah was subsequently converted into a rejection of tobacco smoking in general.

Most of the injunctions directed against other eighteenth-century rivals of the true Khalsa survive in the modern Rahit as interesting relics rather than as reconstituted components of essential behaviour. Who now cares about the minor *panth*s listed as *pañj mel* or 'the five reprobate groups'?[4] In many other respects, however, the early tradition holds firm. The ban on both hair-cutting and smoking is certainly firm as far as orthodox opinion is concerned. These are two of the four gross sins which earn the title of *patit* or 'renegade', and which today require re-initiation if repentance is offered and accepted.

The third element in a standard *rahit-nama* consists of orders for the conduct of Khalsa ceremonies. Once again the distinction between Khalsa and non-Khalsa Sikh emerges. Some of these rituals can, it is true, be practised by the latter as well as by the former. The tone and content of the modern orders is, however, strongly Khalsa, and the principal rite is unambiguous in intention. The prime ritual of initiation is exclusively Khalsa, for thus does one accept its discipline and adopt its outward identity. In the standard modern version of the Rahit, many of the personal injunctions are actually incorporated within this particular rite, recited as portions of a standard homily which must be delivered to all who take *pāhul*.

The fourth element in a comprehensive *rahit-nama* presents the sanctions which are to be invoked in the case of offences against the Rahit. Procedures designed to enforce the Rahit have, in practice, been very difficult to define and even more difficult to apply consistently. This, at least, appears to be

[4]There is agreement concerning three of the five reprobate groups. These are the Minas and Dhir-malias (the followers of relatives of the orthodox line who asserted claims to the title of Guru) and the Masands. The fourth and fifth are disputed. According to *Gur Gobhā* they were *naṛī-nār* (users of the hookah) and *kuṛī-mār* (killers of female daughters). In the *Chaupā Singh Rahit-nāmā* it is the Ram-raias (the followers of a third schismatic claimant to the title of Guru) and the Masandias (those who follow the Masands). Kahn Singh identified the fifth as the Sir-gum, or those who cut their hair (Nabha 1960: 593–4).

the modern experience and there is evidence which suggests that earlier generations suffered a similar problem.

Any Khalsa Sikh adjudged guilty of violating the Rahit is branded *tanakhāhia* and the penance imposed on the offender is called a *tanakhah*. Both terms emerged during the eighteenth century, clearly demonstrating that effective enforcement of the Rahit has long been a major concern within the Khalsa. There are, however, few indications of precisely how enforcement procedures were applied during the eighteenth century. In recent times the process has necessarily been selective, concentrating on important individuals or on issues which happen to be conspicuously present in the public eye. Individual *sangat*s certainly possess the authority to impose penances. This authority is delegated to five chosen representatives (*pañj piāre*) and a guilty verdict requires the performance of a penance if the offender is to remain an accepted member of the *sangat*. In practice, however, this simple procedure is too often frustrated by indifference or circumvented by the internal dynamics of a *sangat*. It is one aspect of the problem of authority; a general problem to which we must return.

In thus defining and briefly describing the Rahit we have necessarily used expressions which indicate that the system is not a static one; that it has in fact continued to evolve during the three centuries which have elapsed since it was first formally promulgated. In theory this pattern of change and development need pose no problem. Although the line of personal Gurus ended with Guru Gobind Singh in 1708, the mystical Guru continues to dwell in the Granth and in the Panth, ever-available for the kind of situational guidance which changing circumstances require. It is, therefore, perfectly consistent for an authorized assembly of the Khalsa to speak as the Guru, provided only that its message does not conflict with anything contained in the Guru Granth Sahib. Given this doctrine of the continuing authority of the eternal Guru, there should be no problem as far as changes to the Rahit are concerned.

In practice, however, the issue is much more complex. This is partly because it can be exceedingly difficult to secure the kind of corporate agreement which will command general acceptance; and partly because serious problems are raised by the eighteenth-century history of the Panth. The first of these difficulties must await our discussion of authority in a later chapter. It is the second of them which demands our attention at this stage.

Inevitably it has been assumed that the essence and substance of the Rahit must have been determined by Guru Gobind Singh during his own lifetime, and that in communicating the Rahit to his Sikhs he was effectively promulgating a definitive version. A large portion would have been delivered on the occasion of the founding of the Khalsa in 1699, and the remainder would have been added shortly before his death. One of the extant *rahit-*

*nama*s reinforces this impression by purporting to record words spoken by the Guru during his stay in Abchalnagar immediately before he died.

It is the *rahit-nama*s themselves which prevent us from accepting this traditional schema. The tradition demands consistency; a pattern which demonstrably derives from the actual utterances of the tenth Guru, and which is thereafter transmitted through succeeding generations in a regular and unambiguous form. This is not the pattern which the early *rahit-nama*s deliver. They constitute a very considerable problem; one which must be solved with reasonable certainty if we are to achieve a satisfactory understanding of the eighteenth-century notion of Khalsa identity.

The best of our early sources is not a formal *rahit-nama*, but it deserves to be included in any such discussion because it incorporates a portion which briefly describes the requirements of the Rahit. This is Sainapati's *Gur Sobhā*, 'The Radiance of the Guru'. As its title indicates, this work proclaims the marvels of the Guru's glory. It is actually an early example of the *gur-bila*s or 'splendour of the Guru' style which acquired a dominant popularity during the eighteenth and nineteenth centuries, and, because it is relatively close to the tenth Guru himself, is a very important source indeed. It is also important for the brief *rahit-nama* which it supplies and no adequate discussion of the early Rahit can avoid reference to it.

Gur Sobhā nevertheless fails to satisfy the need for a comprehensive statement of the Rahit; one which can be unequivocally traced to the actual utterances of the Guru. This is partly because Sainapati had a larger purpose, setting his brief exposition of the Rahit within his denunciation of the arrogant and corrupt *masand*s. More particularly, it is because the actual date of the work has not yet been conclusively determined. The two contending dates are 1711 and 1745. If the first of these can be definitively established, there will be a significant strengthening of the *rahit-nama* sequence. As far as specific identity injunctions are concerned, two come through with particular force in Sainapati's version of the Rahit. Predictably, they are the ban on hair-cutting and condemnation of the hookah.

The examples of formal *rahit-nama* style which usually attract attention first are four brief poems. These relate, in simple Punjabi verse, conversations which their authors allegedly had with Guru Gobind Singh prior to his death. Two of them are attributed to Nand Lal (*Tanakhāh-nāmā* and *Praśan-uttar*). A third is attributed to a Sikh variously called Prahilad Singh or Prahilad Rai; and the fourth to Desa Singh, a resident of Amritsar who claims to have obtained his information from the Guru and from Nand Lal. The Nand Lal of the *rahit-nama*s is obviously intended to be Bhai Nand Lal, a celebrated member of the tenth Guru's entourage and one renowned for his Persian poetry. There also exists a brief prose *rahit-nama* attributed to him. With the same cluster we can also associate the brief prose *rahit-nama* attributed to

Daya Singh (one of the five Sikhs traditionally believed to have offered their heads at the inauguration of the Khalsa in 1699).

There can be no doubt concerning the importance of these six brief works in the history of Sikh doctrine (especially doctrine relating to the Rahit and thus to the nature of the Khalsa). Their significance in this regard is well illustrated by the repeated use which Bhai Jodh Singh makes of them in the relevant chapter of his influential study of Sikh doctrine entitled *Guramati niraṇay*. It is also indicated by some very familiar expressions. From where do the words *savā lakh* and *rāj karegā khālsā* come? They are to be found in the *Tanakhāh-nāmā*. And where do we first encounter such expressions as *gurū khālsā mānīahi, paragaṭ gurū kī deh* ('Accept the Khalsa as Guru, for it is the manifest body of the Guru') or *sabh sikhan ko bachan hai, gurū mānīahu granth* ('Every Sikh is bidden to accept the Granth as Guru')? These lines we find in the *rahit-nama* attributed to Prahilad Singh. They are accordingly works which should be treated with great respect.

Unfortunately they are also works which the historian has to treat with great reserve. This is because it is still impossible to identify them in terms of author, place, or time. The authorship of such figures as Nand Lal and Daya Singh must be rejected, and so too must the claims which each *rahit-nama* makes to immediate contact with the Guru himself. The distinguished Bhai Nand Lal Goya could never have written the kind of verse which these *rahit-nama*s offer, and in all cases the language indicates a significant remove from the Guru's own time and environment. There are, moreover, some conspicuous errors, such as Prahilad Singh's claim that he received his instruction from the Guru in 1696. Had he received it in Abchalnagar (as he specifically claims) he should have supplied a date corresponding to 1708.

Such features separate this cluster of *rahit-nama*s from immediate contact with Guru Gobind Singh, but we must take care not to exaggerate the distance. Other features indicate a relatively early date. The most important of these is the impression which these *rahit-nama*s give of a Rahit still in the process of formulation. Although we may have to detach them from the person and period of Guru Gobind Singh, this does not necessarily mean that we shall have to advance them well into the eighteenth century or the early nineteenth century.

We have here summarized a very intricate problem; one which still awaits a satisfactory determination. Part of our problem derives from the lack of early manuscript evidence. In its absence we shall have to depend upon analysis of language and content; an analysis which has yet to be adequately performed. A reasonable hypothesis seems to be an origin located somewhere in the middle decades of the eighteenth century. In the meantime, however, it remains a hypothesis.

Fortunately, the same does not apply to the only lengthy *rahit-nama* which belongs to the eighteenth century. This is the prose *rahit-nama* attributed to Chaupa Singh Chhibbar, tutor to the infant Guru Gobind Singh and later one of his trusted advisers. An analysis of the *Chaupā Siṅgh Rahit-nāmā* indicates that it was compiled in its present form during the middle decades of the eighteenth century (between 1740 and 1765), and that it is accordingly the earliest of the datable *rahit-namas*. In its extant form it is a composite product mixing sections of classic *rahit-nama* material with anecdotes concerning Guru Gobind Singh, denunciation of the current Khalsa leadership, prophecies of imminent disaster, and a promise of ultimate glory (McLeod 1987: 24–8).

The composite nature of the *Chaupā Siṅgh Rahit-nāmā* points clearly to earlier sources, and it is conceivable that portions of it may indeed go back to Chaupa Singh Chhibbar of the tenth Guru's entourage. These portions are impossible to identify with any certainty, although some parts can be safely detached from the *rahit-nama*'s putative author and firmly located in a later period. The *rahit-nama* must be read as a mid-century interpretation of the Khalsa and its duty, as perceived by a particular family of Chhibbar Brahmans, once influential in the Panth but now pushed aside by coarsely aggressive successors (ibid.: 16–19).

This firm identification is the basis of the *rahit-nama*'s value today. Portions of its prolific content can be offensive to a modern Khalsa taste, and it is easy to identify features which have made it an object of deep suspicion in orthodox circles. Notable in this respect is its claim that Brahmans are entitled to a special consideration in the Panth, a view which is unlikely to commend the source to those who support an egalitarian interpretation of the Panth (ibid.: 24, 151). Such features are nevertheless very valuable, for they sustain the credibility of the *rahit-nama* as a Chhibbar product and enable us to set it within a clearly definable context. Its profusion of detailed Rahit injunctions can thus be tagged in terms of source and period, and once this has been done the injunctions can be interpreted accordingly.

Although the Chhibbar connection arouses orthodox suspicions, it should not be assumed that these suspicions are necessarily valid. It does not follow that the *rahit-nama* will be unrepresentative or untrustworthy simply because of its Brahman provenance. On the contrary, the connection should considerably strengthen its claims, for this particular family had been very close to the tenth Guru, and it can be plausibly maintained that for this very reason the *rahit-nama* deserves sympathetic analysis. The claim is strengthened by features which one might not have expected from a Brahmanic source. Strong emphasis is laid on the prime significance of the sword, on the role of the Khalsa Sikh as a soldier, and on the menace posed by polluting Muslims (ibid.: 40, 42).

Because the Rahit portions of the *Chaupā Siṅgh Rahit-nāmā* are so lengthy

and detailed, it is impossible to summarize them here (ibid.: 32–43). There
are two such sections, one specifying duties which the loyal Khalsa must
perform and the other listing offences which require a penance (*tanakhāh*)
(ibid.: 149–66, 174–90). In addition to their many injunctions concerning
warfare and the sword, the two lists include such predictable items as rules
for harmonious relations within a *sangat*, appropriate rituals, reverence for
the sacred scripture, various means of avoiding pollution, and an insistent
stress on maintaining the hair uncut. Practices to be strictly avoided include
smoking a hookah and eating *halāl* meat.

The *Chaupā Siṅgh Rahit-nāmā* thus incorporates the customary stress on
the *kes* (the uncut hair), but it does not include the Five Ks (the *pañj kakke* or
pañj kakar). The earliest extant version omits them altogether, and when a
later version introduces a fivefold cluster, the actual items which it lists do
not correspond to the *pañj kakke*. Three of the Five Ks are included (*kachh,
kirpān*, and *kes*) but two are missing (*kaṅghā* and *kaṛā*). In their place we find
bāṇī (the Gurus' utterances as recorded in sacred scripture) and *sādh saṅgat*
(the fellowship of the devout). Precisely the same situation is presented by
the brief *rahit-nama*s which we have tentatively assigned to the mid-eighteenth
century. There too we find no reference to the *pañj kakke* in the early versions,
though a reference subsequently appears in a later text of the *Prahilād Siṅgh
Rahit-nāmā*.[5]

This particular instance can be generalized in the sense that other features
of the orthodox Rahit, as understood today, are absent from the eighteenth-
century evidence or are present as prototypes which have yet to attain firm
definition. Others possess a clear definition, but their content or emphasis
is subsequently amended in response to changing circumstances. From this
evidence we must draw the following conclusion. A version of the Rahit was
certainly current during the lifetime of Guru Gobind Singh, but that version
must be regarded as a nucleus, not as the fully-fledged twentieth-century
Rahit. In the meantime (and particularly during the early and middle decades
of the eighteenth century) a process of growth and development took place;
one which had produced the essential lineaments of the modern Rahit by
the end of the eighteenth century.

This process of change and development continued through the
nineteenth century into the twentieth and it still continues today. The Rahit
has never been static. It still responds to contemporary pressures, producing
shifts in emphasis which gradually emerge as significant changes. Two

---

[5]The twentieth-century version of the *Prahilād Siṅgh Rahit-nāmā* has an addendum
attached which affirms the use of the *pañj kakke*. ...

*kachh kes kaṅghā kirapān/kaṛā aur to karau bakhān/
ih kakke pañj tum māno/gurū granth sabh tum jāno/*

interesting (and closely related) examples are provided by changing attitudes towards illicit sexual intercourse and towards Muslims. If one compares modern injunctions with those from the eighteenth century, some interesting (yet unsurprising) differences become evident.

It thus appears that the developed Rahit must be ascribed to an extended period of evolution rather than limited to explicit pronouncements on the part of the tenth Guru. If this is indeed the case, it raises the question of how one identifies sources for the various elements included in the developed Rahit. Three general sources may be briefly postulated.

The first is the traditional source, namely the intention of the Gurus applied during the formative years of the Panth's growth and codified by Guru Gobind Singh as a nucleus of the later Rahit. This source delivered items relating to the importance of the *sangat* and to devotional practices designed to achieve *mukti* or spiritual liberation. Duties associated with the growing militancy of the Panth will also have developed during the course of the seventeenth century, and we must also accept that an outward identity had been defined by the end of the century. Given the insistent stress on the *kes* in all *rahit-namas*, we can assume that the dominant feature of this external identity was its insistence on uncut hair.

Militant conventions and uncut hair point to a second source. This comprises the culture and traditions of the caste group which was progressively moving towards ascendancy within the Panth, particularly after the founding of the Khalsa. This ascendancy had presumably been reached in numerical terms before the ending of the line of personal Gurus, and during the eighteenth century it was to assume a much larger connotation. The Jats have long been distinguished by their militant traditions and by the custom of retaining their hair uncut. The influence of these traditions evidently operated prior to the formal inauguration of the Khalsa, fusing with the purpose of Guru Gobind Singh and thus emerging as significant features of the Khalsa nucleus. During the course of the eighteenth century the same influence accelerated as Jat leadership assumed an increasingly high profile within the Panth.

The third source also affected the development of the Rahit during the seventeenth century, growing significantly in influence during the eighteenth. This was the pressure of contemporary circumstances, specifically the experience of warfare against enemies who increasingly were identified as Muslims. These circumstances served to strengthen the influence of the Jat source, in that they encouraged militancy within the Panth. They stand alone as the source of some notable eighteenth-century injunctions aimed clearly and directly at Muslims.

The Rahit must thus be viewed as an evolving system; one which began to emerge during the earliest days of the Nanak-panth. It thereafter continued to develop formally (in accordance with deliberate decisions) and informally (in response to internal influences and external pressures). The precise distribution of these factors cannot be determined, particularly as all three were intertwined to a considerable extent. It is, however, possible to identify the appearance of certain key items and to reconstruct a loose sequence. This should enable us to describe in general terms the nature of the Khalsa identity at the beginning of the eighteenth century; the pattern of development which progressively enlarged and consolidated the Rahit during the course of the eighteenth century; and the developed identity which the Khalsa carried forward into the nineteenth century.

In so doing, we must take care to set this Khalsa identity within the context of the larger Panth, ever aware that, however dominant the Khalsa mode may sometimes seem, its boundaries have never coincided with those of the Panth as a whole. It all depends, of course, on one's point of view. For some strict members of the Khalsa the two sets of boundaries are indeed coterminous and those who fail to meet Khalsa requirements are ipso facto deregistered as Sikhs. Although no one has ever managed to isolate the strict or 'fundamentalist' sector of the Panth, there can be little doubt that it always constitutes a comparatively small minority. The majority consists of the liberal, the lax, and the ambivalent, all of whom would presumably acknowledge a Panth larger than the orthodox Khalsa.

This means that our basic problem will persist, emerging in each period and generation to frustrate the promise of easy definition which the Khalsa so insistently proffers. We must also remind ourselves that the problem of definition will not be confined to a simple distinction between loyal Khalsa, on the one hand, and clean-shaven Sahaj-dhari, on the other. Punjabi society will not permit such an easy solution, particularly in the villages which are home to a majority of those who call themselves Sikhs. A major aspect of the practical problem is the willingness of many Punjabis to merge identities which the academic and the devout would prefer to keep separate. We shall delude ourselves if we imagine otherwise, just as we so easily misunderstand Sikh society if we insist on keeping our normative categories carefully intact.

REFERENCES

Gian Singh
1970 *Tvarikh Gurū Khālsā*. Second edition. Patiala
Grewal, J.S.
1972 *From Guru Nanak to Maharaja Ranjit Singh: Essays in Sikh History*. Amritsar.
Harbans Singh
1982 *Guru Tegh Bahadur*. New Delhi.

Khushwant Singh
1963 *A history of Sikhs*, vol. 1. Princeton.
McLeod, W.H.
1976 *The evolution of the Sikh Community*. Oxford.
1987 (trans.) *The Chaupa Singh rahit* nama. Dunedin.
Nabha, Kahan Singh
1960 *Gurusabad ratanakar mahan kos* (in Punjabi). Second revised edition. Patiala.

PART five

Innovations: Religious Creativity and Social Change

PREFATORY REMARKS

As stated in the introductory remarks to Part Four, religious traditions are dynamic, marked by both continuity and change. Change may be gradual and reformist rather than sudden and radical. It usually tends to be the former. The history of religions in India, nevertheless, includes many instances of genuine creativity, confirmed as such by the passage of time. A notable twentieth century example is Mahatma Gandhi's reinterpretation of Hinduism as a non-ritualistic faith grounded in truth and love, according to which the service of suffering humanity constitutes true devotion to God (see Chatterjee 1983). Gandhi however maintained that he was an orthodox Hindu, and he owed a great deal to Vivekananda's 'Practical Vedanta' (see below). To take the case of innovation resulting in a new religion, one could mention the Radhasaomi faith from the late nineteenth century (see Juergensmeyer 1991), or push further back in time to the birth of Sikhism in the sixteenth century. Sikhism did not, however, emerge fully fledged, as it were, from Guru Nanak's mind and meditations. It was in good measure a product of widespread social protest and religious ferment in medieval north India (see McLeod 1976). Many new communities of faith came into existence during that period, representing a creative contestation between Puranic Hinduism and Sufi Islam, north and south Indian streams of religiosity, and theistic and non-theistic devotionalism.

The life and teachings of Kabir (d. 1518) are an outstanding, paradigmatic illustration of the intellectual and emotional churning that characterized the times. Born a Muslim or, perhaps, a Brahman, brought up by a Muslim weaver family, Kabir was, according to one tradition (which too has recently been challenged), initiated into spiritualism by a Vaishnava guru, Ramananda (d. 1470), belonging to the south Indian Shri-Sampraday sect, in the holy city of Kashi.

He found little to attract him in contemporary Hinduism and Islam, and much to criticize in their respective institutional frameworks. Kabir gave a message of devotion to the attributeless, impersonal divine (*nirguna bhakti*) in what he considered an illusory world. He derived inspiration from a number of religious traditions, including notably that of Nath Jogis, and produced a genuinely creative synthesis from them (see Vaudeville 1993).

The first reading in this part by David Lorenzen is about the followers of Kabir's teachings organized as a distinct fraternity, namely the Kabir Panth. Lorenzen argues that Kabir's teachings found an enthusiastic audience among non-privileged and marginal social groups, notably the lowliest of low caste Hindus and tribal folk respectively. Social protest thus became a significant element in the world-view of Kabir Panthis. Rejecting the legitimacy of caste distinctions and privileges or disabilities, and questioning the authority of Brahmans and *mullahs*, they could well have grown into a community of a truly new faith but this, Lorenzen maintains, did not happen. Before the Kabir Panthis could settle down to being a distinct religious community, they were overtaken by Hinduization and, in course of time, emerged as just yet another Vaishnava sect. He presents details of the processes at work and of the interaction between the host and client groups. Larenzen concludes by pointing out that even the followers of Kabir and Nanak, not to mention lesser religious leaders (including those of the post-medieval period), have failed in really questioning the legitimacy of the Hindu social order and living up to the original vision of the path-setters.

The post-medieval period has just been mentioned. From the point of view of this discussion, the nineteenth century is of great importance. A most significant event was the permission that the British Government gave in 1813 for the commencement of missionary activity in India. Proselytization had of course preceded British rule, particularly along the west and east coasts of peninsular India (see the introductory essay in this volume), but now it could and did spread to other parts of the country. The impact of Christianity upon the religious beliefs and practices of the peoples of India acted as a generative force. There already were however outstanding individuals who had discovered Christianity by their own search and contacts. Rammohan Roy (1772–1833) was much impressed by the ethical content of the New Testament and deeply desirous of bringing together the best in Vedantic Hinduism and Unitarian Christianity. For this purpose he established the Brahmo Sabha (in 1828), which was later (in 1843) transformed into the Brahmo Samaj. His successors, some of them self-consciously Hindu and others keenly inclined toward Christianity, split over the issue of the synthesis itself (see Kopf 1979).

A weakened Brahmo Samaj yielded the religious space to the mystic Ramakrishna (1836–86) and his famous disciple Vivekananda (1863–1902). His guru's religious syncretism was the most significant element in Vivekananda's inquiries into the praxis of the proselytizing religions of Islam and Christianity. Firmly rooted in the Vedantic tradition, he admired the social egalitarianism of Islam and Christianity's concern for the meek and the humble of the earth (see Radice 1998). While he gave the message of the spiritual conquest of the world to the youth of India, he also showed them the way to social service at home. There is an interesting continuity from Rammohan Roy's consensual theology to

Vivekananda's universal praxis via Ramakrishna's personal experiments with religious pluralism.

Krishna Prakash Gupta's essay on the Ramakrishna Mission in this part poses the critical question of how Hinduism, generally regarded as the religion of renunciation, could have been transformed into a mission of altruistic service by Vivekananda virtually single-handed. Adopting the historical rather than the functionalist approach to the study of this religious movements, Gupta rejects the common but simplistic characterization of the Mission as a response to the challenge of the West. Instead, he explores it in its own terms, that is, in terms of the evolutionary potential of Hinduism. One must also stress, I think, the brilliance and vigour of Vivekananda as a 'religious personality'. I use this term (following Nicholas Berdyaev) to describe a person who is creative in the profoundest sense through an engagement of the spirit to its uttermost in the cause of human weal and welfare. Vivekananda's creativeness is viewed in Gupta's essay from several perspectives, including the original manner in which he yoked sacred *jnana* (gnosis) and secular *karma*. Besides a discussion of the Ramakrishna Mission, the essay offers a critical commentary on some dominant tendencies in the sociology of religion, many of whose conceptual categories are rooted in the Judeo-Christian tradition.

The twentieth century has been witness to much religious creativity in India, particularly in the setting of the Hindu tradition. A distinctively new phenomenon has been the extension of Indian religious movements to the West, such as the Svaminarayan sect in England in the 1950s, which has since grown into one of the largest religious communities of overseas origin in that country (see Williams 1984). Even more noteworthy, perhaps, has been the emergence of such movements in the West with a predominantly non-Indian following. The best example is the International Society for Krishna Consciousness (ISKCON) established by an Indian guru in the USA (see Gelberg 1983). It is arguable that movements like ISKCON or Transcendental Meditation™ tell us more about the stresses and strains of contemporary life in the West, notwithstanding their undeniable impact upon people in India. The achievements of these movements are 'not quite what Vivekananda's' vision of Vedanta as the world religion was all about.

Religious creativity comes in many forms, besides those represented by the two cases noted above. One of the momentous happenings in contemporary India was the appropriation through reinterpretation of Buddhism by Bhimrao Ramji Ambedkar (1891–1956) when he, along with a very large number of his followers among the 'Untouchable' communities, repudiated his Hindu identity and became a Buddhist. Ambedkar, a man of great ability, overcame his lowly origins, acquired a modern education in India and abroad (he studied law at Columbia University where he apparently came under the influence of John Dewey's pragmatism), had a successful career as a lawyer, and engaged in a lifelong struggle to end the exploitation of the 'low' castes. He quite appropriately insisted on the inseparability of Brahmanical religious ideas and the inequities of the caste system. He rejected Gandhi's contention that these inequities were excrescences that had nothing to do with the essential teachings of Hinduism, and could be removed through informed public pressure.

It is noteworthy that Ambedkar's choice of Buddhism was a carefully considered one. Here was a religion of great antiquity that had originated in India, but had then virtually disappeared from the country a thousand years ago even while it had spread (in various forms) far and wide throughout Asia. Its nominal presence in India perhaps made it available for the kind of reinterpretation Ambedkar made without significant resistance from anywhere. And the scope of Ambedkar's Buddhism was vast, bringing together universal moral imperatives transcending established religious boundaries, specific social concerns, and personal commitments. Ambedkar died within a few weeks of the mass conversion. He was unable to work out the details and nuances of the new Buddhism he had fathered. He was not fortunate enough to have someone of his own calibre among his followers to complete the work. Martin Fuchs in the essay that is the third reading in this part of the reader, examines the making of Ambedkar's decision, its broad scope, and also its unresolved inner tensions. Can Ambedkar's bold initiative be said to have been successful as authentic religious creativity, or has it remained basically an exercise in political bargaining? Meanwhile, the Dalits have sought empowerment in other, secular ways too, but 'neo-Buddhism', such as it is, has taken root. Needless to add, a comparison, first, between the Kabir Panth and the Neo-Buddhists as protestant downtrodden peoples, and, second, between Vivekananda and Ambedkar as charismatic modern leaders of reform/liberation movements is of great historical and sociological interest (see Radice 1998 and Gore 1993). The readings presented here should contribute to the making of these comparisons.

REFERENCES

Chatterjee, Margaret.
1983 *Gandhi's religious thought.* London: Macmillan.
Gelberg, Steven J., ed.
1983 *Hare Krishna, Hare Krishna.* New York: Grove Press.
Gore, M.S.
1993 *The social context of an ideology: Ambedkar's social and political thought.* New Delhi: Sage.
Juergensmeyer, Mark.
1991 *Radhasaomi reality: The logic of a modern faith.* Princeton, N.J.: Princeton University Press.
Kopf, David.
1979 *The Brahmo Samaj and the shaping of the modern Indian mind.* Princeton, N.J.: Princeton University Press.
McLeod, W.H.
1976 *The evolution of the Sikh community.* Oxford: Clarendon Press.
Radice, William, ed.
1998 *Swami Vivekananda and the modernization of Hinduism.* New Delhi: Oxford University Press.
Vandeville, Charlotee.
1993 *A weaver named Kabir.* New Delhi: Oxford University Press.
Williams, R.B.
1984 *A new face of Hinduism.* Cambridge: Cambridge University Press.

CHAPTER
13

The Kabir-panth

DAVID N. LORENZEN

The concept of *bhakti* or devotion is a frequent victim of ... anachronistic or de-contextualized analysis. ... The superficial similarity of the devotional sentiments expressed in different stages of Hindu tradition, in say the Vedas and Puranas, tends to disguise serious contextual and functional differences. Nonetheless, from the time of the *Bhagavad-Gītā* [c. 200 BC], we can identify a set or field of associated characteristics which makes *bhakti* Hinduism a legitimate category of analysis. These characteristics, not all of which are necessarily present in any given manifestation of *bhakti*, include: (1) the doctrine of avatars or incarnations of the principal gods, usually Vishnu; (2) a defined contrast between different paths to salvation, only one of which is devotion; (3) the notion that, although the various paths to salvation are partly complementary, *bhakti* is in some sense the best and certainly the only one easily accessible to a wide range of social classes and to women; (4) a concept of salvation (*mukti, mokṣa*) implying a release from the cycle of rebirth (*saṃsāra*), determined by the moral fruits of past actions (*karma*), as well as some sort of permanent union or association (*sāyujya, sahaja,* etc.) with the object of devotion by means of some form of grace (*prasāda*); (5) varying degrees of elaboration and definition of different psychological attitudes of devotion based on human relationships, such as child to parent, woman to lover, slave to master, friend to friend, etc.

Excerpted from David N. Lorenzon, The Kabir-panth and social protest. *In* Karine Schomer and W.H. McLeod, eds., *The sants: Studies in a devotional tradition of India,* Delhi: Motilal Banarsidass, 1987. Pp. 281–302. © 1987 by Berkeley Religious Studies Series, Berkeley, CA.

The mere existence of this set of characteristics does not, however, tell us how it is used and interpreted in specific historical cases. To understand any particular manifestation of *bhakti* religiosity we must ask a number of specific questions about both content and context. First, what is the message? In other words, how is *bhakti* defined? Which aspects of the concept receive special emphasis and which are passed over more lightly? In many cases, including many studies of Kabir, the analysis gets little further than this. Secondly, who is transmitting the message? What is the socio–economic position and personal history of the transmitters? Why do they act as they do? Are they sincere or do they have ulterior motives? Thirdly, to whom is the message being transmitted? What is the social make-up and class base of the audience? Fourthly, when and where and how is the message transmitted? In other words, what is the total historical context of the message, its exponents, and its receivers? Finally, how is the message accepted and interpreted by the audience? How popular is it and how is it understood and utilized? ...

The basic hypothesis of this paper is that the strong element of social and religious dissent in Kabir's teachings, whatever its original intent and function, has been used by the adherents of the *panth*—mostly marginal groups such as Shudras, Untouchables, and Tribals—to express their rejection of certain aspects of hierarchical caste ideology, at the same time that their membership in the Kabir-panth has fostered their actual assimilation within that same society. Insofar as they do internalize large portions of higher caste ideology, they also attempt to raise the social status that others assign to them by adopting Sanskritized customs. Nonetheless, these groups cannot realistically hope that this will dramatically raise their caste ranking in the eyes of others. Even so, the more egalitarian ideology of the Kabir-panth does provide them with a positive self-image: one which rejects the innate and absolute character of the inferior status to which they are relegated by more orthodox Brahmanical Hinduism. Their membership in the Kabir-panth indicates a general acceptance of caste society, but it is an acceptance conditioned by another vision of the ultimate nature of that society and of their own innate worth within it. In this vision the absolute value of the Untouchable is not inferior to that of the Brahman. They accept that it is difficult to change social customs, and that it is generally necessary to respect them, but the true human reality is a different one: one in which each human being is judged on his own merits, not those of his birth in a particular family. The social ideology of Kabir, as transmitted both within and without the Kabir-panth, clearly expresses what Jayant Lele (1981) has called the 'liberating moments' of *bhakti* tradition. ...

Kabir has been commonly portrayed as a religious and social reformer who sought a spiritual reconciliation and purification of Islam and Hinduism, as well as the propounder of an exalted mystical religion of the heart which aimed to do away with vulgar exterior rites and noxious social practices and prejudices. ... Tara Chand (1954) has praised Kabir enthusiastically: 'He has gazed into the mystery of life and seen the vision of the ineffable light. He brings from the world of beyond a new message for the individual and for society. ... He is a mighty warner, an intrepid pathfinder, the great pioneer of the unity of the Hindu and Muslim communities of India and the apostle of the faith of Humanity.'

Other scholars such as P.D. Barthwal (1936) and Hazariprasad Dvivedi (1941), who examined the texts attributed to Kabir with somewhat more caution and attention, early noted that these texts owe considerably more to Hindu than to Islamic tradition, and that they were extensively influenced by the Tantric doctrines of the heterodox Nath sect. Barthwal and, later on, Dvivedi, Charlotte Vaudeville (1974) and W.H. McLeod (1968), have suggested that Kabir's family may have been only nominally converted to Islam from the Nath tradition, or possibly even from Tantric Buddhism. In any case, Kabir was not himself a Nath Yogi, however much he may have borrowed from this tradition. Rather, as McLeod has noted, Kabir represents in many ways the culmination of the Sant or *nirguṇa* tradition (*sampradāy*) which was 'a synthesis of the three principal dissenting movements; a compound of elements drawn mainly from Vaiṣṇava *bhakti* and the *haṭha-yoga* of the Nath Yogis, with a marginal contribution from Sufism' (ibid.: 152).

Although it may be true that Sufism exercised less influence on Kabir than the Nath and Vaishnava traditions, it is still debatable whether he can be considered essentially a Hindu. I have argued elsewhere that, by their very ferocity, Kabir's satires against both Islam and Hinduism go beyond mere attacks on the hypocrisy of their external rites and suggest that he was attempting to stake out an ideological position basically independent of both (Lorenzen 1981). A consideration of Kabir's own social background, however imperfectly known, lends support to this suggestion. Whether or not Kabir's family had been steeped in Nath tradition, it is certain that they were Julahas, a Muslim weaver caste of low status. Like most low-caste Muslims, they were undoubtedly indigenous converts to Islam and not immigrants, though when this conversion took place is not known. The fact that Kabir based his religious message more on Hindu traditions than on Muslim ones at least shows that he had little use for Islam. Granted that he was born in this faith, however, it would have been virtually impossible for him to directly re-enter the Hindu fold as an individual, and almost as impossible for him to have secured the re-entrance of his family or local caste group, since Hindu tradition has generally discouraged conversions from Islam. Furthermore, even when non-Hindu groups have been permitted to join Hindu caste society, they have generally been admitted as castes of the lowest status (ruling groups which became Kshatriya castes are of course an exception). An independent spirit like Kabir is unlikely to have willingly accepted such a status even if it were offered.

This view of Kabir's social situation perhaps can also help to explain the choice of an impersonal (*nirguṇa*) deity as his sole object of worship. Although we know nothing of the social make-up of Kabir's listeners, it is reasonable to assume that they included mostly little-educated members from low castes such as Kabir's own. In the traditional Hindu view, such persons are best suited to a religion based on simple devotion to a thoroughly anthropomorphized deity. The classic example is Vaishnava devotion directed to the avatars of Vishnu such as Krishna and Ram, a religion which has had great success among the common people. Why did Kabir insist on a more difficult and arduous devotion to an impersonal godhead? Some scholars have simply argued that this choice simply shows the intuitive subtlety of Kabir's mind, or even the direct influence of *advaita* Vedanta. Others, with rather more plausibility, have argued that Kabir is merely developing a line of thought present in the teachings of his Sant predecessors. This explanation, however, simply broadens the question. Why did Kabir's predecessors also tend toward the worship of an impersonal deity?

Here we encounter a very interesting fact, namely that nearly all the better known Sants of the *nirguṇa* tradition were non-Brahmans, many from quite low castes. According to tradition, Kabir was one of twelve disciples of the Brahman Ramananda. Several of these disciples represent what Barthwal calls 'an intermediate position between the Saguna [personal or with-attributes] and Nirguna Schools' (1936: 249–69). They include Pipaji, the Khichi king of Gagaraunagadh; Sen, a barber (*nāī*); Ravidas or Raidas, a leatherworker (*chamār*); and Dhanna, a Jat. Among Kabir's more important predecessors should be mentioned Namdev (c. 1300), a cotton-printer (*chīpī*) and Sadhan or Sadan (c. 1350), a butcher (*kasāī*). Most of the prominent *nirguṇa* Sants who came after Kabir were also non-Brahmans. These include Guru Nanak (1469–1538), a Khatri; Dadu Dayal (1544–1603), a cotton carder (*dhuniyā*) and possibly born as a Muslim with the name Daud; Maluk Das (1574–1682), a *kakkaḍ* Khatri; Dariya of Bihar (1674–1780), the son of a Kshatriya (possibly converted to Islam) and the daughter of a seamstress; Charan Das (b. 1703), a *dhāsar* Bania; and others. For Kabir, and these *nirguṇa* Sants as well, *saguṇa* worship implied worship of gods and avatars whose mythology was controlled by Brahmans and authoritatively codified in Sanskrit texts such as the Puranas. Given this situation, it is not surprising that an impersonal deity would be preferred in spite of the intellectual and psychological difficulties It (or He) presented.

The analysis of the interrelations between Kabir, his message, his audience, and the socio–historical environment unfortunately cannot be carried much

further without confronting a number of formidable obstacles. About the
man Kabir we know virtually nothing apart from his having belonged to a
family of Muslim weavers of Banaras. His dates are uncertain, with scholars
about equally divided between 1448–50 and 1518 (or possibly 1504) as
the year of his death. As for his message, most independent scholars accept
that all of the three major collections of writings attributed to Kabir—the
songs contained in the *Ādi Granth*, the Rajasthani *Kabīr-granthāvali* collection,
and the Kabir-panth's own *Bījak*—contain interpolations of material from
other sources. In this regard, the *Bījak* collection seems particularly suspect
although it has had the greatest historical impact among the members of the
panth since most branches (*śākhās*) of the *panth* accept only it as authoritative.
About Kabir's audience, as has been noted, little can be said apart from the
supposition that it must have appealed primarily to people of marginal
social status like Kabir himself. In any case, by the end of the sixteenth century
or even earlier, Kabir's verses had become popular among the common people
over wide parts of north India as is evident from the large number of later
Sants who directly or indirectly acknowledge their debt to him.

As far as the Kabir-panth is concerned, its history before the nineteenth
century is known almost exclusively from tendentious sectarian traditions.
Nonetheless, there exist a sizable number of early references to legends of
Kabir's life that may possibly be products of the early *panth*. Most are today
accepted as true by all branches of the *panth* (see Dvivedi 1965). ...

The general tendency of these legends, which need not be discussed in
detail here, is to make Kabir more Hindu and less Muslim. The principal
legends are those which claim that Kabir (1) descended from heaven on to
a lotus leaf in the Lahartara pond as an avatar of Vishnu (or alternately was
the son of a virgin Brahman widow); (2) became, by a trick, the disciple of
the Brahman Ramananda; (3) was persecuted by Sikandar Lodi, the Muslim
Sultan (d. 1517) and disputed with a Muslim divine named Shaikh Taqi;
(4) saved the temple of Jagannath in Puri from the wrath of the Lord of the
Ocean who instead vented it on Dwarka in Gujarat. Another frequently cited
legend relates how his Muslim and Hindu disciples fought over how to
dispose of his body after his death but then discovered under his shroud
only a pile of flowers which they evenly divided.

In one respect, there exists an important difference between the legends
accepted by the Kabir-panth and those accepted by the Sikh tradition (see
McLeod 1976). In the songs attributed to Kabir in the *Ādi Granth* and the
Kabīr-granthāvalī, reasonably clear allusions are made to his wife or wives,
to a son named Kamal, and possibly to a daughter named Kamali. Various
legends about Kabir and these family members are current in Sikh tradition.
The monks of the Kabir-panth, on the other hand, insist that Kabir remained
all his life an unmarried ascetic. They either deny the authenticity of the

songs in question or interpret them away rather in the same fashion that certain Christian churches do the various biblical allusions to Jesus's brothers. Songs referring to Kabir's wives and children are noticeably absent from the *panth*'s own *Bījak*.

However mythologized all these legends may be, they do clearly illustrate the rapid Hinduization of Kabir tradition. Except in the case of the stories of his family life, or its absence, however, it is not clear to what extent these stories are the product of diffused popular tradition as opposed to being relatively conscious creations of the Kabir-panth. The most that we can say is that today each branch of the *panth* actively fosters them, each in its own variants, often together with fanciful stories of Kabir's former births and a matching, rather eccentric theology. ...

The first serious attempt at an academic description of the Kabir-panth seems to be that of H.H. Wilson in his famous study of Hindu sects first published in *Asiatick Researches* in 1828 and 1832 (see Wilson 1972). Apart from brief discussions in various district gazetteers and the 1891 census report, the *panth* attracted little other attention from outsiders during the nineteenth century. In the twentieth century there have been some studies, such as those noted above. ...

Considering the numerical strength of the *panth* and its strategic social and religious importance, its relative neglect by scholars is somewhat surprising; all the more so when compared to the ample material published on the person, language, and literature of Kabir himself. In the remainder of this paper I would like first to briefly describe the organization and distribution of the *panth*, and then to argue the hypothesis that it has functioned primarily as a Hinduizing agent for marginal groups, mainly Untouchables, Shudras, and Tribals.

According to Kabir-panthi tradition, four of the principal disciples of Kabir founded four distinct branches (*śākhā*) of the *panth*. Surat Gopal (or Sruti Gopal) founded the Kabir Chaura *śākhā* centred at Banaras; Dharmadas the Chhattisgarh *śākhā* centred in eastern Madhya Pradesh; Jagudas (or Jagodas) the *śākhā* centred at Bidupur (Muzaffarpur District, Bihar) and at Shivpur (near Banaras); and Bhagodas (also Bhagudas or Bhagavan Gusain), the Bhagatahi *śākhā* centred at Dhanauti (Chapra District, Bihar). In fact, this historical tradition is very dubious and omits another important *śākhā* of the *panth*, the Phatuha *śākhā* centred near Patna said to have been founded by two other direct disciples of Kabir, the brothers Tattva and Jiva. Some scholars have suggested that all these branches of the Kabir-panth may date from a time considerably later than Kabir himself. Another important *śākhā* of the contemporary panth is that centred at Burhanpur in south-western Madhya Pradesh and founded by Puran Sahab in about 1835. Independent monasteries, some with subsidiary centres elsewhere, exist at Puri in Orissa (apparently quite an old monastery), at Hatakesar in Madhya Pradesh, at Badaiya village about 37 miles west of Banaras, and two separate monasteries at Rusera (Rusada) in Darbhanga District, Bihar (see Dvivedi 1965).

The two principal branches of the *panth* are the Kabir Chaura *śākhā* of Banaras and the Chhattisgarh *śākhā* with rival headquarters in Damakheda and Kharasiya, both in eastern Madhya Pradesh. The Kabir Chaura *maṭh* in Banaras is situated on the reputed site of Kabir's family house and claims to be the original seat (*mūl gaddi*) of the *panth* from which all the other branches derive. The members of the Kabir Chaura *śākhā*, both laymen and monks, on the average come from castes of somewhat higher status than those of the Chhattisgarh *śākhā*. The Kabir Chaura *maṭh* at Banaras maintains its authority over a large number of subsidiary monasteries located in northern Bihar, eastern UP, and Gujarat. It is not clear just how much contact the monks of this *śākhā* maintain with lay members of the *panth*. The Chhattisgarh *śākhā* seems, in this respect, to be much more active. Its chief area of operations is in Madhya Pradesh, especially the eastern (Chhattisgarh) and north-western (Bundelkhand) districts, although it also controls a few centres in Gujarat and elsewhere. The Burhanpur *śākhā* is active chiefly in eastern Madhya Pradesh while the Bhagatahi and Phatuha *śākhā*s control numerous subsidiary monasteries in central and northern Bihar and even Nepal. The reason for this rather curious geographical distribution of the *panth* has not been adequately explained. Mostly it seems to stem from historical accident, although the relative absence of the *panth* from the Punjab and Rajasthan may result from the appropriation of the songs of Kabir by the religious traditions of the Sikhs and Dadu respectively. The absence of the Kabir-panth from all but extreme eastern UP may reflect the historical competition of Islam for the allegiance of the lower castes in this region.

The present size of the total Kabir-panthi population is somewhat difficult to estimate. In the 1901 census the number of Kabir-panthis in the Central Provinces (Madhya Pradesh) was recorded as about 500,000 and in India as a whole as about 850,000. In the 1911 census, the number of Kabir-panthis in the Central Provinces was about 600,000. The all-India census figure is probably a serious underestimate since, in at least some districts, the census-takers seem to have registered as Kabir-panthis only those who claimed this as their caste, a status generally applicable only to Kabir-panthi monks (*bairāgīs*) and not to the lay followers of the *panth*. If the relative percentage of Kabir-panthis in the total population has remained constant since 1901 the 850,000 Kabir-panthis of that date should have become by today (1986) some 2,500,000. Considering that the original figure is probably too low, the total numbers may well be much larger, especially if the *panth*'s proselytizing activities have met with any success.

The question of the social composition and ideology of the Kabir-panth has also been investigated systematically only rarely if at all. The common scholarly consensus is that the *panth* represents merely one of a large number of heterodox sects which have arisen periodically in India to challenge the established religious and social and even political order. According to this view, these sects are in essence movements of social protest in the religious guise appropriate to the population of a pre-modern, traditional culture. It is correctly pointed out that most of these movements, including the Kabir-panth, tend to denounce, with varying degrees of severity, the so-called 'exterior' practices of religion such as elaborate sacrifices, idolatry, and pilgrimages, as well as the degrading social inequalities fostered by the caste system. Instead, they preach a simpler and purer religion of the heart in which ceremony is minimized and all men are considered theoretically equal and individual. K.N. Panikkar has further suggested that the appearance of a large number of such movements in the eighteenth century tends to argue against the theory that 'the emergence of modern ideas and the development of social protest and religious dissent in the nineteenth century... [was] a consequence of the introduction of European ideas and institutions into India'. In his view, this theory 'overlooks the elements of protest and dissent in the Indian intellectual tradition and the potentialities of social development in the eighteenth century before the intervention of the British (1975: 3).

This general scholarly consensus, which classes the Kabir-panth and other sects as indigenous movements of social dissent and protest, undoubtedly contains a large measure of truth. Unfortunately, it also tends toward oversimplification and at times contains an element of wishful thinking. Nearly all new religious movements necessarily arise within a context of serious changes in economic and social conditions, that is to say a situation of socio–economic dislocation and conflict. In part they are protests against these changes and against the social and economic injustices that accompany them. They also, however, embody attempts to come to terms with these changes, to create new value systems in which they can be accommodated and their negative, exploitative impact made bearable. In each movement, the relative strength and specific characteristics of the elements of social protest and social accommodation will be different. They also tend to change as the movements progress.

From this perspective, it is clearly a mistake to evaluate religious (and other) movements simply according to the degree of overt social protest they manifest. Social discontent and the striving toward change are always present, though they may take very different forms and directions. The essential character of any movement basically depends on the values and aims it expounds and the effectiveness of the means it uses to achieve them. In the final analysis, each movement must be considered on its own merits in its own material and ideological context.

The scholarly consensus, which classes religious movements such as the Kabir-panth as pre-secular or pre-political social protest movements, is often supplemented by a complementary theory which seeks to explain their evident change over the course of time. A number of scholars, especially anthropologists and sociologists, have noted that the element of overt social dissidence in new religious movements soon tends to get dissipated via a process that Max Weber called the institutionalization of charisma and Ernst Troeltsch the transition from sect to church. In the case of India, this process is often identified as the transition from cult or sect to caste. Clearly implied is the idea that the process represents a sort of spiritual hardening of the arteries leading to eventual senility. ...

In another paper I have discussed how the monks of the Kabir-panth have Hinduized and Sanskritized the *panth* so that today it is flatly a Vaishnava Hindu sect. ... Since my field work was principally among the monks of the *panth*, the paper did not make a serious effort to relate these Hinduizing and Sanskritizing tendencies (nor the partly contradictory 'Westernizing' tendency) to the ideological and social needs of its lay adherents. In spite of the fact that sustained fieldwork on this question has not yet been attempted, a clear general profile can be obtained from brief references to the proselytizing activities of the *panth* by anthropologists and sociologists and from a few more detailed studies of analogous cases.

The Kabir-panth has two principal sorts of clientele: (1) lower class Hindus who seek an ideology which offers them a more positive status and self image, certainly in their own eyes and if possible in the eyes of others as well, and (2) tribal peoples who are being socially and culturally assimilated into the lower levels of the caste hierarchy and are trying to preserve their self-esteem against almost hopeless odds. In both cases, membership in the *panth* embodies an element of social protest against the hierarchical structure of the Hindu socio–religious order at the same time that it represents a general acceptance of the hegemony of that same order.

The only well-documented example of Kabir-panth activity among tribal populations is that of the Kabir-panthi Bhagats (*bhaktas*) among the Oraon, one of the principal tribes of Chhotanagpur in southern Bihar (especially Ranchi District). In the 1961 census this tribe numbered about one and a half million persons, of whom about one half lived in Bihar. In Ranchi district, they have coexisted peacefully for more than two hundred years with the Mundas. Although the two tribes are linguistically and culturally distinct, they have often joined forces to protest, with limited success, against foreign penetration and domination of their region. Early in this century, the direct religious influence of the alien Hindu social system began to make itself felt in the so-called Bhagat movements. N.K. Bose (1972: 124–49) distinguishes as most significant: (1) the Nemha Bhagats, native Oraons who were instructed in visions to introduce Hinduized customs; (2) the Kabir-panthi Bhagats, initially non-Oraon outsiders from the Chhattisgarh region; (3) the Vaishnava or Bacchidan Bhagats, also outsiders from other regions; (4) the followers of the month-long Manda Parab ceremony (which includes a fire-walking finale); and (5) the Tana Bhagat or Kurukh Dharam movement, which actively got involved in nationalist politics.

All these movements have inculcated observance of essentially Hindu customs and a corresponding rejection of certain traditional Oraon behaviour. The new movements did not completely reject tribal culture, however, and preserved or tolerated many traditional beliefs and practices. They remained distinctively Oraon versions of Hinduism. The Kabir-panthi Bhagats abstain from the worship of idols and other visible symbols of divinity; abandon the drinking of alcoholic beverages or their use as libations, practise vegetarianism, and abstain from animal sacrifice; reject the worship of spirits and minor deities; offer devotional worship (*bhakti*) to a single god; adopt strict personal morality with regard to truthfulness, honesty, non-violence to animals, and religious and social tolerance; employ and respect gurus as spiritual advisors and priests; and wear a rosary with a bead of *tulsī* wood which is given to the devotee at the time of his initiation. Although traditional Oraon life crisis rites have continued to be practised among the followers of the Kabir-panthi Bhagats, they are accompanied by a distinctive Kabir-panthi ceremony known as the *chaukā*. The Kabir-panthi Oraons also have continued to intermarry with non-Kabir-panthi fellow tribesmen, although marriage with Kabir-panthis is preferred (see Jay 1961: 293f.)

These Oraon Bhagats are mostly attached to the Chhattisgarh *śākhā*, but in 1976 the lone *pujari* at the Kabir Chaura *śākhā* shrine at Lahartara near Banaras was also an Oraon.

The other Hindu-influenced Bhagat movements among the Oraon preached a similar message, stressing vegetarianism, rejection of animal sacrifice, abstention from alcohol, and a stricter personal morality, especially with regard to interaction between the sexes. The Tana Bhagat movement, in many respects the most influential, also sought the recovery of economic and political rights and powers lost during the long-term progressive alienation of the Oraons from their lands by outsiders.

A less well-documented case of Kabir-panth proselytization among the Mundas of Ranchi district is mentioned in P.C. Tallent's 1921 census report for Bihar and Orissa. The sect was introduced 'about ten years' earlier by 'a *guru* named Kristo Mohan' from the Chhattisgarh region. This guru made converts of about seventeen families among the Khangar Mundas of the Ranchi and Khunti subdivisions. Tallents remarks:

Conversion does not appear to affect their outward way of life to any serious extent, for the converts continue to eat and intermarry with other Khangar Mundas and observe the same marriage and funeral ceremonies. But they believe in one God, they have ceased to believe in witchcraft or to worship their ancestors, and they have given up dancing. They tell their beads when opportunity offers and sing the hymns of Kabir after their evening meals. Once a year, when their *guru* visits them, they hold a feast and offer sweetmeats, spices, nuts and a piece of white cloth to the deity. The son of a Kabir panthi is not born a Kabir panthi but has to be initiated. Apart from the fact that they usually wear yellow clothes and, unlike other Mundas, salute one another with an embrace there is little to distinguish the Kabir panthis outwardly from their fellow. It is however reported that their conversion has made a marked change in their outlook and manner. [1923: 131].

Although only the Tana Bhagat movement directly pressed for economic and political justice, the appearance of these Hindu or Hindu-influenced movements among the Oraons and Mundas cannot be properly understood except against the background of political and economic changes which occurred in this region during the nineteenth century and even before. In his sharp analysis of the effects of these events on these two tribes (with a comparison to the Santals of the nearby Santal Paraganas District), John MacDougall has argued that the nineteenth century saw an incomplete peasantization of the tribes. Though the Oraons apparently practised rice cultivation even before the takeover of the district by the British between 1770 and 1810, earlier they did *not* constitute a peasant society, understood by MacDougall as a society where:

(1) most of the members are peasants, i.e. settled cultivators with a household mode of production; and (2) there are other groups that (a) extract economic surplus from the peasants, (b) are organized into a state ..., (c) are accorded at least some prestige by peasants, and (d) participate in a civilization to which peasants are linked albeit tenuously. (1977: 311).

In MacDougall's opinion, this profile is not applicable to the Oraons (nor to the Mundas and Santals) before British rule since the tribes did not contribute a significant surplus to the Maharaja of Chhotanagpur, nor did they participate in any meaningful way in the Hindu civilization to which the Maharaja's family was oriented. 'Above all,' he notes, '*adivasi* social structure was not organized on the basis of religiously-legitimated hierarchy. Rather, the major feature of *adivasi* society was that it consisted of isolated, egalitarian villages' (ibid.: 311, 300).

During the nineteenth century, the British dramatically increased land revenue taxes and made extensive changes in the laws governing land tenure. These measures indirectly fostered the flooding of the region by outsiders, or *dikus* as the tribals called them, who were mostly caste Hindus. The net result was that the tribals rapidly fell into debt and lost control of their ancestral lands to the *dikus*. The tribals were forced to work as day labourers on these lands or to sell themselves into virtual slavery on British tea plantations outside the region. Not surprisingly, this situation led to a variety of protest movements, some of which ended in open rebellion against British-*diku* rule. Although many of these movements had a strong religious colouring, economic and political demands remained central to them. The climax came with the millenarian rebellion of Mundas and Oraons led by Birsa Munda in 1895–1900. All the movements which turned to armed rebellion, including Birsa's were put down with brutal force by the British government. Although partial attempts at reform were sometimes made in the aftermath of the rebellions, in general, the situation of the tribals continued to deteriorate. The several Christian missions active in the region also made sporadic efforts to help the tribals, at least the converts, but invariably retreated whenever the tribals' demands threatened a vital interest of the government. Successful proselytization also seriously weakened tribal unity, a side effect recognized and appreciated by the government.

What seems to have happened to the tribals in the course of the nineteenth century is that their society became extensively peasantized in the spheres of economics and politics while their traditional social structure and culture retained considerable vitality. By the early twentieth century, especially in the wake of the defeat of the Birsa movement the cultural ramparts could no longer hold. Their collapse was signalled by the appearance of the several Bhagat movements and proselytization by various Hindu sects. Through conversion to these movements and sects the tribals attempted an accommodation with Hindu society on terms they found more or less acceptable. The new cults did introduce several cultural values at odds with the traditional tribal ones, but they permitted the converts to retain a tribal identity and to preserve as much tribal tradition as possible.

The majority of Kabir-panthis belong not to tribal groups but to castes low in the status hierarchy of Hindu society. Although these people are not culturally on the margins of Hindu society in the same way as the tribals, they do share many of the same economic and political disabilities, and, at least in the case of the Untouchables, they hold a socio-religious status inferior even to that of the tribals. Although the functioning of society depends on their labour, on the whole, they receive in exchange a disproportionately small recompense in terms of money, status, education, and power. In all these senses they too are marginalized human beings.

That the Kabir-panth should appeal to people of this class is not surprising and needs less historical analysis than in the case of the tribals. It would nevertheless help enormously if we could determine to which castes the Kabir-panthis belong and in what proportions, which *śākhās* are associated with each caste, and whether or not the Kabir-panthis in each caste form endogamous subcastes. Unfortunately, this information for the

most part will have to remain unavailable until more extensive fieldwork
can be undertaken. From my work among the Kabir-panthi monks, especially
those in Banaras, however, it is possible to say a little more about the monks'
own caste perceptions.

The considerable extent to which the Kabir-panthi monks are sensitive
to the values of higher caste society was evident from their reluctance to talk
about their own caste origins. The *adhikārī* of the Kabir Chaura *math* would
only say that most of the twenty-five to thirty monks living there were of
Vaishya or 'clean' Shudra origin, but he would not let them talk to me about
their family backgrounds on the pretext that they had abandoned all family
ties when they became monks. The monks at the other *math*s in Banaras,
Bihar, and Madhya Pradesh, on the whole, were equally reluctant to broach
this subject.

Nonetheless, other sources provide partial confirmation of the *adhikārī's*
statements. It is common knowledge that the *mahant*s of several of the major
*math*s of the Kabir-panth in Bihar and eastern UP come from the Koiri and
Yadav (Ahir) castes, two peasant castes whose members are often owners of
their own land. For example, the present *mahant* of the Kabir Chaura *matth*
in Banaras is said to be from a Koiri family, while his predecessor was probably
a Yadav. I did learn subsequently that two or three of the approximately forty
monks resident in this *matth* were in fact from Untouchable families.
They do not receive treatment different from that given to the other monks,
including the obligation to work as cooks in the kitchen of the *math*.

About the lay members of the panth, the *adhikārī* of the Kabir Chaura
math claimed that the majority of those attached to the Kabir Chaura *śākhā*,
or as he prefers the *mūl gaddī*, were of 'clean' castes. My subsequent fieldwork
in north-western Bihar has tended to confirm this estimate. The principal
castes with large numbers of followers of the Kabir-panth in this region are
the Koiris, the Yadavs (Ahirs), and the Kurmis. In some areas the Mahuris,
Sonars, Malis, Gaderis, Kahars, Kumhars, Mallahs, and Tharus provide
substantial numbers of followers as well. Among the Untouchables, only
the Chamars, Dusadhs, and Pasis are important in this regard.

In the Chhattisgarh *śākhā* the lay members of the Kabir-panth seem to,
on average, belong to castes of slightly lower status. In Bilaspur, Raigarh,
and Raipur districts my interviewees said that members of the *panth* were
particularly numerous among the agricultural castes of the Chandnahus
(or Chandranahus), the Gabels, and the Kurmis. The Sahus, Banias, Panikas,
Bairagis, Ravats, Telis and Kostas were also mentioned, together with the
Harijan castes of the Satnamis and Chamars, and the tribal groups of the
Kamvars and Gonds. For the whole of the Chhattisgarh region, Russell and
Hira Lal (1969: 1, 242f.) add the names of the Baghel Rajputs, the Lodhis,
and Kachhis, the Balahis and Koris, the Kevats, the Dhobis, and the Mahars.

One of the strongest supports of the Kabir-panth in Madhya Pradesh is the Panka caste. Russell and Hira Lal identify it as 'a Dravidian caste of weavers and labourers found in Mandla, Raipur and Bilāspur, and numbering 215,000 persons in 1911' (ibid.: 3,324). Today they can be estimated at about 600,000. They seem to be related to 'the Pān tribe of Orissa and Chota Nāgpur, who are also known as Panika, Chik, Ganda, and by various other designations'. In 1911, 84 per cent of the caste were members of the Kabir-panth. The Kabir-panthis form one sub-caste who are contrasted with other Pankas who are called Saktaha (śākta). In contrast to the Kabirhas, the Saktahas eat meat, drink liquor, and ignore other restrictive customs. Intermarriage between the Kabirhas and Saktahas is discouraged but apparently does occur. Among the related Gandas in Orissa (especially near Sambalpur) there are four subdivisions, one of which is composed of Kabir-panthis who do not normally intermarry with the other three subdivisions (O'Malley 1913: 5, 1, 497).

In most cases, however, Kabir-panthis do not form endogamous sub-castes. When asked about the possibility of intermarriage between Kabir-panthi and non-Kabir-panthi members of the same caste, the adhikārī of the Kabir Chaura maṭh said that it could and did occur although marriage with other Kabir-panthis of the same caste was generally preferred. Intercaste marriages are not permitted even if both persons are Kabir-panthis. In the case of a Kabir-panthi marrying a non-Kabir-panthi, the wife is expected to follow the religion of her husband. However, if the wife is the Kabir-panthi and the husband is not, she is encouraged to attempt to convert him by persuasion. The adhikārī stressed that above all this meant abstention from alcohol and meat, for as Kabir supposedly said in one of his verses: 'On account of eating meat and fish and drinking liquor, men will go to hell and their parents as well.'

Most low-caste Kabir-panthis distinguish themselves from other members of their castes first and foremost by their vegetarianism and their abstention from alcohol (and usually tobacco). Kabir's rejection of idolatry and other 'external' religious practices is only partly honoured. The Kabir Chaura monks encourage pilgrimages to the maṭh at Banaras as well as to the subsidiary centres at Lahartara (Kabir's birthplace) and Magahar (the site of his death). The daily service at the Kabir Chaura maṭh has also taken on many of the characteristics of Hindu temple worship, while the Chhattisgarh śākhā maṭh in Banaras gives pride of place to a large image of Kabir which is daily offered prasād in the traditional Hindu manner. Although the monks of all śākhās do express some verbal support for Kabir's attacks on caste pride, few of them I talked to rejected the caste system itself in favour of any idea that all men were created equal.

The emphasis the Kabir-panth gives to vegetarianism and abstention from alcohol needs little explanation. From a Hindu point of view the consumption of alcohol and meat are degrading and polluting practices. Low castes that wish to secure a higher socio–religious status in the eyes of other castes have little other option than to abandon them. ...

To see the religious insight and biting social criticism of Kabir's verses reduced to little more than vegetarianism can hardly help but inspire cynicism. We must bear in mind, however, that except in a very few cases—most notably those of Basava [c. 1106–67/8, founder of the Lingayat sect in Karnataka], Kabir, and Nanak (and perhaps the early materialists)—no influential religious and social critic in pre-colonial India directly questioned the overall legitimacy of the Hindu socio-religious order. ... Even in the cases of Basava, Kabir, and Nanak, the extent to which they questioned the legitimacy of the system is debatable. With some exceptions, this also holds true for the social and religious reformers of the nineteenth and twentieth centuries. ...

REFERENCES

Barthwal, P.D.
1936 *The Nirguna school of Hindi poetry*. Banaras: Indian Bookshop.
Bose, Nirmal Kumar.
1972 *Some Indian tribes*. New Delhi: National Book Trust.
Dvivedi, Hazariprasad.
1941 *Kabir* [in Hindi]. New Delhi: Rajkamal Prakashan.
Dvivedi, Kedarnath.
1965 *Kabir aur Kabirpanth*. Allahabad: Hindi Sahitya Sammelan.
Jay, Edward.
1961 'Revitalization movement in tribal India'. *In* L.P. Vidyarthi, ed., *Aspects of religion in Indian society*. pp. 282–322. Meerut: Kedar Nath Ram Nath.
Lele, Jayant, ed.
1981 *Tradition and modernity in bhakti movements*. Leider: E.J. Brill.
Lorenzen, David N.
1981 The Kabir panth: Heretics to Hindus. *In* David Lorenzen, ed., *Religious change and cultural domination*, pp. 151–72. Mexico: El Colegio de Mexico.
McDougall, John.
1977 Agrarian reform vs. religious revitalization: Collective resistance to peasantization. *Contributions to Indian sociology* 11: 295–327.
McLeod, W.H.
1968 *Guru Nanak and the Sikh religion*. Oxford: Clarendon Press.
1976 *The evolution of the Sikh community*, Oxford: Clarendon Press.
O'Malley, L.S.S.
1913 *Report: Bengal, Bihar, and Orissa; Census of India 1911*. Vol. 5, pt. 1. Calcutta: Bengal Secretariat Book Depot.
Panikkar, K.N.
1975 Presidential address: Sec. III, *Proceedings of the Indian History Congress*, 36th Session. Aligarh.

Russell, Robert V. and Rai Bahadur Hira Lal.

1969 *The tribes and castes of the Central Provinces of India.* 4 vols., Oosterhout, N.B: Anthropological Publications; Originally pub. London: Macmillan, 1916.

Tara Chand

1954 *Influence of Islam on Indian culture.* Allahabad: Indian Press.

Tallents, P.C.

1923 *Report, Bihar and Orissa, Census of India 1921.* Vol. 8, pt. 1, Patna: Government Printing.

Vaudeville, Charlotte.

1974 *Kabir.* Oxford: Clarendon Press.

Wilson, H.H.

1972 *Religious sects of the Hindus.* Varanasi: Indological Book House.

The Ramakrishna Mission

KRISHNA PRAKASH GUPTA

I n the fifties and sixties of the last century, a young Bengali priest, Ramakrishna, went through a series of intensely spiritual experiences. Transcending barriers of doctrine and sacrament, he sought to realize in his own life the inherent identity of various religious faiths by going through the phases of a Hindu devotee, a Muslim believer, and a Christian convert. Such unabashed encounters with divine 'reality' in its diverse names and forms soon attracted a devoted band of disciples. Among them was Narendra, later Vivekananda, who felt impelled to replicate his master's vision and broadcast its message of universal love to the whole world.

Beginning in the 1880s with a small number of faithfuls, Vivekananda slowly translated his personal convictions into a massive religious movement. In 1893 he attended the World Parliament of Religions at Chicago and began to organize Ramakrishna Mission centres for devotion and service.

Today there are more than a hundred such centres all over India engaged in medical, educational, religious, and relief activities. In the work of these centres, the abstract Vedantic precepts have been reformulated into concrete moral practices. From its sharply elitist and escapist orientations, Hinduism has become a vehicle of serving the poor and downtrodden. Vivekananda himself has become an ideal for millions in India.

How has Hinduism, an autological religion of renunciation, been

Excerpted from Krishna Prakash Gupta, Religious evolution and social change in India: A study of the Ramakrishna Mission movement, *Contributions to Indian sociology* (NS) 8 (1973): 26–50. © Institute of Economic Growth, Delhi.

transformed into a mission of altruistic service? Was this transformation merely a situational response to the Western challenge or did it signify a new evolutionary innovation in Hinduism? What has been the significance of this transformation in the broader context of religion and social change in India? This paper will be concerned with these three questions. Our central and consistent focus will remain on the processes through which Vivekananda's ideas were formulated, accepted, and institutionalized. In doing this, we will attempt to link the sociology of religion with the sociology of knowledge. The Ramakrishna Mission movement will be analysed first against the concrete historical situation of India, and then evaluated as a bearer of new ideological norms which ultimately affected various aspects of Indian society. ...

I

ANALYSING A RELIGIOUS MOVEMENT: HINDUISM AND SOCIOLOGY OF RELIGION

A religious movement is supposed to serve the society which has produced it. In this sense, the emergence of any new movement is predicated on a fortuitous mix of complex circumstances: crisis in a society, a series of failures to meet this crisis at lower levels, and the emergence of a prophet who reveals new wisdom to resolve this crisis. However, the sociologies of religion and collective behaviour have failed to define so far that precise set of objective conditions which would invariably lead to the emergence of a new religious movement. One still does not know the exact point at which the crisis-perception of an individual is transformed into a spiritually uplifting experience of the masses.

Despite this grave methodological deficiency, much of the current research on religious movements has accepted some sort of functionalist framework to explain the rise and spread of salvation ideas. Part of this is possibly due to the early bias inherent in the very origin of the sociology of religion which had emerged and evolved in response to the rationalist-positivist and, later, Marxist-materialist denunciation of the role of religion in modern society. Starting from three different theoretical orientations, Weber, Durkheim, and Malinowski had nearly converged on this functionalist defence of religion. In turn, this defence led to a variety of need-fulfilment explanations. The rise of new religious movements, especially as these were studied in the primitive or non-Western world, was increasingly explained in terms of reaction to deprivation and helplessness. Through these reactions, religion was supposed to be serving a very useful function in crisis-management.

This functionalist paradigm was extended to the study of revivalist and reform movements in all major non-Christian traditions. Renaissance experiences in the Hindu and Confucian traditions, for example, were described and explained in a simple need-fulfilment framework: impact of the West, impotency of the native tradition, and the nationalist response to a crisis-situation. In this scenario, non-Christian religions were as a rule not viewed as internally-evolving systems but merely as anxiety-resolving defence mechanisms used by the peoples concerned to meet the Western challenge.

Much of the current sociology of religion, both in its alien and Indian adaptations, has retained this paradigm to analyse religious movements in pre-modern India (Gupta 1974). Viewed in this paradigm, these movements can be easily explained as transitional, imitative, and non-rational. The Ramakrishna Mission movement itself can be considered a response to the missionary challenge in the late nineteenth-century India, and Vivekananda's Practical Vedanta merely as an impassioned attempt at Westernization of Hinduism. The impact of the total movement can then be seen simply in the reaffirmation and revitalization of a dying tradition.

In fact, most analyses of the Ramakrishna Mission, irrespective of their widely divergent ideological perspectives, have not been able to go beyond this framework.[1] At a higher level of generalization, this framework seems to draw its support from the historical evidence. One knows enough about the rapid erosion of Hinduism during the time of Vivekananda creating the objective need to respond through Practical Vedanta, and about his fascination for the Western methods of organization creating the inner compulsion to duplicate the missionary methods. Once this knowledge is placed in the available framework of the sociology of religion, Vivekananda becomes a prototype of the native response to the Western challenge, leading— depending on one's bias—to tradition, to modernity, or to a tradition– modernity synthesis.[2] His importance remains not so much as a bearer of some charismatic innovation as of constituting a passive reaction-type. Nothing of the inner structure and dialectics of Hinduism itself remains relevant in this paradigm. Instead of being a total symbol system, articulated in and through individual behaviour and institutional patterns, Hinduism is reduced to play the role of a transitional defence mechanism.

Such an explanation, I think, seriously distorts the meaning of Vivekananda's breakthrough in pre-modern India. Taken backwards in time,

---

[1]Apart from the voluminous Mission literature, one can see, for example, Datta (1954), Majumdar (1965), and Roy (1970), converging on this supposition, despite their mutually irreconcilable political orientations.

[2]These three evaluations represent respectively the positions of Singh (1973: 43–4), Srinivas (1966: 60, 77), and Saran (1969b: 8–9).

this explanation does not at all explain the genesis of the Ramakrishna Mission movement. In the 1880s one could have hardly predicted that Indian society needed a Vivekananda to reactivate Hinduism. When Ramarkishna died in 1886, he had left neither men nor money to build an organization which could have transformed his simple ethic of love into a creed of institutionalized service. In fact, soon after his death, his disciples drifted into silent meditations and lonely pilgrimages. Some, with the help of a landlord devotee, rented a dilapidated house which became a centre of worshipping the Master (HRMM: 43–56). There was nothing in the objective conditions at this time which would have warranted a radical revitalization of this group—unsure of the Master's Last Will, fighting over the possession of his sacred ashes, involved in rehearsed pantomimes of religious ecstasy, and concerned primarily with personal *mukti* (liberation) (LSV: 126, 154; HRMM: 38–42) into an organized order of activist monks.

Vivekananda himself seemed to suffer under various pressing personal disabilities and social pressures. He was constantly burdened by his Kayastha parentage, meat-eating, and sea-voyage, opposed by the well-organized sections of the English missionaries, enraged theosophists and jealous Brahmo Samajists, reviled and ridiculed by the orthodox Brahmins, Sanatanist Hindus, and Westernized social reformers, and even used and abused by his own rich and poor patrons, friends, and disciples. Behind his success, howsoever one evaluates it, could not have been a receptive society waiting for some religious need-fulfilment.

Similarly, Vivekanada's Practical Vedanta, even though it apparently emerged through the mediation of a Western encounter, was conceived and designed strictly in terms of conventional Hindu thought categories. There was nothing definitive in the Western impact or in Vivekananda's imitation that could have determined and directed the eventual evolutionary pattern of the Ramakrishna Mission movement. When men and societies are ready to receive new ideas, they are ready to receive any new movements. The relative success of one over the other depends less on the adaptations of extraneous salvation models and more on the internal cognitive mechanisms for perceiving, analysing, and resolving crisis situations which ultimately settle the form and manner of adaptation itself. Vivekanada's reformulated Vedanta was Western only in appearance; in essence, it was Hindu both in terms of demands it set upon the reformed *sannyasin*s and the specific mode in which it could institutionalize itself in the Indian society.

It is difficult to understand the full implications of this non-functional Hinduism unless one visualizes the Ramakrishna Mission as an internally consistent evolutionary manifestation of India's pre-modern religiosity and not merely as a native response to some Western challenge. This can be done only by abandoning the current sociology-of-religion framework, and by analysing the genesis and evolution of the Mission on its own terms.

II

RAMAKRISHNA MISSION: RELIGIOUS EVOLUTION IN PRE-MODERN INDIA

In order to place the Mission movement within the cultural–historical context of India, it is necessary first to reconstruct briefly the actual organizational process through which Vivekananda transformed an idea into a movement. This must be followed by an examination of various linkages which were forged in this process between Hindu thought categories and Vivekananda's perception and resolution of an external crisis. One can trace through these linkages the actual development of Vivekananda's Practical Vedanta and its institutionalization in the Mission form.

Origins of the movement

In tracing the origins of the Ramakrishna Mission movement, one is struck by the crucial role played by Vivekananda, not as an interpreter, preacher, reformer, prophet, or orator but as a superb organization man. More than to any objective conditions of Indian society, or to the saintly charisma of Ramakrishna, the Mission owes its success to Vivekanada's uncanny business acumen. As one goes back into the early history of the movement, one finds him cautiously engaged in symbol manipulation and self-publicity, both designed to establish and enhance the Mission work.

Not surprisingly the critical moment for this extra-spiritual flirtation came only when Vivekananda dissociated himself completely from his *guru-bhai*s (brother-disciples) (at the monastery, *math*) at Baranagore. Until then, Vivekananda remained Narendra, a middle-class Kayastha graduate turned ascetic, who was busy fighting a court battle over family property, disposing a piece of land (CWSV: VI, 207; VIII, 285), or disputing Shankara's interpretation of caste (CWSV: VI, 208–14). As a leader of a small group of Ramakrishna's disciples, his concerns did not go beyond a little money for maintenance (CWSV: VI, 443), some advice on meditation and chastity (CWSV: VI, 225), and a plan for raising subscription money for building a memorial temple (CWSV: VI, 239–40). This pattern changed only in 1890 when Vivekananda decided to cut himself off from his friends at Ramakrishna's monastery and set himself adrift on a solitary discovery of India through travel.

It was during these travels that Vivekananda discovered his personal charisma and life's mission. What was nearly a hopeless pursuit of monastic vows in some unknown quarters of Calcutta was gradually transformed in this period—from the beginning of 1891 to the middle of 1893—into a planned programme of Practical Vedanta. As an itinerant monk, Vivekananda came into living contact with the ignorant religiosity of the masses, oppressive opportunism of the Hindu priests, cowardly hypocrisy of the middle-class babus, and the inert little faith of the princes. Confronted with this real Hinduism, he quickly realized the futility of his Baranagore escapism and decided to introduce changes *at points and through media* which would prove most effective in the Indian context.

He began by courting and converting the diwans and rajas of princely states in order to initiate a process of dynamic Hindu interference in the daily lives of the masses (RSV: 38–9; LSV: 224–5). He realized the significance of hierarchy not only as a social fact but as a mental construct for the Hindus; changes can occur only from the top–down. Moreover, the medium of this change can only be religious; social reform or politics can become relevant to a Hindu only if it comes through his religion (see esp. CWSV: VIII, 77). It is significant that religion qua religion was not central in this strategy. Hinduism was viewed here neither as a set of beliefs and practices, nor as a religious collectivity. To Vivekananda, one was not a Hindu simply in one's orthodoxy or religious spheres but in one's very way of life.

These insights soon paid rich dividends. In less than two years after he left his *guru-bhais*, Vivekananda was able to attract an impressive number of disciples, high and low, at various places in India. In particular, he worked with deeper intensity to mobilize two key sources of support: Rajput princes for their glorious tradition of keeping promises, and people of Madras for their deeply-ingrained religiosity. Time once again proved him right. Many of his subsequent successes cannot be adequately understood without the commitment displayed by his valuable patron–clients and devoted disciples in western and southern India.

The first test came when he decided to attend the World Parliament of Religions at Chicago in 1893. His followers at Madras began to collect funds, often begging from door to door (LSV: 273, 278). The Maharaja of Khetri presented him with a purse, a first class ticket, a set of proper *sannyasin* robes, and the famous name Vivekananda (LSV: 281: 283). But this was not all. The real contribution of these people came when Vivekanada reached Chicago and found himself alone and isolated after a brief spell of limited success in public speaking. Although hagiographic writings on Vivekananda have produced vastly exaggerated accounts of his glorious victories in America, the fact is that in less than a year after his arrival, his charisma began to fade. Partly influenced by the inspired propaganda of his critics, who vehemently questioned his credentials, many of his American contacts began to suspect his bona fides (CWSV: VIII, 313). It was then that Vivekananda reacted with a vengeance, aided and abetted by his Indian disciples, and ultimately succeeded in dramatically turning a highly adverse situation into an opportunity for greater work.

His technique was simple, if not quite saintly. He asked his disciples in Madras to convene big meetings, arrange crowds, get influential names associated with these conventions, pass resolutions praising his work, and send this publicity material to important men and newspapers in America (CWSV: v, 31–2, 36). From June to September 1894, several public meetings were organized with great éclat in pursuance of these instructions (for audience composition and texts of resolutions, see VIN: 32–3, 41–60, 301–4, 347–50). Vivekananda himself supplied details of some of these meetings to his important contacts in America (CWSV: vi, 308; vii, 460–5; viii, 316, 319, 321), often suggesting, quite falsely, the spontaneous character of this recognition.

Soon, however, the need for such sponsored publicity vanished. By the end of 1894, Vivekananda was able to establish himself sufficiently in America and, in fact, began to utilize his America establishment for creating an echo-effect in India. His white converts to Vedanta not only succeeded in countering the Christian propaganda against him, they also gave him immense leverage to reach Westernized middle-class Hindus through Westernization itself. Through his careful manipulation, acceptance of Hinduism became an instrument of self-affirmation rather than of defeatism and defence.

In addition to drawing on these psychological sources of appeal, Vivekananda began a concerted drive to organize the Mission work on a sound institutional base. The very detailed instructions he sent to his disciples at Madras, Calcutta, and in Rajputana reveal his business acumen in action. Although at times a confirmed opponent of organization and publicity (CWSV: v, 11, 21, 25, 50; vi, 278; vii, 485; viii, 335–6), he quickly grasped now the importance of systematizing secular aspects of his sacred work (CWSV: v, 52). While sending money to his disciples for buying land and houses for setting up Mission offices, or for starting magazines, he carefully worked out amazingly precise instructions for staff recruitment, leadership, rules of discipline, accounting and budgeting, activity schedule, and even for things like space utilization, room furnishings, cover designs, and subscription drives. An almost complete charter was sent by him to his Calcutta disciples: tying his offer of money with complete acceptance of his conditions (CWSV: vii, 488–95), which has since become a Magna Charta of the Movement (HRMM: 113).

But this purely business style of work soon created tensions among those who were keen to pursue a lonely path of unadulterated devotion to Ramakrishna. Just as Vivekananda had earlier found Baranagore monasticism too unworldly, many of his followers now found his secular involvement too irreligious. Much before missionary scholars or their Indian protégés could debunk Vivekananda as a pseudo-Hindu or a feeble Westernizer, many accusing fingers were raised at him by his own followers. What were the sources, they asked, of his revaluation of Vedanta? How far could secular Mission work be considered consistent with sacred Hindu religiosity? In attempting to reach closer to Ramakrishna by an ethic of altruistic service, was Vivekananda in fact moving away from Ramakrishna's gospel of love and renunciation?

Sources of Vivekananda's revaluation

The controversy on the essential meaning of Ramakrishna has a long inner history in the evolution of the Mission work. In fact, serious differences on the divinity of Ramakrishna had arisen amidst his followers even during his lifetime (LSV: 123–4). After his death, many of his immediate disciples openly protested against Vivekananda's attempt to order them into an organized brotherhood (HRMM: 40–1). This protest soon turned into disguised distrust when he decided to leave these disciples alone, and even began to seek religious instruction from other gurus (LSV: 188). Some of these differences may have finally led Vivekananda to a feeling of mental rupture with his Baranagore colleagues around the time of his visit to America. However, as soon as this rupture ended, differences surfaced once again over the theoretical justification for combining other-directed service with self-centred renunciation (CWSV: v, 53, 75; vi, 263–4, 310–11, 345–6). Back home, these differences often erupted into near confrontations when some of Vivekananda's brother-disciples accused him of importing Western religious motives and methods to sell an unreal and contrived Ramakrishna in India (CWSV: vi, 477–9; vii, 112; LSV: 504–6; RSV: 331–2).

Each time, Vivekananda, with his overwhelming passion and overbearing attitude, silenced his critics (CWSV: v, 95; LSV: 507; RSV: 278). Yet the question of authenticity continued to assail him throughout his life. Often in the midst of hectic activity, serious doubts arose in his own mind on the Vedantic validity of his work, and he fervently longed to seek solitary refuge in personal devotion to Mother Kali. Near the end of his career, he wilfully terminated all his connections with active Mission work and returned to a life of pure meditation.

This return only appeared to confirm the existence of a fundamental conflict between Vivekananda's self-chosen secular vocation and his inner sacred religiosity. During moments of spiritual crisis, he admitted that his work of money-raising and institution-building was merely an artificial superimposition on his true vocation (CWSV: vi, 431–2). From this, one can even deduce that the Movement was primarily a product of his suspended spirituality; that, in effect, he could not have created an order of activist monks, had he stayed strictly within the bounds of his preferred Hindu religious action; and that only after he broke through these bounds was he able to start on a tortuous course of reinterpreting Ramakrishna and imitating the Christian humanist ethic and missionary methods.

One can find enough evidence for this usual impact-of-the-West explanation from Vivekananda's own writings. At a very early stage, he seems to have come under the compelling influence of Thomas à Kempis' *Imitation of Christ* (CWSV: vi, 209; viii, 159–61; RSV: 279, 384). Later, one finds the Barangore *math* expressing an intensely deferential attitude to Christianity under his leadership (HRMM: 57; LSV: 163). During his visit to America, he is seen constantly applauding the West's phenomenal capacity to combine and organize (CWSV: v, 27, 56; vi, 476–77; viii, 299, 328; RSV: 144). All this would seem to suggest that he was operating with borrowed ideas and frameworks to produce a nationalist Hindu version of a Christianized Ramakrishna.

Such an explanation, even though it seems grounded in history and common sense, is totally misleading. The actual processes through which linkages are established in a reformer's mind between selective internalization of the West and a reformulated perception of his own tradition are always much more complex, and can be analysed more appropriately in terms of elective affinities, rather than of imitation. In the case of Vivekananda, it can be easily established that Thomas à Kempis was chosen out of a wide variety of available Western 'stimuli' because it converged with his own notions of religious fulfilment. In fact, Vivekananda clearly says that he was astonished to find via à Kempis that *vairagya* (renunciation) and *bhakti* (devotion) existed even among the Christians (CWSV: vi, 209). There is no suggestion of impact here but only of an affinity. Similarly, there was nothing in the objective American reality of the mid-1890s that would have automatically produced a fusion of altruism and organization in Vivekananda's mind. His experiences in America were actually profoundly disturbing: denial of hotel rooms because of his skin colour (LSV: 328; RSV: 136–7), letters threatening his life (RSV: 335), humiliating discourtesy of his presumed hosts (CWSV: vii, 125), condescending behaviour and arrogance of his Christian friends (HRMM: 85–6), and cheating, hypocrisy, and fanaticism in the name of religion (CWSV: iv, 361; v, 82; vi, 339; VIN: 700). If, out of all this, Vivekananda chose to single out the West's organizational genius as something which Hindus should imitate, this was merely an extroversion of a long-felt inner need, mediated in this case by his encounter with America. In other contexts, he also thought of utilizing 'Buddha's heart' (CWSV: vi, 225–7) and 'Islam's body' (CWSV: vi, 416) to push the same idea of bringing Vedanta to the masses.

The roots of this idea lay in the very evolution of Hinduism. One can trace it back to the earliest Hindu protests occurring against the main trend of Brahminic orthodoxy in India. At this point, it is necessary to digress briefly in order to place Vivekananda's innovation in the structural context of this total development. All Hindu protests in the past have occurred to undermine Brahminic ritual constraints on the individual pursuit of *mukti*. In the ealiest period, these protests took two major forms. The first was articulated through a challenge to Vedic exclusiveness and dogmatism. Buddhism and Jainism typified this protest; the former through emperor Ashoka became a vehicle of large-scale state-supported humanitarian work, while the latter became an instrument of ethical legitimation to various trading class activities. The second form of protest sought to establish a direct man–god relationship through devotion, eliminating the need for any systematic Brahminic intervention. Vaishnavism and Shaivism illustrated this development. In the intermediate period of Hindu evolution, these differing forms of protest were often united through a trans-social (anti-caste) and non-ritualistic (anti-Brahmin) ethic of service and renunciation. Kabir, Chaitanya, Nanak, and Nimbarka together with a host of other saint–poets represented this trend. Devotion and charity became primary modes of religious action. In various ways, these protests established the legitimacy of expressing one's religiosity through altruistic acts like feeding the poor and tending the sick.

Vivekananda's pre-modern revaluation of Hinduism occurred in this pre-Western-impact historical context. By attacking caste parochialism and ritual efficacy and by enlarging the sphere of religiously-relevant action, his Practical Vedanta reasserted once again the specific Hindu form and substance of protest. His selective acceptance of the West played only a minor supportive role in this reform. The West became meaningful to him only in providing an occasion to use a new vocabulary; otherwise, the old medium persisted.

This new vocabulary had several antecedents. Two of these are particularly relevant to an understanding of the immediate sources of Vivekananda's revaluation. The first was expressed in and through economic nationalism; the classic formulation came from Dadabhai Naoroji who had created impressive archetypal symbols to attack British exploitation and focus attention on India's degrading poverty (see Chandra 1964). The second crucial antecedent was created by the new imagery of activist Hinduism. The most popular exponent of this imagery was Bankim Chandra Chatterjee who had reoriented Bengal's inert religious consciousness by his powerful fictional recreations of dynamic gods and rebellious *sannyasins*.[3]

Vivekananda's 'idea' of Practical Vedanta was a product of this 'existence': widespread poverty and revaluated religion. His own growth gradually led him to believe that Hinduism itself could be used to revitalize the society.

---

[3]Bankim's *Krishnacharitra* and *Anandmath* were powerful literary works published in the 1880s which could have exerted direct influence on Vivekananda. The former was a biography of a dynamic Krishna, especially relevant for the Chaitanya-inspired passive devotional religiosity of Bengal. The latter work fictionalized the *sannyasi* rebellion against the East India Company in 1772–4. Both these conceptions—dynamism of Krishna and activism of *sannyasins*—were later used by Vivekananda in his Vedantic reform.

As a child, he saw his father's religiosity translated into an ethic of altruism without strings (RSV: 189); as a young man, his encounter with Ramakrishna completely shook his rationalist pretensions and his vigorous atheism was suddenly sublimated into an unqualified surrender. From Ramakrishna he not only learnt to transcend his reliance on reason; he also discovered that true religion inhered only in the realization of a man–god equation, not in beliefs, rituals, or sects (CWSV: iv, 175–80). Brief spells of unemployment and starvation confirmed in his mind the impotency of a graceless religion perpetuated solely by ignorance and selfishness (LSV: 91; RSV: 10). The only way out was to bring Hinduism back 'into the busy streets from caves and mountains' by creating a new theory and practice of Vedanta.

Vedanta in Theory and Practice

In formulating his theory of Vedanta, Vivekananda utilized two major premises of Hinduism: first, that religious reality is meaningful only at the level of the individual, not of collectivities; and second, that the religious goal of self-realization implies in essence cognitive changes, not institutional reform. Both these propositions were used by Vivekananda to liberate Vedanta from a fixed society-type and transform it into an instrument for creating new religiously-relevant links between human shortcomings and ethical demands.

Proceeding from the first premise, Vivekananda broke through the Western conceptualization of an interactional relationship between religion and society. He argued that religion as a subjectively meaningful act of experience cannot be viewed from the outside impinging upon a society. Technically, the relevant distinction for a Vedantist is not between the religious and social spheres but between the higher and lower forms of reality. From this perspective, one cannot conceive of religion as an autonomous sector of life colluding or contending with other organized sectors of society. Vedanta as *the* religion is thus coterminous neither with Hindu social life nor with India's downfall.[4] As a mode of self-realization, it is culturally neutral and trans-social, having no causal connections with collectively cherished beliefs and institutional arrangements. In this sense, Vedanta cannot be considered either a cause of social decay or a promoter of national prosperity.

This line of reasoning freed Hinduism from its guilt of association with India's poverty. As a Vedantist, Vivekananda could easily separate Hindu religious experience from India's social existence (CWSV: ii, 114–15; v, 22,

---

[4]Conversely, he also questioned the presumed Christian basis of modern West's wealth and power. America and England were to him not 'Christian' as nations (CWSV: ii, 474; v, 77; viii, 213). In fact, during his foreign trips, he constantly exhorted his audiences 'to go back to Christ'. In either case, religion as an inner experience was dissociated from concrete social existence.

145; VIII, 173). Not only this, he could also easily discard traditions on the grounds of tradition itself. As a higher order mode of self-realization, Vedanta permitted him to ignore antiquated scriptures (CWSV: IV, 264, 395; VII, 145, 176, 183), expose the self-contradictory nature of Hindu precepts and Hindu practices (CWSV: I, 427; III, 271; V, 15, 127), accept only as much of the Vedas as was consistent with reason and alter the rest (CWSV: VII, 174–5; VIII, 255), ridicule prevalent notions of caste purity and pollution (CWSV: III, 167, 439; V, 27, 93, 226; VI, 319–20, 458), and condemn the vain erudition and empty ritualism of Brahmin priests (CWSV: VI, 254; VII, 172–3). India's popular religiosity of protecting cows and feeding stones in a temple also looked to him as being anachronistic when god in the form of living human beings was starving 'unattended (CWSV: V, 50, 353; VII, 449–51). Vedanta became meaningful to Vivekananda only as a fully conscious choice to pursue the most appropriate path of religious achievement. To each individual, as to each nation, belonged his own particular form of Vedanta.

This utter relativism was in fact used by him to offer two completely different kinds of Vedanta to his audiences in the East and the West. Both in his articulation of religious symbols and in his prescription of religious action, he chose to concretize Vedanta in terms of culturally relevant situation-definitions. Krishna as an object of spiritual identification was a typical example. In America, Vivekananda drew a portrait of Krishna, the divine object of surrender, who was immersed in his *lila* (divine play) with the *gopi*s (milkmaids) (CWSV: VI, 110–11). In India, this image was changed to project a fighting Krishna, the charioteer of Arjuna, who was vigorously pleading for an activist affirmation (CWSV: V, 388). These distinctions became much more sharp in Vivekanada's total relativization of ethical demands. In America, he told his audiences to practise Yoga and renunciation, instead of supporting missionary humanitarian work (CWSV: IV, 244–5). In India, he exhorted his followers to practise a little *bhoga* (indulgence), inculcate some *rajas* (materialism), and engage wholeheartedly in altruistic services (CWSV: III; 149, V, 379; VI, 458–9; VII, 182). In America, he criticized the machine culture because, instead of solving the problem of poverty, it created only new wants (CWSV: V, 308). In India, he not only upheld the necessity of a material civilization (CWSV: IV, 368) but even thought of organizing monks for industrial purposes (CWSV: II, 466).

These contradictory demands stemmed from the linkages created by Vivekananda between Vedanta's inner self-realization and society's variable outer reality. Through these linkages, the external world became meaningful only in its subjective perception; hence Vedantic demands were always made on oneself, not on institutions. In his framework of social change, one changed oneself rather than society. Both social reform and political agitation were treated as inadequate, if not strictly undesirable, lower-level approaches in this framework.

According to Vivekananda, all meaningful change signified inner growth, not violent reform or passive Westernization (CWSV: III, 213; V, 198; RSV, 421). This was possible only if the masses were given their lost individuality (CWSV: IV, 362; V, 29). No attempt would succeed if it sought merely to imitate some alien models. Problems like widow remarriage, which agitated most Westernized social reformers, did not in fact even exist for the lowest classes (CWSV: V, 29, 74, 333; VIII, 307). Similarly, political agitation for a right to run the government was meaningless unless people knew how to 'run' themselves (CWSV: IV, 368; V, 222; VI, 426). In Vivekananda's Vedantic hierarchy, political freedom without individual *swarajya* was only a lower form of achievement. Quite naturally, his Vedanta never seriously concerned itself with the conventional collectivist demands expressed through various contemporary social–political movements.

While such an orientation successfully universalized Vedanta's message and relativized its demands, it did not satisfactorily solve India's dilemma. Cut off from organized attempts at institutional change, Vedanta's affirmative potential needed both an economic dimension and a social base. There was no doubt in Vivekananda's mind that Vedanta would not— and need not—supply any requisite motive force to produce and push technological advancement in India. India must learn this from the West (CWSV: IV, 155), even though this learning should not be used to create a hybrid.[5] Practical Vedanta stopped at deifying the world and elevating the poor to Godhead (CWSV: II, 146; V, 58, 380; VI, 267; VII, 235, 245–7); the idea of sole indulgence in *artha* (economic–political pursuits) still appeared too demeaning to merit any spiritual consideration. In its externalized manifestation, Vedanta meant an unencumbered transferability from one sphere to another—for example, from *shastra* to selling goods in the market (CWSV: III, 447)—but it did not synthesize the two in a non–dualist frame of reference.

It was partly for this reason that Vivekananda's Vedanta could never really come to terms with the householder's way of life. Although he started with the idea of providing an ethic of social salvation to householders (CWSV: VIII, 267), he could never repose his faith in an ordinary house-holder's ability to transcend his kinship constraints.[6] *Sannyasins* alone could provide a focal point for his reformulated *dharma*. Ideally, rulers and re-

---

[5]It is important to stress the character of 'duality' in Vivekananda's synthesis. Later in India, this duality was perverted into a hybrid. To Vivekananda, Hindu tradition and the West's modernity were to be used separately. Subsequent reformers began to suggest that the former itself can become an instrument of the latter.

[6]Part of this distrust goes back to Ramakrishna himself (CWSV: VII, 262). Vivekananda had added several reasons on his own, such as householders' incapacity to liberate themselves from the limits of ordinary duty for a fuller commitment to altruism (CWSV: V, 92; VI, 356).

nouncers could unite in a common endeavour to aid the latter in their
mission of service (CWSV: IV, 329); otherwise, householders remained both
literally and symbolically only on the periphery of Vedanta.

One can briefly trace at this point the origin and evolution of this idea in
Vivekananda's own mind. In its embryonic form, it seems to have come to
him at the end of his *parivrajaka* (itinerant) life in India. At Cape Comorin,
in December 1892, Vivekananda, according to his own version, first 'hit upon
a plan' to redirect wandering *sannyasins* into villages to teach people
elementary geography and science with the aid of maps, globes, and chemicals
(CWSV: VI, 254–65). This plan continued to interest him throughout the
first phase of his stay in America (CWSV: V, 15, 23, 35; VI, 289). In fact, he
occasionally justified his fund-raising abroad in the light of this plan (CWSV:
IV, 363). Around this time, he also wrote to his disciples to try inculcating
some spirituality and philanthropy among the élites in India in order to use
their vast resources for educating the masses (CWSV: VI, 287).

For several reasons, this early proposal for 'practising Vedanta' could
not be carried out. His disciples lacked both the enthusiasm and training
needed for the work. Moreover, Vivekananda's gradually expanding
establishment in America enabled him to elaborate and systematize his
original plan. Beginning with 1895, he seriously started exploring possibilities
for setting up a society or a college in India to teach people the Vedas and
comparative religion (CWSV: IV, 370; V, 67, 77). Gradually, more details
were filled in and by 1896, he had a full-fledged blueprint for starting two
centres, one each in Madras and Calcutta, in order to train young unmarried
men for secular and spiritual education of the masses (CWSV: V, 124, 217,
223; VIN: 113).

When Vivekananda returned to India in 1897, this blueprint was
articulated afresh through various proposals such as establishment of
institutions to train students as preachers of religious truths (CWSV: III, 223);
mobilization of boys to collect food and clothes to be distributed among
the poor (CWSV: VI, 403); opening of feeding homes and five-year training
courses for *brahmacharis* (CWSV: VII, 159); and setting up of *maths* in every
town and village, headed by *sannyasins*, to impart education in the arts and
sciences (CWSV: V, 371). Behind each one of these proposals lay the same
original idea of moving the disciples of Ramakrishna from sacred to secular
work (CWSV: VII, 168). The role of the householder was neglected both
because of the householders' inherent limitations (CWSV: V, 92, 346; VI, 356)
and of the *sannyasins'* greater success potential in committing themselves
to disinterested altruism and in evoking instant approval of the masses
(CWSV: VIII, 425). Vedanta's affirmation was thus confined only to those
who had already renounced everything.

It is fruitless to argue whether this was the right decision for Vivekananda.

Theoretically, there was no alternative but to establish the man–god equation at levels where the distinctions did not exist. To include the householder qua householder would have implied transvaluation from much lower and more problematic levels. The householder therefore became relevant only in his non-householder roles; the real Mission was conceived and actualized primarily for the *sannyasins*. In effect, this meant reformulation of renunciation and service as two distinct phases of *nivritti* (withdrawal) and *pravritti* (involvement) in the same life cycle. In either case, the choice was visualized only at the individual cognitive level; society came into the picture only as an object for exercising this choice. In the actual evolution of the Ramakrishna movement, one can see this principle constantly at work, the participating individuals move back and forth between sacred *jnana* and secular *karma* but there is no attempt ever to create a Vedantic society. Such an idea, in fact, does not make any sense from a strictly Hindu perspective.

Evolution of the Mission

From the earliest period, the Mission activities have alternated between the religious and the philanthropic. The choice has been dependent upon the *swahbavik* (natural) inclinations of the participating monk. The Mission has merely helped each individual to choose a course of action most appropriate for his spiritual stage of development. There has never been an attempt to completely reorient the direction of the total movement. This has led to the emergence of two completely independent spheres of work, bifurcated in substance and consciousness, between religious self-cultivation and secular social service. This duality has been in evidence at every stage of the Mission's development.

Even in the pre-institutional period of 1893 to mid-1897, when the Mission existed only in the minds of Vivekanada's Indian disciples, there were sharp orientational differences producing two mutually exclusive kinds of Vedantic work. The first visualized religious affirmation primarily through the dissemination of religious ideas; at this level, the practice of Vedanta did not go beyond preaching it. It motivated men to organize publicity conferences, publish religious journals,[7] and propagate Vivekananda's exploits abroad. The second kind of work seriously sought to translate Vedantic religiosity into the language of active altruism. It took men into slums and villages, and often into schools and orphanages. Here, humanistic Vedanta was lived by serving afflicted humanity itself.

[7]Two religious journals were started by Vivekanada's followers during this period: *Brahmavadin* in September 1895 and *Prabhuddha Bharat* in July 1896 (HRMM: 103, 128; VIN: 75, 100). There is absolutely nothing in the pages of these journals in the early years to suggest that the men behind them were even aware of altruism as a valid mode of Vedantic expression.

There is no evidence to believe that these two kinds of work ever inter-penetrated at this stage. Each one was undertaken in response to subjectively defined religious requirements. Right when some of Vivekananda's follow-ers were busy meditating, or holding large public meetings to commemo-rate Ramakrishna's birthday, others were silently working to secure the re-lease of slave boys in Khetri, establishing primary schools in villages, and setting up people's welfare associations in various states of Rajputana (LSV: 640; HRMM: 110). Both these groups of people were trying to serve the cause of Practical Vedanta, even though their ways of doing it were vastly different.

These differences were only more firmly established when the Mission activities were institutionalized from 1897 to 1902. Many of these differences can, in fact, be traced back to Vivekananda's personal lifestyle which constantly alternated during this period between sacred and secular predispositions. During moments of intense spiritual fervour, he consistently went back to the proper observance of religious rites, fasts, and pilgrimages, adhering strictly to all ceremonial details (LSV: 545, 590). His insistence on ritual propriety often extended to his disciples' full training in canonical rules of worship and recitation. Periodically, he also engaged himself in the idol worship of Kali and other goddesses of the Hindu pantheon, sometimes going to the extent of *kumari-puja* (worship of virgins) (LSV: 598, 720–3). On at least one occasion he allowed himself to be worshipped by his own disciples (CWSV: VII, 143). Otherwise, Ramakrishna remained his constant favourite, and he occasionally thought of elevating his guru into a formal Hindu incarnation (CWSV: VII, 493; HRMM: 139).

Counterpoised with this was his purely secular self, always crying to throw away scriptures and ceremonials, and hankering ever after the worship of afflicted humanity. At such times, he not only refused to talk about and discuss the 'sterile' intricacies of Vedantic doctrines (LSV: 644), but himself went out to feed the poor and downtrodden (LSV: 732), lived in the plague-infested neighbourhoods to remove panic and bring succour to the needy (LSV: 557, 643), and even seriously planned to sell all Mission properties to help the famine-stricken masses (LSV: 733; HRMM: 127). During such moments, he would tell his disciples to cut down expenses on worship and memorial meetings and tone up relief work by door-to-door collection of money and materials (CWSV: VI, 403–4).

These two diverse orientations in the personality of Vivekananda instantly reflected in the dual policy directives evolved around this time for institutionalizing the Mission movement. On 1 May 1897, when the Ramakrishna Mission was for the first time formally established as an organized body with a well-defined set of rules and regulations, its objectives specifically included both the spread of Vedantic religious ideas and training for the material welfare of individuals (LSV: 501–2; HRMM: 119–20). Similarly, when the Belur *math*[8] rules were framed in 1899, there was clear emphasis both on personal cultivation through the pursuit of spiritual *sadhanas* (disciplines) and the promotion of educational work for the social and economic uplift of the masses. Disciples were especially cautioned not to turn the *math* into an ordinary temple but to work ceaselessly for such prosaic things as suggesting new ways for food-supply and raising the status of the outcastes (HRMM: 133–9).

In actual practice, some of this idealism 'to *combine* immense spirituality with immense practicality' was diluted but the vision was vigorously sustained. As the aims and objects of the Math and Mission were implemented, it soon became clear that there can be no effective combination but only autonomous development of sacred and secular vocations. Thus, while stress was laid in the monastic sphere on purity and chastity, and on reading of scriptures and practising yoga and meditation (LSV: 539), monks were separately delegated in the secular sphere to commit themselves to relief work in distress areas and to run orphanages and schools wherever needed. Both these vocations continued to persist in the Ramakrishna movement, although the Mission ultimately derived its basic character primarily from the secular work.

As early as 1897, the Mission workers were going from door to door in the famine-hit districts of Bengal to distribute rice, medicines, and clothes to the affected people (VIN: 334–5, 391; LSV: 520, 641). In the following years, special houses were set up to feed and nurse orphans and to provide for their religious and vocational education (LSV: 640; HRMM: 122). During the epidemic of plague in 1899, these monks were engaged in cleaning, flushing, and disinfecting surface drains, removing garbage and enrolling volunteers to distribute printed instructions on the adoption of preventive measures (VIN: 210–11, 321, 382, 551–2). In other areas, schemes were drawn up for organizing shelters for ailing *sadhus* and destitute pilgrims (VIN: 218), and for establishing schools to impart training in handicrafts to widows and orphan girls (VIN: 556).

As time rolled on, both kinds of work were further consolidated, expanded, and systematized. In the beginning, there was a spontaneous drive to set up new *math* and Mission centres in various parts of India, depending upon the availability of local initiative, talent, and funds. Most of these centres were engaged both in propagating the writings of Vivekananda, arranging

---

[8]As a new institution, the Belur Math initially pushed the earlier body, the Ramakrishna Mission, into the background and itself began to undertake both the religious and philanthropic activities (LSV: 503). Gradually, however, the Math and the Mission were differentiated into autonomous monastic and secular spheres and, in 1909, the Mission was registered as an independent body (HRMM: 182–92).

spiritual discourses and devotional meetings, celebrating Ramakrishna's birthday and religious festivals, and in arranging relief operations during emergencies, establishing orphanages and homes for the infirm and the invalid, and starting schools for secular and vocational education.

Initially most of these activities were planned and organized by the devoted band of *sannyasins* with the aid received from lay disciples, private charities, and government grants. In 1909, however, the Mission membership was formally extended to the non-monastic followers of Vivekananda. Its objects were widened to include the study of arts, sciences, and industries, and establishment of colleges, workshops, hospitals, and other charitable institutions. Gradually, the movement was routinized through a set of constitutional rules specifying channels of authority and division of labour, and detailing other managerial and financial aspects of the organization. After India's independence, the movement continued to grow under the patronage of government and public support.

In the last twenty-five years, the Mission has on several occasions launched fund collection drives and has succeeded in significantly expanding its religious and philanthropic activities. It has, however, never seriously concerned itself with campaigns either to convert the religious loyalties of its supporters or to bring more *sannyasins* within its fold. It has continued to strive primarily to set an example and provide an outlet whereby an individual may realize his own latent spirituality in altruism. It has never sought to change the total Hindu society as such and has contented itself merely by working on it periphery. In this sense, the Mission has always been non-functional.

This brings us back to the problem of establishing the internal structural context of the relationship between the Mission as an aspect of Hindu religious experience and India as an aspect of Hindu social organization. At what points have the two interacted? What has been the precise sociological significance of the Ramakrishna movement as a concrete manifestation of Hindu religious evolution in pre-modern India? Has the Mission produced rationality and social change, or is this a wrong question?

III

RELIGION, RATIONALITY, AND SOCIAL CHANGE: SOME
THEORETICAL RECONSIDERATIONS

The dominant stream in the current sociology of religion indicates two major criteria for assessing the rationality-content of a given religious movement: first, how far does the movement signify a differentiation from the society into one of its independent but interacting sub-systems; two, to what extent does the movement act as a leverage for inducing rational changes in a total society. The locus classicus implicitly laying down these criteria was Max Weber's Protestant ethic thesis which attempted[9] to demonstrate both the internal autonomy and the rationalizing implications of the Reformation (Weber 1958). Since then this thesis has been worked out more systematically by Parsons and Bellah who have posited differentiation as a master key to unlock evolutionary processes. (Parsons 1966), and Protestant reform as an ideal type of a pre-modern religious movement (Bellah 1964).

Evaluated on the basis of these criteria, the Ramakrishna Mission would fail on both counts. It has neither succeeded in differentiating itself from the Hindu society into an autonomous sphere; nor has it led to the rationalization of its participating monks or of India. Compared with the Luther–Calvin Reformation, the failure of the Ramakrishna–Vivekananda movement would appear even more galling: The Mission has neither produced a Vedantic church, nor a Vedantic nation, to say nothing of supplying an ethic to support industrialization. Logically extended to its ultimate implications, this failure would suggest that the Mission has indeed been only an irrelevant mix of reaction and revivalism, having no potential for effecting any evolutionary breakthrough in India's transition to modernity.

This line of argument would end either in dismissing Hinduism as an inferior religion with its un-evolving tribalistic enchantment and nativist expressions, or in introducing a Neo-Weberian modification for a sympathetic reappraisal of certain aspects of the Hindu tradition on the old Weberian criteria of rationality. In Indian sociology, these alternatives have generally produced two different though overlapping types of responses. Some sociologists have tried to discover Protestant ethic analogues in India's individual communities or sects, like the Jains or the Lingayats. Some others have argued that Hinduism like Christianity is amenable to change and can easily meet from within the requirements of the modernization process (Srinivas 1966; Singer 1972).

Both these responses are in essence apologetic and highly misleading (Gupta 1974). The first unwittingly shifts the focus of Hindu religious evolution from the dominant centre to its peripheral parts. Unlike the West, the Protestant-type religious movements do not occur in India within or against the main trend; neither do they influence developments at the macro-level, either in theology or in society. Evolutionary movements like the Ramakrishna

---

[9] I am using the word 'attempted' deliberately. Weber's hypothesis, notwithstanding many Neo-Weberian attempts, still remains provisional. In fact, Weber's other writings strongly suggest that it was Western evolution in its totality that ultimately determined the character of the modern Western civilization. From this one can logically conclude: first, that the Protestant Reformation as a religious movement was not a causal but a coeval factor in Western development; second, that it is completely meaningless to look for the Protestant ethic analogues in the religious movements of non–Christian traditions.

Mission are ignored in this response because they do not apparently supply the relevant economic ethic. The second type of response also tries to establish an equivalence between Hinduism and Christianity, not only on an analytical level but also on substantive functional grounds. Pre-modern Hindu religious movements are expected to perform the same role which pre-modern Christianity supposedly performed in Europe. Vivekananda-type reforms are valued in this response not as symbolic expressions of an evolving Hindu tradition but primarily as transitional vehicles for bringing India closer to a Westernized modernity.

One major exception to this kind of thinking is available in Saran who has refused the temptation of demonstrating Hinduism's potential for modernity, both in its original and evolved forms (Saran 1963; 1969b). Through this refusal, he has cleared the way for shifting the ground of discourse back to the structural context of Hinduism. His position has, however, become problematic in its ultimate logical deductions which have led him not merely to refute the relevance of the Western Christian models in comprehending Hinduism but to deny the very possibility of building up a sociology of religion within the religion–society framework of India (Saran 1969a: 41–7). It seems plausible to argue that given the two radically different starting points of Hinduism and Christianity, one can still proceed to establish and compare variable patterns of symbol systems, evolutionary developments, pre-modern breakthroughs, and contemporary dilemmas of the Indian and Western societies.

Once this continuous variability is established, the paradigm linking religious movements and social change can be reformulated to account for both the universalistic and particularistic components of evolution. It is clear that in its present form this paradigm, with its emphasis on differentiation and rationality is not only deeply embedded in the Western experience of Christianity's actual development but also selects from such experience some highly questionable modes of looking at this development. It not only ignores the non-West existence; it also ignores part of the Western experience itself. In order to correct this relativism and bias, it is important to place the paradigm in its proper Christian context and juxtapose it with the parallel framework of Hinduism.

The differences between the two systems can be traced back to their respective starting points. Christianity begins its mission in a hostile environment. In its earliest form, it is identifiable through its autonomous religious communities, existing only as reluctant parts of an external society. God's essence is supposed to be embodied in the Church and its sacraments, clearly differentiated from the secular world. In the course of evolution, the Church, as a separate focus of power, continues to seek and enlarge its role in the central social structure. New religious movements occur when such a search leads to an excessive involvement with this world. A Christian reformer always wants to go back to an unadulterated other-worldly spirituality. He is condemned by the orthodoxy as a heretic. If he succeeds, he establishes his own separate sect and begins the search afresh to enlarge its jurisdiction.

In comparison, Hinduism develops within a peaceful secular setting, having no external forces to contend with. God's divine reality is supposed to be inherent in man's human potential; the dominant mode of religious fulfilment is self-realization. Hindu religious functionaries form some kind of interstitial sub-society, dependent upon the protection of their patron–clients. Having no autonomous sources of wealth and power based on a separate jurisdiction, they try to enlarge their sphere of relevance by creating ritual barriers to salvation. New religious movements occur to break these barriers. A Hindu reformer wants to get back to a simplified man–god relationship without any Brahminic other-worldly paraphernalia. In the short run, he is criticized as unorthodox but gradually his reform is absorbed within the main trend.

Quite clearly, this pattern of development precludes any Christianity-type intra- and intercultural differentiation. As a religion both *in* and *of* society, Hinduism continues to exit and evolve as an optional method by which men can empower themselves to grow in their spirituality. In fact, Hindu scriptures, unlike their Christian counterparts, do not act as a straitjacket but primarily as a leaven in society. The believers are bound only in conscience; rules of law are derived from customs, not sacred books. Religious functionaries can technically provide legitimation to any custom provided it is dictated by contemporary efficiency. There is at no point any cognitive conflict between Reason and Religion.

This stands in sharp contrast with Christianity. Quite early in its evolution one can sense a certain tension between divinely ordained 'theology' and secular–rational 'philosophy'. Over a period of time, various solutions are suggested to resolve this tension. One extreme position is indicated by postulating complete antagonism: religion is irrational. This position was vigorously upheld during the Enlightenment and utilized later by the positivists and the materialists. The other extreme places total reliance on inner faith; outer reason is disparaged because religious truth is supposed to be inviolable. In between, there have been at least three compromise positions: first, that religion and reason are identical, the latter setting forth logically what the former practises; second, that religion and reason are consistent but the former transcends the latter without contradicting it; third, that religion and reason are each true in their own respective spheres.

The sociology of religion has derived its basic ethos from these compromise intra-Christian positions. In the hands of Weber, Christian religion, far from being an antithesis of reason, has become the very basis of advancing it. The appeal of this idea has been so viciously pervasive in the Christian conscience of the modern 'capitalist' West that Marx has still not become an integral part in the 'bourgeois' sociology of religion. But this labelling is meaningless. One can still draw comfort from the small mercy that neo-Weberians do not at least look for the Protestant ethic analogues in the available religious experiences of the Soviet, Chinese, or other 'socialist' societies. Evidently, religion's rationality is at stake only in the non-communist world.

However, once this relativist and biased framework is revised, it will become clear that even though religion has universally become less relevant today in real action contexts, it has not necessarily become everywhere more differentiated or rational. Just as religion's differentiation has been a specifically Western fact, religion's rationality has been a specifically Western idea. Having no antecedent state of a sacred–secular split, religion could not have been differentiated from society under Hinduism. To a Hindu, society is already fully religious; one cannot theoretically reconstruct it on a new religious basis. Similarly, the problem of rationality is meaningless from a strict Hindu perspective. Faith is to be realized within; to a Hindu, nothing could be more irreligious than to persecute a man for his beliefs.

Vivekananda's Ramakrishna Mission has to be viewed in this paradigm. Its precise significance cannot be assessed through its rationality–inducing role as an autonomous sector of Indian society. Such an idea would appear jarring to the Hindu sensibilities of the Mission workers. To them, the external environment is given; change can come only when individuals begin to actualize their own divine potential. In fact, the Mission workers have consistently avoided collective endorsement of any structural reform or political change. To the Ramakrishna Mission, India's independence movement was itself an outer event. Even today, it has no functional relationship with any political party. Similarly, economic development as an institutional process cannot conceivably figure in the religious calculations of the Mission workers. From their perspective, Hinduism already provides for meaningful articulation of various orientations—social, political, economic—at both a social class and a life's phase level. An individual only needs to fulfill his own vocation efficiently.

Vivekananda's precise contribution rests on redefining this vocation both for Hindus in general and for *sannyasins* in particular. At the ideological level, he effected the crucial transition from self-directed *mukti* to an other-directed altruism. In this process, he broke through the Brahminic barriers to ritual salvation and people's nonchalant reliance on *karma-phala* (predestination). Through his reformulation of symbols, god reappeared in this world in the form of Daridra-Narayan. Worship was identified with service. To help the poor became an article of Hindu faith.

This innovation was soon expressed in Bengal's early twentieth century militant nationalism. However, a more crucial development occurred with Gandhi who provided an institutional correlate of a non-acquisitive society to Vivekananda's idea of fusing renunciation and service. From this one can move to India's subsequent vocabulary developed with characteristically Hindu nuances: democracy not as a form of government but as an idea to restore individuality to the masses; secularism not as a process of replacing religion with reason but as a belief in relative validity of different faiths; socialism not as a system of socializing property but as an attempt to uplift the downtrodden. In each case, these concepts of self-identification and social change can be traced back to Vivekananda. ...

But then, the sociology of religion, despite all its faults, has already affirmed with unassailable logic that ideas—religious ideas included—are more important in their unintended consequences than in their original substance. Vivekananda's Ramakrishna Mission is important not because it has modernized a band of Hindu *sannyasins* but because it has almost unconsciously laid down a framework, howsoever one might evaluate it, for India's only possible processes of social change.*

REFERENCES

The following abbreviations have been used in the paper:
CWSV
1970 *The complete works of Swami Vivekananda*. Mayavati Memorial edition. Calcutta: Advaita Ashrama.
HRMM Gambhirananda, Swami.
1957 *History of the Ramakrishna math and mission*. Calcutta: Advaita Ashrama.
LSV
1965 *The life of Swami Vivekananda* (by his eastern and western disciples). Calcutta: Advaita Ashrama.
RSV
1964 *Reminiscences of Swami Vivekananda* (by his eastern and western admirers). Calcutta: Advaita Ashrama.
VIN Basu, S.P. and S.K. Ghosh, eds.
1969 *Vivekananda in Indian newspapers*, 1893–1902. Calcutta: D. Basu & Co.
Bellah, R.N.
1964 Religious evolution. *American sociological review* 29: 358–74.
Chandra, Bipin.
1964 The problem of poverty and Indian national leadership. *Enquiry* 2: 54–106.
Datta, B.N.
1954 *Swami Vivekananda: Patriot–prophet*. Calcutta: Navbharat Publishers.

*[I do not share all of Gupta's judgements or enthusiasms, but recognize the fact that it is perhaps the most interesting discussion of the Ramakrishna Mission by a sociologist.—Ed.]

Gupta, Krishna Prakash.
1971 A theoretical approach to Hinduism and modernization of India. *Indian journal of sociology* 2: 59–91.
1974 Sociology of Indian tradition and tradition of Indian sociology. *Sociological bulletin* 23: 14–43.
Majumdar, R.C.
1965 *Swami Vivekananda: A historical review*. Calcutta: General Printers Publishers.
Parsons, Talcott.
1966 *Societies: Evolutionary and comparative perspectives*. New Jersey: Prentice-Hall, Inc.
Roy, B.K.
1970 *Socio-political view of Vivekananda*. New Delhi: People's Publishing House.
Saran, A.K.
1963 Hinduism and economic development in India. *Archives de sociologie des religions* 15: 87–94.
1969a. Religion and society: the Hindu view. *International yearbook of the sociology of religion* 41–67.
1969b. Hinduism in contemporary India. *Convergence*, 3, 3–10.
Singer, Milton.
1972 *When a great tradition modernizes: An anthropological approach to Indian civilization*. Delhi: Vikas Publishing House.
Singh, Yogendra.
1973 *Modernization of Indian tradition: A systemic study of social change*. Delhi: Thomson Press.
Srinivas, M.N.
1966 *Social change in modern India*. Berkeley: University of California Press.
Weber, Max.
1958 *The Protestant ethic and the spirit of capitalism*, trans. Talcott Parsons. New York: Charles Scribner's Sons.

Ambedkar's Buddhism

MARTIN FUCHS

INTRODUCTORY REMARKS

After a long delay, and still only sporadically, Bhimrao Ambedkar's thinking is beginning to receive the attention it deserves in the general intellectual and academic discourse [see esp. Zelliot 1986; Gore 1993]. This delay has to do, above all, with the oppositional stand which he took—and into which he was pressed—against Gandhi and the Gandhian concept of national reconstruction. But in addition to this, his 'conversion', as it was seen, to Buddhism at the end of his life did not meet with understanding everywhere. From within a rationalist or 'secularist' framework a return to religion by a secular political leader, and above all a reinvention of a religion no longer alive in the society in question, is not easily intelligible. Often it is understood as an opportunistic and strategic move, attending to the traditionalistic or irrational needs of one's mass following. Of course, convinced Hindus take the decision as a vote of non-confidence in their own religion, which it certainly also was. Only in recent years have efforts been made to understand what religion, and the choice of a new one, could have meant for the rationalist intellectual that Ambedkar

Excerpted from Martin Fuchs, A religion for civil society? Ambedkar's Buddhism, the Dalit issue and the imagination of emergent possibilities. *In* Vasudha Dalmia, Angelika Malinak, and Martin Christ, eds., *Charisma and canon: Essays on the religious history of the Indian subcontinent.* New Delhi: Oxford University Press, 2001. Pp. 250–73. © Oxford University Press.

was, as well as for the political and apparently materialist movement he represented.[1]

For those who undertook it, the 'conversion' had a direct practical significance. However, it had also broader social, political, and cultural significance, for it was at the same time an appeal for the reconstruction of society. ... [Apart from] the existential significance, its social, socio-psychological or emotional, and even the cognitive meaning of the turn to Buddhism for converted Dalits, and for the cause of 'Ex-Untouchables' in general ... is also relevant [see e.g. Omvedt 1992, 2003]. More relevant here is its importance as interpretive intervention. In addressing this issue I hope to uncover some of the hermeneutical implications of this event which have been largely disregarded by those authors who see Dalit movements only as straightforward struggles for status, power resources, and social advancement.

What I would like to emphasize in particular is Ambedkar's effort to shift the coordinates of public discourse and the modalities of social interaction in India. This touches upon the quest for alternative options of modernity. There are certain links between the socio–ethical dimensions of Ambedkar's depiction of Buddhism and the thinking of John Dewey. According to Ambedkar himself, Dewey impressed and influenced him strongly while he was a student at Columbia University in New York in 1913–16. Something of the interaction or affinity between the two is reflected in Ambedkar's approach to Buddhism. Ambedkar, like Dewey, pursued the idea of what has been termed by some a *religion civile*: a new religious, or rather ethical, concept for modern civil society. But both thinkers differed in their conclusions in respect of the way they related to the tradition of religion. ...

[1]If one includes the political level, things become even more complicated. The strong and meanwhile often purely ritualistic and opportunistic celebrations around and after the 100th anniversary of Ambedkar's birthday in 1991 met with renewed attacks on Ambedkar. He has been used, especially by Dalit politicians, to forward politics in the name of Dalitness (see, especially, the recent manoeuvres of the Bahujan Samaj Party (BSP), in Uttar Pradesh). Other parties, and most significantly the Hindu nationalist ones, like the BJP (Bharatiya Janata Party) and Shiv Sena, long regarded as organizations of upper-caste and/or the regionally dominant middle-caste interests in Maharashtra and elsewhere, tried to incorporate Ambedkar. They use his sayings out of context in order to win the support of voters from amongst the 'Ex-Untouchables'. Against this, there are increasing attacks (not to mention the continuing atrocities on Scheduled Caste members in rural areas) on the symbol Ambedkar has become, physically on his statues (e.g. in Bombay in July 1997. This led to riots in which the police killed ten people, most of them Dalit), ideologically to undermine his integrity and to demonstrate his anti-nationalist and pro-colonial, pro-British stance, as in the volume written by the leading Hindu nationalist journalist Arun Shourie (1997).

ELEMENTARY RELIGION: BUDDHISM AND SOCIETY

Bhimrao Ramji (Dr Babasaheb) Ambedkar lived from 1891 to 1956. Just two months before his death he underwent public initiation into Buddhism in a self-invented *dīkṣā* ceremony together with a large number of followers, most of them from his own *jāti* of Mahars on 14 October. It is said that along with him around half a million people converted on that day and on the day following. Back in 1935, Ambedkar had publicly declared that he would 'not die a Hindu'. In his last years, in fact up to the night he died, he had been working on a text that he considered should assume the role of a Buddhist bible: The *Buddha and his Dhamma* (Ambedkar 1974: 14f). Published a year after his death, the book still shows parts which have not been worked out thoroughly and are not as trenchant as others. ... He sets out to deliberately rewrite parts of what is treated as the Buddhist canonical tradition in order to give to Buddha's teachings a distinct interpretation. He obviously has a very mixed readership in mind: Dalits, people who have been already practising Buddhism, followers of other religions—and ultimately society at large. ... As with every systematic exposition—and especially one which tries to present in broad outline fundamental teachings on the human condition while at the same time inevitably addressing specific socio-historical conditions—one can discern certain tensions within his basic assumptions.

Ambedkar addresses his contemporaries; people of the modern world. But what does he aim at? Is he attempting a contingent, contextual reading or the reconstruction of an eternal yet forgotten truth? A modern message in an ancient garb—or rather an ancient message for modern men and women? 'If the *new* world ... must have a religion—and the new world needs religion far more than the old world did—then it can only be the religion of the Buddha' (Ambedkar 1970: 13; emphasis Ambedkar's). From the 1930s onwards, Ambedkar had been engaged in evaluating different non-Hindu religions with regard to their suitability as means of offering an escape from the stranglehold of the caste system. Ambedkar did not mean to project a religion for the Untouchables or Dalits, i.e. for *one* community only. One cannot even depict Ambedkar's presentation of Buddhism as that of a religion of resentment, in the sense of Nietzsche's idea, which is supposed to serve the feelings of impotence and revenge of the underprivileged against the powerful. On the contrary, Ambedkar was looking for a broadly humanist and social religion, which he found best realized in Buddhism.[2]

While putting forth his conception of Buddhism, Ambedkar was very

---

[2]Besides, Buddhism was easier to convey to others and to defend against his slanderers than, for example, Islam or Christianity, for it was a religion of Indian origin. Ambedkar had also considered Sikhism as a choice.

conscious of what he was setting out to do. He pursued what one might term a counter-modern modernist project. Like a modern student of society and religion—which he had been de facto since he went to the United States and England for his studies—he thought of religion in the plural, representing competing interpretations of the world. From such a perspective, the respective universalist claims of the different religions appeared as contingent, particularist truths relative to the concepts of divinity on which they were based (1970: 3f; 1974: 226, 229, 231). Ambedkar used the yardstick of modern science, and its universalist claim to reason, and subjected the different world religions to a 'test', as he phrased it (1970: 13f). He did this not in order to disown religion, but rather to find out and reclaim ancient moral insights, which had proved their trans-historical validity, and return them to his contemporaries. This mode of dealing with religion, this way of installing a 'new' religion, takes for granted that religion has been differentiated from other social domains, and developed into a sphere that follows its own inner logic.[3] Only then does it become at all possible to think of making a religious choice in the abstract manner Ambedkar did. He saw Hinduism, against which he fought, as keeping religion directly implicated in the institution of society. The turn to Buddhism thus signified the 'liberation' of religion from social entanglement and social strain, making religion free to address itself to society; to give (individual) guidance and (collective) orientation. Only in this way would a religion, in principle, be able to bridge the gap between divergent experiences and opposite outlooks, between those marginalized and excluded and those who wield the logic of exclusion. Unlike many new religious leaders, Ambedkar is not arrogating any particular religious qualities, or 'charisma', to himself; he only wants to revive a forgotten truth, and the charisma of the Buddha.

To understand the relation between religion and society in Ambedkar's thought, I will sketch some basic propositions of his conception of Buddhism and indicate some of the liberties he took in his interpretation of older Buddhist canons.

Basic Propositions

It is not so much an authoritative set of convictions and soteriological practices that Ambedkar tries to fix; rather, he wants to induce a certain humanistic attitude. Ambedkar's interpretation of Buddhism rests on: (a) the contention that Buddhism is based on 'reason' (or rationalism) and 'experience' and that it is 'in accord with science', (b) its contestation of divinity, and (c) the claim that it recognizes the fundamental principles of social life.

---

[3]For 'spheres of value', or 'orders of life', their respective inner logic and their separation and tensions, as characteristic for the secular process of rationalization ... [the writings of Max Weber are relevant].

'Buddha's religion is not a revelation,' Ambedkar states (1974: 153). Buddhism, he emphasizes, denies the reality of God, understood as creator or as absolute, ultimate entity (in the mode of *brahma*). Ambedkar is certain that the Buddha did not claim a divine or supernatural status or supernatural powers for himself, nor did he claim divine status or 'infallibility' for his word. The Buddha, in this understanding, was no prophet (1970: 3f, 12; 1974: 63, 68, 151, 153, 156–7).

Buddhism, on the contrary, is 'discovery'; is the 'result of *inquiry and investigation* into the conditions of human life on earth' (1974: 153; emphasis mine). '[The Buddha] was nothing if not rational, if not logical' (1974: 255). Consistent with this rationalist attitude, the Buddha is presented as having declared his message open. It can be 'questioned' or 'tested', and his followers are 'free to modify or even to abandon any of his teachings if it was found that at a given time and in given circumstances they did not apply' (1974: 157, 1970: 4).

For Ambedkar, the Buddha was a *mārgadātā*—he showed the way—he was not a *mokṣadātā*, i.e. he did not *give* salvation (1970: 4; 1974: 153, 156). The concept of *bodhisattva*, as far as I can make out, makes a single appearance only in Ambedkar's book on Buddhism and remains rather unconnected to the rest of the text.[4] The concept of *bodhisattva* does not match well with those parts of Ambedkar's argument in which he expresses strong scepticism toward the theory of rebirth, or (personal) identity beyond death. The Buddha, says Ambedkar, 'believed in the regeneration of matter' ('energy is never lost'), but rejected the existence of a soul and thus denied the idea of the rebirth of the soul. He is, of course, opposed to the theory of karmic retribution *beyond* actual life. It would have taken all 'responsibility for the condition of the poor and the lowly' from society or the state (1974, book IV, II: 235–48).

Buddhism helps to realize fundamental values. A religion which abides by a moral standard, Ambedkar declares, must 'recognize the fundamental tenets of liberty, equality and fraternity' (1970: 13). Ambedkar does not mean that the Buddha expressed these principles in such modern language— Ambedkar to some extent respects the difference between religion and society, and between historical epochs—but he thinks that the Buddha fostered thinking along these lines. The Buddha was the 'earliest and staunchest upholder of equality' (1974: 216). He laid the ideal of a 'brotherhood of

[4]At this instance Ambedkar does accept the concept of the ten lives a Buddha has to go through to reach final enlightenment. The *bodhisattva* seems to develop some superhuman qualities. In his seventh life he becomes 'one with Infinity', in his tenth and final stage, he 'attains the infinite divine eye of a Buddha' (1974: 56–7). Ambedkar compares the 'theory of the Jatakas or the birth stages of a Bodhisatta' to the 'Brahmanic theory of Avataras'. While within the conception of avatāra God may be 'very impure and immoral in his conduct', the concept of the Buddha is one of ever greater perfection of purity (1974: 57).

men' before the social actors; the 'men-in-the-world' (1974: 234). Buddhism demanded compassion for every human being, not differentiated according to status or gender. The practice of the 'Noble Eightfold Path'—*Ashtanga Marga* or Path of Righteousness—together with the 'Path of Purity' and the 'Path of Virtue'[5] 'remove(s) all injustice and inhumanity' (1974: 89; also 83–8). Ambedkar argues against an interpretation of Buddhism as a 'gospel of pessimism' and gives a distinct interpretation to the 'Four Aryan (noble) Truths' and to the striving for *nirvāṇa* or *nibbāna*.[6] Suffering is not so much contingent on men's clinging to this world, but, more prosaically, it means living 'in sorrow, in misery and poverty' (1974: 83). Suffering, the way Ambedkar conceives it, is primarily being inflicted by man upon man through pursuit of gain, lastly by 'class struggle' (1974: 168f, 424). The recognition of the existence of suffering is counterbalanced by an '*equal stress* on the removal of suffering' (1974: 90; emphasis mine). *Nibbāna* does not so much mean loosening the relationship with the material world; instead Ambedkar declares: 'It was vain to attempt to escape from the world. ... What is necessary is to change the world and to make it better.' (1974: 78). Again and again Ambedkar contrasts the Buddhist tenets with Hinduism which for him advocates the principle(s) of inequality, dependency, and divisiveness. Ambedkar is also very outspoken in his rejection of the assumption that religion should, or Buddhism would, 'sanctify or ennoble poverty'. Rather, the other way round, 'riches are welcome', but must be subject to *vinaya*; acquired lawfully, without craving, and be used to give to others (1970: 13; 1974: 168, 332, 423, 424).

A Religion of Laymen

Ambedkar himself had put the main emphasis on the *message* of the old–new religion. He paid no attention to contemplation (Zelliot 1992: 194) and he was only little concerned with building it up institutionally, or rather he seemed hesitant to give it a fixed institutional structure and create a distinct body of spiritual and ritual specialists who might attempt to distance themselves from the laity and form a separate body. Ambedkar hinted at his disappointment with the performance of the historical *sangha*, as it was to be observed in the neighbouring countries of India (1970: 16f; 1974: xlii;

---

[5]The 'Path of Purity' or the Five Precepts are: not to kill, steal, speak untruth, drink, and indulge in lust; the 'Path of Virtue', which contains ten articles, is drawn from the traditional *pāramitās*, or states of perfection, like *karuṇā*, loving kindness; *maitri*, extended fellow feelings, etc.

[6]In the introduction to *Buddha and his Dhamma*, Ambedkar even doubts that the 'Four Aryan Truths' (on the existence, origin, and overcoming of suffering and the path to be followed) form part of the original teachings of the Buddha, because they would 'deny hope to man' and thus be 'a great stumbling block in the way of non-Buddhists accepting the gospel of Buddhism' (1974: xli–xlii).

comp. Zelliot 1992: 243f). Although Neo-Buddhist supporters sometimes, and more or less metaphorically, employ the title 'human saviour' for him, it becomes apparent again that Ambedkar understood himself not as a religious leader in the common sense of the term but that he rather saw himself as an educator-*cum*-political leader. The *dīkṣā*, the initiation ceremony he had conducted for himself and others, and for which he conceived the procedure as well as the vow to be spoken,[7] was an initiation into the Buddhist *dhamma* and not, as elsewhere in Buddhism, into the *sangha* (Zelliot 1992: 244; cf. Ambedkar 1974: 328).

The only step Ambedkar himself took to give to Buddhism an institutional base was the founding of the *Buddhist Society of India* in 1955 with its head-office in Bombay. This maintains only loose ties with its local branches and gives little by way of directions (Zelliot 1992: 228f). Of course Ambedkar, already very ill on the day of his *dīkṣā* (14. Oct. 1956), had no time to pursue organizational work, but I think it fits very well with his conception of religion and its social significance not to have an élite body of spiritual virtuosi. In any case, he also lacked the decisive prerequisites for creating a *sangha*. Within his larger *jāti*, the Mahars, renunciation or celibate scholarship and piety had no tradition (Zelliot 1992: 246). And then there was the lack of resources. Buddhist missionary activities would have had to be financed from other sources. He himself had hoped that Buddhists from other Asian countries would step in (1970: 17).

Although over the years a number of *bhikkhus* have been visiting the new Buddhists, especially in Maharashtra—*bhikkhus* who hail from various backgrounds and countries (Thai, English, Tibetan *and* Mahar)—the life of the Neo-Buddhist communities for long has basically been a local affair, run by local leaders. Local residents men as well as women, may conduct (daily, mostly weekly) *vandanās* (paying of deference) at the local *vihāra*, hold speeches on Buddhism, or give some training to children, conduct festivals and processions[8] or collective singing, collect money, plan, and build new *vihāra*s (Zelliot 1992: 226f, 229, 244f). The concept of *vihāra* is now being used for meeting places (-*cum*-shrines) and not any more, or at least not primarily, for a residence of Buddhist monks. Many of the *bhikkhus* who first attended to the new Buddhist communities did not manage or attempt to learn any of the languages spoken in the regions, and thus had been in any case restricted in their interactions with them.

While very exceptional for a new, or reinstated, religious movement, the

---

[7]For the text of the vow, see Zelliot (1992: 215).

[8]The main festival days celebrated amongst the Buddhist community are Ambedkar's birth and death (14 April and 6 December respectively), Buddha Jayanti, and the Dhammacakra Pravartan Din, the anniversary of the initial conversion or *dikṣa* ceremony (14 October).

significance of the lay factor and the decentralized structure of this new Indian Buddhism makes it appear very modern: a self-organized, non-hierarchical, participatory, and non-exclusive community. On the other hand, as Eleanor Zelliot suggests, there may be very traditional roots, or at least a traditional model, for this kind of organization without a clear leadership pattern: the bhaktī movement, still vital in Maharashtra. We only need to think of the *vārkarīs*, who also seem to have flourished on dispersed leadership, a shared tradition, and group singing.[9] However, the Buddhists do not have a geographical ceremonial centre, as the *vārkarīs* have Pandharpur, as point of pilgrimage. 'Neo'-Buddhists have only Ambedkar as their focal point (Zelliot 1992: 244f).

But there are signs of stronger 'professionalization' and 'spiritualization' in recent times. The Trailokya Bauddha Mahasangha Sahayaka Gana (TBMSG), founded in 1979, is acting as an institutional disseminator of Buddhist knowledge. It has introduced the practice of meditation among 'Neo'-Buddhists, but it also does educational work and runs health centres and other welfare projects. Originally founded by British Buddhists, with a parent or parallel body, the '(Friends of the) Western Buddhist Order' in Great Britain, it represents a combination of *sangha* and developmental NGO (non-governmental organization). The number of ordinated and affiliated members from within the group of Mahars seems to be slowly increasing. The intention of the TBM is not to be a monastic order in the traditional sense (e.g. no obligation for celibacy). In consonance with Ambedkar, the TBM(SG) wants to avoid a sharp distinction and division between lay members and *bhikkhus*. Forming an institutionally distinct body, it does not cover the whole expanse of 'Neo'-Buddhist communities in Maharashtra, even less so other places in India. Thus, different models of Buddhist practice coexist in Maharashtra today.

A Religion for Society

Buddhism, in the eyes of Ambedkar, carried a strong social message (1974: 159). Ambedkar took to Buddhism to give a new foundation to society. The central term around which all revolves is *dhamma*. This is not the place to discuss the whole spectrum of connotations this term has received in Ambedkar's writings, and even more so in Buddhist literature in general. What I am concerned with is the special role that *dhamma* is given in Ambedkar's attempt to (re-)construct the Buddhist canon. It is his endeavour to translate the individual's search for salvation from suffering into a social, or even sociological, demand, so that it can form a guideline for society.

[9]The same may have been true of the Kabir-panthis, to which Ambedkar's father adhered. [See Chapter 13 above].

On the one hand, Ambedkar does take account of the concern to strive for purity of body, speech, and mind; to control the passions and reach perfection and to strive for *nibbāna* (1974: 160ff and passim). On the other hand he makes this orientation a very this-worldly one. He rejects the idea of a soul, and with this the idea of salvation after death: *nibbāna* in the Buddhist way of Ambedkar means 'happiness of the sentient being in *Samsara* while he is alive' (1974: 164). Buddha's 'main concern', Ambedkar states, 'was to give salvation to man in his life on earth and not to promise it to him in heaven after he is dead' (1970: 14). While *dhamma* does refer to the control of the individual over him- or herself, Ambedkar is very firm in his resolution that '*dhamma* is social'. 'It is fundamentally and essentially so', he adds (1974: 226). Because suffering, the way Ambedkar conceives it, is primarily inflicted upon man by man, *dhamma* is needed to recognize it and 'to remove this suffering from the world' (1974: 83). 'Dhamma is righteousness, which means right relations between man and man in all spheres of life ... one man if he is alone does not need Dhamma. ... But when there are two men living in relation to each other they must find a place for Dhamma whether they like it or not. ... In other words, Society cannot do without Dhamma' (1974: 226). One may take this as a point of departure in the struggle for liberty (1974: 227).

This is a strong claim with regard to the social message of Buddhism, but it is even more so in a theoretical sense. When there is no *dhamma*, no Buddhism, then there is no society; no society at least that allows (fraternal) coexistence. Ambedkar introduces a remarkable perspectival shift into the interpretation of Buddhism. A religion which originates in a critique and questioning of the prevalent attitude in social life, calling upon men to renounce and transcend the world while formulating principles of ethical conduct for those who remain 'in the world', is here being converted into a *prerequisite* essential to secure *the working* of society.[10] *Dhamma* at one and the same time is seen as a moral code—for both the individual's conduct of life and social interaction—*and* as a constitutional necessity for society. 'Morality in Dhamma arises from the direct *necessity* for man to love man' (1974: 231; emphasis mine). One must distinguish between different levels in Ambedkar's argument—his view of the human condition, an individual ethics, and a social code of conduct he advocates—and bring out some of the inherent difficulties and paradoxes, before one can deal with its 'canonized' social status.

The first difficulty concerns the relationship between society and the

---

[10]Taking the traditions of the 'sociology of religion' one can see in this also an opposition between a Weberian and a Durkheimian perspective on the relationship between religion and society.

moral order, and the part of the individual within it. On the one hand, society is to be based on moral principles (an objective); on the other hand, the moral order for society is already, transcendentally, given. Buddha's 'discovery of *dhamma* was the discovery of a preconceived principle of order *and* was the invention of a system of rules to be followed. Thus one can speak of he 'Buddha's *dhamma*', or 'his *dhamma*' (1974: 83, 227 etc.; see also the title of the book). At the same time, Ambedkar makes the objectivist claim that moral order is something determinable; something which can be 'proved' like the 'order in the physical world' (1974: 170); and the opposite claim that it is something to be achieved constantly, that it 'rests on man and on nobody else' (1974: 172). The moral order depends on 'men's' actions: 'The kingdom of righteousness lies on earth and is to be reached by man by righteous conduct.' (1974: 201) Ambedkar here introduces the concept of *kamma*, for 'man's action', and *vipāka*, for its effect (1974: 172). 'The law of *Kamma* has to do only with the question of general moral order. ... It is concerned with the maintenance of the moral order in the universe' (1974: 172, 173).

Ambedkar emphasizes the law-like functioning of *kamma*. At the same time, every person is ethically free to act. There is good (*kusala*) as well as bad (*akusala*) *kamma* (1974: 172). Bad action, or *kamma*, leads to a 'bad' moral order—indeed, men may even decide to give up *dhamma* altogether: 'Society may choose not to have any Dhamma, as an instrument of Government.'[11] Thus, the moral order which was introduced as something given, and therefore universal, has developed into something which is constantly in danger; something one has to work for; something which needs regular re-enactment. This repeats the issue of theodicy, well known to Ambedkar (1974: 171), which denotes a confrontation of ontological and ethical propositions. Ambedkar uses 'moral order' in two different meanings: as a term for a cosmic mechanism, i.e. the mechanics of the working of *kamma*, which allots differential effects to action, and as the idea of righteousness.

But in what sense is this moral order, the *dhamma*, religious? This question indicates a second difficulty which is implied in Ambedkar's argument. To be more specific: is Buddhism, *in principle*, interchangeable with other religions regarding the depiction of the moral order and the selection of moral principles? Or does the desired relationship delineated before, rational

[11]'Society has to choose one of the three alternatives. ... Society may choose not to have any Dhamma, as an instrument of Government. For Dhamma is nothing if it [is] not an instrument of Government. ... This means Society chooses the road to anarchy. ... Secondly, Society may choose the police, i.e. dictatorship as an instrument of Government. ... Thirdly, Society may choose Dhamma plus the Magistrate wherever people fail to observe Dhamma. ... In anarchy and dictatorship liberty is lost. ... Only in the third liberty survives.' (1974: 226f.)

and secular, between moral order, society and individual, pertain only to Buddhism? As a matter of fact, Ambedkar uses 'religion' in two different ways: on the one hand, as a generic term, as is usual in religious and social studies; on the other hand, *in opposition* to *dhamma*. Ambedkar had started, as we have seen, from a comparison of religions. In his earlier article on 'Buddha and the future of his Religion' and also in several instances in his book on the Buddha's teachings, he takes Buddhism as one religion amongst others (1974: 83, 151, 173, etc.), which distinguishes itself 'only', but fundamentally, by the fact that in Buddhism alone morality has attained a pivotal position, occupying a place which other religions reserve for God. 'Morality has been given the place of God', he states (1974: 173). In the central part of *The Buddha and his Dhamma*, on the other hand, he contrasts Buddhism with religion, presenting Buddhism thereby as non-religion. Religion is 'personal',[12] whereas *dhamma* is social. Religion 'is concerned with revealing the beginning of things', *dhamma* is not. 'The purpose of Religion is to explain the origin of the world. The purpose of Dhamma is to reconstruct the world.' (1974: 226, 229, 231) Religion connotes 'belief in God, belief in soul, worship of God, curing of the erring soul, propitiating God by prayers, ceremonies, sacrifices, etc.' (1974: 226).[13] *Dhamma* does not. Morality 'is not the root of religion',[14] while it is the 'essence of Dhamma' (1974: 231). Hinduism especially is without a moral basis; it is a religion of ritual and observances (1970: 5).

Depending on which formula we take, all religions, or all *other* religions besides Buddhism, are deficient. 'In other words, Buddhism is the only religion which the world can have.' (1970: 13). Only the Buddhist *dhamma*, as an ethics of social action, can, according to Ambedkar, bring morality back into society, thus bridging the gap between different, or opposite, spheres of life. Only Buddhism is able to remould society, to give society a new lease of life. Thus, *dhamma* takes the place of religion, but at the same time surpasses, or undercuts, religion: it transposes the moral impetus—the one which is central for Ambedkar—on to another level. What Ambedkar looks for might be called 'elementary' or 'essential' religion: a rediscovery of the minimum

[12]'Religion, it is said, is personal and one must keep it to oneself. One must not let it play its part in public life.' (1974: 226.)

[13]This describes only the final state of religion which does not include Buddhism. Ambedkar, in line with religious studies of his time, assumes an evolution of the idea of (non-*dhammic*) religion through three stages (1974: 225f). As is well known, Émile Durkheim, too, did struggle with the question whether Buddhism, or more precisely Theravada Buddhism, should be included in the generic term religion, because of the atheism of its basic assumptions.

[14]'Every religion preaches morality but morality is not the root of religion. It is a wagon attached to it. It is attached and detached as the occasion requires.' (1974: 231.)

prerequisites or basic requirements of any moral order, of human sociality; a humanistic, universalistic project.

CANONICITY: *LA RELIGION CIVILE* [CIVIL RELIGION]

Buddhism becomes the universal yardstick against which religions are measured. It is in this sense that Buddhism achieves a canonical status with Ambedkar; canonical in respect to all religions. This, however, implies a peculiar contradiction: Ambedkar looks for a universal religion or ethics in the name of Buddhism, i.e. in the name of a particular religion or morality.

In Ambedkar's conception of religion, which ultimately is geared to contemporary society, two perspectives are mixed: *religion as identity; as acceptance of a particular belief system* or distinctive construction of the world (which may give expression to universalist claims); and *religion as the 'elementary' moral basis of all social life* (which voices universal principles like equality, liberty, and solidarity that precede every particular expression). Ambedkar wants to create a religion for his particular community along with a religion for civil society at large.

What Ambedkar relates to in this second aspect is the idea of *religion civile* as it had first been broached by Jean Jacques Rousseau. But Ambedkar also carries with him all the equivocations this concept contains (above and beyond the combination with a particular religious tradition and community). 'Civil religion', as implicitly invoked in Ambedkar's exposition is meant in the sense of a fundamental, reasonable ... principle of 'sociality', which all men have to accept, and not in the narrow sense of collective ideas and sentiments ('national religion'); a 'religion' which integrates a particular social entity, as Durkheim had in mind in certain instances. That is, Ambedkar seems to be looking for a post-religious religion; a religion which transcends religious distinctions, that is, religious and social discrimination;[15] and also a religion which overcomes the cleft between religion and politics, between morality and society. Buddhism is to provide the grounds from which to draw out this general and foundational principle. Ultimately it is in this that we can grasp the meaning Ambedkar gives to the project of making a traditional faith viable or modern times.

This project of a new civil religion shows a distinctive resemblance to, but also a significant difference from, Dewey's ideas. Ambedkar shared impulses with Dewey, if he did not receive them from him, but Dewey took another route from the common proposition and drew a different conclusion. He was heading for a different and even greater impasse. It is worthwhile to

---

[15]'Buddhism is the only real religion and those who do not accept this *must revise their definition of religion*' (1974: 329; emphasis mine).

briefly compare the two ventures, for this will shed new light on Ambedkar's vision and bring Ambedkar's endeavour into clearer profile.

Dewey pursues the idea of a 'secular religion' or 'sacralization of democracy'. Dewey considers modern secularization not as symptom of moral and cultural decay but as a change of the form of religion. Religion is being liberated from dogmatic doctrines and restrictive institutional patterns (as found in the established religions). Dewey wants to get to, and work out, the implicit rational core of all religious attitudes: to make explicit what he calls 'the common faith of mankind' (Dewey 1962: 87). He thus attempts to cling to the power of ideals and values, generated by the imagination, while speaking against belief in supernatural powers from which the pursuance of ideas and values is to be separated. Already in his earlier writings Dewey had pleaded for the sacralization of democracy, of everyday communication, and of interaction with nature (i.e. of science), and thus for the surpassing of Christianity. The new, secular form of religion would no longer detach ideals and values from reality, thus impoverishing the everyday and distracting attention from intersubjective relationships, as had happened in the old religions. Instead, it would acknowledge what might be termed immanent self-transcendence: the dimension of the imaginary, the human faculty of imagination ... as the site of the religious, and place it within social (and physical) experience. In the eyes of Dewey, religion, the definition of values and ideas and the striving for an integral existence, refers to an *ongoing creative process of idealization of contingent possibilities*. For Dewey it is decisive to see this common core of religion and this process as an intersubjective and interactive one, and it is the experience of communication which becomes central, not only in an instrumental sense. Democracy as an institutionalized 'way of living together' signifies the highest ideal.

For Dewey, this reinterpretation of human experience and action marks the final release of the true religious impulses. But what is missing in Dewey is the interpretation of concrete religiosity. Dewey wants to be religious without following any particular religion. He heads for ... 'an empty universalism'. Thus, Dewey's sacralization of democracy ends in a paradox different from Ambedkar's. While Ambedkar attempted to reinstitute a specific, albeit universalist, religion or ethics as a foundation for society and social relationship in general, Dewey refrained from connecting his concept with any particular religion. He replaced the supernatural symbolism and language which had allowed believers to express themselves and their religious aspirations by an abstract ethics, de-culturalized and de-socialized; a dissociated religion. Against this, Ambedkar's endeavour, itself paradoxical, seems more considered, expressing a genuine (sociological) difficulty.

A general religion of or for society, a common social value base—a 'civil religion'—must be compelling for everyone, but it also has to first gain assent.

The rationalist notion of establishing consent through submission to reason, free of constraints, is not able to cope with this dilemma. Besides, such an endeavour, which opts for a re-entwinement of religion and politics, is indissolubly caught in the dilemma that religion and politics constitute different spheres and follow different inner logics; above all, in modern society. Ambedkar himself did acknowledge that religion and politics operate on different lines and only partly intersect, but he obviously did not apply this observation to *dhamma* or civil religion. He also acknowledged this differentiation in his practical and strategic actions. ...

Dewey's and Ambedkar's options taken together indicate the spectrum of alternatives, and of aporias, of public religion in a modern context; of a foundational ethics for a democratic, 'civil' society.

POSSIBILITIES AND PRAGMATICS: SITUATIONAL CREATIVITY

It is not clear from the text of *The Buddha and his Dhamma* to what extent Ambedkar recognized the dilemma inherent in any attempt to create and institute a 'civil religion'; inherent, for one, in the plea for re-entwinement of politics and religion, but as well in the merging of a particular religious tradition and the idea of a general civil religion. Perhaps it was just the simultaneous search for a community religion of self-respect which made it difficult to realize the dilemma. But it is important to stress that Ambedkar was not a mere utopian, drifting away from social reality and venturing a prefabricated model for society. He was well aware, or became aware in the battles he fought, of the contingency and limitations of institutions and the long way he and the Dalits had to go to overcome these difficulties.

Ambedkar operated on two levels. While bringing out his vision of what I called 'civil religion', wrapped into the terminology of a particular religious tradition, he sounds very rigorous and principled, but abstract. However, the way he operated in the public field appeared different. It seems that in his political action he took Buddhism, or Buddhist civil religion, as a kind of counterfactual foil which was to serve as a referential frame for himself and for his followers. This becomes understandable if, by way of trial, one links it with the pragmatist influences he had been exposed to. On closer inspection, this finds unexpected corroboration in his interpretation of Buddhism.

Ideals are conceded a particular social power by Ambedkar for the struggles he fought. Ideals reveal ... the possibilities which show up in reality 'the hard stuff of the world of physical and social experience', and they show the directions in which action was to be taken. They are thus related to the contingencies of a situation. This way of functioning builds on, and helps to develop and further, the faculty of distanciation and self-distanciation: A 'new vision emerges through seeing ... old things in new relations serving a new end which the new end aids in creating (Dewey 1962: 49).

Ambedkar's distance towards social arrangements showed in his practical actions. He was always prepared, or had to inevitably learn, to modify modes of procedure and alter the institutions he had himself created. He tried out several ways of organizing social change, switching when he realized that a scheme did not suit his ends or that he did not get the expected response. Think only of his strategic shifts between class-oriented and caste- or *varna*-oriented political organizations (Independent Labour Party, Scheduled Castes Federation, Republican Party of India). He had always been aware of the overdetermined situation of those at the bottom of society which gave little space for manoeuvre but made it all the more necessary to broaden this space in every possible way. He always related to circumstances; to the conditions of a situation. Ambedkar developed and kept the ability to transcend institutions by moving to a deeper level of sociality. Following a broad (moral) idea, he acknowledged that he was implicated in interactive relations: it is thus a notion of *situational creativity* à la Dewey.

In Buddhism, Ambedkar found this corroborated, or read it into Buddhism. I distinguish three steps in his argument in this respect. He starts with what he calls 'the doctrine of impermanence'. Society keeps changing just as the individual human being 'is always changing, always growing'. Ambedkar disputes any 'permanent and fixed system of classification of men', as written into the *varna* scheme. On the side of the individual, he sees the relative position of the *gunas* in continuous need of rebalancing and tuning. A human being 'is not the same at two different moments of his life'. It is the composite character of beings and things which make them ever-changing (1970: 10, 1974: 169).

'Being is becoming;' Ambedkar depicts this Buddhist notion with a phrase in which the European dialectical tradition resounds (1974: 169). Thus, questioning traditional concepts of identity opens up space for development. This is the second step I want to distinguish. Ambedkar refuses interpretations of the Buddhist notion of *śūnya* or *śūnyatā* (Pali: *sunnata*) as 'nihilism'. Instead, he emphasizes what we would today call the 'emergent side of things'. 'Very few realize that it is on account of *Sunnyata* that everything becomes possible; without it nothing in the world would be possible. It is on the impermanence of the nature of all things that the possibility of all other things depends.' (1974: 170). A two-pronged moral frame, and this is the third step, can be drawn out from the theory of impermanence: on the one hand, detachment from what is contingent: detachment from property, from friends, etc.; on the other, if not hope, then at least non-pessimism; the possibility for improvement of worldly relationships, and thus a certain 'activist', or pragmatist tinge (1970: 10; 1974: 170, cf. 78, 90).

Ambedkar gives Buddhism an anti-essentialist reading which parallels pragmatism. Ambedkar's thought and pragmatism share basic assumptions: the emphasis on potentiality; on non-manifest possibilities which inhere in things and social relations, and which may come to constitute a social force. It is the power of distanciation, of the (social) imaginary, which allows [one] to discern the possibilities open at a time.

THIRD IDIOM: TRANSLATING AND TRANSCENDING PARTICULAR EXPERIENCES

It is the admixture of identity religion to civil religion, and the principled dilemma of civil religion, as indicated above, which makes for the problematics of Ambedkar's endeavour in the last instance. But in addition to this, on a more pragmatic level, it is the difficulty in transcending the opposition between Hinduism, as a self-proclaimed entity, and Dalit (ness), between two ways of expression, two languages, which threatens to frustrate Ambedkar's cause.

Buddhism in India today has a limited range. Ambedkarite Buddhism particularly is treated as a sect; a young and deviant branch of 'real' Buddhism and the religion of mainly one *jāti*, the Mahars.[16] It has become a communalized affair, and, in the eyes of many, a replication of casteist thinking. We can now see more clearly the difficulties and aporias inherent in the project itself, besides the resistance of the larger society which was not able, or was unwilling, to distinguish between the idiosyncratic religious form (of Buddhism) and the general, 'civil' message and which also in large degree was, and is, not prepared to accept Ambedkar as a 'national' leader.

We find already in Ambedkar signs of wavering in the universalist drive. Not fully accepted or acceptable as moral authority, and fighting for the cause of those most oppressed socially, culturally, and economically in Indian society, he could not but first of all address himself to what is taken as his 'natural constituency'. He himself largely refrained from and even opposed the prevalent racist ideas about the different origins of 'Untouchables' and 'Touchables', which declared the Untouchables or Dalits the original, non- and pre-Aryan, inhabitants of India. However, in an attempt to invent a past and a tradition for his people, he also played with an ethnic notion and fleetingly, in his last public speech on the day after the *dīkṣā* or 'conversion' ceremony in Nagpur, voiced the supposition that the Untouchables are the descendants of the ancient 'Nagas' of the Buddhist days who had been considered as enemies by the 'Aryans' and had been 'suppressed and oppressed' by them (Ambedkar 1993: 75). Even while rejecting the idea of

[16]D.C. Ahir, as reported in Kantowsky (1997), distinguishes five groups of Buddhists in contemporary India: 'survivals of the Buddhist period' (in Ladakh, Himachal Pradesh, the North-east, plus the Baruas of Bengal); 'ethnic overlaps' from Nepal and Burma especially; those attracted to Buddhism as result of the missionary activities of the Mahabodhi society; the followers of Ambedkar; and the Tibetan refugees of 1959 and after.

an Aryan and a non-Aryan race, M.S. Gore argues, Ambedkar still accepted the idea of a distinct Aryan culture 'dominated by the ritual of sacrifices, characterized by warfare, regional expansion and subjugation as well as the absorption of conquered peoples.' (Gore 1993: 240). This meant that he too pursued a divisive strategy in some of his statements and actions—difficult to avoid anyhow under the prevailing circumstances. In this he is part of, and has reinforced, a strong tendency of contemporary Indian socio-political reality. The developments in independent India have further deepened the chasm between the large, newly-defined social categories and imagined communities.

Still, Ambedkar's endeavour to break out of this vicious circle was the most forceful of all Dalit endeavours in his days in India. Other Dalit or 'Untouchable' groups too pursued the idea of a universal (ist) religion and an equitable social order. They founded new religious movements to cut themselves off from Hinduism in its hegemonic forms, while still building on Hinduistic, i.e. in many cases *bhakti*, traditions—the SNDP (Sri Narayana Dharma Pariplana) in Kerala or the Satnamipanth in Chattisgarh, or the Ad Dharm in Punjab—which built upon the veneration of *sant* Raidas. The aspect of group identity remained in the foreground in all these cases. Or some others joined, or let themselves be brought into the fold of, alternative universal religions; Islam and Christianity were the foremost options. Ambedkar, on the other hand, while clear about his anti-Hindu position, did not let any 'Hindu' notions creep into the articulation of a new vision. He chose, or rather revived, a universal religion which was not only 'of Indian origin', but, being defunct in the main part of India at that time, was also not controlled by an established body of religious experts and ritual functionaries. The choice of Buddhism, while being one of the universalist 'world religions', allowed Ambedkar and the Dalits to lead themselves; to go ahead without the consent or approval of others, the leaders of the more established religious communities, and to determine the outline of the moral order themselves.[17]

Ambedkar was not content with reconstructing a specific Dalit tradition or counter-tradition, a 'subaltern' tradition, standing out against the hege-monic mainstream. He rather tried to bridge this distance and transcend parochialism. Buddhism, in the guise of civil religion, for Ambedkar served as a 'third idiom' in the Dalit struggle for recognition, i.e. as a mode of trans-lation that tries to introduce an idiom which transcends the limitations of two conflicting positions, discourses, or frames of reference; in this case between a hierarchical idiom, which makes ontological distinctions between categories of people, and a counter-discourse, which rejects ontological discriminations. This can serve as a strategy to overcome a confrontational

[17]Herein lies one reason for the current conflict between more 'political' and more 'religious' followers of Ambedkarite Buddhism in Maharashtra.

deadlock, or lack of understanding, by changing the level or idiom of communication. It means rewriting, recasting, transcribing in the full sense of
the term not only one's ideas and one's language but *also the boundaries* which
divide, or seem to divide, two opponents. The one who tries to translate his
or her concerns and perspectives has to relativize and transcend his/her own
traditions and language, his or her own frame of reference, as she/he has to
relativize that of the opponent and transform it into the third idiom.

Ambedkar translated the specific experiences of oppression and
marginalization, of the disrespect and stigmatization the Untouchables have
had to undergo, into a language and a social imaginary which others would,
or should, comprehend: into a universalist ethics and a project of social
reconstruction and self-organization which it is not easy to dismiss on
intellectual and moral grounds. Understood thus, it is not very meaningful
to argue about the 'authenticity' of Ambedkar's interpretation of Buddhism
and the sources of his construction, or whether he had engaged with 'Western'
readings of the Buddhist message.

To transcend one's own traditions and mode of expression is difficult
enough, but the whole endeavour requires something even more difficult
at the other end. To be really successful the translation (into a third idiom)
would have to happen on both sides. The position *against* which one is fighting tends to obstruct the endeavour to develop a reciprocal understanding.
The problem is to establish a third idiom *as that* level of discourse to which
both sides, and others as well, may link.

Besides, the danger in this switch to a third idiom (the level of civil
religion) is, of course, that it gets disconnected from the everyday struggle
for survival of the non-intellectual, non-middle class Dalits. Ambedkar's
third idiom transcends the restrictions of instituted coordinates; opens up
an imaginary space. But this kind of translation also serves to transpose the
Dalit struggle. It lies in the nature of transposition that not only are issues
phrased differently from how they are experienced in the original context;
many experiential dimensions are also marked off and excluded by this kind
of translation: they cannot be expressed in the detached language which
Ambedkar's third, mediating idiom has to offer.

Does this mean that the switch to a religious discourse and the choice
of Buddhism displaces the 'real' issues with which Dalits and Ex-Untouchables
are faced today? Does the switch to general (ist) principles of civil religion
overlook the specificity of the Dalit cause? And does the pragmatist approach,
the idea of social possibilities and imaginations, still offer the hope of
coming to grips with the situation of Dalits when Hindu nationalist forces
seem to want Dalit integration into a reformulated, empowered Hinduism,
whereby they may identify with their opponents?

On the pragmatic–political level as well as at the level of principle,

Ambedkar's quest can be seen, and should be discussed much more thoroughly, as a paradigmatic attempt to make cultural traditions meaningful for the modern would and its central problems, through reappropriation and reinterpretation. His effort seems equally a paradigmatic example of the aporia this creates, of the dilemmas into which the attempt runs.

REFERENCES

Ambedkar, Bhimrao Ramji.
[1950] 1970 *Buddha and the future of his religion.* Jullundur (Punjab): Bheem Patrika Publications.
[1957] 1974 *The Buddha and his Dhamma.* Bombay: Siddharth Publication.
[1936] 1989 Annihilation of caste with a reply to Mahatma Gandhi. *In* Vasant Moon, comp., *Dr Babasaheb Ambedkar: Writings and speeches.* Bombay: Education Department, Government of Maharashtra.
[1956] 1993 The great conversion. In Varinder Grover, ed., *B.R. Ambedkar,* New Delhi: Deep & Deep.
Dewey, John.
[1934] 1962 *A common faith.* New Haven: Yale University Press.
Gore, M.S.
1993 *The social context of an ideology: Ambedkar's political and social thought.* New Delhi: Sage.
Kantowsky, Detlef.
1997 Buddhisten in Indien heute: Ein Literaturbericht insbesondere über die Neo-Buddhisten. In *Bauddha Vidyasudhakarah: Studies in Honour of Heinz Bechert on the Occasion of His 65th Birthday,* ed. Petra Kieffer-Pülz and Jens-Uwe Hartmann, Swisttal-Odendorf: Indica et Tibetica Verlag.
Omvedt, Gail.
1994 *Dalits and the democratic revolution: Dr Ambedkar and the Dalit movement in colonial India.* New Delhi: Sage.
Shourie, Arun.
1997 *Worshipping false gods: Ambedkar, and the facts which have been erased.* New Delhi: ASA.
Sponberg, Alan.
1996 TBMSG: A Dhamma revolution in contemporary India. *In* Christopher S. Queen and Sallie B. King, *Engaged Buddhism. Buddhist Liberation Movements in Asia,* ed. Albany: State University of New York Press. Pp. 73–120.
Zelliot, Eleanor.
1986 The social and political thought of B.R. Ambedkar. *In* Thomas Pantham and Kenneth L. Deutsch, eds., *Political thought in modern India,* New Delhi: Sage. Pp. 161–75.
1992 *From Untouchable to Dalit: Essays on the Ambedkar movement.* New Delhi: Manohar.

Intertwinements: Religion, Society, and Politics

PREFATORY REMARKS

The previous five parts of this book of readings have dealt with a set of selected and interrelated themes concerning the religious life of Indians. In Part Five, the interconnectedness of the sacred and the secular, for example in the context of religious movements, was illustrated. We have seen that the notion of the sacred as a world apart, with which the religious person attempts to bond in various ways (for example through ritual, piety, devotion, sacrifice, or magic) does not imply the insignificance of the secular domain. In this concluding part we explore further the patterns of interconnectedness of religious institutions (such as a Hindu temple, Christian church, or Muslim shrine), social structure, and politics.

The perspective is not ideological (implying the holism of the religious point of view) but empirical (focusing on the situation on the ground). To put it differently, the approach adopted here is systemic: social reality is seen to comprise different, interrelated, or overlapping, subsystems, such that one is not reducible to any one of the others (reductionism) or, conversely, the foundation or cause of the others (determinism). Religion does not exist sui generis, prior to society, but is socially constructed. Nor does it stand opposed to politics; religious ideas have been employed widely and at all times to legitimize the privileges of the wielders of power; more so in traditional than in modern, secularizing societies. The Brahmanical notion of *karma* is a very familiar example. Religion has also been in some cases of recent times a crucial resource in the armoury of those who have successfully challenged the prevailing social and power structures. The Christian inspiration of the Civil Rights Movement in the USA under the leadership of Martin Luther King, and the decisive role of the Catholic Church in the overthrow of the communist regime in Poland, have been widely acknowledged.

The first essay in this part addresses directly the question of the nature of the interrelatedness of religion, society, and institutionalized authority. The authors, Arjun Appadurai and Carol Breckenridge, look upon the south Indian temple as a well-defined sacred space in which different aspects of society are uniquely synthesized in cultural and structural terms. At the centre of the temple, conceived as an iconographic, economic, and moral complex, stands the deity as the paradigmatic sovereign. It is from him that the royal power of human beings is derived. As such, the temple is a significant institution in the redistribution of ritual, symbolic, and economic benefits in society. A major source of the economic assets consists of the gifts and endowments that the devotees bestow upon the temple. An elaborate organizational framework is in place to operationalize the redistributive process. In short, the social importance of the temple flows from the many functions and ordered meanings that are associated with it.

What is true of the Hindu temple in Tamil Nadu is also true of the Catholic Church in Goa. This comes out clearly in Rowena Robinson's discussion of how the church articulates and maintains the local systems of power and hierarchy within a village community. What makes the Goan case particularly interesting is the manner in which inequalities of social status characteristic of the caste-based Hindu social order are reproduced in Christian society but not without contestation. Robinson's focus is on the privileges in church ritual held by the élite of the village studied by her. She then discusses the healing practices and beliefs of Catholics descended from Hindu lower caste groups. This is a context in which there is actual give-and-take between the two religious communities. We have, on the one hand, temporal and spatial continuities, and on the other, stress and conflict between the communities and among the Christians. Such a situation, as we will see, is a fertile ground for new socio–religious movements.

The intertwining of socio–religious and political lives of Kashmiri Muslims is the theme of the third essay by Muhammad Ishaq Khan. His data are drawn from a study of the famous holy shrine at Hazratbal (on the outskirts of the capital city of Srinagar) where a holy relic (a stand of hair) of Prophet Muhammad is venerated by the devout on two auspicious days every year. Khan describes the arrival of the relic in Kashmir and the manner of its veneration, which sets Kashmiri Muslims apart from orthodox Muslim communities elsewhere. As in the case of Goan Christians, so too among Kashmiri Muslims, pre-conversion Hindu cultural practices have not been altogether abandoned. Indeed they are an important and cherished element of Kashmiri Muslim identity.

Veneration, whatever its form, has many uses. It is, needless to emphasize, undertaken first and foremost for the experience of spiritual upliftment. Secular favours too are sought, be these personal (e.g. good health and longevity) or collective (e.g. protection from floods and famines). The pilgrims, who come to Hazratbal from all over the Kashmir valley, also use the occasion for minor economic gains. In the 1930s, the shrine emerged as a centre of political activity.

Sheikh Abdullah, the leader of a new political awakening, adopted a secular stance tempered by an explicit use of religious symbols for mobilizing support. The weekly Friday prayers at Hazratbal became the occasion for the Sheikh's stirring political speeches. So successful was this marriage of religion and politics that the theft of the holy relic in 1963 precipitated a major, unprecedented political crisis. Khan discusses at length the significance of the event and suggests that the phenomenon of Hazratbal is meaningful in more than local terms.

The three essays (by Appadurai and Breckenridge, Robinson, and Khan) together illustrate some of the ways in which religion, society, and politics form a complex whole in history and in contemporary times. Those who talk about the privatization of religion, to reserve the public arena for the play of economic and political forces, perhaps overestimate the scope of the processes of secularization. The 1960s, it has been said, were the Indian summer of the secularization thesis. The last quarter of the twentieth century was witness to the reassertion of the forces of religion in public spaces: in some places with welcome consequences and in others in the opposite ways (see Casanova 1994). Either way, it has become apparent that historians and social scientists must take religion seriously as a subject of study.

REFERENCE

Casanova, José.
1994 *Public religions in the modern world.* Chicago: University of Chicago Press.

The South Indian Temple: Authority, Honour, and Redistribution

ARJUN APPADURAI, CAROL APPADURAI BRECKENRIDGE

INTRODUCTION

This essay is an effort to present, in schematic form, a systematic framework within which to understand the cultural principles that underlie the workings of the south Indian Hindu temple.[1] Thus, it does not contain elaborate ethnographic details, cannot discuss many important historical issues, and does not seek or claim to exhaust theological understandings of the divine. Rather, the framework represented here is meant to be generative and suggestive in two senses: firstly, as a fresh perspective from which to view the large body of data that is already available in a host

Excerpted from Carol Appadurai Breckenridge and Arjun Appadurai's article bearing the same title. *Contributions to Indian sociology* 10, 2 (1976): 187: 211. © Institute of Economic Growth, Delhi.

[1] By south India is meant that portion of the Indian peninsula which was the territorial base of the Vijayanagara Empire (c. 1350–1550), and which would today encompass the modern states of Karnataka, Andhra Pradesh, and Tamil Nāṭu: as for the region now covered by the state of Kerala, not enough is known, from our point of view, of the temples in this ecologically and politically distinct region to be certain that our framework might be relevant there as well. After considerable reflection, we have decided not to give any overall definition of the kind, or type, or scale of 'temple' that we believe is comprehensible within the framework we propose. We are confident, however, on the basis of the available literature ... that our model is not relevant only to large Brahminical temple complexes, but seems also to fit 'village' temples, goddess temples, lineage temples, and the like. At the very margin the uncertain cases would be, for example, family shrines and ancestor shrines (*samādhi*), where only portions of our model might apply. ...

of monographic studies; and secondly, to generate further investigation of particular issues in order to verify (or correct) the argument presented here.

Our present knowledge of south Indian temples reflects the disparate (and partial) perspectives from which scholars have so far conducted their studies. A considerable body of information concerning temple architecture, (Kramrisch 1946), ritual, and administration is available. Similarly, much is known about temple economics, temple politics, and the sociological aspects of temple clienteles. What is absent, however, is a unified perspective from which to comprehend this abundance of empirical data.

Although it has come to be a truism that the temple is of fundamental importance in south Indian history and society, much of the existing literature, either tacitly or explicitly, encourages the interpretation that the south Indian temple simply reflects its broader social context. Temple ritual appears to be a mixture of Vedic sacrificial procedures and the logic of domestic worship. The division of labour in the *jājmāni* structure of agrarian society appears to inform the division of ceremonial tasks in the temple (Beck 1972: 44–7). The economic underpinnings of the temple have much in common with the ideas of gift and land tenure in other south Indian contexts (Dumont). Historically, the temples has served redistributive and developmental functions that seem co-extensive with those of the political system (Stein 1960: 163–76). Like sectarian networks and urban formations, temples have been reported to provide the links between caste and lineage organization, and regional/territorial segmentation (Beck 1972; Dumont 19: Part III). As in royal courts, the public ritual of the temples provides contexts for the codification or manipulation of the rights and privileges of groups in complementary or competitive relationships with one another (Beck 1972: 79; Barnett 1974: 117–204). Like caste associations, political parties and institutions of higher education, temples have recently provided the institutional context for the social mobilization of both low-ranked caste groups (Galanter 1972: 227–314; Hardgrave 1969: 120–9) and incipient political elites (Baker 1975).

Faced with this wide range of evidence and arguments, is it to be concluded that the south Indian temple is a mere reflection, however distorted, of its broader social context? The argument of this essay is that, looked at in its own terms, the south Indian temple falsifies the tempting 'reflectionist' hypothesis. Although, taken separately, many features of the south Indian temple mimic other institutional aspects of south Indian society, the way in which these features are synthesized in the temple is unique, both in cultural and structural terms. The bulk of this essay is designed to demonstrate precisely the way in which the seemingly disparate aspects of the south Indian temple form a single, coherent whole.

Since an attempt is made here to develop a general and schematic statement about the south Indian temple, it is important to note the primary database on which this model is founded. It reflects an attempt to establish the common features that emerge from two separate, ethno–historical studies conducted in south India:[2] the first is a study of the Śrī Pārthasārathi Svāmi Temple in Triplicane, Madras city, a relatively small temple with links to the Teṉkalai tradition of south Indian Śrī Vaiṣṇavism; the second is a study of the Śrī Mīnākṣi Sundaresvarar Temple in Madurai, a considerably larger complex, with Saivite affiliations, which was the centre of a vast network of agrarian relations, and was intimately linked to the growth of the kingdoms of both the Madurai Paṇḍya and Nāyaka kings. The elaboration of the differences between these two cases has been deliberately eschewed in order to clarify the underlying similarities.

Briefly, the four principles that we believe are central to an understanding of the south Indian temple (and which are dealt with serially in the four substantive sections of this essay) are the following:

(1) That temple ritual makes little sense unless it is viewed as the expression of homage to the reigning deity who is conceived as a sovereign.

(2) That this sovereign figure stands at the centre of a set of moral and economic transactions which constitute, in a specific ethno–sociological sense, a redistributive process.

(3) That temple endowments provide the organizational framework, within which individuals and corporate groups participate in this redistributive process, and acquire distinct and autonomous shares in its ritual and economic benefits.

(4) That conflicts generated by this process, between various such shareholders, are resolved by an outside agency, whose mandate is to 'protect' the temple, thus fulfilling one of the primary requirements for human claims to royal status.

DEITY AS PARADIGMATIC SOVEREIGN

At the moral, economic, and iconographic centre of the south Indian temple is the deity. This deity, however, is not a mere image or symbol. It is conceived to be, in several thoroughly concrete senses, a person. That the deity is both sentient and corporeal is clear from the diverse and elaborate rituals which constitute worship in the temple. Upon installation, the stone figure of the particular deity which is to reside in the temple sanctum sanctorum (Skt.

---

[2]Carol Appadurai Breckenridge conducted fieldwork at the Śrī Mīnākṣi-Sundaresvarar Temple, Madurai (Tamil Nāṭu) between September 1973 and September 1974). Arjun Appadurai conducted fieldwork at the Śrī Pārthasārathi Svāmi Temple, Madras City, from September 1973 to September 1974. See Appadurai 1981.

mūlasthānam; garbha griham) is vivified in a ceremony known as *prāṇa pratiṣṭai*. Literally speaking, the breath (*prāṇa*) of life is infused into the figure to give it sustenance and nurturance as the permanent and immovable centre of the temple (*mūlavar* or *mūla-vigraham*). Thereafter, during daily worship and on calendric festival events, the deity is bathed (*snānām*), anointed (*apisekam*), fed (*naivettiyam*), adorned (*alaṅkāram*), processed, etc. in a complex series of acts collectively known as pūjā [see chap. 7 above]. Still further evidence of the presence of the deity as a person is his or her eligibility for marriage (*tirukkalyāṇam*), capacity of having sexual relations, desire to take holidays, and willingness to engage in conquest, quarrels, or other playful acts (*tiruvilaiyāṭal*). Such behaviour on the part of the deity emerges in temple festivals (Clothey 1969).

This state of vivification is permanent unless the deity is dishonoured (i.e. an inappropriate person touches it, the ritual process is halted due to conflict among the worshippers, etc.) in which case the deity is thought to leave the figure. *Samprōksaṇa* ceremonies are performed to re-invite the deity to reside in the stone figure. Similarly, ceremonies of renewal (*mahāpisekam kumbāpisekam*) are to be performed at regular twelve to twenty-five year intervals during which time the deity leaves the sanctum in a clay pot (*kumbam*) which is placed on a decorated dais in a separate pillared hall (*yāgasaḷai*) especially prepared for the purpose. Repairs necessary to maintain the walled and fortress-like temple structure are performed at this time.

The problem of how a stone figure can be a person has engaged legal and philosophical scholars for almost the last ten centuries (Sontheimer 1964), and has been peculiarly a subject of contention since the advent of the Anglo–Indian legal system in south India which evolved during the nineteenth century. In the Anglo-Indian legal system, the above qualities and capacities of the deity were interpreted to mean that the deity possessed a 'juristic personality' (Bagchi 1933). By extension, in an ideal sense, the deity was considered capable of 'owning property' known as gifts (*tevatāṉam*) which were given to maintain the deity, and its abode, the temple.

This extensive and thorny legal and scholarly literature, which has resulted in the view that the Hindu deity is a juristic personality, has not exhausted the cultural understanding of the Hindu deity who is worshipped in the temple. More specifically, this literature has not taken into account another enduring feature of the popular conception of the Hindu deity in south India, namely, that the deity is seen to be a very special persona. All the ethnographic evidence, particularly linguistic signs, suggests that the deity is conceived to be a sovereign, i.e. one who is first in rank, who commands resources, and who is generous in ensuring prosperity for the kingdom. Both the temple deity and the reigning king, for example, live in a temple palace designated in Tamil as *kōyil*. Both share a rich pool of ritual paraphernalia (i.e. stylus, drum, sceptre, flywisk, umbrella, elephant, etc.) which accompany them during their processional rounds of the kingdom which supports them. Published descriptions of the role of paraphernalia in temple worship as well as in royal ritual, support this analysis (Mahalingam 1967: 65–7). Both are referred to as omnipresent sovereign (Tam. *iraivan*) or universal lord (*svāmi*). Both maintain a supporting retinue which forms a royal court (Tam. *paricanankal*). And finally, the language of service to the deity is in the idiom of bonded servitude (*atimai*).

Still further evidence that the deity is both royal and sovereign is temple ritual which is described by the term pūjā (Tam. *pūcai*: worship, adoration). Of the numerous descriptions of worship in the scholarly literature (Diehl 1956; Viraraghavacharya 1953: 301–54) [see also Davis 1991], the following cameo graphically illustrates the honouring of the deity as a royal sovereign (Krishna Sastri 1916: 3–4):

The ritual followed every day in the temples of Siva and Vishnu may be generally described as *rājōpachāra*, or the paying of royal honours. Thus, in rich temples there will be elephants and camels with their appropriate paraphernalia, the royal umbrellas and *chauris* mounted on gold or silver handles, palanquins and other vehicles, a troupe of dancers and musicians, a host of other temple servants to wash the god, anoint him with sandal or decorate him with flowers, and so on. Crowns and other rich and costly jewellery, set with gems and pearls ... and often presented by Rajas and Chieftains or other rich devotees, are a special pride of the wealthier temples.

The Brāhmana priest is to purify himself by bath and prayers early in the morning, and then open the doors of the sanctum and gently wake up the god, who is supposed to be sleeping, by chanting appropriate hymns in his praise. Then, after duly worshipping the guardian deities, he washes the feet of the chief deity, bathes the image, clothes it properly, decorates it with the usual jewellery, sandal and flowers, waving incense and lamps of diverse pattern ... in front of the god and finally offering him the cooked food or *naivedyam* and the final betel leaf and nut. At stated intervals the god comes out in procession and perhaps sees to the comfort of his attendant deities. Usually there is an important annual festival, representing in some cases the marriage of the god or some other special event in the doings of the god registered in local chronicles or Purānas. On such occasions the procession is carried on different vehicles, both common and special, the latter being such as the *kalpa-vriksha*, the wish-giving celestial tree of the *kāmadhenu*, the wish-giving celestial cow, or the mythic animal *gandabherunda*. The most important procession will generally be the car festival when the god goes round in the huge car through the main streets where his worshippers live and receives worship and offerings at their very homes.

To understand worship more fully, temple ritual may be discussed in terms of pūjā which is daily, festival which is occasional, and Kāmiyam pūjā or *arccanai* which is 'private'. Each involves the offering of gifts which are honours to the deity.

Pūjā or daily worship consists of sixteen rites of adoration (Skt. *sadopacaram, upacaram*) which honour the deity.[3] They are as follows: *āvākaṉam* (invocation), *stāpaṉam* (fixing), *pattiyam* (water for foot-washing), *ācamaṉam* (water for sipping), *arkkiyam* (water for hand-washing), *apisekam* (anointing) or *snānam* (bathing), *vastiram kaṇṭam cāttutal* (Skt. *vastropavita;* dressing or perfuming), *puṣpancāttutal* (offering of flowers), *tūpatīpam camarppittal* (offering of incense and light), *naivettiyam* (offering of food), *pali* (sacrifice), *hōmam* (oblation through fire), *nityōtsavam* (daily festival), *vāttiyam* (music), *narttaṉam* (dance), and *utvācaṉam* (send-off). Of the above sixteen, *apisekam* (anointing) and *naivettiyam* (feeding) form the central rites offering adoration and honour to the deity, and are, therefore, the terms popularly used to refer to worship. [See chap. 4 above.]

Pūjā is regularly performed one to six times daily depending on the size and centrality of the temple (i.e. small village temples may receive donations for only one *pūjā* whereas larger temples situated in cosmopolitan centres may receive donations for the full complement of services dictated by *āgamic* prescriptions). Of the six daily performances, four are obligatory celebrations: morning (*kāla*), noon (*ucci*), sunset (*sāyaṅkālam*), and midnight (*arttayāmam*). Two intermediary ceremonies which occur between the noon performance on auspicious occasions: *upacantikālam* precedes and *peratōsakālam* follows. All ritual in south Indian temples, whether daily, occasional, or calendrical, reflects this basic model of *pūjā* offered to a sovereign deity, although ritual variations are determined by the specific *āgamic* code which governs a particular temple, as well as other local factors. The ritual codes collectively known as the *āgamas* provide the textual core of worship in south Indian temples (Dasgupta 1955: 17–18; 91; 123, 175; Diehl 1956: 43–55).

Festivals, more appropriately translated from the Tamil as royal feasts (*tiruvilā*), and renewal consecrations (*pratiṣta, samprōksaṇa*, etc.) form the second cluster of rituals in the temple (Diehl 1956: 158–80). Their occasional or calendric nature is what unites these celebrations which are the most visible and public occasions at which the deity is honoured. There are two ways in which dates are set for festivals (Martin 1971: 224–25). The first is by reference to one of the fourteen days in the bright or dark half of the moon in a given month, and the second is by reference to *naksattirams* (star-days or lunar asterisms), the twenty-seven named positions that the moon moves through during a month, with a 28th if needed to fill out the month. Tamil months begin on the 14th to the 18th of the months in the Gregorian calendar.

---

[3]Those rites which collectively form the *upacāram* list vary from author to author, and from temple to temple. The list may be increased or reduced according to how inclusive or exclusive the term *pūjā* is intended to be. Some lists include up to twenty-one rites; others double up related activities such as incense and light in order to include music and dance within the sixteen *upacāram* rites. ...

The monthly cycle of festivals consists of the following: new moon, full moon, the two *ekātasi* days (eleventh day after the new and full moons), and the first day of the Tamil month (Māsappiravesam), all presided over by the chief deity. Subsidiary monthly events vary from temple to temple.

The basic and most elaborate paradigm for all temple festivals is the great feast (Skt. *brahmōtsava;* Tam. *peruvilā*) for the sovereign deity of the temple which occupies ten to twenty days in a month determined to be auspicious in the temple calendar, often the month of Cittirai (April–May). A brief description of this feast will provide a graphic overview of all the other festivals in the temple. The elementary units of the great ten-day festival are two processions (morning and evening) on each of the first nine days of the feast, and one evening procession on the tenth day. The central feature of each of these processions is the *utsava-vigraham,* the metal processional form of the deity, which is a considerably smaller version of the main deity housed in the sanctum and known as the *mūlavar.* Numerous other events embedded in the daily ritual precede and follow the two processions (Diehl 1956: 158–80).

While on procession throughout the kingdom, feasting takes place during brief, pre-arranged halts which the royal–divine entourage makes before the homes or businesses of worshippers who wish to make offerings to the deity. Depending on the size and elaborateness of the feast which has been prepared by the donor for he deity, these halts are known as either *tirukkaṇs* (small and very brief halts in temporarily constructed thatched *pantals*) or *maṇṭapappaṭis* (more elaborate halts during which the deity 'graciously abides' in a stone pillared hall (*maṇṭapam*) where it is fed and entertained).

A third and final category of offerings made by worshippers to the sovereign deity is known as *kāmiyam* pūjā or *arccaṇai.* Since these offerings are occasioned by the needs of private persons, this is known as private worship, and is intended to be for the benefit of the donor alone and not for the benefit of the cosmos. *Arccaṇai* offerings consist of select *upacāram* items, such as flowers, fruits, incense, and saffron, which are presented to the presiding deity while its names and titles are being recited, either one hundred and eight, or one thousand and eight times. *Arccaṇai* gifts may be occasioned by a crisis (illness, court case, sterility, poverty, etc.), a change in status (marriage, parenthood, studenthood, etc.), or gratitude for the intervention of the deity in previous situations (Diehl 1956: 235–6).

If the deity is a royal sovereign, it might be asked, over what does this sovereign exercise rule? The most conspicuous answer to this question is, the Hindu temple. But what is the temple? Spatially speaking, the temple consists of dark corridors (*prakārams*) around which the worshipper must circumambulate in order to reach the womb-like sanctum of spacious pillared halls (*maṇṭapams*), and of numerous subsidiary shrines which house the divine retinue who serve to form a panoply of supporting deities (*parivāram*). But, the temple is appropriately the place where the deity resides. It does not satisfy the question of over what does the deity rule? It might be argued that the deity is a sovereign ruler, not so much of a domain, as of a *process*; a redistributive process. In what does this process consist?

At one normative level, the deity, however paradigmatically and however provisionally, commands resources (i.e. services and goods) such as those which are necessary and appropriate for the support and materialization of the ritual process described above. But these resources are not merely authoritatively commanded and received by the deity. On receipt, they are redistributed in the form of shares (*paṅku*) to the royal courtiers, the donor (*yajamāna*), and worshippers at large. The authority to command and redistribute resources places the deity at the centre of a transactional nexus in which the deity is expected to be generous. Ritual which constitutes worship provides the schematic and elementary unit in which to observe the transactional network where first the deity and subsequently the donor are the object of gifting activity.

WORSHIP, REDISTRIBUTION, AND HONOUR

From one point of view, temple-worship in south India based on the pūjā model reflects an extremely complex process of religious evolution in India, starting from the Vedic sacrificial system, complicated by the developments of the Purāṇic or Hinduistic period, and increasingly embellished with Tāntric elements (Gonda 1970: 85). In both lexical and structural terms, pūjā retains key elements of the Vedic sacrifice (Gonda ibid.: 62–86; Kane 1974; 705–40). However, in trying to understand the essential structural contrast between the Vedic sacrifice and temple-worship, it is useful to consider the contrast, in the language of economic anthropology, between 'reciprocity' and 'redistribution' as types of economic transaction. Marshall Sahlins has argued that the basis of this contrast is the difference between a transaction in which a centre independent of the transactors plays a key role, and one in which this is not the case (1972: 188):

True, pooling [i.e. redistribution] and reciprocity may occur in the same social contexts—the same close kinsmen that pool their resources in household commensality, for instance, also as individuals share things with one another—but the precise social relations of pooling and reciprocity are not the same. Pooling is socially a *within* relation, the collective action of a group. Reciprocity is a *between* relation, the action and reaction of two parties.

This view of reciprocity corresponds closely with the classic analysis of Hubert and Mauss, who suggest that all religious sacrifice has a contractual element, in which men and gods exchange their services and 'each gets his due' (1964: 100). There is no doubt that this reciprocal, contractual model of exchange informs some aspects of temple-worship in south India. But of greater importance in the south Indian temple is the 'redistributive' model of economic relationships (Stein 1960; Spencer 1968). In a wide range of societies, however, redistribution is not simply a matter of pooling resources around an arbitrary centre. Synthesizing a number of previous formulations concerning redistribution, Sahlins has demonstrated the widespread association of political chieftainship with this kind of socio–economic system (1972: 189):

Rights of call on the produce of the underlying population, as well as obligations of generosity, are everywhere associated with chieftainship. The organized exercise of these rights and obligations is redistribution. ...

This 'chiefly' model of redistribution fits the deity of a south Indian temple perfectly. This sharpens the seeming paradox that the chiefly slot is here filled by a deified stone image, which stands at the centre of the temple as a set of moral and economic transaction. This paradox becomes muted, however, when we recall that the deity is strictly and literally conceived as a sovereign person. In what cultural terms is this 'redistributive' situation conceived and organized?

The gift which places the donor in an active transactional relationship with the deity, initiates a process of redistribution (*viṇiyōkam*) of a part of the offerings to all those involved in the ritual process: the donor himself, the staff of the temple (*paricanaṅkaḷ*; courtiers), and the worshippers (*cevārtikaḷ*). This is true in the two main forms of worship, pūjā (daily worship) and *utsavam* (festival/processional worship), but in the third form of worship, *arccaṇai*, which fits better the 'reciprocal' model, there is no real allocation of shares for either the worshippers or the staff: the offering is simply transvalued by being offered to the deity and returned to the worshipper. But, in the case of pūjā and *utsavam*, in which the offering of edible food (cooked and uncooked) to the deity is central, shares in the leavings of the deity accrue to all three categories of participants. The largest garland (*mālai*) worn by the deity during a specified ritual period, and in some cases the silk vestments of the deity (*parivaṭṭam*) are bestowed on the donor, who is also given a share of the leftover food of the deity (*prasātam*) and priority in drinking the water (*tīrttam*) sanctified by contact with the deity's ablutions or meals. Similarly, the staff/courtiers to the deity receive a part (*svatantiram*) of the leavings, generally the food leavings, of the deity. Lastly, the worshippers receive a share in the sacred water and holy food left over from feeding the deity.

This basic apportionment is subject to variation, depending on the particular temple, the particular ritual event, the scale of the celebration, and the largesse of the donor. Although much of the prescription of these shares comes to be customary in particular temples, the role of the donor in initiating the transaction and overseeing the redistribution is, in principle, pivotal. Thus the donor is referred to as *yajamāna* (the Vedic term for the sacrificer) and, in Vaiṣṇava temples, at any rate, the share of worshippers is ascribed to the goodwill of the donor, by the term *iṣṭa viṇiyōkam* (the desired redistribution), particularly in processional festivals.

These redistributed leavings of the deity are known as 'honours' (*mariyātai*),[4] and they are subject to variation and fluidity both in their content as well as in their recipients. Recognized sectarian leaders and political figures are often given some prominent combination of these 'honours'. In Vaiṣṇava temples, an important 'honour' is the placing of the Śrī Saṭakōpan (a gold crown, symbolizing the feet of Viṣṇu) on the heads of worshippers at the conclusion of pūjā and in the course of processionals. Given the public nature of these redistributive acts, the order in which they are distributed amongst a set of individuals is often as important as their content. Finally, particular days are allocated in the temple calendar, during which particular members of the temple-staff, such as the priest, are especially honoured.

But these honours are not simply denotative emblems of culturally privileged roles in relationship to the deity. That is, the receipt of specific honours, in any given context, renders authoritative the individual's share (*paṅku*) in the temple conceived as a redistributive process. Such a share would be composed of: the right to offer service (*kaiṅkaryam*) to the deity, either through endowment or through prescribed ritual function; the right to move the resources allocated for the specific ritual event; the right to command the relevant persons involved in the actualization of the given ritual; the right to perform some single part of a complex ritual event; and, finally, the right to worship the deity, by simply witnessing the ritual. Depending on whether one was a donor, a temple-servant, or a worshipper, and depending on the particular ritual event in question, one's share in the ritual process would have a different concrete content. But the sum total of one's rights, over time, would constitute one's share in the ritual and redistributive process of the temple.

This share is given public expression and authoritative constitution by

---

[4]This term is derived from the Sanskrit word *maryada*, which means literally 'limit' or 'boundary', and in various north Indian languages, as well as common parlance in the south, has acquired the more general meaning of 'propriety', 'respect', 'deference', 'honour'. However, in the context of south Indian temples, the term *mariyātai* has acquired a more specific and generic meaning, whereby it denotes a whole series of objects, actions, and transactions, linking the deity with its servants, worshippers, and protectors, whose substance, order, and context provides a public code for the demarcation of status. ...

some combination of the finite set of substances transvalued by association with the deity, which are referred to as 'honours'. This powerful function of 'honours' in the redistributive process of the temple, as well as the actual mechanics of redistribution in this cultural context, can be seen very graphically in the following letter of complaint to the trustees of the Śrī Pārthasārathi Svāmi Temple from the agent of a group of donors, protesting the misappropriation by some temple-servants of a share of the sacred food (*prasātam*) generated by their endowment:

Respected Sirs:

The third day festival of Rapaththu[5] is being conducted through our family by the Reserve Bank of India, Issue Department, Madras, for the last about four decades. On 23-12-1958, 10 Dosais [rice pancakes], 10 Vadais [rice and lentil fritters] and 10 Laddus [sweetmeats] were given out for distribution in the Thiruvaymozhi Goshti [Public]. Out of that, 2 and 3/4 of each item was given as Swathantram[6] according to rules. The balance of 7 and 1/4 of each items was intended for distribution among the devotees present, according to the well-established usage prevalent in this Temple. Out of this above portion, which are purely intended for distribution [i.e. 7 and 1/4 of each item], 2 Dosais, 2 Vadais and 2 Laddus were stolen openly and kept separately by the Temple Staff. This was brought to the notice of the Amin, but he has refused to take notice. It is pointed out that an ubayakar has every right to see his intention of distribution is properly fulfilled and the trustees are equally responsible to see that Prasadams are utilized for the purposes for which they are intended. ...

The concern of this particular agent of a donor for the proper redistribution of the honours generated, in the form of sacred food, by his endowment, is not unusual or peculiar. Temple servants also can, and do, enter into conflict over honours, as the following example, taken from the Sri Mīnākṣi-Sundaresvarar Temple in the first decades of this century, attests. On 17 January 1923, the Temple Superintendent, M.S. Ramaswamy Aiyar, an appointee of the Temple Committee, sent the following petition, asking for police help, to the Inspector of Police, Madurai Town, wherein he requested police assistance during the M.S. temple car processional which included a stop at the prominent Cellatamman temple. In a long-standing set of conflicts which began circa 1915, violence between temple priests (*paṭṭars*) and the mahouts who trained, tended, and rode the lead elephants in temple processionals, was expected to erupt. The petition read:[7]

[5]This festival is the second half of a 2-day celebration that falls in two segments on either side of Vaikuṇṭha Ekādasi, the holiest day of the Śrī Vaiṣṇava calendar.
[6]The customarily prescribed share of the temple-staff in the leavings of the deity.
[7]*Sinnaswami Nayakkar* v. *The Minaksi Sundaresvarar Devastanam*, Original Suit 69 of 1923, District Munsif Court, Madura.

Some disputes having arisen between the elephant mahouts in the distribution of betels, etc., at mantagappadies, the [Court] receiver has ordered on 8-1-23 that the same should be given to both the mahouts. Still some bhatters and one of the mahouts are throwing obstacles and attempting to create disturbances in the distribution of betels today in the Sellathamman Kovil. The honours and the money have as per practice to be given to the adhikara-parapathyam,[8] and disturbed by him to all the servants as per *mamool* [custom and usage]. As some disturbance is anticipated in the absence of police bandobust as reported by the peshkar,[9] I request that police help be given to enable the temple authorities to peacefully conduct the car festival and other functions connected therewith.

These examples suggest the importance which attaches to temple honours, and the connection between honours and other aspects of the rights of those involved in the temple. The issue of conflict in the temple, and its resolution, is taken up in the last section of this essay, 'Protection and Service'. But before that, it is necessary to appreciate that the most general context for the distribution of honours is provided by temple endowments. These endowments represent the organizational means by which donors carve out a share in the redistributive process of the temple, while retaining significant control over the transactions they subsidize. This feature of temple organization is dealt with in the following section.

DECENTRALIZED AUTHORITY AND ENDOWMENTS

Worship offered to a sovereign deity, as has been noted, permits the donor to enter into a transactional relationship with the deity. This transactional relationship, viewed in terms of honours and shares, links deity–donor–temple staff and worshipper in a larger redistributive system. This redistributive process, however, is not monolithic. The donor who supports worship in its multiple forms in a south Indian temple establishes a number of specific, distinct, and enduring relationships to the deity. Moreover, in principle, every gift implies a distinct donor, a distinct portion of the ritual calendar, and a distinct set of honours and shares for the donor, worshipper, temple-staff and deity. This multiplicity in the link between donors, gifts and ritual may be observed in the enduring organizational distinction between the numerous endowments that support ritual in a given temple.

Religious endowments have been the subject of lengthy scholarly, legal (Mukherjea 1962; Rajasikhamani 1971; Varadachari 1968), and philosophical

---

[8]An *Adhikārā-pārapattiyam* is the temple-servant who, among other things, supervises the torch and vehicle bearers in the processional, oversees the display of lights to the deity, and distributes betel-leaf in the *moṇṭapams*.

[9]The *peskar* is a revenue-agent who represents the temple-trustees, and who supervises the day-to-day ritual process in the temple.

treatises over the last one hundred years. Much of this vast and often erudite literature has attempted to elucidate and to understand the 'law' with regard to endowments with a particular eye to understanding endowments as 'property' (Derrett 1962: 68–72). This legal approach to endowments has been the product of a search largely by the Anglo-Indian Courts for a unified and codified approach to conflict-adjudication in temple disputes. In the absence of a well-defined corpus of Hindu law with respect to religious endowments, a judge-made case-law emerged in the late nineteenth and early twentieth centuries in which endowments were inadvertently subjected to the law of trusts based implicitly, if not at times explicitly, on the English law of charitable trusts.

To view temple endowments (Tam. *kaṭṭalai*) as trusts, however, does not answer the question of their place in the larger context of the south Indian Hindu temple. Temple endowments are special kinds of trusts. They are the elementary units within which resources are mobilized, organized, and utilized in the temple. Thus, resources are *pooled* in so far as an endowment generates one portion of the overall ritual process (namely, a single ceremony in a ten-day festival which is in turn a single event in the annual ritual calendar). But, resources are *separately* enjoyed insofar as that particular portion of the ritual process established by an endowment generates a context in which the donor initiates a transaction with the deity. In and through that context, the donor receives honours (i.e. his or her share of the redistributed pūjā offerings), and maintains exclusive access to such things as the surplus (i.e. cash or crops) generated by the capital or land related to the endowment.

To understand endowments more fully, the following four generalizations may be posited for consideration:

(1) an endowment represents the mobilization, organization, and pooling of resources (i.e., capital, land, labour, etc.);

(2) an endowment generates one or more ritual contexts in which to distribute and to receive honours;

(3) an endowment permits the entry and incorporation of corporate units into the temple (i.e. families, castes, monasteries or *maṭams*, sects, kings, etc.) either as temple servants (i.e. *stānikar*s, priests, assistants, drummers, pipers, etc.) or as donors;

(4) an endowment supports, however partially and however incompletely, the reigning deity. But, because the reigning deity is limited since it is made of stone, authority with respect to endowment resources and ritual remains in the hands of the donor or an agent appointed by him or her.

These four points might be explored further so as to sustain the hypothesis that the macro-organization of endowments argues against a monolithic conception of the temple. Conversely, they reveal the temple to be a complex and radically decentralized organization in which endowments provide the means for linking the temple to its agrarian hinterland or urban context.

Similarly, endowments link the temple to corporate units in society. These corporate groups retain their separate identities while being accommodated in the larger ritual and economic process represented by the temple.

The first proposition is that through an endowment resources are mobilized, organized, and utilized. Resources include land and/or capital (i.e. hard cash, the prerogative to collect certain 'taxes', etc.), and human labour (i.e. the services of cultivators, temple ritual specialists, etc.). Through administrative orders (*sāsanam*), now called deeds, these resources are formally and publicly gifted to the temple. The size of the gift varies from endowment to endowment. Seventy-three endowments, for example, provided the resources for worship in the 1973 ritual calendar of the Śrī Mīnākṣi-Sundaresvarar Temple, Madurai. The resources supporting each of these seventy-three endowments varied: Historically, the donor's share from each of twenty-one villages was attached to the Tirumala Nāyaka Endowment; from five to the Tanappa Mutaliyār Endowment; and from two to the Nāgappa Cheṭṭiyār Endowment. Other endowments included plots of land (i.e. flower gardens known as *nandavanam*, etc.) or cash (i.e. voluntary collections known as *mahimai*, etc.).

That the endowment permits the pooling of resources so that temple ritual events might be sustained is the second proposition under discussion. That is to say that separate and discrete endowments variously provide the resources for specified aspects of worship. Pūjā items (including milk, curds, ghee, honey, bananas, sugar, coconut, turmeric, sandalwood, rice, etc.) for the six daily pūjās in the Śrī Mīnākṣi-Sundaresvarar Temple, Madurai, for example, are provided by a number of different endowments. In 1973, items for morning pūjā (*kālasanti*) came variously and in varying proportions from the following eight endowments: Sirkar, Maturanāyakam Piḷḷai, Venkaṭa Krishṇappa Nāyakkar, Muttiruli, Lekkaya Nāyakkar, Pūcci Nāyakkar, Amakappa Mutaliyār, and Mannarappa.

Festival events follow a similar pattern. Embedded within any given nine to twelve day monthly festival are numerous ritual events. Each separate event is sponsored by a separate endowment. An overview of this process, wherein ritual events are separately sponsored by separate donors, who represent a diverse and geographically widespread body, is provided by the general calendar (*pattrikai*) for the 1974 Cittirai (April–May) Peruvilā or great feast of the Śrī Mīnākṣi-Sundaresvarar Temple popularly known as the 'Wedding Festival'. The donor for the major event for each of the twelve days of the feast is cited or implied under the column which is headed 'place and hall'. They include, sequentially from day one to day twelve: the potters (*kuyavar*), Mutturāmayyar, Kalyāṇakuntar Mutaliyār, Villāpuram Pāvakkā, patrons of the Rāmāyaṇa Sāvaṭi, the Sivaganga Rājā (days six and nine), patrons of the Nāyakkar Maṇṭappati, Kaṭṭu Cetti, Nāgappa Cettiyārs and agents of the

Muttambal Mutaliyār Endowment. A similar chart could be presented to further detail the list of donors for each particular day. Such a chart would list the donors for subsidiary but supporting events which elaborate and complicate the festival celebration.

The importance of the discrete sponsorship of ritual events by separate donors lies in the proposition that ritual events are the contexts in which honours are distributed and received in the temple. The first honour (i.e. *akkira-mariyātai* often involves the receipt of a silk vestment, *parivaṭṭam,* which has been presented to and worn by the deity) is received by the donor (or by someone designated by him or her) as the offerer of pūjā or worship. Following the ritual, the donor offers fees known as honours (*tirukkai-valakkam mariyātai*) in the form of betel nut, money, rice-balls, etc. to temple courtiers and servants. Thus, ritual contexts generate by a donor are the occasions when he, the donor, appropriately participates in the distribution and receipt of honours.

The formation of ritual contexts in which honours are generated and moved leads to the third aspect of endowments, namely the entry and incorporation of corporate units in the redistributive process of the temple. The donor of an endowment generally, if not always, represents a social and economic unit. Such units might be a family, a monastery (*maṭam*), a sect, a kingdom, a guild, or more recently, a collection of workers (i.e. court or bank employees, etc.). The formation of an endowment, as noted above, provides the corporate group an opportunity in which their head-man, a king-like figure, may formally and publicly receive honours. Thereafter, in the formal meetings of the group, the 'headman' receives honours first, and subsequently distributes them to group members. The receipt of honours from the deity by the 'headman', however, is not fixed or static. Each time honours are distributed, the possibility that conflict might erupt in the form of a contender to the role of 'headman' claiming the right to receive honours first in those contexts sponsored by his group, does exist.

In the context of the temple, therefore, two things occur: separate and diverse groups are brought together to generate a process in which a share in any one aspect of an endowment is a share in the redistributive cycle of the temple. Likewise, individual members of a group are brought together to participate in the formation of ritual events in which group members compete for the receipt of honours.

Finally, the formation of an endowment, however partially and however incompletely, contributes to the support of the reigning deity. But, because the reigning deity is made to stone, and is hence limited in its capacity to function as the decision-maker or as conflict adjudicator, authority with respect to endowment resources and labour, ritual and honours distribution, remains in the hands of the donor or an agent appointed by him or her. It is this decentralized nature of the exercise of authority which in principle most poignantly characterizes temple structure and organization. However, tensions and conflicts are not always resolvable by the endowment donor or agent. In that case it becomes necessary to look elsewhere for arbitration.

PROTECTION AND SERVICE

Control over endowment is only one potential locus of conflict in the temple. In addition to donors, conflict can involve trustees, temple-servants and worshippers. In both the Śrī Pārthasārathi Svāmi Temple and the Śrī Mīnākṣi-Sundaresvarar Temple, in the course of the last five decades, major conflicts have erupted between the trustees, between the trustees and the priests, amongst the priests themselves, between the priests and other temple-servants, and between donors and everybody else. This is by no means a unique situation, as a glance at the indices to various digests of court cases will easily demonstrate (Sontheimer 1964: 78–100; Derrett 1968: 482–505). These conflicts often take the form of honour disputes, and given the denotative and constitutive role of honours with respect to the overall share (paṅku) of a person or group in the redistributive process of the temple, they are rarely, if ever, trivial (Barnett 1974: 192–3; Beals 1964: 99–113; Beck 1972: 79; Beteille 1965: 91; Dumont 19: 307–8; Dumont 1970: 230).

Whether they involve donors, trustees, temple-servants, or worshippers, these conflicts involve issues raised by the relationship of service (kaiṅkaryam) to the sovereign deity. The most important fact about these various forms of service, is that they are all relatively autonomous forms of participation in the overall ritual and redistributive process of the temple. Each person or group involved in service of any kind, thus, possesses an inalienable and privileged relationship to the sovereign deity, concretized in some sort of share, dramatized and rendered authoritative by some sort of honour. What holds these various 'servants' together, is not a simple hierarchy of functions, no single pyramid of authority, but rather (1) their shared orientation to (and dependence on) the sovereignty of the deity they serve, and (2) the sheer logic of functional interdependence, without which the ritual process would break down. Even the managerial roles in the temple, such as that of the trustees, are not conceived to be superordinate in any clear hierarchial way. They are authoritative only insofar as they do not disturb any one of the 'shares' which they must orchestrate in order to keep the moral and economic cycle of temple-ritual going.

This should not imply, however, that the temple is an ill-disciplined collection of independent agents. Particular chains of command do exist, as well as particular norms which govern these chains. But these norms, which vary from temple to temple, are legitimated by a shared idea of the past, of hallowed convention, which is based on a fragile consensus. Thus, changes in the social and political environment of the temple tend to fragment this delicate consensus fairly easily. At the best of times, the boundaries within which orders can be given and expected to be obeyed, are tightly defined. When these boundaries are overlooked, and the share of some individual or group is see to be threatened, conflict erupts.

It is at these moments of conflict that we can see how the many groups and individuals who possess shares of some sort in the temple, recognize their privileged interaction with the deity as the *only* really authoritative relationship. Thus, the problem arises of how to arbitrate conflicts that arise at any of the complex interphases of these shares; conflicts most often expressed in the idiom of honour. Informants address this problem by invoking another relationship to the deity: the relationship of protection (Skt. *paripālana;* Tam. *kāppātrutal*). In what does protection consist and who is qualified to exercise it?

Today, the Hindu Religious and Charitable Endowments (Administration) Department of the state of Tamil Nāṭu exercises the mandate of protection, though legal and bureaucratic control of thousands of temples in the state (Mudaliar 1974). In this respect, its role is a direct and self-conscious extension of the classical royal model, which obtained in pre-British south India, whereby the role of the king (*arasan*) was understood to entail the protection of the temple. In this classical model, to protect the temple means to ensure that the services, resources, and rules that define the redistributive process of any given temple are allocated, distributed, and defined, so that conflict does not arise and disharmony does not set in. This royal mandate is a delicate one, for the king cannot *rule* the temple. He is himself a servant (*cevārti*) of the deity, and indeed the human agent of the divine sovereignty enshrined in the deity (Sontheimer 1964: 75-6). But since the deity cannot, by its very nature, arbitrate conflict among its servants, the human king is called upon to fulfil this function.

In fulfilling this royal mandate of protection, the king is only the ultimate recourse. Conflicts may be solved amiably by local assemblies. Nor is the protective function of the king in reference to the deity monopolistic. All organized relationships to the deity, relationships of systematic service, are held to be, in a sense, protective, insofar as they safeguard, maintain and nurture some aspect, however finite, of the redistributive process centred on the deity. Thus 'protection' and 'service' are the two extreme (ideal–typical) poles of all relationships to the deity. Just as the protective function of the king is only the highest human expression of service to the deity, so even the most humble form of service to the deity shares some of the prestigious, authoritative, and autonomous texture of the protective role of the king. In this sense, though separated by many other features, the king and the mahout are together servant–protectors of the sovereign deity.

In purely cultural terms, therefore, we can see in the relationship of human kings to temple-deities in south India, an elegant and symbiotic division of sovereignty. The sovereign deity is the paradigm of royal authority. By serving this deity, in the form of elaborate gifts which generated special royal honours, and by protecting the redistributive processes of temples, pre-British kings shared in this paradigmatic royalty. By being the greatest servant of the sovereign deity, the king sustains and displays his rule over men.

But in operational and empirical terms, this cultural model can become problematic, for it does not clearly specify the boundaries of the temple, both as a political and administrative unit, and as a ritual process. In short, it does not provide a set of rules for temple-control. By temple-control is meant the acknowledged competence of an individual or an agency to authoritatively determine the roles, rights, and resources involved in the ongoing maintenance of worship. Not even the protective mandate of kings can abrogate what are perceived to be appropriate shares in relation to the sovereign deity. Kings are obliged to interact with temples. This is partly because, enshrining the deity, temples are repositories of kingship, in its paradigmatic sense. By extension, they are concentrations of economic, political, and cultural concern for the hinterlands they dominate. But their prerogatives as protectors are always *potentially* subject to challenge from other 'servants' of the deity, who perceive their rights/shares as independently derived form the sovereign deity. To a considerable extent, conflicts concerning shares and rights, often expressed in the medium of honour, derive from this structural aspect of the shared sovereignty of kings and temple-deities.

To understand the impact of British ideas and institutions on this complex and delicate system of indigenous meanings, would be to undertake a historical exercise that lies outside the scope of this essay. Stated briefly, however, the colonial period has considerably complicated the institutional framework within which the shared sovereignty of the king and temple-deity is conceived. Unlike pre-British kings, who transacted with temples through elaborate gifting and occasional arbitration of temple-conflict, the present state has inverted and distorted this relationship. Given the legal–rational–bureaucratic (in the Weberian usage) basis of the present political order, the H.R. and C.E. Department is a 'protector' of south Indian temples in a very different way from its pre-British royal predecessors. It maintains a continuous, centralized and bureaucratic relationship with the temples under its management, and it is therefore, in economic terms, more a 'manager' of temples than an 'endower'. Similarly, the ideology of the DMK, in respect to religious matters, is a confusing mix of modern rationalist attitudes and traditional attitudes of veneration and support. Finally, given the division of the state into executive and judiciary (a distinction that goes back to the very beginnings of British rule), the H.R. and C.E. Department does not have a conclusive role in the resolution of temple-conflict. Not only can litigants take their grievances to the judicial system, but they can contest the actions of the H.R. and C.E. Department in court. In the Śrī Pārthasārathi

Svāmi Temple, for example, throughout the 1950s and 1960s members of the local Tenkalai sect of Śrī Vaiṣṇavas conducted a court battle for control of this temple with the H.R. and C.E. Department; a battle they eventually lost.

Nevertheless, it is clear that officials of the state who have active bureaucratic involvements with particular temples, as well as the staff and worshippers in such temples, share the idea that the government (Tam. *arasu*) is in some fashion carrying on, in its management of temples, the mandate of pre-British Hindu kings to protect such institutions. The persistence of this conception of the relationship between the state and the temple, in spite of significant changes in the social, economic, and political order, suggests its centrality to the south Indian way of ordering the universe.

CONCLUSION

The four principles which we have argued to be at the core of the south Indian temple, both as a locus of meaning and as functioning institution, can be recapitulated as follows. The sovereign deity, honoured in daily and calendrical worship, is the authoritative centre of the temple. Gifts to the deity, and culturally demarcated shares in the leavings of the deity, are the dramatized and public features of a complex redistributive process, in which tokens of precedence are the constitutive features of roles, rights, and resources in the temple. The flexible and dynamic organizational framework for this redistributive process is provided by temple-endowments, through which men and groups establish an enduring connection with the deity, just as they enact their autonomy and interdependence with respect to each other. Conflict among such participants, unavoidable because of the nature of the deity (which is the source of their rights but is also incapable of arbitrating their conflicts), can only be resolved by the 'protective' mandate of human rulers, who thus render themselves indispensable to the deity who is the paradigm of their own royalty.

It is to this multiplicity of ordered meanings and functions, that the south Indian temple owes its immense importance in south Indian society. Particular temples, in particular times and places, represent this complex paradigm in a variety of ways. This concrete variety, however, is itself a testimony to the flexibility and centrality of this south Indian paradigm, whose quintessential sociological expression is the south Indian temple.

REFERENCES

Appadurai, Arjun
1981 *Worship and conflict under colonial rule: A south Indian case.* Cambridge: Cambridge University Press.

Bagchi, S.C.
1933 *Juristic personality of Hindu deities*. Calcutta: University of Calcutta.
Baker, C.J.
1975 Temples and political development. *In* C.J. Baker and D.A. Washbrook, eds. *South India: political institutions and political change*. Delhi: Macmillan Company.
Barnett, S.A.
1974 The process of withdrawal in a south Indian caste. *In* Milton Singer, ed. *Entrepreneurship and the modernization of occupations in south Asia*. Durham, N.C.: Duke University Press.
Beals, Alan R.
1964 Conflict and interlocal festivals in a south Indian religion. *In* Edward B. Harper, ed., *Religion in south Asia*. Seattle: University of Washington Press.
Beck, B.E.F.
1972 *Peasant society in Konku: A study of right and left subcastes in south India*. Vancouver: University of British Columbia Press.
Béteille, A.
1965 Social organization of temples in a Tanjore village. *History of religions* 5, 1: 74–92.
Clothey, F.
1969 Skanda-sasti: a festival in Tamil India. *History of religions* 3: 236–59.
Dasgupta, S.
1955 *A history of Indian philosophy. Vol. V: Southern schools of Saivism*. Cambridge: Cambridge University Press.
Davis, R.H.
1991 *Ritual in an oscillating universe: Worshipping Śiva in medieval India*. Princeton: Princeton University Press.
Derrett Davis, J.D.M.
1962 The development of the concept of property in India, c. AD 800–1800. *Zeitschrift fur Vergleichende Rechtswissenschaft* (Stuttgart) 64: 68–72.
1968 *Religion, law and the state in India*. London: Faber & Faber.
Diehl, C.G.
1956 *Instrument and purpose: studies on rites and rituals in south India*. Lund: C.W.K. Gleerup.
Dumont, L.
1957 *Use sous-caste de l'Inde du sud. Organisation sociale et religion des Pramalai Kallar*. Paris: Mouton. [English translation: 1986. *A south Indian subcaste: Social organization and religion of the Pramalai Kallar*. Delhi: Oxford University Press.]
1970 *Homo hierarchicus: the caste system and its implications*. Chicago: University of Chicago Press.
Galanter, M.
1972 The abolition of disabilities—untouchability and the law. *In* J. Michael Mahar, ed. *The untouchables in contemporary India*. Tucson: University of Arizona Press.
Gonda, J.
1970 *Visnuism and Sivaism: A comparison*. London: The Athlone Press.
Hardgrave, Robert L. (Jr.)
1969 *The Nadars of Tamilnad: The political culture of a community in change*. Berkeley & Los Angeles: University of California Press.
Hubert, Henri and Marcel Mauss.
1964 *Sacrifice: its nature and function*. W.D. Hall (Trans.). Chicago: The University of Chicago Press.

Kane, P.V.

1974 *History of Dharmasastra (ancient and mediaeval religious and civil law)*. 2nd edn Poona: Bhandarkar Oriental Research Institute.

Kramrisch, S.

1946 *The Hindu temple*. 2 vols. Calcutta: University of Calcutta Press.

Krishna Sastri, H.

1916 *South Indian images of gods and goddesses*. Madras: Govt. Press.

Mahalingam, T.V.

1967 *South Indian polity*. Madras: University of Madras Press.

Martin, James L.

1971 The cycle of festivals at the Parthasarathi Swami temple. *Journal of the American academy of religions: Asian religions*. Ed. Bardwell L. Smith.Pp. 223–40.

Mudaliar, C.Y.

1974 *The secular state and religious institutions in India: A study of the administration of Hindu religious trusts in Madras*. Wiesbaden: Franz Steiner Verlag.

Mukherjea, B.K.

1962 *The Hindu law of religious and charitable trusts*. 2nd edn Calcutta: Eastern Law House.

Pathar, S. Viraswami.

1974 *Temple and its significance*. Tiruchi.

Pillai, J.M. Somasundaram.

1948 *Tiruchendur: The sea-shore temple of Subrahmanyam*. Madras.

Pillay, K.K.

1953 *The Sucindram temple*. Madras: Kalakshetra Publications.

Rajasikhamani, V.

1971 *The Tamil Nadu Hindu Religious and Charitable Endowments Act (XXII) of 1952 (with allied act), containing a clear exposition of the scope of the legislation, exhaustive commentary and case law and rules* brought up to December 1971, Madras: Sundaralingam.

Sahlins, M.D.

1972 *Stone age economics*. Chicago: Aldine Publishing Co,.

Sontheimer, G.D.

1964 Religious endowments in India: The juristic personality of Hindu deities. In *Zeitschrift fur Vergleichende Rechlswissenschaft* (Stuttgart) 67, I: 45–100.

Spencer, George W.

1968 Temple money lending and livestock redistribution. *The Indian economic and social history review* 3: 277–93.

Stein, Burton.

1960 The economic function of a medieval south Indian temple. *Journal of Asian studies* 19, 2: 163–76.

Sundaram, K.

1969 *The Simhachalam temple*. Simhachalam: Simhachalam Devasthanam.

Varadachari, V.K.

1968 *The law of Hindu religious and charitable endowments*. Calcutta: Eastern Book Co.

Viraraghavacharya, T.K.T.

1953–4 *History of Tirupati*. 2 vols. Tirupati: Tirumalai-Tirupati Devastanams.

Church and Community in Goa

ROWENA ROBINSON

I n this essay, I present an analysis of church ritual and a discussion of the place of the church within the village community and its role in articulating and maintaining the local systems of power and hierarchy. What we see is that the church is itself embedded within the indigenous system of social ranking, and that its rituals and celebrations become occasions for the demonstration or contestation of rank.

The focus is specifically on the privileges in church ritual held by the village élites, and the contestation of these privileges by the lower social groups. The rites and ceremonies of the Catholic calendar become the focus for demonstrating dominance within the community. I will discuss the structure of the mass and the ways in which it manifests hierarchy, and will look briefly at the ordering of different social groups within the church and at processions. Finally, I will look at the manner in which, in the changing agrarian economy, the church has become the arena of a variety of conflicts between socially mobile caste groups which are trying to translate their newly acquired wealth into honour and respect by seeking ritual privileges within the church.

The lowest castes have never had a significant place in church ritual. The main organizers of most church-centred rituals were the *gauncar*s, who usually belonged to one or other of the higher castes. This was the situation for most of the Portuguese period. After the 1960s, however, there was a significant

Excerpted from Rowena Robinson, Ceremony and conflict in the Church, In *Conversion, continuity and change: Lived Christianity in Southern Goa*. Chap. 6. New Delhi: Sage 1998. © Rowena Robinson.

shift. The *gauncars* completely lost at this time all local administrative authority, which passed into the hands of district bureaucrats and the elected panchayats in each village. The lower castes too had by this time improved their economic position to some extent by taking up jobs outside the agrarian structure.

All these changes together have brought the lower social groups into a position from which they can pose a more serious threat to the high-caste *gauncars*. Thus, while the latter still wield considerable socio–economic power and control the panchayats, both economically and politically, the other social groups have today become more serious contenders. The panchayat is dependent on the votes of all castes and it has to 'listen sometimes' to the voice of the lower castes. The different groups are today in conflict, which is played out predominantly in the arena of the church.

THE CHURCH AND SOCIAL RELATIONS

The Portuguese were aware of the centrality of the temple in the life of the Hindu village communities. Among the Hindus, the ritual privileges enjoyed by various social groups in temple festivities represented their positions within the hierarchical social structure of the village.[1] The *gauncars* organized and endowed the various activities of the temple. They carried the newly-cut sheaves into the temple on the day of the harvest festival. Also, the dancing-girls (*kolvonts* danced first at the houses of the village *gauncars*). The *gauncars* led the temple processions and carried the image of the deity. Such privileges were denied to the lower social groups.

With conversion, churches replaced village temples. The east–west cardinal orientation of the construction of temples was replicated in the churches, as the Council of Trent decreed that the church should face east. In the temples, the shrine was smaller than the antechamber in length, width, and height. As light entered through a single door, the antechamber was tuned into a kind of penumbral zone leading to the darkened shrine, shrouded in mystery.

Santosgaon's village church, as other east-oriented churches, ensures that the central sanctuary is luminously lit in the morning, the usual time of mass, but otherwise remains a kind of dim cavern. The worshipper entering the church turns his back to the west, facing east, the direction associated with the figure of Christ.

---

[1]Authors like Dirks (1987) and Appadurai and Breckenridge (1976) have written similarly about temples in south India. In Santosgaon, there are two small chapels built and maintained out of parish funds. Masses are generally held there only on the occasion of the feasts of the chapel patrons (Our Lady of Sorrows and Our Lady of Piety). Else, they are used mainly for private devotion. Major feasts and rituals (and conflicts about them) centre around the village church and we limit our discussion to these.

Churches also replaced temples as the focus of the socio–religious life of the community. The converts were able to reconstruct their socio–cultural system around the new places of worship. From the very early period of conversion, the missionaries allowed the Catholic higher-caste *gauncars* a variety of honours and privileges in the church-centred Catholic ritual cycle. These rituals are, even today, used to symbolize status in the same manner as might have been found in village temple celebrations.

Today, in Santosgaon, the village church is at the centre of the relations of power and hierarchy within the Catholic community. While these relations are based on caste status, the ownership of land, or control within the local panchayats (socio–politically and economically based), the church maintains and articulates them. Honours in church ritual are important in themselves and because they signify authority or stature in the community. They constitute as well as express social relationships and political authority.

Ritual is not merely reflective of relations that exist independently of it. It constitutes a means of crystallizing ordinary social experience by providing 'a vehicle for significance and display in a way presented by no other domain' (Dirks 1987: 304). That is precisely why different castes spend so much time and effort in their attempts to assert themselves by claiming particular privileges in church celebrations. The possession of these privileges is clearly important in itself as a signifier of status within the community. The church *fabrica* remains in the hands of the high-caste *gauncars*. The privilege of hosting the celebrations for different feasts belongs to the two lay Catholic associations in the village.

The two Catholic associations are the major and the minor confraternities. The major confraternity (*confraria maior*) in Santosgaon is Confraria de Santissimo e Nossa Senhora de Socorro. Only high-caste *gauncars* may be members of this confraternity. The confraternity enjoys the privilege of organizing the harvest feast celebrations and those centred around Good Friday. The confraternity has red capes, which distinguishes its members, which they wear at the feasts that are organized and hosted by them. Members of the confraternity are registered automatically at birth and all the *gauncars* of the village belong to it. They organize and participate in its feasts.

The minor confraternity (*confraria menor*) to which the other groups belong is called the Confraria de São Sebastião e Santas Almas. The Chardo non-*gauncars*, Sudras, and other lower-caste groups are members of this confraternity. This confraternity has blue capes, which are worn by its members during the celebration of the feast that it organizes—that of St. Sebastian. One is not automatically registered at birth as a member of the confraternity but membership can be sought by registering at any time with the parish priest. As far as I could find, all the non-*gauncar* lower castes in Santosgaon were registered members and took part in the celebration of the feast of the confraternity.

... Confrarias [it may be pointed out] were Catholic lay associations that developed in Europe in medieval times. They were religious in character and had cultic and ceremonial aims centred particularly around Holy Week celebrations. In Goa, these associations were established very early as a means of involving lay Catholics actively in church life. Though they were in theory open to all, they came to have an essentially exclusive character. In most villages, the village élites (the high-caste *gauncars*) who held most of the ritual privileges in church celebrations could alone become members of the major confraternity. The other caste groups formed the minor confraternity in the village church. Thus, interestingly, though of European origin, the confraternity system in Goa came to be thoroughly indigenized, embedded in the local system of power and privilege.

CHURCH CEREMONY: THE MASS AND PROCESSIONS

In describing church ritual and ceremony, I will examine the interaction between *gauncars* and the lower castes, the priests and the laity, and men and women. As I have noted at various points in the book [Robinson 1998] ... when it comes to the question of gender, to a certain extent Hinduism and Catholicism seem to converge. This may be perceived in the appraisal of church ritual as well.

Women are excluded from important positions in formal religion: they can become nuns but not priests, and it is the latter who celebrate the mass. They also do not find a place in the formal membership of the confraternities and are, thus, not primarily involved in the organization of important public rituals, though they do help in the decoration of the church and the like on such occasions. However, the drama and the conflict in churches in twentieth-century Goa has not centred around gender relations but rather around castes. ...

The mass follows a particular pattern and consists of specific, fixed prayers. The prayers are led by the priest. The mass consists of two parts. In the first, the word of God, taken from the Bible, is read and then interpreted by the priest. In the second, the elements (bread and wine) are consecrated and communicated to the congregation. They constitute the body and blood of Christ. There are usually three readings from the Bible which are read during the first part of the mass. The first is from the Old Testament and the second from the New Testament. They are read by two members of the laity, while the people sit and listen in silence.

The final text is from one of the four Gospels—Matthew, Mark, Luke, or John—which speak directly about the birth, life, and death of Christ. This is the most important reading of the mass and, not surprisingly therefore, is read by the priest while the people stand and listen. Then comes the sermon, where the priest interprets the readings and localizes them to make them meaningful for the community. The mass does not leave room for spontaneous prayer by the laity. Prayers are led by the priest. Specific liturgical prayers are said during the mass and here are particular postures to be adopted: standing, listening in silence, sitting, or kneeling. ... [See chap. 1 above.]

The Second Vatican Council of the 1960s brought two important changes in the celebration of the mass. Instead of being intoned in Latin, incomprehensible to a large majority of local people, the mass is now said in the local language, Konkani. Second, the priest now faces the people, where earlier he celebrated mass with his back turned to them. Both changes were aimed at bringing the laity and clergy closer, but even now it is the priest who controls the celebration while the laity have a passive role to play.

In the second part of the mass, the priest consecrates the elements which are then said to 'become Christ's body and blood'. At that point in the mass, the people kneel in worship. The elements are then communicated to the people who go up to receive them from the priest. In both parts of the mass, then, the people have an essentially passive role. They sit, stand, or kneel while listening or receiving the elements. The priest says the silent words of consecration and controls the celebration because his is the dominant voice speaking and interpreting. He stands to preach while the people sit and listen, and he raises his arms to bless and consecrate. There is, then, a hierarchical relationship between the priest and the people because it is the priest who mediates between the 'word' and the 'body' of Christ and their reception by the people. He interprets the word of God and consecrates the bread and wine.

This relationship also has a spatial dimension in that the benches where the people sit and the altar where the priest stands are separated by some steps. About thirty or forty years ago, it was common for the first few benches (those, nearest to the altar) on one side of the church to be occupied by the high-caste Chardo men, the *gauncars*. High Chardo women and children occupied the front benches on the other side. Behind them sat the lower-caste women and children. Lower-caste men usually stood at the back of the church.

At the present time, however, these divisions are not seen in the village. People sit more or less where they wish. Yet, at the time of feasts, the benches closest to the altar are still left vacant for the high-caste celebrants and, indeed, even the main altar space may be given over to them. The priest stands at the altar and the benches nearest to him, in front of the church, are occupied by men and women from the highest castes. The place of the lowest castes, at least in the past, was at the back of the church. Thus, the different castes appear to be distinguished by their particular places within the church.

As evidenced later, while the priests control ritual, they do so together with the high-caste Chardo *gauncars*. The *gauncars* are members of the church *fabrica* and of the confraternity which organizes the main celebrations in the church. Thus, the church exercises dominance in collaboration with the high castes who have taken its symbols and rituals and made them their own, using them as a demonstration of their status within the indigenous patterns of hierarchy.

The other castes too are found to use church ritual to demonstrate changing status. They manifest their power either through disputes with the high-caste *gauncar*s, withdrawing from active participation in church feasts, or by joining religious movements outside the church, such as the Charismatic movement. The church remains the central arena where order, hierarchy, and dominance emerge through the differing rights of different social groups.

These rights can be seen in the processions which are part of all major church celebrations in this and other villages in Goa. Appadurai and Breckenridge (1976) and Dirks (1987) describe, for parts of south India, the kinds of processions that take place in Hindu temples. The image of the deity is washed, dressed, decorated, and taken out in procession, usually in a decorated carriage or *rath*. The privileges of washing, dressing and decorating the image may be distributed between different groups given their position within the social order. Other privileges associated with temple rituals include that of organizing and paying for a particular celebration.

It is argued that the deity honoured in such festivals may be viewed as a ruler, and the processions serve to demonstrate his sovereignty over his sacred realm, constituted by the temple and the routes covered by the processions. The privileges of different groups in such processions therefore become indicative of their particular social position within the community. In Goa too during the *zatra*s (temple festivals), the deities of different temples are taken out in procession around the temple and its surrounding areas.

Among the Catholics too in Goa, processions are a central part of church ritual and are taken out particularly on the occasions of the feasts of saints. They played an important part in Catholic ritual in Goa from the early period of conversion. When Albuquerque took over Goa, he and his men went in triumphal procession around the city carrying the monstrance with the Host. At the place of victory, he dedicated a church to St Catherine whose feast was on the day. The saint's rule, and in effect that of the Portuguese, was thus established over the realm. ...

In Santosgaon, the Catholics do not use carriages (*rath*s) in their processions but, in other ways, they have practices similar to the Hindus. In the processions on the harvest feast and (in the past) on Good Friday, the first-class Chardo *gauncar*s play a major role. They lead the procession from the front and, on Good Friday, used to carry the large cross. On the feast of Our Lady of Perpetual Succour too, it is the *gauncar* members of the *fabrica* who carry the image.

Processions start at the side door of the church which is to the right of the altar. The participants go around the square in front of the church and enter it through the main door. The image is taken and placed on the main altar and the procession disperses. As mentioned earlier, the organizers or main celebrants carry the image, leading the procession from the front. Behind them come the women and children. Sometimes, upper-caste women walk just behind the main celebrants followed by lower-caste women, but this is not always the case. On occasion I have seen upper-caste women at the back of the group. Lower-caste men follow behind.

This is the order followed when the Chardo *gauncar*s are the main celebrants. On the feast of St Sebastian, the order changes. On that day, it is the Sudras and low Chardos who lead the procession. The main celebrants among them carry the image. Women and children follow. At the feast I witnessed in 1993, some of the high-caste *gauncar*s walked at the back, keeping a little distance between themselves and the bulk of the participants. They walked in a leisurely fashion as though not really interested in the proceedings as such. In fact, a number of them remained in the church and did not join the procession at all. This is probably because they do not wish to be seen participating actively in a celebration which is organized by those lower down the social scale.

The main privilege that is important in these processions is who carries the image and, thus, leads the procession. Yet, other rights are also involved in feasts. It is the members of the major confraternity who have the right to dress and decorate the image of St Bartholomew or bathe the body of Christ before mounting it on the cross during Good Friday celebrations. They also have the right to decorate the altar during these feasts. The confraternity as a whole pays for the altar-cloths and other decorations used on the feast of St Bartholomew. On Good Friday, the *vangor* which is organizing the ritual in a particular year pays for its costs. For the feast of Our Lady of Perpetual Succour, it is the *gauncar* members of the *fabrica* who organize and make arrangements for the decoration of the church and the image.

On the feast of St Sebastian, the high-caste Chardo *gauncar*s remain in the background. It is the minor confraternity which organizes the celebrations. The main celebrants for the year make the arrangements for the decoration of the image and the church, provide the funds for the celebration, and carry the image in procession after the mass. Other confraternity members come to help with the decoration and arrangements on the day of the feast and take a lead role in the procession, helping to carry the image and walking just behind the main celebrants. Thus, processions and the practices related to them, as seen among the Catholics, may be viewed, in some respects, as bringing together Hindu and Christian ideas. The different rights in processions are used to symbolize status within the community. Through such processions centred around feast days, the church itself appears to become a part of the local social system of the Catholics.

HEALING PRACTICES AND BELIEFS

We move on to talk about the healing practices and beliefs which are held, in particular, by the Sudras and other lower-caste groups among the Catholics. They share these ideas in common with lower-caste Hindus. These ideas bring the Catholics who believe in them in contact with Hindu religious specialists. In Santosgaon, the lower-caste groups, particularly Sudras and Gauddis, continue to maintain access to Hindu religious specialists such as the *gaddhi* (a kind of shaman, usually low-caste). They take all kinds of problems and afflictions to the *gaddhi* which, they believe, are caused by the intervention of spirits in their lives. Spirits are called *bhut, mharus* or *khetro*.

They may, on occasion, turn out to be the spirits of some dead ancestor or other relative but are much more frequently identified as the spirits of persons who have died violent or 'bad' deaths: either through drowning, premature illness, murder, or fatal accidents. The spirits of these people are said to be restless because they died 'before their time'. They are said to haunt the world of the living because they still have 'unfulfilled desires'. People can be possessed by these spirits or harmed by them in various ways.

These ideas seem to have a basis in Hindu notions about demonic and spirit possession. In the Hindu beliefs of the region, there appears to be no radical division or opposition between the forces of good and evil. Rather, there emerges a gradual gradation so that the Hindu pantheon includes both benevolent divinities, and spirits and demons, who have the power of evil over human lives.

With the coming of Catholicism to Goa, a different picture arose. Catholic teaching sees good and evil as being radically and fundamentally opposed. This is seen in the celebrations of the annual church calendar which, as we noted, focuses on the worship of Christ, his death, and passion, and the veneration of Mary and the saints. Christ is seen as conquering Satan and the forces of evil through his life and death on earth. He opened the way for the salvation of men from their sins and suffering, which are seen as coming about through the work of the devil on the individual's conscience. All good, then, appears to derive from God and the saints, while the devil is viewed as being essentially antithetical to Christ and the forces of good.

Among the Catholics in Santosgaon, good things or spiritual and material benefits are seen to be the gifts of God. They are the fruits of prayer and a good life in which one treats one's relatives, neighbours, and all other persons with respect and concern. As part of such activity geared towards living a good life, one should also offer masses for dead persons, particularly one's ancestors. Respect for dead ancestors is part of the complex of good acts that one must perform in order to ensure blessings and benefit for oneself and one's family.

How are misfortunes explained? In the folk beliefs of Santosgaon's Catholics, misfortunes are viewed as the possible result of one's sins or evil actions. To avoid or overcome them, as far as I could gather from indigenous interpretations, one performs certain specifically Christian acts such as confessing one's sins to the priest; praying and giving money in charity. Evil therefore has two referents: the misfortunes that occur in one's life and the evil acts that persons themselves commit by not caring about or behaving responsibly towards others.

Catholics, however, also believe that misfortune may be caused by the entry of spirits into one's life. At this particular phenomenological level there is an overlap between Hindu and Catholic notions, despite any differences that may be found in their religious theologies. Both Hindus and Catholics see the human world as being impinged upon by various capricious forces which must either be avoided or placated to prevent them from doing harm (see Caplan 1987). These spirits are viewed as intervening actively in peoples' lives and causing, in many cases, physical illness and affliction.

This notion, which is also held by Catholics, of the active entry of the spirits of the dead into human life appears to owe much more to Hindu ideas than to Christian teaching, for the latter does not envisage the dead as interacting or communicating with the living actively through possession or through mediums and diviners. At this level, a degree of ambiguity also seems to enter the notions of Santosgaon's Catholics. While the spirits' power for evil is in keeping with Christian teachings, sometimes spoken of by Catholics as being 'devilish' in origin or nature, it is recognized by them that even their own ancestors may do them harm.

This they attribute to the fact that ancestors 'punish' their descendants for their own good, 'to bring them to the right path' and (if they themselves had not lived ideal lives) 'to warn them [the descendants] not to follow in their footsteps'. Again, ancestors who have died 'bad' deaths are remembered, but in a different way. They are not included in the *bhikranjevan*, but I was told that food is kept outside the house on the night of All Souls' Day in the belief that they come to partake of it.

Such notions held by Catholics and Hindus alike are, therefore, in a sense, related to ideas about the need to treat dead ancestors with honour to obtain blessings and keep away potential harm. To deal with spirits of the dead when they possess or harm men, the Catholics have recourse to low-caste Hindu religious specialists as the *gaddhi*. However, such recourse to the *gaddhi* and an elaborate cult of spirit affliction and healing has, in general, been much more part of lower-caste practices. It may be possible that in the past such practices were somewhat more widespread than at present. ...

It is perhaps possible to argue that in recent decades the high Chardos may have withdrawn themselves from such practices and beliefs about 'possession' and spirit affliction in an effort to separate themselves from the lower-caste groups who, particularly since the 1960s or so, have become more of a threat to them and have started posing a challenge. They now speak disparagingly of such beliefs and see them largely as the domain of the lower castes. I know of at least one case where a high Chardo woman recently took recourse to a *gaddhi* because she believed that her husband was afflicted with the spirit of his dead brother, but such cases are rare and when they occur are kept secret. Even low Chardos today claim that they do not hold such beliefs. On their part, too, this may be an attempt to separate themselves from the Sudras. ...

It is mainly the sudden and inexplicable onset of illness or the coming of unexpected misfortune that are attributed to the intervention of spirits or *khetro* by the Catholics. Such afflictions, which are believed to be caused by the spirits of dead persons, are called *variancé* and they are taken to the *gaddhi* for his diagnosis and treatment. *Gaddhis* are to be found in many villages, especially in areas where Hindus dominate. Many Catholics in Santosgaon visit *gaddhis* in Fatorpa and Canacona in the south of Goa.

The *gaddhi* asks the patient and his relatives various kinds of questions. For instance, he asks for the symptoms of the illness that the patient is suffering from and where the family comes from. He often asks if there has been a recent death in the family of the afflicted person or if he/she had been to the house or funeral of a dead person in the period before the illness struck. The *gaddhi* usually asks for a detailed account of the various places to which the patient had been in the days or weeks prior to his/her illness. It is on the basis of such questions that the *gaddhi* reaches a diagnosis and prescribes some form of remedy. These remedies can take the form of offerings, usually of one or two chickens, made by the *gaddhi* to the spirit of the dead person for the relief of the patient. Other means are also followed to make the spirit of a dead person depart from the patient whom it has possessed.

Some cases of spirit affliction and healing among the lower castes came to my knowledge in the village. Here are two examples.

Rosa, a Gauddi girl, was said to be possessed by an evil spirit. She was found one day, some distance from her home, standing under a large tree. When people spoke to her she looked at them with glazed eyes and screamed at them, frothing at the mouth. She was taken home by force as she struggled to get free. Suspecting the influence of some evil spirit, her parents and some relations decided that the best way to get rid of the influence was by beating her. The girl was beaten with a stick as she screamed and cried aloud with pain. Even after this treatment, her condition did not change. It was then thought that it might be a god idea to douse her with water to remove the influence of the spirit. Even after this was done, the girl's condition did not change; and so, after two days, she was taken to a *gaddhi*. He asked how long the patient had been so afflicted. When he heard that the symptoms had appeared some days ago, he asked whether anything had been done so far. The patient's father said that they had tried beating her and dousing her with water but the methods had not worked. The *gaddhi* made the patient stand on some grains of black pepper and crush them with her feet. As she did so, he invoked the spirit to reveal itself. The girl started speaking in a male voice which was identified as belonging to the spirit of the dead person afflicting her. Apparently, under the tree where the girl had been standing, a couple of years earlier a man had been killed and his body buried. The spirit belonged to the dead man. When asked by the *gaddhi* why he had possessed the girl, he said: 'She looked good.' Asked what he would take to release her, he said 'chickens'.[2] The *gaddhi* slit the throats of two chickens and offered their blood to the spirit. The spirit is said to have been appeased by the 'honour' of the offering. By this time, the girl had quietened down and was sitting still on the floor. The *gaddhi* then told the relatives that the spirit had gone and that they could take the girl home, but should remove all the clothes she was wearing and burn them. The girl's demonic behaviour did not repeat itself.

Theo, a young Sudra boy, had for some days been displaying behavioural signs that his parents found very disquieting. He would stand still in one place and stare vacantly into the distance, not responding even when called. He started dropping things and displaying other signs of clumsiness. His parents saw these sudden changes of behaviour in their son and suspected some kind of spirit affliction. The boy's mother remembered that some days earlier he had gone to play and when he returned had told her of having gone past a house where a man had recently committed suicide and of having felt a shiver pass through him as he went by. When his symptoms did not recede even after some days had passed, it was decided to take the boy to a *gaddhi*. The *gaddhi* agreed with the boy's parents that he might have been affected by the spirit of that dead man. Since the boy was not displaying signs of acute possession—screaming or violence—he was only given a small piece of charmed wood to wear around his neck so that he would not be affected by the spirit again. The boy's symptoms apparently decreased and his parents were of the opinion that this was to be attributed to the cure that was given. ...

What we may note is that it is among the lower-caste Catholics in particular that such ideas about spirit affliction and healing seem to have developed more elaborately, which involve visits to Hindu religious specialists. In the examples given earlier, the Catholics who go to *gaddhi*s themselves make various kinds of decisions in cases of suspected spirit affliction. The relatives of a patient may decide to take action to remove the spirit by beating or dousing the patient with water. They may also reach tentative conclusions regarding the identity of the spirit. The *gaddhi* takes note of these suspicions

[2]Chickens, or sometimes goats, are the most common offerings made on such occasions by Hindus and Catholics in the region. It should be remembered that such animal offerings are largely to be seen among lower-caste Hindus and are usually made to lower, non-Brahmanic deities or spirits.

and of the actions already taken by the patient's relatives and might even agree with or confirm their suspicions.

It may perhaps be argued that the continuing vitality of ideas and practices about spirit affliction among lower-caste groups may be related to the fact that they appear to retain a degree of control over the ritual activity involved in these practices. While the high-caste group remains in control of church-centred rituals, participation in such practices perhaps enables the lowest social groups to have some control in a setting which is outside that dominated by the former. In recent times, some of these practices have been drawn into the Charismatic movement. Joining the movement itself has become an opportunity for some lower-caste Catholics to challenge the high Chardos on their own ground, as it were, within the arena of the church.

CONFLICT AND CONTESTATION

In this final section, I will discuss the conflicts that have taken place in the church between the major and minor confraternities. These conflicts, as we shall see, have divided the minor confraternity, with the low Chardos seeking to separate themselves from the Sudras, and both coming into conflict with the high, first-class Chardo *gauncars*. Disputes between the confraternities of the different caste groups are quite common. It is probable that in the past conflicts over the distribution of ritual privileges in the temples took place between different groups in the village. This has certainly been shown for other parts of India, particularly in the south (Dirks 1987, Mosse 1986).

In Goa we do know that conflicts between the Catholic confraternities of different villages were often present during the Portuguese period. However, the missionaries or church authorities to whom such conflicts were referred usually maintained the privileges of the high-caste *gauncars* in such situations (Gomes 1987). Hence, while these conflicts are not something altogether recent, today newer kinds of tensions have started feeding into them. The agrarian context is in a fluid and dynamic state and this has, perhaps, given rise to tensions which are brought into the ritual sphere.

The first major conflict between the two confraternities in recent decades took place in the late 1960s. By this period, a change had come about in the economic position of the various caste groups. Many among the lower social groups had started taking up jobs outside the village and had thereby improved their economic position in a major way. Political changes had also taken place. The high-caste *gauncars* had lost all control over the management of *comunidade* land and other matters. The district administration had taken over control of these lands and other administrative rights had come under the panchayats in each village.

Further, during this period, changes were taking place within the church itself. With the Second Vatican Council of the 1960s, the church was coming to terms with the realities of a post-colonial world and the ideas of democracy and social equality that it had thrown up. It became important for the church to redefine its stance with regard to these issues. ...

In Goa, we have noted how changes in the liturgy sought to bring about a more equal relationship between the clergy and the laity and to enable greater participation of the latter in the mass by having it said in the local language. The Council made it clear that 'the laity are not second-class citizens and the mission of the church is not the preserve of those in holy orders' (Ryan 1968: 237). Another consequence of all these changes, for Goa at least, appears to be the more subdued role the church seems to take when conflicts emerge between different confraternities. It is now less willing to be seen supporting the higher-caste *gauncar*s as used to happen frequently in the past (Gomes 1987). Thus, it is not economic factors alone that have led to conflict between the major and minor confraternities in Santosgaon. Rather, a combination of economic, ideological, and political factors appears to have come into play in generating such conflicts in recent times.

The first time serious conflict broke out between the two confraternities in recent decades, it was focused on the rights centred around the *passe* celebrations. In my book [Robinson 1998: chapter 4], I described the *passe* [the re-enactment and solemn celebration of the crucifixion] as I had witnessed it during the period of fieldwork. However, in the past, the crucifixion had been more elaborately celebrated. Earlier, the *gauncar*s used to take the large cross in procession around the church after the evening service wearing their red capes. They would be met by members of the lower-caste confraternity who carried the image of Mary and wore the blue capes that were allotted to them. The biblical scene described in the gospel by John between Christ on the cross and his mother would then be enacted.

Some time in the late 1960s, this celebration became the focus of much conflict. A serious fight broke out between the *gauncar*s and the Sudra and Chardo non-*gauncar* members of the minor confraternity over who should carry the cross. They came up to attack the *gauncar*s and lunged at the cross, trying to snatch it from the latter. They were stopped with difficulty and the celebrations could not proceed that year. Now that the dissent had come out into the open, a new situation arose. Though the fight had included both Sudras and Chardo non-*gauncar*s, it emerged that the latter did not want to be associated with the Sudras. In the heated exchanges that followed, it emerged that the low Chardos really wanted to be given the privilege of joining the confraternity of the high Chardos—the Confraria de Santissimo e Nossa Senhora de Socorro—and of handling the cross and wearing the red capes that distinguished the latter. They wanted to be given rights in the celebration of the feasts of Our Lady of Perpetual Succour and St Bartholomew. However, they did not want the Sudras to be given all these rights: they should remain in the minor confraternity.

The conflict was brought to the attention of the then Archbishop of Goa, and the church, in the new, post-colonial times more acutely sensitive to any accusation of acquiescing to privileges for any particular social group, stopped the wearing of red capes by the high-caste *gauncars* and the carrying of the large cross in procession. The conflict slowly died down after that. As a result of this conflict, the dominance exercised by the major confraternity in rituals centred around the church was, to some extent, challenged. Today, the situation is complex. We find that while the members of the minor confraternity wear their blue capes on the feast of St Sebastian, on the feasts organized by the high-caste *gauncars* red capes are no longer worn.

Since the conflict though, the low Chardos have largely withdrawn themselves from the organization of the celebration of the feast of St Sebastian, saying: 'We do not involve ourselves in all this. They organize the feast. We keep out of all the arrangements'. Thus, they seek to separate themselves from the Sudras and other lower groups and assert their Chardo status, as it were. The Sudras, on the other hand, have begun to show more ostentation in the celebration of the feast, as we saw in the use of cameras and videos.

The next major conflict that we see in the village is essentially between the Sudras and the high Chardos. In this conflict, the Sudras tried to assert themselves by holding a separate prayer service on the day of the *passe*, Good Friday. This new move by the Sudras was seen as a challenge not only by the Chardo *gauncars*, who drove them out of the church, but also by the low Chardos, who supported the latter. As one of them said to me: 'These Sudras are getting above themselves.'

What gave rise to this new conflict? It seems that the entry of the Charismatic movement into Goa in the early 1980s or so may once again have given new life to conflicts between the different social groups in the village. A brief description of the Charismatic movement may be in order here. The movement is part of a wider Pentecostal movement in Christian groups of all denominations, particularly Protestants, that originated in the late nineteenth and early twentieth centuries. It seems to have welled up more or less simultaneously and independently in various parts of the world. The movement entered the Catholic church in a big way in the 1960s in the United States, when it emerged out of the activities of various prayer groups which were influenced by the Pentecostal stress on the Holy Spirit. Since then, the movement has spread to all parts of the Catholic world.

The Charismatic movement relies on the biblical teachings in the New Testament that speak about the power and gifts of the Holy Spirit. Charismatics believe that they can obtain these spiritual gifts or powers through prayer and can use them in a variety of ways, particularly to heal or cure people of physical ailments or remove afflictions caused by evil spirits. Thus, the stress in the movement is on the spiritual power that Charismatics obtain from the Holy Spirit and its use in healing.

The Catholic church has had an uneasy relationship with the Charismatic movement. In theory, the movement has been approved of by the Roman church. However, in practice, as we see in Goa, while there are some priests associated with the movement, most parish priests tend to oppose the Charismatics because they see their activities as disruptive of the order of church ritual and ceremony and as promoting conflict within the church. In the 1970s, a number of Charismatic groups were formed in various parts of Goa. In Santosgaon, as in many other places, the movement tended to attract Sudra and other lower groups in particular. These groups find themselves socio–economically and politically in an inferior position within the existing hierarchies of caste, status, and power. As we shall see, they bring into the Charismatic movement some of their ideas and practices with respect to spirit affliction and healing.

It is not clear how the Charismatic movement came to India or became widespread here. It appears, though, that the movement was already in existence by the middle of this century among Christians in major cities and other urban areas. From there, it seems to have spread slowly to other places. In Goa, the movement grew out of its initial restriction to small groups of Charismatics. These were probably influenced by the teachings of Charismatic groups coming from outside Goa, possibly from nearby cities such as Mumbai and Pune.[3]

Let me describe the features of the Charismatic meetings I attended. Meetings of Charismatics take place in small groups in the houses of one of the members, or in larger groups when Charismatics from two or three villages might get together. They are usually held once or twice a week, during the evening when people are free from work. Most Charismatics are lay persons, but there are some nuns and priests associated with the movement in Goa. Two priests, in particular, are well-known to be very powerful Charismatics. These are Fr Savio and Fr Rufus. There are, however, some others as well. Most of the priests associated with the movement tend not to be linked with any particular parish but go from place to place organizing the meetings of the Charismatics and working with the various local groups. These priests, however, deny that there is any caste-based aspect to the movement. ...

---

[3]The Charismatic movement can perhaps be compared to various *bhakti* and devotional movements that have spread among Hindus all over India in this century. Many of these too are to be found among the urban populace, but there are also cases in villages where the low castes in particular have been drawn to such movements. [See chapter 13 above.]

Thus, there is nothing intrinsic to the Charismatic teachings or beliefs to link them unequivocally with the lower social groups. We must, therefore, look at them as they are found in the particular context and see how the lower social groups in Santosgaon take over these beliefs and practices and use them as part of their own conflicts with the high Chardos of the village.

One of the meetings I attended was led by Fr Savio and two lay persons, a man and a woman. The meeting began with the Charismatics standing up and singing aloud spontaneous praises to Christ and the Holy Spirit and clapping their hands. There were a few moments of spontaneous prayer by different members. Then came the moment for people who had been cured to give their testimonies. After each testimony, there was another period of singing, spontaneous prayer, and clapping. Later, there was the praying over the sick and healing of afflictions. This brought the meeting to an end. This was the essential pattern of most of the Charismatic meetings.

This pattern, as we see, is different from the mass I have described earlier. In the mass, specific prayers were said and these were led by the priest. In the Charismatic meetings, there was what I call a spontaneity. In using this word, I am referring to several things. First, while there are leaders who open the meeting and often say the first prayer, they are not always (or only) priests but include lay persons as well. Further, after the initial introduction, anyone from the group can take up the prayers 'as they might be moved by the Holy Spirit'. Stress is therefore placed not on a particular order imposed by a priest or anyone else but on how the Holy Spirit moves people during the meetings.

People are encouraged to bring up their own concerns in their prayers. They might pray aloud for their families, their needs, or their illnesses, and so on. No control is exercised to ensure that prayers go in a certain order. Both men and women participate in the prayers and there are no caste or status distinctions to be seen. Most of the members are, in any case, from the lower castes. After each prayer there is a pause during which someone else may speak. If the pause is long enough to assume that no-one else wishes to pray aloud, the leader (or even someone else) may start up a hymn of praise and the meeting proceeds.

Finally, what we saw in the mass was that people had to follow a particular pattern of postures: at certain times everyone had to sit or kneel, at other times everyone had to stand together. An emphasis seemed to be placed on passivity, i.e. on listening or responding to the priest rather than on taking a more active part in the service. In Charismatic meetings, on the other hand, there is a more active participation on the part of the people. Clapping, singing, and sometimes even dancing are seen as accepted forms of worship. No regular order is imposed: people may sit, stand, or kneel during the prayer meetings as they wish or feel themselves motivated to do so. The absence of any clear hierarchy between the leaders and the group, of status distinctions, or of any rigidity in modes of worship make me speak of these meetings as being somewhat more spontaneous in character than the mass or other church rituals.

Why do people join this movement? Which are the kinds of people who join? What are they looking for? As one Sudra man told me: 'In the church it is all very rigid: sit, stand, kneel and all that. When I joined the Charismatics it was so different: spontaneous prayer, clapping, singing. I liked it'. ... The themes of healing and possession emerged repeatedly in what people said to me about their reasons for joining the movement. At one meeting, a low-caste woman told me:

My son was very sick. It was diagnosed that he had cancer. The X-ray had shown that there was a growth in his stomach. My sister came and talked to us. She had joined the Charismatic movement and she thought they could help. They had cured her cough, she said. I decided to take my son to one of the meetings. There, when the time came for healing, three of the leaders of the Charismatic group came and prayed over my son. Nothing seemed to show for some time, but when we got home, my son said that he felt less pain. That week we went to take another X-ray and they found that there was nothing. The growth had gone! From that time, I have been coming regularly for the meetings.

... Lower-caste members seem to have taken to the Charismatic movement and to have merged with it certain ideas about spirit affliction and healing. Mosse (1986) shows for the Tamil Catholics, as Caplan (1987) does for Madras Protestants, that ideas about spirits and misfortune have, in recent times, been integrated with the Charismatic and Pentecostal movements.

In Santosgaon, at least for some lower-caste Catholics, involvement in the Charismatic movement has become a means which they can use to challenge the high castes on their own ground, i.e. within the church. This happened in Santosgaon church in 1991 on the occasion of Good Friday. ... Apparently, on that day a group of Charismatics, consisting particularly of Sudras, had approached the parish priest and asked him if they could conduct a small prayer service in the church after the *passe* and the evening mass. The priest did not know that they were Charismatics and agreed. In the evening, the group of about sixty to seventy Charismatics came to the church to pray. They sat at the benches normally occupied by the laity during church services. They began in the usual manner with praise to the Holy Spirit and singing and clapping.

Apparently, knowledge of what was happening in the church came to Mr Viegas, a first-class Chardo *gauncar* of the village. He quickly went to the house of other high Chardos and gathered a number of men together. About thirty of them came with sticks, stones, and bricks and entered the church. They ... ordered the Charismatics out of the church. The later refused to go, saying that they had asked the parish priest's permission.

Furious, the Chardo *gauncars* went to the parish house and called out the priest. Fiercely they demanded to know how he had permitted all these lower-caste people to come in here and start all their singing and so on. The priest denied that he knew what they were going to do, saying he had just thought they wanted to come in and pray quietly in the church, like many other people do on Good Friday. If he had known, he said, he would not have let them. The Chardo *gauncars* demanded that the church be closed. They went back and there was a fierce scuffle between the two groups, the *gauncars* pushing the Charismatics out of the church and even using their sticks. They threw the stones at them as they were going. No one, however, was seriously hurt. The Chardo *gauncars* made sure that the church doors were closed and locked before they went home.

What are we seeing in all this? The lower-caste Charismatics who came in on Good Friday (and who were members of the minor confraternity) may be said to have deliberately chosen that day to make a statement within the church. It has always been the high Chardo *gauncars* who have controlled the ritual celebrations on that day. The other social groups may only participate in the service or 'pray quietly' at other times. It is not for them to conduct their own service on their own lines or in their own way. This is precisely what the Sudra Charismatics seem to have been trying to do. As one of them said: 'We wanted to have our own service. These people organize everything otherwise. We also want a role in the celebrations.'

The groups which oppose these people see them as a threat to their own privileges, which are maintained by the ordered, hierarchical form of worship generally seen in the mass and in church celebrations. The kneeling, sitting, standing and, generally, ordered worship in church is, in a sense, challenged by the spontaneous prayer and worship, the singing and clapping of the Charismatics. The Chardo *gauncar*'s right to oversee Good Friday celebrations is also challenged by them. The priests also oppose the Charismatics, if for slightly different reasons. ...

In the new, democratic atmosphere, the church is clearly less inclined to openly support the privileges of the high-caste *gauncars*. Yet, while the priest says that he is 'not for or against any group', his position involves an implicit support of the high-caste élites in the village. As one high Chardo said to me: 'The priest would not have let them in if he had known what they were going to do. [This is confirmed by what the priest apparently said when the conflict occurred].' Finally, even the lower Chardos come out against the Sudras in this matter. I quoted earlier one who said that they, i.e. the Sudras, were 'getting above themselves'. This is part of the attempt of the low Chardos to separate themselves from the Sudras and assert their higher status.

These disputes are about privileges within the church, which is itself found embedded in the local relations of power and hierarchy. In the present times, as I have pointed out earlier, new kinds of tensions have given rise to and fed these disputes. Till now, however, the Chardo *gauncar*s of the village, with the tacit support of the church, have managed to put down any attempts to take control from them. Moreover, the socially mobile lower groups have not attempted so much to fight the system itself but, rather, have sought to use their own newly acquired wealth to gain some of its privileges for themselves.

We might conclude by saying that the recent changes within the agrarian economy have not altered social relations in the village radically. However, the situation is fluid and the probability of more such conflicts in the future is very high. For one, we might recall the words of the Sudra informant who, speaking about the possibility of lower-caste control in the panchayat said: 'Maybe things will change soon'. Perhaps, these groups will gain control in the panchayat in the future. If this happens, it may strengthen the position of these groups against the high castes. The fact that the church itself now seeks compromise in situations of conflict may also encourage those lower down the scale to use the opportunity to continue their struggle to gain the privileges they seek in church ritual.

Alternatively, and much more radically, they could opt out, as it were. A strengthening of the Charismatic and Pentecostal movements could bring about a shift: the complete and lasting transfer of religious affiliation to these from the established churches. If this should, indeed, happen, the rules of the game would change entirely.

REFERENCES

Appadurai, Arjun and C. Breckenridge.
1976 The south Indian temple: Authority, honour, and redistribution. *Contributions to Indian Sociology* 10, 2: 187–211. [See chap. 16 above.]
Caplan, Lionel.
1987 *Class and culture in urban India: Fundamentalism in a Christian community.* Oxford: Clarendon Press.
Dirks, Nicholas, B.
1987 *The hollow crown.* Cambridge: Cambridge University Press.
Gomes, O.
1987 *Village Goa: A study of Goan social structure and change.* Delhi: S. Chand & Co.
Mosse, C.D.F.
1986 Caste, Christianity and Hinduism: A study of social organization and religion in rural Ramnad. D. Phil thesis, University of Oxford.
Ryan, Laurence.
1968 The laity. *In* Kevin McNamara, ed., *Vatican II: The constitution on the church.* London: Geoffrey Chapman Ltd.

Religious Devotion and Politics at Hazratbal in Kashmir

Muhammad Ishaq Khan

The *dargah* [shrine] of Hazratbal is situated on the shores of the picturesque Dal lake in Srinagar, a city of great antiquity. Being the repository of the sacred hair of Prophet Muhammad,[1] the shrine attracts over a lakh of devotees from every nook and corner of the valley on the eve of two important local festivals, namely Miladun-Nabi (birthday of the Prophet) and Mi'raj-i 'Alam (the day commemorating the Prophet's heavenly journey, in which he reached the immediate presence of God).[2]

Excerpted from Muhammad Ishaq Khan, The significance of the dargah of Hazratbal in the socio–religious and political life of Kashmiri Muslims. In Christian W. Troll, ed., *Muslim shrines in India: Their character, history and significance*, New Delhi: Oxford University Press, 1992. Pp. 172–88. © Oxford University Press.

[1]The sacred hair (*muy-i muqaddas*) 'is fitted in an erect position in a quartz container. The bottom is held in a silver cap which cannot be removed and the top of the hair is slightly curved. The container is constructed like a thermometer tube, opaque on one side, and the holy hair can be seen only from the side opposite. It cannot be seen from any other position. At the top of the container there is a cylindrical lid tapering to an end. The container is mounted on a round, silver base. Both these parts are fitted into the main cylinder containing the relic. The overall length of the tube, its lid and the base is about five inches and this whole object is used for exposition. It is kept in a gold-embroidered narrow bag fastened at one end by a thin string. This bag is wrapped up in a piece of green velevet and kept in a walnut box.' See Mullick 1971: 117–18.

[2]The holy relic is exhibited on these occasions and also on the eve of the death anniversaries of the four illustrious companions of Prophet Muhammad. During the nights of Milad and Mi'raj the *dargah* presents a luminous scene, when thousands of devotees perform supererogatory acts of worship in addition to the loud recitation of *durud*, *aurad* [benedictions], and poetry in praise of the Prophet.

Not long ago, thousands of pilgrims would flock to the shrine from all parts of the Kashmir valley, carrying with them the flags of famous saints. There is abundant evidence to show that for over the last two and a half centuries the shrine has attracted people from a wide area, and thus has gradually become an important element in the religious life of the people of Kashmir.

Speaking in terms of social history, Islam manifests itself in the *dargah* of Hazratbal more as a system of cultural symbols than as a doctrinal system of the *ulama* [scriptural specialists]. Islam, as Clifford Geertz (1973: 87–125) observes, not only exists in scripture but simultaneously in literature, images, objects, and public discourse or ceremonies expressive of a certain conception of the universe: a belief that a perfect harmony exists between the nature of reality and our habitual ways of acting, thinking, and actual imagining. Owing to its multiform manifestations in actual historical situations, Islam has established channels of communication between high culture and daily life, and, while synthesizing the two, has thereby made allowance for diversity and individuality within its fold. As a culture, then, it would be wrong to consider Islam as the major cause of historical events, but, as Ira M. Lapidus perceptively remarks, 'Islam is not something divorced from, above and beyond events. It is precisely a way of conceiving, of articulating, the ordinary issues of worldly experience—whether in moral, family, economic or political matters' (1980: 101).

In the present preliminary study, I have focused on the meaning and direction given to social action by the *dargah* of Hazratbal because it is a conspicuous element in the religious life of Kashmiri Muslims. An attempt has been made to interpret the facts concerning Hazratbal, not in isolation, but in close relationship with the recent Kashmiri Muslims' political resurgence from their centuries-old torpor.

THE HISTORY OF THE HOLY RELIC AND ITS VENERATION

Khwaja Nuruddin Ishbari, a rich Kashmiri merchant, is reported to have purchased the holy relic for a lakh of rupees from Sayyid 'Abdullah of Bijapur, who had brought it to the Deccan from Medina. Ishbari died on his way home from Bijapur in 1699, but the relic was brought to Srinagar along with his dead body, where its arrival created a state of reverential enthusiasm. So joyous and heart-touching was the reception given by the *ulama* [and others] to the holy relic that they vied with each other to carry the dead body of Ishbari on their shoulders. Men and even women chanting litanies and *durud* flooded the streets and bazaars of Srinagar to glimpse the relic. As a mark of respect to popular sentiment, Fazil Khan, the Mughal governor of Kashmir (*r*. 1698–1701), ordered that the relic be housed at a mosque in Bagh-i Sadiqabad, situated on the western bank of the Dal lake

(Diddamari n.d.). The place has since come to be known as Hazratbal, the abode of the Prophet Muhammad.

Since the sacred hair was kept at Bagh-i Sadiqabad, the place became the centre of pilgrimage for Kashmiri Muslims. From several folk songs and poems composed in Kashmiri in praise of the relic, it is evident that there has always been an endeavour to attribute the privileges of Medina to Hazratbal. This explains the fact that every now and then attempts at diminishing the importance of Hazratbal in the general consciousness were made by the Ahl-i Hadith [a fundamentalist group]. In fact, the 'orthodox' left no stone unturned in generating doubts about the authenticity of the relic. But such attempts at deprecating the sacredness and venerability of the shrine have seldom met with success, for several reasons.

However much doctrinal Islam devalues the veneration of relics, human nature seems to require the existence of such a phenomenon. For devotees, the shrine of Hazratbal, by virtue of its being the repository of the Prophet's hair, is actually a place of interaction and communication between the spiritually alive Prophet and his followers. It is a *sui generis* system of signification. The very layout of the shrine, with an object hallowed by its history and associations combined with the popular practice of reciting *aurad-i fathiya*[3] by the devotees with folded hands, and, significantly, with their faces towards the object, expresses symbolically somewhat distinctive characteristics of Islam in Kashmir. This practice of reciting *aurad* in chorus and of standing during the concluding part of it is not only common on special occasions but even on each Friday after the congregational prayers. It is also common to see devotees invoking the help of the Prophet with their eyes fixed at the particular place in the *dargah* where the relic is housed.

A careful study of the religious behaviour of the devotees at the mere sight of the relic in special gatherings held on the occasions referred to above leads us to assert that the sacred relic has almost been personified by a people who, after embracing Islam, have not given up their ancestral practices of adoring holy relics: this is so natural to the human heart.[4] On such occasions the loud expressions of personal suffering and grief by devotees is particularly worthy of examination, both from the historical and anthropological points of view. As a matter of fact, the Kashmiris, even after their 'conversion' to Islam, could not avoid retaining the essential elements of the local ancient

[3]For the importance of the invocatory prayers in Kashmiri Muslim life, see Khan, 1985: 86–97.

[4]Huien Tsiang, the first Chinese traveller to visit Kashmiri in 631, has written about the tooth of the Buddha which was venerated by the Buddhist monks of Kashmir as a sacred relic. In almost similar fashion, the custodians of a good number of the shrines of the *rishis* in Kashmir have preserved to this day some belongings of various saints as sacred objects. Such relics are exposed to the devotees on their anniversaries. ...

religious culture and ethos while adapting to Islamic forms of life and worship. Thus, the harmonious blending of historical circumstances and Islam emboldens us to assume that the beliefs comprising a given culture have important functions for the social structure and personality of the people and, indeed, continue to survive in spite of seemingly great historical upheavals.

The archetypal quest of every culture finds expression in journeys to places that embody the highest values of that culture. ...

The elevation of Hazratbal to Medina *thani* (second Medina) ... must have sprung not only from the devotees' unbounded veneration of the Prophet but also from practical difficulties in performing the sacred duty of the *hajj*. *Hajj* was beyond their reach owing to the abject poverty in which they lived through centuries of misrule and oppression. A visit to the shrine would, at least, have reduced in the devotees' religious consciousness the apparent difference of the physical barriers between the 'Arab and the 'Ajam. This sentiment is reflected in the following verses (Amin 1964: 6):

Whosoever has seen the sacred hair of Muhammad,
Has had in reality the vision of the Prophet,
[Although] he is entombed in Arabia,
His sacred hair sanctifies the *'ajam*
He reveals the eternal reality of his radiance only to those in Kashmir
Who have an abiding faith and are spiritually illuminated.

No wonder, therefore, that a devotee with a mystical love for Muhammad, at the very sight of the object (relic), feels himself to be under the influence of a divine agency or in the spiritual gathering (*darbār*) of Muhammad. While in a number of Kashmiri *na't* [hymns] a visit to Hazratbal is depicted as a spiritual flight to Medina, the importance of the spiritual gatherings is repeatedly emphasized by the priests in their invocations on festive occasions. It is also interesting to note here that on such occasions a number of Kashmiri verses, in which various blessings for the Prophet are invoked, are recited in chorus by the pilgrims in order to obtain the Prophet's intercessions.

But spiritual gains were not the goal of all visitors to the shrine. Health, procreation, longevity, protection from floods, famines, and other calamities were and are the fruits sought by pilgrims. In a society where the *mullah* reigned supreme, people were made to believe that a visit to the shrine would secure the object of their wishes (see Khan 1983). This is the reason why devotees, not unlike the Hindus, made (and still make) a great display of their veneration while approaching the shrine: lowly obeisances are made, hands are folded, and feet bared to the holy dust of the sacred precincts. Significantly, in a number of Kashmiri verses poets have expressed the yearning of their souls for a pilgrimage to Hazratbal with the main purpose of falling down in adoration at the entrance gate of the shrine.

It is no surprise, therefore, that in course of time crafty, hypocritical, and materialist custodians at the shrine have made much of the credulity, ignorance, and innocence of pilgrims. They have also developed highly structured and ritualistic practices which continue to characterize the *dargah* life of Hazratbal. In fact, the devotees, in accordance with customary practice, continue to make vows and offer gifts to the sacred shrine in return for the granting of desires. The walls of the *dargah* are covered with these offerings. Thus the devotion to, reverence for, and implicit trust in the shrine of Hazratbal is more important to the religious life of a great number of Kashmiri Muslims than any special veneration for the Quran or its teachings. For them, the Prophet is venerated with but little knowledge of his teachings; it is the sacred hair which protects against disease and disaster that is all important. The saviour role attributed to the relic for protecting Kashmiris has also been versified.

What is worthy of note here is that even today gullible devotees are seen touching the hands, body, or even the dress of the custodian exhibiting the relic in the hope of receiving a *baraka* [grace]. This reverence for the sacred hair and its custodians may be seen to have fostered what can almost be termed a patron–client relationship in a system of *piri–muridi* which marked *dargah* life in the past (see chapter 8 above). So tied were devotees to the custodians of the shrine that their services were required at every stage and the conception of a family 'priest' grew to such an extent that the *pir* was almost a permanent member of the household. In fact, *pirs* officiating at the various ceremonies and rituals at home and the shrine became an important organized exploitative agency.

SOCIO–ECONOMIC ASPECTS OF THE PILGRIMAGE TO HAZRATBAL

From the social point of view, the festive occasions at the shrine seem to add something joyous and memorable to the dull lives of the Muslims of the city. *Shikaras* [small boats] and *doongas* [big boats] were engaged by the devotees on the eve of local festivals. Tea and sumptuous dishes were served in boats; those musically inclined played on stringed instruments and drums to the accompaniment of singing songs full of ecstatic rapture.

Before the dawn of the modern era, rural–urban relationships and even inter-village communication were extremely limited; hence social contact was often confined to small isolated groups. The shrine of Hazratbal, of course, provided a rare opportunity for Muslims living in rural areas to come out of their closed social environment and join fellow Muslims from distant areas participating in the festival. This social opportunity also had the indirect effect of making them think in terms of the pivotal importance which the shrine occupied in the Valley.

From the economic point of view, Hazratbal offered opportunities— for buying and selling special kinds of commodities. It attracted merchants and artisans and good business was done. To those businessmen who found it difficult to sell their goods all through the year, the six fairs, coupled with the regular Friday congregations at the shrine, offered a suitable outlet for their surplus products. Even at present petty traders seem to do good business on such occasions.

HAZRATBAL AS A SYMBOL OF KASHMIRI MUSLIM IDENTITY

It is remarkable to note that the *dargah* of Hazratbal has, in the course of its history, evolved a distinctive ethics of its own which is reflected in the numerous poems written in praise of the relic as well as in the organization of *dargah* life. In fact, an elaborate code of etiquette and pageantry, visible on the eve of festive occasions, as well as the influx of devotees from the vast geographical area of the Valley, not only point to the integration of Kashmiri Muslims in the unified socio–cultural setting, but, as we shall explain, even in the political structure.

The importance of the shrine was recognized by Shaikh Abdullah during the heyday of his struggle against Dogra rule, when he brought it under the control of the Jammu and Kashmir Muslim Trust, known as Auqaf-i Islamia, [founded by the Shaikh; see Abdullah 1986: 275ff] in January 1943. Since then and, more particularly, after his expulsion from power in 1953, the shrine became a ready-made platform for the Kashmiri Muslim leadership to further its political objectives. What particularly attached political significance to the shrine were the fiery speeches delivered by Shaikh Abdullah after his release, first in 1958 and later in 1964. A brief description of the political role played by the shrine for almost the whole of the last three decades ... therefore seems to be necessary.

Paradoxically, the first attempt to use the Friday congregation at the Hazratbal shrine for vested political interests was made by the Dogra government in 1931, when some Muslim officers tried to dissuade the people from attending the public lectures of Shaikh Abdullah which were then held at the Jama' mosque in Srinagar. But Shaikh Abdullah's dramatic presence at the scene thwarted the plans of the Dogra officials; in fact he carried the day by exposing the evil designs of the government against the Muslims of Kashmir.

A significant feature of the Kashmir movement in the early thirties was the mobilization of mass support through some of the prominent mosques and shrines of Srinagar. The Jama' mosque was,[5] indeed, the first place in Srinagar where Kashmiri Muslims would assemble for political purposes. The policy of the government that kept the Muslims out of state service, heavy taxation, and the consequent destruction of existing [handicrafts], forced labour, a law severely punishing Muslims for cow-slaughter, and the open oppression by the Maharaja's officials—all these were the main issues confronting Kashmiri Muslims in the thirties (see Khan 1983: 129ff.). Muslim leaders often met at the Jama' mosque to protest against the actions of 'high state officials ... trampling on the rights of Muslims'.

It should be borne in mind that the basic foundations of Muslim resurgence in Kashmir rested on assumptions which were historically correct. After the Mughal occupation of Kashmir in 1586, the Kashmiri Muslim ruling class had virtually disappeared. On the other hand, the Kashmiri Pandits, who were few in numbers compared to the entire population of the valley, were able to join the ruling élite under the four sets of alien rulers, namely the Mughals (1586–1757), the Afghans (1757–1819), the Sikhs (1819–46), and the Dogras (1846–1947).* The economic problems of the impoverished peasantry and artisans who formed the bulk of the Muslim population in Kashmir thus became a focus among the emerging educated middle-class of Kashmir's Muslims. Unlike the elitist character of the Muslim resurgence in the rest of northern India, the Kashmiri Muslim leadership did not project and further the vested interests of certain [privileged] social classes. Nor did the Kashmiri leaders exaggerate the basis of Islamic solidarity or romanticize Islam's imperial past in India, as was done to a marked degree by the Indian Muslim leadership.

However, one result of Shaikh Abdullah's emergence as an ardent champion of Muslim sentiment in the Jama' mosque was the gradual eclipse of the ecclesiastical leadership of the Mir Waiz,[6] followed, strangely enough,

[5]Although the Jama' mosque served as an important political centre in the earliest phase of the freedom struggle in Kashmir, it was actually the mosque of Khanqah-i Mu'alla in Srinagar which remained the stronghold of the Muslim Conference and its successor, the National Conference.

* [It would be more accurate to say that this was true of some Pandits. Most of them suffered like the Muslims did, if not more.—Editor].

[6]The Mir Waiz family of Srinagar wielded considerable influence over the Muslim masses before the advent of Shaikh Abdullah on the political horizon of Kashmir. As a matter of fact, it was the Mir Waiz of the Jama' mosque and that of Khanqah-i Mu'alla mosque who were well-known both for their eloquence and recriminations in their religious sermons. It was the Mir Waiz of the Jama' mosque who parted ways with Shaikh Abdullah in 1933, after ably supporting him in the ferment of the early 1930s. The Mir Waiz of Khanqah-i Mu'alla, on the contrary, always supported Shaikh Abdullah.

by the combination of the religious and political leadership of Kashmiri Muslims in his own person. Consequently, and despite his profound faith in secularism, he not only got into conflict with the Mir Waiz family, but, at a later stage, also with the Congress leadership at the centre.

Shaikh Abdullah was, indeed, the only potent force in this century able to influence Kashmiri Muslim belief towards adopting a secular view of religion, culture, and [politics]. He rejected for Kashmir a theocratic conception of the Islamic state; nevertheless, he used the affective and conative power of Islamic symbols in pursing his particular goals. In his several speeches delivered at the *dargah* and also in his autobiography, he exemplifies a high incidence of Islamic symbolism when he attributes the theft of the holy relic from the *dargah* to forces which aimed at undermining the solidarity of the Kashmiri Muslim community. The solidarity of the community, he believed, was based on the social and religious ties fostered by the shrine of Hazratbal. So aware was Abdullah of the *dargah*'s central importance in the life of Kashmiri Muslims that he apprehended serious implications for their solidarity should the relic be lost. The theft of the relic created a wave of resentment throughout the valley; so it would be worthwhile to examine the nature of response which it evokes as an Islamic symbol in Kashmiri society.

THE HOLY RELIC AGITATION

In the early morning of 27 December 1963 the side-door of the passage leading to the room housing the holy relic was found 'broken open and both locks of the inner door leading to the sanctuary had also been forced open. The lock of the front door of the passage had also been forced from inside. The wooden box containing the Muy-i Muqaddas [i.e. the sacred hair of the prophet] had been taken out from the small wooden shelf' (Mullick 1971: 120).

The news of the disappearance of the relic spread like wildfire throughout the Valley. It is not difficult to recall how angry mobs began to gather the same morning in Lal Chowk and Badshah Chowk, the two busiest business centres in Srinagar city. All offices and shops remained closed. And within a short span of forty-eight hours people from all over the Valley carrying black flags began to pour into the city. B.N. Mullick, the intelligence officer who was specially deputed by Jawaharlal Nehru to recover the relic, gives an eyewitness account of the people's resentment in these words:

There was no end to the streams of people and all the main roads were blocked by thousands of people and the smallest procession was at least a mile long covering the entire width of the road including foot-paths. Administration had completely collapsed and no vestige of it remained visible except the armed political guards. (1971: 128, 130).

The theft of the relic enveloped the Valley in gloom. So tense was the atmosphere that in a special broadcast to the people of Kashmir Nehru appealed to them to remain 'calm, patient and co-operate' with the intelligence officer for the recovery of the relic. So critical was the situation that Nehru even felt that the holy relic agitation might 'seriously jeopardize India's position in the Valley' (ibid.: 124).

Although the agitation started purely on religious grounds, it assumed a political nature when an Action Committee was formed with Maulvi Muhammad Farooq as its chairman. The Committee, while demanding the immediate recovery of the relic, brought to the forefront certain political issues. Among these was the release of Shaikh Abdullah [from detention] and the settlement of the Kashmir problem. The holy relic agitation continued for nine days and came to an end on the evening of 4 January 1964, when the relic was recovered under mysterious circumstances. Mullick writes: 'I cannot describe the process which led to its replacement at the place from which it had been removed on 27 December. This was an intelligence operation, never to be disclosed'. (Ibid.: 142).

IMPORTANCE OF THE SACRED RELIC AGITATION

The sacred relic agitation was undoubtedly an event of far-reaching importance. Not only did it pave the ground for the ushering in of a democratic process in the state, it also brought about a salutary change in the centre's policy towards Kashmir. Mullick records Nehru's conversations in a meeting of the members of the Emergency Cabinet Committee in which Kashmir affairs were discussed:

The Prime Minister started by saying that, even after fifteen years of association, if Kashmir still remained in such an unstable state that even on a simple issue like the *Muy-i Muqaddas* the people could be so provoked as to rise in defiance of the government, then, in his opinion, a new approach had to be made and a radical change in our thinking about Kashmir was called for. He said that he felt disappointed that after all that had been done for the people of Kashmir they were apparently still [i.e. calm] to a certain amount of misgovernment. ... He also felt that Shaikh Abdullah still had a strong hold on the people of Kashmir and in the changed circumstances, no political settlement in the valley could be thought of without bringing him in. It was therefore desirable that he should be released. ... (Ibid.: 172).

It would not be too bold to assume that, by virtue of its control over the *dargah* of Hazratbal, the National Conference leadership has developed against the centre's attitude towards Kashmir a system of self-defence and self-preservation. In this context, an indelible influence of the holy relic agitation on Shaikh Abdullah's mind, likely to escape the notice of historians, needs to be examined here.

It remains a fact that during the agitation the Kashmiri Muslim community showed its solidarity in spite of the differences among various religious and political leaders on some issues concerning the community. What is of significance is that not only the Ahl-i Hadith, in spite of their denunciation of relic worship, but also the Shias played an important role in awakening religious consciousness among Kashmiri Muslims. One can hardly forget the scene of the grand procession taken out by Shias through the city for the recovery of the relic. The procession was led by no less a person than Agha Sayyid of Badgam, the most respectable leader among the Shias of Kashmir. The leading role in the agitation played by another Shia leader, Maulwi 'Abbas, was by no means insignificant.

Although politically, for many years after his release, Shaikh Abdullah remained *hors de combat*, he left no stone unturned, through his sermons at the *dargah*, to bring home to his people the importance of Hazratbal as a symbol of their cultural and religious identity. Besides playing the role of a religious preacher at the *dargah*, he concentrated his whole attention on its construction. In his enthusiasm to rebuild the structure of the shrine on a true Islamic pattern, the Shaikh felt no qualms about demolishing the historical mosque built during the reign of the Mughal emperor Shah Jahan. This building, which was considered one of the best specimens of the famous wooden architecture of Kashmir, as a matter of fact, fell victim to Abdullah's megalomaniac desire to immortalize his political links with the *dargah* of Hazratbal. Shaikh Abdullah toured various parts of the Valley and particularly visited almost every house in Srinagar, raising funds for the construction of the new mosque of Hazratbal. On each Friday he would personally collect donations from devotees visiting the *dargah*, who, as a matter of fact, would also seek the blessings of their beloved leader, now turned into a *darwish*.

Consequently, Shaikh Abdullah was not only able to revitalize the local affiliations of Kashmiri masses for the shrine, but even strengthened his claims for making it an organizational focus for his future political programme. That he was also successful in perpetuating the central importance of the shrine in the religious consciousness of Kashmiri Muslims is still evidenced by the large attendance of people at the shrine on each Friday, and particularly on festive occasions. It is significant that during the first twelve days of Rabi'-ul-Auwal thousands of men and women from various parts of the city make it a point to offer congregational prayers at the shrine. Fridays following the 12th Rabi'-ul-Auwal and Miraj-i 'Alam are grand occasions in the religious life of Kashmiri Muslims. Over a lakh devotees offer midday prayers on these days. Such occasions have generally been utilized by Shaikh Abdullah and, in recent times, by his successor Farooq Abdullah, for a reaffirmation of their resolve to defend the special status of Kashmir [within the Indian Union]. On these and other occasions the National Conference has rarely failed to use Muslim rhetoric in defence of Kashmiri Muslim identity, as well as in condemnation of communal politics in the country. At times the National Conference leadership has been severe in its criticism of the insidious designs of the 'communalists' in and outside the state for their alleged activities in destroying the 'Muslim character' of the state.

It would, however, be wrong to assume that through the *dargah* of Hazratbal the National Conference works its religious–political ideology. Two points invalidate such an assumption; firstly, the National Conference has always induced the people to see beyond religion, despite its use of religious places for political purposes; and secondly, in spite of the strong hold exercised by the National Conference over important shrines and mosques, it has seldom sought religious, or for that matter even social, reform in Kashmiri society. However, its use of the Hazratbal shrine to buttress its claim to ruling the state continues to present a paradox. Consequently, the National Conference has, owing to its arrogation of political functions and prestige through the *dargah* for its policies, subordinated the role of the shrine to its claim rather than to that of religion in the strictest sense. No wonder, therefore, that the Madinatul-Ulum, the only institution established by Shaikh Abdullah at the shrine for imparting religious education, has almost become defunct. The general level of training of *imams* in this institution has always remained low by all standards, owing to the Muslim Trust's preoccupation with the politics of the National Conference. And, indeed, Auqaf-i-Islamia has earned a bad name not only for its politicking but even on account of its malfunctioning. An inevitable result of the twin roles played by the National Conference and its subsidiary wing, the Auqaf-i-Islamia, has been the absence of a stable social and religious life among Kashmiri Muslims.

But there is another side to the picture. Through the *dargah* of Hazratbal the National Conference has made much of the psychological genocide with which Kashmiri Muslims are threatened in the face of the Centre's attempts at undermining the special status of the state of Jammu & Kashmir. Thus it would not be incorrect to say that Hazratbal has created a distinctive approach within Islam in a secular state. It has not only sought to unite Kashmiri Muslims around the leadership of the National Conference, it has even motivated psychological commitment to the avowed struggle of the National Conference for the preservation of their distinct historical identity. That the shrine symbolizes the hopes of Kashmiri Muslims not only for countering attacks on their identity but even for keeping alive their centuries-old aspirations of living in conformity with their cherished cultural and religious ideals is reflected in the fervent invocations of the *imam* of the mosque each Friday.*

REFERENCES

Abdullah, Shaikh Muhammad.
1986 *Atish-i China* ???[in Urdu]. Srinagar: Ali Muhammad & Sons.
Amin, Pir Muhammad.
1964 *Jalwa-i muy-i Shara* ??? [in Urdu]. Srinagar: Bulbul Lankar.
Diddamari, Muhammad Azam.
n.d. *Waqi 'at Kashmir* [in Persian], no. 1843.
Jammu & Kashmir: Government Research and Publication Department.
Geertz, Clifford.
1973 *The interpretation of cultures.* New York: Doubleday.
Lapidus, Ira M.
1980 Islam and the historical experience of Muslim peoples. In *Islamic studies: A tradition and its problems.* Malibu, CA: Undena Publications.
Khan, Muhammad Ishaq.
1983 *Perspectives on Kashmir: Historical dimensions.* Srinagar: Gulshan.
1985 Islam in Kashmir: A historical analysis of its distinctive features. *In* Christian W. Troll, ed., *Islam in India.* Vol. 2. New Delhi: Vikas.
Mullick, B.N.
1971 *My years with Nehru.* New Delhi: Allied.

*[The National Conference lost power in 2003, but it retained considerable following among the Muslim masses of the Valley. The policies of the coalition government that took office after the elections, under the leadership of Mufti Muhammad Sayeed, although fiercely protective of Kashmiri ethnic identity, has not tried to utilize religious rhetoric in the pursuit of its goals.—Ed.]

Epilogue
Religion in India: An essay in interpretation

T.N. MADAN

Books of readings do not have concluding chapters for obvious reasons. In lieu of one, I offer an epilogue here, an essay on religion in India. It focuses on some interreligious conceptual categories and contemporary problems. It should serve to remind the readers of this book of some of the things that they will already have read in it. Both the introductory essay and the epilogue, which frame the readings, reflect my personal conviction about the necessity of religious pluralism as a political objective and its attractiveness as a cultural ideal. As always, what is necessary is clearer than what is defensible. The philosophical doubts about cultural pluralism are far from being settled, but may no longer be evaded. This is not the place, however, to engage even fleetingly in that debate.

I conclude this prefatory note by cautioning the reader that the greater attention given to the Indic religions in this essay in no way constitutes a value judgement about their importance on my part, although it does reflect my greater familiarity with them. I was born and brought up in a mixed (Hindu–Muslim) neighbourhood in the city of Srinagar in the Kashmir Valley. The Kashmiri Pandits knew a great deal about the practice of Islam by Kashmiri Muslims, just as they knew about the Hindu way of life. This knowledge was, however, only observational. There was little interest in deeper understanding of one another's religious beliefs and ethics. Mutual goodwill and social harmony did not seem to be dependent on that. The bonds of vicinage and language seemingly sufficed to cope with acknowledged differences of religion. There were economic ties too but these were contingent. In short, there was mutual interaction and information but not enough knowledge. Subsequently, my studies as a sociologist also have tended to focus on the social dimensions of the religious life than its substantive (philosophical, theological) content.

A final comment. This essay was written fifteen years ago. Today I would conclude it more cautiously, emphasizing that humanism is only one of the varieties of religion in our times. The prospect is pluralistic.

* * * *

Ekam sad vipra bahudha vadanti.
(The Truth is but one, though the learned state it in many ways.)
—Rig Veda
c. 1200 BC

Personally, I think the world as a whole will never have, and need not have, a single religion.

—Mahatma Gandhi
30 May 1913

To write about religion in India without querying the notion of religion as a discrete element of everyday life is to yield to the temptation of words. The point is not that the religious domain is not distinguished from the secular but rather that the secular is regarded as encompassed by the religious—even when considered opposed to it—and not independent of it. The relationship is hierarchical. That is, religion in indigenous cultures is believed to be the foundation of society, and the traditional vision of life is holistic. This is the first principle for any discussion of religion in India.

It is an irony of history that modern intellectuals, Indians as well as Westerners, have generally considered religion (or religiosity) the bane of the good enlightened life in South Asia and indeed everywhere. Considering the abuse of religion in our times, this opinion is not surprising. Thus, Jawaharlal Nehru wrote: 'We have to get rid of that narrowing religious outlook, that obsession with the supernatural and metaphysical speculations, that loosening of the mind's discipline in ceremonial and mystical emotionalism, which come in the way of our understanding ourselves and the world' (1961: 552–53). Needless to emphasize, *understanding* here means comprehension in terms of Western rational thought.

There are other modern Indians who have wondered if the religious label that has stuck to Indian culture is genuine or only spurious. Dhurjati Prasad Mukerji (one of the founding fathers of sociology in India) wrote about fifty years ago: 'Our material conditions, our political subjection, our nationalism conspire in the currency of the story started by the West for its own purposes that Indians, by and large, are ... addicts to religion, that both the body and the soul of Indian culture are annexed and possessed by the Divinity' (1948: 6). He felt constrained to add, however, that those 'progressives' in India who dismiss religion as the opium of the people not only ignore social facts but also 'the historical process by which these have assumed the attached social values' (ibid.: 7).

Contrast these expressions of the negative or apologetic attitude toward religion with the characteristically simple but emphatic expression of faith

Reproduced with minor verbal changes and bibliographical additions from *Daedalus*, Fall 1989, pp. 115–46. © American Academy of Arts and Sciences, Cambridge, MA.

by Mahatma Gandhi: 'For me every, the tiniest, activity is governed by what I consider to be my religion' (1986: 391). For Gandhi and the millions of Indians he represented, religion was indeed constitutive of society. This is as true of Indian Muslims, for whom the ultimate reality is spiritual and for whom consequently there is no such thing as a profane world, as it is of the Sikhs, who deny the separation of spiritual goals from the pursuit of political power, and of the Hindus, who see the cosmos as a single whole, a unity, comprising all creation animated by one spirit.

Let me state here·that I am inclined to believe that the religious, or traditional, view of life has not really been the source of conflict between peoples, that it is its perversion which has been so. The scope of interreligious understanding is, in my opinion, immense, and it is in no way contradicted by the holism of the religious traditions of mankind. And yet one surely may not turn a blind eye to the conflicts between religious communities which have for so long caused untold suffering to innocent people everywhere. The historicity of such conflicts does not, however, constitute an argument against religion or signify its irrelevance; it only points to the unrealized promise of cultural pluralism. The history of India is the history of syncretism among religious traditions as well as conflict between religious communities, and should have a great deal to tell us about both processes. It is therefore important that we read history carefully, for while the clash between obscurantist-revivalist ideologies has turned out to be not only barren but also bloody, secularism (in the Enlightenment sense of the term) has nowhere—not even in Europe—succeeded in providing a comprehensive alternative to the religious worldview. In fact, secularization has entailed the loss of meaning in human life about which Max Weber wrote so eloquently.

Now, all worldviews, whether religious or secular, have their metaphysical foundations, which are the basis and an integral component of social activity everywhere. In India, the root paradigm of all the major indigenous religious traditions is that of the cosmic moral social order, of *dharma*. It is to an interpretation of this that I now turn.

METAPHYSICS: *DHARMA*

Dharma, a Sanskrit word, is generally employed in contemporary writing in most Indian languages to stand for religion, but this usage is not satisfactory. According to Hinduism, Jainism, Buddhism, and Sikhism, the universe is sustained by *dharma*. The great Indian epic *Mahabharata* (c. 400 BC–400 AD) says: '*Dharma* is so called because it protects *dharnat* (everything); *Dharma* maintains everything that has been created; *Dharma* is thus that very principle which can maintain the universe' (Lingat 1973: 3 n2). Today, we do not need old texts or modern philosophers to tell us that 'next to the category of reality, that of *dharma* is the most important concept in Indian thought' (Radhakrishnan 1923: 52). Almost every Hindu, Jain, Buddhist, or Sikh, even if he is illiterate and of humble origin, knows that *dharma* is the foundation of the good life. Whether this is seen naively as an instance of equal social distribution of knowledge, or critically as the hegemonic imposition of the thought of the Brahmins on others, the fact remains that *dharma* is a rich word of everyday speech in India. This does not, however, mean that its meaning is easily conveyed in non-Indian languages. It is broader and more complex than the Christian notion of religion and less jural than our current conceptions of duty. It emphasizes awareness and freedom rather than the notion of *religio*, or obligation.

A concept of multiple connotations, *dharma* includes cosmological, ethical, social, and legal principles that provide the basis for the notion of an ordered universe. In the social context, it stands for the imperative of righteousness in the definition of the good life. More specifically, *dharma* refers to the rules of social intercourse laid down traditionally for every category of actor (or moral agent) in terms of social status (*varna*), the stage of life (*ashrama*), and the qualities of inborn nature (*guna*). Put simply, for every person there is a mode of conduct that is most appropriate: it is his or her *svadharma*, which may be translated as 'vocation.' The emphasis here is upon legitimacy in terms of authenticity; and authenticity flows from one's social position and physical nature; external coercion is of no real value. So much so indeed that the *Bhagavad Gita* (c. 200 BC–200 AD), which is in our times the most widely known text of the Hindu religious tradition, repeatedly exhorts the actor to prefer failure in the pursuit of his vocation to success in someone else's role. Action to which one is born arises spontaneously and is easily performed: it is not a burden. When one achieves such a state of dharmic existence or moral perfection—the mystic Jiddu Krishnamurti called it 'choiceless awareness'—contexts are dissolved, specificities disappear, dualities are transcended, and what survives is a seamless moral sensibility.

Many scholars—Indians as well as foreigners—have commented on the absence of 'natural law' from Hindu thought and its alleged ethical relativism. What I have just said about the dissolution of contexts may be seen to underscore this problem rather than to resolve it. It is therefore relevant to mention here that the Hindu tradition does in fact entertain the notion of universally applicable law, *sadharan* or *samanya* dharma, which is the foundation for all specific *dharmas*. Thus, untruthfulness, wanton killing, stealing, sexual assault, or self-seeking endeavor at the cost of others may never be justified under any circumstances, though the punishment for transgression is not the same in all cases. Similarly, forgiveness, application to work, sincerity, personal cleanliness, and moral watchfulness are virtues that Hinduism calls for everybody to cultivate. The charge of ethical relativism does not really hold. Moreover, the unease of modern scholars when faced with complex Indian traditions is a result of their distrust of pluralism; but pluralism is not a self-evident moral flaw; it is in fact the strength of many non-Western ethical traditions.

Dharma as the foundation of the good life consists of the rational pursuit of economic and political goals (*artha*) as well as pleasure (*kama*). Taken together, these three constitute the goals of life (*purushartha*), and are hierarchically related: the pursuit of pleasure ought to be subordinated to economic and political goals and to *dharma*, and the pursuit of economic and political goals must likewise conform to *dharma*. In other words, one must avoid the acquisition of wealth and the gratification of desires if they involve the violation of *dharma*.

Although only three principal goals of life are mentioned in the earlier texts, a significantly different fourth goal is discussed at much length in the *Mahabharata* and has since remained prominent. This is the goal of *moksha*, or freedom through transcendence from the cycle of birth, death, and rebirth, and therefore from the pursuit of the other three goals. *Dharma*, inclusive of *artha* and *kama*, is a grand design of life, and *moksha* is the alternative. There is no contradiction here. *Dharma* is the basis of the householder's life, which is highly prized. Its repudiation is renunciation, or *sannyasa*. Ideally, however, one may become a renouncer only after fulfilling the obligations of householdership. As for the renouncer himself, he too is bound but by his own *dharma*.

Non-Indian students of the Hindu way of life have been deeply impressed with renunciation as an ideal for personal life just as they have been by the caste system as a framework for social life. Hindus themselves acknowledge the fascination with renunciation, and yet postpone it to the very end of a person's life as its fourth stage, after the stages of study, householdership, and retirement. In fact, only a microscopic minority actually renounce the world. Not only is the renouncer a theatrical figure, dressed in ocher robe, carrying his staff and begging bowl, a living embodiment of self-control and asceticism; he is also an exemplar of values. As the French social anthropologist Louis Dumont has reminded us, renouncers have often been founders of sects in the caste-based Hindu society' (1980: 275, 284–6).

Perhaps because this ideal is so noble and lofty, reverence for it as an ideal is combined with a healthy skepticism about real-life renouncers. Hindu tradition stresses the importance of overcoming dualistic choices and the possibility of doing so without renouncing, by means of detachment and the overcoming of all passions. Sociologically, the householder who follows *dharma* is the true hero. Everyday the renouncer knocks at his front door, asking for alms: by his very presence, he invites the householder to renounce the world. And the householder hears equally often, if not oftener, the muffled yet powerful knock of the sensualist at his back door, as it were, tempting him to a life of pleasure. The householder's heroism lies in the good sense of the middle path, which the *Katha Upanishad* tells us is sharp like the razor's edge (see Madan 1987a).

The middle path (*madhyamika*) is also what is extolled above all in the Buddhist tradition. It comprises 'the noble eightfold path' based on 'the four noble truths.' Gotama the Buddha (563–483 BC), in his first sermon at Sarnath to the five disciples who had stood by him, set in motion, as the Buddhists say, 'the wheel of the cosmic law of righteousness' (*dhammachakka*). The enlightened Gotama stressed the folly of the pursuit of pleasure, for it produces pain and suffering. The first truth of life, he said, is sorrow; the second, that the source of sorrow is desire; the third, that sorrow can be ended if craving is eliminated; and the fourth, that the eightfold path leads to *nibanna*, the 'blowing out' of both desire and suffering. We see that no sooner had the seer stated the truth than he pointed to action in a striking unity of the theory and the art of life.

The noble eightfold path is, then, *dharma* (*dhamma* in Pali). It consists of right views, right resolve, right speech, right conduct, right livelihood, right effort, right mindfulness, and right concentration. This exhortation in all its nobility and severity is addressed to the monk who seeks refuge in the community of monks. Monks and lay Buddhists seek the protection of the Buddha and *dhamma*. *Dhamma* is equally acknowledged as the foundation of the universe by all schools of Buddhism—Hinayana, Mahayana, Theravada, and others.

It would be an oversimplification to treat the Buddhist *dhamma* and the Hindu *dharma* as essentially the same, though they are similar. For one thing, the Buddhist notion of cosmic and moral law is in no way whatsoever linked with any notion of the supernatural, while such an association acquires increasing importance in the history of Hinduism. Moreover, the hierarchical triad of *dharma*, *artha*, and *kama* is significantly restated so as to stress that *dharma* as the cosmic law, or the Truth, absolutely encompasses the righteousness of the ruler. *Dhamma* is indeed called the 'king of the righteous king.' It is this absolutist conception of *dhamma* that resulted in the elevation of nonviolence (*ahimsa*) and compassion as supreme values.

In Jainism *ahimsa* forms the very core of *dharma*; indeed, *ahimsa* is *dharma*. There is also a special use of the term, according to which it denotes a spatial category in Jain physics—the space in which movement takes place. Movement is central to Jain practice in many ways; as moral exertion, it is the essence of life. In its more basic sense, *dharma* in the Jain tradition is the eternal law of respect for life; and for the Jains life is an attribute of practically everything that exists, including earth, water, and wind, so even the wind must not be harmed. As far as possible, nothing must be destroyed.

The notion of destroying or killing to protect *dharma* was, however, developed within the Hindu tradition. The war described in the *Mahabharata* is called the dharmic war. In fact the *Bhagavad Gita* puts forward the notion of *avatar*, or divine incarnation, as a means of destroying the wicked and restoring *dharma*. This idea has been incorporated into the Sikh tradition also.

Sikhs employ the word *dharam* (*dharma*) to describe their way of life, which is the same for all Sikhs irrespective of differences of social origin or personal conditions. It is a universally applicable code of conduct taught by the Divine Preceptor (*guru*) and expressing the Divine Commandment (*hukam*). Nanak, the founder of the Sikh faith, spoke of the five 'domains' (*khanda*) that constitute what I would call 'life space.' Of these, the first is *dharma*, or moral duty. The others are the domains of spiritual knowledge, human effort, divine benevolence, and truth. Sikh men consider it a moral duty to carry a small sword (*kirpan*) on their person to symbolize both the divinity and the individual's determination to kill or be killed in the defense of *dharma*. The congregational prayer of the Sikhs includes a reference to those who 'offered their heads at the altar of *dharma*.'

An examination of the notions of *dharma* in India's cultural traditions reveals that in the earliest formulations it had less to do with supernatural powers or rituals than with human activity and the moral integrity of the actor. The notion of a supreme being or divinity had remained alien to Jainism and Buddhism, but it gradually gained ground in the Hindu tradition. By the time the *Bhagavad Gita* came to be composed, the idea of *dharma* being divinely instituted and protected had become established.

According to the *Manusmriti* (c. 200 AD), there are four sources of *dharma*—namely, the original teaching, remembered traditions, the conduct of good people, and personal judgment. Whether what was originally taught and heard is revelation and, if so, whether revealed knowledge is to be traced to a divine origin are questions that have been long debated within the tradition but need not detain us here. More important, surely, is the mutual relationship between the four sources. A narrow exegesis of the texts might suggest a descending order of preference, but a more insightful interpretation would look upon the sources as a matrix of interacting factors. *Dharma* is not law or custom or conscience but all these in different combinations. Some of the truly significant interpretations of *dharma* have been provided by those who defied tradition and sought to discover it in their own conscience or, to put it differently, in moral reason. This is what Yuddhishthira, the hero of the *Mahabharata*, did; in our own time this is what Mahatma Gandhi did. And surely it is this acknowledgment of the superiority of moral reason to customary usage that underlies the power of the notion of *dharma*: it not only sustains but also transforms society.

PRAXIS: *KARMA*

Dharma as the abstract principle of the social order is a metaphysical concept. As a disposition of the mind, it is a subjective quality. As metaphysics and as psychology, it has practical consequences—namely, the obligation and the tendency to act in a particular way in specified situations. The synthesis of thought and action—of theory and practice—is even more clearly expressed in the notion of *karma*, another key concept of India's indigenous cultural traditions. *Dharma* and *karma* are inseparable and in certain contexts indistinguishable. If *dharma* is the social consensus about the good life, *karma* is the individual actor's effort to live according to it.

Karma literally means action. The *Bhagavad Gita* (3: 24) makes creativity obligatory for the Supreme Being himself, for if he did not act, the world would fall into ruins and there would be chaos. Divine creation is thus the paradigmatic karmic act. For human beings, the emphasis is on tasks to be accomplished, on desires to be fulfilled. The tasks may be traditionally commanded; the desires or goals are often empirically motivated. Traditionally, *karma* is said to be of three kinds—of the body, of speech, and of the mind— but it is best when it is all three together. The karmic act is value neutral. While *adharma* would mean evil, the opposite of *dharma*, the opposite of *karma* is absence of *karma* (*akarma*). It follows that while *dharma* produces *dharma*, the consequences of particular karmic acts may be meritorious or evil. This is the notion of the fruits of action, of compensation or retribution, which was regarded by Max Weber (1958: 118) as 'the unique Hindu theodicy' of the existing social order. He saw in *karma* the nearest that one could get to doctrinal belief in Hinduism, revealing more about his own Christina anxieties, perhaps, than about Indic cultures. Be that as it may, *karma* does stand for what may loosely be called a theory.

In all Indian cultural traditions, human actions have consequences that are inescapable. The fruits of action bring joy or sorrow depending on whether certain actions have been good or evil. Whatever cannot be enjoyed or suffered in the present life must be experienced hereafter in another birth, which may not be a human birth. To be born a human being is a rare privilege because it is only through such a birth that a soul may be freed from reincarnation.

An emphasis on the metaphysics of *karma* characterizes Western scholarship on India in our own time no less than in the late nineteenth century. Within the indigenous Hindu discourse, however, the emphasis is on pragmatics, on *karma in* action or *as* action. This is particularly true of the original Buddhist teaching. According to it, everybody is the architect, here and now, of his own destiny, for better or worse, depending on the moral choices he makes. The notion of karmic legacy is rejected. The Jains do, however, entertain the notion of karmic burden, which they seek to 'burn up' through the practice of severe austerities (something that the Buddha clearly disapproved of). They conceive of *karma* as a substance that accumulates in the process of transmigration and envelops the soul as a form of matter.

The Hindu concept of *karma* is, however, essentially pragmatic. Ask an orthodox Hindu about *karma* and he is more likely to talk of it as ritual than as abstract belief. In his life millennia of experience are summed up. Thus, *karma* will stand for prayer and worship addressed to favorite gods and goddesses: this is the popular ritual called *puja*. Its origins go back three thousand years, when the early Vedic seers, overwhelmed by the power of nature and by its beauty, anthropomorphized it—saw aspects of it as gods— and prayed to these gods for boons and protection. (Incidentally, the Vedic chant is said to be the beginning of the northern and southern Indian classical music traditions.)

Later, in the evolution of Hinduism, *karma* became identified with sacrificial rituals that were believed to produce results simply because the rituals were performed and not because they were offerings to deities or merely mediating links between human beings and supernatural powers. It was against such intense and exacting ritualism, and the attendant power of ritual specialists, that the Buddha revolted two and a half thousand years ago. During the post-Buddhist revival, the great eighth-century Hindu Vedantist philosopher from South India, Shankara, uncompromisingly downgraded ritualism and placed the way of knowledge and wisdom high above it as a means to spiritual good. Seven hundred years later, a devout Hindu householder of North India, Nanak, taught his disciples, the Sikhs, the superiority of moral righteousness over mechanical ritualism. And yet rituals have not wholly disappeared from the life of the Hindus or the Buddhists or the Sikhs. In fact, rituals define these and other religion-suffused ways of life all over South Asia, but they do so in rather flexible ways.

Rituals thus survive as rites of passage. Every Hindu, no matter what caste or community he belongs to, is the subject of rituals at birth, marriage, and death. Such rituals are intended for the moral refinement of the individual. Life-cycle rituals constitute *samskara*, that is, the process whereby one is 'made complete or perfect' and, ultimately after death, transformed into an ancestor. As an ancestor, one is in contact with one's descendants through the rituals of feeding that the latter perform. If the ancestors are not at peace, there will be no births. Rituals protect the seed and the fetus. They give the newborn child her individual and social identity. They bestow on the so-called 'twice-born' Hindus their upper-caste status. In marriage, as a vedic hymn puts it, parental love gives way to conjugal love: love gives, love receives, and with love is the ocean of life filled. The so-called rites of passage are in fact rituals of transformation and continuity in one great chain of being. They are supplemented by rituals that protect the body against disease and physical dangers. There are also the expiatory rituals of atonement and moral purification.

Important as *karma* (in the foregoing sense of ritual) is, it is not self-sufficient. Man is ever in need of divine favour and one seeks this through *puja* and pilgrimage. *Puja*, the Hindu ritual of adoration, may be performed at home or in a temple. Its recipient is one's favorite deity—Shiva, Vishnu, or Devi—iconically represented and treated as an honoured guest. It is bathed, anointed, fed, entertained with song and dance, praised and prayed to, and put to bed. While sacrificial rituals also were performed to win divine favour, *puja* emerged as a distinctive mode of worship characterized by intensity of emotion. Although the home was regarded as good as the temple for this purpose, the latter enjoyed a special status.

Temple art and architecture of ancient and medieval India survive to bear witness to the primacy of the religious over the secular in Hindu society. According to an old Tamil saying, one should not build a house in a town without a temple. Even kings obviously paid greater attention to the temple than to the palace: as a rule the palace had to be lower than a temple and the Brahmins' houses lower than the palace. The temple was the centre of the town. Its spire, visible from a long distance, indicated its very existence. The temples in turn took interest in mundane affairs, using their landed and other forms of wealth to promote the economic well-being of the priestly class and occasionally and derivatively of the larger community as well. As is well known, temples provided loans and promoted irrigation works in South India.

Prayers are also offered at sacred spots such as the source of a river or the meeting place of rivers. Every day in India Hindu pilgrims walk to some such sacred place (*tirtha*), an *axis mundi*, far away from home, to wash off their moral impurities and attain merit. To go on a pilgrimage one becomes a 'wanderer' (a *yatrika*) for the specific purposes of accumulating merit. In a well-known ancient text, we hear the god Indra, presiding deity of pilgrims, pronounce the following exhortation: 'The fortune of him who is sitting, sits; it rises when he rises; it sleeps when he sleeps; it moves when he moves. Therefore, wander!' (Eck 1982: 21). Indeed, going on pilgrimages, particularly to highly esteemed places, and on particularly auspicious occasions, is scripturally recommended *karma*. Thus, every twelve years, on the astrologically auspicious occasion called Kumbha, millions of Hindus visit the holy city of Prayag in North India at the confluence of the rivers Ganga and Jamuna. All of India gathers there, as it were. Walking together, bathing together, or having *darshan* (seeing an image or icon) together, each pilgrim is yet alone in the crowd: being a pilgrim is an intensely personal experience (see Karve 1988: 142–71).

The practice of pilgrimage knows no community barriers. The Jains are the pilgrims *par excellence*, always on the move visiting temples and holy places. The most notable among the latter is Shravana Belgola in South India, where the world's largest monolith, the sixty-foot image of Gomateshvara, a Jain spiritual teacher, sculpted late in the tenth century, is venerated daily and especially at periodic festivals. The Buddhists from India and abroad go on pilgrimage to Bodh Gaya, where Gotama received enlightenment, or to Sarnath, where he preached his first sermon, or to Kandy in Sri Lanka, where the holy relic of his tooth is venerated. Similarly, Sikh pilgrims from India and elsewhere go on pilgrimage to Nankana Sahab, the birthplace of Nanak, in Pakistan. For Muslims anywhere, one of the five key religious obligations is, of course, to visit Mecca if they have the means to make it; but practically every Muslim in India goes on pilgrimage to the shrine of one Sufi saint or another within a reasonable distance of where he lives. As modern means of communication and transportation become available more generally, holy places attract larger numbers of pilgrims (and also secularly minded tourists, since many of these shrines are scenic or architecturally interesting).

For the Hindu in search of liberation from the cycle of birth, death, and rebirth, the karmic store of accumulated merit is a trap—hence the appeal of renouncing all worldly *karma*. But this ideal—itself probably a reversal of an earlier notion that one needs more than a lifetime to fully partake of worldly joys—is difficult to achieve. It is in this context that the teaching of the *Bhagavad Gita* acquires critical importance. Emphasizing the performance rather than the abandonment of *karma*, it teaches the ethics of altruism. If one performs one's duty in a spirit of sacrifice, eliminating one's ego and self-interest one is liberated from the fruits of action even before death. One of the most crucial statements in the *Bhagavad Gita* (2: 47) bears on this point: 'Your entitlement is to *karma* alone, never to its fruits. The hope of such fruit should not therefore be the motive for action, nor should one therefore become inactive.' In the twentieth century, Mahatma Gandhi has been the most distinguished teacher of this view of *karma*. He added a note of caution, however, for those who would endeavor to convert this precept into practice: without surrender to divine will as an act of devotion, the Mahatma taught, the practice of *karma yoga* will not succeed.

AGAPE: *BHAKTI*

Vedic polytheism and ritualism gave way to Upanishadic philosophizing about the metaphysics of the act. There was a transformation then rather than a sharp break, an attempted synthesis rather than a flat repudiation. Still later, the *Bhagavad Gita* acknowledged both ritual and knowledge as legitimate ways to attain self-realization, which, according to Hindu tradition, is the highest goal of human life. To the ways of action (*karma*) and intelligence (*jnana*), the *Gita* added the way of devotion (*bhakti*), thus reviving the theistic element that post-vedic Hinduism had played down. After describing the ways of action, knowledge, and devotion, the *Bhagavad Gita* in one of the concluding verses (chapter 18, verse 66) enjoins the seeker to abandon all three ways and to seek refuge in God so as to be free of the burden of all moral imperfections. This call to total surrender is as much intellectual as it is devotional. It was an idea fashioned by the Brahmins, the guardians of the sacred tradition and the ideologues of Hindu society.

Many centuries later (toward the close of the ninth century) a devotional movement flowered in South India among non-Brahmin groups, who gave it utterance in Tamil rather than Sanskrit, which the Brahmins called the language of the gods. These groups represented a longing for theism after a millennium of Jain and Buddhist influence had swept over India, pushing the existence of God into the sidelines of religious thought and practice. They also expressed a moral weariness about the *dharma*s of caste and gender and sought to transcend such relativism by concentrating on personal devotion to their favorite deities. Shiva devotees took the lead, but Vishnu devotees followed soon later. The latter came to be known as Alvars—that is, those with an intuitive knowledge of God who were engaged in contemplative 'immersion' in him. These devotional movements became widespread, embracing high castes as well as low by the end of the eleventh century.

The best known among the Alvars is Nammalvar. In his 'hymns for the drowning' (to use A. K. Ramanujan's [1981] felicitous phrase), Nammalvar puts forward a novel notion of devotion as the assumption of femininity by the devotee in relation to the one supremely noble man, Vishnu. While the Upanishads taught man to realize his own divinity and the *Bhagavad Gita* advised surrender, the Alvars stressed either the constant companionship of God or separation from him and the consequent longing, amorous in character, for union with him. But the preoccupation is with separation (*viraha*). While other Alvars covered a wide range of emotions, including those experienced by parents, sons, companions, servants, and women in love, Nammalvar sang particularly of the last of these (Ramanujan ibid.: 52).

Is that you, little bird?
When I asked you to go
as my messenger to the great lord
and tell him of my pain, you
dawdled, didn't go.

I have lost my looks,
my dark limbs are pale.
Go look for someone else
to put sweet things in your beak,
go now.

The intoxication of love found expression among the devotees of Shiva in South India. The pangs of separation are typically described thus by Mahadevi, a woman from Karnataka who was a devotee in the twelfth century (Ramanujan 1973: 124, 125):

Four parts of the day
I grieve for you.
Four parts of the night
I'm mad for you.
I lie lost,
sick for you, night and day.
O Lord white as jasmine.

Describing the imagined ecstasy of union, she sang:

He bartered my heart,
looted my flesh,
claimed as tribute
my pleasure,
took over
all of me.
I'm the woman of love
for my lord, white as jasmine.

The most celebrated Sanskrit text of *viraha bhakti* is the *Bhagavata Purana* (ninth century), which was most probably composed in South India. It contains much metaphysics and, laying particular stress on his childhood and youth, tells the tale of Krishna, the most illustrious avatar of Vishnu. Stories of his dalliance with young cowherdesses occupy a central place in the *bhakti* tradition, for the love of these women for Krishna is seen to symbolize the love of all devotees for God or, more abstractly, the longing of the individual soul for merger with the supreme soul, of which it is an emanation. This love, while all-consuming and incessant, is totally selfless and therefore pure. The *Bhagavata Purana* describes nine modes of *bhakti*: 'Listening to the Lord's glory, singing of Him, thinking of Him, serving His feet, performing His worship, saluting Him, serving Him, friendship with Him, surrendering oneself to Him' (de Bary 1958: 333).

The story of the unmarried love of Krishna and the cowherdess Radha

has had wide influence all over India. Many Vaishnava sects owe their origin
to it. In the late twelfth century in eastern India, the poet Jayadeva composed
a religious-erotic poem of great beauty (the celebrated and much translated
Gita Govinda), describing the love of Radha and Krishna, their separation
and eventual reunion. Soon this poem became a part of temple worship
and was set to music. It became an expression of spiritual quest. Gradually
it spread to southern and western India and was incorporated in temple
dance and music.

Later, in the sixteenth century, a Bengali devotee called Chaitanya became
possessed with the love of Krishna and identified himself with Radha
agonizing over the pangs of separation from the Lord. Dancing and singing
along with his followers, he travelled all the way to Vrindavan in North
India, where, according to legend, Krishna had been born and had spent
his youth. This dance-song form of worship with the agony of love as its
theme came to be called *kirtan*. Chaitanya looked upon union with fear
and even hatred, for it is in separation that the devotee, with all his or her
senses, experiences God. In Gujarat, a contemporary of Chaitanya called
Vallabha composed a treatise on aesthetic theory as a commentary on the
love-play of Krishna as narrated in the *Bhagavata Purana*. Vallabha spoke of
the complementarity of 'total love' and 'constraint.' For him, *bhakti* was the
contemplative endeavor of achieving union but the search for it was superior
to finding it, so one must hold oneself back and experience in separation
the love of God in full measure.

Bhakti imagined as conjugal love found its most poignant expression
in the deeply moving lyrics of Mira, a Rajasthan princess of the late sixteenth
century. While for Mahadevi Shiva had been the lover, for Mira Krishna
was the longed-for husband. The pain of separation was no more bearable
for that reason: 'I will build myself a pyre of fragrant wood and beseech
you to set it aflame with your own hand. The fire will consume me and I
will be a heap of ashes. Won't you rub your body with these ashes, in the
manner of the mendicant?'

Intense religious emotion found other kinds of expression also. In the
sixteenth century, Sur sang joyously in Brijbhasha (a dialect of Hindi) of
Krishna, child and young man, and Tulsi composed in Avadhi (another dialect
of Hindi) the epic story of Rama, avatar of Vishnu, originally written in
Sanskrit (c. 200 BC). Tulsi's *bhakti* was that of the servant (*dasa*) devoted to
the service of his divine master. The love of God for the devotee, who dwells
on his own imperfections and therefore on divine grace, is a central theme
of Tulsi's sublime poetry. His *Ramacharitamanas* is a widely read, recited,
and enacted vernacular religious text of India.

Sur, Tulsi, and Kabir, another devotee from a century earlier, are not
only luminaries of the medieval *bhakti* movement but also the three great

pillars of Hindi literature, a fact that draws our attention once again to the all-encompassing nature of religion in India. Kabir's devotionalism was centred not on a personalized god in human form, however, but on an abstract and formless conception of the divine. He considered the religious experience more important than its ground in some conception of a divinity. Alongside *bhakti* Kabir echoed the metaphysics of the Upanishads and reflected in some measure the influence of Sufi ideas on his upbringing as a Muslim.

SYNCRETISM: SUFIS, SANTS, AND SIKHS

Hinduism, Buddhism, and Jainism are indigenous religious traditions: it is from India that they—particularly Buddhism—have spread to others parts of Asia and the world. Buddhism was practically wiped out of India by the eighth century but only after many of its ideas and ideals had been absorbed into Hindu thought. In fact, the Buddha was deified by the Hindus, not by the Buddhists. Jainism has remained very close to Hinduism, especially in the realm of practice. In terms of the number of adherents, however, it is Islam that has become the second most important religion of India. In fact, there are more Muslims in India now (over 120 million) than in any other country except Indonesia.

Islam was brought to India by Arab traders toward the close of the seventh century, within living memory of the prophet Muhammad. Subsequently, the conquerors came and with them, the 'doctors' of Muslim law called the Ulama. They stressed the realization of the true spirit of Islam through submission to 'the way' (*sharia*) God had ordained for his true followers and faith in the example and sayings of Muhammad. Simultaneously, the Sufi seekers of God also came to India. They tended to keep aloof from the kings, but the kings often sought them out. The Sufis evolved their own way (*tariqa*) of realizing God—through love and the intermediary role of saints. The chasm between *sharia* and *tariqa*, between the Ulama and the Sufis, has been a factor of immense importance in the history of Islam in India. While the original tradition emphasized living in faith through the material world, the Sufi quest was essentially spiritual. 'If knowledge strikes the heart,' the Sufis taught, 'it is welcome: if it strikes the body it is a burden.' The idea of realizing the true nature of God, and even attempting to become one with him, was anathema to the Ulama, who denounced many Sufi orders as heretical. The Sufis' quest was, however, very similar to that of the Upanishadic seers: the latter's *soham* ('I am He') was echoed by the former's *anal-haqq* ('I am Truth').

The scope for religious syncretism was not perceived immediately. In fact, anti-Hindu polemics were characteristic of Indian Sufism in the pre-

Mughal period. Leaders of various Sufi orders were active in converting Hindus to Islam. Kashmir and Bengal, where mass conversions took place, were won over more by Sufis than by kings. The promise of syncretism was realized better in areas such as Bengal, where Hindu mythology and cosmology became the vehicles for Islamic dogmas and practices. As Bengal was Islamized, Islam itself became Hinduized. Muhammad's biography became a variant of Krishna's early life (see Roy 1983); Hindu gods rubbed shoulders with Muslim saints. In the heartland of India, two royal brothers, Dara Shukoh and Aurangzeb, the former a disciple of the Sufis, and the latter of the Ulama and the more orthodox Sufis, fought the battle to the finish. The Ulama won. This was perhaps one of the most critical events in the history of Islam in India, and I will describe it in some detail.

Dara Shukoh (1605–1659), son of Shah Jahan, was great grandson of the Mughal emperor Akbar, who had valiantly tried to bring the various religions of his realm together. But the special hall for discussions among scholars professing different faiths that Akbar had had built in his capital city of Fatehpur-Sikri ended up being a hall of disharmony, a Tower of Babel. Not to be defeated, Akbar assumed the role of religious leader and formally promulgated a new religion combining elements of Islam, Christianity, and Upanishadic Hinduism. But this too failed, and Akbar's *din-i-Ilahi* (religion of God), which never made much headway beyond the court except to antagonize the Ulama, died with him in 1605.

In his zeal for religious syncretism, Dara Shukoh was Akbar's true heir and also a scholar of the religious classics of Islam and Hinduism. Taking his stand on the revelation in the Koran that God had sent his messengers to all peoples and given them their scriptures, Shukoh maintained that it was the moral duty of a Muslim to learn from these other religious traditions. He believed that the Upanishads must be the 'concealed scripture' spoken of in the *Quran*. He considered them, as such, the original source of monotheism. Not surprisingly, he translated the *Bhagavad Gita* and a number of Upanishads into Persian. He maintained that the translation was intended to clarify the Quranic revelation, not to devalue it. He also wrote a treatise on comparative religion, in which he compared the technical terms of Upanishadic pantheism with what he believed, perhaps mistakenly, to be their equivalents in Sufi thought. Apart from his Sufi preceptors, Dara consulted Brahmins as well as Hindu mystics and saints on aspects of the spiritual quest (see Mujeeb 1967).

Dara's younger brother, Aurangzeb, disapproved of Akbar and Dara's quest for religious syncretism. Getting the Ulama to pronounce Dara an apostate, for maintaining, among other things, that Islam and Hinduism were 'twin brothers,' Aurangzeb had Dara executed in 1659. For Aurangzeb, Islam and Hinduism were as irreconcilable as truth and error. The Akbar-Dara quest for interreligious understanding was not, however, a total failure. It gradually led to a change in the attitudes of some Sufi orders (notably, the Qadiri with whom Dara was associated and later the Naqshbandi with whom Aurangzeb had his ties). They moved from hostility to tolerance and even understanding of Hinduism. In fact, the exclusive and syncretic tendencies ran parallel to each other, often in the thought and action of the same person. After reading the *Bhagavad Gita*, Shah Abdul Aziz (d. 1824), for example, who was at the forefront of the 'purifiers' of Indian Islam and worked for the return of Sufi orders to orthodoxy, also regarded Krishna as a saint.

If the Akbar-Dara experiment had succeeded, perhaps Hinduism would have evolved in a manner consistent with its monotheistic potential and Islam perhaps would have been absorbed into it just as the Buddhist and Jain heterodoxies had been. But these changes did not occur. The role of Sufism in bringing Islam and Hinduism close together must not be overestimated. Even the outstanding contributions of the gifted Sufi Amir Khusrau in the late thirteenth century to a composite literary and musical culture, and his obvious pride in being an Indian, did nothing to soften his ambivalence about, if not hostility toward, Hinduism.

Some contemporary Indian thinkers, confronting history with metaphysics, maintain that a syntehsis between Hinduism and Islam was never truly possible because their basic value orientations are irreconcilable (Ahmad 1964). The lure of synthesis, according to these scholars, turned out to be elusive. In terms of the fundamentals of belief and practice, their opinion may well be true, but the unthinkable (namely synthesis) did take place in medieval India, and not only in art and architecture, painting and music, language and literature, but also in religion and philosophy—though in a much more limited way in the latter than in the former three domains.

And yet the coming of Islam was indeed a revolutionary event: it broke the ancient bond between India and her indigenous religious traditions. Although Christianity had arrived here with the apostle Thomas, who established the Syrian church in southwestern India, it had not sued for the state, and no Christian kingdoms were established. It is in this sense that the coming of Muslims to India was undeniably a political act, an invasion.

Cultural synthesis at the high philosophical level had its counterpart at the popular level. The latter in fact anticipated the former and was also more successful. Kabir, whom I have already mentioned in connection with *bhakti*, had preceded Dara Shukoh by almost a hundred years. Looking back, social historians consider him the originator of a new religious tradition, namely the Sant tradition. The word *sant* is derived from the Sanskrit *sat* for 'truth' or 'reality,' and means one who knows the Truth or who has experienced Reality.

Rejecting the external authority of the Vedas and the Quran, Kabir, who was brought up in a Muslim family, preached the goal of inner realization based on the love of a transcendent and formless divinity. He was influenced by Vaishnava *bhakti* primarily but also by yogic and Sufi ideas and practices, such as the ideals of self-perfection and the oneness of God respectively, and the meditative recitation of God's name as an expression of one's love for him, common to both Hindu devotees and Muslim Sufis. His followers were drawn mostly from lower, often untouchable, Hindu castes, and included Muslims. The latter saw him as an exponent of the Sufi notion of the 'unity of being' (*wahdat-al-wujud*).

The Sants stressed the fulfillment of essential social obligations such as the need to support one's family through personal effort. Kabir himself is said to have practised the craft of weaving. Although socially involved, the Sants advocated an inner detachment from worldly ties. Seeking a true guru, keeping the company of like-minded seekers, and dedicating themselves to the incessant remembrance of God, they abandoned traditional rituals and rejected caste and religious barriers. Their creed of love embraced humanity as well as the abstract supreme being. Rabindranath Tagore called this the religion of man. Sociologically, the Sant reformation is important because it gave birth to a large number of sects in northern, central, and western India. Many of these sects, including the Kabir Panth, survive until today.

One sect that was to grow into a world religion was that of the followers of Nanak (1469–1539) in the Punjab. Born a clean-caste Hindu, deeply influenced by the Sant tradition as well as by Upanishadic metaphysics, and clearly aware of the teachings of Islam and the practice of the Nath Yogis (members of a Hindu sect who focus on self-perception and inner awareness), Nanak revolted against ritualism and caste rigidities, particularly the former. He also sought to combine elements from the various religious traditions of India and to transcend them. Worship of and submission to the will of God, honest labour, and collective sharing of the fruits of labour are believed to be the principles of his teaching. His companions and followers came to be called Nanak Panthis as well as Sikhs (disciples, or learners), and their religious tradition, the Sikh *dharam*.

Nanak was the first guru of the Sikhs. He was followed by nine others. The Mughal emperor Akbar was tolerant of the new sect and is believed even to have visited the third guru. The political environment after Akbar's death became increasingly hostile under the Naqshbandi Sufi reaction to Akbar's alleged apostasy. Sikh tradition holds Jahangir (Akbar's son) responsible for the death of the fifth guru. Around the same time the social composition of the Sikh community, which had been confined largely to a small number of clean Hindu castes, also changed. The large-scale entry of Jat agriculturalists into the Sikh fold contributed to the shaping of its militant character. The original pietist and pacifist message of Nanak was gradually transformed without being abandoned completely. On the one hand, Hindu ritualistic practices were gradually revived; on the other, the Sikhs came into armed conflict with the Mughals, who considered them rebellious and tried to suppress, if not exterminate, them. The sixth guru, Hargobind, proclaimed himself the spiritual and temporal leader of the Sikhs. Distinguishing between the two functions, subordinating the temporal to the religious, he yet insisted on combining them both in his own person.

Finally, the tenth guru, Gobind (1666–1708), took up arms against Aurangzeb and presented the two-edged sword as the symbol of the deity to his followers. More than any of his nine predecessors, Gobind brought the Sikh faith closer to completion philosophically; he also highlighted the distance between the Sikhs and the followers of the two main faiths through an emphasis on behavioral differences. Obviously influenced by the *Bhagavad Gita*, he presented himself as the protector of *dharma*; also he composed a hymn in praise of the Hindu goddess Chandi, whom he worshipped. He translated the *Bhagavata Purana* and some other Sanskrit texts into the vernacular. At the same time he instituted a ritual of initiation and a code of conduct for his followers. The latter included the injunction to remain unshorn (unlike the Hindus) and uncircumcised (unlike the Muslims). Besides their head and facial hair, the Sikhs were to wear other visible markers of their distinctive identity. He put an end to the institution of personal gurus and declared the Sikh holy book, the *Granth Sahab*, originally compiled by the fifth guru and containing the hymns of Nanak and many Sants and Sufis, as the eternal spiritual guru. Temporal power would vest in the Sikh congregation itself.

Theologically, the Sikh faith is syncretistic. Sociologically, the Sikh community is a reproduction of Hindu society, being characterized by caste distinctions to this day. Politically, it had remained opposed to the Muslims, since the seventeenth century and began to distance itself from the Hindus towards the end of the nineteenth century. Those Sikh 'Sants' of today who are politicians or who patronize terrorists in the name of the unity of religion and politics have hardly any claims to membership in the Sant tradition of which Nanak was a flower or of the Sikh faith to which he gave birth.

Religious syncretism bore witness to the vitality of the religious life in medieval India. But religion was to become perverted in the modern age. The coming together of religious traditions was to give way to the falling apart of politicized religious communities. The encounter of Hinduism and Christianity in the sixteenth and following centuries was to generate one last syncretic movement before the parting of ways—or what seems so just now—between the adherents of different faiths in India.

Bengal, which had seen the coming together of Buddhism, Hinduism, and tribal religions, and later of Hinduism and Islam, and which had also witnessed an upsurge of Vaishnava *bhakti*, was to be the home of an experiment in syncretism in the nineteenth century. Its moving force was Rammohan Roy (1772–1833), a Hindu of wide sympathies and vast scholarship. He operated on two fronts. Convinced of the need for the elevation of the religious life of the Hindus in the direction of a monistic theism, he launched a multipronged drive to synthesize whatever he considered most valuable in vedantic Hinduism, Islam, and Protestant Christianity. He also initiated and supported campaigns to eradicate social abuses of various kinds in Hindu society. The most remarkable feature of his syncretic quest was, perhaps, its rootedness in Hinduism, Roy's great admiration for the moral precepts of Jesus (on which he wrote a book) notwithstanding. His religious philosophy was perhaps too austere and intellectual for the Hindus to accept. Not surprisingly, therefore, the universal religion he dreamed of died with him. His successors split up and the majority returned to the Hindu fold before long.

COMMUNALISM AND SECULARISM

Rammohan Roy had hoped for a sociocultural and a religious renaissance under British rule (which he considered a civilizing force) and as a result of India's encounter with Christianity. The search for syncretism on the part of some was, however, more than matched by the fear of an imperial proselytizing religion on the part of others. The encounter of religious traditions was inevitably linked to the clash of imperialism with nationalism. Given the holist perspectives characteristic of India's cultural traditions, nationalism was presented as a religious quest. Thus, Aurobindo Ghose proclaimed: 'nationalism is not a mere political programme; nationalism is a religion that has come from God' (de Bary 1959: 727).

The dawn of the twentieth century saw political organizations draw upon religious symbolism to mobilize people in the struggle for independence. What is most significant is that the use of such symbolism was resorted to not only by exclusively Hindu or Muslim organizations but also by the multireligious Indian National Congress. This was no less true of the Congress under Mohandas Gandhi (1869–1948), the Mahatma, than it had been earlier when the reins of leadership were in the hands of militant leaders who projected a more emphatic Hindu personality. Bal Gangadhar Tilak (1856–1920) and Gandhi presented new and divergent interpretations of the *Bhagavad Gita* that were reminiscent of old controversies, but unlike some of the commentaries which had been renunciatory, argued a this-worldly philosophy of action.

Gandhi's approach to religious pluralism was transcendental rather than simply syncretic. Throughout his long political career he stressed the inseparability of religion and politics. But, he maintained, religion should not entail sectarianism: 'This religion transcends Hinduism, Islam, Christianity, etc. It does not supersede them. It harmonizes them and gives them reality'. (1984: 54). Gandhi genuinely respected all religions; his outlook on life was influenced not only by Hinduism, into which he was born, but also by Jainism, Christianity, and Islam. Convinced of the truth of all religions and of the limitations of human understanding, he considered conversion an expression of lack of genuine religious faith. He was horrified by the so-called religious conflicts: 'Religion is outraged when an outrage is perpetrated in its name' (1961: 47).

Gandhi set himself three major goals: freedom from British rule, inter-religious harmony, and the improvement of the socioreligious life of the Hindus. He sincerely believed that the goals entailed one another and were pragmatically related. Much to the dismay of secular-minded nationalists, he tied up the national movement after the First World War with Khilafat (the movement against termination of the caliphate) and later with the eradication of untouchability among the Hindus. He never waivered in his commitment to a holist worldview: each religion was all-comprehensive though there were many religions.

The Mahatma's efforts to untie Hindus and Muslims in the pursuit of the national goal of independence from foreign rule failed in the end. His conception of religion as faith wedded to moral reason was not shared by his followers, whether Hindu or non-Hindus. The religiosity which won against him was of the miracle-haunted rustic and the rootless urbanite on the one hand, and of the profit-seeking politician on the other. Extremist elements among Hindus and Muslims alike repudiated his leadership: to the former he was a foe of Hinduism, to the latter of their aspiration for a separate homeland. Nationalism in India became polarized, with Hindus and Muslims generally pitted against each other. Although most Hindus stayed with the Congress, the two turbulent streams of communalism flowed along their separate courses, as the subcontinent lurched forward toward independence. Communalism in the sense of struggle for independence and power on the basis of religious identity rather than on the principle of territory—which is the usual basis of nationalism—thus came to dominate the internal politics of India.

Gandhi and like-minded people, especially the Muslim theologian and politician Maulana Abul Kalam Azad and the secularist Jawaharlal Nehru, could not stem the tide of communalism. India was partitioned in 1947 and the Islamic state of Pakistan was born in the midst of communal riots on an unprecedented scale, resulting in the killing of thousands of Hindus, Muslims, and Sikhs in many parts of the subcontinent but most of all in the provinces of Bengal and the Punjab. Millions became refugees and fled across the newly created international frontiers. Gandhi's dream of a united independent India went up in smoke, but he did not have to suffer long: he was assassinated early in 1948 by a group of Hindu militants.

Instead of cleansing politics of its unsavory aspects, as men of faith such as Mahatma Gandhi had believed it would, religion was reduced to being a mere 'sign of distinction' between politically mobilized human groups. It became a 'shadow' of itself (Dumont ibid.: 315–6). Millions of people felt revulsion toward the political abuse of religion, particularly by leaders who had no use for religion in their own lives. In such a situation, there were many who still believed in the idea of interreligious understanding, but there were numerous others who looked forward to the elimination of religion from public life. Jawaharlal Nehru (1889–1964) was one such rationalist and he committed independent India to the custody of a modern state. Secularism in India has, however, had far from an easy passage. Asked by André Malraux what his greatest difficulty had been since Independence, Nehru had replied, 'Creating a just state by just means,' and, after a pause, 'Perhaps, too, creating a secular state in a religious country' (1968: 145). This was in 1958, eleven years after India had gained freedom.

Nehru was a modernizer who was deeply conscious of the harm that religiosity had done to India. He had written just three years before he became the prime minister of India in 1947 that it was 'with the temper and approach of science allied to philosophy, and with reverence for all that lies beyond' that Indians must face life. He had further observed that 'the day-to-day religion of the orthodox Hindu is more concerned with what to eat, who to eat with and from whom to keep away, than with spiritual values. ... The Moslem ... has his own narrow codes and ceremonials, a routine which he vigorously follows, forgetting the lesson of brotherhood which his religion taught him' (1961: 553).

Nehru's views are important because they are the best possible statement of the liberal secular outlook, which is widely regarded as a precondition of modernization. In fact, what is remarkable is the need Nehru felt to defend religion as philosophy or as a concern with 'all that lies beyond'; otherwise, he was an agnostic and favoured a rationalist, and even a historicist, worldview.

An examination of Nehru's published work brings out clearly his conviction that religion is a hindrance to 'the tendency to change and progress inherent in human society' and that 'the belief in a supernatural agency which ordains everything has led to a certain irresponsibility on the social plane, and emotion and sentimentality have taken the place of reasoned thought and inquiry' (ibid.: 543). But, then, he did not worry too much about religion and its political expression as communalism because 'the real thing' was 'the economic factor' (1973: 203). He expected communalism to recede in the face of a reordered economic structure. But this proved a false hope, perhaps because no real economic restructuring was possible in the short run. Secularism as the basis of the state had therefore to be a policy of strict neutrality on the part of the state in its dealings with citizens irrespective of their various religious faiths. This policy is more a defensive strategy to help tide over the intervening period until the anticipated transition to a truly secularized society than a positive philosophy of life (see Madan 1997).

It is pertinent to recall here that the emergence of secularism in Europe, in the sense of 'disenchantment with the world' (as Schiller and Weber put it), was not only an expression of repugnance toward the corruption of institutionalized religion but was also aided by developments in the teachings of Christianity. The basis for the separation of state and church is to be found in the New Testament itself. The privatization of religion, through the assumption by the individual of the responsibility for his own salvation without the intervention of the Church, was a later development. All this is well known. A similar ideology is, however, absent from the cultural traditions of India. The idiom in which to express the ideal of secularism has, therefore, yet to be constructed. This is not an easy task, because the great majority of the people of India are adherents of one religious faith or another and also because in such matters borrowed ideas do not carry us very far (see Madan ibid.).

As for the vitality of the religious life of the people, it is unfortunate that what attracts attention most is the so-called fundamentalism among Muslims and Sikhs and revivalism among Hindus. There is no doubt that communal politics, which had been weakened considerably in the wake of Gandhi's martyrdom, has become strident again. Nonpolitical expressions of this vitality are also available, testifying to the capacity of the Hindu tradition to continuously spawn not only new cults and sects but also new gods and goddesses. The secularists consider this wholly regrettable because they see such developments as evidence of the persistence of antirational attitudes and social backwardness.

Arguably, their conceptions of rationalism and social advancement are unreasonably restrictive. They fail to realize that religiously minded people are not necessarily bad or stupid—certainly not more than the secularists themselves. It should be realized that secularism may not be restricted to rationalism as understood in the West, that it is compatible with faith, and that it need not be the sole motive force of a modern state. For the secularist minority to stigmatize the majority as superstitious and to preach secularism to them as the law of their being is both moral arrogance and political folly (see Madan 1987b).

What, then, is the way out of the present predicament in the history of religion in India? The question is more easily posed than answered; but it is quite clear that the solution will have to be broadly humanist rather than narrowly sectarian or naively secularist. Maybe Gandhi's approach still has its uses. For Gandhi, religion was a matter of faith but not blind faith. He placed moral reason above scriptural authority. Religion, he maintained, is the source of absolute value and hence constitutive of social life; politics is the arena of public interest; without the former the latter becomes debased. But the multiplicity of religious faiths would generate conflict in the value domain itself. He considered the quest for a single religion neither feasible nor indeed desirable. There was thus no escape from a transcendentalist approach and the quest for interreligious understanding; a simple pluralism advocating respect for all religions would not do.

Gandhi's secularism was a restraint on the state, not because this was expedient but because society would ultimately be reformed by good people and not by governments. In saying so, he reiterated such old and enduring ideas as *dharma*, *karma*, and *bhakti*. He also sought to carry forward the syncretic tendencies that have always been present and that had become particularly salient in the medieval period. In doing all this, he also showed a keen awareness of the spirit of the age in which he lived, as, for instance, when he maintained that morality in our time finds expression through politics.

* * *

As an interpretive essay on religion in India, this has been an exercise in selection. The terrain to be covered is vast and bristles with many complex problems of fact and interpretation. To cut a way through it, I have focused on some points on high ground, as it were, in the hope that, seen together, they would provide a coherent picture. Doubtless there are other perspectives and other profiles. The issue is not that but rather that the interpretation offered here should be based on a fair reading of the history of religions in India. Naturally, I believe it to be so. I certainly have my preferences in relation to the available interpretations, but they are not peculiarly mine. And, as the German philosopher Hans-Georg Gadamer (1983: 105) has emphasized, 'The very idea of a definitive interpretation seems to be intrinsically contradictory. Interpretation is always on the way.'

At this point it seems pertinent to state very briefly that I was born a Hindu and had a Hindu upbringing combined with a 'modern' education—a common enough experience in contemporary India. I became an anthropologist, which means, I guess, that I have tried to look upon my cultural heritage with an attitude that stands in the twilight zone between sympathy and skepticism, admiration and distaste. But, then, there is really no minimum definition of what it requires and means to be a Hindu other than in terms of birth, and that gives me release. Although I do not believe in or do a hundred things that my grandfathers believed in or did, yet I do not feel I am not a Hindu; nor has anybody suggested otherwise. There are no practising Hindus in the sense in which there are practising Christians; there are no 'five pillars' of Hinduism as there are of Islam. But my personal beliefs and behavior are beyond a certain point irrelevant to my concerns as a scholar. If I find that religion is a significant element in the constitution of society in India, that does not mean that I wish it to be so. One does not wish that the Himalayas were or were not there; they *are* there.

What, then, distinguishes the perspective offered in this essay? It is above all the effort to look upon religion not as a reflection or a subsystem of society but as society, viewed primarily in terms of axiologically grounded social action, and as something on the move. Whether in its cosmological, moral, theological, or social aspects, the religious landscape in India has been characterized by pluralism for more than two thousand years. Holism and pluralism are not necessarily in conflict. Syncretic movements as well as interreligious antagonisms have been present throughout the history of India. If anybody should think that my emphasis on syncretism is misplaced, I would ask such a critic to ponder the Sant tradition. If India has ever had a religion that cut across traditional religious, social, and gender boundaries, that combined the intellectual and the emotional, that unified rather than divided people, it is the Sant tradition. It is up to us to realize the potential for good that is inherent in religion.

In the modern age, while conflict between politically mobilized religious communities has become a salient phenomenon in India, conscious efforts have been made to replace syncretism with secularism. Secularism is generally understood as both the limitation of the role of religion in public affairs and the policy of neutrality on the part of the state in relation to the citizens who are followers of various religious traditions. Secularism would have had wider acceptance if it had not been so utterly uncritical in its rejection of religion and its acceptance of a technological view of the world.

Meanwhile, the present is marked by the return of religion to the secular city, as Harvey Cox (1984) has said, and also by a resurgence of violence, even terrorism, in the name of religion (see Casanova 1994 and Juergensmeyer 2000). The secularists, whether liberals or Marxists, seem unable to appreciate that the ideologies of secularism themselves have contributed to the present impasse. The prospect is uncertain. The history of humankind, however, teaches us that, as Èmile Durkheim (1965) observed, there is something eternal about the role of religion as the moral foundation of social life, and that religion is more likely to be transformed rather than eliminated from society. I stand with those who think that in India, and indeed everywhere else in the postmodern age, religion will yet be rediscovered as humanism, and find expression in a variety of ways *excluding* fundamentalism theocracy and intolerance. In the words of T. S. Eliot,

The only hope, or else despair
Lies in the choice of pyre or pyre—
To be redeemed from fire by fire.

REFERENCES

Ahmad, Aziz
1964 *Studies in Islamic culture in the Indian environment.* Oxford: Clarendon Press.
Casanova, José
1994 *The public religions in the modern world.* Chicago: University of Chicago Press.
Cox, Harvey
1984 *Religion in the secular city: Toward a postmodern theology.* New York: Simon & Schuster.
de, Bary, Wm. Th., ed.
1958, 1959 *Sources of Indian tradition.* Vol. 1 (1958), Vol. 2 (1959). New York: Columbia University Press.
Dumont, Louis
1980 *Homo hierarchicus: The caste system and its implications;* Chicago: University of Chicago Press.
Durkheim, Èmile
1965 (1915) *The elementary forms of the religious life.* Trs., J. W. Swain. New York: The Fress Press.
Eck, Diana
1982 *Banaras: The city of light.* New York: Alfned Knopf.
Gadamer, Hans-Georg
1983 *Reason in the age of science.* Trs., F. Lawrence. Cambridge: MIT Press.
Gandhi, M. K. (Mahatma)
1961 *The way to communal harmony.* Ed., U. R. Rao. Ahmedabad: Navjivan.
1984 *All men are brothers.* Ed., K. Kripalani. New York: Continuum.
1986 *The moral and political writings of Mahatma Gandhi.* Ed., Raghavan Iyer. Oxford: Clarendon Press.
Juergensmsyer, Mark
2000 *Terror in the mind of God: Global rise of religious violence.* Berkeley: University of California Press.
Karve, Irawati
1988 On the road: A Maharashtrian pilgrimage. In Eleanor Zelliot, and Maxine Bernsten, eds., *The experience of Hinduism.* Albany: State University of New York Press.
Lingat, Robert
1973 *The classical law of India.* Berkeley: University of California Press.
Malraux, André
1968 *Antimemoirs.* London: Hamish Hamilton.

Madan, T. N.
1987a *Non-renunciation: Themes and interpretations of Hindu culture*. New Delhi: Oxford University Press.
1987b Secularism in its place. *The Journal of Asian studies* 46, 4: 747–59.
1997 *Modern myths, locked minds: Secularism and fundamentalism in India*. New Delhi: Oxford University Press.
Mujeeb, M.
1967 *The Indian Muslims*. London: Allen & Unwin.
Mukerji, D. P.
1948 *Modern Indian culture*. Bombay: Hind Kitabs.
Nehru, Jawaharlal
1961 (1946) *The discovery of India*. Bombay: Asia Publishing House.
1973 *Selected works of Jawaharlal Nehru*, Vol. 5. New Delhi: Orient Longman.
Radhakrishnan, S.
1923 *Indian philosophy*, Vol. 1. London: Allen & Unwin.
Ramanujan, A. K.
1973 *Speaking of Siva*. Harmondsworth: Penguin Books.
1981 *Hymns for the drowning*. Princeton: Princeton University Press.
Roy, Asim
1983 *The Islamic syncretistic tradition in Bengal*. Princeton: Princeton University Press.
Weber, Max
1958 *The religion of India: The sociology of Hinduism and Buddhism*. Trs., H. H. Gerth and D. Martindale. Glencoe, Ill.: Fress Press.

Contributors

Akbar Ahmed holds the Ibn Khaldun Chair in Islamic Studies at the American University, Washington, DC.

Arjun Appadurai is Provost, New School University, New York.

Lawrence A. Babb is Professor of Anthropology at Amherst College (USA).

Carol A. Breckenridge is Associate Professor of History, in the South Asia Programme, Yale University.

Louis E. Fenech teaches South Asian History at the University of Northern Iowa.

Gavind Flood is Head of the Department of Religious Studies at the University of Stirling (UK).

Martin Fuchs is a Researcher at the South Asia Institute, Hiedelberg University.

Christopher J. Fuller is Professor of Anthropology at the London School of Economics & Political Science.

Krishna Prakash Gupta formerly taught sociology at the Department of Chinese Studies, University of Delhi.

Muhammad Ishaq Khan is Professor of History at Kashmir University, Srinagar.

Ravindra Sahai Khare is Professor of Anthropology at the University of Virginia, Charlottesville (USA).

David N. Loremzen is Professor of History of El Colegio de Mexico, Mexico City.

Triloki Nath Madan is Emeritus Professor (Sociology) at the Institute of Economic Growth, Delhi.

W.H. McLeod is Professor of History at the University of Otago, Dunedin (New Zealand).

Jonathan P. Parry is Professor of Anthropology at the London School of Economics & Political Science.

Desiderio Pinto, interested in the comparative study of Islam, was formerly teaching at Vidyajyoti, Delhi.

Jean-Luc Racine is Head, International Programme for Advanced Studies, Foundation Maison des Sciences de l'Homme, Paris.

Rosianne Racine researches popular culture in South Asia and is based in Paris.

A.K. Ramanujan was (at the time of his death) William E. Cowan Professor at the University of Chicago.

Rowena Robinson teaches sociology at the University of Bombay, Mumbai.

Susan Visvanathan is Associate Professor of Sociology at the Jawaharlal Nehru University, New Delhi.

Index